Charles van Onselen is an acclaimed biographer who has been honoured with visiting fellowships at Cambridge, Oxford and Yale. A graduate of Rhodes University, Grahamstown, and St. Antony's College, Oxford, his earlier works on the social history of southern Africa won him, amongst others, the American African Studies Association's Herskovits Prize, the Institute of Commonwealth Studies' Trevor Reese Memorial Prize and the *Sunday Times* Alan Paton Award for non-fiction. He has published extensively in leading historical journals in America, England and France. A Fellow of the Royal Society (S.A.), he has recently been a visiting fellow at Magdalen College, Oxford, and the recipient of an honorary doctorate in literature from Rhodes University. He is currently Research Professor in the Faculty of Humanities at the University of Pretoria in South Africa.

CHARLES VAN ONSELEN

The Fox and the Flies

The Criminal Empire of the
Whitechapel Murderer

VINTAGE BOOKS
London

Published by Vintage 2008

1 3 5 7 9 10 8 6 4 2

Copyright © Charles van Onselen 2007

Charles van Onselen has asserted his right under the Copyright,
Designs and Patents Act 1988 to be identified as the author
of this work

This book is a work of non-fiction. The author has stated to the
publishers that the contents of this book are true.

First published in Great Britain in 2007 by
Jonathan Cape
Random House, 20 Vauxhall Bridge Road,
London SW1V 2SA

www.vintage-books.co.uk

Addresses for companies within The Random House Group
Limited can be found at:
www.randomhouse.co.uk/offices.htm

The Random House Group Limited Reg. No. 954009

A CIP catalogue record for this book
is available from the British Library

ISBN 9780099502821

The Random House Group Limited supports The Forest Stewardship
Council (FSC), the leading international forest certification
organisation. All our titles that are printed on Greenpeace
approved FSC ... paper
pr...
www.rbooks.co.uk/environment

Prin...
CPI ...

For metics old and new

I will rehearse vnto you a fable. There was a fox hauing a sore place on him ouerset with a swarme of flies, that continuallie sucked out hir bloud: and when one that came by and saw this manner, demanded whether she would haue the flies driuen beside hir, she answered no: for if these flies that are alreadie full, and by reason thereof sucke not verie egerlie, should be chased awaie, other that are emptie and fellie an hungred, should light in their places, and sucke out the residue of my bloud farre more to my greeuance than these, which now being satisfied doo not much annoie me.

Holinshead, *Chronicles of Scotland*

to fox To steal or cheat. Brewer's *Dictionary of Phrase and Fable* (1988).

fly a. A familiar demon. b. A spy. (F. *mouche*) *The Shorter Oxford English Dictionary* (1956).

fly *n.* A policeman. U.K. underworld use 1857.

fly cop A sharp police officer, well-informed, streetwise, usually a detective. Underworld use 1859. J.R. Nash, *Dictionary of Crime* (London, 1993).

fly-blown Suspected of venereal disease, low: from ca. 1885.

fly-cop A clever detective: U.S. >, by 1889.

fly-dame harlot 1888. E. Partridge, *The Penguin Dictionary of Historical Slang* (1972).

CONTENTS

LIST OF ILLUSTRATIONS

Every effort has been made to trace and contact copyright holders. The publishers will be pleased to correct any mistakes or omissions in future editions.

LIST OF MAPS

WHO'S WHO IN THE ATLANTIC UNDERWORLD: SOME ALIASES AND NICKNAMES

A

Abrahams, Katia — real name of prostitute, also known as 'Gertie Gordon'; controlled by Joseph Silver in Cape Town 1905 and German South West Africa, 1905–6. Sometimes 'Gertie Abrahams'.

Alford, Annie — one of several aliases adopted by Hannah Vygenbaum, prostitute and bigamous wife of Joseph Silver, 1902.

Anker, Joseph — pimp, informer and rapist, reputedly a cousin of Joseph Silver's in London, 1895–98 and Cape Town, 1902–5.

B

Bach, George — alias of Georges Hayum, Cape Town, 1902

Beck, Adolf — Norwegian born British criminal active on London's South Bank in mid-1890s and later a beneficiary of a case of 'mistaken identity' and given a free pardon. Beck's case cited by Joseph Silver, 1906–07.

Bernstein, Hymie/ Hyman — 'grocer' to the American Club and pimp who gave evidence against Joseph Silver in Johannesburg, 1899 and Cape Town, 1905.

Bertha, Mathilda — alias of Bertha Hermann, ex New York City, Johannesburg, 1898.

Blatt, Mrs S. — trade name of Sarah Rosenblatt.

Bloem/Bloom, 'Annie',   aliases adopted by Hannah Vygenbaum in
    or 'Lena'   Bloemfontein and Cape Town.
'Booter'   Moritz Kleinberg, store-breaker, London
                      and Antwerp.
Brietstein, Haskel   *see* Goldberg, Adolph.
Budner, Salus   brother-in-law of Haskel Brietstein; *see also*
                      Gold, Joe.

C

Corney, Ernest   alias of Ernest Korne, Johannesburg, 1898.
Cosman, J.   alias used by Jack Lis/Silver, Santiago, 1912.

D

Davis, Dave/David   *see* Krakower, David.

E

Elgiman(n), Joe   alias assumed by Silver, in London,
                      1895–98 and later also used in
                      Johannesburg, 1898.

F

Fineberg, Annie   alias of Regina Weinberg, prostitute and
                      long-time consort of Jack Lis/Silver *c.*
                      1895–1906, Bloemfontein, Johannesburg
                      and Swakopmund/Windhoek.

Fierstein, Beile   cousin of Joseph Silver's, married to Leon
   (originally probably   Fierstein. The couple appear to have
   Beilke)   entered Cape Town in 1898, as Mr and
                      Mrs Max Schoffer. Also active in London
                      and Port Elizabeth.

G

Gold, Joe   alias of Salus Budner adopted in
                      Johannesburg, 1898.
Goldberg, Adolph   assumed name of Haskel Brietstein,
                      chronically unsuccessful actor and burglar
                      and Joseph Silver's closest friend in London
                      in 1887–89 and in New York City in
                      1891–95.

Goldstein, Solomon   Russo-Polish pimp, ex Buenos Aires, active
                          in Cape Town, 1900–05 and Buenos Aires,
                          1910.
Gordon, Gertie   trade name of 'Katia' Abrahams, ex East
                          End, London, also of Cape Town,
                          Swakopmund and Windhoek.
Grunbaum, Charles   probable alias of Joseph Silver used in the
                          Low Countries, 1909–10.

H

Haberberg, Sarah   maiden name of Mrs Leibus Cohen.
Harris, Max   Russian brothel-keeper, counterfeiter, pimp
                          and professional gambler, Johannesburg in
                          1898 and in Cape Town, 1900–6.
Hayum, Georges   Parisian-based pimp, thief and white slave
                          trafficker, known by various names in Cape
                          Town, 1902.
Hermann, Bertha   real name of notorious New York madame
                          who, in Johannesburg in 1898, went under
                          the name Mathilda Bertha.
Hirschberg, James   Far Eastern spy, pimp and police informer,
                          Bloemfontein and Johannesburg, 1902.
Hirschberg, William   brother of James H. and business partner
                          of Joseph Silver in Bloemfontein.
'Hirsch Japanese'   nickname of James Hirschberg, Far Eastern
                          spy, pimp and police informer,
                          Bloemfontein and Johannesburg, 1902.

J

Jacobs, Charles   corrupt New York City detective-
                          policeman, 1891–95.
Jacobs, Max   alias 'Scotch Jack', pawnbroker from New
                          York's Lower East Side, in 1900 of
                          Kimberley; later also known as 'Martin
                          Johnson' in Bloemfontein.
Jankelowitz   alias of Hyman Sawicki, German South
                          West Africa.
Johnson, Martin   alias of Max Jacobs.
Josephs, Lizzie   see Laskin, Rachel.

K

Kaplan, Morris   Yiddish translator and American Club
                          'mole' in Johannesburg Public Prosecutors
                          office, 1898–99; later provided evidence for
                          the state in a case against Joseph Silver,
                          Cape Town, 1905.

Kepler, Jacob   probable alias of Jack Lis/Silver upon
                          entering Cape Town in June, 1898.

Korne, Ernest   chemist-gangster associate of Silver's in
                          Johannesburg, 1898.

Krakower, David   Russo-Polish, ex-New York City pimp, real
                          name of 'David Davis', one of Silver's
                          adversaries in Johannesburg, 1898.

Kramer, J.   alias used by Silver, in London, 1895–98.

L

Laskin, Rachel   real name of 'Lizzie Josephs'/ 'Lizzie Silver',
                          intercepted, raped and corrupted by Joseph
                          Silver, London, 1897–98.

Le Cuirassier, Georges   alias of Georges Hayum, Parisian pimp and
                          white slave trafficker in Cape Town 1902;
                          also known as 'George Bach', 'Dacheux' or
                          'Levasser'.

Lees, Joachim   alias of Jack Lis/Silver's, Kimberley, 1900.

Leiss, John   name under which Silver was prosecuted in
                          New York City in Oct., 1891.

Lis, Bertha   name of Joseph Silver's daughter, born
                          London 1888; also used as her married
                          name after she became the wife of his half-
                          brother, Jack Lis/Silver.

Lis, Joseph   real name of Joseph Silver, born Kielce,
                          1868.

Lis, Jacob, 'Jack'   maternal half-brother of Joseph Lis, born
                          Kielce, 1873.

Liss, Joe   alias used by Silver in London, 1895–98.

Ludwig   alias used by Joseph Silver in
                          Johannesburg, 1898.

Lys, Joseph   alias allegedly used by Joseph Silver in the
                          Low Countries, 1909–10.

M

Mande, Michael, usually 'Max'	pickpocket, formerly of New York City, pimp and storekeeper, Swakopmund, 1905.

R

Ramer, Abraham	small time Pittsburgh crook; also an alias used by Joseph Silver in London, 1895, and the Low Countries, 1909–10.
Roland, Jacob	alias used by Jack Lis/Silver when travelling to the United States with his brother, Joseph, in 1914.
Rosenblatt, Sarah	brothel-keeper and prostitute, associate of Joseph Silver's first in Bloemfontein and later in Cape Town, 1902–5.

S

Sawicki, Hyman	Polish pimp operating in German South West Africa, 1905, more usually known as Jankelowitz.
Schmidt, Joseph	alias used by Joseph Silver in Johannesburg, 1898, and the name under which he was reported to the Russian Foreign Minister, Count Muraviev, in 1899.
'Scotch Jack'	alias of Max Jacobs, ex New York City, 1890s.
Silver, Annie	alias of Hannah Vygenbaum, bigamous wife of Joseph Silver, Bloemfontein, 1902.
Silver, Bertha	name assumed by the illegitimate daughter of Joseph Lis/Silver, born London, 1888.
Silver, Charlie	alias of Joseph Silver, Kimberley, 1900.
Silver, Jack	alias occasionally used by Jacob Lis.
Silver, Joe	name assumed by Joseph Lis, New York City, 1891.
Silvermann, Maurice	alias used by Jack Lis, in London, c. 1895–98.
Skratz, Felix	alias used by Joseph Silver, Europe, 1917.
Smith, Jack/Jacob	alias of Jack Lis/Silver used in Johannesburg, 1898, while his half-brother, Joseph was using name 'James Smith'.

Smith, James   alias used by Joseph Silver, London,
                            1895–98. Also the assumed name of an
                            unknown Russo-Polish immigrant in the
                            South African Republic (ZAR), 1895.

T

Taubentracht, Abraham   reputed alias of Joseph Silver used in the
                            Low Countries, 1909–10.

V

Vygenbaum, Hannah   real name of Annie Alford/Bloom/Bloem,
                            one-time partner of 'Scotch Jack'
                            Jacobs/Johnson and bigamous wife of
                            Joseph Silver, Simonstown, 1902.

W

Wallerstein, Sam   actor and pimp, Johannesburg, 1897–98;
                            real name Saul.
Weinberg, Regina   prostitute and long-time consort of Jack
                            Lis/Silver.
Witkofsky/Wilkowski   Ze'ev Wulf Witkofsy/Wilkowski, sometimes
                            Wilf or Wolf. Close friend of Joseph Silver
                            in Johannesburg, 1898–99, and Cape
                            Town, 1900–1905.

Lis Family Tree

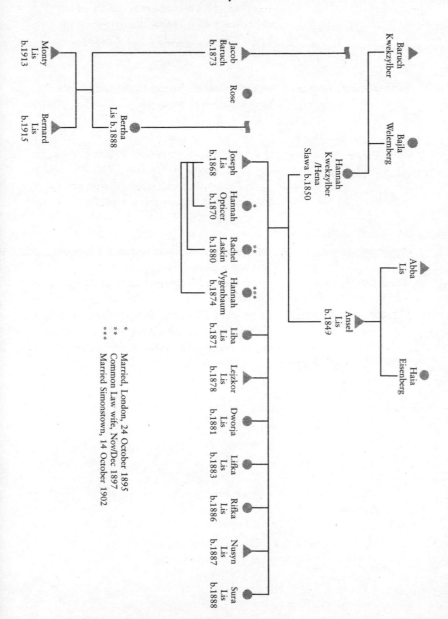

* Married, London, 24 October 1895
** Common Law wife, Nov/Dec 1897
*** Married Simonstown, 14 October 1902

INTRODUCTION

How came they here? What burst of Christian hate, What
persecution, merciless and blind, Drove o'er the sea – that
desert desolate – These Ishmaels and Hagars of mankind?

Longfellow, 'The Jewish Cemetery at Newport'

Potchefstroom, South Africa
1945

SUMMER and winter are writ large; they make bold statements and leave
little doubt as to character. So sharp are their imprints on the consciousness of humans that, in many pre-literate cultures, the life-span of men
and women are measured in summers. Autumn and spring, by contrast,
are more tentative in nature. The shorter seasons are less predictable and
happier posing questions than providing answers. In South Africa, the
fairest days in creation are coaxed out of the highveld sky in October
and March each year. The sun, normally uncompromisingly harsh, blinks
briefly and angled rays scribble shadows amidst pleasant temperatures.

At Witrand – White Ridge – Hospital in Potchefstroom, a small town
seventy miles west of Johannesburg serving as the administrative,
commercial and educational centre of a farming community, first light,
on the last day of March 1945, was imperceptibly slower in arriving
than it had been four weeks earlier. At 6.30 a.m. several African cleaners
appeared at the storeroom, opened the doors and dragged out a bunch
of protesting brooms, buckets and mops. The clanking and cluttering

that followed was ignored by purposeful, white male orderlies making their way around the low wooden veranda of an impressive corrugated-iron structure that housed the wards ranged opposite the store. A jangling of keys announced the unlocking of a large metal door set between a pair of barred windows. There were bars everywhere.

The ruffled roof on the main building had been painted a distinctive dark green by the Public Works Department. A few minutes later an orderly emerged from the unlocked door and scurried away towards the administrative section. On his way back, he fell into step behind a doctor. The District Surgeon entered the ward where, forewarned by the superintendent, he found the corpse of a female patient. He checked for vital signs and, satisfied that she had passed away within the hour, hoisted a clipboard. With the assistance of the orderly, he completed the chillingly direct 'Form of Information of a Death' and a 'Medical Certificate of the Cause of a Death', issued in terms of Act 17 of 1923. The whole exercise took only minutes. Little was known about the sixty-nine-year-old woman.

'Lizzie Silver' had been an inmate ever since the institution, an offshoot of that same Act of 1923, had opened its doors in 1924. Between her admission on transfer from the Cape Province and her death that morning – twenty-one years – no item of biographical significance had been added to her file. It was stated that she was born in Poland, in 1876, but her maiden name was unknown and had been irretrievable. It was as if she wanted no one to know who she had once been; as if some terrible shame clung to her past. It was said that she had been married when admitted to a mental hospital in Cape Town but, since then, there had been no word of her husband. She had suffered from dementia, perhaps aggravated by venereal disease contracted at an early age and had, for some years, been considered 'senile'. Paradoxically, her physical condition remained fairly robust until just before her death when she 'collapsed suddenly'. But her body had been an empty cage for decades. Her mind, personality, perhaps even her soul, had gone by the age of twenty-five. On the day when she was first admitted, in 1901, she was reported to be 'suffering from an attack of mania, excited, incoherent, very restless' and 'not properly conscious of her surroundings'.

Uncertain as to her religion, the District Surgeon suggested that the body be sent to the cemetery for burial at the state's expense as that of a pauper-inmate. A few African assistants, duly summoned, removed the corpse to a makeshift morgue at the far side of the hospital where it lay for some hours. It is difficult to know what happened next but, in most societies, the living are uncomfortable with the idea of putting a body to rest without it first having been reconciled with the soul. For the faithful, no cage is empty; the farewell song of the smallest bird warrants an audience. A few hours later a phone call was made and somebody in town was told of her death. In late afternoon a panel van bounced over the gravel strip leading to the mortuary. The body was removed and driven downtown where an undertaker placed it in a plain wooden coffin.

The next day, amidst the quiet of an autumn afternoon and a mound of freshly dug soil, an elderly Jew intoned a prayer, pleading comfort for the deceased 'who has been gathered unto her people'. The coffin was lowered into grave 140 in the 'Hebrew Section' and men drawn from the communal burial association, the Chevra Kadisha, returned the clods of earth to where Hashem had first placed them. And there, unmarked by plate or stone, half a world from Poland, stood her unadorned grave. The ceremony, like the life around which it had rotated, had been pared to the bone. What else could the man or any of his helpers say? He and the faithful knew as little about the dead woman as did the staff at Witrand.

Her real name was most certainly not Lizzie Silver. Although she had been born in a Polish city, or perhaps a shtetl, it was more likely to have been in 1880 than 1876. She had never married Silver and her maiden name was Rachel Laskin. Like millions of Jews who fled the pogroms of the Russian empire after the assassination of Tsar Alexander II in 1881, she had been spawned in a cohort driven to find the sea and reach for the shores of the New World. But not every emigrant had the resources or stamina to cross the Atlantic in a single effort. Many stopped off in the Old World to gather strength and earn the pittance that would buy them a steerage passage to freedom and opportunity.

Rachel Laskin, aged seventeen, arrived in London in 1897 looking for that ethnic redoubt that could sustain her until she was ready to move on. Its impoverished East End was already home to 30,000 vulnerable Russian and Polish Jews. Like thousands before her, Rachel was destined for the rag trade and became a 'buttonhole-maker'. But sweated labour in the ghetto did nothing for her language skills or purse. She left, found a new position as a domestic servant and moved into a common lodging house.

Most of Whitechapel's dosshouses, notoriously squalid, were in little better shape in 1897 than they had been almost ten years earlier when 'Jack the Ripper' had stalked the streets. They housed thousands of casual workers, employed seasonally, along with those fortunate enough to have obtained more regular employment on breadline wages. The same sordid nightly and weekly rentals attracted hundreds of burglars, thieves, pimps and prostitutes. Lodging houses, gigantic social barometers, charted the fortunes of young women that rose and fell with almost the same predictability as the tide in the nearby Thames. 'White-slave' traffickers constantly monitored them for recruits who could be enticed, or coerced, into a life of prostitution before being exported to burgeoning cities spread across the wider Atlantic world.

No ambitious young woman entered a lodging house without dreaming of how, and when, she would extricate herself. Rachel Laskin was no exception. In late November 1897, a fellow lodger introduced her to a well-dressed young 'draper' newly returned from America who lived in a hired room at St Mark's, Aldgate. He, in turn, introduced her to his cousin, also a partially assimilated Jew, at least as well dressed, who spoke English with the American accent of a New York 'Bowery Boy'. He was, it was said, the proprietor of a hotel in Stamford Street, near Waterloo station, on the South Bank.

He was good-looking, twenty-nine years old, and apparently quite smitten by her. In a few heady weeks she was courted assiduously and responded cautiously, but positively. She was treated to fine meals, taken to the Yiddish theatres where she was comfortable amongst her *landsleit*, countrymen and women, and given small items of tasteful, albeit inexpensive, jewellery. Her beau did not want for cash, and the hotel business appeared to be thriving. There was much talk of Jewish hardship back in the Old Country, and of prospects opening up all around the Atlantic world for adventurous young couples. He apparently knew a great deal about such matters and was in contact with many businessmen in Argentina, Brazil, the United States and South Africa. The romance blossomed and, on a day in December, he suggested that she should meet his relatives – more cousins and a brother who were all in the family business on the South Bank.

They met one chilly afternoon when her services were not in demand at the house where she worked, crossed Blackfriars Bridge and walked towards Waterloo. The American Hotel did not have a pleasing aspect. It was not so much a hotel as a set of interconnected rooms on two floors of a house near a busy thoroughfare leading to the station. Rachel entered the murky warmth of the reception area and was reassured when introduced to a friendly looking, middle-aged woman; a cousin. Later his brother and other relatives joined them for a meal that spilt over into the early hours. The female cousin prevailed upon her to stay the night and she was shown to a room.

She slept undisturbed but in the morning was awakened by the sound of the door to her room being opened by her suitor. He was brutal, clinical, utterly mechanical. With the hotel strangely silent – as if it had been purposefully emptied – and the tempo of the morning traffic rising in the street outside, he assaulted and then raped her. He left, removing what few personal items she had brought with her and locking the door behind him. Unmoved, he kept her there, literally under lock and key, for two weeks.

For fourteen days and nights she was never out of sight or sound. He reappeared at unpredictable times, often wearing different, deliberately confusing emotional masks, to repeat savage psycho-sexual offences in circumstances he alone shaped. She was sucked into a vortex of conflicting emotions and thoughts until it became impossible to distinguish between ambition and despair, dignity and disintegration, good and evil, or love and lust. She was made to beg for the smallest of favours. By the time he finished with her she was a changed person, a different woman, utterly slave-like. He gave her a new name with a built-in twist so that it reflected her new status as a commodity belonging to a beast-man. She was 'Lizzie Josephs'. It was one of the cousins who suggested that if she wanted food, drink or clothing sufficiently badly enough she would venture into Stamford Street, bring back a client and earn it. And, when she eventually did so, her assailant was always there, always watching. When the wintry weather held up briefly he would slouch against a wall, watching. When it rained he would take up a position at a window and watch her. And when she brought in men off the street for hasty couplings he was there watching, forever watching.

Even in Victorian London, where the twin sisters of need and sexual service lurked on every corner near a railway station, 'Lizzie' came across as unusually confused and fear-stricken. In a soulless world it would be nice to think that it was a sensitive co-religionist who drew her plight to the attention of the Jewish Association for the Protection of Girls and Women. That is a possibility. But the information was more likely to have been fed to the JAPGW by rival gangsters located in the same street as the American Hotel. In the underworld of organised prostitution and 'white slavery' professional jealousies and treachery lived cheek by jowl. Just months before the surgical excision of her psychological innards, her rapist had stabbed a neighbouring pimp so badly that the police were summoned and charges laid. A campaign of bribery and violence mounted by the cousins and other gang members ensured that the plaintiff fled to France before the charges were brought to court.

On this occasion, he was less fortunate. In February 1898, he, along with other members of the family, appeared in the Old Bailey charged with rape and 'conspiring together to procure Rachel Laskin to become a common prostitute'. However, he, his brother, cousins and hangers-on, had sufficient resources to retain two of the City's finest barristers. Six weeks later, on technical grounds, they were found not guilty and acquitted. Having exhausted their war chest, they decided to relocate their operations and embark for fairer economic climes. On 8 June 1898, along with several prostitutes, they departed for Southampton and boarded the Shaw Savill liner, SS *Ionic*, bound for New Zealand via a booming southern Africa.

By chance, that very day, the secretary to the JAPGW learned of yet another case of trafficking and, accompanied by an officer from Scotland Yard, went to Southampton hoping to rescue so-called 'white slaves' rumoured to be aboard the *Ionic*. They found the liner at her moorings, boarded her and, as expected, came upon a 'large number of traffickers'. Their search led to an alarming, wholly unexpected, discovery. There, amongst other prostitutes bound for South Africa, was the hapless Rachel Laskin; clearly back in the thrall of her nemesis. So well had he succeeded in his aim to turn her into a commodity-object that, immediately after being acquitted in the Old Bailey, he had simply sought her out and reappropriated her as his property. Astounded by this turn of events, the secretary made an unsuccessful attempt to persuade Rachel and others to break free from the clutches of their masters. Scorned, they disembarked to raucous cheering, hooting and taunts from the pimps lining the upper deck. 'Sad to relate', the secretary noted in his diary that night, 'this very girl who had but a few weeks before prosecuted him for having ruined her was now going with him to her final destruction'. He could not have known how thorough that destruction was to be.

The JAPGW, part of an expanding network of concerned Jews in the Atlantic world intent on combating the evils of organised prostitution and anti-Semitism, dealt with scores of such cases each year. Even so, there was something profoundly distressing about the Laskin case. The secretary somehow knew that she was in the hands of evil incarnate, in the power of a Jekyll and Hyde capable of disposing of her body as readily as he had emptied her inner being. He made a desperate telegraphic effort to try and ensure that body and soul might be reconnected. When the *Ionic* docked in Cape Town two weeks later, before passengers could disembark it was boarded by a rabbi and a senior police officer. Another attempt was made to persuade Rachel and other women to abandon their *souteneurs* but the couples, more cohesive than ever after a period spent together at sea, failed to respond to warnings. Soon all of them boarded a north-bound train.

In Johannesburg, gold mining capital of the world, where men of all colours and cultures outnumbered women by ten to one, he found the perfect environment in which to build an organisation devoted to commercial sex and trafficking in human flesh. In less than six months, he was elected president of the 'American Club' – a 'trade union' of more than fifty pimps, procurers and white-slavers in coded, telegraphic and postal communication with their counterparts in organised crime in Argentina, Brazil, Germany, Great Britain, France, Poland, Russia and the United States. It was the heyday of the transnational trade in prostitutes and, in an expanding western hemisphere, 'commercial vice' assumed proportions akin to modern drug trafficking. A burgeoning supply of steam-driven ocean liners servicing the great migrations underwrote falling passenger fares on most Atlantic routes. Prior to the First World War, international travel seldom necessitated the production of passports and, with Interpol decades away, co-operation between police forces was the exception rather than the rule. The American Club on one occasion filled an order from a downtown brothel for a fifteen-year-old Lithuanian virgin within a matter of weeks.

Cunning and manipulative to the core, he and his lieutenants used assault, blackmail, bribery, corruption and death threats to maintain discipline within their own fractious organisation and extend their power over a ramshackle, venal Johannesburg police force. A consummate police informer, incapable of fidelity, he effectively managed those charged with enforcing public morality and his influence penetrated the Office of the public prosecutor to the point where it became a national scandal. A Prince of Darkness, he could mobilise either public or private forces to enforce his commands.

And her; what of her? A trusted minion, she was elevated to the rank of *madame* and put in charge of two large brothels. A change in status, a chance to appropriate some cash and less overt surveillance saw the final flickering of what had once been an independent personality. Courted by a few pimps resentful of his autocratic rule, she was drawn into a conspiracy to denounce. When her disloyalty and the threat it posed to his position came to his notice, he assaulted her so severely that she never again challenged or questioned his authority. But by then, substantial damage had been done to the gang's operations by his embittered underworld rivals.

In January 1899, a newly appointed independent public prosecutor in Johannesburg, reporting directly to the State Attorney in Pretoria, exploited divisions in the American Club and provisions in revised and expanded legislation to arrest him – and her – on charges of trafficking in white slaves. His detention, and the tensions occasioned by court appearances, further undermined the mind of a woman whose body had by then been invaded by syphilis, Blake's 'invisible worm'.

The young State Attorney, newly graduated from Cambridge and London, sensing that he was dealing with the spectre of a button-hole-maker rather than the substance of a brothel-keeper, declined to prosecute her. He, however, was sentenced to two years' hard labour and banishment from the South African Republic. Convinced that his misfortune was attributable solely to the machinations of others, especially whores, he was confined to the Johannesburg Fort; now the site of South Africa's Constitutional Court. There, three months after his sentence commenced, he, a notorious police informer and pimp attacked and sodomised an African inmate. That offence earned him an additional six months in prison but the gangster's name was immortalised in black South African prison argot. To this very day all informers in South Africa, criminal and political alike, are collectively known as *impimpi* and older males in prison gangs who procure younger men for sexual favours sport a variation on his mother's name, Kwekzylber.

It was perhaps written that he would never serve out his sentence. It was true that, throughout his life, he had consciously sought out frontiers of turbulence in the expanding Atlantic world. But sometimes events simply overtook him, changed his direction and gave new impetus to a career that defied belief, justice and logic alike. With war between Britain and the South African Republic threatening, he was moved from Johannesburg to the very town in which Rachel Laskin was to spend her interminable, dying days. But whereas the iron-clad walls of the Potchefstroom mental hospital held her until she had served out a death sentence, the sandstone walls of the new prison merely shortened his sentence and set him free. In late 1899, in order to tie up as much British manpower as possible away from the theatres of war, republican forces released prison inmates in the hope that the worst of them would make their way to the urban centres of neighbouring southern African colonies and foment further – criminal – trouble. He did not disappoint them. And in the course of so doing, he got another chance to put the finishing touches to Rachel's savage destruction.

Penniless and briefly without access to the women he habitually preyed upon, turned into prostitutes and then loathed as whores, he traced her to the nearby diamond fields where she had been followed by one of his parasitic American Hotel cousins. In Kimberley, benefiting from the presence of troops as well as miners in late 1900, he worked her and two other prostitutes so hard that, within weeks, he accumulated sufficient funds to put down a deposit on a house that would cement his control over its female inmates. With a regular income secured, he used the brothel as the base from which to extend his interests into professional gambling in a city renowned for illicit diamond buying. He consorted with burglars and thieves of the type he had encountered in London, New York City and Pittsburgh long before he met Rachel. He was implicated in the burglary of a jewellery store and the British military authorities used wartime powers to have him deported to Cape Town. She was made to follow.

Recognised in the thriving southern wartime colony of East European gangsters as a dangerously moody, potentially violent man, he found it impossible to re-establish himself at the centre of the temporarily over-supplied trade in commercial sex. He set her up in a small downmarket brothel, some distance from the heart of organised vice in District Six and sought out supplementary sources of income. He became a partner in a nearby café where late-night revellers were sold liquor illicitly before being directed to the brothel. He spent time at the races, gambling professionally, and met several corrupt city policemen. On other days he was employed as a 'banker' in an illegal gaming house in District Six – a role testifying to considerable mental acumen. The gaming house also served as a listening post where he picked up on items of criminal intelligence; he passed these on to members of the Criminal Investigation Department who had been told that he had once been a 'special agent' in the fight against organised crime in New York City, and a 'detective's agent' in London.

So successful an informer was he that – like Vidocq, the French criminal turned police commissioner – he was taken on as a full-time police agent at an impressive salary and sent back to Kimberley with special responsibility for gathering information on illicit diamond buying. Habitual lying and chronic untrustworthiness lost him that position after just three months but, long before that, he had been leading a fraught life. Amazingly, betrayal and deceit seemed to have no effect on him. The pain he inflicted on his victims – male or female – never troubled him. He was entirely without remorse; it was as if he had been born without a centre of moral gravity. The pressures and uncertainties his behaviour occasioned were, however, transmitted directly to Rachel, whom he assaulted and ceaselessly tormented. He exuded alienating and noxious vapours which, like a choking London fog, effectively killed her.

By early May 1901 she was losing what vestige of self-control she still possessed. Confused and disorientated as to time and place she started raving and he was unable to sell her disease-ravaged body to passing sailors. Insane, she had slipped beyond the reach of violence. A mad slave was the ultimate worthless commodity, an object that could bring only ruin to its master. In a perverse way their roles were reversed. Instead of her providing him with an income, she now demanded attention, needing to be cleaned and fed at his expense. Uncertain what to do, he locked her into the house in Keerom Street in inner Cape Town. But a lunatic in a brothel kept him confined to the mockingly named Turnaround Street just as surely as leg-irons had once gripped him in the prison at Sing Sing. The situation was untenable. In the third week of that month he reluctantly summoned a cab and took her to Valkenberg mental hospital, where she was admitted as a patient. In an unguarded moment he let it slip that she was his 'wife'. It was a costly mistake. Years later, the state sued him for the cost of her maintenance. His inability to pay partly shaped his decision, in 1905, to abandon the country. In what had once been a Cape of Slaves, it was the needs of an insane slave – an unconscious act of retribution – that prompted the master to flee the colony.

But pathological misogyny and the need to control, exploit and humiliate white slaves never left the master as he cruised the Atlantic searching out micro-climates capable of sustaining his frightening physical and psychological needs. His travels took him back to America, Britain and Poland, as well as to Argentina, Brazil, Belgium, Chile, France, German South West Africa and Norway. What follows is the search for a nobody, for a boy born Joseph Lis in 1868 and an adolescent raised in a crucible of anti-Semitism at the dawn of the modern world. It is the story of a man and many like him who took to the currents and counter-currents of global migration, using them to explore four continents and a score of countries between 1880 and 1918.

It is a sketch of a person of many names and parts, some of which dated back to the surging sexuality of his early manhood spent in London's East End in the late 1880s. It is the outline of an unfolding personality which, at different moments, assumed the role of arsonist, bank robber, barber, bigamist, brothel-owner, burglar, confidence trickster, detective's agent, gangster, horse trader, hotelier, informer, jewel thief, merchant, pickpocket, pimp, policeman, rapist, restaurateur, safecracker, smuggler, sodomist, special agent, spy, storekeeper, trader, thief, widower, wig-maker and white slave trafficker. It is a picture of a man let loose on, and occasionally goaded into action in an imperfect, marginalising, world. It is the record of a flawed being with a built-in ability to find institutions and processes on the fringes of supposedly normal societies that are tacitly underwritten by decent, ordinary citizens, and it reveals how, just beneath the streets of civilisation everywhere, flow the sewers of avarice, envy, hatred, lust and violence. It's the tale of a man who, as his life unfolded, preferred to call himself Joseph Silver.

I

KIELCE
1868–1884

'As is the nest, so is the bird'

Jules Michelet

IN Poland, once the extended kingdom of Poland–Lithuania, misfortune came in threes. A thriving tolerant state in the sixteenth and seventeenth centuries Poland, like Cinderella, grew to be resented by the sisters Austria, Prussia and Russia. Her fertile open fields and forested plains were the envy of siblings anxious to secure the natural approaches to their own territories. Tsarist Russia, in particular, was wary of un-desirable political messages making their way east from what it saw as an upstart reformist state that lay between it and the two other un-attractive sisters. On three occasions in just over three decades – in 1773, 1793 and 1795 – Moscow, with the approval of Berlin and Vienna, pushed for the division of the greater Polish heartland into smaller, far less threatening, parts.[1]

With continental Europe shaking from a revolution whose epicentre lay in France, 1795 saw the destruction of what, by then, was the Polish republic. Napoleon's rise and defeat occasioned further after-shocks with yet more, albeit smaller, fissions that suited the sisters. But, for all their differing pedigrees, the Grand Duchy of Posen (1815–48), the Republic of Kraków (1815–46) and the Duchy of Warsaw (1807–15) were mere political curiosities incapable of survival in the age of empire. The spectre of old Poland with its enfeebled nobility, however, lived on in the shape of the Congress Kingdom of Poland (1815–64) but it, too, was an ill-fated state. Three European uprisings failed to free Poland from external ambitions, and when Polish nationalists made a direct attempt to shed the Tsarist yoke in 1863, the ostensibly 'independent' Congress Kingdom was simply folded into the Russian empire.

Poland's political aspirations came to rest in the hands of an autocratic Russia: between the will of the Tsar and the whisperings of his largely compliant aristocracy. The masters of St Petersburg foresaw few problems in incorporating the Congress Kingdom into the western reaches of their empire. The Tsarist administration in effect could extend the territory at its disposal for accommodating Russia's most despised ethnic minority. With its dense and expanding Jewish population, Poland was the ideal neighbouring state for the Pale of Settlement – the notorious half-moon-shaped territory stretching from the Baltic in the north to the Black Sea in the south to which Russia had, ever since 1835, confined its own oppressed Jewish population. Although the Congress Kingdom was never formally part of the Pale, it is significant that the Tsarist government permitted Jews to move freely between the territories. This facilitated the migration of impoverished Jews in Lithuania, in the north-west, to the relatively more attractive economic opportunities to be found in the south-eastern and most western reaches of Poland.

Although behind almost all her western rivals in terms of industrial development, the regional dominance and sheer magnitude of Mother Russia's economy encouraged entrepreneurs in the Congress Kingdom to look east. The new linkages spurred Polish industrialisation and urbanisation. Most of the new manufactured goods supplemented more important traditional agricultural products flowing east towards Moscow along a branching network of Polish rail. The domestic economy also benefited from the presence of Russian troops in garrison towns, including several that nestled in the folds of the hilly Świętokrzyskie region of the south-west. By 1890, 70 per cent of the Congress Kingdom's trade was being channelled into the Tsarist domain.[2]

But economic stimulants tend to revive nationalist ambitions, which is why empires in the ascendant crush, rather than encourage, hope or reform. By the mid-nineteenth century, the Romanovs were straying from their tried and tested formula of outright terror and repression and embarking on dangerous experiments with controlled liberalisation. The emancipation of the serfs in Russia, in 1861, sent out precisely the type of signal that Polish ears were likely to misinterpret. Confusion was compounded when, in June 1862, the Jews in Poland also attained full legal equality as part of the broader reforms initiated by the Viceroy, Alexander Wielopolski, in an attempt to stem rising middle-class aspirations. In practice well-meant economic and political realignments had exactly the opposite effect of those intended: they helped to stoke the Polish nationalist uprising of 1863.[3]

On the plains of a phantom Polish state, small streams of economic advance and political progress often burst their banks to further muddy the waters. With three lots of actors – Russians, Poles and Jews – each harbouring suspicions about the motives of the others, the stage was set for a triangulated conflict which, while most starkly evident between 1860 and 1885, persisted until at least the First World War. It was usually the Russian administration or army that sought to play off sections of the Polish nobility, middle classes or peasants against the Jews. For their part, the Poles seldom resisted the temptation to advance their cause or ingratiate themselves with their Tsarist masters at the expense of the Jews. While the rules of the game meant that those with fewest political chips – the Jews – almost always lost, they, too, sought out such advantages as they could in an attempt to optimise the use

of limited space between the Poles and Russians. In essence, these manoeuvrings were but part of longer-standing economic and political clashes that stretched back at least to medieval times. They were set pieces in which the passions of the strongest players were sometimes aroused to violence by the religious beliefs of the most vulnerable contestants. Anti-Judaism and anti-Semitism were exacerbated by the Tsarist administration's affiliation to the Russian Orthodox Church on the one hand and the Polish attachment to Catholicism on the other.

Thrice cursed, Russian-Poland – as the Congress Kingdom was known in the latter half of the nineteenth century – was a country where nothing was quite as it seemed. Neither Russia nor Poland, it was not so much a state as a contested place, a space where centrifugal political forces were held in check only by the proximity of powerful neighbours. In truth, economic and social instability and volatility were features of the entire region stretching from the Baltic to the Carpathians. Even the ancient folds of the Holy Cross mountains in the remote central-south area of Świętokrzyskie were underlain by dangerous fluidities. Nowhere was the fickleness of everyday life more apparent than in the small town of Kielce, half-way between Warsaw and Kraków.

It is uncertain how Kielce – pronounced 'kilts' – acquired its name but explanations abound. Some trace its roots indirectly, back to bee-keepers and hunters who frequented its hills over nine hundred years ago. It is also claimed that the name derives from the term for a peasant hut, or from the word for 'tusk' associated with the wild boar that roamed the forests of Świętokrzyskie. Others are taken with the idea that the name came from Celts who passed through the woodlands during their earliest migrations. But, whatever the etymology, it is clear that by the tenth century, Kielce had attracted the attention of clerics who dedicated a church there to St Wojiech. The Bishops of Kraków, who owned the land, deepened ecclesiastical roots by authorising the building of new fortifications and other churches along the banks of the River Silnica between the eleventh and thirteenth centuries. A regular market and occasional trade fairs helped sketch out Kielce's outline in a rural economy dominated by Polish peasants and noblemen but, with its bishops, churches and crosses, it was clearly also an outpost of the Holy Roman Empire.[4]

Kielce's feudal roots, along with a conservatism and introversion drawing sustenance from agriculture and the Church, made for slow growth. In the fifteenth century, the discovery of copper, iron and lead deposits helped diversify the economy and attracted some foreign artisans, but small mining and manufacturing enterprises did little to change the town's clerical character. In essence Kielce evolved as a market town which, in time, was served by even smaller satellite *shtetlekh* and villages, each of which built its reputation on the specialist production and marketing of fruit, grain, timber, poultry and livestock.

The Napoleonic upheavals, nineteenth-century reforms and the first twinges of industrialisation roused Kielce from a deep rural slumber. Having looked south towards Austria and clerical Kraków for hundreds of years, it was then incorporated into the short-lived Duchy of Warsaw in 1809, and forced to look north. Eight years later, it and the Duchy were swallowed by the Congress Kingdom and made to cast their eyes farther afield, to Russia and the east where their Tsarist ruler sat. Still spinning from sudden political changes, the town had to cope with attendant economic and social shifts. Whereas in the past most changes had derived from slow-moving ecclesiastical sources, they now came from the secular centre of St Petersburg, mediated through a weak, nominally 'independent', state in Warsaw. Not all the new developments met with the approval of the Polish nobility, the *szlachta*, or a peasantry rooted in Catholic beliefs and feudalism.

In 1816, the state underwrote the cost of a college which, for some time, provided the sons of the Polish nobility with academic as well as specialist instruction in mining. A later, longer-lived, more successful high school educated the sons of notables for most of the nineteenth century. Jewish artisans, merchants, traders and pedlars fleeing the viciously competitive and over-traded markets of the north-east and the Pale moved south and west towards the Świętokrzyskie, shoe-horning themselves into the villages surrounding Kielce in the hope of gaining access to the growing market town. These mid-century developments were boosted when, after the uprising in January 1863, the Russians stationed the 28th Polock Rifle Regiment, comprising 2,500 men, at Kielce. Yet more troops arrived when, in 1874, the Tsarist administration – set on a programme of Russification to counter Polish nationalism – stationed the 14th Division of the Russian Cavalry, including a contingent of the feared Don Cossacks, in the small regional centre.

In 1867, the governorship of Radom in which the town had been located since Duchy days, was divided into two and Kielce became the capital of a new and fully fledged province bearing the same name as the town. This state-driven initiative saw the building of several major roads but even they were eclipsed when, in 1884–85, a railroad linking the coal mines of Upper Silesia in the south-west to Deblin in the north-east was routed through the provincial capital. It was the railway that did more than any other development to bring on the first, very modest birth pangs, of industrial Kielce.[5]

In 1870 Kielce, although still clerical, rural and Polish, had 8,000 permanent residents. It was starting to provide a regional economic focus. It boasted an expanding market for agricultural produce, a growing commercial sector and several factories serving the building industry. But, as always, progress was Janus-faced and the town already had a darker side to it. A garrison town, its distillery, breweries, a hotel, a theatre and scores of cheap retail outlets gave Russian troops and Polish peasants alike access to unlimited quantities of liquor and several women of easy virtue. But, blemishes aside, Kielce was becoming a hub which the Church, the Polish nobility and trading classes had, for many centuries, guarded against invasion by their most able and feared commercial rivals – the Jews.[6]

With its clerical origins, Kielce was poorly disposed to those drawn from other faiths. Jews were particularly unwelcome. In 1360, the town's municipal charter made explicit *de non tolerandis Judaeis*, and for a section of the poorest Poles that exclusionary clause embodied a civic and religious principle worthy of upholding for 500 years. On the very day Poland regained its independence, in 1918, the town experienced a pogrom and, more alarmingly still, it witnessed yet another, in 1946 – months after the Holocaust and the end of the Second World War. Ancient, deeply-rooted anti-Semitic prejudice, arguably even more evident and virulent in other parts of Poland and Russia, failed to detract from the town's appeal to increasingly desperate Jewish tradesmen.

The Church and the Polish shopkeepers it served resisted such incursions but, even when Kielce fell under Austrian rule, they were not always successful. In 1761 the Bishop of Kraków had issued a decree expelling a few resident Jews, but they either returned or were soon replaced by others. When Kielce was incorporated into the Duchy of Warsaw and later still into the Congress Kingdom, it became more difficult for clerical wishes to prevail. By 1842 there were thirty-eight Jewish families living in the town. Anti-Semitic feelings boiled over and high school pupils assaulted and harassed Jewish storekeepers until the principal had one in four of the offenders flogged. The Polish merchants, undeterred, returned to the fray and in 1843 persuaded the Mayor to issue an expulsion order which rid the town of its resident Jews. But by 1853 several Jewish tradesmen had eased their way back in and they were soon supplemented by a number of Crimean veterans and co-religionists whom the Russians allowed to settle in Kielce as a reward for Tsarist loyalties. But, for most Jews, the turning point came ten years later, after the political reforms of Count Wielopolski. In 1864, for the first time in history, Jews had a formal, legal, right to reside in the town; by 1897, one in four of Kielce's citizens – some 6,400 inhabitants – were Jewish.[7]

Who exactly were these people that so frightened the Polish merchants and priests of a modest provincial centre? On closer examination 'the Jews', like most of humanity, constituted a diverse grouping. True, when defined only in religious terms they were all 'Jews', but even that description concealed as much as it revealed. Over the centuries East European Judaism had assumed several guises. The once prosperous northern economy of the Lithuanian heartland had given rise to an Orthodox, cerebral and scholarly rabbinical tradition that many saw as a cold and aloof form of Judaism – a Jewishness of the head. This contrasted with the celebratory, quasi-mystical, visceral and warm Jewishness of the heart in the south, which had developed in the courts of the Hasidic rebbes in the Ukraine in the eighteenth century and then spread west to engulf most of Poland. In practice, by 1850 these two traditions had rubbed off on each other to mutual advantage but, around Kielce, most Jewish worship still had powerful Hasidic overtones of compassion, forgiveness and tolerance.

Even so, not all Jews approved of Hasidism, and its conservative opponents – the *mitnaggedim* – continued to wield influence within the *shul* and community. The mystical elements of Hasidism, deriving from the kabbala, were scorned by the *maskilim* – progressive children of the enlightenment, the *haskalah* whose roots lay in eighteenth-century Berlin. This opening of intellectual space, the sense of new possibilities arising from an expanding world, was also evident in Jewish political life during the closing decades of the nineteenth century. *Bundists* – trade unionists – along with nationalists, socialists and Zionists, offered competing or complementary ideologies that appealed in differing measures to Kielce's Jews on the basis of age, gender and, of course, occupation.[8]

Varying traditions made it difficult, other than for mischievous purposes, to see 'the Jews' as a homogeneous mass of humanity. Jews were aware of these distinctions and knew they had consequences that were neither theoretical nor trivial. Differences made for real and painful choices and especially so in moments of crisis, as in the uprisings of 1863 or the First World War. In 1863, the Crimean veterans who had settled in Kielce and enjoyed close economic ties to the Russian army as contractors sided with General Zinger's Tsarist forces. But most Jews, including one who was executed, sided with Polish nationalists and supported rebels with cash, equipment or food. Jews were seldom just 'Jews', they were also 'Polish Jews' or 'Russian Jews' and between those easy distinctions there often lay a world of difference.[9]

Within the multi-faceted inner domain of Jews living in a contested city locked into a ghostly state overseen by a distant imperial master, there was one section of the community seldom openly spoken about – the criminal. All societies undergoing the birth pangs of industrialisation and the wrenching that accompanies the shift from feudalism to capitalism shed groups of people who are difficult to reabsorb into the emerging order. If this was true for much of central and eastern Europe after the sixteenth century, then it is even more true for the nineteenth century Pale and Congress Kingdom where millions of Jews were consciously subjected to additional religious and political persecution.

Not all marginalised or oppressed Jews in Russia's vast rural domains either could or would, despite sustained intra-communal efforts, be reaccommodated in its cities, towns and villages. In the sometimes de-centred universe of the Tsarist empire where it was occasionally difficult to detect an unambiguous and lasting source of legitimate power, the micro-world was characterised by a bewildering array of moral and political contingencies replete with double standards. Why on earth should there not be a minority of Jews – East Europeans who had been socialised in the very heartland of anti-Semitism – who would turn to shady, questionable, practices and, beyond that, to crime?

Jewish criminal associations can be traced as far back as the written record extends but attracted attention in western Europe in the seventeenth century partly because they were expanding their specialised underworld argot. Whereas almost all law-abiding Jews used Yiddish, a richly endowed medieval German dialect, for everyday interactions, and restricted the use of Hebrew largely to prayers and the synagogue, some Jewish criminals resorted to a 'secret tongue' for professional communication. *Mauscheln*, in both written and oral form, drew on Hebrew and other terminology to develop a distinctive syntax supplemented by codes, gestures and oaths. An integral part of an undesirable subculture, this opaque language was later linked to the tempting but elusive notion of an archetypical 'East European Jew'. *Mauscheln* may also have contributed, indirectly, to a notion of 'self-hatred' and ethnically specific psychopathologies. Either way, the argot found a home in the Jewish underworld and industrial cities of nineteenth-century Poland in places like Bialystok, Lódz and Warsaw, as well as in some small towns and *shtetlekh*.[10]

The Holy Cross Mountains held its fair share of the burglars, card-sharps, con men, fraudsters, gamblers, horse thieves, hucksters, illegal liquor sellers, robbers, prostitutes, store-breakers and thieves. After the Wielopolski reforms, however, anti-social elements in the Świętokrzyskie found it easier to gravitate to the urban recesses of Kielce. Many such transgressors were the by-products of the underlying processes at work in the rural economy and some were undoubtedly first-generation offenders. But not all felons are the offspring of immaculate conceptions of such impersonal processes.

Some criminal families – a minority within a minority – develop craft traditions consciously passed from father to son and the offspring thrive as long as the environment provides conditions supportive of anti-social activities. Some malefactors are thus born 'good' but are pushed, or socialised, into patterns of deviance by circumstances that lie beyond their control. Beyond that category, however, lies an even more rare grouping on the fringes of what is already a minority within a minority – those who through genetic predisposition are born 'bad' and then inserted into a familial and societal context especially conducive to anti-social activities. For those born into this, the most unfortunate lot of all, criminal tendencies are reinforced three times over: by their genes, by processes of primary socialisation, and by the shortcomings of society.[11]

In the environs of Kielce, during arguably the sixty-five most difficult years Jews had yet experienced in the Congress Kingdom and Russian empire (1850–1914), there were three generations of the family Lis in which it was almost impossible to disaggregate the component parts of the triple curse that beset them. Perhaps the surname – a post-Napoleonic innovation foisted on Ashkenazi Jews by modernising administrations – hinted at cunning and deviousness since, in Slavic tongues the word 'Lis' refers to 'Fox'.

How long the Lis foxes had roamed the Świętokrzyskie is impossible to tell but tax registers reveal traces in the villages of Bodzentyn, Chmielnik, Dzialoscyce and Opatów in the 1840s. The alpha male, grandfather Abba Lis, sniffed around these *shtetlekh* for years but, like many others, set his sights on settling in the town expressly forbidden to Jews. Forced into a peripatetic existence, he restricted his business to daytime excursions into Kielce. One who clearly recalled seeing him there, and remembered him by name, was the novelist, Adolf Dygasinski, who attended high school in the 1850s. Dygasinski and other sons of the Polish gentry sold their schoolbooks and unwanted items of clothing to Lis and another pedlar named Wilk in order to help settle mounting gambling debts.[12]

Morally tinged transactions centring on new or second-hand clothing became part of a secret family legacy. Abba, his oldest son and at least one grandson retained a formal interest in the clothing trade and, despite their poverty, the Lis men were usually fashionably dressed. The last surviving male in the line, Meyer, was the respected owner of a small men's outfitting store in Kilinskiego Street when the Nazis rounded him, his wife and two children up on 22 August 1942 and sent them to Treblinka along with the rest of Kielce's Jews.[13] Any blemishes Abba Lis may have had were later lost in the painful communal memory that slowly settled over the Holocaust trauma. A century later, when the survivors of the Shoah set about collecting such history as could be retrieved from the horrors of Treblinka, the older Lises were remembered only as respected home-owners who 'raised large families, children and grandchildren', including 'artisans, pious Hasidim, merchants, Torah scholars' and 'in later days, also Zionists'.[14]

For reasons that are not difficult to understand, this was a partly sanitised version of the fate of only the more respected members of the clan. Abba Lis did indeed raise a family which, even by the standards of the day, was large but the history of his offspring was far more complex and uncomfortable than that recalled by later chroniclers. In particular, it was one of his sons, a boy born at a time when Abba was frequently away from home on business and the family perhaps least settled in the Świętokrzyskie region, who gave rise to what was to become the most troubled scion of the family.

Ansel Lis, born in Chmielnik in 1849, was raised in the acute poverty that haunted the family for decades. Little is known of his childhood although he may have benefited from some of the domestic advantages accruing to male children in Jewish families.[15] He may also have gained several insights into how his father earned a living. If not his father, then his peers must have instructed him in the mysteries of *Mauscheln* since he appears to have passed on elements of the 'secret language' to his own sons. His bar mitzvah at the age of thirteen was celebrated in the same year as the Wielopolski reforms, 1862. Twelve months later he was amongst the first Jewish families adjusting to life in clerical Kielce.

The father could not have chosen a more difficult moment for the move to the provincial capital. The nationalist uprisings, a heavy-handed response by Tsarist forces and simmering discontent between the Russo-Crimean veterans and the local Jews, saw a fog of suspicion descend over the town. Abba was seldom there to help the family adjust to the new situation. He moved about the countryside visiting Lódz, Piotroków and Warsaw, introducing his son to other pedlars as well as members of the underworld. Increasingly rootless, Ansel learned about the small, lightweight, high-value items prized by hawkers and smugglers – alcohol, matches, cigarettes and tobacco – and served an apprenticeship in doubtful enterprises characterised by movement, risk and uncertainty.[16]

Shortly after the move, Ansel started taking an interest in a precocious young newcomer, Hannah Kwekzylber, whose family hailed from nearby Staszów. The surname, almost certainly derived from quicksilver, hinted at the mineral-rich Świętokrzyskie. It may, however, also have pointed to hawkers who sold the small quantities of mercury used in the treatment of syphilis. The Kwekzylbers probably had some recent connection to Opatów, a small Hasidic town on a private estate known in Yiddish as 'Apt'. Decades later Hannah's oldest son, a habitual dissembler but always obsessed with his mother, said that her maiden name was Apticer. The tax register records that, in 1864, fourteen-year-old Hannah was already earning a living as a 'tobacco merchant' in Kielce. This, too, may be linked to Apt since the Polish owners of Opatów had, in the eighteenth century, allowed the sale of tobacco on the estate to become a Jewish monopoly.[17]

Very early marriages amongst Jews had been the rule in Poland until at least the 1840s but the youngsters, although soon involved in a tempestuous relationship, were prevented from tying the knot by a shortage of cash and precarious family circumstances. They drifted in the shallows of local business and watched as the inflow of Jews added to the town's merchants and storekeepers. Working on wafer-thin profit margins it took time to make economic headway. In 1866, Ansel, aged seventeen and Hannah, aged sixteen, gathered beneath the canopy and broke a glass before Rabbi Gutman in time-honoured fashion.

By summer 1867 Hannah was expecting her first child. The town's rutted tracks were still etched with crusts of angular snow when, on 16 February 1868, the offspring of 'Fox' and 'Quicksilver' slipped into town under the cover of darkness. For those taken with *aggadah*, the Jewish folklore that still held sway over the minds of many in the less well educated reaches of Poland, 1868 was a year of some significance. Mars was in the ascendant and it was believed that 'people who are born under the sign of Mars will have a blood-related occupation, such as a murderer or a surgeon . . .'[18] It was Ansel who named the boy Joseph. Hannah did not mind. A person without pretensions, a *proster mensch*, she referred to her cub in Yiddish as 'Yossele'.

From the state's point of view, the boy arrived at an inconvenient moment. The Russians were transferring provincial administration from Radom to Kielce and, technically, the birth should have been registered in the nearby Jewish settlement of Checiny. But confusion, a reluctance to engage with officialdom, idleness and winter's teeth prevented the father from venturing there. It was only in mid-November that Ansel did anything about the matter. He dragged two friends to the registry in Kielce, where they testified to having witnessed the boy's *bris* or circumcision. The clerk, unimpressed by the trio's inability to communicate in Russian, dismissed them as 'illiterates', but the child was only the third Jewish birth ever recorded in the capital and the event was of some importance for the community. In 1954, Holocaust survivors, unaware of the trajectory of the later life of the child, retrieved the name 'Joseph Lis' and recorded it in their *Yizkor* book with some pride as the third of fifteen Jewish children born in that troubled centre in 1868.[19]

Over the next twenty years, between 1868 and 1888, when Hannah gave birth to her last child, Ansel reported to the registry office on eight more occasions; usually doing so at the last moment. Not all these visits were, as we shall see, joyful or unproblematic. All in all there were nine children in the Lis lair – five girls and four boys. With the exception of one, Rifka (b. 1886) Joseph grew up having no contact whatsoever with his sisters – Liba (b. 1871), Dworja (b. 1881), Lifka (b. 1883) or Sura (b. 1888). Again, with one notable exception, he was equally distant from his male siblings – Jacob Baruch (b. 1873), Lejzkor

(b. 1878) and Nusyn (b. 1887). Joseph was incapable of forming close emotional bonds with anybody apart from his mother. There were others, too, who struggled to form attachments; it was, in several ways, an unusual household.

Ansel and Hannah Lis had a long but not particularly happy marriage. For two decades they lived in acute poverty, with Ansel failing in all the small ventures he started and being harassed constantly by irate creditors who seldom hesitated to take him to court. His promiscuity and underworld exploits attracted the attention of the police, adding to domestic tension, and on one occasion they were plastered over the pages of the newspaper. A few short-lived enterprises, including a small kosher restaurant, revolved around the provision of food and drink. At times he drank heavily, and he associated with women of easy virtue sufficiently frequently and publicly for the local police to brand him 'immoral'.

The youthful Hannah, too, had an adventurous and perhaps even immoral sex life and did not confine her favours to her husband. In 1873 she gave birth to a *mamzer*: a child born of an adulterous relationship. Although the boy, in keeping with local custom, was registered as Ansel's, the child was, in fact, someone else's. The birth of Jacob did nothing to ease a troubled relationship. In 1892 Rabbi Gutman, one in a line of distinguished and tolerant Hasidic teachers, granted the unhappy couple a divorce, a *get*, on the grounds of mutual 'misunderstandings'. The couple were, however, reconciled in 1912 and Hannah continued to contribute to the upkeep of the synagogue.[20]

This scruffy nest, visited by at least one cuckoo, was home to Joseph Lis. Here, stranded between a distant, ineffectual, father and a lively, louche, mother, he became increasingly aware of what it was to be neglected and poor at home, and marginalised and Jewish in the wider community. Predisposed to disturbing traits that became more evident as he approached adolescence and entered early manhood he, too, was victim of a triple curse. Raised by young parents with a weakly developed moral code, he lived in a town filled with the social hostilities of Polish nationalists dominated by Russian imperialists. Nest, branch and tree hosted what was destined to be a raptor.[21]

Like most first-born males, the boy enjoyed privileged emotional access to his mother during his formative years. At that time it was not unusual for boys to sleep with their mothers; in one recorded instance, right up to the age of ritual manhood, thirteen. By contrast,

husbands were 'prohibited by sacred law' from lingering in the beds of
their wives. Joseph appears to have enjoyed a very close, possibly even
exceptionally close physical relationship with his mother and deeply
resented his father. 'There [was] no avoidance between mother and son,
except that intercourse was forbidden.' From his troubled subsequent
career and deviant behaviour towards women we can deduce that he
developed extraordinarily ambivalent feelings – loving the warmth and
proximity of a Yiddisher mama, but hating her increasing remoteness
as she took on rival, intimate male attachments and produced an
expanding brood of children.[22]

Later siblings, no doubt, found it even harder to get any individual
attention from their mother but, arguably, benefited from the presence
of older brothers and sisters. Again it is perhaps significant that, when
confronted with a crisis later in life that necessitated his adopting a
new and more acceptable persona, Hannah's oldest reached for her
maiden name to fashion himself a new identity as 'Joseph Silver'.
Typical of the times, Ansel was fairly 'remote from domestic concerns'.
By 1905, Joseph and Jacob – Hannah's child by her lover – both
claimed, falsely, that their father was 'dead'. In emotional terms, perhaps
he had always been so for them.[23]

If there were idyllic moments in Joseph's early relationship with his
mother they cannot have lasted long. In 1872, when he was four, she
embarked on her extra-marital affair and that same year he was
dispatched to attend *cheder* along with others of his age. Able and
quick-witted, he seems to have had little difficulty in coping with the
diet of reading, writing and rote-learning meted out by the *melamed*.
He attained considerable fluency and literacy and later claimed, quite
plausibly, to have studied, albeit intermittently, to the age of fifteen. As
the oldest child he did get a relatively good start to his education but
it is impossible to know for how long, or with what diligence, he
attended school.

If the forced separation occasioned by having to go to school came
as a shock to Joseph, more adjustments were forced on him just months
later. In 1873, the *mamzer*, Jacob Baruch appeared in the Lis lair. Perhaps
Hannah was seeking to blur the distinctions between her offspring, or
perhaps there were more practical considerations, but she appears to
have neglected the children and pushed the boys towards one another.
Whatever the reason, the consequences were clear. Five years older than
Jacob, Joseph – who had difficulty forming meaningful relationships –

seemed to be genuinely fond of his half-brother. Jacob, who in moves around the Anglophone world came to be known as 'Jack' or 'Jake', grew up idolising his older, if wayward, 'brother'. Lacking family social-isation of the sort usually associated with *shtetl* life, the boys had anything but a classic Jewish boyhood and grew up as strangers to the synagogue and indifferent to most holy days.

Throughout their later travels in the Atlantic world, the boys contrived to keep Hannah's secret, invariably referring to one another as 'brothers'. It was almost as if they had entered into a pact to keep their mother's indiscretion from view. The exact nature of the blood relationship between them was only ever revealed in public on two occasions. Once, when both were firmly established as professional criminals, a rival gangster-cum-informer who must have obtained his information from a source within the family, drew attention to the fact that they were 'stepbrothers'. On the second occasion, in 1912, it was the perfidious Joseph, anxious to put distance between him and his 'brother' in the face of police inquiries, who admitted that Jack was his 'maternal half-brother' rather than a brother.[24]

The boys were inseparable. By the time Jack went to *cheder* they had taken to exploring the fairs, livestock auctions, river byways and dirty back streets of Kielce where 30,000 head of cattle were traded annually. The nearby slaughterhouse, on the bank of the Silnica, was a place of particular fascination. Notorious for its stench and its unsan-itary condition, the abbatoir served Kielce's twenty-three registered butchers and was invariably a filthy but exciting mess. The slaughtering of the cattle and sheep and hoisting of the carcasses high into the air prior to removing the innards were of as much interest to the curious, or the irredeemably callous, as were the enormous vats fired up for reducing the excess fat.[25]

For Jewish youngsters witnessing the *shechitah* – openly or covertly – the slaughter had additional, ritualised, dimensions. The *shochet* would use a fingernail to ensure that the blade of the knife was perfectly sharp and smooth. Before cutting the windpipe and gullet he would make a blessing, and afterwards the internal organs of the animal would be examined 'to see that there were no perforations, signs of disease or lesions on the lungs which would make the animal *terefah*', or impure. Perhaps it is not surprising that, later in life, Joseph could plausibly pass himself off as an established cattle trader, or that two of his closer gangster associates were butchers by trade.[26]

He also took sufficient interest in the resident cavalry to acquire some knowledge of horses and, years later, passed himself off, again fairly successfully, as a horse dealer when some suspected him of arms-smuggling. Jack, in turn, was so taken with soldiering that when he came of age he voluntarily joined the army at a time when the conscription of Jews had eased but remained the subject of resentment in the community. The fact that Jack joined the army and won a medal awarded to him by 'the Tsar' for his shooting prowess spoke more of his own wild ambitions than it did of Jewishness.[27]

Making excursions into the hidden dimensions of everyday urban life, tinged with elements of danger, is a common feature of a provincial boyhood. In the case of the older Lis boys, however, the business failures of the parents, debt and moral indiscretions invited teasing that was met with customary juvenile responses. Both youngsters were unusually aggressive and short-tempered and Joseph, in later life an occasional prize-fighter, carried several small tell-tale facial scars into early manhood. As ill-tempered young adults, neither of the brothers hesitated to use broken bottles, fists, guns or knives when thwarted. Joseph, who took a sandbag to one gangster and stabbed another, routinely threatened women with murder. Jack, unsuccessfully prosecuted on a charge of attempted murder, was the favoured suspect for another, fatal, shooting.

The boys learned to cope with police surveillance early in life. When Joseph was eleven and Jack six, they lived through an encounter which foreshadowed some of their later, not always successful, criminal exploits. In autumn 1879 Ansel Lis, then the proprietor of an unsuccessful clothing store, noted that Herman Edelman of Gawlika's House had advertised the arrival of a large consignment of fur coats in the local gazette.[28] He then masterminded a plan to enter Edelman's premises at night, using false keys, and to have the goods removed by a carefully selected team of professionals. Under cover of darkness, the consignment of coats would then be transported to remote villages, stored in the houses of distant relatives, redistributed and ultimately sold in Warsaw.

The plan was put into action at 3 a.m. on 12 October but things did not go according to plan. The intruders were interrupted while loading the stolen goods and some smaller items were abandoned outside the store before they could set off in the direction of Piotrków. More problems arose while unloading some of the loot at the village of Vistaka. Yet more coats were abandoned and half buried before the thieves fled.

Before they could reach the last of the supposedly safe houses, however, disaster struck. A vigilant Russian policeman stopped them and they were unable to produce the passports required of travelling Jews. They were searched, found to be in possession of furs they could not readily account for, and arrested. By late November all Ansel Lis's out-of-town collaborators were back in Kielce as prisoners awaiting trial.[29]

Lis did not lose his nerve. On 16 October he asked the Chief of Police in Kielce for a passport to travel to Warsaw on business. The request was denied. Undaunted, he fired off an appeal to the new provincial Governor. The argumentative, rights-based tone of his letter is replicated in similar letters later sent by his oldest son to law enforcement agencies all around the Atlantic world:

> On 16 October 1879, I applied to the Chief of the Police in
> Kielce for a passport that I needed if I were to proceed to

Warsaw and purchase goods. The Chief of Police rejected
my application without providing me with a reason. As a
shopkeeper who pays taxes, any delay in obtaining a passport denies me the right to run my business and trade. I have,
therefore, the honour to ask your Excellency to issue instructions that I be granted a passport, or that I be furnished with
the reasons why I am not to be granted one.[30]

The Governor, in keeping with bureaucratic practice, went back down
the chain of command, to the Chief of Police, for an answer. On 27
October, he got a response:

I have the honour to report that I did not issue a passport
to Ansel Lis because he is suspected of being involved in the
robbery that took place at merchant Edelman's on 12 October.
This information was come by in the following manner.

First, when the men who participated in the robbery were
arrested in the settlement of Vistaka in the Blonsk district,
a guard overheard them making arrangements to let Ansel
Lis know that they had been arrested.

Secondly, one of the accused, Efraim Kriger, told Officer
Greczka, in the presence of witnesses, that Ansel Lis had
written a letter to David Dukat, in Warsaw, inviting him to
bring his accomplices to Kielce to commit a robbery at
Edelman's and that the portion of the stolen goods which
they had not had time to remove from the gates at Gawlika's
were for Ansel Lis.

Thirdly, some of the goods were sold in Warsaw and, at
the time when Ansel Lis applied for a passport to go to
Warsaw, not all those now accused had been moved to Kielce
and Ansel Lis could easily have met with them somewhere
along the way. He could then have arranged to go to Warsaw
and hide any remaining traces of the stolen goods.

Fourthly, Ansel Lis has a bad reputation and is regarded
by the police as being untrustworthy and immoral. He has,
on a previous occasion, also been under police surveillance.[31]

The Governor waited for the police to complete their investigations
and the court case that was to follow. In mid-December, when it was

clear that there was insufficient evidence to prosecute Lis, the Governor ordered that Lis be allowed to visit Warsaw.

The publicity attendant on the store-breaking did not go unnoticed amongst local traders and further alienated the pubescent Joseph, who was becoming increasingly contemptuous of the elders in the community. Ansel's business, cash-strapped prior to the break-in, buckled as trading conditions declined and competition increased. The number of Jews in Kielce doubled from just over 1,000 in 1874 to more than 2,500 by 1881. By 1883, the family business was in deep financial trouble and that year creditors confronted Lis with letters of demand on twenty-one occasions. He was effectively bankrupt and the years between 1882 and 1885 were amongst the most miserable imaginable in the Lis household.[32]

Already badly scarred at the age of eleven, Joseph must have found the twenty-four months leading up to his coming of age at least as indelible. His anxieties gave way to the richer fantasy life of early adolescence, but he continued to be subjected to tensions that were difficult, almost impossible, to reconcile. Fragments pieced together from later life suggest that most of his torment derived from the troubled relationship with his mother arising from her sexuality and perceived immorality. Her betrayal and his abandonment, previously sensed intuitively, were thought through more consciously and attributed to women more generally as he listened, read and was prepared for his bar mitzvah in 1881.

Medieval Jewish folklore abounded with tales about the dire consequences of female sexual immorality. We know that some of the stories with dramatic outcomes, such as the tale of Sodom, burnt their way into the lad's consciousness because he later invoked them in the course of his own struggles with laws governing public morals.[33] Importantly, these moral injunctions were reinforced by the Torah and, more especially, in the words of the prophets. Indeed, so explicit, immodest and lurid were the writings of one prophet considered by early rabbis that they deemed parts unsuitable for public consumption and the *Mishnah* proscribed their reading in the synagogue.[34] The study of these passages – about children being sacrificed by promiscuous mothers, the dangers posed by menstrual blood and the need for ritual cleansing as well as the sexual exploits of foreign males with genitals the size of asses who ejaculated like horses into whores – were supposedly restricted to mature males, well versed in the Torah.[35] But the same passages fascinated curious, sexually charged, adolescents, and for Joseph Lis they had an almost eerie personal resonance. They further primed his interest in female genitalia and reproductive organs and permanently shaped his views about the immorality of women, the need to undertake ritual ablutions at *mikvot*, and the dreadful fate that awaited whores.

These warped templates were laid down during the early 1880s, when Ansel was entering the financial wilderness and Jews throughout the Congress Kingdom were being forced to come to terms with outright terror. Just as Ansel's bar mitzvah foreshadowed the nationalist uprisings of 1863, so Joseph's, in 1881, presaged a time of great insecurity. On 1 March 1881, just days after the boy's birthday, Alexander II was assassinated by an activist from *Narodnaia Volia* – 'People's Will' – a revolutionary grouping which, on its fringes, included a Jewish seamstress. The Tsar's death deepened the economic downturn and there were pogroms in Warsaw well into December. In Kielce, a sink of anti-Semitic vapours, Rabbi Gutman led a delegation to Tomasz Kulinski, Bishop of Kielce, who, rising above the moment, instructed priests to preach the virtues of tolerance and love. Miraculously, the Świętokrzyskie region escaped the worst. But outrages elsewhere in the Congress Kingdom and southern Russia turned the trickle of Jewish refugees into a veritable torrent of emigrants. The mid-1880s saw millions of Jews fleeing the greater Russian empire, making their way to the freedom, safety and opportunity of the west.[36]

Could one envisage more difficult times for a babe to become a boy, a child an adolescent, a man a Jew, a Jew a Pole or a Pole a Russian?[37] Everything in the Lis house, in the town, and country spoke of fragmentation and vulnerability. But, over the centuries, Jews had developed ways of ensuring their survival and well-being. These mechanisms and the unofficial office-bearers they spawned assumed greater importance in the wake of the assassination and pogroms. In many *shtetlekh*, towns and cities a 'fixer' or 'intermediary' – a *makher* or a *shadtlan* – used 'tricks' or 'devices', including bribes and presents to initiate processes that would otherwise never have gained bureaucratic momentum, or to halt undesirable actions by hostile outsiders.[38]

These practices fed on, and into, ethnic stereotypes and eased the day-to-day predicament of East European Jewry. Joseph, already disdainful of elders in the community, could not have failed to notice how bribes removed hostility from Russian administrators, officers or policemen. The underlying problem, however, was that while this grammar of survival had one logic for God-fearing Jews in Poland, it had another for anti-social elements abroad. The actions of *makhers* and *shadtlans*, which arose from within the context of understandable if morally questionable roles in everyday *shtetl* life, informed the practices of Jewish criminals who later fanned out to become collaborators, informers and police spies in the criminal underworlds and intelligence systems of the Atlantic world.[39]

Throughout his criminal career, Joseph Lis remained powerfully attracted to roles in which brazenness, duplicity and slyness were the stock in trade, and to occupations where it was often impossible to tell where the morally problematic gave way to the grossly amoral. The best double agents, it is often claimed, engage in short-term cheating, deception and lying in order to make longer-term contributions to supposedly laudable elevated causes. The worst, however, are born with no centre of moral gravity or alternative vision and master the dark arts in clinical fashion for purely personal gain. For those who would rule the world, or control the criminal underworld, the skill lay in knowing the difference between the two types, and it was not always easy.

Even if Joseph was distant from the regular trade in influence or information during his youth – a branch of commerce in which mind and money habitually trumped muscle – he could not have avoided undesirable haunts during the worst of the family's financial difficulties. Ansel and his friends eased the young man's movement into circles where drinking, gambling and whoring were tolerated, if not approved of. Beyond that lay the murky world of outright criminal activity focused on theft, requiring its own measures of stealth and subterfuge; attributes that came easily to most men in the family.

In the thirty-six months between his coming of age and his leaving home when he was not yet sixteen, the young man got to know several older men who, if they were not already established criminals, were in the final stages of their apprenticeship. Some cousins, drawn from kin strewn across Świętokrzyskie, shared his growing dislike of women. Two later became international white slavers and, despite differences in age, were firmly in his thrall. Principal amongst these was Joseph Anker, eight years older than Joseph Lis.[40]

Others who later came to play an important part in Lis's career, like Leibus and Mendel Cohen, had links to the trade in new and second-hand clothing. The 'brothers' Cohen, actually stepbrothers, were originally 'tailors' from Opoczno, west of Radom, but in later life were better known as audacious European safe crackers.[41] Joseph Moscovitz and Moritz Kleinberg, drawn from the same Warsaw underworld that participated in the break-in at Edelman's, later focused on theft and robbery on both sides of the Atlantic.[42]

But it was yet another 'tailor' who became the most important older man in the youngster's life. Haskel Brietstein, later a mentor and partner in modest criminal exploits in London and New York, greatly influenced Joseph during his most impressionable and tempestuous years. Born in 1855 in the western city of Lódz, the so-called 'Manchester of Poland', nearly fifteen years older than Joseph Lis, Brietstein was raised in the shadow of the large textile mills in the nearby *shtetl*-town of Aleksander-Lódzki.

An amoral romantic drifter, Brietstein married at the age of twenty-two, and when the young man first met him, probably around 1884, he was the father of three children to whom he was closely attached. Like most Jews he struggled to make a living in the economic downturn, which delayed his family moving out of his parents-in-law's home. That, and a longing to become an actor in the then rapidly expanding western Yiddish theatre, primed an interest in emigration at a time when many were abandoning Russian-Poland for the New World. Brietstein's fondness of the young, and Joseph Lis's mounting frustration at being confined to Kielce flowed together at an important, possibly crucial, point in their lives.[43]

Joseph Lis spent at least three, probably more, years in Haskel Brietstein's company before he turned twenty-four. During those years, two of which they spent together in prison, they became intimate friends; upon their release, Brietstein's kin in effect became Lis's surrogate family. An odd couple, they cast themselves primarily as professional burglars and store-breakers; but at a time when Brietstein was also trying to break into the theatre under the stage name 'Adolph Goldberg', Lis's patron had other skills to pass on to his young charge. As a professional assumer of identities and roles Brietstein was paid to deceive, to create illusions. He was an actor, a person capable of faking it, of putting on masks, of conjuring up emotions that could persuade an audience of the authenticity of his feelings.[44]

Burglars and store-breakers, men who shunned company as they went about the business of acquiring property, had little need for acting abilities. But the same was not true of agents, informers, procurers, seducers or spies. For the latter art and skill were vital and deception and plausibility often made the difference between success and failure. For anybody born with emotionally stunted responses and socialised into a disregard of the effect his actions might have on others, the ability to assume, to pretend, to simulate, was central to survival. 'Adolph Goldberg' taught his charge far more than he ever realised and who knows what exactly it was that attracted the younger Lis to Brietstein?

As already noted, Joseph's contact with men who later became leading figures in the Atlantic underworld commenced during a time of great hardship in the Lis household. The fact that none appear to have been arrested, investigated or prosecuted for criminal offences prior to emigration, however, suggests that Ansel, his son and their friends avoided getting embroiled in another débâcle of the Edelman variety. Indeed, over the longer term, Ansel did, as the *Yizkor* book suggested, become a rehabilitated member of the Jewish community. But between 1881 and 1885, when life was at its most difficult, the patriarch looked to his oldest son to bring home cash in whatever way was possible.

Unlike some of the Lis boys, Joseph never took a direct interest in the clothing business or in tailoring, although a decade later he claimed to be a draper when, during one of the impulsive acts he was prone to, he stole a roll of satin. But since he, like most Yiddish-speakers, liked punning, it may have been the proximity of the words 'draper' and 'raper' that appealed to him more than a purported interest in fabric and scissors. He looked elsewhere to find his contribution.[45]

Just as the assumed calling of draper left an indirect clue to life back in Kielce, so repeated references in his twenties to his being a 'barber' and, once, a 'wig-maker' point to an earlier association with the hairdressing trade. Unlike Hasidic or Orthodox Jews, whose long beards and distinctive locks signified their status as God-fearing males, Joseph found no need for such displays. A non-believer from an early age and bisexual by at least his twenties, he had no beard and, but for a small moustache, evinced a lifelong preference for being clean-shaven with closely cropped hair. In this, largely by chance, he was like the biblical prophet whose lascivious writings he secretly savoured.[46] He also came of age at a time when, in smaller Polish towns, clean-shaven delinquent adolescents and pimps were easily identifiable and known as *wurljungen*.[47]

If his first exposure to the barbering profession he later adduced as his own was in his home town, or even if it was abroad, it came at an

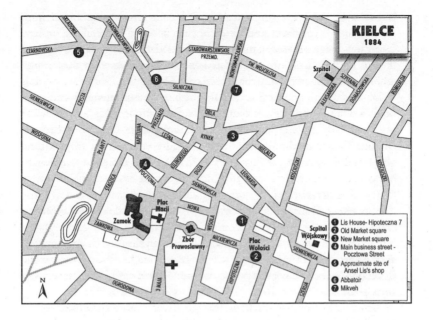

KIELCE
1884

1 Lis House- Hipoteczna 7
2 Old Market square
3 New Market square
4 Main business street -
   Pocztowa Street
5 Approximate site of
   Ansel Lis's shop
6 Abbatoir
7 Mikveh

interesting historical moment. In the latter half of the nineteenth century the guild of barber-surgeons, with its distinctive twirled blue-and-white tubular totem, was only just putting into effect the divorce that would eventually split it into its component parts. In nineteenth-century Russian-Poland, barber-surgeons, or *feldschers*, were trained to use knife and razor to remove minor growths, moles or warts that made the cutting of hair or shaving of beards difficult. But regardless of whether it was in Kielce, London or New York City, barbershops long before – and well after – the turn of the twentieth century were strictly male-only zones deliberately excluding females.[48]

Hairdressing saloons marked out club-like territory, creating space for otherwise illicit discussions and practices that distanced, diminished and objectified women. In Sholem Asch's novel, *Mottke the Thief*, Yankele's barbershop in old Warsaw was the haunt of regular clients as well as pimps. In England and the United States hairdressers, in addition to customary services, often sold alcohol and their premises were used for assignations, betting and the sale of pornography. Yet, despite the heavy air of masculinity that clung to them like the smell of cheap antiseptic, barbershops were also places where men were in close physical contact. Males – sometimes quite young males – groomed and stroked the beards, faces and heads of clients. These movements, undertaken too roughly, were a source of discomfort; performed too lightly, they were likely to be misinterpreted as effeminate. As with the acting, there is no knowing what the adolescent Lis made of this.[49]

Likewise, it is impossible to tell what, if any, difference such legal or illegal labours made to the collective income of the Lis household after 1881. What is clear is that in the midst of their most straitened circumstances, Ansel and his oldest son suddenly received an inexplicable financial reprieve. Whereas in 1883 – the year the railway reached Kielce – Ansel was hounded through the courts by twenty-one creditors, and another seven in 1885, not a single claim was lodged against him in 1884. The year between was wholly anomalous in the financial history of the family; not only was Ansel magically clear of debt, but Joseph found the cash to enable him to bypass the army, acquire a passport and emigrate. On 14 August 1884, with the Congress Kingdom leaking Jewish brains, capital, labour and skills at a rate surpassed only by the ability of a ravenous New World to take it all in, Joseph Lis popped up with the ten Russian silver roubles necessary for the passport that would spirit him away from Poland to England.[50]

In the great global migration that followed on the Tsar's assassination, the poor and the oppressed were drawn overwhelmingly from the ranks of the ambitious, the believers, the chaste, the determined, the good, the healthy, the innocent and the young. They went in their millions and contributed immeasurably to the civilisation and economic development of the western world. But it was an open caravan, free for those of modest means to join without prior questions about faith or competence. Who then could be surprised that an exodus prompted by religious bigotry was joined by the anti-social, the criminal, the godless, the mentally ill, the predatory, the vulnerable or the morally weak?

Anti-Semitism, like other forms of ethnic prejudice, makes few distinctions. The unwanted, too, left the Old World in their thousands and established themselves in the ports and other cities around the Atlantic where their criminal activities became a source of contempt, embarrassment and humiliation for millions. It is a measure of both the strength of anti-Semitism and the depth of communal concern that the Jews stand out amongst other emigrant peoples – the British, French,

Germans, Italians and Scandinavians – for their efforts to guide the flow west of their oppressed *landsleit*.[51]

A fifteen-year-old Joseph Lis is unlikely to have left Kielce on his own but it would not have been out of character had he done so. From what transpired later it seems probable that he left in company of one or more older men – the actor Brietstein or his cousin, Anker being the most likely candidates. The favoured route out of the southern Congress Kingdom took Jews further south, across the border into the Austro-Hungarian town of Brody. From there trains of hope chugged westward to the Galician capital of Lemberg and then lurched north towards Myslowitz where the real journey to Hamburg and the North Sea began. Again, it is probably significant that, many years later, when prohibited from entering the Russian empire legally and getting back to Kielce, Lis told officials in the United States that his place of birth was close by, in Myslowitz, Silesia.[52]

Like most migrants he carried some familiar baggage. These men came from a bifurcated country, half Polish, half Russian, on the margins of a wider empire. Their identities and occupations were even more contingent than usual on the vagaries of authority and power and they would never be free of the label 'Jew'. But Lis had also taken along some very personal items. He was an abandoned child in a clerical town that barely tolerated his presence and had a dislike of those who were supposedly his co-religionists. Through no fault of his own he had become a man at a time when the air was thick with the word 'pogrom'. Now, free of his father, mother and the others, he could experiment with his identity, redefine himself, go where he pleased and perhaps earn a living as he saw fit.

He placed little store on conventional notions of occupation, family or religion. A merchant could, should the need arise, trade in just about anything that took his fancy, acquire goods in many different places and market them through vastly different channels. What precisely was a family? Were not those seated at the front of the *shul* utterly scornful of his parents? A father – supposedly a husband and storekeeper – could be a thief and whore-monger as readily as a patriarch. And a mother? What exactly was a mother? A woman who could be a lover, if not a prostitute, and a hopeless matriarch as readily as a wife. Was not his own 'brother', Jacob, the product of another man's loins? Women were prisoners of their mysterious, rampant sexuality – vectors of treachery and pollution. Were they not merely outlets for male sexual gratification and, in the right circumstances, could their bodies not be bought and sold like any other commodity?

In Hamburg, most travellers sought out Thomas Wilson & Sons, which dominated the passenger trade between Germany and the nearest British ports. Hull, the larger of two principal North Sea ports, was much favoured by emigrants from northern Europe. In effect, the city acted as a gigantic sieve – sorting out those with modest cash resources from those who had least before diverting them into two smaller streams for onward routing. Those with the financial strength to leap the Atlantic in a single jump boarded the train, crossed the Pennines, and positioned themselves in Liverpool for the leap to the eastern seaboard of the United States. Those who needed to put on more muscle before attempting so ambitious a move, or who had other reasons for staying on in the United Kingdom, went south. Brietstein headed for Liverpool. Joseph Lis went south.[53]

II

LONDON
1885–1889

With every day and from both sides my intelligence, the moral and the intellectual, I thus drew steadily nearer to that truth, by whose partial discovery I have been doomed to such a dreadful shipwreck: that man is not truly one, but truly two.

R.L. Stevenson, *Dr Jekyll and Mr Hyde*

SEEN from a distance, nineteenth-century British economic achievement hints at a century of unbroken progress. Viewed from closer up, a more complex picture unfolds. Britain was unrivalled as the 'workshop of the world' by the early nineteenth century, and reforms in the 1830s and 1860s did indeed underwrite advances in many walks of life. Domestic output strengthened the stability of a modest-sized middle class. In England, a burgeoning number of industrial workers primed colonial expansion and imperial consolidation – a trend that became more pronounced after the European powers divided up the African continent at the Berlin Conference of 1884–85. But by then the economic motor that had driven the British push abroad was already spluttering from changes that dated back as far as the Napoleonic wars.

In 1850, when town-dwellers exceeded those living in the country for the first time, Britain – in terms of steam power and steel production – still outstripped its continental rivals and its young challenger across the Atlantic. By the onset of the Great Depression of 1873, British industrial dominance, measured against the same indicators, had faltered. When the depression lifted in 1896 and the long slide in prices was halted, the bulk of the world's manufacturing capacity, driven by electricity and gas, had shifted to the United States and European competitors such as Belgium. Even then, the full extent of the slump was masked partially by geo-political developments that bolstered Britain's performance through hidden earnings. Banking, insurance and shipping provided a financial lifeline for the metropolis while British colonies in Asia and southern African yielded cheap food-stuffs, raw materials and minerals in an era that was given added stability by the international imperatives of free trade and the gold standard.[1]

These underlying shifts in the economy were mirrored in the changing fortunes, demographic patterning and physical growth of the nation's capital. As an industrial centre, London had never compared seriously with its smokestack cousins in the midlands. A commercial, financial and finishing centre whose strength derived from the docks on the lower reaches of the Thames, the inner city had a population of about a million in 1880; this grew to nearly two and a half million by 1910. Greater London, bisected by the river's eastward flow, had for centuries been characterised by a natural north–south divide. Its more affluent nineteenth-century citizens tended to spread out along the sunnier north bank of the Thames while the poorer huddled on the chilly south bank.

By the mid-nineteenth century, however, this blurred north–south divide on the mental map of most middle-class observers was giving way to a sharper distinction between London's east and west wards. While the City and the retail and residential districts of the west continued to profit from underlying strengths in the economy, jour-nalists, novelists and social analysts were becoming aware of how that wealth contrasted with the deteriorating situation in the east. A slow-down in manufacturing, the depression and an East European immi-grant influx after 1881 contributed to growing crime, destitution and poverty in the east, feeding the idea that London had a distinctive, separate, 'East End'.[2]

More of a cultural construct than a geographical entity, it was the Borough of Tower Hamlets that lay east of the City and north of the river that constituted most of the East End. A sweep around its curved northern limits embraced Hoxton and Shoreditch before falling away towards Hackney. In the south, tucked up against the Thames and curling along with bends in the river as far downstream as the West India docks, it included Eastcheap, Wapping, Shadwell, Ratcliff and Poplar. In between these ragged northern and southern arcs lay the heart of the East End, made up of Bethnal Green, Spitalfields, Whitechapel, St George's-in-the-East, Mile End, Limehouse and Bow.

The East End of the 1880s clung stubbornly to the dockland recesses – a warren of interlinked dank alleys, dirty passageways and hidden courts. Roughly cobbled streets often stopped short of their apparent destinations or, more alarmingly still, ran off at unexpected angles. Swamped by thick fog during cold wet winters, it sweated mercilessly on summer's days when breezes struggled to find their way through its bricked confusion. A closely knit mess, it nevertheless sustained nodules of habitation that were identifiably human. Squat cottages, relics of a bygone era, stood marooned between hundreds of cheap lodging houses inhabited by a host of criminals and thousands of casual labourers who returned to them after work in an economy which, for all its professed modernity, still pulsed strongly to a seasonal beat. Formerly dominant, lodging houses were, by the 1880s, being challenged by new model buildings and tenement blocks housing semi-skilled working-class men and women whose year-round labour churned out rent in slightly more predictable patterns.[3]

A few arterial roads were all that penetrated the East End's thick crust of dwellings, shops and small manufacturing enterprises. Commercial Street entered from the north before reaching a junction and splitting into Commercial Road East and Leman Street, the latter pushing on to the docks in the south. Entering from the west, Aldgate Street headed for the same junction and then changed to Whitechapel High Street before moving on east as the Mile End Road. Just east of this major intersection the misleadingly named Brick Lane appeared from the north before, in typical East End fashion, changing its name to Osborn Street and colliding with Whitechapel High Street.

The web of housing suspended between these threads supported the 'dangerous classes' made up of native English, immigrant Irish and other European newcomers. By the late 1880s and early 1890s two sections of the web were sagging noticeably. One was Whitechapel, south of Spitalfields's notorious 'evil quarter of a mile' where, on average, 176 people were crowded on to each acre. The other was closer still to the docks, around Aldgate, where regular employment was more difficult to come by and unskilled labourers rubbed shoulders with huge numbers of the unashamedly criminal. In St George's-in-the-East there were 250 to the acre – more than five times the number to be found in 'respectable' suburbs.[4]

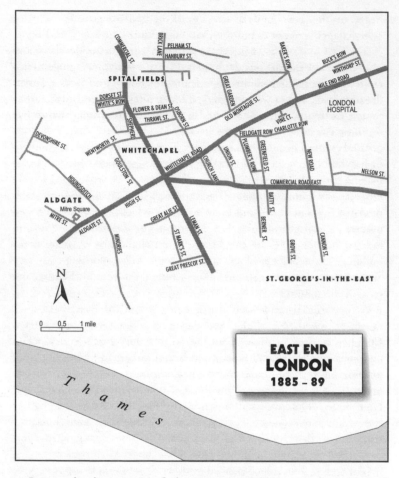

EAST END
LONDON
1885 – 89

Poverty bred poverty and the two areas, along with a corridor of hardship that poked up Mile End Road towards Bow, became home to East European Jewish immigrants after Alexander II's assassination in 1881. While a few long-established Dutch and German Jewish craftsmen and storekeepers were ensconced near the City, numerous incoming Polish, Russian, Romanian and Lithuanian immigrants crammed into Spitalfields-Whitechapel and Aldgate-St George's-in-the-East. The poor with craft skills – boot-repairers, cabinet-makers, shoemakers and especially tailors – sought employment in cramped quarters where it was hard to tell where workshops ended and bedrooms began.

Jewish refugees from the Congress Kingdom sought out casual or seasonal employment as best they could, but were often frowned upon, even by co-religionists, who saw them as occupying the lowest rungs of social disadvantage. They and the Russo-Polish unemployed clustered in identifiable neighbourhoods around Booth and Dorset Streets in Spitalfields. Along with burglars, thieves, pimps and prostitutes, they fought for space with rats and lice in rented rooms costing two to five shillings a week.[5]

When Joseph Lis, just turned sixteen, took leave of his travel companions in Hull and proceeded to London in winter 1885, it was almost inevitable that he would make his way to one of five congested sectors around the principal thoroughfares of the East End which already accommodated between thirty and forty thousand Russo-Polish Jews.[6] Where exactly he went is unknown but, like most immigrants, he presumably arrived with the name of some kinsman who could be relied upon for initial assistance.

'Lis', an uncommon name in England at that time, was seldom encountered in London. But the East End boasted a scion of that ilk in business-cum-residential premises just south of the Whitechapel Road. Lewis Lis, a general dealer, his wife and a dress-making daughter, Mandel, lived at 35 Plumber's Row. The business, which was not in existence in 1881, was viable for a short time and in 1888 Lis employed a clerk, Moses Gourvitch of the same address who, that same year, married eighteen-year-old Mandel. Shortly after 1888, the Lises and Gourvitches of Plumber's Row left Whitechapel, London and England for an unknown destination. The census of 1891 shows no record of them.[7]

We do not know whether Joseph was related to this Lis family or if he lived at, or visited, that address. It is, however, highly unlikely that in a tightly knit, highly localised Jewish community his attention was not drawn to the name by others, or that in his wanderings he failed to spot a signboard or shop window bearing his surname. It is not the only thing that places him in the vicinity. In 1887, when Haskel Brietstein returned to England after a foray abroad, he hired a room in Vine Court, near the Yiddish theatre in Fieldgate Street, only five minutes from Plumber's Row. Moreover, later that same year Brietstein was party to a burglary at a warehouse directly opposite the Lis general dealer's store. It is unlikely that Joseph Lis did not know Plumber's Row well.[8]

Be that as it may, the young man could not have chosen a worse moment to find his feet. Working-class incomes collapsed the year he arrived in London and then got worse. By 1888, 'wages in tailoring, shoemaking and cabinet-making, which had once stood at £2 a week had dropped by half to £1 and £1 5s'.[9] Immigrants were particularly hard hit. As early as 1883 one in four Jews was in receipt of poor relief. In 1885, alarmed by the deteriorating situation, the Board of Guardians encouraged the destitute to retrace their steps. At first the Board underwrote the cost of return passages only as far as Hamburg, but after 1886 it financed some all the way back to Tsarist Russia. By 1887 the number of Jews in receipt of poor relief in the capital had risen to one in three, and every second Jew dying in the greater London area was given a pauper's funeral.[10]

In prolonged storms it is the crafty, the strong or the vicious that are most likely to survive. Economic circumstances brought out traits in the young fox which might have been slower to surface in more benign climates. Predatory by pedigree, animal cunning enabled him to sniff out opportunities to make a living in a singularly unpromising environment. Hunting expeditions took him into terrain that was criminal, male and frequently violent.

One haunt, frequented by burglars, cardsharps, diamond-dealers, furriers, jewellers, thieves, pimps and pawnshop owners, was a gambling den between Aldgate and Houndsditch, owned by a fence, Marks Levy.[11] It was probably here that Lis perfected his skills at faro. Better known to East European Jews as 'stuss' or 'stosh', this is a game of chance in which punters bet against the house on the likelihood of cards emblazoned on an enamelled oilcloth being turned up from the pack. For the house to profit, as it inevitably did, faro demanded a 'banker' with a sharp mind and nimble fingers.[12] There were twenty or more such dens in the East End including the Tower Hamlets Club, in Whitechapel Road, run by an unnamed Polish Jew in 1888.[13] Skills acquired in the East End stayed with Lis and years later, down on his luck, he earned a living as a 'banker'.[14]

Fearless, and blessed with excellent powers of co-ordination, Lis also tried his hand at pickpocketing; yet another skill put to use in his subsequent underworld career. But, subject to upswellings of aggression and bouts of uncontrollable rage, he was equally drawn to the 'manly' arts that had a growing Jewish following. Aldgate, Hoxton and Shoreditch had sufficient clubs and other boxing venues to be known as the 'Cradle

of Pugilism'. Legal outlets, built on the platform provided by the introduction of the Marquess of Queensberry's rules in the 1860s, were often
sited beside notorious rookeries such as the Jago in the hope that the
physicality of the dangerous classes would be channelled into socially
acceptable directions. Amateur outlets, like Jay's Club for Jago Men
near the Old Nichol, however, had to compete for the attention of the
poorest with scores of booths off the Whitechapel Road where prize-
fighters competed for cash purses well into the 1890s.[15]

Lis was lean and muscular. He was slightly taller than most working-
class Victorian men which gave him the advantage of reach and he
took naturally to boxing. By the time he left the East End, aged twenty-
one, he bore several scars acquired in as well as out of the ring.[16] Most
of his organised fights were illegal. When he made one of his periodic
returns to London, in 1898, it was stated that he 'was known to the
police as a prize-fighter'.[17] As with gambling, it was not only the
fighting that drew him in, but the company it attracted. In the mid-
1880s, and well into the 1890s, many part-time East End 'bruisers',
'bullies', 'minders' and prize-fighters were active pimps.[18]

Steeped in the brine of masculinity and violence, he took equally
readily to alcohol and tobacco. Within months of his leaving Whitechapel
in 1889, he admitted to a prison officer that his drinking habits were
'intemperate' and that he was a smoker.[19] Habits acquired in his teens
continued to cling to him and, like blows to the head sustained while
boxing, can have done little for either his physical or mental health.
Although never an alcoholic, it was as if he had a physical need for
beer or spirits.[20] The East End was awash with cheap gin, and Lis,
although aware that liquor tended to accentuate his problems, nevertheless drank and smoked throughout his life. He would, however, have
been made aware that he was not the only person with a darker side
to a troubled personality.

In 1886, Robert Louis Stevenson, influenced by new scientific writings about multiple personalities, published *The Strange Case of Dr
Jekyll and Mr Hyde*. His novel 'featured a murderer with a divided
personality, who encompassed within himself the two social extremes
of London: the urbane Dr Jekyll, who used his scientific knowledge
to create another self, [and] the stunted, troglodyte, proletarian Mr
Hyde, as a cover for "secret pleasures" and "nocturnal adventures"'.
The work was immensely popular and 'despite the author's repeated
denials, contemporary readers and reviewers immediately interpreted

the undisclosed nocturnal adventures and pleasures of Jekyll/Hyde as illicit and violently erotic'. Popular perceptions were woven into the dramatised version of the story and when the play opened at the Lyceum Theatre in the West End, in August 1888, Jekyll/Hyde was portrayed as a 'sadistic sex criminal'.[21] What did Lis make of all this?

It is difficult to know. He was at the stage of life most prone to sexual activity and fantasy, and that alone might have pricked his curiosity. His friendship with the actor, Brietstein, too, may have drawn him to the play. A decade later, Lis and his cousins certainly frequented the East End, and more especially Yiddish theatres as they pursued their low-life projects. It was impossible for him to miss talk of Jekyll and Hyde; especially when the production was closed down after the 'Jack the Ripper' murders for fear that the play might further incite the mentally unstable. Yet, for all that, it is difficult to envisage an immigrant, new to the English language, going 'up west'. Given his age, class and culture Lis's sexual interests and proclivities probably played themselves out closer to home. On Sundays, between Grove Road and Bow Church, young louts blackened their hands with soot in preparation for the 'Monkey Parade' and pawed at the faces and dresses of young ladies attending church. Not all street theatre was so innocuous. The behaviour of adolescent gangs, such as the High Rips and Forty Thieves, was openly predatory and frequently violent. Thugs would surround prostitutes or working women and use whatever force was necessary to relieve them of cash or other items of value. The East End offered easy access to an open-air laboratory where anyone with ambivalent feelings about his own sexuality, or that of others, could experiment.[22]

Lis's problems aside, Jekyll and Hyde's purported 'secret pleasures' were well grounded in the social reality and popular imagination of Victorian London. In the mid-1880s, the 'City of Dreadful Delight' was served by at least 75,000 full-time prostitutes. As elsewhere in the world, poverty drew unskilled females to urban areas and then, unable to provide them with a living wage, recycled them through the streets as 'unfortunates'. Girls, young and naïve, were forcibly entrapped into the profession by men and women established in the commercial sex trade. Other young women, valuing financial independence and personal freedom, chose to earn their living from prostitution. Young prostitutes in their physical prime earned in a single night what most working-class women sweated to earn in a week. In Whitechapel alone, there were several hundred brothels in the great semicircle between Commercial Street and Commercial Road East. Some East End brothels were masked as cigar shops, coffee shops or restaurants. Many more functioned openly from backstreet entrances or in cheap lodging houses.[23]

The dangers that commercial sex and venereal disease posed to the moral and physical well-being of the British armed services and an urbanising population had been a subject for concern since the end of the Napoleonic wars. In the mid-nineteenth century, these issues were placed firmly on the agenda by feminists, middle-class activists and Nonconformists. In 1869, Josephine Butler, outraged by the double standard of the Contagious Diseases Acts which allowed for the compulsory inspection of women suspected of being prostitutes but not their male consorts, launched the Ladies' National Association for the Repeal of the Contagious Diseases Acts. This initiative was supplemented by Ellice Hopkins's White Cross Movement which impressed the need for chastity and moral purity on young men.[24]

These movements gained further momentum in 1879 when Alfred Dyer and 'social purity' advocates revealed that some young British women were being held against their will in continental brothels. By 1882, a Select Committee of the House of Lords was debating whether the age of consent should be raised from thirteen to sixteen and, twelve months later, in the face of public pressure, the provisions of the Contagious Diseases Acts were suspended. The Select Committee, however, balked at the idea of raising the age of consent, thereby incurring the wrath of crusaders for reform who, in turn, captured the support of the new, single-minded editor of a London-based journal, W.T. Stead.[25]

In 1885, Stead, son of a Congregationalist minister, embarked on a poorly thought through publicity campaign involving the purchase of a thirteen-year-old virgin 'on the clear understanding that the girl was destined for despoliation'. His melodramatic findings, published as 'The Maiden Tribute of Modern Babylon' in the *Pall Mall Gazette*, caused a sensation. The journal's offices were mobbed by readers keen to learn about the murky world of commercial sex and thousands of legal and pirated copies of the exposé were printed, and then reprinted. Stead was prosecuted for removing a girl from her parents' custody without permission, under false pretences, but by then victory was assured. The Contagious Diseases Acts, already in abeyance, were repealed and the new Criminal Law Amendment Act of 1885 raised the age of consent to sixteen.[26]

Lis could no more have avoided the spotlight of publicity surrounding the issues of public morality, sexual norms and venereal disease in the capital than he could have avoided one of the capital's notorious pea-soupers. In 1885, the year of his arrival, a demonstration a quarter of a million strong gathered in Hyde Park to witness the launching of the indefatigable Stead's National Vigilance Association. And if the possibilities for pickpocketing presented by a large crowd failed to draw Lis west, then he could not have escaped noticing the sequel to the NVA campaign that played itself out in the East End.

The unlikely agent for this was the heir to a brewery fortune. F.N. Charrington, already dedicated to the causes of chastity and temperance in the East End, was re-enthused by Stead's campaign and recent changes to the law. But, as ever, new legislation brought with it unintended consequences. Because the Criminal Law Amendment Act discouraged street-soliciting, many prostitutes were driven indoors where they became more vulnerable to the predations of pimp intermediaries. Charrington, however, found a provision in the Act that facilitated direct action of the type he favoured. Any landlord whose attention had been drawn to the fact that his property was used to run a disorderly house and failed to evict the tenants, was liable to a stiff fine. Armed only with a little 'black book', which offered him scant protection from 'boxers' and 'bullies', he moved through Bedford, Devonshire, Dorset, Nelson and other streets until – by late 1888 – he had succeeded in closing more than 200 brothels in the East End.[27]

The Jewish quarter was not exempt from the surging tide of concern about public morality. In 1885 the Board of Guardians, horrified by cases of immigrant women being entrapped into prostitution, formed the Jewish Association for the Protection of Girls, Women and Children. The association set up a sanctuary for prostitutes in the Mile End Road; in 1888 it moved to Tenter Street, Aldgate. Such care and vigilance was not misplaced. The *East London Observer* carried several items citing incidents in which girls and married women were either abducted, or drugged by procurers. In July 1888, even the *Jewish Chronicle* had cause to lament this 'dark side of Jewish life'.[28]

Lis, whose head already held echoes of biblical prophecies in which the 'Son of Man' was called upon to deal with whores, and whose heart was filled with a hatred of morally fickle, sexually charged women, found himself in the most inappropriate environment imagin-able. In a way, it was as if he had been transported back to the ancient whoring cities of Samaria and Jerusalem, whose gross betrayals, lasciv-ious behaviour and potential for pollution had been so vividly portrayed by the prophet in the holy writings, the *tanakh*.[29] It is within the broader context of these problematic notions that the young man had an early sexual adventure which, for many years, he seems to have considered deeply problematic.

In 1887, aged nineteen, he either had a one-off encounter with, or entered into a fleeting but loveless liaison with a woman about whom almost nothing is known. For reasons we will have occasion to probe later, Lis contrived to conceal her name and the significance – if any – of their coupling. Her fate, too, became the subject of a profound silence. Indeed, so determined was he to mask the circumstances and moment of this encounter that not even the illegitimate child born of the union, Bertha, was willing to disclose her mother's name, or to reveal the precise date and place of her own birth – if she knew anything about the matter.

In 1908, Bertha, abandoned by her father for the duration of her childhood, told insistent French police officers that her mother's name might have been 'Rose'. Long before and after her encounter with Parisian police, however, she had taken to dissembling about this and related matters. At various times, she claimed to have been born in America or Russian-Poland. What is clear is that she was an illegiti-mate child. There is no record either of Lis's getting married in the 1880s, or of her birth in London, New York or Kielce. Fragmentary evidence hints at her having been handed over for adoption, or informal raising by an East End Jewish woman, shortly after birth. It is possible that her biological mother, at a time when it was not uncommon, had died during her birth.[30]

From late adolescence and into her early twenties Bertha remained in thrall to her frightening father and for several years shared the bed of his violent half-brother, Jack. Significantly, she never did reveal the secrets of her infancy. Lis, who left no truthful account of his only child's birth, once suggested – verifiably falsely – that Bertha was the offspring of a woman to whom he was briefly married, in London, in 1895. If the baby's mother's name was indeed 'Rose', then for Lis it was as if she never existed, as if 'Rose' had become part of the living dead or, more ominously still, had somehow truly departed.

The same obfuscation about dates, to the same end, surrounds what may have been Lis's first meeting, but was probably his reunion, with Haskel Brietstein in late 1887. After their parting in Hull in 1885, Brietstein – who had left his wife in the Congress Kingdom – had taken up with a woman in Liverpool. There, under the stage name, Adolph Goldberg, rooted in a family name a brother in America had taken he 'got up a company to play Hebrew pieces in a theatre'. But things went wrong when in March 1886 his wife, Paulina and their three children left Aleksander-Lódzki to join him in his new life abroad. Paulina, learning of his illicit liaison, wanted no more to do with him, or his unsuccessful dramatic productions. Frustrated by untenable domestic circumstances, Brietstein left for the United States and tried his luck in Philadelphia's burgeoning Yiddish theatre. But that, too, did not work out. By spring 1887, he was back in Liverpool. A second attempt at a reunion with Paulina, by then in Hull, was disastrous. Brietstein stole cash and clothing from his estranged wife and returned to Liverpool by train. Undaunted, Paulina laid a charge of theft. The matter ended in court, back in Hull, where the magistrate had to rule on the then novel question of whether or not a husband could be guilty of theft for removing his wife's property. In a landmark ruling it was decided that he could, and Brietstein was sentenced to six months' imprisonment.[31]

Discharged in September 1887, Brietstein went to London and, as already noted, found a room just off the Whitechapel Road, close to Plumber's Row and New Road. Vine Court was a squalid little enclave notorious for criminal activity. The Board of Works had it scheduled for gas lamps long before the area became infamous for other reasons. On 18 August 1888, days after the knifing of Martha Tabram and two weeks before the other murders attributed to 'Jack the Ripper' commenced, Vine Court was one of eight corner sites selected for the immediate introduction of lamps with 'double illuminating power'.[32]

For Brietstein, the address probably held additional attractions since it lay at the heart of Yiddish culture. The East London Theatre was in nearby Fieldgate Street while the Pavilion Theatre was, quite literally, around the corner from Vine Court. If Brietstein was looking for stage work, however, he was out of luck. In 1887, when a gas lamp had gone out in the nearby Princess Club, panicking patrons, fearing a fire, had stampeded to the exits trampling seventeen people to death. The tragedy cast a pall over Jewish theatre and by the end of that year there was no work to be had for good actors, let alone serial failures.[33]

Down at heel, Brietstein alias Goldberg drew on Polish repertory for inspiration. In a play mirroring the burglary at Edelman's in Kielce in 1879, he and two accomplices settled on a plan of the sort that Joseph Lis would have understood and taken a keen interest in. Goldberg, Simon Cohen and Abraham Levy were later fingered for having broken into Spiegel's warehouse at 34 Plumber's Row during the dying days of December 1887 and removing several overcoats which they planned to sell in London and the west country. It may have been by chance that the principal victim of the theft was Jewish and a tailor, and that his premises stood directly opposite Lewis Lis's general dealer's store at 35 Plumber's Row. But could it also have been mere misfortune that the perpetrators of the crime were arrested after the police had received an anonymous tip-off? In retrospect, the sheer number of coincidences is striking and hints at the presence of some unknown police informer. In January 1888, Goldberg and Cohen were each sentenced to fifteen months in prison and Levy, the oldest of the trio, to eight months.[34]

In some ways, Goldberg's plight was probably symptomatic of East End hardship. In February 1887, the deteriorating economic climate had prompted a parliamentary inquiry into the effects of uncontrolled immigration on the labour market which gave rise to several anti-Semitic statements. The winter of 1887 became the longest and coldest on record for thirty years. Working-class discontent was expressed in marches and huge public demonstrations. In November 1887, just weeks before the burglary in Plumber's Row, the police had to use considerable force to quell disturbances around Trafalgar Square on 'Bloody Sunday'. When its only martyr, Alfred Linnell, was buried that December, it produced the biggest crowd seen on the streets of London since the burial of the Duke of Wellington in 1852.[35]

The new year started on an equally dismal note. January 1888 saw the capital blanketed in the thickest fog in memory. Social reformers sensed that the demoralised and overcrowded East End was on the verge of a potentially violent convulsion. Lis, by then, had more personal concerns. In April, 'Rose' gave birth to the child he never wanted, Bertha. By then he was also aware of another problem that was to plague him for the rest of his life. His face, which eighteen months later was reported as being 'full of pimples' and 'pitted' with small scars, was manifesting the rash and type of lesions associated with secondary syphilis. For him, spring 1888 was most unpleasant.[36]

By then Lis had already completed or was still completing an apprenticeship as a barber. For the next twenty years, when there was nothing to be gained from it, he maintained consistently that he was a barber by profession. In late 1889, Goldberg, also with nothing seemingly at stake, spoke of having first met Lis in a barbershop during the previous year. But, since we also know that, with the exception of the first week of 1888 Goldberg was in prison until the end of the first quarter of 1889, that barbershop meeting may well have taken place after his release in Hull, in September 1887 and before his arrest in January 1888. We also know that after his release from prison in March 1889 Goldberg and Lis emigrated almost immediately to the United States and that a few years later, Lis told an attorney who was probing unrelated matters that he had arrived in New York City, in 1889, already a qualified barber.[37] Regardless of the exact date, Lis could not have earned much as a part-time hairdresser in the East End during a slump when there were many ex-*feldschers* around.

One former *feldscher* Lis may have encountered was Severin 'Ludwig' Klosowski who, as 'George Chapman', was hanged years later for having poisoned three wives. He and Klosowski had much in common. Both were Polish barbers; Klosowski hailing from Radom, the province that separated Kielce from Warsaw. Moreover, Klosowski spoke Yiddish, had a taste for Jewish company and, on occasion, passed himself off as a Jew. More importantly, both had well-developed sexual appetites, an interest in prostitutes, and both were deeply misogynistic. Klosowski worked at a hairdresser's in High Street, Whitechapel, for some months in 1888 before he, too, emigrated to the United States.[38]

In London, locks acquired for winter warmth were shorn with the approach of high summer in June, while the demand for clean-shaven faces came on Fridays and Saturdays with the week's end looming. This meant that hairdressers often took on assistants on a casual basis to help with seasonal or weekend pressures. In late August 1888, C.A. Partridge, owner of a hairdresser's in the Minories, employed Charles Ludwig, yet another woman-hating barber he had met at a German watering hole in Houndsditch.[39] The underlying mainstay of the trade, however, was a stream of boys recruited from local workhouses who served as apprentices. A source of cheap labour, the youngsters were retained only until such time as they were qualified and then promptly replaced by a new intake from the same source.[40] This, together with the way many hairdressers co-operated with pimps, contributed to a barbershop subculture with a hidden potential for sexual violence that also fed back into predatory gangs such as the High Rips. A barbershop was not the ideal setting for an unsettled young man in late 1887 or 1888.[41]

Lis, unsuited to steady employment by temperament, could well have been without work in the dismal winter months leading up to his daughter's birth in spring 1888. Full-time work may only have become possible during the busy summer months that followed. Once the seasonal high passed and autumn set in, most barbers reverted to part-time work, and some found themselves without a position at all. The economic climate, too, remained unpropitious. In July 1888 the women at the Bryant and May Match Company went out on strike. It was in these unsettled times that the trauma which East End reformers had long been expecting played itself out. At first it eased into Whitechapel in a form least expected and almost unnoticed. By the end of that autumn, however, there were few in the Anglophone world who had not heard of 'Jack the Ripper'.[42]

With the benefit of recent research it is possible to see that the terror commenced in late February 1888. On Saturday the 25th, a thirty-eight-year-old widow of White's Row, Spitalfields, who may have been a part-time prostitute, Annie Millwood, was admitted to Whitechapel Workhouse Infirmary with multiple stab wounds to the 'legs and lower part of the body'. She had been attacked by an unknown assailant who had pulled a clasp knife from his pocket. Millwood recovered from her wounds but, a month later, collapsed and died from a heart condition. Her death was a stroke of good fortune for her assailant.[43]

In the very week when Millwood died, Ada Wilson, an 'unfortunate' of Maidman Street, Mile End, was confronted by a man demanding money. Reaching into his pocket, he drew a knife, and twice stabbed her in the throat. She, too, survived but, only days later, on 3 April, another prostitute was less fortunate. Emma Smith was followed into Brick Lane by three men who beat her, raped her and then rammed a blunt stick into her vagina, rupturing the perineum, which led to the infection that she died from before she could provide a fuller description of her assailants. On 6 August Martha Tabram, yet another 'unfortunate', was found dead with thirty-nine stab wounds to the neck, chest and stomach. These four deadly assaults were, in retrospect, seen as the start to the killer's increasingly frenzied, misogynistic mission.[44]

At 1.40 a.m. on the morning of 31 August, a forty-three-year-old prostitute, Mary Ann Nichols was turned out of the lodging house she frequented in Thrawl Street, Spitalfields, for want of fourpence or eight-pence to cover her nightly stay. She was later seen, drunk, in Osborn Street and had then made her way east up Whitechapel Street. At about four that morning a carman discovered her body in Buck's Row, a street running parallel to Whitechapel Road. The murder of a prostitute was unusual but not without precedent. In this instance, however, it was the post-mortem findings that grabbed the interest of the press and public. Nichols's throat had been slit, but she had also been ripped from the ribs to the pelvis. Her stomach lining had been slashed and there were wounds to the vagina.[45]

A week or so later, on 8 September, Annie Chapman, a prostitute, was murdered behind a house at 29 Hanbury Street, scarcely half a mile from the site of the previous murder. This, the second outright murder in a series that were later cast as the 'canonical five' by some authors, was executed with greater ferocity than the first. The victim's throat had been slit with such force that the body was almost decapi-tated. The stomach lining was fully penetrated, the intestines pulled free and thrown over the victim's shoulder. The blade had slashed the navel, bladder, womb and upper part of the vagina. Some body parts were missing. The penny press reported these ghoulish findings with relish and the imagination of the terrified populace slid into ancient prejudices. It was probably the old anti-Semitic canard that Jews used the blood of Gentile children to make matzos, that helped crystallise the idea that only a Jew was capable of such blood-letting. Indeed, but for the presence of a sizeable police contingent, an upsurge in anti-Semitism might well have translated itself into a murderous reaction directed against recent East European Jewish immigrants.[46]

On 18 September the police, pressed for signs of progress in their investigations, arrested Charles Ludwig for being drunk and threat-ening to stab a prostitute, Elizabeth Burns, and a coffee stall owner. Ludwig, the owner of a knife, was found to have a pair of long-bladed scissors and a razor on his person when arrested. But the barber was able to account for his movements on the nights of the murders and, after a brief appearance in court, was discharged.

Growing public speculation as to the identity of the murderer, his alleged knowledge of female anatomy and the real, and supposed, incom-petence of the police, followed. For two weeks marked by simmering tension, the slaughter ceased. Then, on 25 September, the police received a card, one amongst many sent to them and the press, purporting to come from the murderer. Any significance of the content of the note, however, was soon eclipsed by the evocative *nom de plume* used by the signatory. From that moment on the received wisdom was that all the slayings were the work of 'Jack the Ripper'.[47]

Five days after receipt of that postcard, on Sunday 30 September, 'Jack the Ripper' struck twice in one night. Shortly after 1 a.m. the steward of the International Workers' Educational Club, which was controlled by Polish-Jewish socialists and situated just off Commercial Road East, came across the body of yet another prostitute; the third of the so-called canonical five. So recently had Elisabeth Stride's throat been slit that blood was still oozing from the neck. It appeared that the killer had been disturbed before he could complete his gruesome business and leave his trademark signature. Club members raised the alarm and hurried off to find a policeman. By the time they returned, a crowd of threatening and muttering onlookers had assembled in Berner Street. The steward and two comrades, angered by anti-Semitic taunts, laid into the crowd with broomsticks and umbrellas and were subsequently convicted of assault.[48]

The socialists in Berner Street were still coming to terms with the horror on their doorstep when news arrived of a second murder, about ten minutes' walk west of the club. Mitre Square, just inside the bounds of the City, fell within the jurisdiction of a different police division. The body was still warm when discovered. Catherine Eddowes, the fourth victim, had been murdered shortly after 1.30 a.m., just forty-five minutes after Elisabeth Stride's throat was slit. This time the slaughter had been uninterrupted, and bore the Ripper's full signature. Eddowes' throat had also been slit and her face, nose and an ear mutilated. She had been ripped from rectum to breastbone and disembowelled. Her intestines had been slung over her shoulder and at least one section separated and placed beside the body.[49]

The murderer left one clue, possibly two. Policemen examining the body noted that part of the victim's apron was missing. About an hour and a half later a constable found the missing cloth, smeared with blood and faecal matter, in Goulston Street about a third of a mile from the site of the crime. Above it, on the passageway wall, chalked in blurred writing was a message: 'The Jewes are the men that will not be blamed for nothing.' The officer in charge, reading prevailing East End sentiment correctly, and fearing the consequences should the contents of the message become too widely known, saw to it that the words were recorded and then ordered that the wall be washed clean.[50]

The message disappeared, but prejudice and terror oozed freely from Whitechapel's gaping social wounds. While the coroners went about their business as best they could, the press pursued the reading public with factual and fictional detail that left some immigrant Jews and prostitutes cowering in the crowded quarters that stood between them and utter destitution. October crawled by without incident, as did the first week of November. When winter strutted darkened streets with greater confidence the Ripper turned his back on the cold and sidled indoors. On the night of 8–9 November, he indulged his lust for death and destruction; for two hours his actions were illuminated and warmed by a roaring fire.

What was still recognisable of Mary Jane Kelly's body was discovered by a rent collector peering through a broken window at 13 McCarthy's Rents, Miller's Court, Dorset Street, at a quarter to eleven on the morning of the murder. An unsuccessful attempt had been made to remove the head of the victim. There was scarcely a part of her body that had not been butchered, removed, or that had been left in the position intended by nature. The police surgeon noted: 'The whole of the surface of the abdomen and thighs was removed and the abdominal cavity emptied of its viscera. The breasts were cut off, the arms mutilated by several jagged wounds and the face hacked beyond recognition of the features.' The heart was missing and the external part of the vagina cut away. As with one other victim, she had been robbed of what little cash she possessed. But on this occasion, a witness, George Hutchinson, may have got an excellent look at the killer.[51]

Where precisely Joseph Lis or his cousin, Joseph Anker, were to be found during the initial attacks in the first quarter of 1888, during that quiet summer or through the orgy of autumn slayings that followed will for ever remain unknown. One thing is, however, certain; neither the moral ferment that preceded the Ripper murders, nor the ethnic and sexual tensions that followed could have failed to have had an impact on a twenty-year-old preoccupied with the act of copulation, vaginas, reproduction and wombs. Lis's adolescent fantasies and sexual behaviour came to fruition in the Victorian East End. By the age of twenty, one year in every five of his life had been spent in Whitechapel. If the same sum is done, taking as its baseline his coming of age at thirteen, then by 1888 more than half his sexually active life had been spent in the East End.

Not surprisingly London – and more especially Aldgate and Whitechapel – continued to attract and fascinate Lis. A decade after the Ripper murders he returned to the East End where some of his and Anker's more extreme psychosexual assaults did not escape detection and were duly recorded. In a life characterised by ceaseless sexual predation and constant movement, London remained the closest thing to 'home' Lis ever knew. He returned to the city in 1895, living there until 1898 and yet again between 1914 and 1915. By the time he turned thirty, in 1898, more than half his adult life had been spent in the English capital, with most of the time in and around Whitechapel, looking for ways of living off women who were prostitutes, or looking for ways to turn women into whores.

We are left asking if the East End murders moulded Joseph Lis's subsequent actions or, more intriguingly, whether young Lis did not perhaps somehow inform the behaviour of Jack the Ripper? It is a question that can only be addressed after we have traced the rest of his amazing life, searching for clues that might point to that autumn of terror in Whitechapel. For the moment we have to content ourselves with knowing that, at some point before mid-1889, Lis again met Adolph Goldberg, recently released from a London prison, and that shortly thereafter they both set off to start their lives afresh in the New World.

III

NEW YORK CITY
1889–1891

> Hence it came about that I concealed my pleasures; and that
> when I reached years of reflection, and began to look round
> me, and take stock of my progress and position in the world,
> I stood already committed to a profound duplicity of life.

R.L. Stevenson, *Dr Jekyll and Mr Hyde*

LIS (21), and Adolph Goldberg (34) – as Brietstein now insisted on being known – arrived in the dreamland of the East Europeans in the second quarter of 1889. The name of the vessel, the port of entry, date of arrival, destination and the names they presented to immigration authorities – information assembled routinely but later the subject of Lis's dissembling – remain a mystery. Goldberg, a man who brought poor timing and misfortune together in a lifelong marriage, steered them into New York City. On the Lower East Side tens of thousands of working-class and unemployed Jews from the Congress Kingdom and the Russian Pale challenged and jostled longer-established German co-religionists for a place in the sun of the fabled, ever-expanding, New World.

But even in the 'Golden Medina' the Great Depression occasionally blocked out the sun. American economic growth after the Civil War was held in check by federal policy which avoided issuing currency not fully backed by gold. Increased output, inflationary surges and speculatively fuelled growth spurts were often stifled by 'sound' monetary policy as the international supply of gold struggled to keep abreast of demand. An unpredictable choking-off in the money supply produced periodic panics, such as those of 1873 and 1893, and elevated populist demands for bimetallism. Silver, it was argued, should be used alongside gold to usher in new and broadly based prosperity.

For all these uncertainties, the Lower East Side of 1889 retained a bustle and vibrancy that contrasted sharply with the sluggishness of London's East End. With its bold grid-patterned streets already the most densely settled strip of land on earth, and a population density exceeding that of most contemporary Asian cities, the Lower East Side gave immigrants a sense of being part of a new world. American commitment to liberty and republicanism informed a civic culture that championed the values of democracy, egalitarianism and voluntarism. It gave newcomers the feeling that they could triumph over adversity. East European Jews, with an intuitive dislike of crown and empire born of persecution, identified readily with their new order. Accustomed to being confined to the circuits of commerce in the ghetto or *shtetl*, Jews knew the difference between hope and resignation and they fled the Old World for the New in their millions.[1]

With one in three immigrants under the age of sixteen and most of them male, the Lower East Side was charged with raw energy. While the irregular beat of manufacturing tried to pace the economy, the smoother-running conveyor belt of immigration never stopped depositing people along the north-east coastline and the demand for food, clothing and shelter never faltered. Throughout the 1873–96 depression retail demand in New York City remained buoyant. With working men earning, on average, $40–50 a month, and women $25–40, the Lower East Side saw a growing number of cafés, grocery stores, restaurants, clothing, furniture and jewellery stores.

Yiddish-speakers taking the tentative steps from penury to plenty saw eating, dressing and living properly as an integral part of *oystgringen zich* – 'greening oneself out'. For respectable Jews, the advent of relative prosperity and the capacity to consume blurred the line separating weekdays from the Sabbath, posing subtle new questions about their emerging American identity and Jewishness. For those already relegated to the margins of society because of criminal or moral offences, the contest between a religious and secular definition of self was experienced unevenly at best and, at worst, not at all. In a perverse way, it was often easier for a Jew with criminal propensities to adapt to the American way than it was for a law-abiding person who respected the Jewish heritage.[2]

But not even the city's interlocking grid of blocks, streets and tenement houses could eliminate all traces of Jewishness at a stroke or create instant Americans. On the Lower East Side distinctive sights, sounds and smells spewed from every building, mocking attempts at standardisation. Differences in diet, dress and forms of worship all bore testimony to the diverse worlds of Judaism. A small quarter of Romanian Jews around Forsyth and Eldridge Streets in the west gave way to more numerous Galicians who were wedged between Houston and Broome Streets. Further east, stretching south and occupying almost all the streets between Grand and Monroe Streets, were the numerically preponderant eastern Jews of Belorussia, Poland, Russia, the Ukraine and Lithuania.[3]

A palpably male 'sporting' subculture pervaded much of the Lower East Side. Stifling summer heat or bitter winter cold encouraged men to abandon overcrowded rooms and apartments and seek solace in nearby liquor outlets. Bad beer and rotten spirits adulterated with

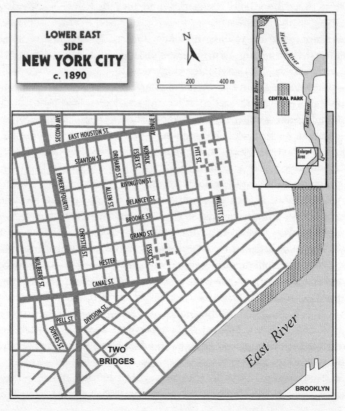

anything from kerosene to soft soap supposedly lifted the spirits. Illicit liquor sales managed from barbershops, retail stores or basement dives competed with thousands of licensed premises belonging to the cronies of the corrupt Tammany Hall politicians who dominated municipal politics. Although respectable Jews eschewed the wild saloon culture of the immigrant Irish, many East European criminals spent their time drinking, gambling and whoring. An 1897 survey listed 230 licensed liquor outlets between the Bowery and Essex, and East Houston and Hester, Streets.[4]

Saloons formed part of a broader patchwork of venues encouraging the young to explore manly elements of popular culture. Bouncers in the lowest dives were recruited from the swollen ranks of prize-fighters while the science of boxing, epitomised by Gentleman Jim Corbett's defeat of John L. Sullivan in 1891, attracted an enormous following.[5] There was hardly a block on the Lower East Side that did not boast a gambling joint including several catering for faro.[6] With the frontier experience and Civil War still looming large in the consciousness of a nation with a constitutionally entrenched right to bear arms, shooting galleries 'with noise-making figures' were everywhere. On nearby Elizabeth Street there was a notorious outlet where any citizen or crook could buy a gun.[7]

Zones of gender exclusivity with their hard-edged expressions of manliness were not, of course, to the taste of all. There were other venues where men could meet women, but even those were firmly locked into the greater orbit of masculinity. Some dancing academies allowed young working women to meet eligible bachelors and the hopeful couples then paired off to acquire American manners and improve their language skills. But many more similar establishments were mere fronts for brothels, gambling dens or saloons where 'cadets', pimps in the making, preyed on the adventurous and innocent alike. Concert saloons and masked balls at Madison Square, especially popular during the late 1890s, provided yet more opportunities for legitimate or illicit introductions.[8]

The most alienated and direct expressions of masculinity, however, were to be found in a myriad overt and covert brothels on the Lower East Side. In 1885, Allen, Broome and Rivington Streets – just three veins running through a tumour of urban poverty – hosted over 200 brothels. Barbershops, cafés, dance houses, hotels, restaurants, theatres, saloons and tenements barely concealed thousands of prostitutes plying their trade singularly or collectively. 'Cigar stores' offered quick lunchtime sexual release for men around Canal Street. Contrary to appearances, Jewish establishments in the quarter were in fact in proportion to the number of Jews in the population as a whole. East European pimps, drawing on a philosophy pioneered by hawkers everywhere – low prices and high turnover – encouraged prostitutes to provide clients with quick oral sex.[9]

But behind their alluring façades everything was not what it seemed in the brothels. True, sex in any number of 'natural' and 'perverted' forms produced the main stream of income but other, equally dangerous, contributions derived from gambling or the sale of alcohol. And beyond the latter lay the dark arts of blackmail, robbery and theft.

Young men between eighteen and twenty-five started their careers in 'vice' on the Lower East Side as 'lighthouses' outside shady establishments either to guide in or warn off the passing vessels of the night. The promising graduated to become 'cadets' and frequented dance academies, shops and theatres where they hoped to make the conquests that would set them up as fully-fledged pimps and procurers. Established pimps and procurers, in turn, aspired to becoming proprietors, property-owners or saloon-keepers who enjoyed easy access to the street lieutenants of corrupt Tammany Hall politicians.[10]

Careers in 'vice' did not preclude youngsters from signing on for simultaneous, parallel courses focused on property rather than people. Smart cadets could also be confidence tricksters, pickpockets or sneak thieves – callings that eschewed physical confrontation – until such time as they had put on sufficient muscle to become burglars, robbers or store thieves. Stolen goods swiftly found their way to fences operating out of furniture shops, grocery stores, second-hand clothes outlets or pawnshops. The best fences operated with the connivance of precinct policemen, so ensuring that the cogs of the black economy remained in alignment with the wheels of municipal government. 'For many years the Eight Ward Thieves' Exchange, at Bowery and Houston, ran a sort of fence's supermarket, and it was eventually succeeded by the Bowery's Little Stock Exchange, the one at which it was rumoured that real diamonds had once exchanged hands for a mere dollar.'[11]

For Adolph Goldberg, with an interest in, but no real aptitude for, burglary, New York oozed opportunity even though the linkages between corrupt policemen and politicians posed unfamiliar problems. However, technical advice and good contacts abounded. In 1888, William Howe and Abraham Hummel, two Tammany Hall lawyers, published *In Danger*. At first glance the book is an attempt to inform the naïve about the numerous pitfalls to be encountered in the city but, on closer inspection, it turns out to be a practical guide for those bent on criminal action. One section provided instructions on how to manufacture state-of-the-art tools for breaking into sealed premises. Another drew attention to 'traveling bags with false, quick-opening sides' and special burglars' vests, replete with various compartments, into which items of value could be stuffed.[12]

Goldberg's brother Joseph, a fence, who ran a second-hand clothing store on Division Street, introduced him to the local burglaring fraternity, including twenty-two-year-old Louis Sturm of Sheriff Street. Goldberg hired a room on nearby Delancey and spent a good deal of time with his relatives. But there was bad blood in the family. Back in Poland in 1885, one of the Brietstein sisters had married a small-time German crook, Rauschauer Budner, who had borrowed about $230 from Joseph Goldberg. But when Budner later appeared in New York, he refused to repay the loan. Unable to squeeze Budner (alias Butner) himself, Joseph Goldberg got two corrupt precinct cops to help him. For a share in the proceeds, Detective-Sergeants Charles Jacobs and Charles McManus agreed to take in Butner on trumped-up charges and to release him should he settle the debt in cash. They arrested Butner who took them to a pawnshop on Orchard where he got $250 for some diamond jewellery, thereby buying his release. This ugly business, relayed to Joseph Lis by either Butner or the Goldbergs, was the source of much ongoing tension in Division Street.[13]

Lis, focused on prostitution if not prostitutes, got a room on Chatham and spent most of his time roaming the Lower East Side. Joseph Moscovitz, yet another older Pole who may have accompanied him and Adolph Goldberg on their journey from London to New York, helped ease him into the underworld of Manhattan vice. Moscovitz, with good connections in Jewish organised crime, introduced Lis to members of the Max Hochstim Association (MHA) who, in turn, ushered him into the murky world of 'cadets' and 'lighthouses' where he encountered dozens of pickpockets of about his own age. Lis, however, had ambitions of his own and no intention of hanging about in the lower ranks of crime.

Years later, Lis claimed to have arrived in New York with 'one thousand American dollars' and said that he had started 'a business as a barber'.[14] He may well have had some start-up capital from an exit-burglary in London and he did spend some time at a barbershop in Suffolk Street, but his main interest was undoubtedly in a small 'cigar store' at 118 Delancey. The shop was a stone's throw away from the headquarters of the Max Hochstim Association, an organisation seemingly dedicated to Jewish charitable causes and voluntary works. Moscovitz introduced him to Joseph Heller, an MHA committee member who, for $75, allowed Lis to place a 'cousin' – actually Heller's whore-wife, Esther – as well as Sadie Wolff and others in the cigar store. It was probably Lis who, for his own reasons, asked Esther to work under the name 'Annie'.[15]

Neither the barbershop nor the cigar store did particularly well or, in retrospect, perhaps they did too well. Lis seemed incapable of managing his new income. In a story that was to become all too familiar, Lis saw himself as the victim of a conniving prostitute. He claimed that he and Esther, whom he subsequently discovered to be Mrs Heller, went to live on Orchard Street and that 'she got possession of my money and everything else that I had'. More pertinently, he 'began to drink' – more likely continued to drink – and spent more time with 'burglars, pickpockets and "flim-flam" men'.[16] Either way, within months of his arrival he was short of funds. He was not alone.

Across the way, Adolph Goldberg, too, was struggling. He had undertaken several small burglaries on his own account, denying the precinct police a share of the proceeds. Arrogance, stupidity, or a combination thereof caused Goldberg and Lis again to exclude Jacobs and McManus when they planned a modest daytime foray to raise necessary cash.

On Sunday 22 September 1889 Lis, equipped with 'false keys' and a 'shoplifters' bag' linked up with Goldberg and together they made their way to Clinton Street where they had targeted a first-floor apartment occupied by a married Jewish couple. They kept the premises under observation until the Rubinsteins left the building. Goldberg remained outside, guarding the approaches. Lis went upstairs and slipped into the apartment. The pickings, however, were exceptionally lean. He popped a dollar-fifty into a pocket and had just picked up a silk shawl when Sarah Rubinstein returned unexpectedly. He saw her, hissed that he would kill her if she made a sound and then spat in her face before pushing her to the ground, running down the stairs, and leaving the building via a rear exit. She picked herself up and followed, screaming. He fled, scaling several wooden fences.[17]

The Fox was eagerly pursued by a growing pack of males which was soon joined by two policemen. Officer Charles Fay eventually cornered and arrested him in a tenement block on Hester Street. Lis appeared before Judge Randolph B. Martine, on 10 October. Not even a parade of witnesses for the defence that included Goldberg and Annie Heller could persuade the jury of his innocence. The jurors, sensing an amateur operation, took his age into account and 'rendered a verdict of guilty of burglary in the third degree with a recommendation to mercy'. Martine sentenced him to two and a half years in the state penitentiary. Joseph Lis, recently of Whitechapel, would not be a free man until 1893.[18]

Adolph Goldberg was soon to see more of the judge. Like a mongrel attracted by the smell of a passing tramp, failure dogged his every step. On 4 December, he and Louis Sturm appeared before Martine charged with the burglary of an apartment on the third floor of a tenement block on Suffolk Street occupied by another Jewish married couple, the Levensons. They had stolen goods worth $300, including a lady's gold watch. Goldberg, who appeared either to know or to learn nothing, had again set up a project without prior police approval. Charles Jacobs arrested them and claimed in court that the accused were 'well known to him as thieves'. Sturm probably got smart and somehow reached an accommodation with Jacobs; Goldberg did not. Sturm was found not guilty and discharged but Goldberg, 'guilty of burglary in the third degree', was sentenced to two years and three months' hard labour in the state penitentiary.[19]

Twice within fifty days in late 1889, Goldberg and Lis, unsuccessful burglars, fell foul of a fairly complex system which they did not acknowledge; a system in which corrupt police farmed out the right to commit offences against property in their precinct in return for a share of the loot. Goldberg never got the point but Lis was already mastering the lesson.

* * *

The holding cells in the Halls of Justice between Franklin and Leonard were better known to New Yorkers as 'The Tombs'. Lis spent forty-eight hours there before being loaded into a Black Maria for the short ride to the station. The train sneaked out of Manhattan, eased across the Hudson and then, stuck to the right bank as it picked up steam and headed north.[20] On the far bank, blue water gave way to streaks of gold and russet where the last of the autumn leaves clung to skeleton trees. The air tumbling down steep cliff-sides was clean and pleasant.

After Yonkers, the river brushed aside the hills and, with broad sweeps, spread out along the valley floor. Only when the river silence was complete did Lis become aware of other sounds. Voices got louder, the journey grew longer and thirty-five miles up the track, the train rolled past a forbidding building and, sighing steam, pulled into Ossining.

The first Americans, reconciled to nature, called the place Ossine-Ossine, meaning 'stone-upon-stone'. The settlers who followed had different notions and renamed it Silver Mine Farm. By the time state prison authorities got interested in the site in the early nineteenth century, all thought of mining had gone and, taken with the tranquil riverside and the project they were embarking on, insisted on seeing the place as Mount Pleasant.

A guard shouted instructions. Prisoners scrambled out, littering the platform in their disorder. Barked into silence and hounded into the outline of a unit, they marched out of the station and up a winding road that climbed parallel to the river. They had gone no further than a few blocks when they were confronted by a stone and iron edifice; 44 feet wide, 476 feet long: four tiers of cell windows housing a thousand inmates grinned down at them. It was easy to see why the name Mount Pleasant had never stuck to the place. Convicts hacking marble from the surrounding quarries saw the place more as the first Americans did and, at the end of the day, it was a variation on the original Indian terminology that triumphed. This was Sing Sing and, in two phrases that did take root in everyday English, it was at 'the end of the line', or 'up the river'.[21]

Its reputation was as gloomy as the airless room that Lis was shoved into. A bloodless face that could have been there when the penitentiary opened in 1827 peered over a register. A mechanical hand positioned a regulation-issue pen above a clean sheet. The first warden, like those who followed, was obsessed with the need for discipline and silence. He said nothing. It had taken two decades for the first warden to be persuaded that inmates might be allowed to smoke. Cold showers, darkened cells, floggings and solitary confinement were the staple fare and, up to 1873, prisoners were still being strung up by their thumbs. The place was as corrupt, overcrowded and 'immoral' as any of its type.

In 1884, the holding capacity of the main block was increased by cramming several convicts into a single cell 'seven feet long, six feet high and three feet six inches wide' with windows 'ten inches wide and twenty-four inches high'. By the time Lis got there, on 12 October

1889, the cramped conditions in which the 1,500 inmates were held contributed to practices the prison doctor saw as being 'too degrading and disgusting to be named'. Efforts at reform through involvement in productive labour led to such widespread abuse that, in 1888, the state legislature was forced to terminate it; in 1889 it was reintroduced in more controlled form. By 1890, Sing Sing was considered to be in a state of advanced decay.[22]

The 'receiving clerk' had been around long enough to note how the intake had changed over time. In the 1860s and 1870s, New York's hardest criminals – muscular, disturbed, armed robbers, murderers and rapists – were sent upstream to the quarries at Ossining. But the new wave of immigration had occasioned a change. By the end of the 1880s younger men more focused on what cunning and deception could deliver by way of property than crude physical force were in the majority. Lis seemed typical of the new brand but, for reasons only he knew, he was keen to ensure that he was not perceived as a Polish Jew who had, until quite recently, been in Whitechapel. The alienated clerk, who had heard and seen it all before, duly recorded the blend of fact and fiction he was presented with.[23]

Lis was five feet eight and a half inches tall and weighed 140 pounds. His eyes were grey, his hair was brown, and his complexion sallow. He had 'a large looking head, but said that he wore a six and seven-eights hat' which offset his size nine shoes. He claimed to be a barber and said that he was literate – positive attributes that might help take the edge off prison life – but went on to lie by claiming that he was living at 190 Sheriff Street at the time of his arrest. Then, showing that the short apprenticeship in New York had not been wasted on him, he alleged that he could no longer recall the name of the officer who had arrested him. He admitted to 'intemperate habits', owning up to smoking and drinking, and the clerk, looking at a face 'full of pimples', took it as evidence of a degenerate lifestyle. Lis said he was 'single', and pronounced himself to be a 'Protestant'. The clerk contemplated what was proffered, took a last searching look at him and then, in a careful and deliberate hand, wrote down his summary: 'features quite Jewish – except nose'.[24]

The clerk was not to be trifled with since he also determined what category a prisoner was assigned to, and in Sing Sing that shaped the quotidian world. Grade C was for those beyond hope – hardened, older prisoners with long or indeterminate sentences ineligible for parole who were to be denied access to productive work, confined to hard labour in the quarries and kept from positions of trust. Grade B prisoners, depending on age, disposition and length of sentence, could acquire basic skills through productive labour and, where appropriate, were allowed to participate in recreational activities including 'choir-singing'. Grade A was for the prison aristocracy. Young men, first-time offenders eligible for parole after they had served a third of their sentences, A-graders were encouraged to improve their education by making use of the library, could attend prison school on weekday afternoons, take on positions of trust, work at productive labour and earn some money that might help them on their discharge. Lis, sentenced to two and a half years' imprisonment without hard labour by a reluctant jury, got an A grading, and Goldberg a B when he arrived to do his two and a quarter years' hard labour, a mere six weeks later.[25]

Not even an A grading, however, could exempt inmates from Sing Sing's most brutalising demands. All inmates had to wear broad-stripe, black-and-white numbered uniforms of the type used by chain-gangs doing public works in the American South. All collective movement was undertaken in unison through the physically intimate lock-step march. Outside formal recreation hours, all prisoners were expected to remain silent at all times.[26]

The silence rule proved impossible to implement. Yet its mere existence and the possibility of punishment meant that inside the main block all whispering lay blanketed beneath a fog as thick as that which enveloped the fortress in winter. Outside, in the yard or beyond, the silence rule, prison uniforms and the lock-step contrived to slot men into an elongated, centipede-like creature. It marched about Ossining, hissing audibly as angled knees creased in unison, stretched and released rough prison fabric to the sound of leather boots crunching on granite pebbles. It was intentionally dehumanising; the effects not easily dispelled back in the cell blocks or in the intimacy of shared stone niches.

In 'The House of Fear' the routine was as dour and unimaginative as the prison floor. Each morning, at 6.15, the bell rang, giving prisoners fifteen minutes to wash, dress and put their cells in order. At 6.30 a.m. the duty officer appeared, unlocked the doors, saw to it that every man produced a night bucket, and assembled his company on the landing. Once the buckets had been taken down and emptied, the men were marched off to breakfast. At 7.30 a.m. the whistle blew and those destined for the quarries were marched out while the foreman, instructors and remaining inmates filtered into the workshops watched by the turnkeys. At 11.30 work stopped for the dinner hour and then recommenced, without break, until 4.30 when the morning's procedures were put into reverse. Companies were marched off to collect their night buckets, back to their galleries, and locked into the cells for the night. Inside each cell men were made to stand close to their barred doors until all had been accounted for and then, once the tally had been verified, the 'all clear' signal was given and prisoners were left to their own devices.[27]

This thirteen-hour nightly incarceration paled beside the confinement prisoners endured at the week's end. Inmates were locked away for thirty-six hours at a stretch between noon Saturday and 6.15 a.m. on Monday. Over weekends hot, unimaginative weekday rations gave way to small portions of cold coffee, stew and rice shoved through cell doors. Some attempted to enliven the sloppy fare by heating it over burning paper placed above brimming night buckets. Disgust and despair swilled through the galleries and prisoners were markedly less tractable on 'Blue Mondays'. Demanding seasonal rhythms, weekend ordeals and unsuccessful attempts at escape or suicide made for pervasive melancholia and cases of outright insanity.[28]

Survival depended on clinging to benefits derived from the grading system or additional privileges earned through 'good behaviour'. Lis and Goldberg guarded their own with considerable success. Within their all-male environment, as in society beyond, good conduct was predicated on attitudes and values as well as unstated ideas about gender. The ambivalent roles played by prison trusties brought out, changed, or modified existing personality traits. Lis, opportunistic and self-centred, found himself between the pressure from prison officers to collaborate and the impetus from some inmates to resist. Cunning and duplicity enabled him to reconcile these tensions, and somehow he became both an exemplary inmate and a convict fairly at home in Sing Sing's brutal homoerotic sub-culture.[29]

A Grade A prisoner, he was exempted from hard labour and a member of the inner circle cultivated by officers in a climate rife with favouritism. Inherently disposed to manipulating authority and power, Lis thrived. Along with about a hundred others on 'light duties' he may have tended the ill in the sick bay, carried messages as a 'hallway boy', cut hair in the barbershop, shelved books in the library, prepared food in the kitchen or dished out rations in the dining hall. It is not clear what exactly he did do but it may be significant that, on his release, he switched from calling himself a barber – an unambiguously male occupation harking back to the East End – and, for a while, saw himself as a 'waiter' – a calling less gender-edged. In Grade B, Goldberg, a 'clothes dealer', worked at sewing and, on his release, reclassified himself as a 'tailor'.

In prison, Lis, increasingly ambivalent about his own sexuality, found himself in roles entailing elements of nurturing and serving – caring functions which, in the society beyond Sing Sing, were more readily, although hardly exclusively, associated with women. Young trusties were made to serve older, tougher, more 'manly' inmates at the behest of those who ultimately exercised most power of all – the uniformed, corrupt prison guards.[30] It is unknown whether Lis, with his marked dislike of women and loathing of prostitutes, saw 'light duties' as having recognisably female components or, if he did, what this did to his sense of self-worth. What is known is that, when viewed from a structural as opposed to an interpersonal vantage point, neither B nor C-grade convicts had reason to regard A-graders with genuine affection, since they failed to embody the values of 'manliness' most admired in the prison confines. These, and other, ambiguities of the psyche contributed to the bouts of depression he was becoming prone to.

A boxing enthusiast, Lis had reasons of his own for being contemptuous of a few of the less physically inclined trusties. When boredom drove him to the library, he discovered that visits were not cost-free. The inmate in charge dispensed books only to those who smuggled in tea, tobacco or other small items suitable for use as prison currency. Haynes, alias Hallen, a former schoolmaster who presided over classes that met for three-quarters of an hour at the end of the day, was a more appealing character. Haynes coached the illiterate Goldberg to the point where, by the time that he left prison, he could write in Yiddish and sign his letters with a flourish. Lis was equally taken with Haynes's insights into the American constitution and legal knowledge, and learned much from him about the rights of the accused and criminal court procedures. More impressively still, Haynes was a master of the art of prison survival, a notorious 'stool pigeon' of the sort that Lis could admire.[31]

The system encouraged collaboration and it counted in Lis's favour when, as scheduled, he appeared before the warden in June 1890 – nine months after entering Sing Sing and almost a third of the way through his lengthy sentence. Both the principal keeper and prison doctor attested to his good behaviour and, a few weeks later, the warden addressed a letter to the Governor of New York State recommending executive clemency. But the wheels of the administration in Albany turned at the familiar bureaucratic pace and it was October before Lis heard that his sentence had been commuted by six months.[32]

Read in fading light filtering through a cell window the news was cheering, but not overwhelming. It assumed a better hue a few weeks later, when Goldberg, too, had his sentence commuted. Fate had pushed them together and it intended keeping them together when they left prison within a day of one another in October 1891. But during the autumnal weeks that followed, the chill in the house of stone became more intense and Lis found it difficult to urge body and mind through the mindless routines of prison life. A miserable paradox beset him. Instead of being cheered by thoughts of time served, he was overcome by depression when contemplating time yet to elapse and things to come.

Lis's mood swings, as much a by-product of syphilis contracted in Whitechapel as a response to the immediate situation, deepened. So, too, did his strange affinity with Goldberg. It was at about this time – as the two contemplated possible new starts – that Lis recommenced the experiments in semantics which led him to adopt the surname by which he became known all around the Atlantic world – Silver. Its deepest roots, as already noted, lay with the woman who troubled him most in his life, his mother, Hannah Kwekzylber. For the moment, however, he was getting most of his comfort from another, male, source. The words 'gold' and 'silver' lent themselves to coupling even if some might have thought it closer to 'horse and carriage' than 'love and marriage'. It was an amusing game played in an age debating the virtues of bimetallism but it was also one which, in his mind, gave him quasi-kinship status within the extended Goldberg family. In 1898, in a different context, he gave Goldberg's brother-in-law, Salus Budner, the alias 'Joe Gold'.

On 12 October 1891, Lis stepped out of the prison stripes that had never quite moulded themselves to his body and slipped into the suit that had brought him to Ossining. Without the lock-step he could walk freely, but his spirits dragged. The cost of a rail ticket had taken a huge chunk out of his prison savings. It was chilly on the platform and it seemed like a winter's month in the cells before the train from Albany lumbered in. He clambered aboard and took a last look at the tree stubble on the hill opposite the prison. The locomotive chugged out past the House of Fear and then settled down to a brisker pace, following the Hudson. He was not sure where he was going; it hardly mattered.

The train charged down the valley but it could not go fast enough for him; he wanted Sing Sing, New York and the United States behind him. The idea flashed through his mind that he should perhaps return to England. A few cousins he could trust had recently abandoned Poland but run out of funds in London. Perhaps he should join them? They were, after all, part of his own family, real flesh and blood. But the horrors of Whitechapel were all too recent, part of a personal history he wished to conceal for ever. It was 'Joseph Silver', a new persona searching for new opportunities, who disembarked at Grand Central. But the past clung to him like the smell of wet dog and, in the end, it was Adolph Goldberg's friend that went back into the Lower East Side.

*   *   *

Lis got himself a room near the barbershop close to his former pimping haunts but, true to his nature, it could have been at either of the addresses he used over the fortnight that followed – 161 Broome Street or 177 Chrystie. He visited the 'cigar shop' on Delancey to reclaim some items he had left when he was sent to prison. On the way in, he saw Sadie Wolff who had never got on well with him. Annie Heller gave him the key to a box she had secured for him at the time of his arrest. The whores seemed to bother him less than they had before he went to Sing Sing, and Joseph Silver prepared himself for a fresh start.[33]

He found part-time employment in a restaurant and earned some cash but the lure of London and the East End again made itself felt. Perhaps he really could return there in his new guise? Lis had been a Polish Jew in Whitechapel – a persona in a place he wished for ever to conceal – but Silver, with his emerging accent, was more of an American. He persuaded a 'barber', Frank Miller, to act as his witness in perpetrating a small but vital fraud. On 15 October 1891, three days after his leaving Sing Sing, they went to the New York County's Superior Court where 'Joseph Silver', a 'restaurant-keeper' took the oath of citizenship as a prelude to obtaining a passport. The recording clerk, perhaps chosen for his understanding attitude in such matters, paid no attention to detail. Miller did not live at the address he offered the court. 'Joseph Silver' was equally mean with the truth. He lived, he said, on

Broome Street and was originally from 'Imperial Russia'. His date and place of birth, the date on which he had first set foot in the United States three years earlier, and his port of entry, all remained unrecorded.[34]

Concealment of past, naturalisation and personal transformation were effected at the stroke of a pen. 'Joseph Silver', American citizen, born fully formed in a courtroom, emerged grasping naturalisation papers that never, ever, left his clutches as he later criss-crossed the Atlantic. The clerk's inked scratchings helped give birth to a new legal persona while a stain of lies spread over the earlier, messier parts of Joseph Lis's life. Gone was an illegitimate child abandoned in London; and gone were two years only just completed, in Sing Sing. It was a small Manhattan miracle and the future looked assured.

But then, three days later, Goldberg materialised. He got a room on Stanton and, back together, he and Lis established the cost of steamship fares and debated ways of raising cash. They identified a place not far from the Williamsburg Bridge and acquired burglars' tools, two sets of false keys and a new, purpose-made canvas bag for carrying loot. Goldberg, ever hopeful, took charge. On 27 October they collected the equipment and headed for the elbow in the East River. They were early and stood about talking on the corner of Jackson and Madison, not noticing that they were being observed. Detective Charles Jacobs took it all in. Needing to kill time, they wandered off, south of Canal Street, followed by Jacobs. Somewhere along the line Jacobs came across officers McManus and Long and, by the time they headed back to Madison three detectives were on their tail. They entered the building, but it was not their day. They were disturbed and re-emerged minutes later, still conversing. Five minutes later they went back in, but when they again emerged empty-handed they were arrested on suspicion of conspiring to commit a burglary. They were taken to the Attorney Street station, searched, and found to be in possession of the usual professional paraphernalia. It was all painfully familiar. The two nights spent in the squalid Attorney Street lock-up were depressing. On 29 October, they appeared in the police court only to have the matter referred to a Grand Jury, and hear bail set at $1,000 each. They didn't have 1,000 cents. The next day Jacobs and the other detectives arrived to take them across to the Tombs but, on the way, stopped off at a saloon so that they could sit down and talk the matter through like adult men. They were told that it would cost them $250, each, to get off the charges they faced.

In the Tombs, Goldberg spent several days in a feverish, but unsuccessful, attempt to raise cash. His counter-offer of $65 was dismissed out of hand. Frustrated by Jacobs's refusal, Goldberg resigned himself to the situation and instead let his thoughts run to revenge. Lis, master of the collaborative arts, sensed his chances ebbing away and, self-centred as ever, decided to abandon his partner. He got a message to 'a friend, a lady' – almost certainly Annie Heller – to raise most of the money probably from the Max Hochstim Association, and had it delivered to Jacobs and McManus. When the prisoners appeared before the Grand Jury, on 4 November 1891, Goldberg told the jurors that the three arresting officers were corrupt and that they had demanded money in return for his release. Lis said nothing, insisting only on his innocence. By the time Jacobs got round to testifying, he was no longer certain that the canvas bag found on the accused at the time of the arrest belonged to Lis.

Goldberg knew that he had probably secured himself a one-way ticket up the river. When they appeared before the Court of the General Sessions a few days later, Joseph Lis – whose name had helpfully mutated from Lis to Liss, then to Lees and finally to John Leiss – was discharged. Goldberg, who changed his plea from not guilty to guilty was sentenced to a year's imprisonment. 'John Leiss' had never been found guilty of an offence, 'Joseph Lis' was an unknown previous offender, and 'Joseph Silver' had had nothing whatsoever to do with the burglary. Emboldened by his success, he set out to consolidate his position with Jacobs and McManus:

> After being discharged, I went to the detectives to get some trinkets that had been taken out of my pockets. They told me that, since I was smart enough to keep my mouth shut, I could do everything in the world if I would only do the right thing by them. They gave me their address, and informed me that should I get into trouble, I should send for them.[35]

Goldberg's blunder had, rather unexpectedly, left Lis with the one key that was prized above all others in New York City underworld – one that opened a small side door in Tammany Hall. It had all been worth while and Silver's emigration plans were shelved.

IV

NEW YORK CITY
1891–1893

... he could understand the mind of a burglar, because, as
a matter of fact, the mind and the instincts of the burglar
are of the same kind as the mind and the instincts of a police
officer. Both recognize the same conventions, and have a
working knowledge of each other's methods and of the routine
of their respective trades. They understand each other, which
is advantageous to both, and establishes a sort of amenity
in their relations

Joseph Conrad, *The Secret Agent*

HEAVILY dependent on cheap labour for growth since the time of slavery,
not even the powerful American economy could escape a mauling by
the Great Depression. Throughout the 1880s and 1890s riots and
strikes – often led by a cohort of partly assimilated workers standing
on the backs of recent arrivals – testified to working-class hardship. In
heavy industries all round the country, including mining, railways and
steel production, determined capitalists, sometimes aided by a small
army of Pinkerton agents, inflicted crushing defeats on organised labour,
giving rise to deeply embittered workers.

In New York State where, unlike neighbouring Pennsylvania, there
were few heavy industries, a broadly similar process was at work. Tens
of thousands of East Europeans worked in light manufacturing enterprises centred on the Jewish immigrant quarters of the Lower East
Side. But bakers, cigar-, cigarette-, cloak-, garment- or hat-makers in
sweatshops and other enterprises were vulnerable to the economic logic
that flowed from a glut of cheap labour, seasonal work and the

depression. Long hours and low wages caused angry strikes as fledgling labour movements, dominated by more established workers, struggled to establish themselves amidst surges from the incoming tides of immigrants.

Jewish workers, although drawn together by an overarching sense of 'Yiddishness' nevertheless struggled to overcome the particularism of Old World backgrounds. Many reached for familiar ideologies as they repositioned themselves in the fiercely capitalist environment of their adopted country. The 'Pioneers of Liberty' and others, intoxicated with anti-Tsarist Russian populism, looked to anarchism and terror, the adjunct of the 'propaganda of the deed', to advance their cause. Others drew on *bundist* or socialist roots to contribute to new labour movements like the United Hebrew Trades. Most imported ideas eventually either dribbled away or were channelled into broadly based movements or political parties where their effect was greatly diluted. New York's conservative middle class viewed the advent of these more radical organisations with some alarm and took them as a sign of the pressing need for reform but, at the same time, were privately cheered by the existence of a formidable machine that kept their municipal affairs operating within the broad parameters set by orthodox American party politics.[1]

As he negotiated the closing months of 1891, the slump in 1892 and one of the steeper dips within the depression in 1893, Joseph Lis was comforted by the thought that most of his day-to-day business was underwritten by the police. Although Jacobs and McManus were only small cogs in the machine that drove the city he knew that, provided he behaved sensibly, there would be no unscheduled second trip up the river. Tammany Hall somehow reconciled criminal activity with public order and good governance and he was free to pursue his own interests. A middle-ranking pimp, most of his regular income came from crimes against people; from 'protection' money handed over by frightened prostitutes. Other income derived from crimes involving property – burglary, robbery and theft. Seemingly discrete, both streams of income were informed by the overlapping information fed him by other young and equally opportunistic gangsters.

Immediately after his release from prison Lis's energy went into crude efforts to acquire cash. Fortunately, most of these exploits – but by no means all – were recorded thirty-six months later in an extraordinary, partly truthful interview with one of the only two employers he ever worked for formally. Hours after reaching an initial understanding, he went back to the detectives. With Jacobs and McManus watching from over the road, he entered a Chinese laundry, leapt over the counter, grabbed the cash box and then ran off to a saloon on Essex Street, where the three of them sat down to share $50.[2]

Having passed a first, nervous, test, he exposed his partners to more ambitious projects:

> Then I located a place at ——— Street, where there was living a rich man. I went to the detectives and told them that if they wanted to make some money they should go along with me. We went to the place in the night time. The detectives stood guard on the corner of Pitt and Broome Streets; for the purpose that, should there be an outcry, I would run into their hands. I got in through the window. I got watches, diamonds and cash to the amount of five hundred dollars. The next morning I pawned the goods and divided the money with the detectives.[3]

Before long, Lis identified a favourite target of his: a jewellery store, this time on Houston. What followed was an operation later to be repeated on several other continents with minor modifications. It was destined to become something of a criminal signature:

> I informed the detectives and made arrangements to meet them. We met, and they went with me and tried the key in the door, so I could open the door the next morning. Two or three days later I went with two detectives and stationed one at the corner of Ridge and Houston Streets and the other at the corner of Pitt and Houston Streets. When the man went out to dinner I opened the door and robbed the place of about twenty-five watches. I sold some of them to ——— who keeps a dive at 41 East ——— Street, and I pawned some of the goods and I divided the money with the detectives.[4]

Having possibly already betrayed Adolph Goldberg on two other occasions – on either side of the Atlantic – Lis seldom hesitated to entrap his criminal associates.

> A man named ——— lived at ——— R[ivington] Street. I told him how I could make a couple of thousand dollars, and

invited him to go with me at night time. He accepted the
invitation. I gave him a lot of burglar's tools to carry. I had
arranged with detectives [Jacobs] and [McManus] to wait
outside on the street. The man walked a little behind me.
The detectives jumped on him and kept him at headquarters
two days. I went and told his wife that by paying a sum of
money he would be released, and if not he was liable to get
a couple of years. His wife raised fifty dollars and paid it to
the detectives in a saloon near the Tombs. The burglar's tools
were not shown to the judge and the man was discharged.[5]

In receipt of an income that allowed him to underwrite all his physical needs, Lis was by now also operating in a psychological climate
totally attuned to the process of 'splitting'. He could, at one and the
same time, do and say things completely at variance with one another.
At one level, he was working with law enforcers who could, no doubt,
be bent to assist him in intimidating or threatening prostitutes as well
as helping him with his personal or professional vendettas. At another,
he was working in the Max Hochstim Association.

From late 1891 to early 1893, Lis lounged about saloons keeping
the company of lighthouses and pickpockets, or working with older
pimps as he solicited customers for Rosa Schmidt and Sadie Wolff who
shared a tenement with him on Orchard. The vice business, too,
demanded traits which, if he had not already mastered them, he quickly
developed as he and other cadets set about seducing or, when necessary, drugging and raping young women destined for the trade in
commercial sex. By their own admission, Jacobs and McManus were
aware that Lis was involved in these 'unsavory professions' but, rather
than get involved directly themselves, they remained content to take
cash payments in exchange for extending their protection to prostitutes. Like Lis, they were capable of combining cynicism and pragmatism in equal measure. As Lis later recalled:

At Number —— Norfolk Street a man kept a saloon. I met
a boy pickpocket who had some money, and I informed
detective [Jacobs] of this, and suggested that he arrest the
boy and give him a bluff, and we would get some money
out of him. The detective arrested the boy and took him as
far as Houston and Chrystie Streets, where I met them and

told the boy that it was best to square it with the detective. The boy told me to run quickly to the saloon and tell his friends that they should raise money enough to get him released. I got fifty dollars, and the boy was never taken to headquarters and I divided the money with the detective.[6]

Very rarely, as on the day he set up the man on Rivington with burglar's tools, Lis would intervene on behalf of those who worked with or for him. On 3 December 1891 Nelson Trebos, a Russian 'barber' of Orchard Street and Adolph Fischer, a German 'upholsterer' of Stanton, were picking pockets on lower Broadway when they heard an enormous explosion in the nearby Arcadia Building. An unstable young man from Boston, Henry L. Norcross, had walked into the office of the banking magnate, Russell Sage and demanded a million dollars in cash. When the demand was rejected out of hand he detonated a dynamite bomb, instantly decapitating himself but only injuring the financier.

Within minutes a crowd gathered. Jacobs, McManus and a third officer arrived and watched as the pickpockets, profiting from the commotion, worked the crowd. Fischer dipped into a dress pocket, removed the woman's pocketbook and passed it to the waiting Trebos, but the two were arrested before they could flee. As Lis later recalled:

> The same day [3 December 1891] a crank went into Russell Sage's office and threw a bomb, and while the crowd had collected there two pickpockets were caught by Detectives [Jacobs], [McManus] and [McNaught]. They were held for trial, and I saw the detectives and gave them money to release them, and when the time came for trial only one detective appeared, and his evidence was not sufficient to convict them.[7]

This was just one of thirty-three cases involving Lis, Jacobs and McManus between November 1891 and April 1893. Several of these cases were independently corroborated by a leading city lawyer in 1895 and some – including that of Fischer and Trebos – can be verified to this day by reference to documents held in New York City's Municipal Archives. So successful was the partnership between Burglar-Detective Lis and Detective-Burglar Jacobs that the relationship took on an additional social dimension that almost transcended business requirements. Jacobs and the corrupt New York Police Department helped deepen the spilt in the Jekyll-and-Hyde personality of Lis-Silver.[8]

Jacobs, the son of immigrant Jews, was born in New York in 1861. He was thirty and seven years older than Lis when they became partners in 1891. Raised in a German-speaking home and educated in his mother tongue, Jacobs was equally fluent in Yiddish which he refined on the streets of the Lower East Side. Cunning and thickset, Jacobs joined the police in the early 1880s and was, for a time, assigned duties around the German theatre.[9]

In 1884, the city's corrupt Chief of Police, Thomas F. Byrnes, reorganised the police force and appointed Detective-Sergeant Jacobs to a newly established elite investigative unit. Jacobs, one of only twenty Jews in the NYPD in the early 1890s, earned $400 a year more than did an ordinary patrolman. A 'burglar cop' as opposed to a 'square cop', like most men in the ranks at the time, Jacobs was an active supporter of the Democratic Party.[10] Byrnes saw in him the potential for more sensitive duties and put him in charge of extraditions across state lines. In 1893, at the lowest point in the depression, Jacobs was sent to report on anarchist and socialist meetings where Jewish activists often delivered speeches in German or Yiddish. Jacobs was instrumental in getting the anarchist-feminist, Emma Goldman, charged with 'criminal incitement', and was later made to arrange her extradition from Pennsylvania when she fled the state. On Byrnes's instruction, Jacobs collected Goldman in Philadelphia and, on board the train back to New York, told her that he was a Jew and then tried to persuade her to become an informer. She responded by flinging the remains of a glass of iced water in his face.[11]

Jacobs, a creature of the moral twilight, thus occupied a profoundly ambiguous role at an extraordinary moment in the city's history. As a detective present at the birth of the modern criminal investigation department, he lived and worked in a precinct enveloped in an ethical fog. Arrogant, opportunistic and venal, Jacobs was encouraged to cultivate criminal and political informers in a climate of conspiracy. Lis, with a penchant for conspiracies and criminal behaviour was drawn ever more deeply into this amoral existence where it was difficult to tell a criminal-policeman from a policeman-criminal. Lis, whose capacity to distinguish between good and evil had always been seriously impaired if it existed at all, and whose sense of self-worth had been at its lowest ebb in Ossining, began to feel better about himself and defined his role in more flattering terms.

He was no longer a troubled young man who had fled the East End after some crazed vigilante had tried to cleanse Whitechapel of whores, or an amateurish burglar who had been incarcerated in Sing Sing, but someone engaged in mysterious, secret work. He was an integral part of an order under constant threat from gangsters and prostitutes. Although not a regular policeman like Jacobs, he, too, served the city and wider society and, in that sense, was not unlike a Pinkerton man. That was it; he was an 'agent'! It was nomenclature he became attached to for a decade. Trow's *New York Directory* confirms that from 1891 to 1893 'Joseph Silver', 'agent' resided at 344 East 4th Street.[12]

For his part, Jacobs slotted into Byrnes's scheme which allowed captains, and those serving below them, to parcel out precincts between them as personal fiefdoms operated for private gain. As 'bagmen', Jacobs and McManus retained 20 per cent of the cash proceeds from burglaries, robberies or thefts before passing on a share to their superior officer, Captain Devery. It was estimated that, in the early 1890s, the NYPD received about 10 per cent of the value of all robberies committed in Manhattan. Like other 'bagmen' Jacobs also collected pre-determined sums from brothels, gambling dens and liquor outlets before taking his cut and passing on the balance as 'protection money'.[13]

Byrnes presided over two bureaucratised, parallel, articulating structures – the one a visible law enforcement agency, with state-defined powers, designed to protect the public by preventing crime; the other a shadowy underworld style outfit with rules and procedures that allowed officers to encourage and benefit from crime. As head of the former, Byrnes, once a detective, set up the NYPD's 'Rogues Gallery', a collection of photographs of the country's most wanted criminals in which Lis's mugshot featured as number 1473. In the latter, phantom, organisation Byrnes's senior officers could purchase promotion by adhering to an established scale of tariffs, and protect ill-gotten gains by listing assets in their wives' names. It was a system in which those lower down the ranks were the ones who interacted most directly with criminals, and during the course of these exchanges distinctions between the personal and professional were further blurred.[14]

Detective Jacobs, a gangster with publicly conferred rank, and 'agent' Lis, a gangster with quasi-official, self-designated status, negotiated the business of their overlapping enterprises at watering-holes along the western margins of the Lower East Side. Max Cohen's saloon on Bowery was one venue; Flynn's, on the corner of Bowery and Pell, another. Lis particularly liked meeting at a noisy pub on Delancey, near the offices of the Max Hochstim Association, where they both knew the proprietor, Ike van Leer. Jacobs preferred a slightly more respectable venue, where law-abiding citizens and better fare offset the more familiar smells of stale beer and unwashed company. Mike Lyon's restaurant, between Houston and Stanton, famous for never having closed for a minute in thirty years of trading, was his meeting place of choice. There were occasions, however, when their negotiations were so fraught with risk that neither wished to be seen in public. Lis was a welcome guest in Jacobs's modest home on Mulberry.[15]

The intimacy of the Mulberry Street visits can be gleaned from the records of a police court hearing in 1895, when Jacobs was quizzed about his relationship with Silver:

Q. How long have you known S[ilver] (the burglar)?
A. Since the day of the arrest in Madison Street. I believe it was in October 1891.
Q. How many such people are you acquainted with?
A. I know a great many of them.
Q. And you recognise that as one of the established methods of the police department, cultivating the acquaintances of criminals that you may catch other criminals.
A. It is absolutely essential to our business.
Q. How many times did you see S[ilver] in those two years?
A. A thousand times.
Q. Did you ever write to him?
A. I think that I wrote him letters when I wanted to see him.
Q. How did you address him?
A. J[oe] S[ilver.]
Q. Friend Joe?
A. Yes, sir; it requires a little 'jolly' to keep these people in line.
Q. You used to meet him in a restaurant?
A. Yes, sir; he came to my house a hundred times and knows my children and my wife. I always received him with the utmost courtesy and acted to him like a man should to anybody. He sat at my table. I let him eat there when he was hungry. I have sat with him in public restaurants many times.

Q. This place, 'Lyons' where you say you met him, do you meet other thieves there?

A. Oh, yes, sir.

Q. Did you give him your address in writing?

A. Oh yes, I told him to send any letter, because I told him that any time he wanted to see me that he could either write to the post-office or police headquarters; that if he had anything he wanted to give me *urgently*, if it was in the afternoon, to direct it to the post-office box, because every afternoon I am downtown.[16]

Jacobs's 1895 testimony was notable for another reason. As in a supplementary account provided by Lis that year, there was no mention of the pair's involvement in the more sordid aspects of organised crime. In both their versions, there is a strange silence about any involvement with prostitutes or protection rackets between 1891 and 1893. Reluctant to concede their engagement in crimes against property, they were even more determined to keep silent about crimes against people, especially those involving women. As will become evident, there were good reasons for this. At the time, however, neither of the partners wanted to reveal anything about other associations that fed into Tammany Hall.

For Jewish gangsters running organised prostitution rackets the most convenient meeting place was Silver Dollar Smith's, a saloon opposite the Essex Street Market Court. The place got its name when the owner 'Charles Smith' (actually Finkelstein or Solomon) had thousands of coins studded into the floor of an establishment which was guarded by, amongst others, Monk Eastman. If Lis did not know Eastman, who went on to become one of the most notorious gangsters on the Lower East Side, he would have recognised the boxing heroes of the day who frequented the saloon, including Jack Dempsey, Tom Sharkey and John L. Sullivan. Other regulars who would have interested Lis less were political notables like 'Cross-Eyed' Murphy and 'Big Feet' Louie Gorden.[17]

Max Hochstim and a few East European friends contributed to the crust of respectability that shielded 'Silver Dollar' from his harshest critics. Like most respectable immigrant associations – *landmanshaftn* – the MHA devoted some of its energy to organising winter balls, summer picnics and other outings for newcomers to the city. Later it mutated into the New York Independent Benevolent Association, a funeral society which arranged for the burial of pimps who had been denied a resting place beside ordinary, God-fearing Jews. Even in the early 1890s, however, it was clear that the MHA was closely involved in crimes against both people and property.[18]

Hochstim owned the Sans Souci 'concert saloon' on Third Avenue where prostitutes from the Alhambra Hotel enjoyed the exclusive right to solicit for custom. The Russo-Polish cadets and lighthouses of the MHA supplemented their incomes in the usual ways and, during the worst of the depression in the 1890s, scoured mill towns in adjacent states buying, seducing or otherwise procuring the supply of fresh young prostitutes needed on the East Side. Frank Moss, the politically ambitious attorney who took charge of Lis's affairs in 1895, noted that, throughout his association with Jacobs, 'members of the Max Hochstim Association were always on hand when any money was at stake'.[19]

The real power in the Silver Dollar saloon, however, lay with a second, even less visible, grouping. Whereas the MHA was part block-based voluntary ethnic association, and part loosely knit criminal fraternity, the Essex Street Courthouse Gang had no such pretensions. It was a dedicated professional criminal outfit with political aspirations that embraced the 10th assembly ward.[20] Martin Engel, principal sex merchant in the quarter and 'honorary treasurer' of the MHA, had first made money through a thriving wholesale poultry business on the Lower East Side. He, Hochstim and Silver Dollar, however, had moved into loan-sharking, putting up bail for the scores of prostitutes that passed through the courthouse. Engel never looked back. He and his brother acquired some of the largest brothels on Allen, including a notorious 'fifty-cent' house, for close on $50,000. By the early 1890s, owning property valued at $200,000, Engel started standing surety for big-time criminals with links to city politicians and Tammany Hall. His friends included Chief Byrnes, Inspector McClaughlin, and Captain 'Big Bill' Devery of the 11th precinct as well as Jacobs and McManus. When Jacobs was eventually arrested, in 1895, it was Martin Engel who put up bail of $1,000.[21]

Engel's ability to pierce the cordon of municipal politics owed something to pragmatism in Tammany circles which, at first glance, seemed impenetrably Irish. Some of the same openness was evident in the career of Timothy D. – 'Big Tim' – Sullivan. The son of an alcoholic Irish father, 'Big Tim' worked his way up from bootblack and newsboy to become the owner of several successful saloons in lower Manhattan.

A lifelong supporter of the Democratic Party, he had won a bruising election to the state assembly in 1889 after Thomas Byrnes had accused him of keeping company with burglars, thieves and murderers. A populist of note, Sullivan extended his political base on the Lower East Side by incorporating several young Jewish hoodlums into his entourage, including Monk Eastman, 'Beansy' Rosenthal, Arnold Rothstein and Jake Wolff. By helping to bring out the Democrat vote and stuffing ballot boxes, these deracinated thugs helped ensure a resounding Tammany Hall victory in the 1892 municipal election. Not surprisingly, 'Big Tim' Sullivan was an honorary vice-president of the Max Hochstim Association.²²

In the early 1890s, New York thus presented a face to the world that was, simultaneously, quite exceptional and utterly prosaic. Its local government was easily recognisable in that the cousins – crime, law and politics – were seldom far apart. In older systems, where well established ruling classes liked to keep up public appearances, greater efforts were often made to keep the cousins apart even if, in private, they could barely keep their hands off one another. On the brash Lower East Side, however, the cousins were happy enough to share intimate moments. Jacobs and Lis were aware of the overlapping interests of the Essex Street Gang, the Max Hochstim Association, the NYPD and Tammany Hall but, for obvious reasons, tended to act on them in very different ways.

Jacobs, formally on the city payroll, with a clear interest in keeping politics, the law and crime in alignment, was a Tammany man through and through. For him the Democrats' victory in the 1892 election was reassuring in that it promised to keep the machine intact for another two years. The unexpected deepening of the depression in 1893 and the radical anarchist and socialist challenge that it gave rise to, however, threatened that stability and drew him away from criminal pursuits towards the fringes of radical politics.

As a criminal on the city's informal payroll, Lis cared very little, if at all, for politics. As some of his surviving letters demonstrate, he was capable of picking up the platitudes of the day and, if necessary, recycling them to senior state officials in the form of special appeals for 'justice', but this was almost always undertaken for opportunistic and utterly self-serving reasons. He kept abreast of current affairs but any interest remained strictly subservient to his obsessive pursuit of prostitutes and possibilities for theft. Jacobs's gradual shift from criminal to political work after 1892 did not bode well for their partnership and, in order to take out some insurance, Lis started taking note of the challenge to Tammany Hall emerging from an old civic organisation with a new leader.

In 1880 the Presbyterian Church on Madison Square was happy to welcome a new minister, the Reverend Charles Parkhurst. Raised in rural Massachusetts and a graduate of Amherst, Parkhurst was at home amongst 'Mugwumps' – upper middle-class Protestants with Republican sympathies. For more than a decade, he was content to look after the spiritual needs of his congregants, who included the Republican Governor of the state, Thomas Platt. But, by the early 1890s, he felt that he could no longer ignore the social pathologies of mass immigration and Tammany Hall corruption. The Society for the Prevention of Crime (SPC), a body with vaguely defined law enforcement powers dating back to an 1870s state charter, presented itself as an obvious vehicle for change. In April 1891, Parkhurst assumed leadership of the SPC on condition that its members accepted an extended and revised agenda that would require a far more radical approach to the many problems associated with liquor and 'vice'. It was a decision that set the society and its 'agents' and private detectives on a collision course not only with the city's brothel-owners and saloon-keepers, but with police and Tammany Hall politicians.[23]

Parkhurst's first foray into public life was on 14 February 1892, when he blasted away at Tammany Hall from his pulpit, complaining about 'the polluted harpies that, under the pretense of governing this city, are feeding day and night on its quivering vitals. 'They are,' he suggested, 'a lying, perjured, rum-soaked, and libidinous lot.' His sermon was carried in full by the supportive *Sunday World* but the initiative backfired when he was summoned to appear before a Grand Jury and was unable to substantiate his claims. Sceptical observers sympathised with Thomas Byrnes, a Democrat but not a Tammany member, who dismissed Parkhurst as a sensationalist in search of publicity.[24]

Stung by this reproach, Parkhurst prepared a second, more damaging attack. Advised by Attorney Frank Moss, an activist with Republican credentials, he hired C.W. Gardner as the SPC's 'Chief Detective' to obtain the evidence that would back his charges. Parkhurst, Gardner and Erving, a foppish socialite, disguised themselves and toured the *demi-monde*. These excursions, which the clergyman handled with aplomb but which later attracted some opprobrium, were subsequently written up in book form by Charles Gardner as *The Doctor and the Devil, or Midnight Adventures of Dr Parkhurst*.[25]

Armed with sworn affidavits, Parkhurst resumed his position in the pulpit and, on 13 March 1892, launched another blistering attack on Tammany Hall. A second appearance before a Grand Jury brought vindication, a sham reorganisation of sections of the police, several high-profile raids on disorderly houses and a series of show trials. But Tammany struck back. Gardner was framed, arrested and prosecuted for promoting the prostitution of his former wife. The conviction was eventually overturned in a superior court but he emerged humiliated and penniless from an eleven-month stay in the Tombs. Parkhurst, having secured his redoubt in Madison Square, moved about more confidently and, in the months that followed, continued to blaze away at Tammany helping to prepare the climate for a yet more serious assault on the bastion of municipal power.[26]

Lis and Jacobs's 1891–93 joint venture was rooted in a corrupt municipal system, but Tammany Hall was also under growing pressure to implement reforms. The underlying possibility of a shift in municipal power unsettled their partnership and there was further deterioration when Jacobs was redeployed to political work on the Lower East Side. Co-operation became difficult and then, at some point in the first quarter of 1893, there was a parting of the ways potentially so serious that Silver felt it wisest to leave town for a while. It was Sadie Wolff, one of the women in the house he lived in on Orchard, who noted that Lis, with another prostitute, had left New York City.

The bitter strike at the Carnegie steel mills in Pennsylvania in mid-1892 had caught Lis's attention since working-class hardship often paved the way for the recruitment of young women as prostitutes. With Goldberg still away upriver, but due for release, Lis and 'Rosie' Schmidt made their way to Pittsburgh. When Lis returned unexpectedly to the Lower East Side, some months later, it was in vastly altered circumstances and he was to help prime the pump for an extraordinarily turbulent period in the city's politics.[27]

V

PITTSBURGH
1893–1894

> He talked to himself, indifferent to the sympathy or hostility
> of his hearers, indifferent indeed to their presence, from the
> habit he had acquired of thinking aloud hopefully in the soli-
> tude of the four whitewashed walls of his cell, in the sepul-
> chral silence of the great blind pile of bricks near a river,
> sinister and ugly like a colossal mortuary for the socially
> drowned.
>
> Joseph Conrad, *The Secret Agent*

AT first glance the Appalachians appear to run from West Virginia in
the north-east to Tennessee in the south-west. But that is misleading.
On close examination it is clear that the northern extremities belong
rightfully to the Alleghenies whose foothills extend even further north
and east, into the pitted and scoured basins of western Pennsylvania.
Anybody setting out due west from New York is bound, after 350
miles, to confront the Alleghenies and the large watercourses that drain
its foothills. These rivers flow into the Ohio which, ever swelling, flows
south and west until it meets the mighty Mississippi.

Pittsburgh sits astride steep hills at a point where two such rivers
meet to form a third. The resulting Y lies on its side – its open mouth
gaping east towards the Atlantic while the thickened stem points west,
towards the remote Pacific. The upper jaw, the Allegheny River,
connects to the lower – the Monaghela – in downtown Pittsburgh
and after joining, they flow west as the Ohio. The confluence formed
a natural fortification for the colonists who erected Fort Pitt on the
site in the mid-eighteenth century. The settlement was well placed to

exploit cross-continental trade routes linking the east to the interior.

Left to its own devices, the heart of Pittsburgh might have pulsed to a mercantile beat and the town might have developed into a city dominated by gentlemanly commerce. But the river scalpels had exposed much of western Pennsylvania's mineral bounty, sources of wealth readily exploited by those intent on developing heavy industries in America at a time when the industrial revolution in Europe had lost some of its impetus. The proximity of large reserves of high-quality coking-coal, limestone and iron ore drawn largely from central Pennsylvania sealed the fate of the river city's natural environment.

The first iron foundry opened in 1806. As the century unfolded, production shifted from iron to steel, and by 1892 steel production surpassed that of iron. This transition from base commodity to a product of higher value was accompanied by the progressive consolidation and rationalisation of the industry. The number of firms dropped from 167, in 1870, to 50 by 1895. The crucial marker in this process was the 1881 Carnegie–Frick merger, but the same trend could be detected amongst other entrepreneurs, including the Mellon family.[1]

Viewed from afar the smaller number of enlarged steel works looked like cathedrals of capitalism devoted to the worship of production quotas. Progress, however, came at a cost. Large factories, sited on strips of floodplain where the rivers had brushed aside hillsides, vomited a mess of fire, smoke and steam that left Pittsburgh and its surrounds dripping in dirt and soot. Inside the mills, modern practices forced unbelievers to bend the knee before the altar of efficiency.[2]

Pittsburgh survived the worst years of the Great Depression in somewhat paradoxical fashion. On the one hand, the profitability of steel never faltered and the pace-setting Carnegie Works made a profit of $3 million in 1893 and $4 million in 1894. Business confidence mushroomed in the downtown area where corporations erected buildings and office blocks that helped drive up land prices. Middle-class residents took to using electric tramcars to escape from older and congested inner-city neighbourhoods and establish themselves in a suburban world spreading outwards from the Ohio into the area between the two rivers known as the East End. The still better-off, including the very rich, moved north of the Ohio into the even more elegant residences of Allegheny City.[3]

On the other hand, declining wages, redundancies, a longer working day and an influx of unskilled African-American and European immi-grants drawn from the Deep South, Italy and Poland further undercut a working-class which, for the better part of half a century, had been dominated by Irish and Scottish labourers. Hardship and poverty was evident in the Strip, Lawrenceville, the Lower Hill, the Upper Hill and Polish Hill – neighbourhoods on the southern bank of the Allegheny with easy access to the largest employers, including the American Steel and Hoop Company, the Pressed Steel Car Works, the Pittsburgh Machine Company and the huge Fort Wayne Railroad workshops.

By the turn of the century, Pittsburgh was the seventh largest city in the United States and foremost amongst the nation's steel-producing centres, the changing fortunes of its classes mirrored in its shifting settle-ment patterns. Any turbulence in residential quarters after 1880,

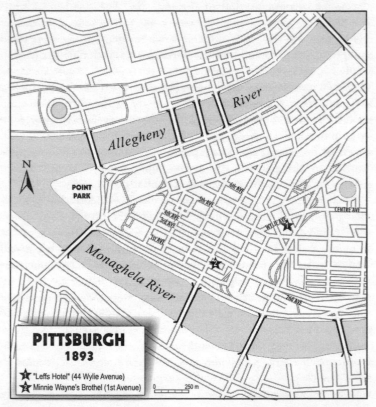

PITTSBURGH
1893

⭐ "Leffs Hotel" (44 Wylie Avenue)
⭐ Minnie Wayne's Brothel (1st Avenue)

however, paled beside confrontations at work as mill-owners contemplated twenty fat, and labour twenty lean years. Between 1887 and 1894, Pittsburgh ranked behind Chicago and New York as a site of serious labour unrest. Bitter struggles and overt industrial warfare were epitomised by the strike of 1892 when the beleaguered Amalgamated Association of Iron and Steel Workers, an old craft union representing skilled workers, challenged the Carnegie's use of unskilled, non-unionised, labour.[4]

A lock-out at the Homestead plant, on the banks of the Monaghela, set in motion a train of events disastrous for everyone bar the Carnegie company. Strikers used dynamite to secure their positions while the company, under the direction of the hard-nosed Henry Clay Frick, deployed 300 armed Pinkerton agents to confront the employees and supplement the National Guard which had been mobilised. A murderous barge and riverside battle followed. Nine Pinkertons and ten workers lost their lives while scores more were seriously wounded. In New York, Emma Goldman and her lover, Alexander Berkman, a Russian immigrant and anarchist of the 'propaganda of the deed' school, were outraged. Berkman proceeded to Pittsburgh where he made an unsuccessful attempt to assassinate Frick. The state forces gained ascendancy and the strikers were defeated.

In the court cases that followed, the commonwealth of Pennsylvania was represented by, amongst others, District Attorney John S. Robb and workers suffered further setbacks. In the decade that followed, the Homestead works shed 25 per cent of its craft workforce in favour of cheaper, unskilled, immigrant labour.[5] The strike strengthened the grip of industrialists, and workers got mixed messages. For craft workers the strike was a disaster, but for anyone willing to offer their labour cheaply in longer shifts western Pennsylvania offered a new opportunity, albeit one in hell. There was no shortage of folk willing to stoke furnaces. In the American south slavery had left African-Americans vulnerable to the vagaries of the market, and in parts of central and eastern Europe declining economic opportunities and political repression had prefabricated any number of desperate unskilled labourers ready to move on and take their chances in Pittsburgh.

As the rich moved out to Allegheny City and the middle class made for the suburbs of the East End, thousands of African-Americans, Italians and Poles jostled for positions in the downtown area. African-Americans, who preferred service positions in the inner city over positions in the steelworks, settled around the Hill, within walking distance of work. Some Russo-Poles squeezed into the Strip on the southern bank of the Allegheny, displacing longer-established German and Irish workers. Others, mainly Jews, settled around Center Avenue, on the Lower Hill, where their Yiddish facilitated interaction with established German Jews and where they were in a cultural and social environment that catered for dietary and religious needs.[6]

A demoralised, ethnically diverse and structurally vulnerable proletariat trying to field initiatives from a state legislature dominated by rural conservatives with powerful links to the new industrial elite was in no position to mount a political challenge to the entrenched two-party system. Republican power simply dwarfed Democratic reform initiatives. Organised labour's energy was divided between workplace initiatives coming from the Amalgamated Association of Iron and Steel Workers or the Knights of Labour, while at home campaigns on issues such as temperance were driven by the Anti-Saloon League which was especially active in the mid-1890s. A lack of political focus made space for a Tammany-Hall-style machine to gain control both of municipal politics and of the economic spoils of a city rising on the back of growing corporate profits.[7]

The Flinn–Magee partnership, which dominated local government in the 1880s and 1890s, was truly remarkable. Lincoln Steffens contemplated their Republican machine and noted simply; 'I know of nothing like it in any city. Tammany is in comparison a plaything and in the management of a city Croker was a child besides Chris Magee.' A fourth-generation American with good family connections, Magee started out by being elected city treasurer. The position gave him an appetite for public office and when 'Boss' Tweed's ring was broken in New York City, in the 1870s, he spent time in Manhattan studying Tammany's magic as well as its mistakes. On his return, Magee discovered an ideal partner and a foil in William Flinn – a Protestant Irish immigrant contractor of Catholic stock whose interest was the single-minded pursuit of profit.[8]

Together, they formed a devastating combination. As Steffens saw it; 'Magee wanted power, Flinn wealth. Each got both these things; but Magee spent his wealth for more power, and Flinn spent his power for more wealth.' They kept Republicans in power by incorporating adjacent county structures into city politics while being careful to keep key Democrats on the city's payroll. Between them they rewrote municipal statutes in ways that obviated the need for overt corruption. In

Pittsburgh, unlike New York, most of what the machine did was within the bounds of the law. 'How could they commit a crime? If they wanted something from the city they passed an ordinance granting it, and if some other ordinance was in conflict, it was repealed or amended.' The city's infrastructure was upgraded, even when there was no need for its bridges to be replaced.[9]

Machine-manufactured legislation made looting legitimate. Graft in Pittsburgh centred on diverting public funds into contracts and franchises and, at the bottom end of the feeding chain, allowing vice to flourish at ward level. In this more sensitive domain Magee took even greater pains to ensure that structures under their control functioned in ways that made it difficult to link the activities of those higher up to the 'businessmen' lower down:

> ... he nominated cheaper or dependent men for the select and common councils. Relatives and friends were his first recourse, then came bartenders, saloon-keepers, liquor dealers, and others allied to the vices who were subject to police regulation and dependent in a business way upon the mal-administration of the law.[10]

Financial tribute paid by vice dealers found its way into party coffers only after having passed through the hands of intermediate, legitimate businessmen for laundering.[11]

At neighbourhood level the basic infrastructural requirements of organised prostitution – the hiring of premises, the furnishing of brothels and provisioning with alcohol – were supplied by members of the ward syndicate. Syndicated interests extended right down to the prostitutes themselves. Steffens noted that

> These women may not buy shoes, hats, jewelry, or any other luxury or necessity except from the official concessionaires, and then only at the official, monopoly prices. If the victims have anything left, a policeman or some other city official is said to call and get it – there are rich ex-police officials in Pittsburgh.[12]

In effect, organised prostitution in downtown Pittsburgh was subject to punitive indirect taxation collected through 'legitimate' commercial outlets which owed their position in the market to the machine. While the system milked a few upmarket bordellos servicing supposedly respectable upper middle-class businessmen, it pressed harder on one-and-two-dollar establishments catering for 'clerks, mechanics and railroad men', and weighed heaviest of all on 'fifty-cent' houses catering for an 'immigrant and unskilled clientele'.[13] Determination to avoid paying taxes, however, is almost fundamental to human nature. The harder ward syndicates pressed sex merchants for taxes, the greater the propensity of brothel owners to acquire provisioning from cheaper 'unauthorised' suppliers. The need to outflank the syndicates was especially pronounced during the worst years of the depression, 1893–94.

In Pittsburgh, then, little was as it seemed. The city's affairs were run along diabolic lines, manipulated by hidden operators who had bypassed the customary ethical checks wired into civic administration. The city offered a near-perfect environment for anyone with anti-social tendencies and whose moral balance was out of kilter. For Silver, living in a world filled with real and imagined conspiracies, in which revenge and vendettas were the order of the day, it was a home from home. He had only one problem with the Flinn–Magee machine: it excluded him. Getting into its workings might be difficult.

It is not clear what precisely he or Rosa Schmidt had in mind when they boarded a Pittsburgh-bound train, or what the nature of their relationship was. He had more or less weaned himself of his more intimate relationship with Goldberg although they continued to correspond and share a dislike of Charles Jacobs. A predator, capable of scenting trouble half a world away, Silver was naturally drawn to the dynamite and disputes of Pennsylvania. Perhaps they thought that Rosa's name would appeal to the city's German-speakers. They moved into downtown Pittsburgh realising that without capital, police protection or endorsement from the ward syndicates it would be impossible to run an independent operation. Silver found her a place in a one-and-two-dollar establishment; Minnie Wayne's on the south side, in First Avenue. It was within a seven-to-twelve-block walk of the clusters of German, Russian and Polish immigrants to be found in the lower city.[14]

Location and competitive pricing ensured a reasonable turnover and Minnie Wayne, an ambitious and independent *madame*, worked the women hard. With Schmidt settled, Silver used the dives in the Jewish quarter slightly further uptown as a base for his drinking, gambling and pimping. One modest-sized hotel with a large billiard room owned

by two brothers was the favoured meeting place of small-time underworld figures. Casper Leff, a baker by trade, had started out with a
confectionery store on Tunnel Street in the fifth ward but had, in 1890,
bought the premises on Wylie. Despite generally unpropitious times,
Leff did fairly well and in 1893 extended the pool room to become a
hotel which he ran with the help of his brother, Louis. Leff took a
personal and professional interest in prostitutes, and the hotel became
the headquarters of a small cosmopolitan gang, centred on Wylie
Avenue.[15]

Leff's sidekicks included Abraham Ramer/Reimer, a low-life German
and two East Europeans, Barney Davis and Philip Hack, who hung
about the hotel gambling and directing clients to nearby brothels.
Ramer, in particular, appears to have made a great impression on
twenty-five-year-old Silver, who later paid him the compliment of stealing
his name. Davis, supposedly a 'diamond peddler' but in reality a fence,
was for a time also a trusted friend of Silver's; he was also taken with
Hack, who was out on a suspended sentence for a burglary committed
at Schaefer's Jewelry Store on Fifth Avenue. The only non-Jew in the
gang was the elusive Thomas Carson, about whom nothing is known.

In April 1893 Leff started extorting cash from proprietors and
madames circumventing the ward syndicate's liquor concession. His
henchmen called on brothel-owners known to be selling unauthorised
liquor and 'persuaded' the owners either to take cut-price liquor from
Leff's own outlet or risk prosecution if he told Flinn–Magee politicians
about their infractions. In fact, Leff had only one political contact –
Burns, a minor ward politician, elected alderman and magistrate. It was
a racket based largely on bluff.

It was while doing these gang-rounds that Silver met the sisters Fanny
and Gussy Bernstein, then aged sixteen and thirteen; women he was to
encounter again in distant Atlantic cities. In addition to his share in
the Leff scam, Silver may also have done some freelance work as an
arsonist at the time. In Pittsburg as in New York, unsuccessful traders
used the notorious 'Jewish Lightning' to defraud insurance companies.
The prostitute Sadie Wolff later claimed that Silver had been convicted
of arson and imprisoned in Pittsburgh – a statement which, although
strictly untrue, may have pointed in the right direction.[16] Silver was
certainly cash-strapped at a time when he claimed to be considering
getting married and his problems were compounded when a favoured,
but unnamed, client 'ill-treated' his 'sweetheart'. Schmidt complained

to Wayne but the *madame*, putting client before prostitute, refused to take the matter further. Silver got the Leff gang to visit Wayne's brothel.

One night in May, he, Leff, Ramer and Joseph Frank set out 'to see the sights'. They called at several brothels and, on each occasion, the money to buy beer was handed to Leff who was known to, and feared by, proprietors. Suitably fortified, they entered Minnie Wayne's whore-house where, as the insider, it fell to Silver to buy 'illicit beer'. Leff, of 'immoral habits', sampled the pleasures of the house in ways so scan-dalous that the details were later deemed unfit for publication. The trap set, Leff sent Silver and Hack to see Burns to lay a charge against Wayne for selling beer from unlicensed premises. Wayne was then unexpectedly approached by Barney Davis, a 'friend', who offered to assist her with her legal problems. When Wayne appeared before Burns, bail was set at $2,500, and paid by Davis. The proceedings were adjourned and Davis pressured Wayne for an interim financial 'accommodation' in lieu of the money put up for bail. Having succeeded in getting most of the money from her, Davis told her that, for an additional payment of $100, he and Carson could 'fix' the witnesses and persuade Burns to drop the charges. What happened next is unclear but the prosecution never followed through so Davis must have been fully repaid.[17] Wayne, however, was not without friends and it may be significant that, later that year, she started referring to herself as Mrs Wayne. She also enjoyed better access to the machine than did Leff. Her attorney had Carson, Davis, Hack and Silver charged with being party to a 'criminal conspiracy'.[18]

A barbershop quartet reduced to solo parts, the four appeared before Alderman Toole's court, on 22 June 1893, in the presence of 'a large crowd, including men and women of shady reputation'. Davis, who had the funds to retain counsel, realised the gravity of the charge and was defended by Charles C. Montooth, a junior partner in a firm that had been prominent in the legal aftermath of the Homestead strike. Silver, enamoured with the legal expertise he had acquired in Sing Sing and without funds to retain counsel, defended himself in court.[19] The hearing 'was a loud and riotous mixing of imperfect English, bad language, ugly charges and evidence of various kinds of depravity'. Sensing a conspiracy within a conspiracy, Silver decided that the waters would be muddied best if Leff's name was dragged into proceedings at every turn.

Montooth, protecting Davis, did not hesitate to mention Leff as the gang leader while Wayne's attorney, determined to highlight Silver's personal animus, was equally happy to draw attention to Leff's role. Leff, who was following proceedings from the gallery, was so incensed at being exposed that he laid a counter-charge against Silver. It also emerged that Davis, instead of handing $50 to Burns, as promised, had given him only $25. When the court rose Silver was arrested and charged with perjury. Unable to raise bail, he, Carson, Hack and Davis were committed to the police cells.[20]

Rosa Schmidt did her best to protect Silver by raising money. Four days later he was released on bail – a luxury that was not extended to his co-accused. Having fallen foul of Leff and still without counsel or connections to the machine, he estreated bail and fled.[21] He reverted to the name Lis, crossed the state line and re-emerged in New York City hoping that Charles Jacobs would leave him enough space in which to operate. Back on Delancey Street his return was noted by Sadie Wolff, who lived in fear of him. The Max Hochstim Association helped ease him back into the organised prostitution rackets in hard times. It was not the best moment for a return to the Lower East Side. The Society for the Prevention of Crime led by the Reverend Parkhurst and Attorney Moss was heightening its campaign against organised vice and corruption in the New York Police Department. Although nothing like the Pinkertons, the agents of the SPC were becoming a force to be reckoned with. Lis kept a low profile in the face of disconcerting news from Pittsburgh. A determined Wayne had succeeded in getting Leff and Schmidt's names added to the list of conspirators and the police were widening their search for him.

Lis lay low for several months, accumulating funds for some unknown project as conditions grew steadily more unsettled. SPC initiatives made policemen on the 11th precinct, including Detective Jacobs, skittish. The SPC forced the Board of Police Commissioners into closing down a score of bordellos between East Houston and Canal, which gave rise to a messy sequel. On 27 October 1893 several brothel-owners and prostitutes appeared before the respected Judge Voorhis at the Essex Street Market Court in the presence of Moss and four agents scheduled to give evidence for the prosecution. Max Hochstim himself appeared along with so many other pimps and underworld elements that the crowd soon reached menacing proportions. During the proceedings, Moss told Voorhis that a defendant had been tipped off about his impending arrest by Hochstim. Hochstim objected from the gallery. The judge had Hochstim hauled down before the bench for 'a scathing lecture' and then ordered him to leave the court.[22]

On the courthouse steps Hochstim addressed a crowd of between two and five hundred men, most of them members of the Max Hochstim Association. When Moss and the SPC agents emerged, a great murmuring arose and the crowd followed the agents down Broome Street. As they entered the Bowery and boarded a tramcar, they were set upon and assaulted by a mob.[23] The Board of Police Commissioners, under pressure from the public, asked Chief of Police Byrnes and Captain Devery to report on the alleged unwillingness of the police to go to the rescue of the retreating agents. Clouds of words descended over the nervous 11th precinct. It was against this background, just a week later, that an officer from Pittsburgh arrived with a warrant for Lis's arrest. Charles Jacobs, the officer responsible for interstate extraditions, arrested Joseph Silver on Sunday, 5 November 1893, and handed him over to officer J.R. Holland from Pennsylvania for the long ride back to Pittsburgh.[24]

Silver, child of a betrayer and himself a serial betrayer, lived in a world in which betrayal was endemic; yet somehow, beneath the skein of narcissism and pseudo-morality that encased him, he felt himself deserving of fidelity. Casper Leff, and more especially Jacobs, became objects of undying enmity. Ten days after his arrest Silver appeared in court where it was alleged that, at some point after his departure, he had sneaked back into Pittsburgh to put up 'straw bail' for Rosa Schmidt so that she would not be detained while doing his bidding. Alderman King recognised him as the man who had put up the bail and 'an additional charge of perjury was made against him. He was committed for trial'.[25]

Undaunted, Silver – in what was to become a standard move – retained the best legal advice his money could buy. John S. Robb, admired by Pittsburgh's captains of industry for the role he had played as District Attorney in the Homestead strike, was on nodding terms with members of the Flinn-Magee machine.[26] The additional charge of perjury was dropped, and Schmidt's name was removed from the list of conspirators. But that was as far as Robb's successes went. Davis, Hack, Leff and Silver appeared before Judge Collier and thirteen jurors on 17 November 1893. Of Thomas Carson, who had also jumped bail, there was no sign. On 21 November, the jury found all four guilty of criminal conspiracy but recommended Davis to the court's mercy.[27] Montooth, acting for Davis who was out on bail, filed a motion for a retrial. Two days later Leff's attorney did the same, as did Robb, acting for Silver who was held in the court lockup. Only the unfortunate Philip Hack, without the resources to retain counsel, was left in the cells.[28]

Casper Leff, the wealthiest of the defendants, used the week that followed to get his brother to tidy up his affairs and then fled city and state alike. On 1 December, Silver and Hack were each sentenced to fourteen months for 'criminal conspiracy' and made to pay a nominal fine of six cents each to meet the costs of the prosecution. Hack, under a suspended sentence, was given an additional year. Davis received a fine of $400 and a day's imprisonment in Riverside, Pennsylvania's Western State Penitentiary in nearby Allegheny City.[29]

Silver and Hack, too, were immediately taken across the Ohio to the penitentiary which boasted 'an admirable type of modern prison architecture': 900 prisoners were housed in a facility designed to accommodate half that number in cells measuring eight feet by eight feet with a ceiling of eight to ten feet above them. Warden Edward S. Wright, who had been there twenty-five years, enforced a Sing Sing-type silence rule. When he retired, debating change, he noted that 'some prisons' were already permitting 'five-minute conversation at the close of each meal'.[30]

Silver, knowing the drill, led the way. As always, he avoided giving any details about his family or the period spent in London in the late 1880s. He claimed to be married but, if he was, there was no record of it and he never again saw Rosa Schmidt. With a new identity and Whitechapel five years behind him he reverted to being a twenty-six-year-old 'Hebrew' from Poland, and a 'moderate' drinker. He had been to secondary school, could read and write, and had once served a full apprenticeship as a barber. He was relieved of his certificate of naturalisation, a ring, two cuff-links, a watch-and-chain, and $19 in cash and told that, provided his behaviour was satisfactory, he would be released on 31 December 1894. That date burnt its way into his consciousness. Hack, who was pardoned not long after his admission to the grim riverside penitentiary, described himself as a salesman hailing from Pittsburgh.[31]

The Allegheny–Ohio was not the Hudson and the regime at Riverside was less arduous than that in the 'House of Fear' but, for all the difference it made, he might as well have been in Ossining. Without Goldberg, time went by more slowly and, denied an inflow of new inmates to tell him about the NYPD and what was happening on the Lower East Side, he was more given to brooding than in Sing Sing. As usual, he collaborated with the prison authorities and was never subjected to internal discipline. His prison record states that both his mental and physical health were 'good' throughout his stay in Riverside. But while his underlying syphilitic condition did not cause much overt physical discomfort, it was progressing and contributing to his mood swings. He reported sick twenty-four times in fourteen months.

Silver craved information about New York's 11th precinct and Charles Jacobs. Outwardly calm, inwardly incandescent, the furnace within him needed constant stoking if Jacobs was ever to be consigned to the fires of hell. But confined to the damp hosiery section of the workshops, he spent his time making socks and only occasionally gave vent to his feelings in letters, in Yiddish, to Adolph Goldberg. Goldberg, who shared his loathing of Jacobs, sent back scraps of kindling. But first prison gossip, and later smuggled newspapers, produced sufficient coke to keep a thousand Pittsburgh mills burning night and day. Suddenly, he saw how best to incinerate Jacobs.

Throughout 1893, Parkhurst, more liberal than some of his members, struggled to broaden the social base of the SPC. In essence, he attempted to turn the society into a non-partisan movement embracing other religious and secular organisations. He was not entirely unsuccessful: by the mid-1890s the SPC boasted several Catholic and Jewish members. More notable was the way in which the society's activities started to feed into an emerging trend in city politics. In Manhattan and other boroughs, middle-class voters were moving away from head-on particularist assaults on Tammany Hall, and becoming more enamoured with broad-based reform sentiments swept along by strong moral undercurrents. The SPC was, at last, taking shape as the right movement, in the right place, at the right time.[32]

In the fall of 1893, the New York State legislature, in Albany, in which Parkhurst's parishioner, Thomas Platt, served as party leader, fell under Republican control. New York City, however, remained a cause of concern for state Republicans because most Democrats were comfortable with machine politics. More worryingly still, because the Board of Police Commissioners supervised the Bureau of Elections, Croker and his Tammany supporters had the potential to influence the outcome of state as well as national elections. It was not only the Republicans who were troubled. Alarmed by the way in which the NYPD had become integrated into the underworld economy of the Lower East Side to the detriment of middle-class citizens and traders, the Chamber of Commerce petitioned the state legislature to appoint a committee to inquire into electoral fraud, voting irregularities, organised 'vice' and the ambiguous role of Byrnes's police.[33]

The Chamber's petition, presented to legislators in Albany in early 1894, found a sympathetic audience in the Republican senate but R.P. Flower, the state's Democratic Governor, took a different line. Twice he vetoed an appropriation to cover the costs of any inquiry. Denied funding, the Republicans outflanked him by persuading the Chamber of Commerce to meet the costs of counsel. Left without a political leg to stand on, Flower approved a committee chaired by Senator Clarence Lexow, a Republican, and backed by New York City reformers W.T. Goff, Frank Moss and others. It was the presence of Moss, legal adviser to the Owners and Businessmen's Association of West 27th Street, as well as the SPC that gave Revd Charles Parkhurst most to cheer about.[34]

The Lexow Committee met for the first time on 9 March 1894, and held its final meeting on 29 December of that year; two days before Silver's release from prison. The committee spent five weeks prying into electoral fraud; the remainder of its effort, captured in six volumes of evidence, was devoted to an exploration of Tammany's reach, the institutionalisation of corruption, and links between members of the NYPD and the 'vice' merchants of the Lower East Side. In an era of mass literacy, testimony from underworld sources dominated the national and local print media while the proceedings – often minor 'show trials' – on occasion assumed positively theatrical proportions.[35]

Flushed from their redoubts, Superintendent Byrnes's officers, from inspectors and captains all the way down to men on the beat, were publicly exposed. Amongst the linkages that came under the spotlight was the association between certain senior officers, the Essex Street Market Court gang and the Max Hochstim Association. Confronted by a challenge with out-of-town support, Byrnes's men defended themselves as best possible. Those with good memories recalled how the force had its own way of dealing with threats; how Charles Gardner of the SPC had once been framed and made to spend a year in the Tombs before being vindicated. Arrests, sudden departures for Chicago and lies of all kinds became part and parcel of proceedings around the Lexow Committee. Perhaps the most important reminder of the power and reach of the police surfaced in the unlikely shape of fat Matilda Hermann.[36]

Born in the highly contested terrain of Alsace-Lorraine, 'Matilda' or

'Bertha' Hermann emigrated to the United States in 1882, and used experience gained in France to open a brothel in the 'Tenderloin'. A woman of great financial acumen, by 1891 she and a sister ran four brothels and owned two properties in West 3rd Street. Known to police as the 'French gold mine', she had paid $30,000 in bribes to Byrnes's men by the time she received a subpoena to appear before Lexow.[37] Alarmed by what she might reveal, the NYPD collected $1,700 and, on the night before she was due to testify, got a plainclothes officer to call on her and bundle her into a cab. She was whisked out of the city, across the state line and into Jersey City. She was pushed aboard a Canada-bound train and routed through several cities before being tracked down by state officials. On the way back, in Philadelphia, she, and the Deputy Sergeant-at-Arms of the New York Senate were arrested on trumped-up charges by policemen well disposed to colleagues back across the Hudson. It was only after the intervention of the Chief of Police in Jersey City and a local magistrate that the witness and her escort could proceed to New York.[38]

Silver, later a neighbour of Hermann's in another part of the Atlantic world, knew from personal experience how the NYPD hunted down and 'extradited' its enemies to friendly forces in adjacent states. Watching from within Riverside, he nevertheless sensed the opportunity to strike back at Jacobs and McManus. But how was it to be done? As a man known to have links to organised prostitution he was probably not well placed to do it himself. Moreover, the committee would complete its inquiries long before he was out of prison. But all was not lost. The names of both detectives were mentioned before Lexow on more than one occasion and the committee learned how burglary and theft fitted into the operations of 'bagmen' like Jacobs and McManus. As Lexow later reported:

> It has been conclusively shown that an understanding existed between headquarters' detectives, pawnbrokers and thieves, by which stolen property might be promptly recovered by the owner on condition that he repay the pawnbroker the amount advanced on the stolen property. In almost every instance it also appears that the detective, moving between the owner and pawnbroker receives substantial gratuities from the owner of the property for the work done in his official capacity.[39]

None of this was lost on Attorney Frank Moss and members of the 'Parkhurst Society'. The well-publicised hearings of the committee fed back directly into New York's mayoral election of 1894, reaching well beyond Parkhurst's 'Mugwump' constituency. With Lexow already in the driving seat at Albany, Parkhurst redoubled his efforts to build a civic alliance to underwrite reform. In mid-October, just six weeks before Joseph Silver's release, he went to the Lower East Side as a guest of the Good Government Club X and pleaded with immigrant Jews to support the reform-minded millionaire candidate, William L. Strong. Silver was almost never moved by formal, public appeals to religion. But he could not fail to notice that the SPC was becoming more open to working with people drawn from the city's ethnic minorities, including Jews.[40]

When William Strong defeated the Tammany candidate for Mayor in November 1894, conditions in New York were about as propitious as they were ever likely to be for a strike against Jacobs and McManus. Lexow's report was being prepared for release, the Tammany men were in a rare moment of retreat, the SPC was stronger than ever and Byrnes's officers were facing the possibility of having to deal with a new – potentially hostile – reshuffled Board of Police Commissioners. For a man with vengeance in his heart, December 1894 offered prospects that were not displeasing. Silver made a decision as audacious as it was implausible: he would become an 'agent' for the 'Parkhurst Society'. All he had to do was to persuade Moss that he had something special to offer and Jacobs and McManus would fall. He was released from Riverside on 31 December, and went directly to New York City. 1895 promised to be an interesting year.

VI

NEW YORK CITY
1895

Revenge is a kind of wild justice.

Francis Bacon, 'Of Revenge'

. . . the air of moral nihilism common to keepers of gambling
hells and disorderly houses; to private detectives and inquiry
agents . . .

Joseph Conrad, *The Secret Agent*

THE records of the Western State Penitentiary, in Pennsylvania, are clear:
Joseph Silver, in for criminal conspiracy, was released on 31 December
1894. But from that point on, and for the ten weeks following, everything is blurred. Out of choice and desire for revenge, he got sucked
into machine politics in New York at a particularly fraught moment in
the history of Tammany Hall. It was a world in which the chances of
politicians competing for power were affected by the actions of their
agents and detectives; one filled with calculated silences, conspiracies,
double-crossings, fake evidence, feigned ignorance, orchestrated disappearances, press leaks, staged interviews, lies and truncated inquiries.
For a man with so much of his past to conceal it was dangerous terrain
and it is one of the many ironies of his life that, for a time, the name
of this creature of the dark was emblazoned across the front pages of
the *New York Times*.

The Lexow report was made public on 15 January 1895. By then,
the NYPD was reeling from blows inflicted by the legislature, in Albany,
and the unexpected defeat of Tammany in the mayoral election of

November 1894. Although groggy and unsteady, the NYPD was hardly down and out. With Mayor Strong contemplating appointments to a new, non-partisan Board of Police Commissioners, Thomas Byrnes, who had signalled his intention of retiring, held on as best possible. He and his officers punched back at Parkhurst, the Society for the Prevention of Crime (SPC) and their allies. It was an unusual contest in which the contestants were, for a short time, fairly evenly matched.[1]

The police and Parkhurst people later agreed that Silver made his way directly from Pittsburgh to New York and immediately made contact with the SPC. But there agreement ends. Nobody knows when or how he first approached the SPC. It seems that, before his release, he was corresponding with Goldberg about the need for them to get even with Detective Charles Jacobs. Jacobs later stated, repeatedly but erroneously, that Silver had been released from prison on 1 February, and one newspaper recorded that Silver himself told a Grand Jury that that was the date of his release from Riverside. Frank Moss never contested these assertions, but later implied that the SPC had made contact with Silver earlier than 1 February because 'his society had the man Liss watched all the way from Pittsburgh after his discharge from the Allegheny prison'.[2]

The date is important because, if it could be verified, it would provide a clue as to how much thought Silver, the SPC and police put into the planning and sequencing of events that followed. As things stand we have to assume that Silver found himself a room back on Delancey and that in the second week of January he made his way to the United Charities Building. He was shown to the offices of the SPC and engaged Attorney Moss, with anything but charity in his heart. The Fox understood the risks and, plausible as ever, made it his business to draw in and convince the counsellor of his plan.

Moss was not well disposed towards Jewish immigrants on the Lower East Side. In his 'mugwumpish' view they had displaced older, law-abiding communities. Months later he noted, rather sourly, that in Allen Street the Methodist church had sold its 'building to the Jews, who use it for a synagogue', and that in Division Street an established Quaker community had given way to 'the merchants of New Israel': here families such as the Goldbergs ran their second-hand clothing stores. The East Europeans were, in his opinion, the worst of the lot: 'the criminal instincts that are so often found naturally in the Russian and Polish Jews come to the surface here in such ways to warrant the

opinion that these people are the worst element in the entire make-up
of New York life'. Frank Moss had no reason to be well disposed to
a Polish, Jewish interloper like Joseph Silver.[3]

He had other things on his mind. All was not well in the ranks of
the society's agents. His detectives were hardly of Pinkerton calibre; not
that all the national detective agency's men were out of the top drawer
either. His agents were not well paid, and the mixed bunch could not
always resist the temptations put their way. His superintendent, Alexander
Wishart, a former police captain from New Jersey who had been in
charge of agents during the Bowery disturbances a few months earlier,
was not going to have his contract renewed for reasons Moss 'did not
care to make public'. It was 'no reflection whatever' on Wishart, Moss
suggested, but prostitutes like Sadie Wolff believed Wishart had been
dismissed because he, like Byrnes's officers in the NYPD, had extracted
'protection money' from brothel-keepers. With the release of the Lexow
report imminent, that sort of news was disconcerting since it was being
whispered that the Mayor was going to appoint Moss and others to a
reconstructed Board of Police Commissioners.

The ambitious and impatient Moss's concentration sometimes lapsed
when listening to underworld figures offering to help the SPC for their
own opaque reasons. George Appo, a former pickpocket who had
appeared before the Lexow Committee as a star witness, was one such
criminal Moss had partly misjudged; Silver was another. Silver was a
counterfeiter, a counterfeiter of emotions, putting women's bodies and
men's desires together for money, pretending it was love. He and Moss
had no respect for one another, but history had readied them to interact
on a willing-buyer meets willing-seller basis.[4]

He provided Moss with an abridged, carefully edited version of his
life, avoiding any mention of his four-year stay in Whitechapel, or of
his problematic relationships with prostitutes. In Silver's version his
story began in Poland and moved directly to his arrival in America.
He had arrived in New York City in 1889, with $1,000 to acquire a
barbershop, but had been ensnared by a mercenary *shadchan*, a matchmaker, who had led him to the false Annie/Esther Heller. It all came
to a sad end with his descent into crime and his encounters with
Detectives Jacobs and McManus. His spell in the Riverside prison had,
however, persuaded him 'to reform' and offer his services to the SPC.[5]

Moss found the ideological feast impossible to resist. Here was a
young man, with a profession, who had tried to establish himself on

the Lower East Side only to be misled into a life of crime and vice by co-religionists. But Silver, having repented, was ready to help entrap corrupt policemen. The society had long been interested in Jacobs and McManus, and hoped to 'show the dealings of men like them with thieves'.[6] Moss's legal training did not, however, desert him entirely. He waited to have thirty-three instances of alleged collaborative burglary investigated and later recorded that 'several of them were sustained by corroborative proof'.[7] But, after that there was no stopping Attorney Moss. He tucked in. If there was subsequent cause for discomfort it never showed. Nor were misgivings expressed when he outlined his dealings with Silver – coded as 'J.S.' – in a book published in 1897. Public confidence and private doubt are staple fare for political aspirants. 'This man Silver,' he told a reporter in early March 1895, 'decided to make an honest effort to reform after his release from the penitentiary in Pittsburgh, and came to our society.'[8] 'Silver was an unfortunate man,' he told another, 'who took to burglary through force of circumstances. When he was released from the Pittsburgh Penitentiary a year ago he thought his career carefully over, and decided that he might as well confess and mend his ways.'[9] But 'confession' was a minor part of what Silver had in mind.

With Moss safely on a hook baited with anti-Semitism, Silver reeled him in. He proposed a project drawn from past experience – a burglary actively involving the NYPD detectives. This time, however, the crime would be witnessed by SPC agents and the sharing of the spoils would make it impossible for the officers to distance themselves from the joint venture. It was a crude scheme bearing the imprimatur of revenge and was fraught with ethical, legal and moral problems. These difficulties did not concern Moss since it was a project that he knew about, and approved. As he put it after the burglary: 'Silver has been working hand-in-glove with us since [his release from prison] unknown to the police, and had helped us work up a clear case against McManus and Jacobs'.[10]

Now that Moss's public ambition to do good through evil was aligned with Silver's secret wish to conjure evil from good, the project was placed on an official footing. It was life on the ethical frontier, municipal politics at its most sordid. Moss introduced him to Wishart's successor, Superintendent Arthur B. Dennett, a man who, in press circles, was known as 'Angel' Dennett because of the honourable role he played in the Lexow proceedings. Dennett, in turn, introduced him to agents

Whitney, Lemmon and Feffer. They were briefed about the nature and purpose of the project and the dangers he faced were impressed on Silver. Days later he purchased a .38 calibre revolver and had it licensed by the city authority. Next to his certificate of naturalisation the licence to carry a gun in New York was his most treasured document. It is difficult to believe that this firearm was acquired without the active, or at very least passive, approval of the SPC.[11]

But the acquisition of the revolver was only one of the aspects surrounding Silver's links with the SPC that was unclear. Was he ever an authorised and armed agent of the SPC at a time when Moss acknowledged that Silver was 'hand in glove' with the organisation? Did Parkhurst know that Moss, Silver and other agents were involved in a scheme to entrap Jacobs and McManus? These were questions to which neither Moss nor the Reverend Charles Parkhurst ever provided satisfactory answers. When later quizzed about Silver's status by a hostile reporter from the pro-Tammany *Sun*, Moss refused to expand; 'He did say, however, that Liss had never been a duly accredited agent of the society.'[12] What exactly 'due accreditation' involved is unknown; on another occasion, Moss claimed that Silver was 'in training' as a detective. If he was 'in training', it is unlikely that he was not on the payroll. He certainly submitted stubs for expenses he incurred in a way that one associates with employees rather than with casual collaborators.[13]

We also know that when Silver eventually fled the city one of his last acts was to call on Dennett and obtain a testimonial, signed by the superintendent, which was sufficiently appreciative for Silver to produce it as part of his defence in a court case in another country.[14] The Reverend Parkhurst himself was equally unhelpful once the troubles around the burglary erupted. Asked by a reporter from the *Recorder* whether he knew anything about a man 'named Joseph Liss who is said to be an agent for your society', Parkhurst replied, 'Liss! Liss! Never heard the name before in my life.' Pressed about Jacobs and McManus, he was quick to respond: 'Ah, yes, I've heard about them frequently before.'[15]

Lis, in a transitional phase, saw himself becoming more like Silver. He was a lad who, due to shocking parental neglect, had got off to a bad start in life followed by a horrific young manhood in London's East End. With prison life behind him, he had fewer self-doubts and sensed a different person, one capable of doing good, emerging. He was, in a phrase he used nine months later, a 'detective's agent'. Ten years after that, in a grandiose flourish driven by neurospyhilis, he informed German authorities that, while he was in New York, he was an officer in the 'secret police'.[16] If he was not, in Moss's words, 'a duly accredited agent', he certainly acted like one and definitely saw himself as having authority. But as ever, there was a fractured self. Within weeks of returning to the Lower East Side he was terrorising prostitutes, extorting $25 a month as 'protection money'.[17]

But, whatever his status, by the time Silver left Dennett and the agents at the United Charities Building to return to his room on Delancey, he knew what was expected of him. His immediate task was twofold. First, he was to re-establish contact with Jacobs and McManus and win back their trust. It would not be easy. A good deal had happened during the intervening eighteen months, including his extradition and a deterioration in the political climate. He mulled over these issues at his favourite watering holes – Ike van Leer's on Delancey, August Gloistein's, James Murray's on Grand and Max Cohen's on the Bowery. His second task was to identify premises that could easily be observed by SPC agents during a burglary and monitor the occupants' movements.

He sought out Jacobs where he would feel least vulnerable – his home. Their meeting in Mulberry Street took place over a meal during the last week of January and went reasonably well. Jacobs, however, suggested that future meetings take place in Lyons Restaurant where he was to be found after midnight on week nights, or at any of the saloons near the Goldbergs' second-hand clothing shop off the Bowery. Between their first, tentative, encounter and the second week of February, Jacobs, by his own admission, met with Silver on at least five occasions. At one meeting they were joined by the fence, Joseph Goldberg and Charles McManus. Silver used these early encounters to find out how the detectives had got on during his year in prison and to build confidence.[18]

The year 1894 had not been a good one for either Jacobs or McManus. Both had been named as 'bagmen' before Lexow, and McManus had got into a mess when a bent detective in Brooklyn named Zundt had received a 'reward' for recovering a stolen watch, only to be told that he would have to split the proceeds with Manhattan police – one of whom was McManus. McManus was reduced to the ranks for a while but, with Tammany in control, it was just weeks before he was reinstated. April had been another bad month. Patrick Higgins, one of several crooks in the detectives' stable had been party to assaulting and robbing a visitor from New Haven. When the Connecticut police sought Higgins's extradition, Jacobs had to hire counsel and perjure himself. Higgins had avoided extradition but the New Haven police were still deeply displeased about the matter.[19] The detectives were understandably skittish and the publication of the Lexow report made it difficult to regain their trust. In order to speed up the process Silver kept his eyes and ears open for underworld information that he could feed to Jacobs. But it took time, since he had been out of the city for a while. Then, about ten days into February, after a period of intense but fruitless interaction with the detectives, two things came to Silver at the same time – a snippet of information for Jacobs and a possible target for the burglary.

The janitor in his building let a room to Samuel Cohen; a man nobody seems to have known much about. Silver established that the newcomer owned several watches, which was unusual for someone occupying such modest quarters. In retrospect, Cohen seems to have been a petty criminal of the type Silver habitually associated with. The intended victim, his rooms and the portable nature of the belongings appealed to Jacobs and McManus as well as to Dennett and his agents. The idea of a corrupt Jewish detective watching a Jewish burglar-agent stealing from a Jewish thief in order to further the public good would have appealed to Moss. For Jacobs and McManus it would just be a day at the office. These ideas were still taking root in Silver's mind when he had a second lucky break. He bumped into two shoplifters from Pittsburgh and established that they were working the patch without having obtained clearance from the detectives. Jacobs and McManus could put such information to good use. They would either arrest the men and be seen to be doing their public duty, or reach an agreement with the newcomers and share in the proceeds.

On the evening of Monday, 11 February, Jacobs opened the front door of his home to find Silver hawking treachery. Over dinner he was told about the thieves from Pittsburgh and it was put to him that, if he and McManus took up a position in the saloon opposite Simpson's pawnshop on the corner of Bowery and Delancey early that Wednesday morning, Silver would make the shoplifters known to them. He also told Jacobs about his plans for Cohen and asked that the detectives take up their positions outside Delancey later on Wednesday morning.[20] The following day, Tuesday the 12th, is smothered in silence. Silver probably spent it with Moss's men. Dennett and the agents familiarised themselves with the set-up around the building on Delancey to ensure that when the time came they would not be spotted by the detectives. They also talked through what would happen after the burglary. Given what followed, however, it seems that Silver did not tell the SPC officers about his prior arrangement to meet Jacobs and McManus at the pawnshop early the next morning. Either that or, less likely, he and the SPC agents agreed that there was no point in exposing Parkhurst's men to possible detection in what was a separate exercise with an uncertain outcome.

Wednesday morning, first thing, was anticlimactic. Jacobs and McManus assumed their positions in a saloon opposite the pawnshop shortly before eight o'clock. With Silver concealed conveniently nearby, everybody watched the shop entrance for close on two hours. Eventually, Silver gave up, went into the saloon and told them what they already knew – that it looked as if the men were not going to put in an appearance. It was disappointing but hardly a disaster; hopefully, things would improve later that morning.[21]

By mid-morning Agents Dennett and Whitney, who had been in place for some hours, were wearying of their task when Jacobs and McManus suddenly appeared and swept down Delancey – only to disappear. Some time elapsed, they returned, made another sweep and disappeared for a second time. A few minutes later they reappeared and took up positions opposite number 8 Delancey, pacing up and down the sidewalk. Shortly afterwards Silver, too, appeared. After glancing down the street, he entered the building. He soon re-emerged and, without looking around, turned and made off in the direction of the Bowery. The NYPD detectives moved off in one direction while the SPC agents, satisfied that things were going to plan, moved off in another.[22]

Whitney, making certain he was not being followed, walked to a pre-arranged meeting place where he linked up with Silver and they then hurried back uptown. They boarded a train at Grand Central Station that took them across the state line to a destination north-west of New York City, pointedly avoiding Jersey City where the NYPD had such good connections. They disembarked at Paterson, a textile-producing centre that appealed to Russo-Polish gangsters, went to a telegraph office and sent a message to Jacobs's home address: 'Everything all right: letter will follow. Joe.'[23] They got something to eat and found themselves a place to stay for the night.

In New York late the same afternoon, or so it was later claimed, Cohen found that the door to his room had been forced, saw some burglar's tools lying around and realised he had been robbed. That evening he went to police headquarters on Mulberry Street, to report the burglary and, shown pictures from Byrnes's 'Rogues' Gallery', identified mugshot number 1473 as belonging to Joseph Lis/Silver, the man he thought might have robbed him. The officer on duty, it was said, at once dispatched Detective Hickey to investigate but he soon returned, having 'failed to find the slightest injury to the door'.[24] Byrnes later said that Hickey's investigation – which had the look of a cover-up – had taken place at his behest and that he, personally, endorsed the view that there had been 'no robbery at 8 Delancey Street'.[25] Despite this, and most puzzlingly, the duty officer allegedly went on to type a note for whoever might be assigned to the case the following day, pointing out that: '1473 [was] today identified by Samuel Cohen as having committed a burglary there. Arrest by Inspector McLaughlin's instructions.'[26] Neither this important note nor other relevant police documents were ever produced in court.

In Paterson, early the following morning, Thursday, 14 February, the Parkhurst men changed hotels. SPC agents were entitled only to modest allowances and the manager of the United States Hotel remembered allocating room 26 to Silver and Whitney.[27] Beyond the reach of Byrnes's men, they composed the letter they had promised Jacobs. Part of this awkwardly worded letter was later alleged to have read as follows:

> *Charles Jacobs:*
> Dear Friend,
> Burglary I committed yesterday morning in Delancey Street
> did not turn out as profitably as we expected that it would.
> Only got nine watches, three fitted gold ones, some chains,
> two pairs of opera glasses, and several other small things.[28]

In the latter part of the same communication, or perhaps in a separate telegram, there was also a sentence from Silver stating that he would soon be sending Jacobs and McManus $50 each as their share of the spoils.[29] Regardless of the form the message took, the content was clear enough. It, along with a similar note to McManus, was sent by registered mail to the detectives' homes. That same afternoon, their wives took receipt of the notes.[30]

But the Parkhurst men had overplayed their hand. The sudden departure for New Jersey, a telegram and a flurry of registered letters reeked of a set-up, of 'a job'. When Jacobs and McManus arrived home to find letters informing them that they were to get $50 each they smelt a rat and started taking necessary precautions. The next morning, Friday the 15th, they took Inspector McLaughlin into their confidence, telling him that they had been set up by agents working for Moss and the SPC. McLaughlin then told Byrnes. It was at this point that the NYPD adopted the position, in public, that they had always been aware of the SPC's involvement in an alleged burglary, and that they had gone along with it to see where it would lead. The police also set about reordering their documentation and the accounts of what had happened at 8 Delancey, to make it appear that no burglary had ever taken place. This was not as easy as it seemed; in addition to messy paperwork they had to bring Cohen and the building's janitor into line.

Aware of their damning personal histories with Silver, Jacobs and McManus, on their own initiative, then took the cover-up further and tried to ensure that Silver would never appear before a Grand Jury or a court. To achieve that, they had to lure him back across the state line and deal with him in an appropriate manner. McManus suggested to the saloon-keeper on Delancey, van Leer, that he go to Paterson and persuade Silver to return to New York so that they could all sit down and work through the situation. But realising that this move might be monitored by Moss, they got a second, unnamed colleague to precede van Leer and report on the presence of any SPC agents.[31]

But, even before the NYPD counter-offensive got under way, Moss's men were making their next move. Silver and Whitney handed two packages to Wells Fargo, each containing a letter and $50 in cash, with instructions that they be delivered to police headquarters in Mulberry Street.[32] With the receipts in their pockets, it was decided that Whitney would return to New York, leaving Silver back at the hotel. Whitney took the train to Grand Central but, according to an unnamed witness who was never called to give evidence, not before he had been spotted in the company of 'Angel' Dennett and Silver.[33]

On Saturday morning, 16 February, Jacobs and McManus received the packages and, suspicions confirmed, refused to take delivery of them and had them returned to Paterson unopened. McManus sent van Leer scurrying to Paterson. He was to tell Silver that the parcels had been returned unopened because they should have been sent to the detectives' home addresses, not police headquarters. Van Leer was also instructed to persuade Silver to accompany him back to New York so that matters could be talked through.[34]

Jacobs and McManus later claimed that it was at about this time that they spotted Samuel Cohen in 'Big Tim' Sullivan's saloon and followed him to a meeting with Dennett and Whitney. But it is by no means certain that such a meeting ever took place. What *was* important was that Jacobs and McManus saw Cohen and seem to have suggested to him that it would be unwise to pursue the burglary charge, or to appear as witness should the matter reach court. Cohen, a man with an unusual predilection for opera-glasses and gold watches, got the point.[35]

Back in Paterson, van Leer was having some success with Silver. Without easy access to his SPC principals, Silver had some hard thinking to do. From what van Leer said it was clear that Jacobs and McManus had not swallowed the bait. No money had changed hands and it was unlikely that Moss would ever be able to prove that the detectives had been involved in any crime. He was now vulnerable to the NYPD counter-offensive and the only thing he had on his side was time. Caught between the two great fires of New York City politics – the SPC and the NYPD – he did as he always did in such circumstances: he looked after himself. He decided to abandon Moss and use such information as he did have to try to bargain himself out of the mess through face-to-face-discussions with Jacobs and McManus.

Late on Saturday afternoon he checked out of the hotel, without leaving a contact address or message for Dennett's men, and accompanied van Leer back to New York. From that moment he was, as far as the SPC was concerned, 'missing' for reasons that could only be speculated about. Back on the Lower East Side, van Leer left him at a safe house and went to tell the detectives what he had accomplished. From Jacobs's account, as reported in the press, it is clear that he and McManus remained concerned that Silver might still be in secret contact with Moss or Dennett, playing a double game.

To avoid being set up by Dennett and his agents, Jacobs and McManus told van Leer that, on a day they would determine, he should meet with Silver and then take him on a long, circuitous tour of the Lower East Side. The detectives would then pick up the trail, shadow them and, when satisfied that they were not being followed, would link up with Silver and van Leer on the corner of Avenue B and 8th Street. They could then go to a coffee saloon on Bowery and Houston where they would sit down and negotiate.[36]

That meeting was short, tense and unproductive. Both parties were nervous and spent most of their time trying to determine what it was that was driving their adversary and what the next move was likely to be. Silver, it was said, acknowledged openly that he was driven by the desire for revenge. But not all was lost. Contact had been made and, believing they might make more progress on an individual basis, the old firm of Jacobs and Silver agreed to meet a few hours later, at midnight, on the corner of Chrystie and Houston. According to Jacobs, the second meeting never took place. Silver, thinking better of it, either did not appear or failed to reveal himself.

The following morning, Jacobs, feeling the heat, went out to look for Silver. At an old hang-out on Norfolk, he established that Silver had spent the night there. A day or two later, on leaving his house he was confronted by Silver, 'who seemed to spring from the ground'. Startled, Jacobs steered him away from Mulberry Street, in the direction of the East River and they swapped notes on the corner of Stanton and Willett. Realising they were both in a very tight spot, they started searching for a compromise. Only Jacobs's account of the discussion survives, but he later claimed that Silver offered to leave New York if he was given $700. Jacobs said that it was a large sum, that he needed to speak to McManus, and that it would take time for them to get the money together. They parted, agreeing to meet again later that day, feeling more confident that they were dealing solely on an interpersonal basis although Jacobs later suggested, almost certainly falsely, that all meetings were arranged and observed by SPC agents.[37]

When they met again, two days later, Jacobs produced $250 in notes which, he said, showed that he was acting in good faith and trying to find a solution. Silver responded by saying that the *City of Paris*, in port, was scheduled to sail for Europe later that month and that if they reached an agreement he would leave on it. Still believing they were making progress, they agreed to meet the following day. That meeting, the last one-on-one meeting between them, took place on the corner of 4th Street and Second Avenue at 6.00 on Sunday, 23 February, and went very badly. Silver said he had given the matter more thought and that it would take $1,000 rather than $700 to get him to leave. Jacobs claimed he told Silver that $1,000 was beyond his reach and by the end of the meeting had got him to accept a compromise of $500 in cash, the cost of a steamship passage and an overcoat, a hat, two suits, shirts, collars, neckties and a pair of shoes. In return, Silver would recover incriminating documents in the possession of the SPC. The offer of clothing, always important for Silver, gives a ring of authenticity to Jacobs's claim. Although agreement seemed within reach, both parties felt they could probably never meet the asking price. How could the detectives raise that sort of money from their own resources in forty-eight hours? And how could Silver re-engage with Moss and retrieve papers kept in the SPC offices? It was more in hope than in anticipation that they agreed to meet again, at Flynn's saloon, the following evening.

By Monday the 25th, both sides were tiring; nerves were becoming jangled. They had met on five occasions over more than a week and neither was giving way. The *City of Paris* was due to sail in days. Moreover, both were in trouble with their principals. Jacobs and McManus, who had dragged McLaughlin into their business for the sake of a few watches, were not making progress in their private initiative to rid the city of a loose cannon. Silver, whom Moss and his men had last seen a week earlier, had left the SPC stranded amidst a delicate political operation. It is difficult to know how much goodwill was left as the parties made their way to the corner of the Bowery and Pell that evening. It was Jacobs and McManus who lost their nerve first, knowing that they needed to make a definitive move if they were to get Silver to the point where he would board the *Paris*.

There would be no more talk. McManus, it was later reported, took up a concealed position within the saloon while Jacobs stood outside, pretending to read a newspaper, watching for SPC agents. Jacobs said that, when Silver arrived, he saw a Parkhurst man leaving Flynn's who gave Silver a signal by 'rubbing his chin with a handkerchief'. Silver, expecting to meet only Jacobs, followed him into the saloon. Jacobs at once turned and said, 'Well Joe, what are you going to have to drink?' It was the signal for McManus to emerge. They then arrested Silver. They searched him and found a .38 revolver, three pages of notes covering meetings with Jacobs and McManus, a list of expenses incurred on SPC business, and a letter by Silver to Adolph Goldberg in 'Hebrew', post-marked Pittsburgh and allegedly stating; 'Now is the time to get even.'[38]

The detectives took him to the cells at the Essex Street Market Court station. They had their man, and could now work on him with purpose and urgency. But who *was* this man? And, more pertinently, what charge would they prefer? Was this not the same 'Joseph Liss' who figured in Byrnes's 'Rogues' Gallery' and who, on the instruction of McLaughlin, was wanted for the burglary on Delancey; a break-in the police said never happened? If 'Liss' was booked and charged with burglary would this not precipitate the court appearance Moss and his agents were working towards? Clearly, he could not have been arrested for burglary, nor could he be held under the name Lis, Liss or Silver. When they got to headquarters they booked a 'Don't Know', a 'John Doe', for 'disorderly' behaviour. Silver, already 'missing' for more than a week as far as the SPC was concerned, was now well and truly missing; he was an offender without name.[39]

Jacobs and McManus were up against the clock. They had only days in which either to arraign their 'John Doe' or cut him loose, and only forty-eight hours before the *Paris* sailed. Throughout that night and the morning of 26 February, they worked the good cop/bad cop routine. It was best, they suggested, for Silver to take the lesser amount offered and start a new life 'on the other side'. Failing that, he could always admit to being part of a SPC conspiracy and stay on in the Lower East Side where they would look after him. If all else failed, things would get messy and Jacobs, using his powers of extradition, would put him aboard the *Paris* with or without his approval. But the Polish mule, unable or unwilling to distinguish carrot from stick, refused to budge.

Silver realised time was on his side. A professional gambler, he clung to what he had and waited for Jacobs and McManus to arraign him. His eyes took in the judge at the Essex Street Market Court and the Stars and Stripes, but his help did not come from on high, or from the constitution. It came from an earthly source, from one of the agents of doubtful provenance employed by the SPC. In court on entirely another matter, Agent Lemmon of the SPC happened to catch a glimpse of the man he and his colleagues had been searching for, for more than a week.[40]

Lemmon hurried off to tell Dennett, and for ten days there was not a newspaper in the city that did not carry lengthy reports on a contest which, at one level, was just a legal wrangle between two Lower East Side nonentities – a corrupt native-born detective, Charles Jacobs, and an immigrant burglar bearing a grudge, Joseph Silver. They were, however, mere foot soldiers in far more important battles between

Thomas Byrnes and Frank Moss, between the New York Police Department and the Society for the Prevention of Crime and – in its most distant dimension – between Richard Croker's Tammany Hall Democrats and William Strong's reform-minded City Hall supporters.

When Moss learned, on the afternoon of 26 February, that Silver was being held in the cells at Essex Street, he sent a letter to Byrnes 'informing him that a certain "John Doe" was confined at Headquarters and that I would hold him personally responsible for his safety. I insisted that he should be allowed to communicate with his friends.'[41] This misleadingly worded letter, in which Moss placed some distance between himself, Silver and Silver's 'friends', elicited a note in reply from Byrnes, who, probably quite truthfully, claimed to have no knowledge of the man's detention and said that he was at liberty to communicate with whoever he wanted to. That evening Silver wrote to Dennett giving him a doctored account of what had happened since he left Paterson.[42]

Who knows what Silver told Dennett? The letter, too, was never again seen but it was enough to convince Dennett and Moss that the next day had to be spent in Essex Street where Silver would be arraigned a second time. Moss and the agents' unexpected appearance in court on Wednesday morning threw Jacobs and McManus into disarray. Unable to claim they had a 'John Doe' on their hands, and unwilling to pursue a charge of burglary that might compromise themselves and McLaughlin, they were forced to come up with charges or see Silver set free. According to Moss, 'after thinking about it for a long time, the detectives preferred three charges, two of bribery and one of carrying concealed weapons'.[43] Moss used the opportunity Justice Grady gave Silver to respond to the charges to put the two detectives on the witness stand, but it was insufficient to prevent the charges being referred to a Grand Jury that Saturday.

As Silver was whisked away, Moss, Dennett and Whitney hurried to the office of the City Recorder with a request for an urgent audience with the senior judge in the Court of the General Sessions, John W. Goff. Moss was pushing an open door. Goff, an anti-Tammany Democrat had, along with Moss and W.T. Jerome, formed the legal team appointed to lead evidence before the Lexow Committee. Goff was familiar with police shenanigans on the 11th precinct. *Prima facie* evidence linking Jacobs and McManus to the Cohen burglary persuaded the Recorder to issue a warrant for the arrest of the detectives on the complaint of Dennett. Goff telephoned Byrnes and instructed him to have the detectives present themselves at his office. Byrnes, annoyed by these un-expected developments, arrested Jacobs and McManus and personally escorted them across to Essex Street where they were charged with being party to a conspiracy to commit a burglary at 8 Delancey. The detectives were, reportedly, 'astonished' by these events.[44]

Astonished, but hardly paralysed. By the time they were arraigned before Goff in the Court of the General Sessions for a preliminary grilling by Moss at midday, word had already been sent to office-bearers in the Max Hochstim Association and other interested parties on the Lower East Side that two detectives known to take protection money from brothel-owners and prostitutes were in trouble with the law for an alleged burglary, and that they would need cash for bail if they were to avoid spending a night in the cells.[45]

Moss, face to face with his quarry on the very day that Parkhurst was calling on the Mayor to discuss the composition of a new board of police commissioners and debate a successor to Byrnes as Chief of Police, used the courtroom to reveal the extraordinary links between Jacobs, McManus and Silver.[46] The proceedings concluded with Goff setting bail for Jacobs and McManus at $1,000 each, and directing that the charges be examined by a Grand Jury the following Tuesday. Martin Engel, 'poultry dealer' and treasurer of the MHA, arrived to put up Jacobs's bail while Charles Rabb, 'a Tammany politician' of Allen Street, home to Jewish prostitutes, placed the bond for McManus.[47]

With both sets of adversaries scheduled to appear before grand juries within a week, the intervening period was spent in frantic legal and political preparation. Moss used the sensation created by Byrnes's arresting his own men to further shape public opinion and remind the press of McManus's earlier problem with the Brooklyn police and stolen property. Prompted by Moss, the police in New Haven became very forthcoming about the meddlesome role that Jacobs had played when they had sought to have the burglar Higgins extradited.[48] Back in his office, when not fending off press queries, Moss did the paperwork to defend the SPC's agent and was no doubt relieved to discover, if he did not already know it, that Silver was the owner of a licensed firearm.

Jacobs, McManus and friends were no less active in press circles. They gave lengthy, confusing and misleading accounts of their inter-actions with Silver. They also picked up on Moss's prevarications about the subject to suggest that Silver was an authorised agent of the SPC, and that he had been party to the conspiracy that had played itself out on Delancey. On 28 February they found the money to retain Tammany's preferred attorneys – Howe & Hummel. Howe lost no time in addressing a letter to the foreman of the Grand Jury investigating the charges against Silver, requesting that his clients, Jacobs and McManus, be afforded the 'courtesy' of putting their case personally. The letter was then leaked to journalists Howe kept on the firm's payroll.[49]

Out of sight, the NYPD fixed things so as to suggest that, whatever had happened on Delancey that day, it could not have been a burglary. It was already on record that Detective Hickey, sent by Byrnes to investigate immediately after the burglary, could find no sign of forced entry. The police now also encountered unexpected problems in finding the complainant.[50] When they visited the contact address Cohen had given, they found no one by that name; only an old Republican police adversary, Ralph Nathan, a man who had presented damning evidence about vote-rigging before Lexow.[51] Almost as mystifying was the way in which the janitor, Frank Engelhardt, his wife and daughter had become hopelessly confused. By the time the matter got to court Mrs Engelhardt and her daughter were of the opinion that Cohen and Silver had been close friends, while the janitor was no longer certain that he could tell the difference between Cohen and Dennett. To the best of his knowledge, no burglary had ever taken place at number 8.[52]

Most of these things happened before the grand juries even met; prompted by information and misinformation bled into the press and rumour mills by opposing attorneys. Moss and Howe needed no reminding of what was at stake – the nature of the links between the NYPD and Tammany Democrats, and the composition of the new Board of Police Commissioners.[53] The Jacobs–Silver débâcle raised the political temperature and Moss was exaggerating only slightly when he suggested that the story was 'big enough to make the entire city crazy with excitement'. One person who needed no convincing that events outside the courts were starting to eclipse common sense was Byrnes. He went to see Moss who was referring publicly to his detectives as 'scoundrels', and complained about the 'sensational course' being pursued.[54] But this private approach, too, Moss was quick to make public. At about the same time a rumour surfaced that Moss and Dennett were to be arrested on a charge of conspiracy in relation to the burglary and that it was Moss who had provided Silver with the $100 used in the attempt to bribe the detectives.[55]

By 1 March, damaging public squabbles had forced the parties to take their horses to market for trading, in secret. A conference was held – between whom is not clear – in the District Attorney's office. It was agreed that, instead of a Grand Jury looking at the charges against Silver the following morning, the charges against Jacobs and McManus would be examined first.[56] The charges against Silver then disappeared from public view although the accused, whose bail had been set at $3,000, remained in custody.[57] Whether Silver's incarceration was a function of lack of funds on the part of the SPC or whether it actually suited Moss to have the agent behind bars is impossible to tell. The next day, Silver was brought before Judge Cowling and the Grand Jury as the principal witness in the ongoing investigation against Detectives Jacobs and McManus.

The hearing occasioned great excitement on the Lower East Side. It was, in the words of one journalist, a case of 'diamond cut diamond'. But the problem for *Daily Tribune* readers, as for most mortals, was 'to determine which diamond had been cut'.[58] Fragments of truth and falsehood filled the air until the jurors all but choked in confusion. There was an unstated agreement that neither party would allude to links between them, the Max Hochstim Association or the 'unsavoury professions': it was a contest between two men involved in crimes against property. By one o'clock everybody was flagging and the judge, noting that the detectives had not had the chance of addressing the jury, ordered that the court would reconvene the following morning to hear Jacobs and McManus.[59]

But the detectives, who had been so fulsome before the press corps and whom Howe had been so keen to get into the witness box, were never tested before the judge. When the Grand Jury reconvened early on 3 March, the first witness was Inspector McLaughlin. He told the jury that Jacobs and McManus had been instructed by him to take part in the 'burglary' on the explicit understanding and in full knowledge that all the proceedings on Delancey had been orchestrated by the SPC. This proved decisive. Members of the jury – battling to make sense of a case in which the original complainant, Cohen, had stuck his head into the courtroom, caught sight of those assembled and then fled never to be seen again – dismissed the charges against both Jacobs and McManus.[60]

Outside the court, the war of words raged on. The Grand Jury ruling did not let the detectives fully off the hook since they had to face a further examination by the Recorder before the matter could be put to rest. Goff examined Jacobs and McManus on 5 March but, for reasons that were not made public, concluded that the evidence did not warrant 'holding the defendants or resubmitting the case to the Grand Jury'.[61]

And still the waters of revenge boiled, as if the removal of the source of the heat made no difference. Encouraged by Tammany friends who were meeting their legal costs, and heartened by what they saw as the diminishing resolve of Moss who was appearing on a *pro amico* basis for his agents, Jacobs and McManus decided to retaliate. Within hours of the charges being dismissed, and with Silver still behind bars, they laid a charge of conspiracy against Dennett and Whitney. The two agents were arrested in the early hours of 6 March and eased into the Tombs where they, and Silver, were represented by Moss who now saw his own neck on the block. He got them a hearing in the police court where Justice Grady ruled that, since the charges of burglary against the detectives had been dismissed, the defendants must have been bent on entrapping Jacobs and McManus and that the charge of conspiracy should be examined by a Grand Jury, unless the charge of bribery against Silver was disproved. Unlike when Silver had been up on his own and the SPC could not find bail of $3,000, this time Moss had no difficulty in persuading a private benefactor to come up with three amounts of $1,000 in bail, for Dennett, Silver and Whitney. By late that afternoon the three were out and Attorney Frank Moss was back in very deep discussion with his former boss, Recorder Goff.[62]

The whole legal mess, together with a second, interwined, Parkhurst initiative against Byrnes and the NYPD, was referred to 'an extraordinary Grand Jury'. The jurors met on 13, 14 and 15 March – and layer upon layer of complication was added to the proceedings. When Howe pursued what had gone on amongst the SPC agents in Paterson a month earlier, Moss struck back by getting Silver to try to persuade Joseph Goldberg to recount how Jacobs and McManus had once helped extort money owed to him by his brother-in-law. Each blow struck was a blow parried. It was, as the *New York Times* portrayed it, a contest 'Fought at Close Range'. By 18 March the jury had had enough and refused to indict Dennett, Whitney or Silver, who walked free. Silver had learned a crucial lesson, one he never forgot: there was no limit to what a good, well-connected lawyer could achieve. The circus had run for a month and at the end of the day neither Tammany Hall nor the SPC had emerged triumphant.[63]

These contests, capable only of producing losers, were followed by the reform-minded Strong and those whom he had identified as members of the new Board of Police Commissioners that would bring Byrnes and the NYPD to heel. Amongst the new commissioners-designate was a thirty-three-year-old Republican civil servant with political ambitions by the name of Theodore Roosevelt. In May, just six weeks after the last of the public encounters between Jacobs and Silver, Roosevelt assumed his position as president of the Board assisted by three citizens selected for their willingness to serve in a non-partisan capacity. Unsurprisingly, Moss was not among the new appointees.

Roosevelt, lately a cowboy on the Dakota frontier, lost no time in setting his sights. On 18 May he wrote to Henry Cabot Lodge, 'I think that I shall move against Byrnes at once. I thoroughly distrust him, and cannot do any thorough work while he remains. It will be a very hard fight and I have no idea how it will come out.'[64] In the end, there was no contest. By the month's end Byrnes, a man 'who more or less legalised crime, or more precisely kept it within acceptable limits by using some criminals to oversee or suppress other criminals, giving each a protected area in which to operate', had tendered his resignation.[65] His sudden departure sounded the death knell for Jacobs and McManus.[66]

Roosevelt recognised the need for more sensitive, ethnically attuned policing on the Lower East Side. A keen boxer in the grand era of the sport, he had high regard for 'the Maccabee or fighting Jewish type' – a description which could, in part, have described Silver. During Roosevelt's short stewardship of the Board of Commissioners, the number of Jews in the NYPD grew from less than a score to nearly three times that number in just twenty-four months. Clear water flows from dark swamps.[67]

On the surface the demise of Byrnes and those like him was attributable to Roosevelt and his new commissioners. Seen in broader context, however, it was a by-product of the struggles between Democrats and Republicans, between Tammany Democrats and the SPC, between William Howe and Frank Moss and – in its remotest dimension – between Jacobs and Silver. Driven by the need to get even with Jacobs he had, almost inadvertently, got caught up in the struggle for control of municipal politics and institutionalised corruption.

'Silver', a weak persona born after a lengthy stay in prison and with no real interest in civic well-being, was left with nowhere to turn to. A minor but notorious figure in police and criminal circles, he was of no use to Roosevelt who needed good policemen, or to Moss, who needed better underworld informants. He was marginalised by the Max Hochstim Association and even the Goldberg brothers were wary of him, although he remained on good terms with their brother-in-law, Budner. 'Silver', an identity born in a moment of hope, had been stripped down to the more familiar personality of Joseph Lis.

Left to his own devices he set out his stall, trading on the only thing he retained: a reputation as a dangerous 'agent' of indeterminate status who, in some secret capacity, might still be attached to the SPC. Lexow had increased the hazards for corrupt policemen and in the wake of the hearings the price for 'protection' of prostitutes had escalated.[68] Within weeks of being discharged by the Grand Jury, still passing himself off as a 'Parkhurst agent', he started to prey on prostitutes around Delancey, including Lillie Bloom, Sadie Wolff, and the sisters Fanny and Gussy Bernstein from Pittsburgh. At a time when the protection money paid to patrolmen had doubled from $5 a month in 1893 to $10 in 1895, Silver demanded $25 per month from Bloom. He had reverted to the type of menacing, predatory existence he had employed back in London, in the East End, in the mid-1880s. The prostitutes were utterly terrified of him and, when they got the chance to contribute to his downfall many years later, when he was at the very pinnacle of his criminal career, they did not hesitate to denounce him.[69]

He was not the only one to increase pressure on the women working the streets or living in brothels. Lexow-led reforms and the change in police commissioners prompted large operators, including Bertha/ Matilda Hermann, to abandon the city and relocate their enterprises in settings all round the Atlantic world, from Argentina to South Africa. Indeed, with its gold mining industry expanding at an unprecedented rate the Witwatersrand was a popular destination and the first wave of pioneering pimps and prostitutes bearing notorious or highly distinctive names – like Mortke and Rosie Goldberg, 'Jack Rand' or 'Sadie Afrikander' – were already spreading stories about the promise of Johannesburg or Kimberley.[70]

Silver, locked into an inner universe where he could be both an 'agent' and an extortionist, was finding it difficult to survive. Sadie Wolff later claimed that it was at about this time that he was again arrested, and that he fled to Pittsburgh only to be brought back to New York by the police to face charges for living off the proceeds of prostitution.[71] She may have confused events surrounding his earlier extradition to Pittsburgh, but, either way, it was a difficult time for him. By summer's end it was almost impossible to make a living. He decided that it was best to leave America for a few months and link up with some of his criminal cousins who had emigrated from Poland.

On the first day of August, he called on Dennett, who provided a testimonial stating that Silver had worked as an agent for the SPC and that they had parted on good terms. Two weeks later he used his status as a naturalised American citizen to apply for a passport. Carefully he ensured that the information he supplied was an interleaved text of truth and falsehood. He claimed to have been born on 14 March 1869, but in Warsaw rather than Kielce. He swore that he had arrived in New York on 16 February 1885, aboard the SS *Bothnia,* and had worked continuously in the city for ten years as a barber. This concealed the fact that he had first got a passport in Kielce, in 1884, and that he had spent four years in Whitechapel. It was also at variance with the more truthful account that he had given Frank Moss when he claimed that he had first arrived in New York City in 1889. His lies were compounded by the fact that the *Bothnia* was not in port on 16 February although it had arrived in New York two days later but without a passenger remotely like Lis in age, name or status. He also stated that he wished to travel abroad for six months and that, after that, he would be returning to the United States.[72]

Silver left on an unnamed steamer on a day in September 1895, bound for an unknown European port using a name which shipping manifests refuse to reveal. It was late September, the season was changing, the breeze stiffening, and the Atlantic starting to heave and sigh to the rhythm of winter swells. He wondered whether he was doing the right thing – going from west to east, from the light of the New into the darkness of the Old World when most Jews were moving resolutely in the opposite direction. He was going from a city where his name was on the front pages of the newspapers to a place where, ten years earlier, over forty-eight months, he had done such awful things that he wanted them obliterated from official records for all time. He was leaving a young society with an open economy in which the demand for sexual services was paramount, for an ageing society and sluggish economy where the supply of prostitutes for destinations around the Atlantic was becoming more important than domestic demand.

Procurement and pimping were, however, very different branches of the profession. Each made demands on the character, and each was locked into its own matrix of dangers. 'Silver' was more of a New Yorker, a Lower East Side man with a lighter touch; a pimp who could point you in the direction of a good time. Lis was a Londoner, an East Ender, a creature who had lived off women in Whitechapel during the very worst of times. As the ship ploughed east he was aware of how in dress, manner and speech he remained Joseph Silver, but deep within him he felt the exciting stirrings of the older Lis. By October 1895 he was back in London, not far from Waterloo station. But who was he?

VII

LONDON
1895–1898

Descended from generations victimised by the instruments of
an arbitrary power, he was racially, nationally, and individ-
ually afraid of the police. It was an inherited weakness, altogether independent of his judgement, of his reason, of his
experience. He was born to it. But that sentiment, which
resembled the irrational horror some people have of cats, did
not stand in the way of his immense contempt of the English
police.

Joseph Conrad, *The Secret Agent*

BY 1895, the industrial economies of the northern hemisphere were
shrugging off the lingering effects of the Great Depression in which
they had been mired for two decades or more. Britain – still the financially hegemonic power of the western world – was expanding its
formal and informal empire around the Atlantic and elsewhere. On the
Latin American perimeter the combination of liberal ideology and free
trade mesmerised the emerging markets. Export-driven economies in
Argentina, Brazil and Chile made energetic efforts to maintain favourable
trading balances and service growing debts as a stream of primary
commodities and partially processed goods, directed northwards, struggled to match the much larger flow of capital goods and manufactures
to the underdeveloped south.[1]

In Britain, accelerated growth in invisible earnings from banking,
insurance and shipping gave the City added muscle in managing the
periodic crises in Latin America occasioned by faltering debt repay-
ments in an international economy based on the gold standard. Such

bouts of turbulence, however, had to be offset against developments elsewhere where there was mounting evidence of real and sustained growth in areas that fell squarely within Britain's sphere of influence. In southern Africa the discovery of diamonds in the Cape in the 1860s, and gold in the Transvaal in the 1880s, contributed to the underlying strength of the City. By the mid-1890s it was becoming clearer that the Witwatersrand was set to become a major producer of the metal that underpinned international trade and that gold would dominate South African exports for decades to come. Indeed, 1895 saw an investment boom in Rand-based gold mining shares.[2]

With the industrialising United States a magnet in the west and labour-hungry economies expanding rapidly in the southern hemisphere, albeit in ways that were not always sustainable, the Atlantic world drew in human capital from the Old World at an unprecedented rate. Millions of migrants, including hundreds of thousands of Jews keen to put the Russian empire behind them, crossed Europe's muddied boundaries to the Atlantic shoreline where they positioned themselves for the journey to the New World or the southern colonies. With modern undersea cabling and the telegraph serving as direction-finders, and steamships propelling them, shoal upon shoal of hopefuls took to the water. But – as in most mass migrations – many did not make it. Thousands, exhausted by the mental and physical effort of reaching the coast, were too afraid, too emaciated or too financially stretched to brave the open ocean and remained in the economic shallows of European port cities where specialist predators picked off the weakest.[3]

In London, employers were in need of semi- or unskilled labour that could turn out mass-produced goods for expanding markets. In the docklands of the East End the production and processing of boots and shoes, chemicals, cigarettes, clothing, furniture and wood, hats, matches, paper and printing, umbrellas and textiles wore out any number of workers each year. In the bespoke and ready-made clothing trades, thousands of Jews from central Europe and the Russian empire, familiar with needle, scissors and sewing-machine, were prime candidates for 'sweating'.[4]

Small-scale employers entrenched in dark recesses of blackened houses, dirty workshops and soot-encrusted factories, with a penchant for exploiting the strong and the young, were not the worst or most dangerous of dockside predators. Lurking just beyond their premises lay even more calculating, specialised feeders capable of consuming female bodies and souls alike. Predatory males, in flattering guises, intercepted prospective female employees with false offers of assistance before they reached factory gates, or waylaid the desperate or the weary with glowing tales of prospects for a better life.

Some middle-aged feckless fellows were easily fobbed off. Other predators, young and handsome, sometimes supported by a plausible female cast, were more difficult to detect and deflect. Bearing cash and gifts, well-dressed 'bachelors' affected a sporting demeanour, seemed knowledgeable about the workings of the city and made it clear they were in search of wives or lovers. By 1895, the chancers and small-time confidence tricksters who preyed on gullible women were giving way to a growing number of gangsters and white slave traffickers. The latter, familiar with the contours of the widening world and the migration patterns that fed into it, were ready to recruit, seduce or rape young women as a prelude to putting them on the streets before exporting them as commodities, as white slaves.

Such extreme male predation had been the subject of private and public concern for decades. The first, largely ineffectual, international conference on white slavery had taken place in Liverpool, in 1875. As the pace and volume of international migration picked up, the attendant problems became more urgent and visible in European port cities. In 1885, members of the Anglo-Jewish elite in London, led by the Rothschilds and Montefiores, founded the Jewish Ladies' Society for Preventative and Rescue Work. Concentrating on the East End, they founded places of refuge for vulnerable women at Charcroft House in Mile End and Sarah Pyke House in Aldgate.[5]

But with the flow of impoverished, poorly educated migrants showing no sign of abating, the emphasis on rescue work was soon supplanted by a new focus on pro-active, preventative, work. The Jewish Association for the Protection of Girls and Women (JAPGW), established in 1896, used paid agents, male volunteers and religious leaders to liaise with the state as well as the railroad and shipping companies that controlled the docks and railways stations. It set out to provide women with protection at the European end of migration as well as at distant Atlantic destinations. This expansion in the scope of the work was underwritten by a substantial grant from the JCA – the Jewish Colonisation Association founded five years earlier to facilitate Jewish emigration by Baron Maurice de Hirsch, scion of a prominent Bavarian banking family.[6]

Bearing secrets only he knew, Silver slipped into England in September 1895, through an unknown port and under a name that cannot be traced. Twenty-seven years old, with neatly cropped hair, he sported a moustache that failed to divert attention from a face slightly pock-marked by secondary syphilis. Although cash-strapped after his American misadventures, he remained neatly attired and had the frame of a well-built man at the height of his physical power. He maintained an interest in boxing and was perhaps still marginally involved in the prize-fighting that was increasingly frowned upon. He kept his licence to carry a gun, but appears to have abandoned the revolver he had used as a Parkhurst 'agent' and reverted to the clasp knife he was more comfortable with.[7]

Physically formidable, with the syphilis in its dormant phase, he was mentally better equipped for a predatory existence than he had been when he had fled London as a twenty-year-old. Prone to mood swings which sometimes gave rise to life-threatening outbursts, and liable to impulsive behaviour, he had nevertheless acquired insights and skills that gave him more confidence in his day-to-day business. The quality of his spoken and written English had improved and the acquisition of a slight Bowery accent allowed him to adopt an American identity whenever it suited. His repertoire had grown.

During his second stay in London Joseph Silver was, at various times, also 'Joe Eligman', Abraham 'Kramer' or 'Ramer', 'Joe Liss' or 'James Smith'. He tended to steal and amend, rather than invent, names. 'Eligman' and 'Kramer', or 'Ramer', were borrowed from former associates in the New York or Pittsburgh underworld. The seemingly banal James Smith – who dared to share Silver's initials – appears to have been the alias of an unknown London-based Russo-Polish Jew involved in the white slave traffick who was sent to southern Africa in 1896. In 1903, Silver, ever self-serving, went on to denounce this James Smith to the police in the Orange River colony.[8]

Whatever name he employed, he knew that he would be severely tested in the new setting. In New York, a demand-driven economy for sexual services overseen by ethnic associations gave him ready access to prostitutes. Prostitution there fitted into city machinery manned by corrupt police who worked with Tammany. London was different. Although it, too, thrived on the never-ending demand for commercial sex, a relatively sluggish economy and modest wages made for smaller returns. Gangs with extensive, well-established links to corrupt policemen and politicians were almost unheard of. The capital's location, at the far western end of European migration paths, ensured that there were better returns to be made from intercepting vulnerable young women, turning them into prostitutes, and then exporting them to destinations spread around the Atlantic.

Ever curious and innovative when it came to women's bodies, Silver knew that high returns meant high risk. He lacked the capital and manpower to start up an 'import – export' agency and had few contacts in his new environment. The deception, seduction or raping of young women in an established social order was fraught with danger. For all that, it took him just thirty-six months to build a business with associates in Argentina, South Africa and the United States. So financially well off was he by the end of that period that he could hire the finest barristers in the City to help keep him and his associates out of prison. He created a classic family business, fashioning his stepbrother and cousins into a specialist unit of the sort that London lacked at the time. He obtained cash from burglary, extortion and theft, until he was in a position to get prostitutes to work for the firm on a regular basis. London saw the first flowering of his business acumen and heralded more 'achievements' to come.

Devoted to crimes against people, he cast himself as a detective's agent, draper or hotel proprietor and, when dealing with stolen property, as a jeweller or watchmaker. He chose not to base himself in the East End. Instead he 'worked' mostly from Belvedere Road, Great Windmill or Little Portland Streets – addresses on the South Bank or in the seedier parts of the West End where there were pockets of Jewish garment workers. The main business, however, was on Stamford Street, near Waterloo station. Here he worked his way up from unsuccessful burglar and petty thief in 1895, to pimp and extremely well-heeled white slave trafficker by 1898. Ever secretive, he also kept a small room in St Mark's Street in Stepney, at the lower end of Aldgate. This was close to Sarah Pyke House, where he and his associates could monitor Jewish prostitutes. It was also close to familiar old haunts in Whitechapel.

His upward trajectory, marked by an uncertain start, got under way with a family reunion in a house at 134 Stamford Street, in a squalid quarter south of the river sandwiched between Blackfriars and Waterloo Roads. In a street filled with brothels often fronting as cheap lodging houses or hotels he was reunited with his stepbrother, Jack, whom he had last seen as a twelve-year-old. After his bar mitzvah Jack had been

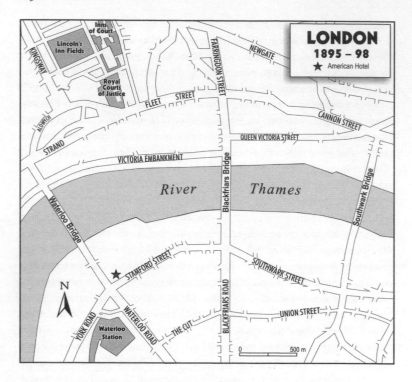

LONDON
1895 – 98
★ American Hotel

drawn into the Russian Army. Although the 14th Cavalry Division was based at Kielce, he had probably served his time with one of the regiments posted around the greater Warsaw military district, or even further afield. The spell in the army had done little to instil discipline into what was still a wild lad. He had, however, been awarded a medal, 'in the name of the Tsar', for his shooting prowess. Like his older stepbrother, whom he adored and remained loyal to for most of his life, Jack was dangerous, impulsive and violent.[9]

On leaving the army Jack made his way to London, where his career assumed a familiar shape. In 1893, aged twenty, he met and seduced Regina Weinberg who, then fifteen, was put on to the streets to earn a living while he pursued other, potentially more lucrative, interests. He had a penchant for burglary and the theft of jewellery and is alleged to have resorted to one of the criminal clichés of the day when he once hid a diamond in soap. More a gun than a knife-man Jack, who was later prosecuted for attempted murder and suspected of yet another murder, came to favour a revolver over a rifle. In London, thinly disguised as Maurice Silvermann, he was his older brother's devoted henchman.[10]

Two older cousins – on their mother's side – either frequented the house in Stamford Street or lived there. Both worked closely with the Lis brothers and assisted in running the family business. Beile (originally probaby Beilke) or 'Temma', had married the ineffectual Leon Fierstein and was eight years older than Joseph. Supposedly a 'lodging-house keeper', she was actually a hardened procuress. She helped oversee younger pimps and procurers who went into the East End where they either sought out new recruits or followed experienced prostitutes who had passed through Sarah Pyke House but then found it difficult to obtain work and could therefore be persuaded to re-enter the profession.[11]

The other cousin drawn from the same cohort as Beile, but with prior American exposure, was Joseph Anker. A pimp and procurer who sometimes posed as a draper or a mantle-maker, Anker resented the Fiersteins and longed to own his own business. As deceitful and treacherous as any in the family, but perhaps a trifle more cowardly, he welcomed the arrival of his young cousin from New York, whom he saw as a counterweight to the pushy Beile and useless Leon. Silver, quick to read the micro-politics, gave his cousin an important part to play in a restructured set-up and Anker, who ended his days as a baker in Cape Town, repaid him by being loyal to him for almost a decade.[12]

Silver, alpha male in a troop of nocturnal hunters, sought to consolidate his position by acquiring the female partner who could confirm his status, meet some of his polyvalent sexual needs, and help lure other women into prostitution. Since the choice of partner was a business rather than a personal decision it did not take him long to settle on a victim. Within eight weeks of his arrival he entered into what was to be the first of several marriages of convenience over the decade that followed. How exactly the unfortunate Hannah Opticer was snared is unknown, as is her fate in the longer term.

She was Polish and from Apt, just a few miles east of Kielce. Like a subsequent victim, she was presumably spotted working in the rag trade in the East End; she was sufficiently proud of her father's status as a master tailor to have it recorded on her marriage certificate. Perhaps she thought that Silver might be a good catch since, at the time, he sometimes posed as a successful draper recently arrived from America. Like another victim, it seems that Hannah had been lured out of the East End and was already living in the house in Southwark when the trap was finally sprung. If so, her marriage would have culminated in a series of horrifying psycho-sexual assaults. On 24 October 1895, Silver, a 'Detective's Agent' of 134 Stamford Street, a widower at the age of twenty-seven, married Hannah Opticer, twenty-five, a spinster, of the same address, at the Lambeth Registry in the presence of Joseph Anker and Leon Fierstein.[13]

It was not a marriage made in heaven; nor did it last very long. What Hannah did to earn a living in Waterloo may be imagined but is not known. The civil and criminal records yield no further information about her under either her married or her maiden name. She may have assumed, or was given, a professional *nom de plume* – possibly 'Annie' like Esther Heller before her – prior to being sold abroad. It is possible that her husband reverted to being a 'widower' once she was out of the way but, either way, there is no surviving documentary record of her, alive or dead. Maybe it did not matter all that much; two weeks after the wedding her husband was in police custody.

William Griffin, umbrella manufacturer in an age that prided itself on the quality of its products, had branches at three outlets on the north bank, between Tower and Westminster Bridges, not far from Southwark. At a time when a good umbrella cost thirty shillings, Londoners had their umbrellas repaired by craftsmen known as 'mushroom-fakers' assisted by unskilled immigrant female workers. Since the case was not reported on in the press we do not know what drew Silver there but, once on the premises, he fell prey to impulse and on 8 November 1895 he was arrested for the theft of an umbrella.[14]

Neatly dressed, he told the police he was Abraham Ramer, a watchmaker who, they noted, commanded reasonable spoken and written English. No one asked about his marital status or enquired after his address, but they attempted, without success, to see if he had a criminal record. If, under another name, he had once stolen a watch in the East End back in 1888, then there was no detective from Whitechapel to recognise him. When he appeared before Magistrate Loveland-Loveland at the Marlborough Police Court thirteen days later, he was sentenced to three months' imprisonment, with hard labour, in Wormwood Scrubs.[15] Silver was released two days after his birthday, on 18 February 1896, but, instead of the release heralding an upturn in his career, bad luck continued to dog him. Still sniffing out women in the rag trade, six weeks later he met Eleanor Finkelstein.

Finkelstein, a twenty-four-year-old 'needlewoman', could not have understood how dangerous her new friend was or what his real business was. 'Abraham Ramer' took great interest not only in her, but in her employers' affairs. In late March he persuaded her to help steal a roll of satin, valued at £6, from a Hoffer and a sable coat belonging to Henry Raven. It was a variant on burglaries undertaken by his father in Kielce, in 1879 and, more pertinently, of that by Adolph Goldberg and others in Plumber's Row, Whitechapel in 1887. It was as poorly executed as the Rubinstein burglary on the Lower East Side, in 1889. Then he had ended upriver; this time the road led to Pentonville.

By April Fool's Day he was in police custody, and on 21 April 1895 he appeared before the Common Serjeant at the Central Criminal Courts. The prosecutor at the Old Bailey took a kindly view of the illiterate needlewoman and saw Finkelstein largely as a victim. The charge relating to the theft of the coat was separated from that of the satin. She was granted bail of £50 and instructed to reappear at a later date. But the prosecutor chose not to pursue her. The magistrate took a stern view of Mr Ramer and his criminal record and sentenced him to nine months' hard labour.[16]

Pentonville in high summer was no better than the Scrubs in midwinter. Built north of the City near King's Cross in 1840, the prison was originally designed to accommodate a thousand inmates who were expected to adhere to a silence rule and remained masked. Initially a holding facility for those awaiting transportation to Australia, the prison had moved with the times and by the mid-1890s was a 'modern institution' with an emphasis on cleanliness and discipline enforced by the usual regime of spare rations and hard labour.[17] Silver's arrival in Pentonville was at once noted by members of the extraordinarily mobile Atlantic underworld. Sadie Wolff, who seemes to have followed him almost round the world, learned of his presence while visiting a friend in one of London's female prisons and later gave a garbled account of his recent escapades. Other, potentially more serious adversaries also picked up on 'Abraham Ramer' and he had sufficient time to reflect on the fact that the name had outlived its usefulness in East End circles.[18]

While he was in Pentonville, relationships back in the house at Stamford Street deteriorated. Jack managed on Regina's earnings and the proceeds of small burglary jobs and they got on well enough with the family and the young pimps. The problem lay with the professional jealousies of cousins Anker and Beile. In October, Anker had gone secretly to Mrs Harris, the matron at Sarah Pyke House, and told her that 'Beile Fierstein, of 134 Stamford Street, had recently got hold of six girls whom she had obliged to go on to the streets' and that 'one of the girls had been at SP House'. Mrs Harris reported what she had been told to the 'dock agent', Sternheim, but he said it was unlikely that their employer, the Jewish Association for the Protection of Girls and Women would do anything about it. It was curious advice which later earned him a sharp rebuke from the committee. The Fiersteins escaped police scrutiny but it was clear that, without Silver there, the partners lacked discipline.[19]

He was far more professional after his release from Pentonville. In January 1897, he discarded the name Ramer and extended his repertoire to include 'Eligman' and 'Kramer'. He controlled his impulses, eschewed personal involvement in burglaries and concentrated on the commercial sex trade. Business picked up and he had pimps swarming around Waterloo soliciting customers for a growing number of prostitutes. He rotated women between houses and extended the lucrative white slave trade by 'exporting' women around the Atlantic to new and old contacts. He tightened his control of the enterprise. The Fiersteins moved out of 134, which he took over; he then opened a second brothel there, fronting as a restaurant, which he sold at a profit to the delighted Anker. Still expanding, he hired a set of interconnected rooms at 167 Stamford Street under the name James Smith. A touch nostalgically, he named this 'The American Hotel'.[20]

With the major outlets clustered around the station, Silver spent most of his time on the South Bank protecting a business supporting ten pimps, procurers and white slavers as well as a score or more prostitutes. But the East End retained its endless fascination for him and he instructed his men – Simon 'Monkey Jack' Kumcher, Jacob 'Curley' Shrednicki, Jack Strakiosky and Morris Zimmerman – to concentrate their efforts on procurement in and around Whitechapel. Dressed in fashionable suits and wearing fob-watches, he and Jack kept the young Polish bullies under control and backed up their authority with knives and guns. He kept in good physical shape, visiting the boxing booths between Vallance Road and Mile End Gate where outlawed prize-fighting yielded the odd windfall.[21]

He maintained an interest in Yiddish theatre, a by-product of his friendship with Goldberg. Some of the poorest-paid Jewish actors and actresses occasionally doubled as pimps and part-time prostitutes. The connection between drama and commercial sex became ever more pronounced during the mass migrations and expansion of the Atlantic world. In London, as elsewhere, pimps and white slavers monitored women in the theatre very carefully. But there was no reason for him to cross Blackfriars to keep abreast of new trends in Yiddish theatre.[22]

In 1897, S.M. Hyman, variety agent for the Empire Palace and Theatre Royal in Johannesburg, opened an office at 182 Stamford Street. It was a propitious moment. South African theatre, riding on the back of the mid-nineties boom, was drawing in northern hemisphere companies and presenting Yiddish productions for audiences composed largely of immigrant Lithuanian Jews. Johannesburg-based syndicates facilitated these exchanges and one of the East End's most famous sons, the actor turned diamond magnate, Barney Barnato, was contemplating building a lavish new theatre on the goldfields. With 'the Rand' on everybody's lips, many talented actors of the day, including some with underworld connections, passed through Hyman's office on their way south. At least one of these actor-pimps, Saul Wallerstein, got to know Silver well.[23]

Actors and flashy agents, transcontinental migrants gliding about like some new species of swallow provided the preening pimps and white slavers of Stamford Street with a continuous stream of information about the ever-changing socio-economic conditions in port cities all around the Atlantic world. Excited chattering did nothing to ease rivalries amongst highly competitive males. Knowledge of successes by other ponces could ruffle feathers and unleash unforeseen, sometimes violent, confrontations.

Henschel Joseph, based in the brothel next door to the American Hotel, hailed from Warsaw and had started his career as a pimp in London before doing a tour of duty in Paris and returning to the capital. In mid-1897, he and his whore-wife, Bertha Golgowski, embarked upon a scheme to ensnare two Polish immigrants – Golgowski's own sister and a friend, Goodman – into prostitution. For some unknown reason Silver took exception to this and, when he next saw Joseph, he told him so. An argument ensued, Silver drew a knife and stabbed him. The police were summoned and 'James Smith' was arrested. Shortly after that, in a move reminiscent of Anker's earlier denunciation of Beile at Sarah Pyke House, the JAPGW somehow got to hear of the situation and managed to rescue Goodman. Joseph retaliated by pressing charges against 'James Smith' but was then subjected to so sustained a campaign of bribery and terror by the Silver gang that he, Golgowski and the hapless sister fled London for New York, leaving Silver a free man.[24]

To keep the business expanding, Silver needed new prostitutes. Ageing, disease and familiarity were occupational hazards for prostitutes and popular brothels had to have a never-ending supply of healthy younger women with sexual energy capable of feigning the relative inexperience that would please the fragile egos of their clients. By late 1897, probably earlier, he was already supplying another ex-New Yorker, Sam Stein, and other Polish-American brothel-owners in South Africa with young women who had served an apprenticeship in the American Hotel. He, Jack, Anker and the other cousins extended their East End procurement operations to meet domestic, and insatiable, foreign demand.

As 'drapers' newly arrived from America, Anker hired a room in Osborn Street, Whitechapel and Silver one in Stepney, literally around the corner from Sarah Pyke House. Jack, a Polish 'leather merchant', was based in Sidney Street, also in Whitechapel. Their methods were crude and direct. Posing as older and supposedly respectable tradesmen they identified girls, cultivated avuncular friendships with them and then introduced them to eligible bachelors – Jacob Shrednicki (26), a 'tailor' and Simon Kumcher (22) a 'jewellery dealer'. 'Curley' and 'Monkey Jack' entertained the women, escorting them to the theatre and wooing them with displays of diamonds and jewellery. Once their trust had been won and there was talk of marriage, they would be invited to meet family members at a house in Portland Street, Soho. Knock-out drops of the sort that Silver would have seen on the Lower East Side would then be administered to the women who, in their drugged state, would be raped by their 'lovers'. The women, shamed by what had transpired, would be drawn ever further into the control of the gang before they were made to work as prostitutes. This plan, with variations, was used on two occasions during December 1897, with devastating consequences for three women.[25]

In mid-December, 'Silvermann' met Bernard Baumwoll, a fellow leather merchant formerly from Warsaw, in Commercial Road. Baumwoll had a seventeen-year-old sister-in-law, Taube Gordon, and was also acting as guardian for her friend, Fanny Rosenbaum. Rosenbaum, sixteen going on seventeen, had been in London for about eighteen months. Neither woman spoke English fluently and both appear to have led a sheltered life of the sort not uncommon amongst immigrants. Rosenbaum's closest family was a brother, Auscher, who shared his rooms in Holloway Road with their stepbrother, Simon Zudik. Silvermann, assuming the role of *shadchan*, read the situation and identified what he considered to be the weakest link in the chain. He offered Zudik £3 if he would arrange for Kumcher to meet Gordon.

A few days later Auscher Rosenbaum and Zudik took Silvermann and Kumcher to Baumwoll's house, where they were introduced to the young women. They all proceeded to the house in Holloway Road where Zudik's wife served them drinks. Kumcher showed Taube a marquise ring and told her it was his hope eventually to marry her. Nothing further transpired but, a few days later, the young women again saw Kumcher; this time he also introduced them to Shrednicki. With the customary formalities behind them and the women no longer being escorted by Auscher Rosenbaum or Zudik, 'Monkey Jack' and 'Curley' used the opening weeks of 1898 to woo the women with ever greater intensity. They assured them of their affection, wore diamond jewellery, and escorted them to the Yiddish theatre in the East End. Once they were fully at ease the women were introduced to the equally unthreatening, older, Joseph Anker.

Increasingly emboldened and trusting in relationships which they had kept secret from the elderly Baumwoll, the girls agreed to meet their beaux at the house in Portland Street. Beile, a friendly female face, met them at the door, escorted them into the kitchen and said to them, 'Do not fear anything. They are fine boys and they are going to marry you.' Anker, equally reassuring, told them, 'They are good boys; they will go away with you abroad; they will make a good living and they will be good to you.' Then, in suitably affirming conspiratorial tone, he asked whether Baumwoll knew of their romance and was happy to learn that he did not. Kumcher and Shrednicki then appeared.

The hostess, offering drinks all round, disappeared into a recess and reappeared with a honeyed concoction which a police surgeon later testified to as consisting of 58.5 per cent alcohol, some sugar, and an unidentifiable substance 'smelling like cloves'. But the girls were reluctant to drink alcohol and it was only at Beile's insistence that they swallowed the spirits which, they said, burnt their insides. Ever helpful, Beile suggested that the spirits be washed down with beer, which she was quick to produce. Before long they complained of feeling befuddled and ill, and Shrednicki and Kumcher suggested they go upstairs to lie down and recover. 'Curley' eased Rosenbaum into a room and raped her, while across the landing, 'Monkey Jack', raped Gordon.

When the women came to their senses, their attentive beaux re-assured them and confirmed their intention of marrying them. They agreed to meet again a week later, and the girls were escorted to the door where a cab was summoned to take them back to Whitechapel. Morally stranded and unwilling to confide in Auscher or Zudik, let alone Baumwoll, the girls returned to Soho the following week. This time the niceties were dispensed with and they were again raped. Rosenbaum, sensing their long-term fate, summoned all her courage and told her distressed guardian what had happened.

On 6 February the women were examined by a doctor at Marlborough police station, who confirmed that they had been raped. Baumwoll preferred charges and the following day Anker, Fierstein, Kumcher and Shrednicki were arrested and taken into custody for 'unlawfully administering spirits of wine and beer' to Gordon and Rosenbaum 'so as to stupefy them for an unlawful purpose'. It was an alarming devel-opment which Anker and the others – banking on the girls' shame silencing them – had not foreseen. The Lis brothers were informed and, within hours, 'Silvermann' called on his brother tradesman and compat-riot. He told Baumwoll that he had been to the police cells and spoken to Kumcher, who, in return for having the charge withdrawn, would marry Gordon and 'make over all his money and jewellery to her'. Baumwoll reported the offer to the police, who laid a charge against Silvermann for attempting to procure Taube Gordon.

On 12 February, after an appearance in the Marlborough police court, the headline in the *People* ran; 'Revolting Story – Poles Accused of Drugging Young Girls'. The story attracted the attention of ordinary Jews in the East End as well as the Anglo-Jewish elite. The Board of Guardians urged that a 'Committee of Gentlemen' should establish Baumwoll's credentials. Reassured that he was respectable, the JAPGW appointed a lawyer to track the case through the police court and Old Bailey.[26] With the cousins Anker and Fierstein, as well as Kumcher and Shrednicki in custody, it was left to the boss to mount a defence. Silver drew on his American experience as an agent and remembered that a good lawyer, like Frank Moss, could do almost anything. He hired a solicitor and obtained the services of 'two very able barristers'. The family got priority and Anker and Fierstein were better represented than 'Curley' and 'Monkey Jack'. Silver's master-stroke was to hire a private investigator who was sent to Warsaw to probe Baumwoll's background with a view to discrediting him. The Lis brothers then mounted the usual campaign of bribery and intimidation.

They got Solomon Rosenbaum – no relation – to call on Zudik and explain that 'his life would be worth nothing if he dared give evidence for the prosecution'. Rosenbaum then went on to threaten a second witness, Simon Sudey, with death if he testified against the accused. When Zudik – filled with remorse for the role he had played in the girls' downfall – refused, he was twice attacked. Zudik then brought a charge of assault and Rosenbaum was convicted, but on the way out of court Zudik was attacked by another gang member specialising in death threats, Morris Zimmerwich.[27] Still not content, the Lis brothers deputed Frankel, yet another Stamford Street thug, to visit Baumwoll's neighbour, Kruger, and offer him £25 to testify that he had seen men visiting Taube Gordon and Fanny Rosenbaum and that they had been taken into a 'private room', thereby 'trying to prove that the girls were immoral before the alleged violation'. Such testimony would have supplemented disconcerting news about Baumwoll's background that the agent had found in Warsaw. Kruger, however, was no less honourable than Zudik and he, too, was assaulted for his trouble. Frankel was prosecuted, convicted and fined for assault.[28]

The failure to secure courtroom objectives during street skirmishes in Whitechapel was troubling for the foot soldiers but, back in Waterloo, it was beginning to dawn on their commanding officer that the JAPGW was drawing them into a more extended battle. Indeed, even as the Gordon–Rosenbaum case unfolded before the courts during February and March 1898, the police net was closing around 'James Smith'. From what followed it was clear that Silver had been directly involved in the spine-chilling events that accompanied the East End campaign mounted by the gang in the closing months of 1897.

It was about then that a fellow lodger had introduced the luckless seventeen-year-old buttonhole-maker, Rachel Laskin, to Anker, a 'draper' recently returned from the United States. He, in turn, introduced her to his cousin from New York City who, after a brief courtship, lured her across the river and into the American Hotel where, after an ordeal lasting two weeks, her life was to change for ever. It was only a combination of chance and design that led ultimately to her discovery by agents of the JAPGW.[29]

By the third week of February 1898, Silver's family and their acolytes were involved in two sets of cases before police courts. Given what was occurring outside the courts, the prosecution struggled. By late March the charges, by then before the superior Central Criminal Court, had been consolidated to draw Anker, Beile Fierstein and 'Smith' into one case, and Anker, Fierstein, Shrednicki, Silvermann and Kumcher into another. In addition, Shrednicki, 'Smith' and Kumcher each faced separate charges for the rape of Rosenbaum, Gordon and Laskin. In essence those in the gallery of the Old Bailey were witnessing the JAPGW – backed by the finance capital of Baron de Hirsch, the Montefiores and Rothschilds – ranged against the filthy lucre of 'Jewish' gangsters buoyed by the international trade in white slaves. Each party retained the best barristers money could buy; men with impeccable credentials. Charles Matthews (Sir Charles Matthews, Director of Public Prosecutions by 1910) and Guy Stephenson appeared for the prosecution; while the defence was represented by the equally formidable trio of Messrs Geoghegan, Hughes and Symmons. It promised to be an epic fight, but it was not.

With witnesses of unimpeachable integrity at a premium, the cases for the prosecution faltered and then failed. By 2 April, Anker, Fierstein and Smith had all been found not guilty of 'conspiring together to procure Rachel Laskin to become a common prostitute'. On the same day, Smith – enamoured with the American system of justice and the fifth amendment – had refused to give evidence that might incriminate him and, serendipitously, touched on a point in the law of evidence that was in the throes of being reworked in the English legal system. He was found not guilty of having raped Laskin. Matthews and Stephenson were dismayed. More bad news for the JAPGW followed.[30]

Six weeks later, again at the Old Bailey, Anker, Fierstein, Shrednicki, Silvermann and Kumcher were found not guilty of 'conspiring to cause Fanny Rosenbaum to become a common prostitute' when 'no evidence was offered'. 'Curley' Shrednicki was found not guilty of raping Rosenbaum and Kumcher was found not guilty of the rape of Taube Gordon. Yet again, no evidence was offered. The JAPGW recorded these outcomes in suitably restrained terms. 'The Committee, while regretting that they did not secure a conviction would point out that these trials resulted in putting the traffickers to very heavy expenses, in their detention in prison for so many weeks, and in the breaking up for the time being of their opportunities in this country for the continuation of their nefarious pursuits.'[31]

Vice had trumped virtue, deepening Silver's half-admiring, half-contemptuous view of the courts, law and justice. But he and the others had a narrow escape. The brothels around Waterloo were wound down and plans made to relocate the company's human capital. Jenny Stein, 'wife' of Silver's distant southern African associate, Sam, collected several of the older women, including one Lena Kuhbeck, and saw them safely aboard Union Castle steamships and escorted them to South Africa. Members of the inner family circle, the youngest prostitutes, and the white slaves were dealt with differently. Anxious to elude JAPGW agents and the police, Silver avoided the established carriers south and obtained berths for himself and about twenty others aboard Shaw Savill's SS *Ionic* which, bound for New Zealand, would put in at Cape Town. But fate, it seemed, had decreed that he and the JAPGW agents should meet just one more time.[32]

On 8 June 1898, Samuel Cohen of the JAPGW and a detective from Scotland Yard investigating an unrelated case of white slavery went to Southampton to examine the *Ionic*'s passenger list. They walked into a score of familiar pimps and prostitutes who, recognising Cohen, assumed a threatening attitude towards the men. The two officials retreated amidst torrents of abuse hurled at them by a 'large number of traffickers'. The Stamford Street gang was taking its leave of England, the JAPGW and Scotland Yard.[33]

As the *Ionic* slipped down Southampton water and into the Channel, Cohen got a final glimpse of Rachel Laskin – 'going to her final destruction' – standing beside his adversary.[34] He told Claude Montefiore about the brothel floating down the African coast towards a British colony said to be of immense economic promise. Montefiore 'sent a cable to Colonel Hanbury Williams, a government official and friend of his in Cape Town, advising him of the arrival of the traffickers there, and asking him to kindly enlist the officers of the Cape Town police to have their future movements watched.'[35] Weeks later, Cohen recounted the tale of the 'draper', 'James Smith', to one of the moving forces in the National Vigilance Association. Alexander Coote agreed to disseminate any information he had about what they believed to be a Polish-American monster. When Coote met the Russian Foreign Minister, in early 1899, he told Count Muraviev about a man who, in truth, few in the world as yet knew about. Muraviev promised to help. In 1899, for reasons never made clear to border guards at the time, one 'Joseph Schmidt/Smith' an American citizen, aged twenty-five, of medium height, with brownish hair and a thinnish face, was declared a 'prohibited immigrant' in the Russian empire.[36]

Even before the turn of the century the name 'Joseph Lis', an unknown Jew from Kielce, had in different guises come to the attention of the authorities in far-flung places. His name would soon also be known to President Kruger of the South African Republic and to his nemesis – a young attorney by the name of Jan Christiaan Smuts who, in the very months when 'James Smith' was entrenching himself in Waterloo, was completing his studies at the Middle Temple on the opposite bank of the Thames. On a good day, the two could, without knowing it, have encountered one another on Blackfriars Bridge. They were destined to meet in a titanic struggle, but that was in the future. Silver was, for the moment, confronted with another problem – how to deal with Colonel Hanbury Williams.

VIII

JOHANNESBURG
1898

But no journalist who keeps his eyes open, nor any man who knows the town can be ignorant of the appalling system of compulsory prostitution that obtains.

Editorial, *Standard & Diggers' News*, Johannesburg,
12 November 1898.

I don't know what makes me suddenly want to write to you this morning unless it be that Johannesburg always makes me think of your poem, 'Perhaps in his infinite mercy, God may remove this man'. Here's this great fiendish hell of a city sprung up in ten years in our sweet pure rare African velt. A city which for glitter and gold, and wickedness – carriages, and palaces and brothels, and gambling halls, beats creation.

Olive Schreiner to Edward Carpenter, Johannesburg,
13 November, 1898

OUT in the colonies, the wishes of London notables were not to be trifled with. Hanbury Williams took Montefiore's request seriously. Sensing that he was ill-equipped to cope with the arrival of a horde of East European marginals on his own, he sought counsel. Alfred Bender, the Hebrew Congregation's recently appointed young, rather scholarly, spiritual leader was an anglicised product of St John's College, Cambridge. But Bender was equally uncomfortable with the idea of confronting a

Russo-Polish rabble and they secured the services of a few policemen who, in June 1898, accompanied them to the dockside to intercept James Smith, friends and family.

Cape Town, in midwinter, was cold, wet and windy. The Shaw Savill liner put the churning Atlantic behind it, veered to port and, with the bow spitting spray, nosed into Table Bay. Craftsmen, farmers, tradesmen and shopkeepers bound for New Zealand, some with female companions but most without, grasped the rails as the *Ionic* drew in to the quay. The gangplank was lowered and non-English immigrants could be seen and heard on the lower deck. Amongst the latter were familiar faces, but their names remained unknown to their fellow passengers just as their real names, even now, remain hard to wrest from the ship's lengthy manifest.[1]

The leader of the group was Mr Joseph Silver, a 'jeweller' who had an interest in Miss Rachel Laskin, supposedly twenty-six years old. They chatted to two other couples who were not amongst the most refined of the ship's company – Mr Joseph Anker, another 'jeweller', accompanied by his 'wife', and Max Schoffer, a 'joiner', and his wife, probably Leon and Beile Fierstein. The whole group, including a 'dealer' by the name of Jacob Kepler – Jack Lis – had acquired tickets from the same outlet in London at the same time. There were others capable of exciting the Rabbi's curiosity but who remain impossible to identify.

The captain of the *Ionic* gave the colonel and his party permission to board and speak to the passengers. Bender and Williams concentrated their efforts on Laskin, but also talked to the other women, hoping to persuade them 'to abandon the life of shame to which they were going'. This unusual encounter later gave rise to a myth amongst prostitutes that Silver had been forbidden entry to Cape Town. Williams and Bender left and their friends back in London had to content themselves with the knowledge that the colonial police had 'put themselves in communication with the police in Johannesburg'. They might as well have addressed a message to the Pope, popped it in a bottle, tossed it into the sea and hoped that it would be found and acted upon.[2]

Silver knew about policemen and could not have cared less about the colonel or the colony. Cape Town was a sleepy provisioning centre that had experienced a spurt of development when diamonds had been discovered around Kimberley in the late 1860s. It had a small, domesticated, white middle class, serviced by a settled coloured artisanal working class composed of people of mixed descent whose origins could be traced back to the seventeenth-century slave economy that focused on the export of meat, wheat and wine. The city did not offer the unsettled social conditions necessary for a business of Silver's type. The object of his attention now lay 800 miles farther north, on an elevated plateau 6,000 feet above sea level, at the end of a railway track not yet fully six years old.

Ever since slavery ended in the 1830s, the area to the north, between the Vaal and Limpopo rivers, had been dominated by migrating European farmers. Disgruntled Boers, drawn from Dutch and other stock, had turned their backs on an anglicised Cape liberalism born of mercantile interests which, they felt, suckled too readily at the breast of British imperialism. The Zuid Afrikaansche Republiek (ZAR), in which a conquering white minority presided over an indigenous majority of black pastoralists, was founded on the principle that there would be no racial equality in Church or state. But the pursuit of racial purity had not ensured progress. An economy based on agriculture but without access to markets, and a society held together by a makeshift ideology of Christianity, paternalism and republicanism, did nothing to fill the state's coffers. This deep – almost feudal – stupor gave way to manic intensity in the 1880s.

In 1884, a reef was uncovered at Barberton in the eastern ZAR – a development foreshadowed by earlier discoveries of alluvial gold. With a minor rush already under way, there was more excitement twenty-four months later when the largest continuous low-grade gold reefs in the world were discovered on the Witwatersrand. At the helm of the republic's affairs stood President S.J.P. Kruger, elected in 1881, who was to remain in office throughout the 1890s. Kruger found himself in the unenviable position of having to adapt policies that had been designed to nudge agricultural producers into the industrial age, to the needs of an economy dominated by mining and predicated on foreign capital served by an unruly, urban-based, immigrant proletariat composed of black and white men without their wives.[3] All he had to assist him were a small number of Dutch advisers and civil servants whom he had recruited during an earlier visit to the Netherlands. So a Cape-born president was advised by a corps of urbanised Hollanders who, while politically conservative and opposed to British imperialism, were nevertheless social liberals reluctant to endorse legislation limiting the use of alcohol, gambling or prostitution.[4]

At the heart of the resulting confusion stood Johannesburg. A tented diggers' camp of 3,000 people in 1886 had, by 1896, given way to an unattractive city of 100,000 inhabitants. A core of modern business premises and a few state buildings were surrounded by hundreds of shops, saloons, offices, bars, restaurants and beer gardens. The commercial hub, characterised by the rectangular layout of its blocks and streets, gave way almost immediately to inner-city housing. Low-slung residences, some of brick, but many more made from brick and corrugated iron and painted in drab colours, spoke of a colonial sprawl that contrasted with the northern hemisphere's crowded three-storeyed lodging houses and tenements. Beyond this were the white working-class suburbs. Even further away, stretching to a treeless horizon, lay mining villages with 'boarding-houses' and cottages catering for skilled white artisans, and beyond that – on the very edge of the known world – were the dormitory black compounds housing unskilled African migrants in their tens of thousands.

By the mid-1890s this artificial encrustation on a set of attractive rises had spread for about twenty miles in an east-west direction along the ridges and hollows of the Witwatersrand. Both the Rand and the unlovable mixture of humanity it had attracted had, for some time, been the object of apprehension and envy in certain foreign circles. The root cause was not difficult to determine.

In 1886 the ZAR produced less than 1 per cent of the world's gold: by 1898, the figure was 27 per cent. Britain, the dominant power on the subcontinent, already controlled the world's largest diamond deposits, in Griqualand West. Joseph Chamberlain, British Foreign Secretary and capitalists like Cecil Rhodes were not comfortable with a Boer republic commanding gold production and the routes to imperial expansion in Africa. In 1895 they conspired to overthrow the Kruger government, launching the poorly planned, unsuccessful Jameson Raid. The attempted coup alarmed Kruger. Benefiting from an upsurge in domestic support, the President addressed the mine-owners' needs with renewed urgency.

The 1897 industrial commission of inquiry focused on problems impacting directly on production costs but also drew attention to the Witwatersrand's social deficiencies. An urgent need for social reform made the President willing to abandon his Dutch advisers' liberal policies on alcohol, gambling and prostitution and adopt those that were closer to his own, inherently conservative, religious convictions. Kruger hoped that industrialisation's discreet lovers – Calvinism and capitalism – could be brought together publicly to

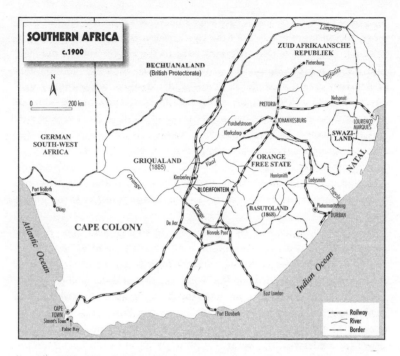

benefit white family life. But achievement of this complex objective was thwarted by accumulated administrative and legislative problems as well as the deep-seated and pervasive corruption of the police. It was while searching for a solution to these problems that Kruger settled on J.C. Smuts as his State Attorney.[5]

In Smuts, Kruger found the blend of Calvinism and modernity his reform-minded administration needed. Raised in a Christian home and destined for the ministry, Smuts had gone on from a childhood spent on a farm in the Cape to complete a first degree at Victoria College, Stellenbosch followed by extraordinarily successful legal studies in Cambridge and at the Middle Temple, London. He returned to the Cape in 1895 and, like many Afrikaners, had his anti-imperialist sentiments awakened by the smash and grab politics of the Jameson Raid. Newly married, Smuts was running a modest legal practice in a building he shared with another young advocate in Johannesburg, Mostyn Cleaver, when Kruger appointed him State Attorney just three weeks before Silver disembarked in Cape Town.

History set Smuts and Silver, separated by twenty-four months in age, on a collision course. There was a perverse asymmetry in the character, socialisation and lives of the two ambitious, impatient and tough-minded protagonists that extended beyond the intersecting of the legal and criminal professions. The differences were endless – country boy and urban creature, studious youth and extrovert adolescent, frugal aesthete and avaricious hedonist, wise counsellor and cunning manipulator, conservatively attired functionary and flashily dressed gangster. But the outcomes of great battles are seldom determined solely by the qualities of opposing generals; the terrain on which they encounter one another is often decisive. The ground on which the two adversaries assumed positions after Silver and his henchmen had strutted into Johannesburg's railway station, in late June 1898, initially favoured the insurgents.

Silver was confronted by significant personal challenges. A rank outsider, he needed to know the personal strengths and weaknesses of potential underworld rivals who inhabited a world beset by betrayal, lies and treachery. And, since the worlds of the gangster and the police intersected, he needed to plot precisely the fault lines of power. It was hell's playground, and he was totally at home in it. His success in capturing control of the city's law enforcement machinery as well as its most powerful underworld structures within six months spoke of an evil genius at the height of his powers. He had boundless energy and an unlimited ability to manipulate people and situations to his advantage. His voyage of discovery offered a fascinating panorama of the city.

It was a man's town. Even in the inner core, around the Market Square, where the ratio between the sexes was most balanced, there were two white men to every white woman. Beyond that the situation was as promising, with ten black men for every woman. For a mass-marketer accustomed to prostitutes turning 50-cent tricks on the Lower East Side it was a dream come true. A blind cab driver could tell what line of work most of the women were involved in.[6]

But there was something else that made him feel that he was the right man, in the right place, at the right time. For all its would-be Englishness, inner Johannesburg exuded an international air and its dusty streets were more like something out of the dry American west than the damp European east. There was a palpable ethnic element that made it feel like the Poland of his youth; many people were unmistakably Jewish. Dismissed by anti-Semites as 'Jewburg', the city had, right from its inception, played host to fully half of southern Africa's

Jewish population. What Silver found most promising was the presence of 7,000 or more poor East European Jews from Lithuania, Russia and Poland who had used the tide of globalisation to carry them to southern Africa.[7]

Known collectively – but misleadingly – as 'Peruvians' by locals who disliked them, this rag-bag of unskilled immigrants hung from the lowest rung of the class ladder. In a new society, their callings as hawkers, traders or assistants in eating-houses and liquor stores placed them in close proximity to African miners and, in the white haze of colonial prejudice, their Russian and Polish identities had become elided. Yet other Peruvians, even further out in the social cold, brought up the rear of this ragged bunch as burglars, confidence men, gamblers, liars, petty thieves, pimps and touts. But whatever walk of life they came from, they had needs Silver could profit from.[8]

During the eight weeks he spent in the Constantia Hotel, a stream of friends, business associates and gangsters passed through, who either bought him drinks or cadged them from him. These meetings familiarised Silver with gambling outlets, house rentals, the price of brothel furnishings, the vagaries of liquor-selling and the state of Yiddish theatre. Amongst frequent visitors were Sam and Jenny Stein, partners in the export traffic routed through the American Hotel. Sam he had known since 1891, when they had met as cadets and pickpockets back on the Lower East Side. A compatriot, friend and flesh-salesman, Sam now saw himself as a 'merchant' in the same cheeky way that humorous Argentine white slavers referred to themselves as 'fur merchants'. Reflecting on old times, Stein told him that the Manhattan underworld and Max Hochstim Association was well represented locally. Jenny knew Silver from London visits, and feared him.[9]

David Krakower – 'Dave Davis' – was a *landsleit* from Bowery days. They remained on reasonable terms and he lent Silver £17 to open his first, modest outlet – a New-York-style 'cigar shop' close to the hotel, on Kerk Street. For all that, Silver was wary of Krakower, who had taken up with Sadie Wolff, who knew about his history as a Parkhurst 'agent', as well as of his recent spells in prison, in England. Wolff, who had once paid him protection money, was terrified of him.[10] Another old-timer was Adolph Goldberg's brother-in-law, Salus Budner. A crude, violent fellow but a city slicker by comparison with most 'greeners' and Peruvians, Budner was already earning a living as a pimp and would clearly be of use to him.[11]

Leopold Priziger was a sinister friend about whom little is known, other than he, too, had once been in New York and was a butcher by trade. Abbatoirs and butchers, a central feature of a childhood in Kielce, had always fascinated Silver, and Priziger became party to some highly confidential information. Silver's most trusted lieutenant of all in Johannesburg, however, was the one we know almost nothing about. Where and when he first encountered Ze'ev Wulf Witkofsky, a Polish Jew, is unknown. It could have been in Whitechapel in the 1880s, in New York in the 1890s, or both. Like Krakower, 'Wilf' Witkofsky had taken up with a woman whom he had given the name Woolf, but who was unrelated to Sadie Wolff. Unlike Sadie, Rosie Woolf was completely trustworthy and firmly controlled by her pimp-husband.[12]

Budner, Stein and Witkofsky did most to brief Silver about prevailing business conditions. Americanised Russo-Polish Jews did not have a controlling share of the competitive trade in commercial sex, and the underworld was plagued by chronic instability. As in other Atlantic cities, organised prostitution was dominated by the 'French' – a sloppy formulation that embraced Brussels as readily as Paris. Comedians and newspaper reporters sometimes referred to the area bounded by Bree Street in the north and Anderson in the south, Kruis in the east and Sauer in the west, as 'Frenchfontein'. Of the ninety-five brothels listed in a municipal survey in 1895, thirty-six were 'French'. The city's most popular brothel – Sylvio Villa – opened in the mid-1890s and only closed in 1906. In its heyday the place had a male manager, a *madame*, four pimps, and ten prostitutes who on the Saturday after pay-day could deal with close on a hundred black and white clients between 8 p.m. and 1.30 a.m.[13]

The French pimps and white slavers worked out of saloons like the Golden Lion and the *Ne Plus Ultra*, but what Silver found most re-assuring was the presence of a colony of Franco-Americans who had fled Manhattan's 'Frenchtown', around Greene and Wooster Streets, after the Lexow report. Amongst these was Bertha Hermann, now 'Mathilda Bertha' – the infamous 'French gold mine' of *Satan's Invisible World* who had paid $30,000 in bribes to the NYPD. She and François Saubert, now 'Francis Benjamin', ran several brothels including one at 19 Sauer Street. The presence of such experienced operators spoke not only of profitability, but of a well-developed system of police protection. Quite unintentionally, protected houses sometimes cast protective shadows over adjacent buildings. It was not by chance that Silver's

notorious 'Green House', a would-be *maison verte* of the French variety
was sited at 20 Sauer.[14]

The other, comparatively low-profile group revealed by the city's
1895 survey was that of the 'Germans', who, it was claimed, operated
at least twenty brothels. As with the 'French', however, it was hard to
know what the term meant. After all, Bertha Hermann, who hardly
boasted the most obvious of 'French' names, was actually a native of
Alsace. Many of Johannesburg's 'Germans' were actually German-
Americans who, like Hermann, had fled New York after Lexow.
Nevertheless, such confusion assisted the Yiddish-speaking Silver who
had something of a predilection for Saxon names. During his meteoric
rise to power as a businessman gangster on the Rand he used both old
and new names, including Eligman, Ludwig and Schmidt.[15]

The French and Germans accounted for two out of three brothels
and operated fairly openly even after Kruger had secured the passage
of Law Number 2, the Ontucht Wet, or Immorality Act, through the
Volksraad in 1897. The law, to all intents and purposes a dead letter,
was ridiculed, with some justification, as the 'Untouched Law'. There
were two, related reasons, for its moribund status. The first harked
back to Kruger's earlier reliance on 'liberal' Dutch advisers. The second
was Dr F.E.T. Krause, Dutch-educated son of a German immigrant,
whom the widely disliked 'Hollanders' had appointed as the city's First
– as in principal – Public Prosecutor.

Trained in Amsterdam, the First Public Prosecutor, F.E.T. Krause was
of the view that the state should attempt to control rather than eradicate commercial sex. It was a view that was to bring him into direct
conflict with the Cambridge-educated Smuts. For Krause, prostitution
was a sad but 'necessary evil', and he saw his role as Public Prosecutor
as discretionary and regulatory. This interpretation assumed even greater
significance in 1897 when, again following continental practice, Krause
assumed control of all personal interactions with the city's corrupt
detectives and policemen.[16]

The ramshackle *Zuid Afrikaansche Republiek's Polisie* also did little
to implement Law No. 2 of 1897. The problems with the 'Zarps'
started at the top, with a weak Chief of Police. Commandant G.M.J.
van Dam, persuaded by Krause's views on public morals, had actually ceded control of the men directly responsible for implementing
the law to the Public Prosecutor. The idea that the implementation of
legislation governing public morals was discretionary took root only

too easily in the minds of inexperienced officers and many ordinary policemen.

Only *burghers* or naturalised citizens were eligible to serve in the ZAR police. This meant that, for the most part, van Dam had to rely on illiterate or poorly educated sons of the least successful farmers. Command of little more than their mother tongue, Afrikaans-Dutch, left them poorly placed to deal with international criminals raised in Babel. Moreover the Zarps were demoralised, poorly paid and, in 1895, had had to go on strike to get their wages. The officers, only slightly better paid and more experienced than their men, were often naturalised 'outsiders'. Official hesitancy in the prosecutor's office was passed on from the police chief to his officers, and then on down to men on the beat. For a New York Tammany veteran it was paradise.[17]

This promising situation, however, needed careful handling. Johannesburg was hardly virgin territory, devoid of vested interests. In addition to the French and German operators there was an unruly bunch of 50 to 100 Russo-Polish pimps and white slavers that needed reorganising. Most of them were about Silver's age and known to him from the Lower East Side but were already working within established networks. It was this motley assortment of 'Jewish' racketeers who owned the 'American' and five 'Russian' brothels captured in the municipal survey.

The 'Bowery Boys', who took their name from the notorious Manhattan gang of the same name, were a loosely knit, flashily dressed bunch dealing in crimes against people and property. Within twenty-four months of their arrival in 1896, these low class Americans had taken over western Commissioner Street where their cafés, restaurants and saloons were fronts for brothels. A press report claimed that this 'refuse of the great Republic' conducted a nightly 'reign of terror' on turf where only the bravest ventured. But they were a fractious rabble whose querulousness manifested itself in public displays of disunity. One Sunday in 1897, revolvers were used in a shoot-out on Commissioner Street that failed to draw a single Zarp. This lack of focus and discipline left them playing second fiddle to other racketeers. The more diplomatic, less aggressive, French and Germans cultivated and promoted a champion who brought the pimps and police together into something approximating a system. It was this man that Silver had to come to terms with if he were to succeed.[18]

'Ernest Corney' – real name Korne – was a New Yorker who arrived on the Rand shortly after the Jameson Raid. In 1896, he and four compatriots floated the Speer Medical and Chemical Company Limited to 'carry on the business of chemists and druggists', importing all manner of industrial, medicinal and pharmaceutical preparations, patent medicines, as well as surgical and scientific apparatus. Launched at an unpropitious moment, the business failed and a year later Corney was in financial trouble. By then, however, he had met Fred H. Brennan – Doctor of Medicine and Master of Surgery from Trinity University, Toronto, and a member of the College of Physicians and Surgeons of the state of Ontario. Brennan's practice spanned Frenchfontein and he supplied his patients with abortifacients and medicines for venereal diseases including syphilis, then known as 'Contagious Blood Poison'.[19]

In March 1898 Brennan and Corney refloated the Speer company as the American Medical and Chemical Company in which they were principal shareholders, with Brennan, chairman of the Board. The new company's retail outlet, the American Pharmacy, was run by Corney, who lacked qualifications as a pharmacist. But it did not matter since the pharmacy was, in large part, a front for a sinister grouping, 'The Company', comprising Brennan, Corney, and Corney's 'Private Secretary', Charles Winter. The Company was devoted almost solely to organised prostitution. Its chief executive, Corney, was a gangster whose interests lay in buying, letting or subletting houses to the Bowery Boys, or to French and German gangsters. But he was no mere real-estate dealer – he offered clients a service that added real value to any deal by ensuring that the houses were 'protected' by Zarps.[20]

The one-time owner of the American Hotel met the owners of the American Pharmacy not long after his arrival in the city, in June 1898. Within four months Silver – who was interested in chemicals, including those used in the treatment of syphilis – was closely involved in deals with Brennan and Corney that revolved around the commercial sex trade. By then, in a burst of manic energy that belied his contagious blood disease, he was in the final phases of consolidating a business empire that easily transcended that of the formerly dominant French or Germans. It was an astounding achievement that contained within it the seeds of self-destruction.

The foundations of his new enterprise had been laid by the Steins. Using telegraphic codes known to merchants in the white slave trade they imported prostitutes from Europe at a rate that struggled to keep pace with the demand of local brothels. The Union and Castle shipping lines, whose ships plied the Southampton–Cape Town route, were indirect beneficiaries as pimps and *madames* escorted 'fresh goods' and 'remounts' on the journey south.[21] Working-class women were intercepted in London with promises of employment as actresses, barmaids, dancers, domestic servants or waitresses in South Africa. Some, like Rachel Laskin, were seduced or raped prior to departure and ended working as prostitutes in Johannesburg's bars, beer halls, cafés, cigar shops, dance halls and restaurants, or on the outer fringes of Yiddish theatre.[22]

Silver acquired a string of such cafés, cigar shops and restaurants and, like Al Capone in another era, was astute enough to use those with potential as genuine retail outlets to service the core business. In Commissioner Street, a café run for him by Hymie Bernstein was a meeting place for pimps and prostitutes but also supplied all Bowery Boy brothels with groceries.[23] This profitable venture became an institution in the city and survived as a front for gambling and vice into the post-bellum period as the 'American' and 'Little Yankee' Café.[24] It may also have prompted brother, Jack, to take a share in another, less successful grocery store after the South African War.[25]

Silver expanded his interests to take in dives, drinking joints and gambling dens which, although linked primarily to brothels, often brought in substantial income in their own right. Nor did he confine his interest to central Johannesburg. Within months of his arrival he was active in Germiston on the East Rand, a town notorious for illicit liquor syndicates. Extending outwards, he moved even farther afield and opened a brothel right under Kruger's nose in Pretoria where French pimps and prostitutes had alerted him to new business opportunities.[26]

Rapid expansion posed unforeseen organisational problems. In London he had run a successful business with the help of the family. Johannesburg was different: instead of running a family business he was increasingly reliant on former confidants and outsiders to help run enterprises. It is difficult to know where all his assistants came from, but one of the threads linking them can be traced back to the Empire Palace and Theatre Royal that had opened its agency back on London's South Bank, in 1897.[27]

One of the Stamford Street gang who ran a business on the East Rand, and who didn't like being relegated to the margins, was Jack Strakiosky whom Silver put in charge of a 'café' in Germiston.[28] Close by was Gustav Shakt, a twenty-two-year-old actor born in Riga with

American experience who, between roles in Yiddish theatre, earned his living as a pimp.[29] In Pretoria, Silver's interests in the Empire Café on Market Street were taken care of by Boris Alexander, a former musician in Johannesburg's Theatre Royal. Like Strakiosky, Alexander disliked being marginalised and resented his small share of the café's profits. When the time came, he and Strakiosky were quick to bite the hand that had once fed them.[30] Saul Wallerstein, with links to the seedy world of entertainment, may have known Silver's old friend, the actor, Goldberg. A noted Yiddish comic talent, Wallerstein was part of the Oriental Opera Company of New York when it visited Johannesburg in 1897.[31]

Morris Kaplan, Silver's most important informant, was no thespian. Official, part-time interpreter of Yiddish in the magistrates' court until mid-1898, Kaplan kept a low public profile and used former colleagues to remain abreast of what was happening in the charge office and Public Prosecutor's office.[32] It may have been Kaplan who first introduced Silver to H.E. Cuyler and W.A. De Klerk, policemen entrusted with enforcing the Ontucht Wet.[33] They, in turn, introduced him to the officers in charge of the morals squad. From within this nexus Silver got the names of businessmen and corporations like the Banque de l'Afrique du Sud, the mine-owner Charles Rudd, or others who let properties to gangsters for organised prostitution.[34]

From a few hired premises, Silver developed a fiefdom of interconnected businesses which by late 1898, were spread over twenty blocks in the south-western corner of Frenchfontein and the adjacent theatre district. Within this informal fortress he owned and operated at least half a dozen gambling joints, which benefited from their very close links to a score of police-protected brothels all within easy walking distance of one another.[35]

The oldest of the gambling joint/brothels, originally in Fox Street, near the *mikveh*, dated to 1896 when it was managed by Sam Stein with the assistance of Robert and Esther Shoub. The Shoubs, well connected in the Argentine and French underworlds, ran it as a 'faro' or 'stuss' house with the help of a former Lower East Sider, twenty-year-old Max Harris. By 1898, when Silver took control of the 'Green House', it was located besides Bertha Hermann's brothel at 20 Sauer Street. Protected by shotgun-wielding gangsters, the place was so successful that Silver, with the help of Harris who fancied himself as a counterfeiter, had false coins struck bearing 'a décolleté bust on the obverse and the name of the house on the reverse side'. These counters were as good as the coin of the realm within parts of Frenchfontein, where they circulated in brothels and gambling joints controlled by the Bowery Boys.[36]

The Green House was not the biggest money-spinner for Silver and Stein. They owned several larger brothels which had displaced similar outfits owned by Frenchmen working with a few African pimps who had linked up with abandoned 'continental' whores to cater for the lower end of the market.[37] New York-style low-price, high-turnover, non-racial brothels catering for miners were advertised by word of mouth, or through the distribution of printed cards bearing the names of women. These houses were staffed by older prostitutes on their way out of the trade, along with a few young white slaves. Resident *madames*, who handed half the receipts to the partners, used ticket systems to keep track of customers passing through the establishment and to monitor turnover. Silver also got police on his payroll to extract protection money from any woman operating independently on their patch.[38]

The three principal such establishments were on Anderson Street and Kruis Street. At 45 Anderson, the day-to-day business was in the hands of Florence Maude de Lacey, a former barmaid, who was responsible for training the inexperienced Rachel Laskin in the finer arts of house management. After serving a short apprenticeship 'Lizzie Josephs', as she was known, was sent to run the house in Kruis Street but, untrustworthy or unable to manage on her own, she was recalled to the Green House where Silver and the pimps could keep a closer eye on her.[39]

Laskin was symptomatic of the partners' managerial problems. With expanding businesses staffed by fractious prostitutes in towns miles apart, all attracting hundreds of unruly customers at night, they found keeping control of operations difficult. Without sufficient family to draw on, Silver was up against unruly, small-time pimps who prevented the emerging system from working optimally. What was needed was an umbrella organisation, like the Max Hochstim Association, that could draw in independent-minded elements and provide overall guidelines for the commercial sex trade. Using a combination of charm and outright terror, he got the Bowery Boys to join the new organisation. He hired premises at 10 Sauer Street and, in a city already filled with ethnic associations, launched the seemingly innocuous American Club.

The American Club was, from the outset, devoted exclusively to the needs of pimps. An all-male sodality, it dimly resembled *hevrot*, voluntary associations in eastern Europe, or *landmanshaftn*, Jewish hometown associations in the New World. Its fifty or more members included many with Polish names and one or two English-sounding ones, like Jacob Smith. With the help of Stein and his brother, Jack, Silver was elected chairman of the 'pimps union' and Salus Budner, with the humorous *nom de plume*, Joe Gold, was made its secretary. What most of the members did not know, however, was that within the ranks of the overarching executive they had elected there was an un-appointed secret cabinet, the system within the system, designed to safeguard Silver's empire.[40]

In organisational terms, the secret cabinet was Silver's crowning achievement. Since the moment of his arrival in the city, it had taken 130 days to turn a ramshackle gambling and prostitution network into an integrated organisation and knock the Bowery Boys into a disciplined unit with a recognisable, yet only partially revealed, command structure. It was an extraordinary achievement. The novelist, Olive Schreiner, although never mentioning him by name, was astounded by what was happening. Success on so large a scale, however, almost invited a spontaneous counter-reaction – from within the criminal fraternity or the citizenry at large. By the closing months of 1898 it was apparent to all but the most short-sighted that the underworld of the world's mining capital had undergone a qualitative change, and that sections of the public were at the mercy of flashy 'American' gangsters.

On 30 September, Emmanuel Mendelssohn, editor of the pro-government *Standard & Diggers' News* ran an editorial on 'Blackguard Syndicates' drawing attention to ways in which legislation governing prostitution and the sale of liquor to Africans was being violated. A week later he penned another leader under the tell-tale rubric, 'A Foul Tammany'. Independent prostitutes, 'no matter how unostentatious their dwellings or behaviour', were being 'hounded down', he suggested. The 'wretched victims were virtually enslaved and sweated'. Underworld 'interests extended to syndicates and organisations for other crimes including illicit gold-buying'. If the syndicates were not broken up, 'the town and the government will want to know the reason of it'. Shown the way, and with the role of the Public Prosecutor and police also under question, Johannesburg's Protestant clergy took five days to organise themselves and find their way to the President's office in Pretoria.

The Reverend Meiring's delegation was met by Kruger and Smuts, who had been State Attorney for barely four months. The President was told that the existing legislation was a dead letter. Neither the prosecutor nor the police had done anything to eradicate brothels in the city or to restrict the scandalous public activity of pimps or prostitutes. It was widely believed that some women, the so-called 'white slaves', were being held in brothels against their will and the law offered them no protection. Kruger promised that the State Attorney would attend closely to their complaints.[41]

Smuts, who had spent his first weeks in office reorganising the secret service for the coming conflict with Britain, applied his mind to a war against organised crime on the Rand. His counter-offensive was mounted between mid-October and 31 December 1898, and planned with military precision utilising secret service techniques rather than those usually associated with conventional law enforcement agencies. Silver had taken just over four months to construct a criminal empire: it took Smuts about half that time – just seventy days – to position himself for a devastating counter-attack. The stage was now set for a fight to the death between J.C. Smuts and Joseph Silver.

JOHANNESBURG
1899

There are more things in Johannesburg than are dreamt of in the ordinary man's philosophy. For instance there is here a large and thriving colony of Americanised Russian women engaged in the immoral traffic, who are controlled by an association of *macquereaus* of profound Russian pedigree embellished by a flashy embroidery of style and speech acquired in the Bowery of New York City, where most of them, with frequent excursions to London, have graduated in the noble profession.

Standard & Diggers' News, Johannesburg,
7 December 1899

THE demolition of Silver's business empire was the achievement of J.C. Smuts and, as we are about to see, F.R.M. Cleaver. Its dismantling was no less complex than had been its assembly. To understand its eclipse requires entry into an underworld of byzantine complexity in which the stitching of conspiracies was so finely woven that, at times, it was impossible to tell woof from warp. By exploring these minutiae, we can attain a better understanding of Silver's universe, observe how his mind operated when under pressure, and gain a better idea of how he responded when challenged.

Within days of the President and Protestants meeting, in October 1898, Smuts familiarised himself with the deficiencies of Law 2 of 1897 and drafted amending and supplementary clauses. His new bill included provisions for countering organised prostitution and white slavery. Clause 4 made it an offence to hold a woman against her will in a brothel, or in any other place, for purposes of commercial sex. Wise to the ways of 'slave-owners', he also made it an offence to withhold the personal belongings or clothing of women engaging in prostitution, or to threaten them with legal action to recover the value of clothing they had been provided with. It indemnified any woman against prosecution for theft who, in attempting to regain her independence by leaving a brothel, removed apparel. The bill enabled public prosecutors to act against any owners of properties that were suspected of, or known to be used for, immoral commercial purposes.[1]

From the State Attorney's subsequent actions, there is no doubt who his major quarry was. Still, Smuts knew that the best arsenal in the world would be of little use unless he had a prosecutor in Johannesburg who was willing to enforce the letter of the law. The prosecutor would also need a few incorruptible policemen capable of generating the intelligence and muscle power necessary to break the hold of the American Club. With the bill waiting its first reading, he addressed these difficulties.

On the face of it, he was confronted by an intractable problem. F.E.T. Krause, Johannesburg's First Public Prosecutor, had persuaded the ineffectual Chief of Police, G.M.J. van Dam, that prostitution was a necessary evil and that, like their continental counterparts, they had to control rather than eradicate commercial sex. Smuts, already shaping a secret service preparing for war, circumvented the problem by creating a new position that bypassed existing personnel and structures. Johannesburg would have a new Second Public Prosecutor: although based in the same building as Krause, he would report directly to the State Attorney in Pretoria and be responsible for implementing all morals legislation. The man he had in mind for the position was drawn from his cohort at the Inns of Court, and eerily like Smuts.

At twenty-eight, Ferrar Reginald Mostyn Cleaver was a year younger than his mentor. The product of a Christian home and a farm upbringing in a remote mountainous region with the same love of 'manly' outdoor living as Smuts, Cleaver, too, had been educated locally before completing his legal studies in England. Like Smuts, whom he had met first in London, Cleaver had returned to South Africa in 1895 to practise as an advocate and, as a modernising Afrikaner, he too had been radicalised by the Jameson Raid, become a naturalised *burgher* and a strong supporter of Kruger. More pertinently, his courage, energy and ice-cold resolve mirrored exactly those of the famous Smuts. Neither van Dam nor the offended Krause – who deliberately referred to Cleaver in provocative terms as 'my assistant' – had reason to like him.[2]

Cleaver, in office by November 1898 and secure in the knowledge that he was safe from attempts to undermine him in Pretoria, could not have cared less about Krause. He discovered an additional source of support in the Fourth Public Prosecutor, an old school friend, James Skirving. Cleaver saw off Krause, who sought to neutralise his efforts and limit his powers by lodging a complaint with Smuts.[3] Van Dam and the Zarps were more difficult to deal with but his position improved when, in mid-November, Smuts persuaded a nervous legislature that the Rand's detective force should be controlled by the State Attorney, rather than the Chief of Police.[4] A few hand-picked 'special morality police' were assigned to Cleaver, and he was given permission to recruit two experienced undercover agents from the Rand Private Detective Bureau.[5] Decades before federal authorities in the United States assembled a corps of 'untouchables' to deal with the menace of the syphilitic Al Capone, Smuts and Cleaver had created their own force to deal with a man just as dangerous.

At first Cleaver made little progress. Smuts, impatient to pull down the houses of sin, continued to centralise power. He got the corrupt detective heading the morals squad, J.J. Donovan, dismissed for failing to obtain successful prosecutions. Then, with things still looking bleak, Cleaver got a break. In October 1898, at about the time that the churchmen went to see Kruger, Silver used two constables on his payroll, Hendrik Cuyler and Willem De Klerk, to extend his control over several prostitutes based in the south-western corner of Frenchfontein. Increasingly arrogant and self-important, he demanded that Sadie Wolff, Lillie Bloom and other prostitutes known to him from his days as a Parkhurst agent on the Lower East Side pay him protection money.

Wolff, whose *souteneur*, David Krakower, had paid public tribute to her by hosting a New York-style ball in her honour, resented having to pay a man she knew, from bitter experience, to be an insatiable predator. But Krakower was wary of confronting Silver and it was only when he learned that two other pimps, Henry Rosenchild and Morris Rosenberg, were experiencing the same problem that they took action. They broke away from the American Club and turned to Ernest Corney for assistance. Corney not only enjoyed better links with the police than Silver but had access to any number of properties. Corney got Krakower and Wolff a new house at 38 Bree Street.[6] Silver knew at once what was at stake: the American Club was up against Corney's 'Company' and would have to out-bid it. He waited as Krakower, emboldened by having independent access to the police, embarked on tit-for-tat retaliation. Krakower persuaded an increasingly disaffected Lizzie Josephs to swap allegiances and pay him, rather than Silver, protection. It was an underworld squall and Silver did not want to move too quickly. But another of his adversaries stirred.[7]

Cleaver sensed that if he moved first against the Krakower faction, he might be able to squeeze its members into giving evidence against Silver and Sam Stein and, in so doing, destroy the American Club. As he prepared to do this, two opportunities presented themselves. First, Donovan, smarting from his dismissal as head of the morals squad, claimed that he had been unable to execute his duties because of Krause. Donovan told Smuts that Krause had refused to issue him with warrants to arrest prominent brothel-owners. This fed into Smuts's – and Cleaver's – suspicions about the First Public Prosecutor and, in order to counter them, Krause threatened to prosecute Donovan for perjury. Smuts was happy to entertain this, since the case would bring new evidence into the public domain and help justify his decision to create an unusual position for Cleaver.[8]

Second, with Donovan out of the way and his position temporarily filled by his brother-in-law, Lieutenant Tossel, the gangsters were uncertain where the locus of power within the police lay. With a new law in the offing, an independent prosecutor in place and private detectives nosing about, the situation was becoming threatening. Silver adopted a strategy which, he hoped, would ease problems with the police, minimise Corney's influence and thwart the embarrassing Krakower–Laskin liaison. In retrospect, his strategy only strengthened the hand of his principal adversary, Cleaver.

Silver used an emissary to arrange a meeting with senior members of the Company in order to discover who the next permanent head of the morals squad was likely to be, establish what it would cost to secure protection for his own enterprises, and help reduce unnecessary volatility in the underworld. The meeting, held in the American Pharmacy, produced results that any member of the Max Hochstim Association would be proud of.

Donovan's successor was likely to be an English-speaking, naturalised *burgher* with morality squad experience, Michael Thomas Murphy. Lieutenant Murphy, who earned £25 a month at a time when Silver was netting in excess of £2,000 a month, was a reasonable man, well known to Brennan, and his partner, Corney, and not averse to doing business. Shortly after Murphy's appointment, Corney treated Murphy, a Justice of the Peace and two clerks of the court to dinner at the Sylvio Villa brothel.[9] What appealed most to Silver, however, was Murphy's involvement with the two constables already on his payroll – Cuyler and De Klerk. Cuyler was by then so comfortable with the Bowery Boys that he had his photo taken outside the American Club along with half a dozen pimps sporting new bicycles.[10] It was agreed that Silver would pay Murphy £1,000 for protection and that the money would be handed to Murphy by Ernest Corney's private secretary, Charles Winter.[11]

Winter made the payment. By mid-November 1898, Murphy was also on the American Club payroll. As so often in business deals, however, it was not what had been agreed upon that caused the problems which followed, but what had been left unstated. Corney believed that the deal did not jeopardise the Company, whose primary asset remained the houses run by the numerous French pimps. Silver, in turn, felt that he was free to expand his operations by closing down or incorporating independent pimps and prostitutes, including French ones. Murphy and his constables continued to extort money from 'independents' on Silver's behalf, or on their own account.[12]

Towards the end of November, Murphy ran into a problem. One Saturday night, shortly after midnight, two uncorrupt and zealous constables in plain clothes – S.G. Maritz and C.J. van Vuuren – entered a 'cigar shop' and encountered two prostitutes who, unbeknown to them, were protected by the American Club. Convinced that the place was a brothel, they returned to the charge office and, benefiting from the new dispensation, obtained warrants for the arrest of the women. Silver was irked and told Murphy he did not want the women languishing in prison. When Maritz and van Vuuren appeared in court two days later they were amazed to find their testimony contradicted by Murphy. According to Murphy, the constables could not have seen the women at the cigar shop at the time suggested because, at midnight that same night, he had been taking statements from them about another matter. Confronted with conflicting evidence the magistrate dismissed the case, leaving observers with the impression that the constables had perjured themselves. Murphy had got the women off the hook, but he had made himself two committed, formidable enemies.[13]

S.G. 'Manie' Maritz was no ordinary Zarp. Brutally honest and brimming with nationalist zeal, Maritz went on to become a general in the

South African War at the age of twenty-five, the leader of an unsuccessful rebellion against the government of the day in 1914 and, later
still, as a result of his interactions with Silver, one of South Africa's
most notorious anti-Semites and neo-Nazis.[14] Dismissed as a liar and
told that he might be charged with perjury, Maritz went to Pretoria
and appealed to Smuts. The State Attorney, seeing a way of strength-
ening Cleaver's hand, instructed Maritz to return to Johannesburg, report
to the Second Public Prosecutor as a 'special' morality constable, and
face the charges laid against him and van Vuuren. At the same time
Maritz was given instructions – perhaps not even with Cleaver's knowledge – to infiltrate the Company. Shortly after his trip to Pretoria he
became a boarder in Corney's home at 17 Leyds Street. Cleaver had
acquired two more allies.[15]

This amazing world of intrigue was about to merge into a single
more or less integrated stream of events before an astounded and

JOHANNESBURG
"FRENCHFONTEIN"
c. 1898-99

1 Globe Theatre (1891)
2 1st Empire Theatre (1894)
3 Gaiety Theatre (1895)
4 Theatre Royal (1888)
5 Standard Theatre (1891)
6 Rissik Street Post Office
7 The American Club
8 The Green House

The original corrugated iron-structure at Witrand, dating back to the 1890s which, in 1924, formed the core of the mental hospital that housed 'Lizzie Silver'/'Rachel Laskin' until her death in 1945.

Synagogue, Kielce, *c.* 1910.

Derelict synagogue, Checiny.

Street scene, Dzialoscyce,
Kielce district, 1988.

Leman Street, East End,
London, *c.* 1885.

Frying Pan Alley, East End,
London, *c.* 1885.

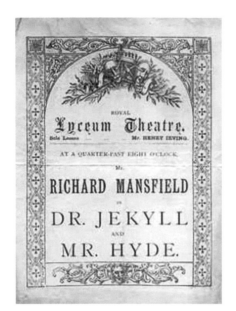
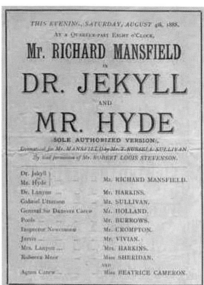

Billboard, Lyceum Theatre, August 1888.

Dorset Street, Whitechapel, London, *c.* 1890.

Lock-step march, Sing Sing Prison, New York State, *c.* 1890.

Sing Sing Prison, New York State, *c.* 1900.

Ellis Island, New York, *c.* 1900.

Rivington Street, New York City, Lower East Side, *c.* 1900.

Allegheny Court House and Jail, Pittsburgh, *c.* 1890.

Pittsburgh, *c.* 1893.

Liberty Ave, Pittsburgh, *c.* 1900.

uncomprehending public. On 24 November, François Saubert and 'Madame Mathilda Hermann' of New York fame appeared in the magistrates' court charged with running a brothel at 19 Sauer Street. Donovan repeated his allegations about Krause's unwillingness to issue warrants against the owners of certain houses. In a move without precedent, Krause took the stand to refute the former head of the morals squad's testimony. After this well-publicised response, Krause took no further action against Donovan. The same hearing, however, gave the public some insight into conflict between, and within, gangs of American, German and French pimps. These revelations lent credence to Krause's argument that his office had to be very certain that it was getting genuine complaints, rather than maliciously planted information from rival gangsters, before proceeding against brothel-owners. Smuts took further comfort from these public developments.[16]

Within hours of the Hermann case, Cleaver got permission for Krakower, Rosenberg and Rosenchild to be arrested and charged with having committed 'theft by means of fraud' for taking protection money from Lizzie Josephs and half a dozen other prostitutes. Still on the back foot, Krause handed the case to his closest office ally – the Dutch-trained Third Public Prosecutor, Cornelis Broeksma. But when it was heard, on 7 December, Broeksma ran into unexpected problems. Krakower's attorney, L.E. van Diggelen used evidence presented in the Hermann case to raise doubts about policies in the prosecutor's office, to question the competence of the morality squad, and to suggest that there was a conspiracy against his client. The hearing groaned beneath the weight of contradictory evidence and the charges were dismissed. The outcome placed Krause under yet more pressure and played into Cleaver's hands.[17]

Silver, anxious to keep his criminal record hidden and his deal with Murphy secret, saw in this development confirmation of Cleaver's growing influence. He had been worried that Lizzie Josephs/Rachel Laskin might reveal what had occurred back in Stamford Street – it was a chain of inquiry which might, one day, lead back to the East End in the 1880s. Laskin's ties to Krakower, a growing embarrassment, had assumed menacing proportions. They had unleashed some old demons and, well before Krakower's appearance, Silver had ferreted Josephs's out, marched her back to the Green House and beat her so severely about the head that she had reverted to being his 'slave'. That assault may have contributed to her increasingly parlous mental condition.[18]

When Maritz and van Vuuren appeared in court charged with perjury, also on 7 December, it was apparent that the recolonised Lizzie Josephs had been very active.[19] She had persuaded one of the cigar shop prostitutes to suggest not only that Krakower was in cahoots with Maritz and van Vuuren in collecting protection money but that, on the night in question, she, Murphy, Cuyler, De Klerk and Silver had been at a dinner in a brothel in Kruis Street! Laskin's perjured testimony helped shift blame for the cigar shop débâcle from Lieutenant Murphy to Krakower and increased the pressure on Maritz and van Vuuren. But the magistrate, unpersuaded by Josephs's testimony, ruled that the papers be forwarded to the State Attorney and, when the hearing resumed a week later, the charges against the constables were left pending.[20]

Silver was troubled by the Maritz and Krakower cases. Both hearings had seen evidence hinting at his role in the American Club and pointed to the existence of white slaves, thus confirming allegations made by the *Standard & Diggers' News*. Behind the scenes, did the Company and Krause still wield great influence? Could it be that the old continental view that prostitution was a necessary evil that needed to be controlled rather than eradicated had some life in it yet – despite the fact that the gazetting of new legislation, Law No. 23 of 1898, was now only days away? It was this plausible – but flawed – reading of the situation that informed his next, bizarre move. Bombastic, grandiose behaviour driven by his underlying neurosyphilis prompted a rare, rash public intervention.

On 10 December 1898, the *Standard & Diggers' News* late edition carried a letter from a man at the apex of his career, a man who aspired to having his business, if not legalised, then at least grudgingly tolerated as it was in other modern cities around the Atlantic. It was also the letter of a dangerously violent man who made and broke prostitutes at will.

Sir,

Your remarks in a leaderette of this morning's issue regarding the Expulsion of Pimps, is a very commendable one. It would mean nothing less than relief from a gang of bandits and ruffians. It is the moral duty of every well disposed man to assist us in our efforts to remove this undesirable element from the town.

My name having been freely mentioned as one belonging

to the pimping fraternity, to that I can only express my desire
to hold a mass meeting during the next few days with the
object of discussing the desirability of having these shame-
less ruffians driven out of our midst.

Johannesburg has of late become the refuge of the above-
mentioned class, and the unrivalled home in South Africa of
people who trade on prostitution, and unless we take some
further steps to remove them, they will before long eat themselves into the community so deeply that the cure will be an
impossibility.

I appeal to the large section of your readers to support
my efforts in this direction so that the special detective force
will be enabled to make practically a clean sweep of them.

All the members of the special police force in their desire
to carry out their duties [should] leave no stone unturned.

Thanking you, sir, in anticipation, I am, yours etc.

JOSEPH SILVER.

Observant readers would have noted that it was not the first time that
Mr Silver had intervened to influence policies on prostitution. Back in
September, before the clergymen had gone to see Kruger, he had popped
up at a public meeting to discuss the shortcomings of the law. He was,
he said, a citizen of the United States. Then, in the manner of an urban
sophisticate, he advocated that prostitutes be taken up in 'reformatory
institutions' or be confined to one particular locality within the city.[21]

Cleaver, meanwhile, was almost beside himself with frustration. He
had to cope with sniping from Krause and his office allies, as well as
fend off attempts by corrupt morality policemen to undermine his larger,
secret project to rid the city of Silver. Recent developments and their
attendant publicity heightened his impatience as he waited for the
government printer to produce the gazette that would allow him to use
the powers of Law 23 of 1898. After weeks of waiting, the gazette
appeared on 15 December.[22] Within hours of the law being promulgated
he had Krakower, Rosenberg and Rosenchild re-arrested – this time on
the new, and far more serious, charge of having procured women for
immoral purposes. They were arraigned on 29 December and it was
soon evident that this time not even van Diggelen would save them.
Cleaver, who personally led the prosecution, prepared the case with
exemplary thoroughness. When the hearing was adjourned until 6 January

1899, the pimps, on the advice of their attorney, started plea bargaining. Amidst great secrecy, Cleaver agreed to forgo charges in return for evidence against the 'King of the Pimps'. He also persuaded van Diggelen to assist him and work with other, junior, state prosecutors.[23]

Cleaver's moves unhinged not only Silver but some in the prosecutor's office, and many in the morality squad. It was a sign that Smuts and the new man were set on an uncompromising course that would render everyone in organised crime vulnerable. For the first five days of 1899 the air was filled with menace. Murphy, ready to counterattack with a double-bluff, persuaded Cuyler, De Klerk and J.J. Nel to lay false charges against Donovan. They claimed that Donovan had tried to incite them to lay false charges against Murphy! Donovan, discredited and already facing several charges, had to contend with new problems.[24] Silver, now beyond plotting, wanted action: he told Murphy and police on his payroll to find and thrash his enemies into submission.

This mock showdown took place in the Northwestern Hotel on the evening of 6 January. Cuyler, De Klerk and some of their uniformed friends found Donovan, Corney, Maritz and van Vuuren playing billiards and started 'chaffing' them about their style of play. The ploy worked and an almighty fight ensued. The Company thugs were brutally assaulted with Smuts's hidden agent, Maritz, coming in for particularly close attention. Maritz, ever the nationalist, saw it as an attack by 'Afrikaners' on 'Afrikaners' orchestrated by the hidden hand of 'the Jew' and it kick-started his anti-Semitism. In the short term, all he wanted to do, however, was to free himself of Smuts and Cleaver's project so that he could deal with Cuyler on his own terms.[25]

The real showdown started on the stroke of eleven on 10 January 1899. Cleaver slipped into the new Rissik Street Post Office and sent Smuts a 'top-secret' telegram requesting a warrant to search 10 Sauer Street where he hoped to find the minute books of the American Club. He left, went back to the office and waited for the private detectives to report on the whereabouts of his quarry. Ninety minutes later, he sent Smuts a second telegram asking for warrants for the arrest of Sam and Jenny Stein, Joseph Silver, Lizzie Josephs and others, as well as a warrant to enter the premises of the Rand Safety Deposit Company, where the gangsters kept copies of leases, receipts, steamship tickets and other documents.[26]

By late afternoon he had what he wanted. He instructed Maritz to ready a posse of armed 'special police' who were not to be told what their mission was until the last moment. The city streets took for ever to clear. Eventually, at 8.45 p.m., with the last breeze of the day dying away, Maritz and his men mounted their steeds and moved slowly down Commissioner Street. Heading westwards, they swung south in a long lazy loop and then, accelerating fairly sharply, suddenly turned into Anderson Street. At number 45 they burst in and netted almost all their suspects in one swoop. Knowing that the Bowery Boys often carried guns, Maritz took no chances. The following morning it was reported that 'the arrests were effected by force of arms, loaded weapons being held before the accused's eyes'. Silver, Lizzie Josephs, Sam Stein, along with four women in charge of larger enterprises – Annie Schwartz, Bessie Weinberg, Florence Maud de Lacey and Lillie Bloom – were all taken into custody. The only one missing was Jenny Stein, and Maritz knew where to find her. He and a few constables went to the Empire Theatre where they effected two more arrests.[27]

It was a good start. Cleaver had the prey within his grasp but would he be able to hang on? Which police could he trust? Would the other prosecutors help or hinder? And, would the magistrates hold the line when the accused appeared in court? At 7.30 a.m. the following morning he was back in the post office, asking Smuts for permission to arrest morality squad constables should the need arise, and warning that van Dam was on his way to complain about how the police were being used. He arranged secure detention for the prisoners and, in mid-morning, asked Smuts to ensure that they were not granted bail when they appeared in court later that day.[28]

Silver arranged for the accused to be represented by a young 'law agent', Max Nathan. They appeared before the magistrate at a no-nonsense hearing that afternoon. The accused had the charges put to them by James Skirving, Cleaver's friend, and heard that state witnesses would include Sadie Wolff and Maritz. Nathan, hoping to secure bail for his clients, made much of the fact that Maritz was no longer a member of the uniformed morality police and was facing possible charges of perjury. The magistrate, unmoved, denied bail. Silver, the most experienced of the gang, was not unduly perturbed when they were led away. He may, however, have started to take more notice when, on the way out, it became clear that they were not going back to the police holding cells, but were being escorted to the far more formidable Fort.[29]

Located on a small hill, the Fort peered down over Park Station and, beyond that, to the inner city. After the Jameson Raid the cells were strengthened and by 1898 the entrance was commanded by massive doors leading to a slanting tunnel surrounded by huge earthworks. Yet, for all its forbidding face, the inside of the prison did not pose much of a psychological challenge for a graduate of Sing Sing. Prisoners of all ages, colours and of both sexes mixed freely. Unlike Pentonville, prison labour did not depend on the usual mindless Victorian devices – the crank, shot drill or treadmill. For three months, until his case came to trial before the High Court in Pretoria in April 1899, Silver found it a perfectly acceptable place from which to run a coldly calculated and wide-ranging campaign of intimidation.[30]

This *grande peur* – 'organised terrorism', as Cleaver had it – percolated through all levels of authority. Predictably, Cleaver himself was the initial target. It started with a blend of inducements and demands. He was offered bribes of thousands of pounds if charges were dropped or modified. The sweeteners were replaced by blackmailing letters and, when these too failed, he was threatened with 'shooting irons', the Commissioner Street six-gun special.[31] Lower down, the Zarps were dealt with in similar fashion. Cuyler and De Klerk, suitably intimidated, continued to collect tributes from French and Jewish prostitutes for several weeks. Only the hot-headed Maritz remained unbowed. In late March, once the preliminary examination was concluded, Maritz sought out Cuyler the night before yet another police perjury hearing and assaulted him so severely that he and his partner De Klerk agreed to change their earlier stories and to present new – truthful – evidence against Murphy.[32]

The divide between American Club loyalists and the break-away dissidents in the rival Company deepened. Inside the court Krakower's legal team wrestled with the prosecution, while outside Bowery Boys assaulted one another.[33] Spontaneous eruptions soon gave way to focused intimidation. Silver's instruction to 'fix' Krakower before his own trial commenced fell to Budner, Witkofsky and another American Club pimp, Max Spiro. In late January, they found Krakower in Commissioner Street. There was much pushing and shoving and the loyalists then went to the police to lay charges, alleging that Krakower had attempted to get them to commit perjury and had assaulted Budner. When that matter went to court in early February, however, Krakower was again defended by van Diggelen and the initiative backfired when Budner was charged with perjury.[34]

Undeterred, Silver's henchmen continued to terrorise women thinking of giving evidence against the boss. They worked their way through Frenchfontein threatening prostitutes and raising demands for protection money from anyone tempted to peel off from the American Club and support the Company. Lena Kuhbeck, a Stamford Street veteran, got special consideration and was asked to pay just £11 rent and £2 protection each month. But her closest associate, Krendel Muscowitz, was so terrified that she fled to Delagoa Bay. Another prostitute, Lena Landau's protection doubled from £5 to £10 a month at a stroke. Not everyone was so lucky.[35]

The women Silver loathed most were those he had encountered as a Parkhurst agent four years earlier, some of whom might also have known something about his earlier life in London.[36] They aroused in him the sort of fury and disgust he had experienced as a young man in Whitechapel. Budner, Witkofsky and two others were dispatched to deal with Sadie Wolff. What exactly they did to the poor woman is unknown but she was so badly roughed up that her assailants were each sentenced to a fine of £50 or four months' imprisonment. Unable to pay they, too, were dispatched to the Fort where, for a time, they were even closer to their leader.[37] But it was Lillie Bloom formerly of New York who got the most terrifying glimpse of what Silver might do to a wayward woman. In late February, just days after the preliminary examination in which Bloom had appeared as a witness for the prosecution, Silver talked the prison authorities into allowing him to venture downtown in the company of a policeman. They made several stops and then called in at 30 Anderson Street, where they summoned Bloom. Silver manoeuvred her behind a partition separating the premises from the house next door and then, within sight but out of earshot of his police escort, told her – in Yiddish – that if she gave evidence against him again he would 'open up her belly'.[38]

If the threat was mere brothel braggadocio, the discourse of the *demimonde*, then it might not have troubled whores hardened in the furnaces of organised crime on both sides of the Atlantic. But it did. The prostitutes genuinely believed he was capable of murdering them. Lillie Bloom, Sadie Wolff and five other Jewish prostitutes signed affidavits swearing that they knew him to be an extremely dangerous man, that they had heard him swear revenge, and that they feared for their lives.[39] They were not the only ones who thought him capable of such deeds. Smuts and Cleaver, cool, level-headed men, were as convinced. Skirving's view was that if Silver were again let out of prison the lives of Bloom and others were in danger and a mistake could have 'fatal consequences'.[40]

The Grand Fear lasted twelve weeks and took its toll. On 19 January, Cleaver was forced to ask Smuts for more 'specials' as the morality police remained corrupt and deeply divided.[41] On the 31st, Krause, engaged in his own struggles with Smuts and Cleaver, could take it no longer. Citing 'strain' as a reason, he took several days' leave to escape mounting pressure. And just weeks after the conclusion of the trial Cleaver, too, became deeply depressed and had a nervous breakdown.[42] Two days after Krause fled the city, on the very day scheduled for Silver and Stein's first appearance in the Third Criminal Court, the two accused handed an eleven-page petition to Magistrate Dietzch. The letter, written by Silver, was filled with the legal phrases of a man conversant with different systems of justice. It contained a ringing appeal for justice to be done to a common man, the victim of a conspiracy by Corney, Donovan, Krakower, Maritz, van Vuuren and Sadie Wolff. It revealed an intimate understanding of micro-politics amongst the police and in the prosecutor's office. It was a cunning, pre-emptive bid to be granted bail.[43]

The preliminary examination, held in Johannesburg over seven days in early February, caused a sensation. The case for the state drew damaging testimony from Krakower and Wolff as well as other pimps and prostitutes. The prosecution presented the court with minutes of meetings held in the American Club and presided over by Silver. Club members, placing some store on fraternal solidarity, addressed one another in trade union fashion as 'Brother'. On 10 October 1898 members debated a grant to 'Brother Abraham Goldstein' who was in financial distress; there was also discussion about a reduction in rent for some houses and of the need to keep strangers at bay, a demand for more disciplined behaviour, and the introduction of a new member, 'Brother Joe Bernstein'.[44]

Silver, protecting his war chest for the battle to follow in Pretoria, conducted his own defence. His vigorous and pointed cross-examination of compromised witnesses such as Cuyler and Krakower, or prostitutes such as Sadie Wolff, was surprisingly effective. Skirving conceded that 'Silver seemed to have a peculiar and extensive knowledge of the Public Prosecutor's department', but said 'he was at a loss to know how he arrived at it'.[45] Even Magistrate Dietzch, under instructions from Smuts not to grant bail, was not entirely unmoved.[46] But these manoeuvrings came to nothing. The hearing concluded with the accused again being denied bail and committed for trial.

The denial of bail came as a shock. Silver realised just how determined his adversary was. He got rid of Nathan and retained Attorney Ballot and Advocate Lohman to launch an urgent application for bail in the High Court. The application was heard, *in camera*, before Justice Morice in Pretoria over three days in mid-March. It, too, was unsuccessful. Smuts employed an advocate, another school friend of Cleaver's and a graduate of the Inner Temple, Louis Jacobsz, to oppose the application. Jacobsz used the affidavits, including Lillie Bloom's, to convince the court of the threat that Silver posed to state witnesses.[47]

March was spent in the Fort with no sign of relief, let alone a date being set for the trial in the High Court. There was a brief flicker of hope when Jenny Stein, who had been granted bail a few weeks earlier, tried to do some of Silver's bidding. But there were limits to what she could achieve. Cleaver soaked up time tidying up cases that might weaken the High Court's focus on the main business. Corney was prosecuted for letting premises for immoral purposes and preparations were made to bring Brennan to trial for an abortion that had gone wrong. More importantly, a successful action was launched against Lieutenant Murphy.[48]

In early April, Silver moved an application to secure bail for Laskin in the belief that she, too, might run errands. But when 'Lizzie Josephs', 'pale and in delicate health' appeared in the magistrates' court on 5 April, she was told that the High Court had already considered, and rejected, such an appeal.[49] The hearing produced one bit of news: Silver, Lizzie and the Steins were committed for trial at the Pretoria High Court, on 18 April. By then, they would have been in prison for more than three months. He decided to employ a familiar strategy when he met his tormentor face to face. He would spend every penny he possessed to make sure he obtained the finest defence money could buy.

John Gilbert Kotzé was a maverick, a man accustomed to life's vicissitudes. A graduate of London University and called to the bar at the Inner Temple, he was appointed a judge in the ZAR High Court in 1874 at the age of twenty-seven. Politically ambitious, he had opposed Kruger in the 1893 presidential election without resigning office and, by 1895, had incurred sufficient debt to have to borrow thousands of pounds from a leading mining house. Escalating political tension after the Jameson Raid raised his temperature. In 1898 he became totally estranged from the government when he denied Kruger the right to amend the constitution by means of a resolution in the Volksraad. He paid for his opposition. A constitutional crisis followed and he was relieved of his position as Chief Justice. Back in private practice, a lucrative fee for a High Court appearance was most attractive, and he agreed to represent Silver.[50]

Smuts and Cleaver were undaunted. Kotzé would be opposed by Louis Jacobsz, himself a former judge.[51] Alert to the prosecution's needs, Cleaver persuaded Smuts not to allow Morris Kaplan, the state's official, Johannesburg-based, German and Yiddish translator, who had strong ties to the Bowery Boys, to appear before the High Court in his customary role. He was also, in all likelihood, Silver's best source of information in the prosecutor's office.[52]

Silver and Stein's hearing, before Justice Esser and a jury, took place over five days. As at the Old Bailey, proceedings were under-reported. The *Transvaal Leader* noted: 'we dare not publish the evidence that was heard by the Judge and jury; it was too revolting . . .' [53]

The secretary to the American Club, Budner alias 'Joe Gold', was called but his off-beat humour did nothing to help the defence. Jacobsz paraded Bowery Boys who had defected to the Company. Max Cohen, former Lower East Side saloon-keeper – now a 'speculator' and 'horse dealer' – along with 'butcher' Leopold Priziger, provided damning evidence. So, too, did Hyman Bernstein a 'grocer' and Jack Strakiosky who had been relegated to Germiston.[54] Their testimony, which foregrounded Silver's actions, left the evidence against Stein blurred. 'Lizzie Josephs' was predictably ineffectual. Eighteen years old, under enormous stress and about to face separate charges for keeping brothels at different Johannesburg addresses, Josephs, whose true identity as Laskin appears never to have been uncovered, did little to help Silver's case.

When Esser handed down his findings on 26 April, and sentences two days later, the courtroom swarmed with reporters. Stein, found not guilty on all counts, was discharged – a verdict that helped Kotzé save face in a case that he obliterated from his official memory. Stein chose not to leave the country at once. Indeed, he lingered on the Rand for another two months, deferring to Silver and leaving one with the impression that he was tidying up unfinished business. When he did eventually leave South Africa, shortly before the outbreak of war, he crossed the Atlantic. First in Rio de Janeiro, and then later in Buenos Aires, he resumed a career in organised crime that lasted for another three decades until eventually he was deported to Europe in 1931.[55]

Silver was found guilty on five counts under the Ontucht Wet of 1898 – a law that, in all but name, had been written to snare him. He was sentenced to the maximum term provided for – two years' imprisonment with hard labour. He was not unduly distressed; the sentence paled beside the two years and three months he had spent in Sing Sing for a single, botched, burglary. But Esser was not done with him. Invoking clause 3 of the new Act, the judge ordered that, on completion of the sentence, he be banished from the ZAR. Silver found that unacceptable and resolved to contest it. The legal brotherhood – Smuts, Cleaver and Jacobsz – celebrated their great victory.[56]

The fourth estate, too, was enthused. Even the pro-British section of the press congratulated Cleaver. Esser's decision was lauded along the length of the Witwatersrand. Silver's enemies spanned the world and news of his conviction was flashed abroad. Within twenty-four hours of his sentence the press reported that 'The conviction of the notorious "Joe" Silver, the "captain" of the Russo-American *macquerots*, has been received with mingled feelings in local New York circles, Bowery Section.'[57] In South Africa little interest was shown when, shortly afterwards, it became known that the State Attorney had dropped all charges against Lizzie Josephs. Perhaps Cleaver and Smuts somehow knew that they were dealing with a ghost from Whitechapel, with the woman who had once been Rachel Laskin.[58]

That compassionate act may, however, later have been conflated and confused with other post-trial developments in an atmosphere filled with propaganda and misinformation on the eve of war. Even Cleaver's mother – the author Marguerite de Fenton – with whom he was sharing a house at the time, became a victim of rumour and uncertainty. Years later, still fuming, she wrote, 'Silver was condemned to two years' imprisonment with hard labour – he deserved hanging – but a few weeks after his incarceration he was pardoned. Only himself and one other knew why.'[59] If Mrs Cleaver was pointing to her son's *bête noire*, F.E.T. Krause, she was almost certainly mistaken. Silver had certainly not been pardoned and, by 30 April, he was back in the Fort, in Johannesburg.[60]

But there *were* some puzzling movements around the case even after he was reduced to swapping notes with Stein during visits to the Fort.

The banishment clause in the new legislation made no mention of rulings having to be approved by the President. Yet, quite inexplicably, the papers were placed before Kruger and his executive for approval, on 7 June 1899.[61] It was only after the banishment had been confirmed that Silver abandoned hope of finding a legal solution to his problems. A few days later he sent Stein to the prosecutor's office to retrieve items confiscated at the time of his arrest. He noticed that his American documents – the certificate of naturalisation, passport, and a licence to carry a gun in New York – were missing. He at once wrote to Cleaver requesting the return of the documents.[62]

Some believed that Silver had managed to circumvent justice. In September, just days before the outbreak of hostilities, the Reverend J.T. Lloyd wrote to Krause probing the unthinkable. 'It is publicly announced in Great Britain, on platforms and in newspapers,' he complained, 'that Joe Silver was released after two months incarceration.'[63] Krause did not bother to reply since Lloyd's fears, like Mrs Cleaver's, were unfounded. But it was another straw in swirling winds heralding war.

Not everybody focused on propaganda. For law-abiding Jews the American Club raised painful issues. In May, the chairman of the *Chevra Kadisha*, in Johannesburg, Bension Aaron, called a meeting to establish a vigilance group which visited brothels to rescue 'Jewish girls from a fate worse than death' and established links with like-minded associations abroad. The community did as others around the Atlantic did and 'unclean ones' were prevented from burying their dead amongst respectable people; pimps were confined to a fenced-off section of the Braamfontein cemetery.[64]

Cleaver's fight against white slavers did not end with the assault on the American Club. There were other raids in which police were called upon to rescue women being held against their will. Later that year the state prosecuted David Levinsohn and Bessie Levin for decoying fifteen-year-old Fanny Kreslo from Vilna Krevo, in Lithuania, to Johannesburg, and forcing her into a brothel at 35 Anderson Street where she was made to service a stream of African, Asian and European clients.[65]

Silver's organisation left a lasting impression on the minds of Smuts and the local underworld. In 1908, when Smuts was back in the Transvaal as Colonial Secretary, he discovered that the city still had Bowery Boy-style brothels and gambling joints, and that the owners were former American Club members who had reconstituted themselves as the Immorality Trust. For a decade after the South African War, New York City, Russo-Poles and Silver continued to cast a shadow over Commissioner Street. But Silver's legacy cannot be confined to the Rand, or measured in decades. While in the Fort, in the weeks leading to war, he perpetrated a sexual assault that has left its mark on the underclass and remains imprinted on prison argot to this day.

In early August 1899, while moving about the prison yard, he made his way to the tailor's workshop – an area frequented almost exclusively by African convicts. He positioned himself outside an empty cell facing the workshop and, when a black inmate, 'Jim', entered, grabbed him and shoved him into the cell. He then called to yet another black prisoner, 'Jan', to close the door behind them. With Jan and yet another African convicts – partners, perhaps – peering through the surveillance slot, he sodomised 'Jim', pulled up his trousers, and handed his humiliated victim a shilling.[66]

'Jim', swearing it was the first time he had experienced such an act, reported the rape and a charge was laid. The racial dimension of the case may have caused the head warder to raise an eyebrow but the nature of the offence could hardly have come as a surprise. Consensual and forced acts of homosexuality were commonplace among black prisoners and, more especially, among the 'Ninevites', a black gang whose name would have intrigued Silver who had long had more than a passing interest in Old Testament passages that explored sexuality. The rape may or may not have been his only such experience while in the Fort. But his actions remained etched in the consciousness of the Ninevites, who to this day designate those responsible for procuring their 'boy-wives' in prison as AmaSilva.[67]

Six weeks later he was back in court, charged with having committed an 'unnatural offence'. One of the few Bowery Boys still in town to witness the proceedings before joining other refugees at coastal cities, was the American Club's 'grocer', Bernstein. He saw Silver's law agent, Mathey, use a characteristic conspiracy theory to try to persuade the magistrate that his client was the victim of a plot by Jack Donovan with whom he had a very public quarrel. Dietzch was unmoved by the accused's tale, supported by black witnesses, and sentenced him to six months' additional hard labour to take effect after his sentence and prior to his banishment.[68]

But by then the sap was rising, as were Silver's spirits. He knew that the power of the ZAR, like the winter just past, was waning and that the war would give him the best chance yet of regaining his freedom. The prison officers, too, sensed their growing vulnerability and, realising that the Fort might become the focus of British agents or troops, wanted the site cleared of criminal riff-raff. Fifteen days before the declaration of war, on 26 September, it was decided that Silver, two other whites, and twenty-three black long-term inmates should be moved to a newly completed and far more secure prison facility, at Potchefstroom. Things could have been much worse.[69]

Potchefstroom, fifty miles away, was a small town on the banks of a modest river serving a prosperous farming community. But any bucolic charm was lost on Silver, an urban mutant more interested in the fact that it was less than 200 miles away from the Cape border and the diamond-mining metropolis of Kimberley. The warders, rural Afrikaners, were unaccustomed to dealing with hardened criminals and, within days of his arrival there, he attempted to escape. Little is known about his bid for freedom, other than it was said later to have earned him ten lashes which, if administered, were light enough not to leave scars.[70] His timing was unfortunate: war came soon enough. Days after hostilities were declared, on 11 October, ZAR armed forces took over the administration of the town. Anxious to secure all available manpower and to flush human detritus in the direction of the British, the Boers released the prisoners.[71] To the extent that this was a calculated move by men fighting for their independence, it was not entirely unsuccessful. Silver was to cost Britain and her southern allies thousands of pounds in the administration of justice.

Putting behind him a year in which he had reached the height of his profession as well as plumbed the depths of duplicity, penniless, with only the clothing he wore and a few documents proclaiming him as an American citizen – he turned south, towards the Cape. Fate, using war as her instrument, had rescued him. How could he be anything other than optimistic? Ahead of him lay Kimberley where he was bound to find friends. And he was not really without resources. There was always Rachel Laskin.

X

KIMBERLEY
1900

A fox may steal your hens, sir, . . . If lawyer's hand is fee'd
sir He steals your whole estate.

John Gay, *The Beggar's Opera*

WARS surge through urban areas the way floods engage with abandoned watercourses in semi-desert regions – they boil through existing sluices until they rip away at old sandbars cutting new and deeper channels. When the fury abates, the furrowed brows of the old courses reemerge with a few new creases. When the Zuid Afrikaansche Republiek declared war, on 11 October 1899, a wave of fear transformed thousands of ordinary citizens, along with hundreds of gamblers, pimps, illicit liquor traders and 'white slavers', into something more marginal: refugees. Flushed from their usual haunts by approaching troops, the middle and working classes, along with 'Peruvians' and others, used the railway to escape from danger. They disembarked, confused and vulnerable, in the nearest city on the east coast, Lourenço Marques, then under Portuguese rule, or, further south, in an arc of 'British' cities – Durban, East London, Port Elizabeth and, especially, Cape Town.

The South African War of 1899–1902, an imperial initiative to acquire political mastery of the economic resources of an integrating subcontinent, was fought and co-ordinated to secure two objectives. The first, under a succession of military commanders – Sir Redvers Buller, Lord Roberts, and later Lord Kitchener – was to achieve swift, decisive victories on the field of battle. In the end this took longer to achieve than anticipated, requiring nearly half a million men, as the struggle mutated from conventional warfare to guerrilla conflict. The second was to purge the refugees of criminal and 'undesirable' elements, and use the interlude prior to the return to 'normality' to put in place legislation more in keeping with the class structure of a modern industrialising economy. The latter task fell to the High Commissioner, Sir, later Lord, Alfred Milner. The link between the two projects was Imperial Secretary, George Fiddes, appointed 'civilian advisor' to Roberts at Milner's insistence.[1]

For two years and more, as military confrontations shifted from orthodox battles along strategic routes inland to isolated engagements on South Africa's desert-like periphery, Milner busied himself with tidying up the class composition of the white society that would re-emerge on the Witwatersrand. Much of his time at the coast was spent overseeing refugee committees, raising funds for the destitute and planning the sequence and terms on which civilians would be allowed to re-enter Johannesburg. Freed from electoral accountability, arch-imperialists and trusted jingoists formulated martial law to privilege industrial and commercial capitalists along with the British middle- and working-class men of an Anglicised, post-bellum world.

Nobody got to understand the new rules better than the thousands of low-class 'Peruvians' who had sheltered in the crevices of the Rand's pre-war economy. Milner's agents singled them out, along with recent Russian and Polish Jewish immigrants, for the most unsympathetic treatment of all. In London, the Colonial Secretary, Joseph Chamberlain, tried to seal off the supply of impoverished East Europeans still trying to make its way south. With war-ravaged whites anxious to redefine their identities more precisely once hostilities ended, there were renewed fears about the dangers of Asian and other 'alien' immigration that dated back, most recently, to 1893. When the Cape's Immigration Restriction Act of 1902 was introduced, there was heated debate as to whether Yiddish, the lingua franca of poor Jewry, was a 'European' language. It took until 1905 to persuade the legislature that Yiddish qualified – an achievement due largely to pressure from prominent Jews and shipping companies afraid of losing access to their markets. Patronised by their better-established English and German co-religionists, and the butt of British prejudices, Peruvian refugees were amongst the very last whites to be assisted, and among the first to be excluded.[2]

During the opening weeks of the war Russian Jews, alone among European refugees in Delagoa Bay, were refused assistance by embassies in the Portuguese colony. In Durban and East London the reception of

Peruvians was no more civil. In Port Elizabeth not even those with cash could secure shelter. 'Many [refugees] are able to pay for accommodation but are unable to get a place,' the local press noted. 'They are chiefly Polish Jews and boarding houses will not take them in.' In Cape Town, where Milner held views on Russo-Poles that were only saved from being deemed anti-Semitic because of the cosy relationship he enjoyed with notables in the Anglo-German community, things were no better. With the Jewish community swelling from 5–6,000 to nearly 10,000 within weeks, the poor and unemployed had to eke out a living on hastily contrived public works. In January 1900, Milner used funds from the Lord Mayor's appeal in London to ship out 350 'foreign Jews'. The *African Review* took leave of the refugees by labelling them 'illicit liquor-sellers', while in England the *Daily Mail* welcomed them by noting that the ship was 'alive with them' and reporting that its officers were unhappy that monies raised by the Lord Mayor's fund should be used to transport 'foreigners' to Europe when there 'were hundreds of English people utterly destitute . . . who begged . . . to be allowed to sail'.[3]

Nature compensated the strategic town of Kimberley for its plain, dust-encrusted nature by adorning it with extraordinary wealth. Situated on an arid plateau as hellishly hot in summer as it was snipingly cold in winter, Kimberley stood in relation to diamonds as did Johannesburg to gold. Huge 'pipes' shaped like ice-cream cones had been shoved into acia scrubland, their blue volcanic dirt yielding gemstones of inestimable value. Uncovered in the late 1860s, thousands of claims worked by under-capitalised diggers had given way to an enormous monopolistic enterprise presided over by the moving figure behind the Jameson Raid, Cecil Rhodes. It was the same enterprise, De Beers' Consolidated Mines, that oversaw the transformation of Kimberley from tented camp to company town.[4]

Until gold was discovered, Kimberley was the foremost industrial city on the subcontinent. Granted municipal status in 1878, it had electric lighting by 1882: half a decade before much of London. The town sprouted white working-class suburbs and closed compounds for black workers, prison-like structures designed to retain cheap labour and minimise the theft and sale of illicit diamonds. By 1885, Kimberley had a rail link to Cape Town and Port Elizabeth. The prospects of its 50,000 inhabitants were enhanced when gold was discovered on the Rand in 1886, and in lesser quantities in Southern Rhodesia in the 1890s.[5]

For the Boer forces of the Zuid Afrikaansche Republiek and its ally, the Orange Free State whose capital, Bloemfontein, lay only 100 miles east, there was some satisfaction in laying siege to Kimberley. The town was of strategic importance, commanding a key route leading to the Witwatersrand, and housed industrial resources and workshops that might be used by the British. More importantly, it was the centre of power of an arch-enemy, and no sooner had they drawn their net around the city than, to their delight, they learned that within it they had caught Cecil Rhodes himself.

The siege of Kimberley, an operation that lasted for 124 days and ended on 15 February 1900, was the first of the major sieges to end, with the other two, at Ladysmith and Mafeking, continuing until 28 February and 28 May. Throughout the siege Rhodes, master of all he surveyed, was embroiled in a personality-driven clash over martial law requirements with the British commander in the town, Lieutenant-Colonel R.G. Kekewich who, years later, took his own life. When the siege ended, the town, although still subject to martial law, gradually reverted to normality.[6]

But 'normality' is an elusive concept in mining towns – even one in which a company as powerful as De Beers exercised great control over the lives of its employees. Throughout its early years, the town suffered from heavy drinking, reckless gambling and casual sex. It was still in its infancy as the gemstone capital of the world when Barney Barnato enjoyed his earliest experiences with prostitutes and illicit diamond buyers who, it was said, were 'Polish Jews'.[7] Although the outbreak of war saw some *demi-monde* elements head for the coast, a good number of burglars, cardsharps, confidence tricksters, professional gamblers, illicit diamond dealers, pimps and prostitutes remained. It was claimed that, when Bloemfontein fell to Lord Roberts in March 1900, Rhodes arranged for liquor to be transported by rail to the city while De Beers recruited a flotilla of prostitutes who were sent across the veld by horse and cart to join the wild celebrations of the British troops. The revelry that followed, it was said, gave rise to an outbreak of venereal disease.[8]

One of the women making that journey to Bloemfontein may have been a confused, and infected, Rachel Laskin. But, if she did venture into what by then was the Orange River Colony, she did not stay. It was much closer to mid-1900, when the tide was still lifting British spirits, that her rapist-lover, pimp-husband, parasite-torturer found her in Kimberley. How he tracked her down is impossible to tell, but it was probably somebody in the family who told him where she was.

It was almost certainly Joseph Anker, who had been in Kimberley for some weeks, who introduced Silver to Sam Rabinowitz. Rabinowitz, a Russian emigrant capable of the deepest treachery, had an appealing criminal résumé. An *agent provocateur* and brothel-keeper, he was also, in order of preference, a burglar, a confidence trickster, an illicit diamond buyer and a thief. Like most people in his line of work, he was in constant contact with the shadier elements in the police force whom he supplied with information in return for business favours. Not all information he put the police's way, however, was rooted in crime. It was alleged that he set 'false traps' for illicit diamond buying (IDB) and that, because of it, 'many innocents suffered prison'.[9]

Silver and Rabinowitz could have been twins. Both traded in the twilight zone where ambitious and greedy policemen swapped notes with mendacious and narcissistic criminals. Because policemen-criminals and criminal-policemen were difficult to tell apart morally, it was hard to know who was driving the bargain and to what end. Bazaars of betrayal were highly volatile, centred on short-term considerations, and prone to collapse. But even in wartime Kimberley, with many of the main players away at the seaside, there were enough interested parties to keep the market going; one of them being Max Jacobs.

Jacobs was from New York's Lower East Side, where he had once run a pawnshop on Orchard where Goldberg, Silver and others had disposed of stolen goods.[10] After Lexow, he had been sucked out in the Atlantic backwash and deposited in Scotland, where he had picked up the sobriquet 'Scotch Jack'. Newly arrived from Glasgow, where he had twice been sentenced for theft during the first three months of 1900, he started a brothel in George Street.[11] His Scottish management was appreciated by British troops who added yet another dimension to a *demi-monde* which already sported a small contingent of *karayuki-san* – Japanese prostitutes who had made their way to south Africa via various tropical islands spread across the Indian Ocean.[12]

How much of his recent experience Jacobs confided in Silver, or vice versa, is unclear. From what transpired later, however, it is clear that they lived to regret the smallest disclosures and this fed into a mutual loathing. But for the time being, the relationship was unproblematic. Silver was trying to re-establish himself, hoping to return to Johannesburg after the war.

Laskin was staying at 67 George Street when he re-invaded her – body, mind and spirit. She earned enough to keep them and by the end of 1900 he had skimmed off enough to put down a deposit on number 69, the house next door. He had always disliked prostitutes flaunting themselves on the streets and insisted on the whores keeping themselves clean and indoors. Without easy access to white slave supply lines, he kept Laskin working at 67 and either coerced or persuaded two other prostitutes – Alice Donaldson and Maggie du Toit – to work from the newly acquired property. In addition to this, he and Rabinowitz became partners in a gambling den.[13]

While Laskin and the others remained closeted indoors, Silver drifted through nearby dives in search of clients, underworld contacts, detectives and IDB 'traps' who cruised wateringholes with only their eyes protruding, like crocodiles. Rabinowitz introduced him to several plain-clothes police, and by September 1900 he was providing them with sufficient snippets of gossip about crime for the over-confident to trust him and value the assistance. Incredibly, the police either knew nothing of Silver's past or, more likely, made the mistake of thinking that they could control him. He did not embark on a hastily contrived or impulsive venture – a fate that had previously befallen him when cash-strapped,

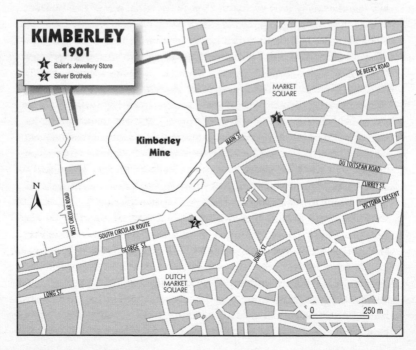

in London and New York. With a few minor successes behind him, he identified premises that might yield something bigger. But the crocodiles remained menacing. He sent a telegram to Jack in Port Elizabeth, inviting him to join him. 'Joachim Lees', had no trouble in obtaining a permit from the military and arrived, with an unknown accomplice, in mid-September.[14]

Not much is known about the store-breaking that followed other than it was planned and executed with the assistance of Anker, Jack and a mysterious fourth. The target was a jewellery store belonging to Martin Baier, a watchmaker, of Jones Street; the objective easily disposable uncut diamonds, emeralds and opals. But the job was botched. Entry was effected but only about £25 worth of stones taken: they may have been interrupted. A day later, on 26 September, the press noted that 'Charlie Silver', a 'European Traveller' resident in the city, had been arrested in connection with the robbery. Anker and Rabinowitz, with Jack hovering in the background, approached Louis Flavien Lezard to defend Silver.[15]

Lezard, born in London, was twenty-three years old. His parents had emigrated when he was a lad to open a jewellery store in Kimberley. Arrogant, bright and pugnacious, he was articled to local attorneys when he was called up to serve in the Bechuanaland campaign of 1895–96. He was hauled in for disobeying orders: 'carrying dispatches to the main camp by himself instead of with another soldier'. Back in Kimberley and qualified, he was again called up to serve under Colonel Harris during the siege but got into more trouble for 'seizing for the pot eleven pigeons belonging to a Chinaman'. He was court-martialled, found guilty and was lucky to escape with a reprimand. When the siege lifted he opened his own practice and bought one of Kimberley's finest houses for £3,000. Without 'money or influence' he was introduced to Silver, who became one of his very first clients.[16]

Lezard, however, thought he had been around long enough to have seen it all. Small-time immigrant crooks held overnight on minor charges were rabbits in his poacher's snare. He demanded ten guineas, in advance, before agreeing to represent Silver. On 27 September, his client appeared before the magistrate, but the preliminary examination was held over until 4 October, when Lezard succeeded in getting the prosecutor to withdraw the charges. Silver liked what he saw, settled his account and, like Lezard, thought no more of it until somebody told him that the police, unhappy with the outcome, were going to lay another charge.[17]

Plagued by this rumour, he approached Lezard and asked whether a person could be prosecuted twice for the same offence. Whatever Lezard told him was soon academic since, hours later, he was re-arrested and charged with theft of jewellery. Anker and Rabinowitz again appeared at Lezard's office with a request that he defend Silver. Still wary, he agreed but this time demanded a £25 deposit. Silver appeared, on 9 November, bail was set at £200 and the case remanded to the following morning. Since Lezard refused to stand surety for bail, Anker, Rabinowitz and Jack Lis were forced to try and raise the cash. Between them they collected £125 but Lezard refused to advance them the bridging amount and insisted on the full sum before he would proceed. Anker, ever faithful, produced the balance from a post office savings account and Lezard eventually agreed to prepare a defence.

His client was released on bail the following morning, but Lezard warned him that he would face a protracted and searching preliminary examination. He also told him he would need an additional deposit to cover prospective fees. This issue was only resolved when it was agreed that any further legal costs be offset against the bail already lodged with the sheriff. With his fees covered, Lezard was assisted by witnesses who, unbeknown to him, included a stepbrother, a cousin, and underworld compatriots. Silver and his kin knew how to 'persuade' potentially hostile witnesses. By the time the preliminary examination drew to a close, on 24 November 1900, it was clear that the police evidence was not going to hold and the prosecutor declined to press charges.[18]

The family celebrated; but it was a Pyrrhic victory – they were dealing with the uniformed branch, not detectives. The police, thwarted for a second time, set about exploring other ways of getting their man. It took them less than ten days. On 7 December, they had Silver re-arrested and charged with living off the proceeds of prostitution with further, separate, charges pending against Alice Donaldson and Maggie du Toit. A familiar cycle was set in motion. Lezard was approached for assistance and agreed to lead the case for the defence on the understanding that any fees would be recovered from the balance of the bail money.

Lezard twice got the case remanded at his client's behest. On 16 December, 'Joseph Silver', a first-time offender in the Cape Colony, was found guilty of living off the proceeds and sentenced to a fine of £10, or six weeks' imprisonment with hard labour. The fine was paid at once but the police, still smarting, had one more trick up their sleeve.

On leaving court he was re-arrested, under martial law, by officers of the Provost Marshal for living in town without a military permit as an 'undesirable'. The war, which had pulled him out of prison in Potchefstroom jail, was about to push him in an unknown direction. As a 'Peruvian', he was almost beyond reach of an attorney in a military regime bent on cleansing society of lower-class East Europeans. He was shocked, and his brother and cousin, fearing that they too might be deported, fled.

Lezard, however, continued to fret about fees. When next he saw Silver, on 21 December, he told him that legal costs, to date, amounted to about 100 guineas, and that the cost of the recent case of living off the proceeds had yet to be factored in. In the end, or so Lezard claimed, it was agreed that he was owed £157 10s. Any subsequent interventions with the military authorities, located out of town, would entail yet more charges at an unspecified 'special' rate. Silver asked Lezard to get him released on bail and obtain him a permit. Lezard tried. He made several trips to the military to seek an audience with the Provost Marshal but failed. The situation became so bleak that his client gave him the names of two detectives, Kingsbury and Nelson, who might be able to establish what the army's intention was. Lezard eventually got to see the Provost Marshal, but it was a disappointing meeting. The military saw no reason to release Silver on bail, or to come up with a charge. The Provost told Lezard to return and make further representations. Lezard did so, on two more occasions. Each time he was told that his client would not be granted bail and that no specific charges had been formulated.[19]

Christmas and New Year passed without charity from foreign God or pagan spirit. The holding cells saw daytime temperatures in the upper thirties. A boy raised in Polish winters could be forgiven for thinking he was in hell. By late January, Lezard was no closer to getting him out of the cell. And then, all of a sudden, it happened. One morning, an officer threw open the cell door and told him that he was to be deported within hours. It did not matter where he chose to go, provided only that he stayed away from Kimberley. Perhaps, after all, Lezard had somehow contrived to get him out of prison. He gave them the name of his preferred destination and got a message to Laskin, telling her to meet him there. On 27 January 1901, without being given the opportunity to tidy up his messy personal affairs, he was put on the 'down' train. The train, slowed by the precedence given to moving

military supplies, took for ever to reach the junction in the heart of
the Karoo. At De Aar, the line branched, as if anxious to reach the
coastal destinations of Cape Town, East London and Port Elizabeth.

The train chugged out of the dreariness of De Aar towards Beaufort
West, which gave no clue to the approaching splendour of the Cape.
The journey gave Silver time to reorder old hatreds and new resentments. The Provost Marshal, egged on by resentful uniformed police,
had treated him poorly, as had his attorney. Lezard, who levied excessive charges and owed him money, had been singularly ineffectual in
his dealings with the military. When Silver disembarked at Cape Town
he could not possibly have foreseen that, when he next boarded an 'up'
train, the state would have placed him in a position where the rulings
of the Provost Marshal no longer mattered, the Kimberley uniformed
police would have to show him some respect, and he could deal with
that Mr Louis Lezard with singular confidence, in the highest courts
of the land.

CAPE TOWN
1901–1902

To betray, you first have to belong.

Kim Philby

THE sharp end of the African continent plunges into the southern seas off Cape Aghulas, splitting the Atlantic from the Indian Oceans in a way decreed by man rather than God. This and the fact that the colonisers clambered ashore from the Atlantic rather than the Indian Ocean, has had a profound effect on southern African history. Three hundred and fifty years of white minority rule ensured that in what was to become 'South Africa' finance, trade, language and religion were inextricably linked to the Atlantic world. It need not have been so. Long before the Portuguese were mapping the southern Atlantic, the Chinese were probing the eastern extremities of Africa. But Oriental initiatives never took root and South Africa, like much of the continent, remained and, for the most part, remains 'western' in outlook.

Yet there were moments, especially when it was in need of cheap labour, that southern Africa *did* glance reluctantly eastward. Many of the Cape's seventeenth-century slaves came from south-eastern Asia, leaving the colony with people of mixed descent – so-called 'coloureds' – as well as remnants of Malay cuisine and tell-tale words embedded in the indigenous, Dutch-derived language of Afrikaans. Likewise, in the 1860s, the coastal colony of Natal obtained indentured labour from India for its sugar plantations. In Natal, Indian cuisine and language had less effect on English-speaking settler 'South Africans' than did Malay on deeply rooted Afrikaners at the Cape. These imperfectly digested eastern precedents, in a country struggling with a profound black–white social divide, had renewed pertinence in the aftermath of the South African War. In 1903, Lord Milner gave Rand mine-owners permission to import cheap indentured Chinese labour at a time when the gold mining industry was languishing for want of a sufficient supply of low-cost African labour.

The emergence of smokestack industries in the north was viewed through narrowed eyes in the bucolic Cape. While diamond and gold mining centres quickened the pulse of port cities dominated by English-speakers and offered new markets for agricultural products to Afrikaner farmers, many agreed that industrialisation had sucked too many adventurers, criminals and semi-skilled workers into the country. A concern about the assimilability of outsiders, linked to a scare about Asian immigration dating to 1893, took on added significance in the South African War as immigrants moved south as refugees. In the western Cape, refugees were joined by other newcomers from Eastern Europe waiting for the reopening of the goldfields. The problem of accommodating these sojourners was exacerbated by a post-war economic downturn as demobilised soldiers and workers of all colours were subjected to a wage squeeze and made to compete for positions in a turbulent labour market.

The Cape Legislature, struggling with an upsurge of anti-alienism and concerns about 'Peruvians', passed an Immigration Restriction Act in 1902, and took its time to recognise Yiddish as a European language. In a brittle society, obsessed with defining outsiders and ethnic rank-ordering, it was difficult to know whether Russian and Polish Jews were 'eastern' or 'western'. 'This is the most prominent section of those who stand on the border-line between white and coloured,' it was suggested in the columns of the *South African Jewish Chronicle* in 1905. 'The raw Russian Jew is, of all Europeans, the one who has the least of the European and the most of the Oriental about him.' For some, Peruvians needed to be grouped alongside aliens such as Chinese, Indians or Malays. Not surprisingly then, there was an element of panic in the way Russo-Polish Jews scurried to become naturalised citizens after the war.[1]

While Jews in the Cape increased from about 3,000 in 1891, to close on 20,000 in 1904, most of the increase was as a result of the refugee influx. Cape Town, increasingly racially segregated in its residential patterns and social practices, dealt with its 5–7,000 Peruvian refugees in much the same way that urban centres everywhere did – by nudging them along existing fault lines of class and colour. Like many Atlantic ports, which showed their contempt for the newly-arrived by designating the quarters closest to the docks as 'Ends' or 'Sides' of the city proper, Cape Town, too, had a runt suckled on harbour water. Its mongrel had never outgrown its administrative designation; it was known simply as 'District Six'.[2]

Cape Town's more elegant suburbs, such as Oranjezicht and Tamboerskloof, were tucked in around Table Mountain and could peer out through the summer haze towards Robben Island and shelter from the sheets of winter rain driving in from the north-west. Middle-class suburbs kept to the lower slopes. Suburban residents in Claremont, Observatory and Rosebank lived in comfortable homes, and took trams along Main Road, or the railway parallel to the road, to get them into town. Closer to the city centre, lower down still and on much poorer soil, the working-class suburbs of Salt River and Woodstock lay prostrate beneath the lashing of the coastal winds. Beyond them, wedged between Woodstock and the shoreline, its head pointing towards the docks and the lower reaches of the city proper lay, largely unloved, District Six.

Shaped a bit like a cloak hanging from a hook, District Six dangled from a nail marking the spot where a Dutch castle had once stood on the shore of Table Bay. Hanover Street, stretching down its middle, ran north-south for about thirty blocks. Planned in Napoleonic times as a military quarter, its patterned street outline was interrupted at the city end by a few nondescript lanes posing as 'terraces'. The district had departed from the official plan and, by late Victorian times, had assumed a distinctive character. A tightly integrated commercial, trading and residential area by 1900, its cosmopolitan population was squeezed into three-storey tenements and numberless smaller cottages housing hundreds of artisans, shopkeepers and workers.

Like most harbour-front areas, District Six had a large disreputable, raffish element. Its underclass, which pre-dated the war, was made up of sun-shy elements: nocturnal predators who occupied cracks and crevices during the day only to emerge at dusk. At night, the weaker amongst them scurried out into poorly lit passageways, turning over human detritus. The redoubts of the strongest were not difficult to identify. Scores of outwardly unremarkable business premises and houses, some with only partially concealed entrances, contained brothels, gambling dens or dives run by illicit liquor sellers.[3]

After 1900, District Six's hundreds of God-fearing East European working-class Jews, whose presence pre-dated the war, suddenly found themselves living cheek by jowl with scores of flashy, up-country 'Bowery Boys' and thousands of impoverished Peruvians. With the economy and immigration in alignment, those living on the upper reaches of the mountain looked down in dismay as a moral eclipse set in over the low-lying parts of the city. The passage of the Betting Houses, Gaming Houses and Brothels Suppression Act of 1902 – the 'Morality Act' – merely confirmed the suspicions of those in Bishopscourt and elsewhere. An upsurge in low-price, high-turnover, cross-racial commercial sex fuelled a moral panic amongst those struggling to reconcile emerging notions of what it was to be a white 'South African'. It became an offence for a white prostitute to take a black man as a client, with sentences of up to five years' imprisonment and twenty-five lashes for anyone promoting such 'illicit sexual intercourse'. Amongst the first, prominent, offenders to be sentenced under the new Act were several members of the former American Club.[4]

For the Act to be effective, however, the state needed functioning law enforcement agencies – something it manifestly lacked. In 1900, the capital's Urban Police Force consisted of 300 men. About a hundred were based in the Wale Street and Sir Lowry Road stations, thirty-five looked after the Docks and only fourteen were deployed in District Six and Woodstock. Throughout the war, and for some time thereafter, the police were without a commissioner and, in 1901, the Acting Commissioner complained of a shortage of both officers and men. Overwhelmed by the wartime influx of criminals and refugees, the situation deteriorated to the point where even those in parliament could see the problem. The years 1901–2 saw a recruitment drive in Ireland and Scotland and by 1903 the number of police in the peninsula had doubled. But it hardly solved the problem. With a constable earning barely £100 a year, many of the new recruits were not of the requisite calibre.[5]

The situation was exacerbated by the absence of a specialist arm for dealing with hardened international gangsters. A dedicated Criminal Investigation Department (CID) capable of liaising with police in other cities and states was not established until 1901. The new Act was an added burden and shortly after its passage – ignoring what had happened in Johannesburg – Cape Town's 'Morality Police' were called into being to curb organised prostitution. But, even in numerical terms, they were not up to the task. The morals squad, under Sub-Inspector Thor Osberg and Sergeant David Charteris, started out with sixteen men in 1902, but was already down to six by 1904.[6]

Here was the devil's brew thirty-two-year-old Silver was addicted to – a poorly paid police force composed of tyros trying to enforce morals legislation in a city with an underworld in the thrall of Russo-Poles. But how exactly to partake of it? He had few contacts with enough resources to start a large house of his own, and no males in the family to draw on. He was well known by former Bowery Boys, which would make it difficult to be an effective police informer since 'In order to betray you first had to belong'. In the end his fate was decided by two factors: his late arrival in the city and the presence of somebody he knew but who, unfortunately, also knew him.

Max Harris, a twenty-four-year-old Russian 'plumber' and 'tinsmith', had arrived in the Cape in 1897 and gone directly up-country. In Johannesburg he had been spotted by Silver and Stein, who got the ex-Argentines, Robert and Esther Schoub to teach him how to run a modern Jewish gambling den and whorehouse. Put in charge of the Green House, he had been a full-time gambler and pimp, and part-time counterfeiter.[7] In wartime Cape Town he and a Russian friend, Lipschitz, had sold cheap furniture to brothels until he met a divorcée from Warsaw running a small brothel at the dock end of District Six. He persuaded Leah Weinstock to help set up a larger 'restaurant'/brothel, opposite the Taymouth Castle Hotel.[8]

The Taymouth, like three other hotels within walking distance, was run by a former policeman, Rogers, who, on leaving the force had no difficulty in obtaining a liquor licence. He was, however, more than a publican; he was a gateway between the outer world and the underworld, affording detectives and off-duty policemen the opportunity to trade information with small-time crooks, gangsters and informers.[9] One of his regulars was David Charteris of the Urban Police, an ex-shunter and Glaswegian policeman who, even before the new 'Morality Act', was responsible for implementing the Police Offences Amendment Act of 1898 outlawing prostitution. Charteris had developed an extensive network by conveying messages between prostitutes held in police cells and the *madames* and pimps who put up their bail money. It was while running precisely such an errand that he was first directed to Weinstock's 'restaurant'.[10] He became a frequent visitor, calling after dark to cadge drinks. During these visits he learned that the emerging power in the *demi-monde* was the real proprietor of the restaurant, a man it took time to meet: Harris. Charteris got on well with Weinstock and their association contributed to the expansion of Harris's 'vice' interests in 1901 and 1902.

Harris was introduced to influential local property owners Frank Ricardi, an Italian immigrant of thirty years' standing and Israel Roytowski, a Warsaw Pole who had been in the colony for fifteen years. They, along with hidden contacts in the police, allowed Harris to increase the number of houses and prostitutes under his control. The property owners used Harris as a broker for deals with other pimps, including Francophone Jews managing relatively upmarket brothels who had fled Paris after the Dreyfus affair, and several even more secretive countrymen who operated from a club downtown. Within eighteen months of his return to Cape Town, Harris had interests in several gambling houses, liquor outlets and, along with Ricardi, a share in the Winter Gardens where smaller theatre companies put on Yiddish productions.[11]

Harris's success, predicated in part on loan-sharking during the recession, excited hostility in police and, especially, underworld circles. Whereas Charteris and his corrupt associates could stay afloat on salaries and – like the Great Whites in the bay – wait for the best moment to glide in and take a bite of the spoils, those without steady incomes found it difficult to control their appetites. Professional gamblers, liquor sellers and pimps struggling in over-traded markets resented the overhead costs Harris inflicted on them regardless of whether these came in the form of interest, rent or 'protection'. Harris himself, sensing the problem, once noted: 'There are jealousies between various keepers of brothels, just as between other men of business.'[12] He could have taken his analysis further. Such jealousy was most pronounced amongst those who had themselves once been top dogs and then slipped back down the order. He was aware that he had several such enemies in District Six but the one he feared above all was the one for whom he had once worked back in Johannesburg.

Silver hated Harris. Seven years his senior and more experienced in every way that mattered, Harris to Silver was an *oyfgekummener*, a parvenu pig. He suspected – with good reason – that Harris and Charteris were the ones most responsible for keeping him out of the police-protected organised prostitution racket in District Six for eighteen months.[13] He made alternative arrangements and rented a strategically located house in the city bowl. The brothel, at 46 Keerom Street, was close to the courts and, by putting up bail for prostitutes, he brought in some cash as a loan shark. More importantly, the proximity of the house to the Wale Street Police Station and the court complex gave him the chance to feed snippets of underworld gossip to the newly formed CID. Two officers he met in this way, and who became especially important to him, were Detective George Easton and Captain Samuel Lorimer.

Sketched crudely, corrupt power in wartime Cape Town centred on the Wale Street Police Station, whence it flowed outwards through two huge cables. The first started in the offices of the morality squad, with Osberg and Charteris directing it into a District Six sub-station where Harris redistributed it into the myriad microcircuits of the commercial sex trade. The second exited from the offices of the CID, with Lorimer and Easton routing it into the city bowl where Silver fed it into smaller circuits, including several linked to burglary, gambling, illicit liquor selling, illicit diamond buying and other crimes against property. Theoretically distinct and well insulated, in practice the cables crossed in the upper parts of District Six, giving rise to friction and fraying with the accompanying danger of short-circuiting.

Silver set up a second enterprise within walking distance of the house in Keerom. A partner, David Feldman, found premises on the corner of Riebeeck and Bree Streets for a 'café' where late-night owls, cab drivers, sailors and soldiers wandering up from the docks could buy sex or liquor long after legal outlets had closed their doors. Just as an earlier venture, in Johannesburg – the American Café – had deferred to Boer republican ideals, so the new enterprise was made to accommodate to changing political times and named the Empire Café.[14] Neither the café nor the house eased financial woes rooted in Silver's Kimberley experience. He owed his cousin Anker and Rabinowitz money for bail that they had advanced, while what little cash he did possess was in the hands of the attorney, Lezard. He wrote to Lezard asking that any money owed him be forwarded immediately. When he had had no reply by early February he sent a bluntly worded telegram: 'Never received money. Please state reason.'[15]

The attorney saw things differently. He argued that the £200 recovered from the court for bail had not even covered his fees. In fact, Silver owed *him* money. Silver did some calculations, wrote back requesting an invoice, and suggested that Lezard should be 'ashamed' of his fees. The correspondence took an ominous downturn. Again he wrote to Lezard, pointing out that only the lack of a military permit kept him from going to Kimberley to collect his money and concluded: 'Hoping that no trouble will come between us, and you will soon return my £110.'[16] Lezard did not bother to reply and the matter continued to rankle but Silver was then overtaken by more pressing personal problems.

In early May 1901 Rachel Laskin, not yet twenty-one, started taking leave of her senses. Sustained personal abuse, aggravated by disease, left her nearly totally unhinged. She was increasingly disorientated and unpredictable and had to be confined to the house in Keerom in much the same way that she had once been kept prisoner in the American Hotel in Waterloo. After a few days of rest and seclusion it seemed that her condition might stabilise, if not improve. But Silver's rickety businesses meant that the pressure was unrelenting. On 19 May, while serving late night customers a drink, he was arrested by a plainclothes officer for selling liquor after hours. The following morning there was more confusion and excitement when George Easton, acting on instructions, arrived to take stock of the liquor kept on the premises.

Laskin, perhaps dreading another round of assaults, court appearances and perjured statements, started raving. Within days she was incoherent. Unable to control her through violence, Silver bustled her into a cab and took her to the Valkenberg Asylum. Persuaded that she might be insane, a clerk – Ernest Rigg – told him to obtain a temporary order from a magistrate so that she could be committed under the Lunacy Act, pending examination. When he returned, the clerk demanded more information before she could be admitted. She was, he told the clerk, 'Lizzie Silver', a European immigrant of three years' standing, born in Poland, Jewish, twenty-five years of age and a 'housewife' most recently of Kimberley and Cape Town. And there he left her, in the Cape of Slaves – a human being without her name, identity, dignity, personality, kin, sound body or mind. A few days later, on 26 May, the medical superintendent confirmed that the woman he examined was indeed insane, noting, in passing, some early signs of paralysis of the sort later associated with syphilis.[17]

But even as Silver discarded what was left of a woman he had hunted down in Whitechapel, he inadvertently erred by implying that she had been his wife – a 'housewife'. The clerk, a bureaucrat to the core, seized on this. While the state would accept her as a patient, it was unwilling to accept responsibility for her maintenance while her husband was alive. After she was formally committed, Rigg informed Silver that it would cost him 4s. 6d. per day for as long as she was confined to hospital. A twist of fate had reversed their roles. Whereas once he had forced her to use a healthy young body to underwrite his parasitic lifestyle while he was making good money, and denied her any legal status, now that he was financially strapped his putative 'wife' was making him pay for the upkeep of her useless, diseased mind and body.[18]

The day Laskin was committed he and his partner appeared before Assistant Resident Magistrate Broers, for selling liquor on a Sunday. Feldman, pleading not guilty, was surprised when the charge against him was withdrawn. Silver, too, pleaded not guilty but then squandered his chances by putting a string of irrelevant questions to the crown witnesses. Easton testified to the nature and quantity of liquor kept on the premises. By then Broers had heard enough and, despite a plea for leniency, sentenced Silver to a fine of £25 or three months' imprisonment.[19] He paid the substantial fine and the nine months that followed were amongst the hardest he had known. Without a woman like Laskin to live off he was like a slow-moving shark in an aquarium, grinding along the bottom feeding off scraps scorned by those darting above. He hung about the courts putting up bail or paying the fines of the loathsome dockside streetwalkers who could no longer command places in brothels. Short-term loans barely yielded a living and the few small windfalls that did come his way – getting a woman off the streets and placing her in a house – added little. It was frustrating for a man who, only a few years before, was chasing down 'fresh goods' amidst an endless supply of young females negotiating the open jaws of London's East End or the Lower East Side.[20]

Some former associates made forays into Belgium or France, returning with 'slaves' but for Silver District Six remained largely off limits.[21] With Harris and Charteris still tightening their grip he had no way of obtaining a more formal toehold in a quarter where he was feared. Yet District Six was where he felt he needed to be. He had long been drawn to public baths and fascinated by young women or prostitutes seeking ritual purification. He hung about the *mikveh* in Lower Hanover Street and frequented the Winter Gardens in nearby Ayre Street where his actor-pimp friend, Sam Wallerstein, performed, or the smaller hall in Williams Street which also put on Yiddish theatre.[22] There were other attractions. Most pimps took an interest in burglary, theft and fencing and he needed to convert information into cash by taking it back to his CID contacts. One source was Solomon Koskes, a Pole who ran a 'boarding house' in Tennant Street, popular amongst Jewish pimps and prostitutes.[23] He used to call in there and on one or two occasions acted as a scribe for illiterate prostitutes remitting money back to the Old Country while picking up professional prattle and doing a little discreet loan-sharking. Another source was the Woolf brothers' barbershop in Caledon Street which pimps and prostitutes used as a 'post office'.[24]

In this murky world where nothing was as it seemed he clung to any information he got. He exaggerated only slightly when he later suggested that during this time he had 'been in the employ of the police in Cape Town' and received a 'good discharge'.[25] But with the CID having no professional interest in prostitution – the business of Osberg and Charteris – much of the information he obtained on vice in late 1901 and early 1902 was of limited use. Some of it, along with the names of a few new contacts, had to be kept in storage until he was better placed to use it. It only added to his growing annoyance and frustration at being excluded from the mainstream.

Max 'Scotch Jack' Jacobs was a major irritation. Since Kimberley, he had been back to Aberdeen and done more time for burglary before taking up with an ambitious German Jewess – Hannah Vygenbaum – who, for the benefit of British clients was by then passing herself off as Jane Wilson. The couple had set up a house but, lacking capital, had abducted a young woman; they escaped prosecution only because the police had failed to work the case up sufficiently well. Instead, they had been charged with keeping a brothel. Silver liked the lively Vygenbaum, advised her how to deal with the police, and sensed that she was tiring of Jacobs. She, in turn was not averse to his company and once had her photograph taken with him. Normally he would have moved in at once but instead he contented himself with a waiting game.[26]

With coastal markets for commercial sex almost saturated, there was a falling off in the importation of 'fresh goods' from Europe. Unlike in Johannesburg, where coerced prostitution had pushed Smuts into drafting legislation that dealt explicitly with white slavery, Merriman's 1902 Morality Act did not address matters such as the confiscation of clothing, or female indebtedness. These anomalies strengthened Charteris and Harris's near monopoly and increased underworld resentment. It was at about this time that Silver met someone who disliked Harris almost as much as he did. And, in that strange world, too, an enemy's enemy was always a potential ally.

Solomon Goldstein running the tide of misfortune, had sailed into Table Bay before the war. A Russo-Pole, he claimed that after leaving the Old Country he had made a fortune from selling furniture to brothels in Buenos Aires and that by the mid-1890s his assets were worth £16,000. He had 'married' Minnie Trautman who, like many *madames* in the Argentine, was more of a genuine business partner than were whore-wives elsewhere in the Atlantic world where 'wives' tended to be less assertive with their brothel-owning 'husbands'. But the business had failed because, Goldstein alleged, she had developed expensive tastes and lost all 'his' money. The real story may, however, have been more complex since the Trautmans were an especially powerful family in the Buenos Aires underworld and he may have run foul of rival gangsters.[27] In any event, Charteris and Harris made it difficult for them to regain their footing in an over-traded market. At one stage Trautman was reduced to trawling the streets for clients under the name 'Salisbury' and paying protection money to Harris, who passed on a cut to Charteris.[28] A developing monopoly restricted entry to the market, and when Goldstein met Charteris in a bar in District Six he warned him that his operation was becoming like Tammany Hall.[29] Goldstein, too, was forced to circumvent Charteris and took to professional gambling – an activity that fell into the province of Lorimer and Detectives Easton and Bassett.

A friendship between Goldstein and Silver – based on common resentments – resulted. They tried to stay within the penumbra of the CID and avoid members of the Charteris–Harris syndicate but it was not always easy since the police had the run of the city and their otherwise separate worlds collided at the racetrack. Goldstein, a bookmaker, and Silver, whose provincial childhood left him with some knowledge of horses, spent a good deal of time and effort following the races.[30] The problem was that the morality police were using the races to disguise their ill-gotten gains. Osberg was so interested in 'very good horses' that he had stables built, while Charteris cultivated the image of an especially lucky punter. These overlapping pursuits later became so embarrassing that Charteris had to speak to Silver about it.[31]

The danger of criminal interests short-circuiting was not confined to chance meetings at the races. Forced to look beyond large-scale organised prostitution, Goldstein and Silver started exploring the possibilities of making money from the faro or 'stuss' houses located in District

Six. Their intermediary was Silver's former enforcer in the American Club, Wilf/Wulf Witkofsky. Witkofsky and his whore-wife, having discovered that the city was over-traded, had argued over who should be first to leave before they linked up in London. In the end she had left and Witkofsky, like Silver, was reduced to card-sharping and gambling. In January 1902, Witkofsky outlined their plight in a letter to Rosie Woolf:

> If I had gone to London when you were in Cape Town by what percent would we have been better off? It would not have cost me so much without having any pleasure. You must not be surprised that I have spent so much money. One walks about the town, have no place to go to, and where ever one goes it costs money, and if we [Silver and Witkofsky] did not play cards, I should have been where Lizzie [Rachel Laskin] is [Valkenberg Asylum]. A man, who does not care for his wife [like Silver], does not trouble about it, but I have only to think of the moment when I should receive a letter and when I do not receive any I go nearly mad.
>
> I have spent very much money in Cape Town. I at least lose it in cards. But you do not spend your money, you do not lose your money in cards, but you waste it. I would not have so much aggravation if you did not spend your money on such foolishness. You sent me with Adele, a present. I know it cost money, but I tramped it under foot and threw it in the dirt box. And so all your money will go . . . No further news from me, your never forgetting husband who sends you his compliments and who kisses you from the distance. Wolf Wilkoski [*sic*]. Joe [Silver] sends his compliments.[32]

Despite his disapproval of the way in which Laskin had been treated, Witkofsky helped ease Goldstein and Silver into his illegal gaming circles. Smart and very experienced, it was not long before they were in demand as bankers in faro games at the busier, dock end of District Six. But not even that was unproblematic. Successful gambling operations needed specialised premises and the most suitable houses were already under the control of the ubiquitous Harris, Frankie Ricardi and Issy Roytowski.[33]

So another vexing paradox arose. Goldstein and Silver resorted to gambling out of financial weakness, in the hope of raising the capital that would allow them to get into organised prostitution, while Charteris and Harris's financial strength – derived from brothels – made them think about diversifying into professional gambling. An underlying convergence was taking place between seemingly discrete areas of special-isation. When Witkofsky opened a gaming house of his own, he had to turn to Harris for premises and ended up paying protection money to Charteris.[34] No matter how hard Captain Lorimer and his CID informers strove to stay within their own circle, some hidden force kept dragging them into the orbit of the morals squad. The resulting East European dominance of increasingly integrated underworld activities makes it easier to understand why, in 1902, betting, gaming and dis-orderly houses were later lumped together in omnibus legislation. What the new law failed to do, however, was to head off the collision of the planets that eventually occurred.

No matter what direction Silver turned in, his plight worsened. Gambling, informing, loan-sharking, liquor-selling and pimping were insufficient to make ends meet. The £7 a month he had to make for the upkeep of Laskin crippled him. He even talked to Philip Polikansky, a respected tobacco manufacturer, about the possibility of doing work that his mother, Hannah, had once done – selling cigarettes on commis-sion. By late 1901, the demands of Rigg were unbearable and he wrote to the Resident Magistrate requesting that the amount he was expected to pay each month be reduced. But the magistrate took advice from Wale Street, and Lorimer and Easton both let him down. 'I cannot think of recommending a man of Silver's class to receive any conces-sion whatever,' wrote Lorimer, who was having difficulty controlling his informer. And throughout these troubled times Silver knew that just a few hundred miles away was an arrogant attorney who owed him £100. Lezard's contempt reminded him: 'The Devil makes his Christmas pies of lawyers' tongues and clerks' fingers.'[35]

But it is at the worst of times that things turn, almost imperceptibly, for the better. Towards the end of 1901, while sharing a meal with prostitutes at Koskes's boarding house, or drinking the imported German beer he favoured with pimps in District Six, Silver chanced upon two snippets of information. The first was about Daniel Roach, a burglar who was later to play an important role in Silver's sweep through sleepy southern colonies. Roach, a ship's carpenter from Hartford, Connecticut, took a room in Chapel Street, District Six, in mid-1901, having just completed nine months' hard labour for shop-breaking in Monmouth, Wales.[36] Despite a Catholic upbringing, Roach, like many in the fraternity, harboured no anti-Semitic prejudices and linked up with a dapper English Jew by the name of George Beck.[37] Between them they soon knew all the Jewish fences in the quarter, including Marks Levy, who had once run a gaming house in Houndsditch.[38] Roach, who operated under a bewildering array of aliases with flashy Irish touchs, had precisely the credentials that appealed to Silver.

The second was about Leon Alexander, a pimp and white slaver with an unusual love of music. Alexander, a Russo-Pole, was to have an immediate effect on Silver's fortunes. Alexander was part of a *ménage à trois*, living with two sisters who hailed from Odessa.[39] Within months of their arrival in the Cape he, his 'wife' Dora and 'sister-in-law' Hannah, were running a string of cheap non-racial brothels around the docks and by late 1901 were being investigated for having lured a naïve nineteen-year-old woman, who objected to taking African men as clients, into a life of white slavery.[40] Alexander, however, also had an interest in diamonds and it was that which drew him to Silver's attention. What follows is partly conjecture since Lorimer and Easton, anxious to protect their informant, never mentioned Silver by name, choosing to refer to the man who put them in touch with Alexander only as 'the third party'. But the 'third party' fits the preceding and subsequent history of Joseph Silver so completely – no, so perfectly – that there can be no doubt that it was him.

In January 1902, the 'third party' informed the CID that Alexander, armed and reputedly dangerous, was in search of illicit diamonds. Lorimer contacted his counterparts in Kimberley, who sent detectives Murray and Saunders south to work with Easton. The 'third person' introduced Murray, posing as a De Beers overseer, to Alexander and it was agreed that they would meet at the White House Hotel the following day to conclude the deal. Murray, who had sealed several diamonds into a bar of soap, met Alexander as agreed, sold the diamonds to him, accepted his money, and then left. Easton and Saunders moved in on the armed suspect, arrested Alexander, and confiscated the money. The entire operation went off without a hitch. The detectives were delighted and there was a sequel in the local magistrates' court when Leon Alexander was sentenced to two years' imprisonment with hard labour – a sentence confirmed, on appeal, in the Cape Town Supreme Court on 24 April 1902.[41]

Alexander's prosecution was a triumph for Lorimer and the CID. It was also a significant, but ambiguous, achievement for the 'third man' since betrayal did not lend itself to repetition. Silver, already marginalised by the Charteris–Harris ring had, in effect, also worked himself out of a job as a CID informer. At about the time Alexander's sentence was being confirmed in the Supreme Court, Silver suggested to Lorimer that he get him a position in the CID at Kimberley. This was not simply ghetto *chutzpah*, it was part of a more grandiose notion harking back to his earlier role as an agent and ultimately attributable to his underlying neurosyphilis. Frozen out of a career in Cape Town, he now saw himself as a 'secret policeman' in Kimberley.[42]

His timing was as good as his reasoning. He was detecting changes in the political climate that presaged the coming of the Betting Houses, Gaming Houses and Brothels Suppression Act later that year. Commercial sex was about to be confronted by a set of new problems. The real market for prostitutes lay in the industrial north, and a sleepy port city was best left to Charteris and Harris.[43] It was a matter of time before the military relinquished control of mining centres and the richest prize would then fall to those who had first muscled their way back into the market. The only problem was that Silver no longer enjoyed easy access to his compatriots in what had once been the American Club.

Silver knew that everything now depended on the Philadelphia-born Lorimer and used his Bowery Boy accent to underscore their common American roots. He may also have exploited one of the captain's personal weaknesses since a few years later Lorimer, too, was confined to the Valkenberg Asylum with syphilis, and indeed died there in 1913. He nagged Lorimer remorselessly. When the offer finally did come it felt like the day on which he was discharged at the Old Bailey. Lorimer would get the military authorities to grant Silver a permit to travel north. The terms of the job beggared belief. He would be officially employed as a policeman, assisting Kimberley detectives by acting as an informant and illicit diamond buying trap. This meant, as Captain Lorimer reluctantly admitted some months later, that he would have 'to associate with very bad characters'.[44] No problem there. In return he would receive a housing allowance of £11 a month and a salary of £100 a month! This exceeded what a constable on the beat earned in a year.[45]

In May 1902, Silver boarded the 'up' train in one of the starkest reversals of fortune imaginable. Three years earlier he had been boss of the American Club, the mastermind of organised crime on the Witwatersrand, with tentacles stretching into Britain, eastern Europe and the United States. Eighteen months later, having been convicted of white slavery and sodomy, he had been down and out on the diamond fields from which he had been banished under military escort. Now, dressed in the gentlemanly mode he favoured, he was a plainclothes officer of the law. How he processed the implications of his metamorphosis is impossible to know. Part of the problem lay in the hopelessly skewed Jekyll and Hyde components of his personality: a poorly developed impulse to do good was swamped by the evil of his anti-social proclivities. As 'policeman', he found it impossible to resist extorting money or indulging in other criminal behaviour, while as 'criminal' the need to close down the opposition and settle scores by providing information to the police was almost overwhelming. But the paradise of paradox was beckoning; he was in a position, paid for by the state, which demanded that he be criminal and policeman simultaneously.

Rational, without delusions of the sort on display in Valkenberg, he must have known he would have difficulty maintaining this balance. But was it meaningful to distinguish between criminals and policemen in the world he inhabited? Did not Samuel Lorimer and others like him – all struggle with the same problem? What divided 'right' from 'wrong'? Was it not all a matter of the angle from which you approached things? Only one thing can be known with certainty. As the train eased into Kimberley Station, one vendetta had long been in place: with Lezard.

XII

KIMBERLEY–BLOEMFONTEIN
1902

I then said; 'I hear that Bloemfontein was swarming with Peruvians'. He denied this . . . but he called on the Assistant Provost Marshal who said my information was 'absolutely correct', that there were between 300 and 400 of them now in Bloemfontein. They either walk (one had tramped from De Aar!) or they bribe the railway officials at Norvals' Pont, or they dress in khaki and bribe soldiers to let them travel in trucks: the A.P.M. says that as he catches them he sends them back, some after a dose of imprisonment. I begged the Governor to assist us in Johannesburg by doing all he could to clear them out.

Alfred Lord Milner, *Diary*, 11 June 1900

SILVER'S fleeting encounter in Cape Town with the manufacturer, Polikansky had reminded him of his mother, a 'tobacco merchant', and in Kimberley he adopted the status of 'cigarette salesman' to hide his role as undercover agent. Under police surveillance, he hired a house at the ragged end of town and undertook his official duties reasonably well. It is true that the Kimberley police were never satisfied with his very uneven performance, but he nevertheless left them on terms which he portrayed as being 'good' to the police in Bloemfontein weeks later. Indeed, when some years after his departure from Kimberley a detective gave misleading evidence against him in a Cape Town court, implying that he had only used his diamond fields property as a brothel, the Chief Detective in Griqualand promptly wrote an unsolicited letter to the secretary of the Cape Law Department setting the official record straight.[1]

He had, however, returned with more on his mind than cigarettes and diamonds. Within days, he retained Coghlan & Coghlan to press Lezard for details of the legal costs incurred in the period leading up to his expulsion from the city. Throughout May and June 1902, his attorney prodded Lezard, sending him letters asking, then demanding, an account. Lezard responded by freezing, pen poised. More prodding followed and by late July Lezard could bear it no longer and he put pen to paper. 'I must now give you notice,' he wrote 'that, unless your client forthwith takes steps to enforce his threatened action, I shall make application to the High Court for an order for perpetual silence against him.'[2] Coghlan had to make the next move. His client, litigious and seldom on the right side of the law, sensed they could not be denied the relief they sought. Like most gangsters, he relished the opportunity to have his rights publicly endorsed. He instructed Coghlan to retain an advocate and issued a summons.

The case was heard in mid-September, two weeks after his contract with the police had ended and final judgement was delivered only in mid-December, by which time he was at an advanced stage of withdrawal from Kimberley and well into the next phase of his extraordinary migration. On the first occasion, the Judge President found for the plaintiff and ordered Lezard to present his client with a detailed account of services and fees. When Lezard produced his statement, the court found that instead of money being owed to the plaintiff, the defendant was owed a sum of £52. At the second hearing, the court ordered Silver to pay the attorney the sum as determined, a recording fee and the substantial legal costs of the defendant.[3]

It was a predictable, if not a pretty, outcome. In keeping with his generally more cautious approach, Silver gave thought to his change of career. Shortly after receiving his first salary from the police, he took the unusual step of sending Rigg £10 towards the upkeep of Rachel Laskin. At first glance this might be construed as part of a desire to make a new start, as concern for his common law wife. In retrospect, however, it had little to do with that. Sensing the end of the war and the coming of British hegemony throughout the region, it was a necessary precaution to ensure that his wider field of operation was not compromised. Failure to keep up payments for Laskin would eventually have come to the notice of the police, leading to legal complications that might jeopardize his chances of returning to Cape Town.[4]

His formal employment in Kimberley, one of arguably two formal jobs he held in his life, lasted four months. During that time he helped trap two illicit diamond buyers but his depositions were so unreliable that, by the end of August 1902, the Detective Department saw no further point in employing him. But the closing of one door saw the opening of another. The signing of the peace treaty, on 31 May 1902, signalled the advent of a new era and the British, keen to show signs of a return to normality, lifted martial law in the adjacent Orange River Colony two weeks after Silver lost his position. The road to Bloemfontein, and perhaps even the Rand, was opening. A move to the Orange River Colony would give him a chance to regroup his forces prior to re-entering the Transvaal, a country from which he had been banished by the Kruger government but never by a British administration. It was time to embark on coastal recruitment before resuming business inland. In Cape Town, pimps and prostitutes were unsettled by the measures in Merriman's morality bill. With some cash and a few family members to draw on, Silver sensed opportunity. He telegraphed Jack, suggesting he go to Johannesburg to assess the situation and then instructed the faithful Anker to proceed at once to Bloemfontein.

Silver went to Cape Town and flitted about Koskes's boarding-house and other promising sites. It did not require much more than the advance of a train fare to recruit Sarah Rosenblatt and a few other war-weary prostitutes to his expeditionary force. He was in a hurry, keen to get up-country before the rest of the fraternity awoke to the fury of the approaching Merriman storm and fled north. But the women, who needed plausible stories to convince the military, risked being intercepted by rival pimps if they were left unaccompanied, so he nosed around 'Peruvian' circles in search of a suitable escort. William Hirschberg was the man for the job. Silver knew him from the Rand, where he had once sold illicit liquor to Africans and been convicted of robbery. They had met again in Kimberley where Hirschberg, too, had been deported as an undesirable. Amazingly, these difficulties had not disqualified him from finding employment in the Special Cape Police as a photo enlarger.[5] Hirschberg aspired to owning a brothel and hoped to link up with a brother in Johannesburg, who had breezed into the country after a series of breathtaking adventures in the Far East. Silver gave him £25, told him to proceed to the junction at Naauwpoort where he would collect yet more prostitutes from East London and then escort the entire party to Bloemfontein.[6]

With Hirschberg as manager-pimp of one brothel, he looked around for a woman of spirit to manage a second house. Whether Hannah Vygenbaum had already left Scotch Jack when Silver approached her, or whether it was his renewed interest that sparked their separation is unclear but, either way, it deepened his and Jacobs's hatred of one another.[7] Vygenbaum, with some capital and by then working as 'Annie Alford', was no pushover. In the end he had to deceive her in order to procure her support. He offered to marry her and agreed to her taking a half-share of any profits in their business. When told that insane 'Lizzie Josephs'/Rachel Laskin had never legally been his wife, and unaware of his earliest marriage to Hannah Opticer back in Lambeth in 1895, she agreed to the move north.[8]

But Silver was in an awkward position. His bride-to-be believed that he was single, while the clerk at Valkenberg and the Cape Town police believed he was married to Laskin. To avoid a second, apparently biga-mous marriage, he could not risk getting married in the city. Undeterred, he bought a ring and persuaded Vygenbaum to get married on the far side of the peninsula, on the False Bay coast, at the old naval base of Simonstown. On 14 October 1902 they were married before a magis-trate who had witnessed many a sailor's wedding. Silver, a thirty-four-year-old 'bachelor' from Kimberley gave his occupation as 'agent' while Annie Alford, twenty-eight, was a spinster of Cape Town. He signed the register in a bold hand and she, in unsteady Hebrew script, wrote something approximating 'Hannah'. The bride was given away by a prostitute he knew from New York and Johannesburg, Annie Schwartz, a mother of two, who signed the register using the more matronly name of Mrs Lakfish.[9]

They went back to District Six and a day later, accompanied by Sarah Rosenblatt, Kitty de Lange and one other, boarded the up train. In Bloemfontein, Silver, his wife and two 'sisters' checked into the Phoenix Hotel. Anker, unable to attend the wedding because of prior business commitments, was already living in a boarding-house in Fraser Street.[10]

The crescent-shaped Orange River Colony which sprawled over the arable high plains of southern Africa was a world apart from the gold-fields 300 miles north, or the diamond fields a hundred miles west. Devoted to grain and livestock farming, it was the agricultural heart-land of the highveld region, struggling to define its boundaries in the belief that, one day, a nation would follow. Its capital, harbouring the nationalist dreams of sullen Afrikaner landowners and voiceless black peasants, was located in the south of the new colony. As with most political mirages, Bloemfontein tried to make up in size and order for what it lacked in economic substance. Conceived of as a capital in the 1840s, its broad streets and large squares bore testimony to cheap land. The inner core, consisting of fifteen blocks running north–south and perhaps ten stretching east-west, was slow to develop. Although the telegraph had linked it to Kimberley in 1874, not even its electrical impulses detected economic charge until gold was discovered by its republican neighbour in the mid-1880s. When the railway eventually reached Bloemfontein in 1890, its citizens, perhaps for the first time, became aware that they were part of a spinal column stretching from Cape Town to Johannesburg, and the town developed more rapidly.

By 1903, there was a rustic majesty to the capital of the former Boer Republic. The inner city with its gnarled trees hosted two-storeyed sandstone buildings boasting arches, clock towers and gently curving windows. But there was a disconcerting quality to it. Large gaps between municipal and state buildings reflected the optimism of town planners let loose amidst too much space. Amongst the official buildings were a few hotels: solid two-storey constructions with pitched corrugated-iron roofs and wrought-iron balustrades on upper floors from behind which peered wooden sashed windows. Nearby, shops squatted beneath yet more corrugated iron, some with their names painted in large letters across the roof. The arrival of the up and down trains each day, bringing mail and visitors, was as close as the place got to having a life. The town aspired to being a dignified small state capital with gravitas.[11]

By 1903, there were 15,500 European residents living in bungalow-type houses; the more stately ones outlined by large shaded verandas. Not even the new imperial overlords bothered to count the Africans who, as in most South African towns, lived in a 'location' on the outskirts of the town. But even the figure of 15,500 had been inflated by war, since fully 3,500 were bored soldiers waiting to be transported home and demobilised. The town's small commercial and professional elite welcomed the Tommies' spending power, but was more interested in re-establishing its relationship with the agriculturalists and black labourers of the surrounding countryside. The white farmers offered long-term stability, had a suitably deferential attitude towards townsfolk and made good use of the churches and well-regarded schools.[12]

A Jewish community of about sixty families consisted of the usual acculturated Anglo or German elements. Although without the services of a rabbi, or even a synagogue, the Jews met regularly in an unused Sabbatarian chapel or the town hall; they were led by a J.H. Levy, a respected ex-Dubliner who served as their warden. Respectable members of middle-class trading families, for whom the presence of Peruvians was a great embarrassment, they knew little, if anything, of an urbanised universe that had spawned Jewish gangsters, pimps, prostitutes and white slavers. The news that a man of Silver's ilk was trying to buy or hire a house in the town would have been rather like being told that the Tsar was in search of a *shul*.[13]

For several days the visitors in the Phoenix did nothing untoward. The ladies, like most Victorians, spent their time indoors while Silver, assuming responsibility for his party, familiarised himself with the layout of the town. He took note of the pedestrian flows and showed some interest in the principal stores and their wares. Most daytime activity centred on the railway station, at the east end of the town, while at night the shopping area, to the west, had a deathly hush. Reassured that the town would be viable as a temporary base, he took the up train for a daring dash into Johannesburg to visit his brother Jack.[14] They discussed business and he told Jack that in Bloemfontein he had spotted Regina Weinberg, the fifteen-year-old that Jack had seduced in London. Shortly before the war she had taken up with an American pimp, Samuel Wax, and accompanied him to the coast as a refugee. Jack, however, considered her to be his property. The journey back to Bloemfontein occasioned no problems, suggesting that the military permit system was working very imperfectly.[15]

'Houses of ill fame' were no novelty in Bloemfontein. Three months before Silver set foot in the place, the Commissioner of Police noted that a dozen premises were suspected of being used for 'immoral purposes'.[16] With every sixth or seventh adult in town a soldier, it was hardly surprising. The brothels were low-key, amateurish operations run in residential backwaters by marginalised women working without pimps. But Silver had his usual formula in mind – another New-York-style low-price, high-turnover operation run by professionals for a multi-racial clientele. His business therefore needed to be in the town centre, where pimps could contact their clients. The middle class was horrified by the arrogance of the American gangsters who took over their town and destroyed the 'cloistered quiet of Bloemfontein'.[17] The new business was so crass that its impact was felt even by other crooks. Before October's end Silver had bought a house in Fichardt Street, off

Baumann Square, near the station and close to the former chapel where Jews gathered for *shabbes*.[18] Like his *maison verte* in Johannesburg, the premises were painted green and sublet to partners at a rental of more than £30 a month at a time when most tenants were paying just £8–£10 a month for a house.[19]

His partners were Annie Vygenbaum, – now restyled 'Annie Bloom' or 'Annie Bloem' in the manner that appealed to the punster in him – Sarah Rosenblatt and her pimp. Bernard Struzack, an irascible Pole Silver had met in District Six, had a liking for pictures of the sort that appealed to most men and few women, styled himself a 'Director of Cinematographs', and owned a circular panorama which the viewer stepped into from below to savour the images.[20] They agreed that, managed properly, the panorama, supported by nearby barbershop and saloon proprietors, could divert a stream of clients to the Green House and decided that a shooting gallery only three blocks from the station was the ideal location. Silver, still flush with funds, negotiated terms with the owner, Mr Church, who later became alarmed when, seeking to conceal their links to the panorama, the Poles insisted that they were the real, and sole, owners of the shooting gallery.[21]

With a front in Maitland Street secured in his own name and his wife, Annie Bloem, in Fichardt Street, Silver set about consolidating his interests in a manner reminiscent of his *ante bellum* frenzy. Intent on a monopoly, he scouted around for a second house and eventually found one in St George's Street, not far from the corner with Fraser Street. He bowled the owner over by signing a lease for an unfurnished property, at £25 a month, for three months.[22] In order to avoid being caught as the lessee of premises used as a brothel, he sublet it to the impecunious William Hirschberg. Keen to get the second house up and running, he lent Hirschberg some money and arranged for two Cape women with mock-English names, Nellie Moore and Rosie Cleghorn, to be issued permits. Hirschberg, given five pounds, was sent to Norval's Pont where he collected the women before escorting them across to Bloemfontein.[23] But Hirschberg had difficulty paying the rent and so he, too, looked around for a business partner. His choice of 'Scotch Jack' Jacobs was unfortunate. But it was a business not a personal decision and it worked for some weeks in late 1902.[24]

Working feverishly Silver had set up three businesses, staffed by specialists, in a matter of weeks. It remained only to safeguard his investments by taking out insurance of the usual kind; this took just days. More plausible than ever as a former policeman until recently deployed in Kimberley, he won over Detective John Egley of the CID. He persuaded Egley that he was an unparalleled source of information on the recent influx of unsavoury characters into a town more accustomed to pigs and ploughs than pimps and prostitutes. Although he later denied it, he was probably also behind a petition which demanded that Egley's friend, Detective William Reid, be promoted. As we shall see, it was not the only petition he promoted in *post bellum* South Africa. At a time when there were few representative structures in place for the white electorate, petitions and memorials were widely resorted to in the hope of influencing the British authorities. By November 1902, there were elements in the CID who believed that Silver was an ally in the fight against crime in general, and vice in particular. It was a dangerous game that had cost several policemen their careers.[25]

The insurance worked well for ten to twelve weeks; not least because the premium was so easy to pay. Every week in late 1902 saw the up train disgorging Americanised pimps or Russo-Polish white slavers waiting for the magical day when they could continue their journey to golden Johannesburg. Most had criminal records and he rifled through their past, removing any useful fragments that could be auctioned off to the police. For a man bearing deep resentments it was payback time for those who had shunned him in District Six. He was ruthless, betraying even some of the low-level escorts, messengers or scouts that he was intent on using in his own ventures. Hymie Bernstein (American Club 'grocer'), Samuel Grohus ('no occupation') Benjamin Friedman ('no occupation'), William Hirschberg (photo enlarger), Joseph Kollerstein (landlord), Mathew Horwitz ('picture dealer') and Struzack ('Director of Cinematographs') were all exposed.[26]

There were other gangsters, some with international experience, hoping to do a little business locally before moving on. Scotch Jack Jacobs, by then known as Martin Johnson, was one. Samuel Wax, who had fooled the military authorities into thinking that he was a *smous*, a hawker, working for the South African Trading Company, was another.[27] But right in the midst of this northerly migrating horde were some of the most notorious white slavers of all in the Atlantic world; men with reputations at least as daunting as Silver's own. Not one of them escaped his notice and a month later, still currying favour, he passed on their names to the authorities. But these names meant little to ill-informed police in a farming centre and they earned him little credit. His Judas list, a veritable 'who's who' of national and international sex traders, included that of Albert Dickenfaden, the so-called King of the White-Slave Traffickers. Amongst lesser known names were also some belonging to 'thiefs and pimps' who had crossed him personally.[28]

An influx of gangsters on this scale could not fail to attract the attention of the public at large. In bars and barbershops, at the shooting gallery, on street corners and in the Market Square, the talk of the town was all of pimps, the panorama and the houses in Fichardt and St George's Street. Local Jews faced the classic anti-Semitic dilemma – if they denounced godless East European Jews, male renegades of Tsarist oppression and clerical hatred, they would be seen as disloyal and, if they failed to do so, the sins of the minority would be attributed to the ethnicity and religion of the majority. The community decided to tackle the problem head on; a choice less easy to make in large cities like Buenos Aires, Cape Town, New York or Rio de Janeiro. The decision was prompted, in large measure, by two exceptional community activists.[29]

In November 1902, Samuel Goldreich, the Anglicised founding father of the South African Zionist Federation, checked into the Masonic Hotel. A man of strong views, Goldreich spoke to communal leaders including Henry Levy, proprietor of the Bloemfontein Mineral Water Works, 'Official Contractors to H.M.'s Imperial Forces and Hospitals'. Levy told him there were several pimps based in Sach's boarding-house, and that properties belonging to Jews were being used as brothels. Goldreich wrote to the Colonial Secretary, H.F. Wilson, complaining about the American pimps: 'The expulsion of this vermin is not only highly meritorious, but would be gratifying to the Jewish community here, and for the South African Zionist Federation.'[30]

But the wheels of British administration turned no faster than those of the Boer bureaucracy. A month later, Levy had to remind Wilson about Goldreich's plea. Underterred by official inaction, Levy and the community took the matter into their own hands. Readers of the *Bloemfontein Post* were told that 'Anyone known in any way to assist in this traffic incurs public exposure and the expulsion from the congregation'.[31] Well before that point was reached, however, low-level gang war had broken out, and the press, in a manner reminiscent of the *Standard & Diggers' News* campaign in *ante bellum* Johannesburg, complained of 'A Reign of Terror'.[32]

In mid-November Silver, increasingly bombastic and self-confident, started giving more thought to a scheme to raise cash and further ingratiate himself with the CID. Even by his own standards, this plan was utterly bizarre. He confided in Hirschberg – who, as we saw, was in partnership with Scotch Jack – that he was exploring the possibility of a break-in at either Stein's, or McCulloch's, jewellery store.³³ On 21 November he took the coach to Kimberley and checked into the Johannesburg Hotel. He spent most of the next day, Saturday, closeted in discussions with George Beck and Daniel Roach, who had travelled north from Cape Town.³⁴ They debated the pros and cons of his plan but pointed out that neither of them had the funds or a military permit that would allow them to leave the Cape Colony. Beck later said that Silver told them, 'I will pay your fare and get you through without a permit.'³⁵ And somehow he did. By the following day they were all back in Bloemfontein, in the Green House.

The following morning Silver disappeared, returning at midday to take the men to lunch at a restaurant. At eleven that night, he reappeared to wake them and told them to ready themselves. He produced a parcel containing the 'jemmies, drills, chisels etc which form the outfit of the up-to-date burglar'. Beck expressed reservations about their safety, but Silver 'took out a revolver and said, "You need not be afraid, I have this with me"'. They then set off for McCulloch's, in Maitland Street.³⁶ A back door was crudely forced; a second jemmied, with little more subtlety. They broke open several boxes and removed brooches, rings and watches but the real effort came with the breaking open of the safe, from which a 'large amount of cash' was taken. 'Their operations extended over some considerable time', carrying on well past midnight. Then, in the small hours of the morning, there was an unusual occurrence. That two patrolmen should walk past a jewellery store at that hour was understandable. But that, of all the policemen in Bloemfontein, those two should be plainclothes officers is more difficult to explain. That one of those officers should be the very man that a public petition was then punting for promotion, Detective Reid, and the other his superior officer, Inspector Richard Ovendale, nudges coincidence towards conspiracy. It reeked of New York City, 1893; of Detective Charles Jacobs.³⁷

Noticing a light on in the shop, the detectives went to the rear of the premises. They saw that a door had been forced and, listening carefully, heard noises indicating that the intruders were still at work. One or both of them lost their nerve. Unwilling to confront the burglars, they sent for reinforcements and a 'strong posse' was deployed in 'an ambush at the back of the premises'. If there was a conspiracy, somebody had parted from the script. The intruders emerged, saw the assembled force and charged directly at the officers, unsettling their men. 'A rather rough melee ensued', the three burglars attempted to escape and a policeman panicked. A shot rang out but, instead of finding an intruder, the bullet struck Ovendale, leaving him with a slight flesh wound. Beck and Roach were overpowered but Silver, pulling clear, bolted down Maitland, doubled into St Andrew's, then hared off towards the nearest safe haven. The posse, including Ovendale, gave chase but 'Bill Sykes was a fine runner and succeeded in making good his escape'. Silver had taken refuge in his and William Hirschberg's brothel, in St George's Street.[38]

The press – reacting in a way perhaps envisaged by the conspirators – found much to commend in the police work although the editor of the *Post* became a touch over-enthused. Two days after the arrest of the hapless Beck and Roach, he devoted his leading article to 'The Burglary'. 'For many weeks past', he noted, there had been 'a noticeable increase in the number of female undesirables in town' who were linked to a 'small gang of professional criminals' from the coastal cities and Johannesburg. That, in itself, was not necessarily bad news. 'The growing town of today,' he opined, 'cannot expect to be the same quiet *dorp* of former days.' It was, therefore, gratifying to record the 'smart denouement of Monday night's incident'. He was proud 'to congratulate the Police Department' and 'particularly the Criminal Investigation branch of it, on their diligence and ability in the public service'.[39]

These were strong sentiments, swiftly expressed. In a small community, where an editor interacted with civic leaders and readers on a regular, face-to-face basis, unfounded opinion could become the cause of embarrassment. The views came to haunt the editor and caused him to assume a more prominent role in the events that followed than might otherwise have been the case. Part of his predicament could be traced back directly to his editorial, which had failed to address the question that was on everyone's lips: who was the 'third man'? In theory there were any number of people who could determine the missing man's identity – the detectives, Beck and Roach, or their accomplices before and after the event. Most people would, like the editor, have placed their faith in the police but neither Reid nor Ovendale, both trained observers, had recognised the third man. Beck and Roach who, as we shall see, had almost immediately been given assurances that somebody was looking after their interests, adhering to their professional code, failed to put a name to the man until almost Christmas. Nor, for several weeks, did anybody else come up with the identity of the missing man. The fraught – almost terror-stricken – silence that descended over the town after the burglary was, of course, engineered by that very elusive third man.

His rules were clear: carrots for the strong, sticks for the weak. Having shaken off his pursuers, he had taken stock of the situation. The most important thing was to ensure that Beck and Roach did not lose their nerve and force the hand of the detectives. The best way of achieving this was to ensure that they were provided with a good legal defence that could not be traced back to him. He got Hirschberg to approach attorney J.P. van Zyl to defend them. Van Zyl agreed and Beck and Roche, true to their calling, remained silent as the grave. The third man was safe.[40]

XIII

BLOEMFONTEIN
1903

There is no occupation that fails a man more completely
than that of a secret agent of police. It's like your horse
suddenly falling dead under you in the midst of an uninhabited and thirsty plain.

Joseph Conrad, *The Secret Agent*

THE great silence lasted a month, from 24 November, the night of the
burglary, until 23 December 1902. For four weeks the police made no
progress in identifying let alone arresting the third man. His brothels in
Fichardt and St George's Streets operated unhindered, and when law-
abiding Jews in neighbouring houses complained to the owners, they
were told that the 'law can be bought'. Those silly enough to persist in
complaining were 'in fear of their lives'. Hirschberg, already an accessory, and of a nervous disposition, kept quiet as did his/their partner,
'Scotch Jack' Jacobs. Outside the jail, where the third man operated with
ease, his will reigned. But, inside the jail, where it was difficult to penetrate and he was confronted by other professionals, his influence was
muted. Beck and Roach fretted as Christmas approached. On 23 December
they cracked, making statements naming Silver as the missing third man.[1]

He now faced the problem, as identified by Yeats, that 'Things fall
apart; the centre cannot hold', and continues, more ominously, 'Mere
Anarchy is loosed upon the world'. Denying his role in the burglary in
the face of Beck and Roach's admissions was pointless. The best he
could do was to try to minimise his part in it. That was going to be
difficult given that there were two others who knew that he was an

accessory. Hirschberg and Scotch Jack were both of a volatile disposition; each as capable of perfidious behaviour as he was. From the moment it was known that Beck and Roach had capitulated, it was a matter of time before one of the remaining parties lost his composure. Feeling the pressure, the cobra struck before the mongoose could lunge.

He spent Christmas and the days thereafter preparing as any lawyer would, deciding on strategy and tactics, finding witnesses and putting them through their paces. The object of the exercise was to remove Hirschberg, Scotch Jack and Samuel Wax from circulation by providing the police with affidavits testifying that they were pimps living off the earnings of the prostitutes in Fichardt and St George's Streets. Not only would this keep them busy but, if they were charged and found guilty, it would help discredit their evidence in subsequent court appearances. Annie Bloom, whom nobody knew as his quasi-legal wife, would testify that her former lover, Scotch Jack, was a pimp. 'Nellie Moore' of St George's Street, would lay a parallel charge against Hirschberg. Silver and Struzack would buttress the women's statements with affidavits swearing, truthfully, that both men were pimps.

On 31 December, while Hirschberg and friends were ushering in a night of revelry Silver and his friends descended on the police station. Avoiding Egley and Reid, they gave their statements to Inspector J.H. Bromley. Bloom claimed that Scotch Jack, alias 'Martin Johnson', had been her pimp for eight months and that she had 'been giving him money out of [her] earnings the whole time', but that two weeks earlier he had 'kicked her so severely' that she had been 'obliged to go to hospital'. If the assault could be corroborated – which it may well have been – it would be interesting to know who the assailant really was. Nellie Moore's tale was as sad. Hirschberg 'had been living with [her] for the past six or seven months', and she had given him her 'earnings all this while'. Struzack, short and sharp, stated that all three men were pimps and provided their addresses. Silver stated that 'all three of the men [were] ex-convicts' and that at 'the present time they are living in brothels and on the proceeds of prostitution'. He gave details of their criminal records, stating, 'I have been in the employ of the Police at Cape Town and also at Kimberley, receiving good discharges from both – I only left the service in Kimberley in November this year.'²

Incredibly, Bromley knew nothing about Silver, a man whom police in Cape Town, Kimberley and Johannesburg knew as little about. The four affidavits, oozing lies, were handed to the prosecutor and – in a town where a month had elapsed in a case where an officer had been wounded and no arrest effected – it now took only hours to act. The echoes of the New Year were almost still audible when Hirschberg, Scotch Jack and Wax were charged with living off the proceeds and 'frequenting houses of ill-fame'. The devil's dictation ensured that 'Mere anarchy was loosed upon the world'.

Trapped between the state and Satan, the pimps were in an unenviable position. In court they faced a fine or a term of imprisonment and beyond it lay unknown terrors that Judge Joe might inflict on them. They thought it best to hire a lawyer, disclose their dealings with Silver and hope, by drawing the court's attention to the hidden hand, to avoid street justice. The civic-minded R.M. Cuthbertson was their attorney. The court's first sitting, shortly after New Year's Day, was adjourned. They were arraigned for a second time before the Assistant Resident Magistrate on 5 January 1903. But Cuthbertson found it almost impossible to represent them. Scotch Jack could not contain himself: he interrupted proceedings until the magistrate had him marched to the cells for contempt of court.³

By the time the court reconvened, on 7 January, Cuthbertson had won his client's co-operation. He quizzed Bloom until it became clear that she was Silver's wife and living with him at the Green House – a revelation with potentially serious consequences. Swimming against a rising tide of untruths, he questioned Silver about the petition to get Reid promoted, but he denied all knowledge of it. He got each of the three accused to raise evidence that incriminated Silver not only in a conspiracy to get them convicted, but in the burglary at McCulloch's. But Silver was set to triumph. The prosecutor, strangely well disposed towards him, gave him the chance to counter defence evidence with damning, deceitful, testimony about the criminal records of the accused and their female consorts. Cuthbertson could not divert Magistrate Bell's eyes from the charges and, when all three of his clients were found guilty and sentenced to a fine of £20 or three months each, he gave notice of his intention to appeal.⁴

It was a messy outcome. Cuthbertson had exposed a bit of the underworld, pointed to the identity of the third man, and revealed the divisions amongst gangsters. Contrary to Silver's and CID expectations, the case against the pimps had raised rather than lowered tensions amongst the Americans in a town with too many crooks and too few cowboys. The press, playing catch-up, started harping on about a 'Reign of Terror', implying that Silver lay behind most civic ills and suggesting that 'the police [were] not altogether blameless in the matter'.[5] With a show-down imminent and bloodshed threatening, Silver and Hirschberg felt the need for more guns. Each slipped into the post office and, on separate days, telegraphed Johannesburg for reinforcements. In the week that followed the same scene twice played itself out at the station. The down train steamed in, a man with a hat alighted, picked up a leather bag, looked around to get his bearings and then spotted his brother. The pair then left the station.

Jack Lis, fresh from a charge of assaulting a woman in Port Elizabeth, was a veteran of gang warfare, having earned his spurs in the East End. In some ways, his brother's war was also his war since he had a personal grievance to settle with Samuel Wax for having appropriated Regina Weinberg, or Annie Fineberg as she now called herself.

James Hirschberg travelled as 'James Lee' although in white slaving circles he was known as 'Hirsch Japanese'. In the mid-1890s, when Britain was taking an interest in the markets of a weakened China, he had refused to serve the Tsar and gone to the Far East. With Japanese–Russian rivalry centred on acquiring eastern ports he used his language skills and found his *métier* as a Japanese spy.[6] Armed with 'several passports' he was based at Port Arthur, where the Russians detained him for four months, and had then moved to Vladivostok. When the Russians extended the Chinese Eastern Railway to Vladivostok, he retreated to Peking where he was, he said, a hotelier. When the Boxer Rebellion broke out, in 1900, he became a member of a Highland Regiment and then switched to the Welsh Fusiliers and had received 'a nasty wound in the side from a fragment of shrapnel' before leaving for southern Africa.[7]

Lee now claimed to be an agent for the Empire Tea Company, running a café on a site the American Club had once used as a brothel, and was on good terms with detectives monitoring organised prostitution on the Rand. In the year 1903, Chinese indentured labourers were first employed in the Witwatersrand gold mines and, not long thereafter, a few Japanese prostitutes appeared in Johannesburg.[8] It is clear that 'Lee's' real identity was known to Silver and that his sudden arrival in town worried him.[9]

Silver continued to monitor the ebb and flow of the tide at the station compulsively, paying the same attention to detail that white slavers gave to ships entering Atlantic ports. Most up and down trains

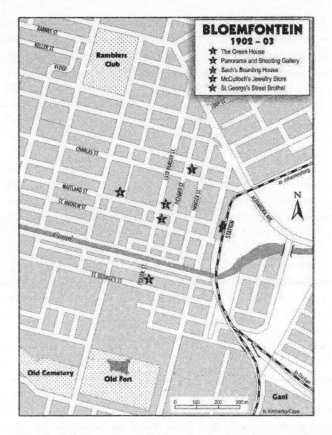

brought men who could be steered in the direction of the brothels but, on one occasion, he also intercepted an unaccompanied woman. In the second week of January he met the down train, and spotted Margaret Finn, a twenty-four-year-old Jewish prostitute. She left the station and he fell in directly behind her. When they were no longer being observed, he asked whether he could show her to 'a nice boarding house'. Realising he was a pimp, she accompanied him to the shooting gallery where, within earshot, he and Struzack had a discussion in Yiddish. He asked his partner if he considered her 'to be nice looking, and whether she could make money in his house'. Struzack did, and they went to Fichardt Street.

At the Green House, he introduced Finn to Bloom along with two other women and told her that she should start work immediately. But it was a lazy summer's afternoon and by sunset she had earned nothing. When darkness fell Bloom introduced her to a 'gentleman' visitor whom she serviced and, after that, she had a few other clients but it was a disappointing start. He reappeared around midnight and, while settling up for the day, she asked how much the 'gentleman' had paid and was told that he had been charged £5. Bloom kept back a pound for herself, handed him two, and gave Finn two. A 60 per cent overhead charge was unacceptable, and Finn told him she wanted to leave. He told her she could either stay on in the house or leave town. When she questioned his ability to control her it triggered a chilling reply, hinting at his darkest secret: '*My dear girl, if you do not remain here I will kill you, I will murder you. You don't know who I am! I am Joe Silver.*' Alarmed, she threatened him with the police and he responded, '*Police! I'm not afraid of the police; I am one of the biggest police here! They cannot do any harm to me.*' Sensing that he was capable of carrying out his threat, she retreated, stayed the night, and when the opportunity presented itself, fled. But then wisdom deserted her. Ignoring the choice she had been given, she stayed in town and found herself a place at Hirschberg's on St George's Street. It placed her squarely in the enemy camp.[10]

But he did nothing. The morning and evening press – the *Friend* and the *Post* – had been very vocal in asking why the Attorney-General and police were incapable of identifying the third man, or closing provocative sites of organised prostitution. Silver and others in the gang countered by threatening members of the press.[11] Cuthbertson and Botha, a fellow attorney, declared publicly that if the police did not act, they would bring a private prosecution against him. The authorities were in a very difficult position. If they moved against Silver they risked losing other vice prosecutions as well as the case against the two McCulloch's store burglars.[12]

Tension was reaching breaking point. The administration was looking askance at the Police Commissioner, the public and the CID were at loggerheads and rival gangs were sizing each other up. And at the heart of it all stood the Hirschberg and Silver brothers fingering holsters beneath tailor-made suits. Bloemfontein was looking like Dodge City, with armed men stalking the Market Square. The police were the first to blink. On 16 January the *Friend* reported a police spokesman as saying that several prosecutions against pimps and prostitutes were pending. Hours later, Silver was arrested on charges which, for some time, remained unclear.[13] For several days, Cuthbertson and his colleague, Botha, had been taking statements from pimps in St George's Street, hoping to launch a private prosecution. They had taken their affidavits to the police station and when the officers on duty refused to issue a warrant for Silver's arrest they had gone to the Resident Magistrate, Ashburnham, who had issued the warrant.[14]

The arrest was not unexpected, but nevertheless caused consternation in the Green House and fury at the panorama, where it was interpreted as the work of the Hirschberg faction. Struzack stormed out to make his way to St George's Street but, before he got there spotted Scotch Jack and two sidekicks on Douglas Street. He drew a knife and followed them, spraying invective until, losing all control, he charged. He aimed for the chest, they claimed, but succeeded only in wounding Jacobs in the fleshy part of the arm. Scotch Jack and the bodyguards bolted, followed by Struzack throwing stones. They retreated to the police station to lay a charge, but Struzack – as confident as he was crazy – quickly overtook them.[15]

When they got to the charge office they found Struzack engaged in animated discussion. The sergeant was in no hurry to attend to them and pointedly took a statement from Struzack first. But, even after they had made their statements it was not clear whether their assailant would be charged. When Bromley of the CID appeared, Jacobs was asked to produce his military permit and Struzack sauntered off.[16] The penny dropped. They retreated to a doctor, where Scotch Jack got his wound attended to and then sought out Cuthbertson. He advised them to tell Assistant Resident Magistrate Bell what had happened and to seek a warrant for Struzack's arrest. Bell heard them but said they would have to go to the police station to collect a warrant, which he would then sign. That, too, did not work. When they reached the charge office they found Reid, who refused to hand them a warrant without Bromley's approval. When Bromley eventually reappeared he said he would not give them a warrant since he was dealing with the matter himself.[17]

That evening the Fichardt Street gang, led by Struzack, went to the charge office where they made an energetic but unsuccessful attempt to get Silver released on bail. Bromley was running out of ideas. As senior CID officer he doubled as public prosecutor, was having to deal with the private action brought by Cuthbertson and, that afternoon, had already thwarted the wishes of a magistrate. He was out of his depth. He refused to release Silver and hurried off to consult the

Attorney-General, H. F. Blaine.[18] The Attorney-General was not happy. The jewel in the crown was a successful prosecution in the high-profile McCulloch burglary. But the administration of justice had become a circus and everything was being compromised by the mess that the CID had got itself into through its dealings with Silver. The lack of hard information on Silver had reached ridiculous proportions and Blaine resolved to remedy it. He gave Bromley some instructions and the inspector then left.

News of the Douglas Street stabbing and the sequel were greeted with outrage in the morning press and wholesale public incredulity. The *Post*, bowled over by Struzack's 'effrontery', was of the opinion that it pointed to 'a state of affairs of the most extraordinary nature' and asked if the time had not arrived for 'an inquiry . . . into the whole matter'.[19] Thoughtful citizens were still turning this over when they learned from the *Friend* that, that morning, the Attorney-General and Public Prosecutor had been involved in exchanges in court which seemed to point to special protection for Silver and to double standards. When the case was remanded for a day, Cuthbertson and Botha were amazed to learn that Silver was out on bail of £20 – an astounding development given that the St George's pimps had been denied bail when confronted with very similar charges.[20]

The big fish had wriggled free and swum away but was not yet in open water. The *Post*, having uncovered Silver's 'scandalous and flagrant' past in the old South African Republic, led the way. He was hardly clear of the court when the paper ran a damning editorial. 'The public can scarcely be expected to acquiesce patiently in the theory that Silver is being made use of to break a gang'; 'Silver *is*, in the minds of many, the gang'. The police lent 'indiscreet protection to a man whose infamies were notorious', a person who was permitted to 'purchase immunity by treachery and intrigue'. He was an *agent provocateur* who 'deliberately engineered the robbery at McCulloch's', 'suborned others to assist him', and then turned 'King's Evidence to procure their conviction and immunity for himself'. The newspaper was disgusted that the police could 'descend to the employment of such a filthy instrument as this man Silver for its purposes'. The matter reeked 'in the nostrils of the public and the sooner the law applie[d] a disinfectant the better'.[21]

A veteran of bad publicity on three continents, Silver coped with this frontal assault as best possible. The pre-judging of his motives in the *Post* was serious, but his doings in Bloemfontein were attracting press attention in neighbouring colonies. That spelt more trouble. If his past became widely known and the subject of yet more official embarrassment it would have a damaging impact on forthcoming court appearances. On 20 January, the *Post* reported that he had once been deported from Kimberley under martial law, the *Times of Natal* ran a sub-leader on 'This Unclean Creature' and, in Johannesburg, the *Star* carried items pointing to his role in the recent troubles.[22]

The Attorney-General and Public Prosecutor, shunning public and press, regrouped and struck back across a wide front. On 19 January, the day that Cuthbertson and Botha confronted Silver, they prosecuted Bloom, Rosenblatt and Kitty de Lange of the Green House for 'residing in, and assisting in the management of a brothel' and each was sentenced to a fine of £5. The action against Bloom, not known to the prosecutor or police as Silver's partner and wife, produced a most unexpected sequel.[23] Hannah Vygenbaum – variously 'Annie Alford', 'Annie Bloom' and 'Annie Silver' in the press – believed that her husband could have intervened to prevent her being prosecuted. She, too, felt betrayed and there was a sudden, if temporary, rupture in their relationship. On the afternoon she was convicted, it was reported that 'Annie Alford is to proceed against Silver in the High Court on a charge of bigamy'. But such was the web of deceit he had spun that even that action was based on the false premises that the other wife was Laskin, in Valkenberg, rather than Hannah Opticer whom he had married in London in 1895.[24]

On Tuesday, 20 January, Bromley revealed that it had been decided not to press charges in the Douglas Street stabbing case. The charge against Struzack, he claimed, was a 'trumped up one' and Martin Johnson alias 'Scotch Jack' had 'probably inflicted the wound himself'.[25] Later that day Silver was back in court facing Cuthbertson and Botha. The attorneys had recruited Regina Weinberg – Jack's disaffected 'wife' – to give evidence for the prosecution. As 'Annie Fineberg', partner of Samuel Wax, she stated that she had known Silver in Kimberley and Cape Town, and that he had always been a pimp. There were, she said, 'a number of women he [had] lived on' and then with a viciousness that could have come straight from Silver's repertoire she said that one of them 'was in the madhouse in Cape Town'.[26] Silver looked to Bromley to come to his aid, but was left stranded. During the course of the morning Blaine and Bromley had decided to cut their losses. Bromley asked for an adjournment, 'in order to procure the attendance of other witnesses at present in Johannesburg and this was granted'. Silver was released against bail already posted, but it was clear that he was on his own.[27]

Outside the court Silver noticed that he was being followed by men in plain clothes and, sensing his cause was lost, decided on flight. Ironically, it was a woman rather than a man who thwarted him. As the *Post* reported that evening: 'he was at the railway station this afternoon while the up-train was in, and apparently was about to board it, when he was handed a writ restraining him from making any use of any money deposited in the Bank of Africa in his name, or other property, pending the hearing' on a charge of bigamy.'[28] Yet, even as he was being served with Vygenbaum's writ, his CID contacts and gang members were extending his vendetta against her former lover. Blaine and Bromley, still not understanding how deeply Silver had penetrated the lower ranks of the CID, had Scotch Jack arraigned before Bell for a second time and charged with 'living on the proceeds of prostitution'.

St George's Street prostitutes and junior officers in the CID, egged on by Struzack, queued up to testify against Jacobs. Once Egley stated that he knew the accused as a pimp and had arrested him in a brothel, Cuthbertson and Botha – appearing for the defence – withdrew. Scotch Jack was left to defend himself. He pleaded with Botha to reconsider. He got the Hirschberg brothers to testify on his behalf. He had Detective Reid hauled into the box, forcing him to deny having said, 'For God's sake Jack, don't kick up any more row, but make friends with Silver. If you make friends with Silver everything will be alright, and then we can stop all the things going on in the paper.' He tried to persuade the court that 'Silver was trying to work up a case against him', and that 'all the evidence was untrue'. He argued for a remand and for bail. All to no avail. The magistrate 'was sorry the previous conviction was not a lesson to him' and sentenced him to 'three months' imprisonment with hard labour'. In the two months he had crossed Silver, Jacobs was fined, stabbed, and imprisoned.[29]

Silver, the fox, felt re-nourished. The following morning he was back before Bell, confronted by Cuthbertson and Botha's charges. His behaviour was instinctual, almost primitive. Bromley put Margaret Finn on the stand and she provided a harrowing account of what had transpired on the night when Silver had threatened to murder her. Her testimony did him great harm and his loathing of her was conveyed, as if by osmosis, to his brother Jack in the gallery. When Bromley tormented him with questions about past prison sentences it triggered a Bowery Boy reflex and he refused to answer. Bell warned him to avoid contempt of court, and to answer or risk imprisonment. He could take no more and was led to the cells for the night.[30]

The following morning, having thought the problem through, Silver was back in court. Bromley poked the same painful questions at him. Had he not been convicted of burglary in New York City and imprisoned in Johannesburg? And were the women who appeared with him in photographs placed before the court not the prostitutes Lizzie Silver and Annie Alford? He decided that wholesale perjury was the best defence and denied everything other than to agree that Alford was going to the High Court to recover £500 that she claimed to have lent him. When Bromley was done Silver fought back by trying to discredit Finn, alleging that he was the victim of a conspiracy by Beck and Roach. Nothing helped. He was found guilty and sentenced to £20 or three months' imprisonment. There was no sign of Vygenbaum, and Sarah Rosenblatt had to come up with 'the necessary sovereigns'.[31]

Presumably Silver left court angry and complained to brother Jack that pimps and a whore like Finn had ruined his career as a secret agent of police. He went to Fichardt Street, changed clothes and slipped a sandbag into his pocket. He made his way back to the centre of town and caught sight of 'Hirsch Japanese' talking to a Johannesburg-based detective. Suddenly it was clear how his past had been revealed.

James Hirschberg remembered Silver seeing him talk to the detective and then moving off in the direction of the Market Square. Near the square he hailed a cab. As he entered it, he was struck from behind by a blunt instrument. He fell, clutching his head but before he could recover received a second blow – across the face – causing his nose to spew blood. Later he claimed that he also felt sore about his neck and arms in a way that suggested that he had been kicked. A passer-by dragged off his assailant who ran off, pursued by an alert uniformed constable who caught him amongst the 'houses between Fichardt and East Burger Streets' and arrested him.[32]

Within weeks the town had witnessed a shooting, a stabbing and a sandbagging. With Blaine and Bromley slow to lead, the CID prepared the documentation for a deportation programme. But, even then, not all were convinced where the problem lay. Egley made a statement naming half a dozen pimps which, although including Struzack and most of the St George's Street gang, said nothing about the Silver family

– Joseph, Jack or Anker. It was left to the more senior CID officers to identify members of the Fichardt Street gang. 'A more dangerous man' than Silver, Inspector Ovendale argued, 'would be hard to find throughout the length and breadth of South Africa'.[33]

The press moved to repair its relationship with the administration and police, who had been involved in 'a misdirected alliance with the biggest, astutest and most unscrupulous scoundrel of the lot'. If the fourth estate 'had allowed Joe Silver and his abominable following to get a foothold in Bloemfontein without protest', it would have 'been guilty of gross and unpardonable treachery to the whole community'.[34] In truth, the press *had* played a more important role than the police in ensuring Silver's downfall. He appeared before the Assistant Resident Magistrate on 23 January, charged with assault, and again chose to defend himself. There was 'applause in court' when he was refused bail, 'but it was promptly suppressed'.[35]

Back in the cells, he called for the only attorney in town willing to defend him, J.P. van Zyl. Van Zyl was willing to deal only with legal strategy and it was left to Silver and the family to handle what needed doing outside the court. He sent a message to his brother, Jack, stressing that Margaret Finn should not be given the opportunity of giving evidence against him a second time and asking him to arrange for another low-life, Samuel Grohus to appear as a witness for the defence.

The prosecution got off to a poor start the following morning when Margaret Finn failed to appear. Nobody knew where she was and she was ruled to be in contempt of the court. Grohus popped up for the defence, alleging that it had been a 'fair fight' but presented evidence 'in a very evasive manner' and had to be called to order frequently. The accused reiterated that it had been a 'fair fight'. The bruises on Hirschberg's head, he suggested, were unintentional and could only have come from a ring he had been wearing at the time. The burden of the defence, however, fell to van Zyl. Much was made of the prosecution's inability to trace the man who had allegedly 'rescued' the victim and of the sustained press campaign argued to have prejudiced his client's case. But Bell found Silver guilty and sentenced him to three months' imprisonment. The magistrate agreed to the case being reviewed by the High Court and bail, set at a stiff £300, was paid instantly.[36]

For six days Silver skulked about town, exploring other possibilities and dealing with unfinished business. He found Vygenbaum and, in his own inimitable way, persuaded her to reach a private settlement. She abandoned her legal action to recover £500 she said he owed her and left for Cape Town. It was another straw in the wind but a final decision had to wait until Jack, now out of town, returned. He got back in time to hear the result of his brother Joe's appeal to the High Court. On 30 January 1903, Justice Fawkes held that the lower court had arrived at the correct decision and Silver was led away to serve three months' imprisonment.[37] By then he had decided that investment in the Green House warranted a three-month stay and he asked Jack to take care of his interests. It would be awkward to be locked up with Jacobs, Beck and Roach, but he was only a week away from his thirty-fifth birthday and had done time in far tougher institutions than the provincial Bloemfontein jail.

A few days later Jack Lis's earlier, out-of-town business was clarified. Margaret Finn appeared in court on 30 January, charged with contempt of court and was sentenced to a fine of 50 shillings, or seven days' imprisonment. Her testimony proved the brothers had lost none of their ability to terrorise women. On the day she was supposed to appear as a witness for the prosecution in the 'Hirsch Japanese' case, someone in Fichardt Street had threatened to kill her if she gave evidence. She left town hurriedly but the brothers were taking no chances. Jack Lis boarded the up train with her and in Johannesburg he 'dogged her footsteps to the extent that she had to take cabs to evade him'. So consistently did he stalk her that she felt she could not do without the protection of the St George's Street pimps and returned to Bloemfontein, Lis still on her tail.[38]

In the days that followed Jack Lis made frequent visits to Johannesburg, returning with prostitutes who were cycled through boarding-houses and the Green House. The police, only dimly aware that they were dealing with cousins, prepared to have Anker and Lis deported and in the second week of February they were forcibly removed from town. It left Silver without help.[39]

The British administration, relieved as an overloaded ox-wagon to encounter a stretch of downhill, gathered momentum. It used Merriman's 1902 Cape Morality Act – the same law that had sent the pimps and prostitutes scurrying north – as a template for new legislation. An Ordinance 'To provide for the Suppression of Brothels and Immorality and to Amend the Police Offences Ordinance, 1902', was promulgated in mid-March 1903. The Ordinance contained a clause which recorded the one-time terror of Whitechapel's passage through the colony that summer. Clause 12, the Finn clause, specified penalties for any person who by 'threats or intimidation procures or attempts to procure any woman or girl to have any unlawful carnal connection within or without the Colony'.[40] In July 1903, Ordinance 46 in the Transvaal, provided for the 'Suppression of Brothels and Immorality' and, weeks later, in Natal, the Criminal Law Amendment Act was passed.[41] The clutch of 1902–3 acts, forbidding white prostitutes from taking black men as clients, were enacted over twelve months and their passage brought British colonies into alignment on the issues surrounding colour and commercial sex.

Silver was *not* the hidden architect of the racial codes that foreshadowed South Africa's later morals legislation, laws that paved the way for the infamous 'Immorality' Act 23 of 1957, a hallmark of the apartheid era presided over by Afrikaner nationalists prohibiting *all* sexual intercourse between black and white. Legislation governing large-scale commercial sex can be traced back to the surge in urbanisation following the mineral discoveries but the Zuid Afrikaansche Republiek's Ontucht Wet No. 2 of 1897 pre-dated Silver's arrival in the country by many months. That said, there can be no doubt that Silver and his Americanised cohort pioneered low-cost high-turnover commercial sex, including inter-racial sex, in southern Africa in the mid-1890s in ways that deeply disturbed colonial administrations at a time when the very idea of what it was to be a white 'South African' was being reshaped.

Morals legislation in the Cape Colony, Natal, the Orange River Colony and the Transvaal in 1902–3 bear the imprimatur of organised crime fashioned on the Atlantic periphery by marginalised East Europeans, lawless refugees hardened in the cauldron of Russian oppression and clerical hatred. White Afrikaner nationalists of the apartheid era had racial demons of their own that grew out of experiences with an indigenous black African majority but the racist coding embedded in their legislation governing commercial sex and morality derived, in the first instance, from the British administration's exposure to organised crime in cities and towns at the turn of the twentieth century. Within that, much broader, context Silver had clearly played a central role.

In February 1903, however, his mind was focused on what implications the case pending against Beck and Roach held for him. But, unknown to him, he was already being stalked by another hound from a completely different angle – Rigg. The clerk of Valkenberg was like a fox terrier with a rat. Unlike the police who had so much trouble in keeping up with Silver, Rigg needed just one sniff of an address to chase down his quarry. On 13 February the Colonial Under-Secretary in the Cape Colony wrote to the Colonial Secretary of the ORC, claiming that Silver was indebted to Valkenberg for maintenance of his 'wife', enquiring after his current financial position and pointing out that legal steps were being taken to recover an amount of £80. The ORC authorities, aware of transactions pending between Silver and 'Annie Alford', spent four weeks uncovering his savings. But, by the time they found an account in the Bank of Africa containing £1,000 sterling, it was too late. The money had already been transferred to van Zyl for safe keeping. The best the ORC administration could do once he had been released from prison was to note that he was negotiating the sale of an unoccupied erf in Bloemfontein that belonged to him. The rat appeared to have eluded the fox terrier.[42]

George Beck, 'printer', and Daniel Roach, 'tailor', appeared in the High Court charged with 'shop-breaking and theft' on 20 February. All items stolen by them had been recovered at the time of their arrest. What the third man had kept by way of cash when he ran away that night is unknown but, as noted, he had £1,000 in his account. The state chose not to call Silver as witness and restricted the king's evidence to that provided by McCulloch, Reid, and two junior policemen. Whatever that quartet sang was enough to convince the judge. Each of the accused was sentenced to five years' imprisonment with hard labour. For reasons that will become clearer later, they were freed from prison after serving three years. Soon after their release, they were again involved in criminal activities on the Witwatersrand.[43]

If Silver experienced a twinge of regret at having set up Beck and Roche it soon passed and he returned his attention to Max Jacobs, alias 'Johnson'. Two days after Beck and Roach were sent down, he wrote a letter to the Commissioner of Police calculated to sabotage an attempt by Scotch Jack to obtain early release on medical grounds. 'Johnson', he claimed, was shamming asthma attacks. It was a ploy that he had previously employed, with success, while in prison in Glasgow. He listed the names of Johannesburg-based pimps, thieves and white slavers who, he claimed, would soon be signing a plea for clemency on 'Johnson's' behalf.[44] Jacobs, however, had other plans and, in late March, he escaped and got himself aboard an up train. Blaine telegraphed Johannesburg requesting his arrest and extradition under the Fugitive Offenders Act. Jacobs, however, retained an attorney and advocate and claimed that he was a victim of perjury, wrongfully convicted and imprisoned. The Crown Prosecutor in Johannesburg, however, was not swayed and on 7 April 'Johnson' was re-arrested and sent to the 'Marshall Square Charge Office pending the departure of the evening train'. But when the lawyers got to hear of this, they obtained an urgent interdict prohibiting their client's deportation prior to an appeal. The attorney went to the holding cells and persuaded the sergeant to release his client until the appeal was heard. Jacobs could not believe his luck. He clambered aboard the first train bound for Delagoa Bay, Mozambique, and took a steamship to Europe.[45]

Silver spent his time in prison trying to secure his release. Although he was morally crippled, incapable of sensing rhythms of care or compassion, like others he had learned to mime sequences about family values, health and religion. He could not acknowledge that his family was utterly dysfunctional or that he had fewer religious convictions than a camel caught up in a pilgrimage to Mecca. Only part of his representations had an element of truth, and that related to his physical well-being and undiagnosed neurosyphilis. He had not been well for years. He suffered digestive pains and strange aches in joints that flared up unexpectedly. The spirochetes that had lodged in the soft tissue of his brain and been dormant for more than a decade, were taking a physical as well as a mental toll. For the first time he was experiencing difficulty in judging the length of a line when writing and sensing where the right-hand margin was. In a letter to the Commissioner of Police, days earlier, several of the words at the ends of lines had started to 'curve round' and 'fall off' the page, cascading down the right-hand margin of the paper.[46]

On 21 March he summoned van Zyl and, with his attorney's help, dictated a petition to the Lieutenant-Governor, Sir Hamilton Goold-Adams. 'Your Excellency's petitioner is very much broken down in health in consequence of imprisonment,' he pleaded. If the administration was in doubt about his plans, he would like to assure it that he was 'desirous of leaving this colony and of joining his child in the Cape Colony' on his release. Perhaps, he suggested, the Lieutenant-Governor could 'pardon him and cause him to be released from the remaining period of the sentence'? And, while the authorities were applying their minds to clemency perhaps they could see fit 'to liberate

[the] Petitioner before the next Jewish holidays'? In one letter he had become a Jew and acknowledged he was the father of a daughter, Bertha.[47]

Goold-Adams gave the petition short shrift. Silver would have to see out the remainder of his sentence. The date of release, 23 April, seemed as far away as ever. Yet, even at this low moment the need to betray was like a reflex; he could not help himself. Shortly after April Fools' Day he reported to the authorities that one of the warders was supplying inmates with cigarettes. 'An inquiry resulted in the statement being disproved and Silver's being sentenced to a short additional term of imprisonment for making the false statement.' For several days the clock stopped.[48]

The ORC gave him fourteen days to dispose of fixed property. Watched by detectives, he sold off the vacant erf, the house in Fichardt Street and then tidied up his affairs with van Zyl. In the second week of May 1903, and for the second time within thirty-six months, he was banished to Cape Town under armed military escort. He was running out of urban space and, with the entire country covered by legislation that owed much to him, should probably have given thought to moving on. But nothing caught his fancy. Ahead of him lay the difficult Vygenbaum and the corrupt micro-economy of District Six. There were other, even less pleasant, things to contemplate – such as Laskin and, standing right behind her, the clerk of Valkenberg.

XIV

CAPE TOWN
1903–1904

> Prosecution seemed to me as grotesque a simplification as defence, and judging was the most grotesque oversimplification of all.
>
> Bernard Schlink, *The Reader*

HE had some money, a 'wife' from a bigamous marriage, and a loyal half-brother. Solomon Goldstein was a friend of sorts and he knew Captain Samuel Lorimer of the CID. But Silver also had an appalling record with up-country police and a still-growing reputation for treachery in the underworld. It was an unpromising situation for someone living in the cramped space between crime and law enforcement. There was not much to go on and a lesser man might have been tempted to proceed to the docks. He was an information vendor but, like a foreign hawker in an unfamiliar city, had to find space for his stall. He lounged about on threadbare chairs in the poorly lit lounges of boarding-houses such as Koskes's and Tivoli's talking to low-class whores in need of pimps. Slowly he eased himself back into the soiled bars and saloons of the Taymouth Castle and other hotels until burglars, detectives, fences, ex-policemen, stool pigeons, thieves and white slavers became more accustomed to his presence.[1]

It was a start but, like grease on harbour water, ugly stories about the break-in at McCulloch's and 'Scotch Jack' had spread everywhere and he was in need of a little solvent. Before long two 'Peruvians', Erlich and Gilvinski, were doing the rounds collecting signatures for a petition requesting that Beck and Roche's sentences be reviewed. It did not matter whether or not the petition influenced the Lieutenant-

Governor and, some months later, Beck and Roche were indeed released before their sentences had been completed. What mattered was that the initiative helped restore some of Silver's credibility with men like Marks Levy who had once been Roach's fence.[2] Back at listening posts crackling with the static of suspicion, he pieced together what had happened since his departure twelve months earlier. From what he heard and saw, the continuties were greater than the changes; there was more space than he'd expected.

The 'Morality Act', promulgated on 1 December 1902, had occasioned a flurry of police activity. With the eyes of the Acting Commissioner of Police and the legislature upon them, Sub-Inspector Thor Osberg and Sergeant David Charteris had been put in charge of a 'morals squad' comprising sixteen poorly paid constables. Although the statistics assembled at the Wale Street Station are questionable, they were particularly active during the first twelve months and a good number of brothel-keepers and prostitutes were prosecuted. The campaign to clean up *post bellum* Cape Town brought stiffer sentences and a minor exodus of pimps and prostitutes – several of whom, in any case, wanted to return to the Rand. By late 1903, with the middle-class moral panic showing no sign of abating, the Acting Commissioner declared the campaign a success and reduced the morals squad from sixteen to four constables.[3]

But the Act had not been an unqualified success: there had been unintended consequences and ambiguous outcomes. The further criminalisation of moral offences had deepened police corruption and nudged prostitution slightly up market, into the hands of more professional operators. Stiffer sanctions had combined with a greater police presence to increase overheads. Harsher legal provisions and heightened police activity had given corrupt officers the opportunity to extract more protection money from brothel-keepers and streetwalkers. But the Act had also increased problems for venal policemen. Corrupt officers, in order to maintain credibility, were under greater pressure to produce successful prosecutions. This was not as easy as it seemed. The more protection lent to brothel-owners and women on the streets who paid bribes, the lower the number of convictions. This decline in numbers had to be offset by leaning even harder on those who could *not* afford to pay. In short, a corrupt system necessitated balancing the amount of protection offered against the number of prosecutions going through a charge office supervised by superior officers.[4] Nor did the dangers end there. Venal operations were liable to be reported to the Commissioner by brothel-keepers and prostitutes lower down the chain who were unable to pay protection. Increased income and conspicuous consumption fuelled suspicions, unleashing professional jealousies amongst those confined to more prosaic functions. A corrupt policeman's lot was not a happy one.

Osberg and Charteris came to appreciate the principles underlying their operations more fully in 1903–4. Charteris traded power for cash faster than a bartender could short-change a late-night drunk. Using Max Harris as middle man, he acquired interests in businesses run by the landlords Frankie Ricardi and Issy Roytowski, and the brothel- and gaming-house owners Solomon Goldstein, Charlie Mabon and Wolf Witkofsky. By late 1903, he was collecting protection money from a dozen brothels in an arc between the lower city and upper District Six.[5] He did not confine himself to 'cherry-picking'. He and Harris branched out, taking a percentage from streetwalkers who were avoiding voracious landlords or greedy pimps. This offered two advantages: it increased earnings and, by drawing in constables on the beat, lessened the dangers of whistle-blowing. Protected prostitutes used the password 'Tommy', which ensured their release if they happened to be arrested.[6]

Charteris's arrangements with his superior, Osberg, were never made public but neither was unduly perturbed by what they were doing. They had an amicable relationship and were often seen at the races. Osberg, who had traces of a Swedish accent, was frequently to be found in the dives of District Six. In retrospect, it would seem that, sensing the direction in which the market was moving, he developed a niche. While Charteris and Harris busied themselves with rowdy East Europeans he concentrated on more classy, upmarket, establishments run by 'French' gangsters, many of whom were French-speaking rather than French. Nevertheless, there were dozens of Francophone brothel-keepers, pimps, white slave traffickers and hundreds of 'continental' women spread throughout the city. Unlike the East Europeans who seldom bothered with assumed names, aliases and nicknames were *de rigueur* for the French. Their true identities remained hidden except when in their downtown club where, at the heart of the French connection, unknown to the Anglocentric CID was Georges Hayum.[7]

Born of Jewish parents in Paris in 1868, Hayum was a brothel-keeper, thief, pimp, and white slaver, well known in Europe where he operated under a bewildering range of names – Bach, Dacheux, Levasser and Le Cuirassier. His mother was a notable member of the Parisian underworld and they enjoyed considerable political influence in important circles. Forty-eight months after being deported from South Africa, in 1904, an undercover American agent investigating the white slave traffic in Paris was told that 'a Commissaire of Police who had taken George Le Cuirassier into custody and endeavoured to secure his conviction, lost his job . . .' At the time, Hayum's mother, 'La Mère Dacheux', was running an establishment that distributed women to brothels as far apart as Argentina, China, Manchuria and the United States.[8]

Hayum's recent problems dated to 1895, when he was sentenced to six months' imprisonment in Paris for fraud. More trouble followed in the wake of the Dreyfus affair. The anti-Semitic *Libre Parole*, exaggerating Jewish involvement in the white slave traffic, labelled it the work of 'Hayum, Israel and Company'. Undeterred, soon thereafter he was sentenced to fifteen months' imprisonment for corrupting the morals of minors. District Six scuttlebutt, however, had it that, before fleeing the French capital in early 1903, he had been involved in the theft of £4,000.[9] While waiting for the heat in Paris to dissipate, he kept a low profile, running his business as an international sex trader with exemplary care. He chose not to live in Cape Town and hired a 'farm' at Lakeside, near Muizenberg on the False Bay coast, where he employed a manager, Valentine Dufis. Hayum imported women from Marseilles and frequently travelled up the coast to Durban, where he collected prostitutes who passed through the farm before being sent to District Six.[10]

In Cape Town, under the name Bach, Hayum retained Dempers & van Ryneveld of St George's Street to take care of his legal affairs. On the face of it the attorneys were men of good standing, running a respectable practice. Herman J. Dempers came from a distinguished family in Caledon which he represented as a Member of Parliament and had voted for the morals act, while Anthony van Ryneveld was a Justice of the Peace.[11] Dempers, however, was none too fussy when it came to clients, or too concerned about legal niceties. Like Silver, he seemed to take an interest in public baths and owned a property in District Six which he let to 'Bach who used it as a "boarding-house"'. If he was unaware of the nature of Bach's business – as he later claimed – he failed to persuade the Public Prosecutor: in August 1903 he was prosecuted and fined for allowing his premises to be used as a brothel. Perhaps significantly, the morals squad failed to bring a simultaneous prosecution against the 'German' proprietor of the boarding-house, a certain elusive 'Mr George Bach'.[12]

On closer inspection, the failure to prosecute Bach was not very puzzling. Hayum had installed his lover, Agnes-Marie Bach and a dozen women in the property at 12 Muir Street where they were overseen by a Peruvian minder and pimp named Goverovitch. Like the notorious Bertha Hermann, Agnes Bach hailed from Franco-German Alsace-Lorraine and, as 'Madame Sarah', had – with the passive assistance of Thor Osberg – transformed the house into one of the city's more expensive brothels.[13]

The existence of two rather than one node of police corruption relating to prostitution in the city – Charteris's and Osberg's – was a godsend since it opened possibilities; more especially so when Lorimer's detectives were looking askance at the morals squad. Silver, who looked down on Harris who had helped marginalise him, and up to Hayum's larger network, moved into the space between with the ease of a rat taking up occupancy in an abandoned outhouse. Having done his reconnaissance work, he spent several weeks in mid-1903 sniffing about for suitable premises. As during his previous stay, his first venture was not located in District Six, but in Bree Street, in the city's lower reaches, near the docks. His new venture, the Alliance Café – like its predecessor the Empire Café – was situated so as to intercept late night revellers in search of liquor and sex. It was not long before the business came to the notice of the authorities. This led to prosecutions, but it also allowed him to renew his acquaintance with the CID.[14]

Sam Lorimer, whose first taste of professional success had come with the Alexander illicit diamond-buying case eighteen months earlier, had every reason to remember Silver. Like most policemen, Lorimer believed he was more in control of informers than they were of him. Undeterred by tales of Silver's Orange River escapades, he was constantly looking for information from the underworld, including any generated around the new morals squad. What human frailties Silver detected in Lorimer and exploited is not clear, but his hold over him appears to have grown over time. From the moment Silver returned to the Cape in 1903 until the time he left in 1905, Lorimer protected him with acts of omission and oversight. Their understanding went further than just the two of them. Shortly after the opening of the Alliance Café, Silver and his brother were told of a business opportunity two blocks away. Rogers, an 'American Negro' pimp, wanted a partner in a 'lodging house' busi-

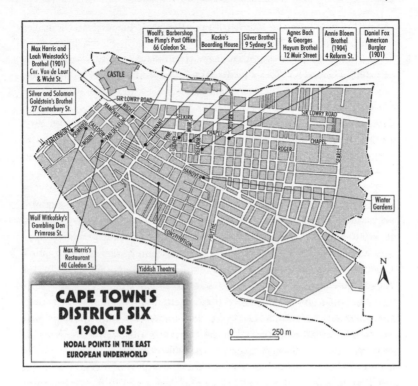

Max Harris and Leah Weinstock's Brothel (1901) Cnr. Von de Leur & Wicht St.

Silver and Solomon Goldstein's Brothel 27 Canterbury St.

Woolf's Barbershop The Pimp's Post Office 66 Caledon St.

Koske's Boarding House

Silver Brothel 9 Sydney St.

Agnes Bach & Georges Hayum Brothel 12 Muir Street

Annie Bloem Brothel (1904) 4 Reform St.

Daniel Fox American Burglar (1901)

Wolf Witkofsky's Gambling Den Primrose St.

Max Harris's Restaurant 40 Caledon St.

Yiddish Theatre

Winter Gardens

CAPE TOWN'S DISTRICT SIX
1900 – 05
NODAL POINTS IN THE EAST EUROPEAN UNDERWORLD

0   250 m

N

ness at 100 Hout Street. Not long thereafter Jack Lis and Regina Weinberg, reconciled after quarrels in Bloemfontein, moved into Hout Street. Clients from the Alliance Café were doubtless directed to prostitutes in Rogers's brothel.[15]

According to the morals squad the house in Hout Street was a 'rowdy' place. During the last quarter of 1903 Jack was twice prosecuted for the sale of illicit liquor but what worried the police far more was the way he dealt with customers who got difficult. A powerfully built man with military experience, he was seldom far from a revolver and, some time after he and his brother had left Cape Town, Lorimer expressed his reservations to a colleague in another colony: 'A man was murdered in front of the door,' he noted, 'but the murderer was not brought to justice although on several occasions information was received by me that [Jack] Lis was the murderer; but I could never get sufficient evidence to lay a charge against him.' Who knows how far the Lorimer-Silver writ ran? It may have run as far as Jack, but certainly not Rogers.[16]

The Lis brothers were content to confine their business to the lower reaches of the city and steer clear of the Charteris–Harris monopoly. With the exception of one, desultory, attempt by Jack to win the right to supply liquor to Harris's principal gambling and prostitution outlet, they restricted their commercial operations to the area around the docks. Silver's secret occupation as police informer, however, demanded that he circulate more widely. So, while Jack kept an eye on the Bree and Hout Street outposts, he, with the help of his once estranged 'wife' – by then renamed 'Lena Bloom' – tried to insinuate himself into the underworld of District Six.

It was not easy. Harris suspected Silver of informing but, fearing him, remained on amicable terms. Others in the cartel were equally uncertain what to make of Silver's relationship with Bloom. Was she, as some claimed, his wife? Or was she simply another brothel-keeper trying to avoid paying protection? This confusion forced Bloom to stick to the less lucrative margins of the main quarter although she was still vulnerable to predatory raids by Charteris's men who needed to maintain their flow of morals cases through the courts. It was delicately poised. Once Charteris, not knowing who he was dealing with, assaulted her, smashing personal possessions and then arresting her. Harris, sensing trouble, hastened to repair the damage and offered her a loan to get her business re-started.[17] Silver let it pass, but it convinced him of the need to disguise his operations more carefully so he took on Goldstein as a front man, a partner who could deal more directly with the cartel. Solomon Goldstein and Minnie Trautman not only moved freely around the edges of the Charteris circle but were trusted by the Osberg–Hayum syndicate. By October 1903, Goldstein, Silver, Trautman and Bloom were secret partners in a brothel at 27 Canterbury, a property rented, via the monopoly, from Issy Roytowski.[18]

But the new venture came at an unpropitious moment. Sensing prosecutions under the Morals Act were falling off, a coalition of clergymen under the leadership of Mr Ross of the Evangelical Church Council, raised fresh objections to brothels in District Six. Amongst those most strongly opposed were down-market joints, like the one in Canterbury Street, run by East European Jews. The complaints, like pebbles in a pond, gave rise to concentric circles of pressure. Corrupt police, under renewed pressure for convictions, raised protection fees from middlemen. The middlemen passed on rising costs to landlords, who promptly charged brothel-owners more. The brothel-keepers then pressed harder on prostitutes, who either passed on the costs to customers or had to increase turnover by taking in more clients at established prices.

In the closing months of 1903, these changes were felt in the Charteris–Harris circle before they were sensed in the Osberg–Hayum ring. In theory, the effects of price hikes could be contained if nobody panicked, if everybody kept faith in the system and the ripple effects were not compounded by greed. But the theory failed to hold up in practice. Charteris, Harris and Roytowski passed on their increases but the women in the Canterbury Street brothel, led by the formidable Trautman, either could not, or would not, pass on the costs to customers. Trautman resented paying £12:10s. a month protection. Independent-minded and possibly beyond the control of others, she may have acted on her own but it is as likely that she acted with the encouragement of one of the partners who had a taste for drama, disruption and the law; one who, only months earlier, had won a civil action against a cocky Jewish lawyer in Kimberley. Trautman decided to contest a rent increase through a civil action against Roytowski.[19]

Trautman's legal initiative destabilised the entire system, causing an uproar amongst the gangsters. Roytowski was successfully prosecuted but then, in a second action, Trautman failed to retrieve rent he owed her. Roytowski lodged a counter-claim, which Trautman lost. These contests, which Silver savoured because they unsettled his *bête noire*, Harris, were soon dwarfed by more sinister actions. Goldstein, seemingly incapable of controlling his wife, was singled out for attention. Unknown underworld agents assaulted him. 'I was nearly killed,' he swore, by men whom he either could not, or would not, name.[20] It was a salutary warning but what frightened wayward elements even more was the belief that they were vulnerable to deportation at the hands of Charteris or Osberg. A perception took root that corrupt officers, exploiting anti-alien and anti-Semitic sentiments, were using provisions of the Morality and Immigration Restriction Acts to deport those who ran foul of their operations. The first to go was 'French' pimp, Charlie Mabon. He was followed by Jack Lis's partner, Rogers. East Europeans who had fled Tsarist oppression wondered who would be next. There was a world of difference between being sent to New York or Paris, and being handed to the Russians in Odessa or St Petersburg.[21]

The Goldstein assault, court cases and the threat of deportation dented the confidence of a few hardened gangsters. After the Roytowski case, Goldstein and Witkofsky fled north. They did so knowing that

only a few months earlier, in mid-1903, the Transvaal had passed a
new, racist, Immorality Act of its own modelled on the Cape and
Orange River Colony Acts – part of the clutch of laws which owed
much to the earlier doings of Silver and former members of the American
Club.[22] Not all coastal birds were equally well placed for the flight
north. Some, like Max Harris, were too gorged on rich pickings to get
airborne. Roytowski, clinging to his assets, was alleged to have said
that 'he did not care at all' about the new laws and 'that he could pay,
like Mr Dempers'. So, instead of fleeing, he contented himself with a
hurried application for naturalisation and noted, with some pleasure,
that it was not too long before certain former business associates were
seen gliding back into the peninsula.[23]

Silver, once banished and twice deported, was another who could
not easily go north. With the exception of Durban, he had exhausted
urban venues in which the police would tolerate his peculiar interests.
That, and his desire to protect his American citizenship, made him
reluctant to apply for naturalisation and he remained more vulnerable
to deportation than many of his peers. It was an awkward situation
and while his partner, Goldstein, was up country, he set about reposi-
tioning their enterprises. He retained his interest in cheaper outlets that
were difficult to protect such as Bloom's, or 'Mrs Blatt's' – the same
Sarah Rosenblatt who had gone with him to Bloemfontein and who
had, since then, moved a little up market. By the time Roytowski's
problems were public, he was customising changes to two properties
that would be more professionally run and attract a better class of
customer. These projects, which bore the fingerprints of Goldstein and
Hayum, drew him closer to Osberg and helped push him even further
away from Charteris and the East European faction.[24]

Goldstein's influence was apparent in alterations brought about at
9 Sydney Road, District Six, but similar changes may have been effected
at another house in the lower reaches of the city, at 28 Longmarket.
A peep-hole in the front door enabled the *madame* to cast an eye over
would-be clients before admitting them to choose one of six prostitutes. Unauthorised policemen, drunks or customers who looked as if
they did not have ten shillings for 'short time', or £3 to stay the night,
were excluded by metal bars guarding the front portal. Inside, fittings
were refurbished in a way that would have appealed to a former furni-
ture-supplier from Buenos Aires.[25]

Hayum, too, assisted. The two properties, collectively worth about

£2,000, were purchased with funds raised through Dempers & van Ryneveld and, within months Silver paid off most of the mortgage on the Sydney Street house. With an average gross income of £150 each, per week, the houses did exceptionally well. Reception rooms had printed cards bearing the names of the ladies of the house; a move away from the low-price, high-turnover strategy. Obscene pictures, of the sort he had used back in Bloemfontein, bore testimony to a more continental-style operation but it was the female personnel who were perhaps most revealing of new influences. Asked whether he ever kept 'Jewish girls' in Sydney Street, he allegedly replied no: 'they gave too much trouble and he kept only German and French girls', a mixture from Alsace-Lorraine via Marseilles and Muizenberg.[26]

It must also have been at about this time – possibly with the financial assistance of, or even in partnership with Dempers who hailed from the spa town of Caledon – that he acquired a stake in a new venture that revealed an old obsession. The purchase of a half-share in the Caledon Street Baths, within easy walking distance of the brothel in Sydney Street, underscored a concern about the polluting potential of prostitutes who failed to maintain necessary standards of cleanliness, or who avoided ritual purification. The business, he later said, brought in about £10 a month.[27]

By late January 1904, Cape Town's 'French' sex traders trusted Silver sufficiently to allow him to hide at their 'farm' when a problem in District Six necessitated his having to lie low for a few days. He saw a lot of the secretive Hayum who refused to go into the city, except on Sundays, when he went to Muir Street to check on the week's takings. Indeed, so cautious and disciplined was the Frenchman that once, when Osberg needed to see him urgently, he had to be lured into town by coded telegram.[28] It may also have been during a visit to Hayum's farm at Lakeside that he agreed to accompany 'Le Cuirassier' up the east coast since, months later, a prostitute who had no reason to lie made a statement claiming to have once seen Silver in Durban.[29]

The smattering of French Silver commanded improved as he interacted with Hayum and Agnes Bach who, like him, aspired to a monopoly and never hesitated to inform on rivals in Muir Street.[30] 'Madame Sarah' ran her *maison* with a rod of iron and her 'German and French girls' retained little of what they earned and enjoyed almost no freedom. A few years later an ambitious entrepreneurial Jewish 'girl' – of the type that Silver said caused 'too much trouble' – complained that the women in his houses were treated 'like slaves'. It was no coincidence that the French *madame* put in charge of Sydney Street, not unlike Laskin before her, was given the trade name 'Josephine'. The new 'Napoleon' needed not only to control but to own his women.[31]

But while Silver's interest in the top end of the market was deepening, problems elsewhere continued to demand attention. He found his brother a partner to replace the deported Rogers, who may have been blamed for the corpse discovered outside the Hout Street 'lodging house'. Morris Gilbert, a Russian, was another naturalised American from the Lower East Side who had, he said, been a 'diamond merchant' in New York City. He and Jack set up a new dive, the Riebeeck Restaurant in Dock Road. It was a classic low-life hangout.[32] At the same time Silver made Goldstein a partner in the Alliance Café, even though Goldstein remained exiled in Johannesburg.[33] Theirs was now a formal alliance; an alliance for what, and against whom was not yet fully clear.

The Charteris–Harris empire was by then centred on large premises the partners had acquired at 40 Caledon Street. Harris and Leah Weinstock, who shared a cottage in nearby Vernon Terrace, let rooms in the house to pimps and prostitutes although it was not a dedicated brothel, more of a multi-purpose recreational centre. An unlicensed restaurant sold sufficient alcohol for it to be the envy of underworld rivals and it housed the largest illegal betting-house in the city. Its faro games were so popular amongst East Europeans that, at one time, 'there were as many as 150 people in the room'. Unlike up-country operations, where Peruvians relied on electric alarms or spies to give them warning of police raids, Harris had no need of such precautions.[34] Looking round for new challenges, he also started manufacturing counterfeit coins. This, together with a developing interest in illicit diamonds, was a dangerous departure from the usual line of business since it fell within Lorimer and the CID's sphere of competence, rather than that of Charteris and the morality squad.[35]

From his position on the Rand, Goldstein heard of Harris's continued progress; Silver had to live with it close up. But the Charteris–Harris syndicate was beginning to overreach itself. Goldstein and Silver's business interests were becoming more closely aligned with Lorimer's professional duty. The alliance, originally just a low-key understanding between a detective and his informer, was extended to include Goldstein and, together, they became largely responsible for Charteris and Harris's subsequent downfall and Osberg's public disgrace.[36] Immediately after the Roytowski cases, the Acting Commissioner, Colonel Robinson, had received a report from CID that 'certain allegations had been made by persons interested in brothels and by prostitutes to the effect that the police were receiving "protection" money from brothel-keepers and prostitutes'.[37] Lorimer's sources for this were almost certainly Goldstein and Silver.[38] In fact, Robinson had interviewed Goldstein at the time but found the exchange unhelpful since he could not 'get at the real motives of the man'.

In January, by which time Goldstein was on the Witwatersrand, Robinson received a letter from 'Labor Omni Vincit', in an envelope postmarked 'Johannesburg', alleging that Harris was taking protection money from prostitutes. Two day later, the Attorney-General received a letter, also from Johannesburg and written in a similar hand, signed 'Pro Bono Publico', making the same allegations. Robinson was disposed to act cautiously since he did not wish to undermine the morals squad on the basis of flimsy allegations proffered by unknown parties with hidden agendas.[39] After these early complaints nothing further happened for some months.

But behind the façade of normality the brickwork was crumbling. While Harris and Silver interacted professionally, Harris remained convinced that Silver was working for Lorimer. But since his largest source of income came from prostitution protected by Charteris, he was not unduly concerned. Nor were Charteris and Osberg. They viewed Silver as a business associate of Hayum's branching out into independent, unprotected ventures in Longmarket and Sydney Streets and the morals squad continued to make up their numbers at the expense of the women in Silver's 'French' maisons. On 18 January 1904, Susan Josephine was prosecuted for keeping a brothel at 9 Sydney, and sentenced to £25 or three months' hard labour. On 15 February it was the turn of Marguerite Degland of Longmarket Street and, on 31 March, that of Jenny Durant of Sydney Street.[40] In all three cases it was Charteris who made the arrests, further fuelling Silver's dislike of him and his partner in Caledon Street.[41]

The Longmarket and Sydney Street arrests fed Silver's paranoia and he began to suspect that Charteris, perhaps at Harris's behest, might be manoeuvring to have him deported. On 21 March, Dempers & van Ryneveld lodged his application for naturalisation. The application was supported by A. van Ryneveld and one H. Botha, justices of the peace who swore that, to the best of their knowledge, he had never been found guilty of serious offences, including rape. The papers were forwarded to the urban police in the usual way and Acting Detective Richardson 'reported favourably on the applicant'. The application was 'endorsed by Inspector Easton who handed the papers to Inspector Lorimer', who sent them on to the new Acting Commissioner, R.M. Crawford, 'with an endorsement to the effect that nothing was known against the applicant'.[42] Dismissed later as 'oversights', the police endorsements showed how successfully Silver had inserted himself into the CID.

Three years earlier Easton had been principal witness in a case in which he had been convicted for illicitly selling liquor from the Empire Café. Lorimer's lapse of memory was even more amazing. While the state was exploring Silver's ability to pay for Laskin's upkeep, Lorimer had informed the Resident Magistrate that he could not think 'of recommending a man of Silver's class for any concession whatever'. And, in April 1902, days after the Alexander diamond case, Lorimer had Silver taken on as a 'special agent' in Kimberley: this had resulted in his contract not being renewed and a sensational sequel in Bloemfontein.[43] Behind this official amnesia lay an explanation that Crawford was perhaps not fully aware of – Silver was a CID informant; Sam Lorimer's favourite nark. Given police backing, the application for naturalisation was a formality and, weeks later, it was approved by the Executive Council subject only to the submission of a 'Declaration of Allegiance'. This potential hurdle, too, was negotiated without difficulty.

By March 1904, the Russo-Polish quarter was racked with tension But, as can happen when history plays the joker, it was an unforeseen occurrence that formed the turning point. At a quarter to ten on the night of 22 March, Harry Beresford and Colin Cowan of the morals squad spotted a Russian immigrant, Rosie Zeeman, who had been working late, making her way back to District Six. With the need for arrests escalating because of the church campaign, the constables, both recent immigrants, could have mistaken her for a streetwalker. But they may also have felt that she was a working-class woman who could be stitched up to prove their commitment. Ignoring protestations, she was arrested, bundled into a cab, and taken to the Wale Street Station. She was charged with soliciting and the arresting officers told the recording officer that she lived in the house where other prostitutes lived – at 40 Caledon Street, the Harris house.

The following morning a bewildered Zeeman appeared before a magistrate in the Loop Street Court, where she was convicted and sentenced to a fine of £5 or 30 days' imprisonment with hard labour before being marched off to the house of correction. But within hours her employer, responding to enquiries from worried family members, tracked her down, paid her fine and secured her release. Zeeman's wrongful arrest and prosecution was the cause of great indignation in the Jewish community which may itself not have been entirely immune to concerns about possible deportation. Amidst what appeared to be the start of a moral panic embracing even the law-abiding sections of the community, Jewish citizens presented a petition to the Attorney-General. On 1 April, the matter became public. The editor of the *South African Review*, writing when Jews could still hear the echoes of Zola's *J'accuse*, ran an article on the incident under the headline: 'Outrageous Conduct of the Police – a Respectable Girl Shamefully Treated'.[44]

Crawford, Acting Commissioner, made some enquiries within the morals squad. Osberg and his men offered an unsatisfactory explanation, calling into question the woman's integrity and hinting at a dark plot to discredit the morals squad. Crawford was still contemplating their responses when, on 8 April, the *Review*, mirroring growing frustration in the community, ran a second article criticising the calibre of the police. Crawford broke ranks and took a personal interest in the matter. He interviewed Zeeman personally, formed an opinion and handed the matter to the CID for further investigation. It was Lorimer's head constable who reported back that '"Rosie Zeeman is not the class of woman she had been condemned to be".'[45]

The brass in the morals squad were still obfuscating when, on 15 April, the *Review* ran another full-page story on 'The Police Outrage on Miss Rosie Zeeman'. The article singled out Charteris and Osberg as policemen of 'questionable character' and suggested that, since the story first broke, Zeeman had been harassed and shadowed by plain-clothes policemen to the point where she was afraid of going to, or returning from, work. Crawford accelerated his enquiries and, on 21 April, the morals squad was disbanded and all plainclothes police ordered to return to uniformed duty. Responsibility for enforcing the Morality Act would henceforth fall to Lorimer and the CID. A day later Cowan was arrested for perjury and, some weeks later, the exonerated Miss Zeeman was fêted at a concert organised by the Jewish community.[46]

The sudden switch in police responsibilities for the Morality Act derailed the gravy train that had been doing the rounds of upper District Six ever since the war. Charteris, Osberg and their constables who had happily chugged along parallel tracks stopping at Harris and Hayum's stations, suddenly found themselves being routed through junctions commanded by the CID. All previously greased and protected lines became suspect and subject to outside inspection. Bent coppers and gangsters were made to pause and rethink who might best provide protection. This need for readjustment was not, however, confined to the former morality squad and its clients. The same strictures were brought to bear on another relationship that dated back to 1901 – that between Captain Sam Lorimer and his most important, best-protected informant.

XV

CAPE TOWN
1904–1905

Madness alone is truly terrifying, inasmuch as you cannot
placate it either by threats, persuasion or bribes.

Joseph Conrad, *The Secret Agent*

SILVER'S application for naturalisation was processed, without problem,
weeks before the Zeeman case. Even as the case was breaking, he continued
to benefit from special treatment as the CID used him to curb Max
Harris's underworld empire which had expanded beyond prostitution.
On 18 April 1904, three days before the morals squad was disbanded,
Lorimer, acting on information provided by an insider, staged a raid on
Harris's gambling den at 40 Caledon Street. Amongst those caught
playing claberjus and faro were Harris, Marks Levy and Absalom Klein.
The three were convicted and each sentenced to a fine of £150, along
with their clients who were fined £5 each. Yet among the names of the
convicted there was again one tell-tale omission: on the night of the police
raid the role of banker for faro had been filled by Lorimer's man.[1]

In the long run Lorimer's new responsibility for the Morality Act
doomed his relationship with his secret agent, who could continue
either as a CID informant, or as a brothel-keeper, but not both. Deep
down, Lorimer knew it, and his informant, too, must have sensed it.
They had grown to know each other; both were moody men and
consummate betrayers, and both were suffering from the mid-stages
of neurosyphilis which heightened their instabilities. One was a
policeman, the other a criminal; the question was – who had the
greater capacity for treachery, who would be first to defect?[2] In the

short term, however, their partnership persisted because of a common dislike of a third party – Harris. Lorimer wanted Harris, the biggest gangster in town, prosecuted not only for professional career reasons, but because he resented the way that Charteris and Osberg had benefited financially from their association with him. Silver, on the other hand, despised Harris and the morals squad for denying him access to the larger sex market. As long as Harris controlled the 'vice' racket Lorimer and Silver's partnership could survive.

Without protection, Harris was vulnerable to attack from the CID. Lorimer did not hesitate to move. Almost a month to the day after the gambling raid, on 17 May, Harris appeared in court charged under clause 32 of the 1902 Act with 'living on the earnings of prostitution'. He now faced the prospect that John X. Merriman had envisaged when he had introduced the bill, advocating the use of the lash so as to get at the 'wretches through their skin'.[3] Harris did not lose his nerve, retained a bluff ex-policeman, the 'law agent', W.B. Shaw, to defend him and told him whom he suspected of providing the police with inside information. He and his agent then made a bold and cunning move to try to minimise the damage. They got Leah Weinstock – in effect Mrs Max Harris – to approach Silver and pay him £40 'for writing the statements of the (defence) witnesses because they could not speak English'.[4] It gave rise to the most extraordinary situation; in effect, Silver was working simultaneously for the prosecution and the defence! By day he fossicked around for Lorimer, collecting evidence that could help the state put Harris away and build a case against Charteris and Osberg. By night, he worked on statements of the defence witnesses that might help his paymaster, Shaw, and Harris.

When the hearing commenced at the Wale Street Magistrates' Court, on 26 May, the gallery was filled with underworld elements who knew that nothing was as it seemed. What looked like just another case of vice was, in truth, a contest for the control of the political economy of an immigrant neighbourhood. Would Harris – a nominally religious Russian Jew, vulnerable to deportation at a moment perceived to be filled with anti-Semitic potential – take the rap on his own, or would he shop Charteris, a corrupt Scottish policeman?[5] There was no immediate answer. Harris instructed his attorney to mount an orthodox defence but Shaw found himself up against an extremely well prepared prosecutor. The crown had traced Fanny Miller, a former *madame* in Primrose Street and brought her down from Johannesburg to give evidence. More damaging testimony from Silver's old friend, Wilf/Wulf Witkofsky, followed. By the end of the day Harris was not sure they had a winning strategy. As his position deteriorated his thoughts turned to betrayal and revenge. As he put it in another case, weeks later, when Charteris was on trial:

> Since my arrest I have been reckoning things up. I do not want to fall myself and allow the prisoner [Charteris] to be a free man, because I have fallen through him and *many other people have fallen through him*. They have been arrested and convicted through him. *I knew in my heart, and he knew in his heart, that they were innocent but for him*.[6]

Silver must have gained early insight into the changing defence position and passed on the information to Lorimer. When the court reconvened on 6 June, Shaw rose and told the magistrate that, 'Our defence is that we are acting as agents for the police. We have assisted them to carry on their business and to buy public houses. We are going to prove that up to the hilt in mitigation.'[7] If this statement took the magistrate or the gangsters by surprise, it did not leave the CID or prosecutor flat-footed. That evening Charteris was arrested and charged with 'living on the proceeds of prostitution'. Osberg, too, was picked up on a charge of 'conspiring to defeat the ends of justice'.[8] But the arrest did nothing to help Harris, who was found guilty and sentenced to two years' imprisonment and fifteen lashes. However, Harris, too, was syphilitic and despite medical opinion that he was fit enough to be lashed, was spared a flogging.[9]

Charteris's trial, watched officially by Lorimer for the CID, commenced in late June 1904; that of Osberg days later. In both hearings Harris appeared as principal witness for the state and, in both cases, Silver's name was mentioned frequently in the context of nefarious transactions. But, in a universe where 'good' and 'evil' were so hopelessly intertwined neither the prosecution nor the defence was willing to risk putting Silver on the stand.

In the case of Charteris, the magistrate took the view that he had been an equal partner in running brothels and that '. . . he could not let him off lighter than Harris, and the sentence of the Court would therefore be that the accused be imprisoned for a period of two years with hard labour, and receive fifteen lashes'.[10] On appeal, the sentence was reduced to fifteen months' imprisonment with hard labour. In a colonial society, where white men were citizens and disenfranchised black men routinely flogged, not even the courts could get at 'the wretches through their skin'. Osberg was the unexpected beneficiary of unnecessarily salacious evidence presented by 'the vilest reptile in Cape Town', Alec Goverovitch. 'Madam Sarah's' coachman left a very bad impression on jurymen who, after a short deliberation found the Swede not guilty – a verdict greeted 'with an outburst of cheering more vigorous than usually accompanied an acquittal'.[11]

Throughout these trials, which ran for nearly three months between May and July, Silver ran five brothels. The 'French' *maisons*, in Longmarket and Sydney Streets, operated with women brought into the colony via Suez and the east coast by Hayum. The three in District Six, staffed by East European women who entered the country via the west coast, were overseen by his 'wife', Lena Bloom, who had lost her battle for independence. Two of the brothels were in Chapel and Reform Streets. The third, Black Sophy's, in Primrose Street, reputedly the oldest brothel in the city, bore the name of a guano island that lay off Lüderitz, in German South West Africa.[12]

Immediately after the Osberg trial, in July 1904, Lorimer told Silver to sell the houses in Longmarket and Sydney Streets.[13] It was the beginning of the end; a low-key signal that his services were no longer required. But how could he be certain Lorimer was serious? Surely the CID would not risk going up against him? He could hardly be expected to dispose of his principal assets. It was just another game of bluff and disguise in a world of smoke and mirrors. So he 'sold' the houses to fictitious purchasers and got Dempers to register the properties in the names of the new owners.[14] Number 9, Sydney Street went to an untraceable 'S. Cohen'. In the Longmarket case, his punning got the better of him and the joke was taken further. The house, he said, belonged to Helena Nieman – Helena Nobody. Lorimer's superior, Davis, saw through the subterfuge even though he failed to detect the humour. When Davis asked who Cohen and Nieman were, Silver said, '. . . with a smile; "You don't want to know them, the houses are very quiet"'.[15]

Acting Commissioner Crawford was less inclined to patience than his senior officers. In the wake of the Zeeman case he wanted the city's remaining gangsters and vice spots cleared out as soon as possible.

Lorimer felt the pressure but was unable to act against an agent who knew not only all the men on his formal and informal payroll, but his department's entire *modus operandi*. Lorimer stalled, had the houses in Longmarket and Sydney Street watched and the women prosecuted. And then, working on the principle of setting a thief to catch a thief, he got hitherto official policy reversed and looked for a private detective to snare his former secret agent. He found the man he needed not far from District Six.[16] Robert Levy, like many West European immigrants, was not particularly well disposed to lower-class *Ostjuden* or 'Peruvians'. For a time he had been a partner in a family carting business but the enterprise had faltered. In May 1904, he was approached by someone in the police who told him that the CID was looking for a German-speaker. His official position was oxymoronic and Levy later described himself as a 'private detective' *in* the Urban Police.[17]

In Levy, Lorimer found the hook; the bait he acquired elsewhere. From his dealings with Silver, who had reverted to being a 'barber' for official purposes, Lorimer knew that 66 Caledon Street played a central part in the Russo-Polish underworld. Woolf's barbershop was an intelligence centre, a post office, for District Six brothel-keepers, pimps and white-slavers. Who better to introduce Silver to Levy than Woolf?[18] Woolf, the pimps' postmaster, mentioned to Silver that he had found a prospective buyer for the houses in Longmarket and Sydney Streets. Silver, under pressure, was sufficiently interested to ask Woolf to arrange a meeting. On 28 July, Woolf was talking to Levy outside the shop when they saw him approaching. They exchanged greetings and went into the shop, where Silver said to Levy, 'I suppose that you have come about the property?' Levy said he was acting for a third party living in Johannesburg, and Silver asked whether his principal was aware of 'the nature of the properties'. Levy said that he was, and he agreed to show his successor, Lorimer's new man, the nearest of the properties, just five minutes away.[19]

They went to see the properties, Levy conversing in German, rather than Yiddish. Silver pointed out the special safety features that might appeal to a newcomer to the trade, and the visit ended with him telling Levy that 'he wanted to sell the places as he had a daughter in England, and wanted to turn over a new leaf'. Levy argued that there might be some difficulty in transferring properties that were not registered in his name and that his principal 'would want to know whether everything was in order'. Silver assured Levy there would be no problem;

'they could send their lawyers to Mr Dempers' office and find out all about it there'.[20] He met Levy again, a few days later. But Levy had had no response from Johannesburg. Silver suggested that, in future, he might be contacted via PO Box 1601, Cape Town, and wrote down the address in Levy's small notebook. They parted – Silver returning to District Six, and Levy heading off to Lorimer at an unknown destination.

The hands of the state, usually spotlessly clean in public, are invariably washed in private. Cleanliness and discretion are what taxpayers pay for, what citizens want. In mid-August the Public Prosecutor issued summons charging 'Joe Lis' and 'Annie Bloem' with contravening Section 22 of Act 36 of 1902 by unlawfully keeping brothels at 9 Sydney and 28 Longmarket Streets. The summons could hardly have come as a shock. Nor was the letter that Silver wrote to Lorimer, on 18 August, unusual; he frequently wrote to the authorities alleging conspiracies or making legalistic points. And yet this time there *was* something different: it had a strange tone of desperation, of resignation, about it.[21] It was addressed, without irony or malice, to the 'Hon. Captain Lorimer'. He started out, refrain-like, by reiterating his desire to 'turn over a new leaf', and then, in supplicatory tones, continued, 'Have mercy on me not to hand me over into the hands of lawyers. Have pity on me for my only daughter's sake who is at present laid up in a Hospital at London'. The letter then took on an unusual, medieval, quasi-religious twist: 'Do not give me up to the fury of an angry mob who would like to see me burned at the stake.' He prayed for a personal audience with Lorimer which would 'cause that summons to be withdrawn against me'. Then ended, head bowed, 'Believe me, I am Sir, your most obedient servant, J. Silver.'[22]

But was that all there was to it? His letter, without hint of anger or menace, was – even by his own highly manipulative standards – remarkably subservient. Why did Lorimer submit only a typewritten copy of the original, doubtless handwritten, letter to the court? 'There is no occupation that fails a man more completely than that of a secret agent of police,' a Pole once observed. Lorimer, once a mentor, ignored the letter and it was like a horse 'falling dead under you in the midst of an uninhabited and thirsty plain'.

Silver liked what he had seen of Shaw in the Harris trial. If Lorimer was again going to set Jew against Jew, *similia similibus curantur* – like cures like – then he would set ex-detective against detective.[23] The following day Shaw wrote to the Attorney-General suggesting it was inappropriate for 'Bloom', who had been a witness for the crown in recent cases, or Silver to be prosecuted. He was of the opinion that, if the state persisted in its actions, then Silver, like those before him, should be accorded a preliminary hearing rather than be sent for summary trial. He also gave notice that, if the case was to be heard by Resident Magistrate C.W. Broers, he would object and ask that Broers be recused since it was well known that he was 'prejudiced in favour of the police'.[24]

The Attorney-General did not respond and Silver feared the consequences. The prospect of the unpredictable, 'Lena Bloem'/'Bloom' giving evidence was particularly worrying. Her hidden resentments and knowledge of his history made her a potentially hostile and dangerous witness. *Similia similibus curantur*: silence had to be matched by silence. When Silver appeared in court, on 23 August, there was no sign of his 'wife'. Nobody reported Hannah Vygenbaum missing. Prostitutes, drawn from the ranks of the marginalised, often changed names and slipped out of town to pursue their profession elsewhere. The case was remanded for two days and he was granted bail of £100. Lorimer searched, unsuccessfully, for the co-accused, who by then was in contempt of court. When the case was reopened, on 25 August, there was still no sign of 'Bloom' and despite an intimation from Shaw, weeks later, that she might perhaps be made to reappear should circumstances change, she remained without trace in her usual settings.[25]

On 30 August, the Attorney-General at last replied to Shaw. 'Bloom', he reminded the law agent, had been warned not to keep a brothel and had persisted. Silver's past was less easily disposed of. Hiding behind a technicality the Attorney-General argued that, 'although his name was freely mentioned in the [recent morality] trials he was not called to give evidence, and that there was no reason why proceedings against him should be stayed'.[26] On the same day Silver petitioned, again unsuccessfully, for Broers's recusal.[27]

The trial commenced the same day but, for reasons that will become apparent, the hearings did not conclude until the third week of September. The delay contributed significantly to the pressures the accused was operating under. The first day in court went well for him but only because of the private campaign of terror he had waged and which his agent must have been aware of. The defence had learned that Hymie Bernstein, ex-American Club 'grocer', had sworn an affidavit as to Silver's criminal record, and that he would be giving evidence for the prosecution.

It was unthinkable. Either Silver or his brother Jack called on Bernstein who was staying in Caledon Street, and persuaded him to think the matter through. By the time Bernstein got into the witness box, he was seeing things more clearly. He did not even recognise the accused, or know anything relevant to the case, and was declared a hostile witness.[28] His amnesia was helpful and the trial was adjourned until 5 September. But before it could resume, Silver had become the accused in a second, unrelated, trial and then found himself closely monitoring the outcome of a third case, involving a charge of 'attempted murder'. Under mounting pressures, which may or may not have had anything to do with the sudden disappearance of Vygenbaum, Jack Lis seemed to be unravelling ever more rapidly.

Jack Lis's new Riebeek Restaurant had started off well enough but some weeks into the venture he and the partner his brother had found for him, Morris Gilbert, started suspecting each other of stealing. Jack had looked around for a second enterprise to invest in. In June 1904, with Harris no longer controlling District Six, he and a certain H. Abbot applied for and, rather surprisingly, were granted a wholesale liquor licence. Much later the civil servants responsible claimed that the licence had been granted 'in error' and he and Abbot received a partial refund but, for some months, they owned a bottle store at 5 Caledon Street.[29] However, things went from bad to worse at the Dock Road restaurant. More cash seemed to go missing each day and Jack, already suspected of having killed one man, was finding it difficult to curb his temper. One night he plucked out a revolver and threatened a sailor and by the third week of August he was facing another, separate charge of 'assault and robbery' which, for reasons maybe the CID knew, the state was unwilling to pursue.[30]

On the evening of 1 September, Jack and Gilbert had another set-to about 'takings and expenses'. The next morning, the quarrel resumed. He confronted Gilbert: "'Have you got some money of mine which you have stolen?"', to which Gilbert, responded, "'What is the matter with you; are you joking?"' Gilbert later claimed that he then reached into his jacket to take out a sixpence – to show that it was all he had on him – and was about to put it back into his pocket when the first bullet spat at him. It sizzled its way through the inside of his coat, setting it on fire. He ran to the window, broke a pane and was about to put his head out and holler for help when the second bullet hit him in the wrist. He yelled, 'Police! Murder!' and, between shouts, found time to blow on a police whistle. The shouting and whistling attracted his wife and stepdaughter, a sailor and a passing constable who rushed into the house, broke down the locked door, and put out the fire in the jacket before arresting Jack.[31]

It was *The Pirates of Penzance*, but the police failed to see the funny side. The Lis brothers were a menace; Jack was charged with 'attempted murder'. Silver, appreciating the seriousness of the charge, followed Gilbert to the police station and attempted to talk to him before he could make a statement. That failed; so he went back to the restaurant and tried to get Mrs Gilbert to talk to her husband before he could complete his statement. That, too, failed. He then suggested to her that she make a dishonest statement claiming that the partners 'were struggling and your husband had the revolver in his hand and fired it to frighten my brother'. If that happened, Gilbert would get 'about three months' and he, Silver, 'would stand good for it if it costs £50'. When that ploy, too, failed he waited for the preparatory examination and slipped into a seat behind Gilbert in court. He then leant forward and, in agitated Yiddish, whispered what the police were told were threats into Gilbert's ear.

The crown charged Silver with 'attempting to defeat the ends of justice'.[32] For the remainder of September he moved between courts as the CID sought to run the Lis brothers ragged.[33] But the race for justice is a contest for stayers rather than sprinters. The accused hired experienced lawyers and their trials were stretched so that the brothers benefited from disproportionately drawn-out proceedings. In *Rex* vs. *Joe Silver*, the evidence was largely inconclusive, and he was found not guilty. In *Rex* vs. *Jack Lis* the cigarette manufacturer, Philip Polikansky, was called by the defence to testify for the accused.[34] This ruse served no more purpose than it had on a previous occasion, but the evidence of other more important witnesses was so unsatisfactory that the crown withdrew the charge. By then the state, having managed to claw back the liquor licence that it had granted Jack 'in error', had started proceedings to have him deported.[35] Jack decided to skip the country and boarded a mail vessel for Southampton.

Favourable outcomes in the Gilbert cases were a relief, but Silver's fate was more closely bound up with the charge of brothel-keeping.

The crown groomed a second surprise witness. Morris Kaplan, one-time Yiddish translator in the Johannesburg magistrates' court and pimp with Bowery Boy connections had, in an unlikely turn of events, become a clerk in the charge office at the Bloemfontein Central Police Station. He arose, as if out of the bosom of Table Mountain, to present damaging testimony about the Green House and produced the photos of the accused in the company of 'Bloom' and Laskin which, in turn, gave rise to questions about prostitutes and wives of a sort that were of interest to the indefatigable clerk of Valkenberg, Ernest Rigg.

Kaplan's evidence paled beside that of the CID detectives from Cape Town and Kimberley and 'Private Detective' Levy. But beneath the orchestrated drama of the courtroom lay the real trial – betrayer against betrayer. It was Lorimer against Silver and, as Harris once put it in a different context, in 'their heart of hearts they knew it'. 'I am Inspector in charge of CID, Cape Town,' Lorimer announced to the court. 'I know the accused', and 'I have known him for about 2 years and 9 months'. Then, taking the plunge, he added, 'I cannot say of my own knowledge how he has been employed during that period'.[36] It was a calculated lie, born of official deviousness. Lorimer was in danger of slipping into a realm that lay beyond bribes, persuasion or threats. It was Shaw's sharp questioning which revealed that, two years earlier, the CID had sent Silver to the diamond fields on 'government service' that dragged Lorimer back from the edge. This sensational admission caused such consternation in the press corps and Attorney-General's office that, a week later, the Chief of the Detective Department, Kimberley, wrote a long letter of explanation to the secretary of the Law Department.[37]

With treachery hanging above the court like fog off Mouille Point, Shaw did his best to defend his client. Marks Levy of Houndsditch, fence, gambler and property owner told an unlikely tale about one 'Charlie Sacks' (sic) who might have been the real owner of the brothel in Chapel Street. But the real problems emerged when the accused himself took the stand. As happened so regularly when Silver found himself caught in the fire of cross-questioning, he dived automatically for the non-existent American fifth amendment:

'I decline to answer whether I was in Bloemfontein in 1903.
I decline to say whether I lived in a place called the Green

House there. I decline to say whether Annie Bloem kept a
brothel there. I decline to answer whether I ever appeared
before a court in Bloemfontein. I decline to state who the
person appearing in the smaller photo with me is [Rachel
Laskin]. I don't remember being in Johannesburg in 1899.
I don't remember being sentenced in Transvaal to 2 years
hard labour for an offence against the Morality Law. I don't
know Potchefstroom. I decline to say whether I ever
attempted to break out of jail. I have no marks of corporal
punishment on my body. I decline to state whether I know
two men named Beck and Roach. I decline to say whether
I know Gilminski of Tennant Street, nor Erlich of Roeland
Street. I don't remember getting these men to sign a petition regarding Beck and Roach who were then under sentence
in the Orange River Colony'.[38]

Adrift in the moral doldrums nothing stirred. Then on 22 September,
he was found not guilty of living off the proceeds of prostitution but
guilty of keeping brothels in Longmarket and Sydney Streets and
sentenced to three months' imprisonment with hard labour. Shaw immediately gave notice of appeal and bail was set at a massive £1,000 –
£500 provided by the accused, with two other, unnamed but nervous
parties each agreeing to stand surety, at short notice, for a princely
£250 each.[39]

It is easy to speculate about, but difficult to know, who came to
Silver's assistance. Herman Dempers, the Member of Parliament, was
presumably one person afraid of publicity but not averse to helping,
given the equity that had accrued on the unsold properties. But, wherever the secret funding came from, it did not come from Georges Hayum.
Reading the signs, Hayum had left Cape Town for Durban, from where
he was deported in mid-September.[40] Hayum, unlike Harris, perhaps
acted precipitately. Harris, released from prison in April 1905, on condition that he leave the colony, boarded a ship for Durban but then disembarked at Port Elizabeth before sneaking back into Cape Town by rail
and winning an order from the Supreme Court allowing him to stay in
the colony.[41] Hayum's departure heightened the sense of the underworld
emptying and did nothing to ease three weeks of waiting as counsel for
the defence prepared the appeal. Chief Justice Sir Henry De Villiers was
on the bench when Silver's bail was halved, on 24 October. But that

was the end of the Chief Justice's sympathy. He was not persuaded that the original summons and indictment had been 'vague' and 'bad in law', or that Broers had allowed the admission of 'illegal evidence'. The appeal was rejected and Silver was sent to do hard labour for three months, from 15 November 1904 to 15 February 1905, at Tokai, near Lakeside.[42]

With only an occasional breeze from False Bay nosing its way up the sweltering slope on which the prison was located, it was an unpleasant summer, although the long southern twilight made for pleasant evenings. He had no visitors but someone informed him that Jack was still trying to get his lawyers to reclaim money laid out for the liquor licence.[43]

On his release instinct sucked him back into the low-life of District Six. He hung around cab ranks speaking to drivers and coachmen who doubled as pimps, men who knew where there were new or unattached whores who could be muscled in on to provide him with a living. He went down to the harbour and watched single women disembarking from the passenger liners that made him think of other places, other times. Cabs, ships and trains were part of the pimp's lottery, and there was no knowing when your number might come up. He took his meals in the cheapest joints and drank in the lowest dives.

It was an alienating, lonely experience, reminding him of being in prison where he had not received a single visitor. In truth, he had no family who could visit. In late November 1904, Jack started an eighteen-month sentence for larceny in Wormwood Scrubs while Silver's daughter, also in London, turned seventeen. Visits to the port and the departure of other gangsters prompted the desire to leave; he felt like running but could not settle on a direction.[44] He called on fat Sarah Rosenblatt – 'Mrs Blatt' – in the hope of raising a few pounds but his reputation preceded him, and it was difficult to get business going. Everybody was afraid of him. He trawled through ethnic connections, speaking Polish, hoping that talk of the Old Country might deflect tales about his recent past. At the very lowest end of the market he linked up with some elderly women including a hagged forty-five-year-old Hungarian prostitute, Bertha Linczock, who worked out of a house in Primrose Street.[45]

At the watering holes men were talking about German South West Africa, where a serious native revolt had prompted the colonial power to mobilise its troops. Chatter centred on making money by provisioning the army with food, horses or livestock. It was said that the smartest entrepreneurs were already exploiting the new market and that horses, in short supply, were being brought in from as far afield as South America. A provincial boyhood spent hovering around the abattoir and a market packed with horses and other livestock made Silver feel that he had some of the requisite experience. Moreover, where there were troops there would always be a need for prostitutes. He saw an opportunity opening up and started assembling an expeditionary force of his own.

He liked butchers and Max Rosenberg, born in Vilkomir, Lithuania, was a butcher by trade who had emigrated to the Cape in 1899 and drifted around the margins of District Six leading a bohemian life before applying for naturalisation in 1903.[46] Another to succumb to the appeal of the south was Fischel 'Phillip' Krell, who ran a small transport business in the city. Krell, and his wife, Rosa Silberberg, a seventeen-year-old prostitute from Warsaw, were keen on the idea of a move north.[47] He also got to hear about a small band of prostitutes from Brazil moving through the port on their way to German South West Africa. Almost all of them were Jewish and from Poland or adjacent parts of the Austro-Hungarian Empire and he knew three of them. Fanny and Gussy Bernstein, Russo-Poles, were teenagers when he had first met them in Pittsburgh. They had moved to New York where they linked up with yet another immigrant, Rosa Müller. In 1895, while working as a Parkhurst 'agent' on the Lower East Side, he had milked all three for protection money. In Cape Town the women heard what they already knew – that he was a dangerous man who kept white slaves and acted as a police agent. It was a distinctly unpromising situation, but not one that he could fully ignore. He hated them in the way that he disliked all whores, and they loathed him in the way that they detested all parasitic pimps. It was an orgy of resentment fuelled by a sad history of bitter personal experiences.[48]

At about the same time, he met another prostitute from Rio de Janeiro who reminded him of the darkest period of all in his life but who, by the same token, mesmerised him. 'Gertie Gordon' who also liked to call herself 'Katia' – or Gertie Abrahams, to give her her real name – came from an East End family and there was something about her that spoke of Rachel Laskin in London in 1898, or of the woman who had given birth to his daughter, Bertha in Whitechapel, in 1888. She was only seventeen years old, had taken to prostitution and then, in order not to bring 'shame' on the family name had emigrated to

Brazil and now aspired to running a house of her own. From the moment he first met her, in early 1905, he set about inveigling himself into her professional life.[49]

With the economic recession deepening, the thought of German South West Africa was becoming ever more attractive and then, as if he needed prodding, the state added impetus. On 7 April, the Assistant Treasurer of the Cape Colony summonsed Silver for the 'payment of the sum of £92–7–0 due by the defendant for the maintenance of one Lizzie Silver at the Valkenberg Asylum for the period 28 May 1901 to 28 February 1903'. But he was not willing to move without Gordon and gave notice of his intention to defend the action. The matter was set down for the Cape Supreme Court on 28 June.[50] Krell and Rosenberg, already in his thrall, urged him to seize the moment and go north where they could all link up with his brother Jack and daughter Bertha. The matter was settled when Gordon agreed to set up a brothel and he advanced her the steamship fare. He then persuaded Bertha Linckzock to join them. When he entered the Supreme Court on 28 June, he cared little about the processes or outcome. He had started out with an attorney but had then not bothered to get him to brief an advocate. It no longer mattered.

The Vampire of Valkenberg led the evidence against him. Clerk Rigg took the court through 'Lizzie Silver's' admission, in 1901, and provided a meticulous account of every financial transaction that followed. But for the constitutionally argumentative, judicial proceedings are irresistible; contestation is all, outcome secondary. Silver took the stand and, confident that there was no Annie Vygenbaum to gainsay him, referred freely to 'Lizzie Josephs' as 'my wife'. Incarcerated and insane, Laskin was accorded the status she had searched for when he had courted her as a 'button-hole maker' in Whitechapel. Counsel for the plaintiff, a Mr Nightingale, knew him well and asked pertinent questions about properties belonging to him. 'I have owned large properties in Cape Town,' Silver admitted. 'I bought them when the boom was on, but I lost.' 'I bought a property four years ago and sold it to the Jewish synagogue.' 'I bought properties in Sydney and Longmarket Streets,' he said, but then at once countered, 'I did not let them as brothels.'[51]

The pastiche of truths, half-truths and outright lies continued. He had a 'twelve year-old', sickly, school-going daughter in England who accounted for most of his expenses. In fact she was seventeen and earning an income. His own income was derived largely from a share in the 'Caledon Street Baths and that brings in about 10 pounds a month'. He had never 'been in Johannesburg'. He was, in short, just another immigrant fallen on hard times. The judge, unmoved, granted judgment for the plaintiff, with costs. He left the court owing the crown £150.[52]

But the state was trying to board a ship which, although not clear of port, had cast off. Even before the hearing Crawford, by then Commissioner of Police, had noted that: 'several well-known foreign Jewesses, prostitutes', had 'left for German South West Africa'.[53] What neither he nor the court knew was that on 30 June Silver, too, had left for Swakopmund aboard the *Crown Prince* with a return ticket, valid for three months. A week later, when the Sheriff of the Court appeared at Vernon Terrace in District Six to attach Silver's goods, he discovered that the pirate had evanesced.[54] At this belated juncture the state suddenly focused on the problem of the 'return ticket'. Sir John Graham, secretary to the Law Department, wanted to know from Crawford how Silver had become a naturalised citizen. The answer was that, a year earlier, the papers had passed through the hands of Richardson, Easton and Lorimer of the CID. All three of them had approved the application, since 'It was not suspected that the applicant was identical to the Joe Silver who was so well known to the Police'.[55] That, of course, was a state lie. The application had been approved *because* he was known, *because* he was their secret agent.

As the steamer surged through the wintry sea, Silver had time to reflect on seven years spent in southern Africa. In Johannesburg, he had shaped the disorganised Bowery Boys into the American Club – an import agency and price-fixing body for East European pimps. His cohort had modernised the vice trade by using printed cards and privately struck metal coins in a low-cost/high-turnover/non-racial business. This retailing success had been built on the back of an industrial revolution while the colonists were trying to redefine their own identities as 'South Africans' and that, in turn, had fed into new, racist morality legislation. In a truly bizarre way, then, irreligious Americanised Jews who had fled Tsarist and clerical anti-Semitism in Poland and Russia had helped shape the emerging definition of what it was to be a 'white' South African. At the personal level, his impact as a police informer and sexual predator *extraordinaire*, too, had been felt and he left two words – *AmaSilva* and *impimpi* – that would always bear testimony to his presence. It was a problematic legacy and, some months later, he conceded that he 'had led a very bad life in South Africa'. He also claimed, however, that he had left the Cape Colony hoping 'to become an honest and a respectable man and to bring over my family'.[56] Nothing could have been farther from the truth. But the *Crown Prince* was approaching its moorings in Swakopmund, and everything pointed to stormy weather.

XVI

SWAKOPMUND
1905

In this world, shipmates, sin that pays its way can travel
freely, and without a passport; whereas Virtue, if a pauper,
is stopped at all frontiers.

Herman Melville, *Moby Dick*

ANCIENT inhabitants and modern Namibians alike will tell you that
God had run short of creative ideas and impetus by the time he reached
the south-western part of Africa. It is, they say, the country that God
forgot. And it is true that nothing could be further from the romantic
notions that the ignorant might entertain of 'Africa' than this angular
block carved out of desert and semi-desert. The territory's only extensive natural border is in the west, where the brown face of the interior
gives way to the glistening sand of the Atlantic; and in the south, where
its jaw nuzzles up against the Orange River.

Like Chile and Patagonia, this south-western part of the continent
aspires to reconcile fire and ice but in less dramatic fashion. The cold
Benguela current expels its chilly breath along the length of the coast.
Beautiful banks of cool fog wallow just off the parched shoreline, or
are nudged inland by gentle breezes towards plants that slake their
thirst from precious droplets of clear water. By mid-morning the sun
triumphs over the chill of the ocean and the interior lies beneath the
bluest of canopies.

Abandoned watercourses, craters, canyons, yellowed dunes sculpted
into scimitar-like perfection by shifting winds, rock-strewn river beds
and crusty salt pans sprawl across seemingly dead horizons. The most
forbidding northern section of the Atlantic shoreline is termed, with

brutal honesty, Skeleton Coast. Behind it, the Namib desert swallows thousands of miles of sand until it gives way to less arid soil supporting a stubble of acacias and hardy grasses. At night clear skies boast glittering stars studded into the very roof of the universe. Every aspect of the place refutes God's supposed amnesia. Desolation and starkness are wrought into an eerie beauty.

Most nineteenth-century European powers, including those who had probed its shoreline for half a millennium, had no abiding love of the place. By the time imperialist vultures settled on the map of Africa for a formal division of the continent, in Berlin in the early 1880s, the continent had already been pulled apart by the British, French and Portuguese. Bismarck, however, remained unconvinced of the value of immediate colonial expansion and it was only when he saw the need for a diversion from domestic policy considerations in the mid-1880s that he was prompted to consolidate German-held territories in Africa.[1]

Late nineteenth-century Germany was unified, prosperous and healthy even though the benefits of its industrial revolution had been spread unevenly. It acquired African colonies largely to keep its political cachet in western Europe. Gunboats with predatory names like *Hyena* and *Wolf*, moving in the wake of pioneering traders, found landing spots on the coast, depositing a few colonial troops, *Schutztruppe*, to secure the terrain. In 1884, a territory that hitherto derived its name from a reference point on the compass suddenly acquired a new character and became the German South West Africa protectorate. Representatives from trading houses followed to help open up the country to farming and mining. With barracks and stores acting as outer markers, the colonial administration pushed large concession companies to make land available to settler farmers and small traders, and to help prod indigenous people into reserves so as to free other tracts of 'crown' land for development and permanent settlement.[2]

The indigenous peoples were unconvinced by policies designed supposedly to protect them. Bibles, bullets and bookkeeping inflicted enormous losses on the Herero and Nama peoples spread over the central, eastern and southern parts of the country. Most of the decade that followed on the declaration of the protectorate saw small-scale armed revolts and native uprisings as *Schutztruppe* struggled to tighten the imperial hold on inhospitable terrain granted to Germany by statesmen who had never seen the place. By the mid-1890s only three settlements of note had been secured, two of them on the coast. The ancient Portuguese 'Narrow Bay', Angra Pequena, renamed Lüderitz, served as the southernmost port of the new colony. Further up the coast, at a point roughly opposite the site chosen for the capital, stood the aspirant harbour town of Swakopmund. About 130 miles inland, due east, lay Windhoek – the 'windy corner' – where the fort established in 1890, the *Alte Feste*, benefited from its central position and a permanent supply of fresh water.[3]

The turn of the century was marked by the arrival of hundreds of farmers, inn- and storekeepers, who dispersed through the central and southern parts of the protectorate. This, and the development of an embryonic mining industry, added muscle to a military skeleton that was the mainstay of the economy. Much of the progress the military found difficult to regulate. The extension of credit to tribal peoples produced an alarming upsurge in foreclosures on cattle as well as land alienation. Colonialism facilitated the dispossession, impoverishment and proletarianisation of the indigenous population.

In January 1904, the Hereros rose in revolt and killed 123 Germans, most of whom were traders. In October the Hereros were joined by Namas under the leadership of Hendrik Witbooi. The administration responded by pouring troops into the colony: the policies they enforced were so akin to genocide as to make no difference.[4] The Herero were dismantled with great cruelty and the robber economy which had given rise to the revolt was given added stimulus by an unexpected upsurge in military expenditure.[5] For several months South West boasted a bubble economy. It was a small bubble, but nevertheless recognisable as one of the sort that had appeared periodically along Atlantic shorelines ever since the 'voyages of discovery'. Like most nineteenth-century powers the German administration was aware that economic prosperity, in itself, was insufficient to ensure a lasting presence. Long-term success required the reproduction of aspects of metropolitan culture and its social structure, but Germany was haunted by the linked issues of class, race and sex. In an age much taken with scientific advance, Darwin and eugenics, Berlin was conscious of the problem of racial 'degeneracy' and the responsibilities it entailed.[6]

Governor Theodor Leutwein (1898–1905) and his successor, Friedrich von Lindequist (1905–7), both had reservations about the increasing rate of cohabitation and intermarriage between white males and black women. In 1898, the supposed dangers of miscegenation prompted Leutwein to ask the Deutsche Kolonialgesellschaft – the Berlin-based,

German Colonial Society – to underwrite the cost of transporting from the German countryside 'strong and healthy girls' who had 'considerable experience in domestic work', and were 'unpretentious in their manner of living', to South West. By 1907, 500 unpretentious 'prospective brides and female relatives' had been shipped to the colony; many settled in the popular southern farming region. It helped ease the shortage of marriageable European women in a protectorate which, in 1907, still had fewer than 5,000 white inhabitants.[7]

But the appearance of working-class women in the remoter parts of the colony did little to ease the discrepancy in the sex ratio of the territory's few urban centres. The arrival of thousands of troops and hundreds of itinerant traders and transport riders intent on supplying the army exacerbated the problem. Military barracks, inns, lodging houses and municipal camping sites were crammed with tradesmen as well as the adventurers, crooks, demobilised soldiers, cheats, liars, opportunists and thieves who swirled in the wake of the South African War of 1899–1902. Given the numerous white men without access to white women at a time of great hardship for indigenous peoples, there was a predictable increase in the number of black prostitutes in towns.[8]

Sexual services across the racial divide did not excite the administration unduly so long as it was confined to the lower end of a market composed of itinerant foreigners. Its own officials were, after all, drawn from a culture in which prostitution, while not encouraged, was tolerated and regulated; as it was in the new colony. For the same reason, prostitution would not have earned the disapproval of the military who came from a tradition in which the army was serviced by brothels and female camp-followers. It was the particular configuration of class and colour in a colonial setting that prompted the military to look beyond black prostitutes to service its officers and men. Shortly after the outbreak of the revolt, the army encouraged East European prostitutes in Brazil to make their way to South West Africa and establish themselves in the garrisons at Swakopmund and Windhoek.[9]

Swakopmund was a booming centre in an economy growing at an unprecedented rate when Silver, Krell and various prostitutes arrived there in July 1905. Its success was all the more remarkable given its inauspicious start. The name of the place on which the town stood was, not to put too fine a point on it, 'arsehole'. Early Nama inhabitants, seeing the river pushing debris and sediment into a clear sea had proclaimed it *Tsoakhaub* – an anus, *tsoa*, depositing excrement, *xoub*.[10]

Despite early setbacks, by 1895 there was a regular mail coach service between the coast and Windhoek. The town ceased to be the backside of nowhere when an undersea cable linked it to Cape Town and London, in 1899. The telegraph and the steamship connected Swakopmund to Europe and, for those more interested in human trafficking, placed it firmly in the Atlantic world.[11]

Even then, the port was slow to develop. In 1900, fewer than two dozen ships a year cast anchor offshore. Those that did, had cargoes unloaded by Kroo tribesmen, from Liberia, who used lighters to guide goods ashore through menacing surf. In 1903, a stone breakwater was constructed in an effort to build a harbour. The Mole functioned for less than thirty-six months before being silted up by the Benguela current. It was replaced by a wooden jetty that witnessed more prosperous times.

The number of ships calling had increased from 31, in 1903–4, to 128 in 1904–5. Silver and Krell, passing themselves off as 'horse dealers', watched as animals lifted from the decks of ships were lowered on to rafts before being towed ashore by huge steel cables. Between 1904 and 1906, tens of thousands of horses were imported from the Argentine, South Africa and, of course, Germany.[12]

The same uneven economic dance, a stately pavan giving way to a frenzied wartime jig, marked the rhythms of the town itself. A mineral water factory and brewery, built in 1899, served the barracks, a few houses, an inn or two and the lodging houses that provided settlers, soldiers, sailors, shopkeepers, officials and tradesmen with rudimentary shelter. A few prefabricated structures and stone buildings sported large windows that stared out into the desert sun. In 1900, the entire settlement had fewer than 500 civilians. The construction of the railway to Windhoek, completed in 1902, and the uprisings that followed, accelerated development.[13] A larger brewery, Swakopmunder Brauereigesellschaft, was built in 1905, along with two new hotels. The state and trading companies, too, either put up better buildings or, as with the magistrates' court, extended existing premises. With a civilian population of just on 1,500 and hundreds of troops, Swakopmund was, by far, the largest town in the protectorate. Indeed so central was it to the economy that many importers treated it as their primary business site and dealt with Windhoek only as an outpost of secondary importance.[14]

Amongst those viewing developments were a small number of Jewish settlers and co-religionists who travelled the territory doing the retail and wholesale trading they were famous for throughout southern Africa. In 1905, the Swakopmund Hebrew community, comprising seventy people, was formally constituted and the event was considered noteworthy enough for it to be telegraphed to the *Jewish Chronicle* in London. At first glance, these Jews looked like those in any other Anglo-German community, or like the 'Port Jews' of coastal communities in Europe or the Levant. Upon closer examination, however, they were closer to 'Frontier Jews' – rugged individualists with a disregard for conventional morality born of social isolation.[15]

Their leader, Solomon Stern, on good terms with the administration, was indeed of German origin but several of his deputies had backgrounds of the sort which, elsewhere on the subcontinent, would have qualified them for the epithet 'Peruvian'. Michael Mande, more commonly known as Max, was drawn from the same cohort of East

Europeans as Silver. Like Silver, he had served an apprenticeship on Manhattan's Lower East Side where he had started out as a pickpocket. Later, he became a pimp to a 'wife' with a penchant for wearing male trousers who followed him to London, Cape Town and Salisbury. Stern's sidekick and partner in the town's small public baths that were notorious for allowing the sexes to bathe together on the same day was the colourful Charney Schwartzmann.[16]

Beyond these mavericks lay an even tougher Jewish element jostling for a place on the frontier with international riff-raff discarded at the end of the South African War.[17] One or two, such as Hugo Friedman, had established themselves in the south where they were involved with the notorious 'Robin Hood' bandit and gun-runner, Scotty Smith.[18] Morris Davidson was a shady 'livestock dealer' in Swakopmund who dealt with anything on four legs, and once sold Silver a pig which he must have slaughtered and eaten. There were others, based in smaller settlements such as Karibib and Okahandja, while Max Rosenberg soon made contact with a Russian butcher in Windhoek, Sam Klotz, who specialised in dealing with stolen livestock.[19]

But, even amidst such formidable company, Silver stood out as someone special. Not only was he vastly more experienced than his gangster peers but his neurosyphilitic condition was propelling him to ever greater heights of self-importance. He was boss of all he surveyed and approved of what he saw in the arc that lay between Swakopmund and Windhoek. The miserable isolation of latter-day Cape Town was behind him. He was no longer alone and brimming with entrepreneurial energy. He wired Jack and asked that he and Bertha, his daughter, join him in addition to their younger sister, Rifka and her trader husband, Wolf Tuchmann, and their two small children. There was room for all in Swakopmund, the frontier of possibility. In the interim, he and Krell, Katia Gordon and Rosa Silberberg would set up a house in Windhoek to cater for the sexual needs of hundreds of civil servants and soldiers. The two women, supplemented by prostitutes imported from Cape Town, could be shuffled between the coast and the interior so as to avoid their clients becoming jaded.

But the dangers Silver faced in the new setting tended to be overlooked while he was in buoyant mood. There was a mismatch between the nature and size of the economy and his abilities, expectations and expansive style. He was the product of large cities with a huge, troubled personality difficult to hide in a town-and-countryside operation.

Complex urban societies provided him with some anonymity and cover. Just six blocks in New York City held more apartments, people and stores than all the settlements of German South West Africa put together. He operated best in maze-like surroundings where the police, riddled with corruption, inefficiency and inter-departmental rivalries were relatively easy to manipulate. South West differed not only from metropolises he was more familiar with, but from the rest of southern Africa. The protectorate had no established civil society; it was an ersatz colony only partially subdued by a military administration supported by a more rudimentary police force.

There were other differences, equally important but perhaps not fully thought through. As in metropolitan Germany, prostitution was legal in South West Africa even if ownership of brothels and pimping were not. The protection this afforded women in the commercial sex trade influenced the attitudes and expectations of prostitutes who were less inclined to put up with the excesses of bullying male parasites. Silver was more accustomed to dealing with servile prostitutes and 'white slaves'. It was a problem, since Gertie/Katia Gordon and Rosa Silberberg had made it clear that they wanted real partnerships or, at worst, considerable independence.

From the moment that he, Krell and the two young women set foot in the colony, perhaps even before, the group was beset by tension. He dominated the hopelessly ineffectual Krell, exercised some control over Katia, but could do little with the feisty seventeen-year-old Silberberg. She considered Silver to have an unhealthy influence on Katia, who was more or less the same age as she was, and took no nonsense from the besotted Krell. It was almost as if Gordon and Silberberg had entered into a secret pact to manage their own brothel, an aspiration that hardly suited the pimps. The net result was that Silver and Silberberg were often at loggerheads, with Krell and Gordon caught up on the margins of conflict. This psychological dynamite survived the cool trip north. Unpacked, in desert heat, it started sweating.

In any place larger than a village Silver would have raised cash from a burglary or store-breaking. Instead, he set about getting to know the local players and developing a hold on them. For a time he, and later Katia, stayed in the home of the trader Stern where they met Mande and Schwartzmann. He liked staying at Stern's not only because of the chance it gave him to talk business, but because it housed the public baths which catered for his need to mitigate the polluting propensities of whores.[20] It was Mande, whom he may have known from New York, who interested Silver most. A 'general merchant', Mande, Warsaw-born and educated, prided himself on his British connections. Silver flaunted his own cosmopolitan experiences and talked up the abilities of his brother-in-law who would be joining him.[21] Within days he persuaded Mande to advance him a substantial sum, in cash, for use as venture capital. This windfall strengthened his position over Krell and the women. It also, however, made the lascivious Mande, who was very taken with Silberberg, a *de facto* partner in any new enterprise. This financial web spread four months later, when Mande entered into yet another, independent, partnership with the trader Wolf Tuchmann.[22]

Having secured his working capital, he and Krell left to join Gordon and Silberberg who had gone ahead to Windhoek to explore the housing market. The train clawed its way along a narrow gauge track which lost itself in the successive nothingness of Arandis, Usakos, Karibib and Okahandja before finding its way to the capital. They took rooms in a boarding-house belonging to a Boer named De Wet and tracked down the women. But it was not a happy reunion. Silberberg was full of *chutzpah*. She and Katia had taken rooms in Hanke's House and then gone right ahead and hired furnished accommodation in a large house, almost perfectly suited as a brothel, near Mittel Street. The house, which belonged to a trader, Pasenau, had seven bedrooms, a kitchen, and two outside rooms for servants. Four rooms had been let to post office employees but their lease was about to come to an end. The women had also taken it upon themselves to approach Pasenau's legal agent, George Thiemann, to canvass the possibility either of hiring all the rooms in the house or of purchasing the property outright, and had deposited 4,000 marks with him.[23] Silberberg was getting beyond her station but Gordon, too, was hardly blameless. She had reiterated her wish to run a brothel of her own and, when asked where she would get the staff to run so sizeable an establishment had responded, 'My Joe is surely going to get me the girls.'[24]

Silver knew how to retrieve the situation and got Krell to go along with the idea. They went to the agent and he explained the difference between the real and imagined purchasers of Pasenau's house. He asked Thiemann if there would be legal problems if the house were occupied by prostitutes and was assured there would not.[25] Thiemann was easily talked into accepting 20,200 marks of Mande's money for outright purchase of the house. The deal done, Silver went to Pasenau and asked that the deposit given to him by Silberberg be returned to him, the real owner of the property. Pasenau gave him 4,000 marks, which he pocketed. Silberberg never again saw so much as a pfennig of a sum which, she believed, she had handed Thiemann for a house that *she* was going to purchase.[26] With the title deeds in his pocket, Silver told them that he and Krell would lease them the property for three months, at 1,000 marks a month, and that they would be left free to run the business as they saw fit. It was a rental which, if extended at the same rate, would cover the cost of the purchase of the house in less than two years. Outmanoeuvred, on the path to 'slavery', Silberberg and Gordon agreed to terms.[27]

He and Krell then returned to Swakopmund where he told his secret partner, Mande, how the money had been invested. A week or so later, having given the women time to come to terms with the situation, he returned to Windhoek intent on tightening his hold on the prostitutes. He moved into a small inn, not far from the Pasenau house, run by Gerhard and Anna Schroeder and made a point of befriending the proprietor and his brother-in-law. The Schroeders ran the sort of establishment he fully approved of – rowdy, with lots of drinking. The clientele was composed mostly of drifters in search of the sort of female company that Silver could easily introduce them to.[28]

At the Pasenau house, he got the essential points across as quickly as possible. He impressed on Silberberg the need to run the house profitably and pay the rent on time. It would not be easy. The women were charging 10 or 20 marks for 'short time' and 100 marks for rare, nightlong, stays. The brothel was in competition with another low-cost house owned by the clerk of the court, Herr Walter, and an establishment run by some black women frequented by low-life types of the sort to be seen at Schroeder's. The sting in the tail, however, was reserved for Katia. He told her that all her earnings were to revert to him. How this was enforced is best left to the imagination, but in the weeks that followed Gordon reported having had a serious disagreement with him and that Silberberg laid a charge of assault against Silver.[29]

Having established control, he set about making sure that the brothel operated at full capacity. He patrolled the station knowing that, with accommodation at a premium and women still flowing in, the Atlantic world would not fail him. Intercepting women was only a bit more taxing than clubbing seals at Swakopmund and it was a measure of their desperation that the Bernstein sisters and Rosa Müller – spotted earlier in Cape Town – ended up in the Pasenau House. Fanny and Gussy Bernstein, ex-Pittsburgh and New York, had linked up with Feldmann, also from the Lower East Side, who had later married Karl Müller, a professional wrestler. But the marriage had been short lived and, as 'Rosa Müller', she had moved on to try her luck in Johannesburg, Pretoria and Cape Town. They knew Silver only too well and lived in terror of him.[30]

With the brothel filling up nicely, Krell persuaded Simon Ablowitz, a fellow Pole and former electrician whom he had employed as 'coachman' in Cape Town, to move in as a resident pimp. Krell hoped that, in addition to drumming up business, Ablowitz might side with him and Silberberg in any dispute with his partner. Ablowitz was soon joined by another Pole, Hyman Sawicki who, under the name Jankelowitz, was doing a little part-time carpentry for the garrison. With two resident pimps and a half-dozen prostitutes, the house provided Walter's brothel with a little competition.[31]

By August 1905 the house was fully functional but, in staffing it, the mastermind had violated his own rules. A year earlier, he had been of the view that 'Jewish girls' were to be avoided because 'they gave too much trouble' but now he had a house full of ambitious young Polish Jewesses. It was Lucifer's lodging house. Silberberg, bitter at the loss of the deposit, was contemptuous of Gordon who was his informer as well as 'slave'. It was a house divided, steered by inexperienced girls. Gordon, protected by the boss, widened the gap by attempting to pull rank on Silberberg. Once, having been indisposed and unable to meet her quota, she demanded that Silberberg give her cash equivalent to three nights' work. The request scorned, tensions rose further.[32]

His very presence gave rise to other problems. Gordon, and to a lesser extent Silberberg, were subjected to a fusillade of complaints from the rear rooms. The Bernstein sisters and Müller, locked into a wretched situation, never ceased telling the younger women about Silver's propensity for treachery and violence. Internecine conflict poisoned the atmosphere in the house which, in economic terms, under-performed. Grim tales of the proprietor, part history, part prophecy, echoed through under-utilised bedrooms and were conveyed back to him by Katia. He found the rumours unsettling: they reminded him of his darkest secrets and raised irrational fears of exposure.[33] The house was fraught with menace; it was a place in which the whores he hated copulated at will with strange men and traded in muttered lies and truths that could do immense harm in uncertain times. It was a mad, almost medieval, environment that in some ways harked back to pre-industrial Europe just as surely as it was rooted in a chaotic, modernising spasm of German colonialism in Africa. It was the classic setting for identifying and, if need be, punishing a witch. The question was: who would it be? Who would the master of the house or his white slave point to?

For unknown reasons, Katia found it difficult to do as much business as she should have. Indeed, with the notable exception of the more fluent German-speaking Müller, most of the women struggled to meet their commitments. Twenty-seven-year-old Müller's success was difficult to emulate. An experienced, energetic redhead with a fine collection of jewellery, including some diamonds, she alone had an identifiably German name appreciated by patriotic clients. Her colleagues all kept their assumed maiden or married names that were recognisably Jewish. Even Silberberg, who had been forced to forgo her name, Rosa, in deference to Müller, had adopted the new first name 'Rachel'. Whatever the reason, Müller's earnings were above average and she saved about £100 which, she said, she would be forwarding to someone unknown to the other women in Cape Town. So marked was her financial success that it bridged some of the differences between Gordon and Silberberg who, united in their envy and resentment, singled her out for a stream of complaints to the proprietor. He knew that Müller knew about his career in Manhattan and about Rachel Laskin, and it fed an underlying paranoia. He, Katia, and even Rosa Silberberg were in agreement that the 'Red One' needed to be worked over, made to toe the line and relieved of her fancy diamond earrings and savings. Even as a very young man, back in London's East End, Silver had had a special – almost biblical – dislike of whores, especially streetwalkers who went about in public, parading their immorality, flaunting their rings and other jewellery.

The plot against Müller gestated for some days until it emerged in early September 1905. The final plan was so diabolical that it could not conceivably have come from two eighteen-year-old women, though they were more than willing to play a wicked part in its implementation. The idea was that of a person whose hatred of women was so intense that he had once assaulted, detained and raped a woman, forced her into prostitution and driven her insane. It was a notion born of a man who loathed prostitutes so intensely that he routinely assaulted them, causing two he had married to disappear without trace. More pertinently, it was the brainchild of a man infected with syphilis who saw the vagina as the fount of all evil. It was a glimpse into the mind of a madman who, under intense pressure, had once threatened to 'open up the belly' of a prostitute who would give evidence against him.

Silver and his accomplices agreed that they would persuade two of Müller's regular clients to overpower her, use chloroform to sedate her, and then insert powdered 'blue vitriol' into her vagina while they stole her prized diamond earrings. Hydrated copper sulphate or 'bluestone' as it was better known, was the choice of a man who had kept the company of chemists and experimented with chemicals as a prelude to sexual assault.[34] In his new guise as livestock dealer, he knew that blue vitriol, used as a preservative for curing hides, would be easily procurable. It was, however, more likely to act as a painful irritant rather than the permanently corrosive agent he may have hoped for. When the authorities eventually got to know of the conspiracy they ordered a search for the chemical but all they could find was a bottle of sublimate – mercuric chloride, a white crystalline powder used in the treatment of syphilis; being toxic, it could be used in larger doses as a disinfectant, insecticide or rat poison.[35]

Gordon and Silberberg identified two Boers, Joubert and Rossouw, who, after being briefed, expressed some interest. Encouraged by this, the women approached a medical practitioner in the hope of procuring an anaesthetic. But the doctor could see no legitimate use for this and refused to supply them with ether or chloroform. He may have suspected that the anaesthetic would be used in a robbery of a different kind involving off-duty soldiers. Mercifully, the delay proved decisive. The Boers had second thoughts, the conspiracy fizzled out, and even Silver became distracted when the two women heard of a less dangerous way of making money.[36]

The war had brought any number of drifters and transport riders to the capital, and many were left stranded once the principal conflict subsided. A dozen or more ne'er-do-wells, aged between twenty and thirty, constituted a loosely knit group which an official in the magistrate's office flatteringly referred to as the 'Kässbar gang'. If ever it was a gang, then it was one singularly lacking in discipline, hierarchy and leadership. Its members were, for the most part, involved in petty crime including horse- and stock theft, and spent a good deal of their time either drinking at Schroeder's inn or in the company of low prostitutes. Cosmopolitan by any standard, the Kässbar grouping included several Americans who would have been equally at home in the wild west or the Pasenau house. One of them was the mysterious Franks; others included 'Alabama Joe' McKenna, Charles 'Shorty' Ryan, George Howard, Harry FitzGibbon and James Murphy who preferred to travel under the name 'Woody S. Allen'. Others close to the core included an Australian, Andrew Livingstone; a Frenchman, Henri Sourd; a New Zealander, Harold Thompson; a Scot, Charles Smith; two South African Boers, Basson and van Blerk and Max Rosenberg's friend the butcher and 'livestock dealer', Sam Klotz.[37]

In mid-September 1905, somebody who moved amongst these 'Internationals', as the press came to dub them, came up with the idea of using a false key to enter Schroeder's inn; the safe would then be removed and explosives would be used to blow it and empty it of its contents. To do this, however, the proprietor would have to be lured from the premises on the night of the robbery. The plan and crime that followed were the worst-kept secrets on the frontier. It is difficult to know how Silver got to hear of the scheme. Perhaps he heard from American visitors at the Pasenau house drinking with an ex-Bowery Boy. But Rosenberg and Klotz may have been another source. Silberberg, whom the court later found to be a 'credible witness', was of the opinion that Silver was directly implicated in the robbery right from the outset. If he was not – and the prosecutor chose not to pursue charges in that regard – then only a most bizarre twist of fate made him an accessory to what followed. But all that lay in the future.

On 13 September, Silver was arrested for living off the proceeds. His arrest could not have come as a surprise since, three weeks earlier, almost all the women in the house had been called in to provide statements about his current and past activities. He was convinced that his misfortune could be laid at the door of Walter, clerk of the court, whom he had met while drinking at Schroeder's. It was a slightly paranoid male-centred view that underestimated the hostility of the women he was dealing with.[38] He and Walter did not get on, he explained to Jack, because of the clerk's rival establishment. It was just professional jealousy.[39]

The air was thick with conspiracy but Silver nevertheless sought professional help from a young Jewish attorney, Jacques Sanders, who got him out on bail of 1,000 marks. The trial was set for 10 November.[40] Supremely self-confident, he underestimated the gravity of his position. He went to the Pasenau house and instructed Ablowitz and Jankelowitz to join him on the coastal train leaving at three that afternoon. He had

faced similar charges in the past and got off fairly lightly. Living off
the proceeds was an occupational hazard, something one made provision for, like bail. Sanders seemed competent, Silver would be well
defended and was about to become the beneficiary of a Kässbar initiative. On the train, he settled back but once or twice, when they passed
through settlements with small stone-built stations, he caught sight of
what in the distance appeared to be corrugated-iron camps, dark spots
amidst the pale desert sands.

In Swakopmund, he headed off to find his brother. Jack, under the
name 'Hyam Goldstein', had served eighteen months for the theft of
clothing in London. On his release in April, he had rushed to
Johannesburg to reclaim his 'wife' but Regina Weinberg, unable to
pay a fine for an infringement under the new Morality Act, was in
prison and he had been forced to mark time for two months as a
'second hand clothing' dealer.[41] He and a certain David Mehr had then
opened a general dealer's store on mining property at Driefontein, near
Boksburg, on the East Rand. The idea had been that they would sell
groceries as a front while providing indentured Chinese labourers with
other, more interesting illegal products – such as alcohol and opium.
But the business had become indebted to wholesalers and, late in
August, Jack decided to slip out of town leaving Mehr with a promise
of money once Weinberg was back in business, in German South West
Africa.[42]

Silver was pleased to have his brother and 'sister-in-law' around. He
bore Weinberg no ill will even though she had given evidence against
him in Bloemfontein. In their circles, evidence given in the heat of battle
was a professional hazard, no offence intended, none taken; provided
the stakes were low. Jack introduced him to Sam Gilbert, an East
European pimp who had followed him to the frontier and confirmed
that they were about to be joined by the Tuchmann family and the
teenage Bertha.[43] Silver introduced Jack to Krell and Mande and told
him about his coming court appearance, and the trouble he was having
with the women in the Pasenau house. He also let Jack into the secret
about the Schroeder project, and said he would have to leave town for
a few days. They agreed that Regina should proceed to the Pasenau
house as soon as possible, but that Jack and Gilbert should remain in
Swakopmund. The arrival of his brother, a man with military experience and yet another henchman, boosted Silver's already overblown
ideas of importance and power. He felt in control of professional

gangsters who, in a frontier society at war, could take on even more ambitious projects. In late September, he and Jack mooted the idea of running guns to Hendrik Witbooi's rebels operating in the south of the territory. For the time being, however, that would have to wait.

With his trial looming and the Schroeder project coming to the boil, he belatedly started extending his cover. He bought fifteen horses from Morris Davidson and told Ablowitz and Jankelowitz – or 'the Boys', as he preferred to call them – to give him a few days' start and then move the animals along the line of rail to Karibib where he would meet them at Rosenmann's inn. He boarded the train for Windhoek and, on the way out of Swakopmund, noticed another of the dark desert stains he had seen on the way down.[44] Suddenly, he realised what it was. It was something he had first seen around Potchefstroom during the South African War, when the British had rounded up Boer women and children and put them in camps where they had died in their thousands. What he was seeing was a *Konzentrationslager*, a concentration camp, housing what was left of the Herero nation, starving and dying like flies.[45] What could such a camp have meant to one unstable East European Jewish gangster in a German colony on the margins of Africa in 1905? How could he have known that the 20th century would become the century of the concentration and extermination camp; that systematised murder was not the prerogative of one people in one place? Or, that one day, in September 1942, his nephew, Maier Lis, his wife and children would be rounded up in their small shop in Kilinskiego Street, back in Kielce, and sent to Treblinka.[46]

But there was something droll about the trek across hundreds of miles of the Namib desert by the 'Boss' and his 'Boys'. Every now and then, about a day's ride apart by horse, a suited New York City gangster with a Bowery Boy accent would disembark from the train and 'distribute fodder [along] the railway line' at Rossing, Trekkopje, Ebony, Aukas and Usakos. A few days later, two fat Polish pimps would appear, huffing and puffing, leading fifteen mistreated horses. It was a crazy expedition led by a madman and marginals trying to conceal future and past misdeeds at the extremities of the earth. It was a minor odyssey in the annals of exile-driven crime somewhat reminiscent of Butch Cassidy and the Sundance Kid who, at almost that very moment, were out robbing banks in Chile.[47]

At Karibib, Rosenmann had a hundred oxen from Ovamboland he wished to sell. The Boss said that he could sell the animals on a commission basis. Shortly thereafter, he boarded the train for Windhoek, where he arrived on either the fourth or fifth of October and booked into Schroeder's inn. When the Boys got to Karibib, he told them to get the haggard horses back on the road and make their way to the capital – a journey that would take them as far as they had already travelled. It was a journey almost as futile and demanding as that of the Boss. The route took them past more dark stains in the sand: the camps at Okahandja and outside Windhoek.[48] In town, the Boss, still dissembling, disposed of some horses through attorney Sanders. Most of his effort, however, went into persuading Schroeder to go and assess Rosenmann's oxen which, he said, could be acquired at a very competitive price. Eventually, unable to resist, Schroeder relented and, at 3 p.m. on the afternoon of Friday, 6 October 1905, he and a friend left for Karibib by train, leaving his wife in charge. The Boss joined Krell at the Pasenau house.[49]

Business at the hostelry picked up the minute the proprietor left town. Henri Sourd and some friends appeared for a Friday afternoon's drinking. Sourd, originally from Lyons, had worked at the horse depot in Swakopmund before becoming a house painter in the garrison at Windhoek. Several layabouts in town had an idea of what was about to happen. In the messy, unsatisfactory investigation that followed, half a dozen or more Kässbar types provided each other with alibis for the evening of 6–7 October.[50]

By ten o'clock Anna Schroeder had had enough of their carousing. Ignoring a request to remain open, she closed the bar. Most of the group hung around the building and, suspecting trouble, she instructed an employee to be vigilant. But the man could not have been very conscientious and Fräulein Schroeder must have slept the sleep of the dead, since the early hours saw much activity in and around the inn. An experienced burglar – someone with experience of false keys – unlocked the front door. Several men entered and removed a safe which contained over 2,000 marks in cash. It was loaded on to a two-wheeled cart and driven off into the night.

On the outskirts of town, close by the Catholic mission station, the safe was unloaded in a dry river bed where an American blacksmith, George Howard, took charge of opening it. Someone produced two artillery shells to blow the safe. But the charge was hopelessly excessive; most of the safe's contents went up in smoke and the unexpected thunder in the night was followed by a steady rain of bent and pitted coins. Gang members scrambled about in the dark, collecting such coins as they could before they were dispersed by the approaching sun. A few days later a schoolgirl, on the way to the mission, found a pile of coins hidden in a handkerchief, and for weeks thereafter battered coins circulated freely in insalubrious quarters.[51]

It was hardly Butch Cassidy, but then there were no Pinkertons either. It took the police weeks to pick up on the plot and it was only in December that they made any real headway. In the end it was Sourd who became the fall guy for what was clearly a more extensive conspiracy. He was sentenced to a lengthy period of imprisonment, deported to Germany, and served his time in Lower Saxony. Back at the Pasenau house, the Boss was not amused. His face, Rosa Silberberg told the police, assumed an expression of pain when told that the proceeds of the robbery lay burnt and scattered in a dry river bed. He, however, remembered things differently. 'Nobody in the world,' he later wrote to the investigating magistrate, 'felt more sorry for Mr Schroeder than I,' since, 'I liked the man and his family as friends . . .'[52] It was another setback and, maybe, another moment to sit back and take stock. But the Boss who had outwitted South African authorities for five years never doubted his ability, or that of the Boys, to outsmart the Germans. He remained confident and, unlike almost everybody else, without fear.

XVII

WINDHOEK
1905–1906

> For what are states but large bandit bands, and what are
> bandit bands but small states?
>
> St Augustine, *City of God*

THERE was a further deterioration in interpersonal relations in the
Pasenau house after the Schroeder robbery. Silver's financial position
was tenuous and it occasioned a tense meeting between the four partners. It was agreed that they needed new attractions if the business
were to be viable. Mande would be pressed for more cash and Krell
and the Boys would go to Cape Town to secure 'fresh goods'. But by
then Krell, Silberberg and Ablowitz were already involved in a separate plot of their own.

Rosa Silberberg impressed upon Krell that Silver was probably going
to be sent to prison and that they should attempt to secure as many
assets as possible; she was particularly keen that his half-share in the
house be transferred into her name. She remained intent on owning
and running a brothel of her own and, to this end, continued to cultivate her special relationship with Max Mande, who was becoming
increasingly distanced from his own whore-wife. The three conspirators – Silberberg, Krell and Ablowitz – agreed to remain in contact via
Mande, and to communicate in the ancient *mauscheln* code used by
pimps and white slavers.

In Swakopmund, with the clock running down the weeks to Silver's
trial for living off the proceeds, there was a veritable convention of
double-crossers, perjurers and thieves. Like politicians at a party conference in a tacky seaside resort, pimps and traders, dressed in the suits

and felt hats that distinguished them from ordinary folk, strutted their stuff. Silver, exercising the customary mixture of charm and blackmail, worked on Mande until he agreed to come up with more money for the Pasenau brothel. Krell siphoned off 4,000 marks from Silver which he and Ablowitz would use for the purchase of prostitutes in the south who, in telegrams and letters routed via Silberberg, would be referred to as 'apples' – a telegraphic code which Russo-Polish Jewish criminals had, in one of the great ironies of East European history, borrowed from the Okhrana, the Russian secret police.[1]

The Boss, anticipating the arrival of the Tuchmann party who had left London for Hamburg to wait on the arrival of the *Erna Woermann*, used the intervening time to plan his defence for the upcoming trial. The plan was tried and trusted. The women who had the misfortune of being closest to the Lis brothers – Katia and Regina Weinberg – would deliver such perjured evidence that it would be impossible for him to be convicted of living off the proceeds. He would muddy the waters further by getting his lawyer, Sanders, to write to Gordon and Silberberg informing them that they were prostitutes and that he wanted them to vacate his premises. If the lies and evictions did not do the trick, there was always the possibility of a witness disappearing.

On 15 October, he reappeared at Rosenmann's in Karibib, a one-horse town which had once seen fifteen of his nags. Not surprisingly, nothing had come of the Schroeder deal and, a week later, Rosenmann had sold the cattle to the garrison at a profit. Having reactivated his status as a 'livestock agent', Silver returned to Windhoek but chose not to stay at Schroeder's. Instead he went directly to the brothel, where he coached Katia and Weinberg in their lines for his trial on 10 November 1905. The following day he instructed Sanders to write to Gordon and Silberberg, telling them that they should vacate the premises when their lease expired on 3 November. All seemed well.[2]

A week later, when the Boss was already back in Swakopmund, the letter was delivered to Gordon, who was in the know, and a furious Rosa Silberberg, who was not. His return to the coast may, however, have been a mistake. Silberberg, sensing that she was about to lose her prize, had already struck back at him. On 27 October, she went to the public prosecutor and accused Silver of assault, of being party to the Schroeder robbery, of plotting the 'bluestone' vaginal attack and of coaching witnesses for his coming trial. By the end of the day the police had other supporting, if less damaging, statements from three other women in the Pasenau house – Katia, Regina Weinberg and Wally Ewert. Battle for ownership of the house commenced.[3]

The public prosecutor, Dr Kornmeyer, opened a docket on the 'horse trader Lis and associates in Windhoek' with the intention of investigating new, possibly more wide-ranging charges. Kornmeyer had been on to Silver before Silberberg's approach and was already in receipt of a letter from the Cape Town CID. Detective George Easton had sent him a copy of his quarry's criminal record hinting at earlier, more serious offences committed in the Transvaal but maintaining absolute silence about his service as informer and policeman.[4] The CID could be as parsimonious with the truth as any Polish pimp. Kornmeyer, confronted by real stature of his opponent, moved with greater urgency. He wrote to the German consul in Johannesburg, asking him to get the Commissioner of Police there to provide him with additional information. In Windhoek there was a focus and professionalism that had been wholly lacking in the supposedly more developed southern colonies. More pertinently, Kornmeyer issued a warrant for the arrest of Gordon and telegraphed the coastal police to have Silver taken in at once.[5]

The Boss could not have been more surprised by his arrest, on 29 October 1905, than if the Atlantic had parted to provide him with safe passage to New York. Without access to a network of informants in the prosecutor's office, there had been a failure of intelligence. He had overreached himself and was out of his *métier*. The tyranny of distance and a small bandit state on a war footing had caught him cold. But he was not about to give up. The Swakopmund police were suspiciously accommodating. Business interests, he told them, demanded his immediate return to Windhoek. But he understood their position: they would probably have to refer the matter back to Kornmeyer. Perhaps the best way round the problem was for him to get men of standing in the community to stand surety for him in order to demonstrate good faith? Max Mande was sent for and, within an hour, he and other 'businessmen' came up with 10,000 marks – 500 pounds sterling – in 'caution money' which they would deposit with the police if Silver were allowed to proceed to Windhoek.

The urgency and amount of money involved transcended the problems of a pimp. It was as if the business consortium who had so readily put up bail were involved in another, unknown, transaction in which more than a property in Windhoek or the fate of a pimp and a few prostitutes was at stake. The police, responding to the pleas of local notables, conveyed their offer to Kornmeyer. A storm of telegraphed messages broke across the neutral Namib – the Swakopmund end counselling conditional release and the Windhoek end, ever more firmly, denying it on the grounds that the prisoner's return to the capital could well facilitate collusion amongst witnesses. Kornmeyer had won the first encounter of what was to become a classic, extended game of desert chess.[6]

But the margin of his first victory was not as wide as he would have liked. The Swakopmund police had requested that, if Silver was to be held, he be held in the capital. It was therefore something of a compromise when, just hours after his arrest, he was put aboard the train for Windhoek. A journey under armed escort was no novel experience, nor were thoughts of escape. All along the way he saw concentration camps. Thirty or more Hereros a day were dying in the camps, and General von Trotha had told the *Swakopmunder Zeitung* that they sought 'the destruction of all rebellious native tribes'.[7] While it was obviously reassuring to be a white, it was troubling to contemplate imprisonment in German South West Africa.

In the interim, Kornmeyer had been very busy. The police had confiscated letters and telegrams linking Silver to the brothel and had also obtained copies of earlier, telegraphic, correspondence. The Post Office was told to intercept and monitor all incoming or outgoing correspondence of suspects, or witnesses, until further notice. Everyone of note connected to the impending trial was snared in a country-wide, wartime communications net. Kornmeyer already had Weinberg in custody and, before the Boss could get to the capital, Katia alias Gertie Gordon, a woman clearly in Silver's thrall, was picked up and placed under police protection.[8]

With Gordon sealed off and a net in place in a country beset by the tyrannies of distance, Kornmeyer baited the trap. He obtained a written assurance from Silver that he understood that he was being investigated for a possible charge of perjury and then cut him loose – waiting to see where he would go, what he would do. True to nature, the Fox responded with an action so unexpected that it remains impossible to understand fully his next move. Knowing why the shadowy coastal importers who had put up his bail were so keen to ensure his mobility, he sneaked aboard a train that took him 600 miles south of Windhoek, towards where 'rebellious native tribes' were still engaging the German army. Jakalswater, a rail siding, had nothing to do with prostitution and little to do with livestock. It was incomprehensible that he should waste two days at a cattle outpost at a time when he should have been in Windhoek preparing his defence. On 2 November, under the mistaken impression that Katia would have been released, he sent her a telegram: 'Get Max [Rosenberg] to meet me in Okahandja.' Indefatigable, he boarded another train and retraced his steps to the northern front. It is impossible to tell who won the second encounter of desert chess but, as we shall see, it may have been the Boss.[9]

Rosenberg, with American experience, was the most independent-minded and smartest of the Boys. He stayed put. Frustrated, the Boss moved further down the line, to Karibib, where Rosenmann, too, must have been puzzled by his movements. On 3 November, he sent three telegrams to Windhoek. The first, to Rosenberg, dripped menace: 'Come at once to Okahandja. I leave here tomorrow morning.' By mid-morning, suspecting he was being ignored he sent another to Regina Weinberg: 'Send Max to meet me. I will be at Windhoek tomorrow night.' The third, to his counsellor, Jacques Sanders, was greased in supplicatory tones: 'I am arriving tomorrow night. If possible; please wait for me.' The following morning he left for Windhoek, again partially retracing his steps. Kornmeyer, who had read all the telegrams, had won their third encounter.[10]

The iron horse rumbled east, stopping to fill its rounded metal belly with water at Okahandja. Of Max Rosenberg there was still nothing to be seen. Having been implicated in stock theft with Sam Klotz, he was lying low.[11] The train turned south, pushing on towards Windhoek, Kornmeyer and the court case. It was to be his last ride as a free man on the continent which had been his home for seven years and which, he had hoped, would have been so for several years more. Two days later Bertha and the Tuchmanns disembarked at Swakopmund. But they were destined never to see him face to face; they saw him only through the bars of a military prison.

That night he rested in one of his customary haunts but the following morning, 5 November 1905, Kornmeyer, tiring of the game, reeled him in.[12] With the Boss and Katia in custody, and the police pushing ahead with inquiries on the charge of perjury, the gravity of the situation was brought home to all in the Pasenau house. Silberberg, who had police informants of her own, became nervous about the project to gain control of the brothel and import more women. She wrote to Krell, back in Swakopmund, telling him that their adversary was in prison, that the Cape Town CID had written a damning report on Silver, and warning him not to send any telegrams.[13]

If Silberberg was jittery, Gordon was frantic. She was no Rachel Laskin but knew, better than most, how unforgiving the Boss was when thwarted. Having been locked away on her own for several days before her puppeteers' return, the princess in the play became unsure of her lines. It is not clear what cash or sexual inducements Katia held out to her jailers but she rose to the challenge. With the help of the prison administration she subjected Kornmeyer to a barrage of vexatious questions. While just one of her unsuccessful ventures is recorded, there is no way of knowing whether or not she did in fact find some way of communicating with the Boss prior to his trial.

On the day she was arrested, 30 October, the police discovered that they were unable to detain her in holding cells that were hopelessly 'over-crowded'. They put in an official request to the court that more suitable accommodation be found. But nothing happened. She stayed in the police cells and was hardly isolated. On 3 November, she was handed the telegram the Boss had sent from Jakalswater and responded with a written message smuggled to someone in town. It occasioned a rebuke for the police from the administration, which noted that prisoners were not allowed to receive or send any form of written communications. By then, however, Gordon was on to a more ambitious project.[14]

On the afternoon that Silver was placed in custody in the nearby military prison, she suddenly fell ill manifesting symptoms of an intestinal obstruction so severe that the prison doctor, Dr Dünschmann was convinced her life was in danger. Since surgery might be needed at any moment, he recommended an immediate transfer to the military hospital. But the surgeon-major had no suitable accommodation for a female patient and told the police that she should be kept in the holding cells until Dünschmann was ready to use the operating facilities. This proved unnecessary. In the next four days the patient experienced so complete and rapid a recovery that, the night before the trial, she staged an unsuccessful attempt to escape. The following morning, as the Boss's trial got under way, Kornmeyer released her on bail raised from 2 to 3,000 marks.[15]

Silver, in whose mind American judicial processes reigned supreme, found the German system as well as the outcome of his trial totally unacceptable. The prosecutor, Dr Hintrager, building on the foundation laid by Kornmeyer, got the Bernstein sisters, Bertha Linczock, Rosa Silberberg and Rosa Müller to give evidence for the state. They testified to the appropriation of the house, the nature of the lease, his record as a pimp elsewhere and his exploitative treatment of Gordon. Sanders could do little to counter the onslaught and attempts to conjure up irrelevant testimony from peripheral witnesses for the defence were utterly ineffectual. Given the last word in his defence, Silver drew attention to what, he said, was a conspiracy by prostitutes; a view on this occasion not entirely without merit. The judge, however, concluded that he had lived off the earnings of Gordon and sentenced him to a year's imprisonment. He awarded the state the costs of the trial.[16]

It was the longest sentence handed down to Silver since that day, in 1889, when he was told he would be spending two and a half years in Sing Sing. He was not the only one dismayed at the sentence. The prosecutors, having perhaps got an inkling of why the Swakopmund importers had been so keen to allow him to visit a war zone before the trial, were equally dissatisfied. So when Sanders gave notice of appeal fourteen days later, Kornmeyer, too, suddenly lodged an appeal.[17] The possibility that he might have to serve a sentence in an institution more attuned to dealing with Africans than Americans had not entirely eluded Silver. The day before the trial, with the prison leaking notes faster than a rusted freighter taking water, he had sent a telegram to Mande in half-Boss, half-pleading tone: 'Tomorrow my trial comes on. Please see to my family's wants until further orders.' Mande, who was taking a very personal interest in Silver's daughter, was already providing support to the Tuchmann family. By the time the sentence was handed down, the full horror was clear. Silver sent a badly scrawled, utterly grovelling note to Kornmeyer, signed 'yours very respectfully', requesting an early interview in order to discuss what was 'a very important matter'.[18]

With Silver behind bars and a further charge of perjury pending, Silberberg sensed her moment had at last arrived. She and most of the women stayed on in the house but, hours later, he gave Sanders instructions to call at the brothel and collect three months' rental, 'payable in advance'. Showing remarkable composure, she used mirror writing and 'thieves' Latin' to tell Ablowitz to go ahead with the original plan and obtain fresh 'apples'. She wrote to Mande and Krell, advising them to skip the country and head south. Krell did as she suggested, but Mande, facing financial ruin, sent her a letter, begging her not to make any further moves against the Boss.[19] Her spirited attempt to cobble together a coalition with three absent men came under pressure from two different quarters as they awaited the outcome of Silver's appeal in January 1906. Kornmeyer, monitoring correspondence, started taking increased interest in Krell and Mande. Lacking her courage and fearing the Boss, they were incapable of holding a line. By early December the police were searching for Krell in connection with the widening perjury charges, and had already questioned Mande. Mande, soon thereafter, attempted to get Stern and other less respectable Jewish notables to intervene on Silver's behalf with the Governor.[20]

The Boss, aware of Silberberg's game, tried to counter her moves. He issued a summons, ordering her to appear in court so that he might force her to pay rent. More ominously, in mid-December, he sent for Jack, and his sister, Rifka, who checked into the Hotel Stadt Windhuk. It is inconceivable that Jack did not call in at the house to discuss the rent but, in a system where prostitution was legal, women were hard of hearing.[21] The sudden appearance of two unknown members of the Lis family made the prosecution edgy. The Lis siblings were hauled in to explain the nature of their business. The police feared that Rifka would pose as Silver's spouse in order to mislead the court of appeal about his relationship with Gordon. But it was the presence of Jack, a past master of the black arts, that they found most alarming. The police were not reassured and gave him three days to leave town or face deportation.[22] The indefatigable Kornmeyer pushed inquiries further and within ten days had established that Jack was living off the earnings of Regina Weinberg.[23]

With pressures from the prosecution starting to get to the extended Lis family, Mande and those who had advanced money for the purchase of the Pasenau house, and other, even more risky ventures, feared they might lose all unless they took counter-measures. Mande exerted pressure on the ineffectual Wolf Tuchmann who already owed him money. He persuaded him that it would be in their interests if the Boss were to have his share in the Pasenau house put in Tuchmann's name. Tuchmann, stranded at the far end of the world with a wife and two small children, asked Jack to put the idea to Silver on his next visit to Windhoek. Everybody wanted the house. The Boss saw through the scheme instantly and his decision was relayed back to Swakopmund, where it occasioned great acrimony within the family.[24]

After this clumsy attempt to acquire the property, the Boss sidelined

Mande and Tuchmann and spoke only to Jack about his business. With Krell away in Cape Town, the problems of ownership, rent-collecting and the sale of the house deepened and mutated. Some time after Silver's fate was decided, Krell handed over his affairs to his feisty 'wife'. This produced a final irony. The house was re-registered in the names of Silver and Silberberg before it was sold, months later, at a substantial loss, for 14,000 marks. But even the 7,000 marks represented a substantial profit for the Boss. The real loss was, of course, sustained by Mande and some very unhappy partners.[25]

The Boss, stuck in prison, adjusted his repertoire from menace to manipulation. He wrote a six-page letter to Kornmeyer culminating in an appeal for an interview. Most of his effort went into outlining how Silberberg, through a series of calculated lies, had wrongfully accused him of threatening her with murder, of being party to the planned attack on Rosa Müller, and being in on the theft of Schroeder's safe. It was a craven communication and contrasted sharply with his aggressive efforts to get Sanders to deal with the rent and other issues relating to the house. The latter, too, were largely unsuccessful. His domineering, know-all approach to the law and a willingness to lie increased the distance between him and Sanders. With the date of the appeal yet to be set, attorney–client confidence was wearing increasingly thin.[26]

Christmas came and went. By the end of the first week in January 1906 Silver still had no idea when his appeal would be heard. He was starting to despair when, on the 9th, the gods glanced in his direction, even though they failed to smile. The Governor, Friedrich von Lindequist, visited the military prison and exchanged a few words with inmates. Silver seized the opportunity to complain about the delay in setting a trial date. Von Lindequist must have been persuaded since, later that day, Silver was told the appeal was set for 17 January.[27] The trial was a disaster. To the Boss's 'horror', the appeal was heard by Acting Chief Justice Schottelius, rather than the Chief Justice. Schottelius, too, refused to hear irrelevant testimony from peripheral witnesses and found Silberberg a 'credible witness'. By then Kornmeyer had copies of Silver's criminal record in the Cape as well as Transvaal. Judge Schottelius, under great pressure from the prosecution, tripled the sentence to three years' imprisonment. He imposed an additional fine of 1,000 marks which, if unpaid, would become another three months spent in prison. The convict was also to be banished from the colony on completion of his sentence.[28]

Schottelius's judgment was as comprehensive as it was damning. He traced the way the house had been acquired and the punitive nature of the lease imposed on Gordon and Silberberg. He noted that Gordon had been 'forced to hand over the greater part of her earnings to him'. This, the judge rightly saw as being of a piece with the accused's criminal record. But Schottelius then went on to outline a further reason for his savage sentence – a reason which, at face value, seemed to transcend both the charge and the evidence presented. The judge argued that 'the activities of pimps' were the source of 'many other criminal offences' in the territory, and that '*the prevailing unrest in the protectorate*' demanded that '*a special effort be made to protect the population*'. He could not have had the Schroeder robbery in mind since it had not involved other pimps, nor could it be directly related to 'native unrest'. The judge appeared to have had other concerns, relating to security of the settlers. Could it have been that he had some private, out-of-court knowledge about the mysterious trip to Jakalswater? If not, was three years' imprisonment for brothel-keeping and banishment from a remote colony an appropriate sentence?

If there were covert dimensions to Silver's operations or in his connections to the shifty Swakopmund importers there was no hint of it in the official correspondence. On the day after the trial, stunned by a sentence increased on appeal, he sat down and addressed a letter of complaint to the judge. 'I am ignorant of the law' and uncertain how exactly to proceed, he suggested. But, 'in the mean time I give you notification that I am not satisfied with the result of my case, and I wish to be granted an interview to lay the facts before you'.[29] In a second letter, to the Governor the same day, having recovered some composure, he was less modest about his legal knowledge. Von Lindequist, he suggested, should acquaint himself with a recent case in which Adolph Beck had been wrongly accused, on the basis of mistaken identity, had subsequently been released, and was paid compensation by the British government. He made his usual appeal for an interview and complained about Ablowitz and Jankelowitz – the 'Boys' – not being allowed to appear as witnesses for the defence.[30]

Kornmeyer relaxed his grip. Six days after sentencing he dropped the charges of perjury. Others remained cautious. The police, unaware of wrangling over the ownership of the house and unconvinced of the prison service's ability to hold on to their prize, worried about Jack's persistent, if unsuccessful, attempts to get to see his brother. It smacked of an escape plot and they urged the administration to have Silver transported at the earliest opportunity. Jack, despite having been warned to stay away from Windhoek, true to form, went to the brothel and threatened Silberberg to the point where she was forced to seek police protection.[31] The Boss, denied access to his brother and uncertain that his letters were getting to the authorities, started experiencing mood swings so severe that some started to question his sanity. Struggling to maintain focus under great pressure, and 'after much praying and persuasion', he decided to write a second letter to the Governor within a week, his bunched handwriting again revealing his neurosyphilis.

The opening lines, addressed in madly flattering terms to the 'Baron', were probably not meant for the Governor at all but for his immediate persecutors in prison. 'Before beginning my letter,' he wrote, 'I wish to make myself understood to Your Excellency, that I am neither mad, nor a lunatic, nor a demoniac, I am by my sound and full senses . . .' Less promising material followed. Drawing on Jewish folklore about the destruction of Sodom, he cast von Lindequist as the 'Angel of the Lord' whose task it was to 'find out and destroy the court'. He was in possession of a dark 'secret' which, if only he could convey it personally to the Governor or his emissary, would clarify the 'mystery' surrounding the delay in his trial. And, if von Lindequist was labouring under the misapprehension that he had been sentenced only to imprisonment and a fine, then the time had come for the Governor to learn the full truth. 'I have been sentenced to die an unnatural death,' he wrote, 'and gagged in the bargain in order that I should be silenced and the secret should not come out.'[32]

This tormented outpouring, at the intersection of pain and paranoia in the highways of his mind mirrored his earlier, psalm-like lamentation to his police handler in Cape Town at another moment of intense pressure. But if his moments of greatest stress produced biblically inspired, heavenly discourses then less pressured communication remained decidedly more earthy. He clearly was not raving mad; his moods ebbed and flowed, but his behaviour was becoming very erratic. Within hours of the 'Angel of the Lord' failing to visit destruction on the court, he wrote a second letter so filled with 'insults to the authorities and court officials' that guards refused to forward it to its probable recipient, his brother.[33]

The rage lifted and seventy-two hours later he produced a more cunning and composed letter which he may have been written suspecting that it, too, would be intercepted and read prior to being passed on. It not only dealt very carefully with legal matters, but displayed contrived concern and warmth for absent kin. 'How is my dear family getting along?' he asked. He told Jack to 'try to do [his] best to cheer the family up', concluding, 'I send my best regards and many kisses to the children, your affectionate brother, J. Lis'. To Issie and Annie – Rifka's children – he was just 'Uncle Joe'.³⁴

Kornmeyer, a flesh-and-blood panopticon, did indeed scrutinise the letter. With ownership of the Pasenau house still being actively contested, he turned his attention to the surrounding issues.³⁵ He returned Gordon's caution money but, almost simultaneously, took new steps against Jack.³⁶ When Lis reappeared in Windhoek on 6 February, to discuss the crisis mounting around Mande and Tuchmann, he was arrested for living off the proceeds of Regina Weinberg's earnings. Kornmeyer then tightened the screw by asking the Cape Town police for a copy of Jack's Cape criminal record. Still not satisfied, he approached Berlin for permission to have Silver transported.³⁷

A jackal with a leg in a snare, Jack Lis twisted and turned. He demanded to be allowed to appear before a court, simultaneously urging Gordon and Weinberg to come up with enough bail. But Kornmeyer was in no hurry. More than a week elapsed before Jack appeared in court. He was warned not to leave the protectorate and released on payment of 1,000 marks: about £50. Free at last, he sought shelter amongst the rest of the pack in Swakopmund. Two weeks later, Kornmeyer received a letter from Samuel Lorimer.³⁸ It told of how Jack Lis was suspected of murder, triggering yet more concern in Kornmeyer, who was developing the fullest picture yet of the criminal potential of the Lis family. Police surveillance was extended to include all gang members, and in Swakopmund there was a new round of questioning.

Two prostitutes, Lena Ebener and Sylvia Melchior alleged that most underworld business in the harbour town was transacted at Stern and Schwartzmann's house or in the adjacent public baths. Several prostitutes, including some that had been rotated through the Pasenau house, had taken rooms there and were on intimate terms with off-duty policemen. It was also said to be common knowledge that Silver had paid the same communal leaders a large sum of money to intervene on his behalf with the German authorities in order to have his pending transportation order rescinded.³⁹

Mande's stone-built residence, distinctive amongst so many prefabricated structures, came under scrutiny. He had provided Bertha Silver
and the Tuchmanns with accommodation and, once Gordon and
Weinberg had fled Windhoek, they, too, had moved into the house.
Bertha, many believed, had already become Mande's lover before his
wife had died unexpectedly and Mande now described himself as being
'engaged' to Bertha. Bertha, however, did not confine her favours to
Mande but entertained 'ships officers' in his home.[40]

In Swakopmund, civil servants, police and prison staff interacted
even more freely with the public than they did in Windhoek, where
Kornmeyer tried, not always successfully, to isolate the Boss from his
Boys. Perhaps it was loose, semi-official talk about the real reason
behind Silver's transportation which prompted three unnamed pimps
on the periphery of Silver's gang to flee the colony and make their way
to New York via London. Indeed, it may have been the same embarrassing loose talk that caused Kornmeyer later to maintain a discreet
official silence about that strange earlier journey to Jakalswater. In any
event, Berlin was slow to respond to Windhoek's request to have Silver
transported and it took until the second week of February to get the
Boss as far as Swakopmund.

Silver had long given thought to the possibility of attempting to
escape once he was clear of the desert and back at the coast amongst
friends. Hours before getting to Swakopmund the family put in motion
a scheme that focused on the district surgeon. In 'the middle of the
night', Dr Zachlehner awoke to find Bertha in his bedroom. She got
straight to the point. Her father, scheduled for transportation, was
due to arrive the following morning and, when he disembarked, would
complain of fever. If the district surgeon was willing to write a certificate testifying to the fever her father would not be put aboard the
ship and Zachlehner 'could do with her whatever he wanted'. But
one man's nectar was another's nitric acid. When the train arrived
the following morning, Zachlehner was not surprised when the prisoner 'announced that he was sick with a fever'. The doctor examined him, could find no symptoms of fever and authorised his
transfer.[41]

There was a last throw of the dice. Before being put aboard a German
East-African liner for Hamburg, the Boss tried to bribe a warder as
part of an attempt at escape. Here, too, the groundwork had been laid
before he even left the capital. But Sergeant Hauk must have known

that getting out of the harbour town unseen would be virtually impossible, and refused to be drawn into the plot. Hauk did not, however, consider the approach serious enough to warrant reporting – a further indication of alarming fluidities within parts of the system beyond the immediate scrutiny of Kornmeyer.[42]

On 11 February 1906, Silver was escorted out through the surf to where the *Bürgermeister*, under command of Captain Fiedler, lay waiting for him and a dozen passengers.[43] In keeping with regulations, he was taken below deck and confined to quarters.[44] As the vessel eased up the coast, he was hidden from the family standing on the old Mole. 'The Boss' took with him secrets that had probably eluded Kornmeyer. What was the 'mystery' surrounding his trial, and why had he been given such a harsh sentence upon appeal? What was the purpose of that journey to Jakalswater? As the *Bürgermeister* slid north another liner, bearing a remarkable letter from Berlin, was slowly making its way south. It was a letter devoted almost entirely to Silver and destined for the desks of Governor von Lindequist and the state's Public Prosecutor.

In early March, during a visit to London, Gustav Stein, a zealous German patriot, chanced upon the three unnamed pimps making their way to New York. He was not certain what to make of the tale they told him, since it could have been 'based partly on the boasting that gangsters are known for'. He nevertheless felt that the information of a 'dangerous gang' with 'enormous capital' 'smuggling arms and ammunition' warranted a 'thorough examination'. On his return to Germany, he wrote a letter to the Colonial Society in Berlin, which received it on 8 March. Whatever misleading statements and misinterpretations the letter contained, it was not short of detail:

> Their headquarters are in Swakopmund, under the leadership of a certain Joseph Lis (or List), English Joe Lees, also named Silver whose brother is Jochen Lis. It is said that Joe Lis is at present serving a 12 month prison sentence because of his activities as a pimp. He is said to be a dangerous criminal. He is said to have been able to enter the circles of the officers and, through his generosity in handing out champagne, to have very close contact with them. This was of the greatest advantage to him for his purposes.
>
> In this way, too, he managed to win the whole of the

police force in Swakopmund and Windhoek over to his side, so that he could carry on with his activities undisturbed for a whole year, which yielded enormous sums of money for himself and his accomplices.

The whole gang is said to consist of about ten persons, most of them Jewish pimps, who are staying in those places where the garrisons are stationed; some of them also stay in Cape Town where the goods are passed through. The goods are then transported overland to a place which Joe Lis would determine, where it was delivered to the Negroes.

Since the imprisonment of the leader the business is said to have gone down slightly. Some of the participants have even left the Protectorate for some time which resulted in quite a bit of correspondence which could expose them since it has been left lying at the post offices. Three of the gentlemen are here at present, on their way to America. It is through them that I have learnt about these matters. They think that Jochen Lis is incapable of conducting the business as well as his brother. Although they still have a large amount of goods in stock, they prefer to sacrifice it and get themselves to a safe place.

It is said that Joe Lis practises his art of bribery even in prison, so that he lives there in a princely style. He wears his own clothes, does no work, has a cell to himself for sleeping and the cell is equipped with everything to make him comfortable. He procures his meals, wine and cigars from a restaurant, and spends his days in the company of senior prison officials or with his lover and his relatives. His lover is said to be a prostitute by the name of Gertie who runs a brothel in Windhoek. He is said to have drawn the money from this source of income (said to have amounted to hundreds of thousands of marks) and used this to finance his smuggling business.[45]

Much of this is at variance with what is known from other sources about Silver's stay in the colony. 'Enormous capital' and 'hundreds of thousands of marks' are not easily squared with family squabbles about money and the Pasenau house, or the farcical sequel to the Schroeder robbery. Likewise, the accounts of a supposedly luxurious lifestyle in prison, and his hold over army officers and 'the whole of the police force' are clearly overblown. They sound like bandit-braggadocio but that does not render them entirely devoid of truth. Grandiose statements are characteristic of the early stages of neurosyphilis so they may well have come from the Boss's own richly textured imagination at the time. But, even after these reservations are noted, a hint of truthfulness clings to many of these allegations, perhaps even that of arms smuggling.

'Truth,' Tacitus tells us, 'is surrounded by mystery.' Writing history is complicated because it is not only that which is recorded that is important, but that which is not. How many undocumented journeys did the Boss make to remote parts of the colony where there were other traders of East European origin? What was the significance of his brother's military background and familiarity with firearms? What had turned Mande, just a pimp, into one of Swakopmund's foremost traders? What did the Boss have on Mande that made him so compliant? Why did Mande refuse to abandon the territory when things started going wrong? How did Sourd obtain the artillery shells used to demolish Schroeder's safe, and what exactly was the role of the pimps who worked on a part-time basis within the garrison? Had Schottelius been briefed secretly about the Boss's possible role in arms smuggling and increased his sentence? We will never know and, in the absence of answers, a lesser test has to be posed – what did the authorities in Windhoek make of Gustav Stein's astounding letter?

Surprisingly little, it would seem. Von Lindequist did not comment on, or reply to, the letter forwarded to him by the Vice-President of the German Colonial Society – an association his administration had close ties with and held in high regard. Nor did Kornmeyer, another not given to bureaucratic oversight, comment in any detail. All that appears to have happened is that the state prosecutor at Swakopmund made a few low-level inquiries. It was as if Kornmeyer was just going through the motions. Officials at the coast evinced even less enthusiasm. Several were so uninterested that they had to be sent reminders before offering replies that either avoided the issue of culpability, or were otherwise unhelpful. By April Fools' Day 1906, the South West African administration, which had steadfastly ignored allegations of gun-running by gangsters linked to frontier traders in a time of war, appears to have lost all remaining interest in the matter.[46]

Kornmeyer tidied up what was left of the mess. Early in March,

Gertie Gordon and Regina Weinberg, anxious to shake off police attention, moved to the southern port of Lüderitz where they based themselves in a brothel owned by Erna Kruger. Somewhat puzzlingly, they
remained in contact with the Lis family in Swakopmund and Jack
allegedly took the unusual step of getting legal authorisation for
Weinberg to take delivery of unspecified 'goods' arriving in Lüderitz
by steamship. It was a strange thing to do since, if the goods were prostitutes, they were imported at a time when he was already facing a
charge of 'living off the proceeds'. If Gustav Stein was correct, however,
there may have been more arms than legs amongst the goods. At the
end of that month Gordon, Kruger and Weinberg were all deported to
Portuguese East Africa. Why?[47]

The departure of the breadwinners deepened the family's financial
plight. Jack Lis suddenly tightened his control of Bertha for reasons that
are not clear. It may have been partly motivated by the desire to look
after his niece and marginalise Mande, in keeping with the instructions
of his brother. But he may also have been starting to take a more
personal, intimate interest in her. Mande's interest in Bertha waned and
there was no more late-night entertaining of free-spending ship's officers. Bertha spent her nights lodging in rooms in the 'Fuchsberg House'
paid for by her uncle.[48]

Jack, armed with power of attorney to represent the absent Boss,
was put under renewed pressure to make over Silver's share in the
Pasenau house to the indebted Tuchmann and therefore, indirectly, to
Mande who would foreclose in an attempt to recover the money he
had lost. Mande got Stern, leader of the community, to convene a
meeting of Jewish notables to arbitrate in the matter of Tuchmann
versus Jack Lis. Tuchmann was awarded 1,480 marks – about £75 sterling – by the communal court on 28 March 1906.[49] Jack, unmoved by
ethnic solidarities, ignored an agreement endorsed by self-appointed
judges of doubtful legal standing. But the judges, important property
owners and traders in their own right, had other ways of pressurising
him. Cash and credit remained at a premium and he found himself
squeezed between his brother's and Tuchmann's wishes. In the end he
was left with only two ways of raising money – recovering the 1,000
marks he had paid Kornmeyer as 'caution money' when he was arrested
for 'living off the proceeds', or selling the house: and that would neces-
sitate the agreement of Silberberg.

With his own business, in Johannesburg, in liquidation and an award of costs and damages against him in Swakopmund, he wrote to Kornmeyer.[50] 'Prolonged illness and unemployment, as well as expenditure incurred in maintaining my family' have, he suggested, 'got me into serious financial trouble'. He 'humbly requested' that 'the money deposited for bail' be returned to him.[51] But the prosecutor was unmoved. The charge of 'living off the proceeds', like the stench of a blocked sewer, lingered.

Between April and June 1906, various lawyers dragged the issues relating to the Pasenau house through the courts. Kornmeyer observed, with growing frustration, as Jack, working to instructions provided by his brother from Germany, got ever more entangled in agreements and repudiations relating to the sale of the property. Silberberg and her friends continued to entertain clients, including several policemen and soldiers from the garrison. At last, in mid-May, an agreement was reached and the house was sold, at a loss, to the firm of Gericke and Hill.[52] The sale came as a relief to all concerned but, in the background, unfinished business smouldered. In early April, Tuchmann, at Mande's suggestion, had launched a civil action to force Jack to pay him the 1,480 marks awarded him by the 'communal court'. Several attorneys took the courts through a series of fairly predictable manoeuvres as Jack used legal filibusters as best he could to protect the Boss's dwindling assets.[53]

Kornmeyer watched with customary patience, never for a moment taking his eye off Jack. A Swakopmund colleague of his, putting a civilised gloss on events, reported that 'Jack Lis intends to leave the colony shortly in order to be able to see to the education and training of his niece, Bertha Lis'.[54] But uncle and niece were not yet in agreement. He wanted them to go to Europe while Bertha, after discussions with various prostitutes, was much more taken with talk about the far-off delights of Rio de Janeiro. Kornmeyer was tiring of the game. He wanted all of them out of the colony: as soon as possible. Days after the last case relating to the Pasenau house concluded in Windhoek he obtained orders for the deportation of Jack and his friend the pimp, Sam Gilbert. A week later, the 1,000 marks of caution money was returned to Lis and the charge of 'living off the proceeds' dropped. Still Jack hovered, waiting for the Tuchmann business to play itself out. Kornmeyer instructed his official to make certain that Lis, and anybody who wanted to accompany him, be expelled at their own cost, to a port of their choice: by 6 June, latest. But that date, too, came and went.[55]

A few days later, Jack, Gilbert, Bertha and an unsubtly named colleague, Lizzie Manlove, boarded the SS *Prinzessin* in Swakopmund 'to settle in Delagoa Bay'.[56] It was the same east coast destination that Gordon and Weinberg had chosen a few weeks earlier. It was a sign that Jack's wishes had trumped Bertha's; the 'family' was bound for the Old World. Lourenço Marques, in Mozambique, was the port of call for pimps and prostitutes moving between Marseilles, Durban and Cape Town. The journey was not a particularly happy one. Short of cash, they sought to disembark in Cape Town but the authorities told them that the port was closed to 'undesirables' and the Chief Immigration Officer, suspecting that they might disembark elsewhere, telegraphed his counterpart in Durban. All four were denied entry into Natal.[57] With the rudiments of an integrated criminal intelligence system slowly emerging in British southern Africa, they sailed on to the neighbouring Portuguese colony. Nobody now knows precisely how long they stayed there, or whether they were aboard the *Prinzessin* when it left for the Horn of Africa and other Mediterranean ports on 24 June 1906. But from a prison, somewhere in Germany, the Boss tracked their movements.

XVIII

NEUMÜNSTER AND PARIS
1908–1909

'For indeed I [Joseph] was stolen away out of the land of
the Hebrews and here also I have done nothing that they
should put me into the dungeon'.

Genesis, 40:15

ON 1 March 1906, or close to that date, the *Bürgermeister* turned its
back on the North Sea and eased into the lanes on the lower Elbe,
probing for a resting place in Hamburg. With the bow in familiar
waters, Fiedler steered a south-easterly course before cutting back the
engines to allow his vessel to glide to a halt besides the waiting wharf.
Happy chatter emanated from several cabins as passengers sensed the
moisture of metropolitan Germany after months in Africa. The prisoner knew the place and it reminded him that he was moving in the
wrong direction; for East Europeans Hamburg was a point of departure, not arrival. The port was supposed to quicken his pulse and accel-
erate time. Instead, it was a darkened doorway leading back into the
Old World where minutes dragged into hours, hours into days, days
into weeks, and weeks into years. Twenty years earlier, aged sixteen,
he had had a sense of excitement on being hurtled outwards by
centrifugal forces. Now just weeks after turning thirty-eight, centripetal
power seemed to crush in on him.

Echoes from departing passengers gave way to prompts from
approaching guards who appeared on the deck above. They exchanged
pleasantries with Fiedler, explained the procedure, and then plunged
below. From their numbers it was clear that not everybody was destined
for the same penitentiary. The 'internationals' were separated and

Schroeder's safe-robber, Sourd, was dispatched to Celle, in Lower Saxony. Then, they came for Silver.

He was escorted down a sagging and stiffening gangway, conscious that his feet seemed to have a mind of their own and that he was taking slightly more pronounced steps when walking. It was not just the swaying of the ship giving way to the flagstones that led to the station that caused it; there was more to it, but he put it out of his mind. It was twenty-three days since he had been bundled on to a train in Windhoek and he was again aboard a train, this time bound for Schleswig-Holstein. The train trundled north for an hour and then, two-thirds of the way to Kiel, stopped amidst a thicket of factories. He was told to get out and the guard, more relaxed amidst familiar surroundings, led him through several streets until they came up against a wooden door of what looked like an enormous *Schloss*.

Neumünster's central prison administrative block, unveiled a year earlier, was disarmingly benign. A two-storey brick building, its upper offices were set in a garret tucked in beneath a pitched slate roof. A raised edifice, boasting a clock and an ornate turret-like structure, provided the focus for protruding wings. Almost all the windows were on the upper levels. At ground level a cavernous mouth, guarded on either side by small barred windows, emphasised that it was an entry rather than exit portal. Just as surely as the mouth of the Elbe had taken him in, he was being swallowed by jaws of ever-diminishing size.[1]

The outer door closed surprisingly quickly behind him. Inside, moving towards the belly of the beast, they passed a small oval garden; the final pretence of civilian life. To the east a few nondescript buildings housed more administrative functions and some storerooms. To the west stood a chapel, its sharply pointed façade topped by a huge metal cross, reaching heavenwards in a penitential gesture. Yet with the exception of his short, unhappy stay in Potchefstroom, he had always been a model prisoner and past experience had long since underscored the need for quiescence.

Beyond the church, inside an elongated brick complex three storeys high, with a spiked lookout, loomed the main cellblock. It was, and still is, a structure of intimidating proportions. If its exterior was mildly frightening, the inside was forbidding. A state-of-the-art prison barely twelve months old, it was designed for the new century, built to leach the mind of anti-social tendencies rather than punish the body. Staggered iron gangways, set at sharply raked angles, paused on metal platforms at first-floor level before climbing to yet more landings on the second and third tiers. At each level, separate concreted doorways led to each of 150 cells. Angled iron, squared corners and grey paint – a universe where God, geometry and time met – was the best civilisation could offer the deviant or the dispossessed. He felt the doorway's teeth brushing his prison garb as he was eased into the cell.

Silver had always been a stranger to fear, and God he had almost never encountered. It was not so much that he was courageous or daring in any conventional sense; just that he lacked the anxiety most people experience when confronted with danger or the unknown. It was not the discipline, the inmates or the place that got to him; it was time. It was time suspended. Between short bouts of exercise or leisure and slightly longer periods in the workshops, he sat around waiting for sleep to offer some respite from the world. The prison authorities, for whom he had no respect despite his collaborative tendencies, had plotted his time with the accuracy and efficiency Teutons were famous for. He was, they said, to be released at 2.00 p.m. on 17 January 1909 – if that day ever dawned.

The days shuffled by. The nine remaining months of that year were dismal. In November, he was notified that the legal agent in Windhoek, Thiemann, had paid the court his outstanding fine of 1,000 marks, thereby staving off the need to serve an additional month. The following year was worse. In mid-September 1907 he was told that he was liable for the cost of his transport to Germany. Despite the proceeds from the sale of the Pasenau house he was penniless.[2] In between terse official letters there were occasional notes and possibly even a visit or two from his family of two. Jack and Bertha kept him informed of their movements around the wider Atlantic world.

His reading of their exploits was coloured by his altered mood. The underlying restlessness and desire to explore new frontiers was still there, but the domineering behaviour that had characterised his stay in South West Africa had abated. Bouts of apathy, depression and listlessness underlay what prison officials mistakenly took for the sort of mellowing that sometimes precedes 'rehabilitation'. They could not have been wider of the mark. Although diminished in intensity and no longer driven by the energy of youth, or as vulnerable to silly bouts of impulsive behaviour, his anti-social thinking and tendencies remained largely intact. In his new setting, however, he could reflect more deeply – and critically – on the path his troubled career had taken.

His most damaging encounters with the law could all be traced to the same root: the need for money and his lifelong abomination of whores. It was the never-ending quest for money and his near-compulsive interest in prostitutes that had led inexorably to brothel-keeping, pimping and white slavery. If he wished to avoid falling into the same old trap, he would have to uncouple the need for cash from his dependence on whores.

The moderation in his behaviour after 1908 was not because prison had 'taught him a lesson'; it could not, and had not. Alterations in behaviour, body and mind were primarily a function of the progression of neurosyphilis and the way he adapted to it. The bombast that had been such a notable part of the Boss's final days in Africa faded, giving way to more intense bouts of depression and inactivity. His hand-writing showed further deterioration, he was starting to walk with a higher step, and his hair had begun to thin and fall out in tufts leaving him with an almost moth-eaten appearance. He was also becoming impotent. After this, his last lengthy spell in an ordinary prison, he never again took up with a woman in the same personalised way that he had been involved with Heller, Opticer, Vygenbaum or even Laskin. If Schleswig-Holstein marked a turning point in his career – and in some respects it did – the prison's contribution was largely indirect, almost unintentional.[3]

Adept at languages and with an ear already attuned by his southern stay, he benefited from three years of informal language instruction. As he was compliant and anxious to please, interactions with warders and inmates improved his spoken German. The ability to converse more freely allowed him, a Russian-Pole, one of the despised *Ostjuden*, to present himself as a rather more assimilated, higher-caste native of metropolitan Europe. Indeed, only a few months after his release the police paid him the generous, if unintended, compliment of describing him as a 'German Jew'.

The state remained doggedly interested in his mind. But measuring improvement in behaviour is an elusive science. How was Rüstow, the prison director, to know whether Silver was genuinely on the path to rehabilitation? What could he have had to go on, other than reports of compliance and an enhanced ability to communicate in a man intel-ligent and literate? So, when the Colonial Director in Berlin enquired as to whether 'the trader Joseph Lis' had made sufficient progress to be considered for early release during the second quarter of 1908, what was he to say? Rüstow supported the idea and Rip van Winkle stirred. The question of parole escaped notice in South West Africa but Silver had hardly been forgotten. In August 1909, eight months after the date originally set for release, Kornmeyer, perhaps still fretting about gun-running allegations, wrote to ask about the fate of his adversary. Rüstow replied: 'Following the decree by the Colonial Director of 12.08.08 . . . Lis was released from prison . . . on 18 August, 1908, at 11.45 a.m. He stated that he was going to stay with his brother, in Paris, at 57 Rue Rambuteau.' Silver, who had developed an antipathy to many things German, had left to link up with his family.[4]

In Paris he at once noted how much more adventurous and in-dependent-minded Jack had become during their time apart. There was an air of confidence about his brother, who had acquired contacts and skills that lifted him beyond pimping and white slavery and placed him squarely in the Atlantic-wide world of armed robbery, break-ins and fencing. It was an exciting development which chimed with his own desire to work with small groups of men on carefully chosen and planned projects. Ageing, disease and changes in personality meant that he was slowly relinquishing his position as leader. Now his brother was more like an equal, a genuine partner in crime.

After being expelled from Lüderitz in 1906, Jack and party had spent some time in Delagoa Bay. From there they made their way up the east coast, passed through the modern marvel of Suez and disembarked at Marseilles before moving on to Paris. France, secure as one of four powerful financial and industrial powers in the world, was midway through its *belle époque*. The Third Republic, benefiting from a period of uninterrupted growth, was recovering its equanimity and poise after the Dreyfus affair.[5] A full recovery from deeply rooted anti-Semitism was, however, slowed by new ethnic insanities in Russia. The Khisnev pogrom of 1903 and a failed revolution, in 1905, gave new impetus to Jewish emigration which had, in any case, never faltered since the moment of Tsar Alexander II's assassination. Formerly bypassed as an exit destination for those trying to reach the United States, Paris became reluctant host to some of the Old World's most hated, least skilled and poorest refugees.

In 1906, 10,000 East Europeans, sensing that Britain's Aliens Restriction Act might be closing one route to New York, poured into Paris through the Gare de l'Est. In the half-decade that followed a further 15,000 put the darkness of the Old Country behind them and entered the City of Light. The influx continued, at reduced rate, until the outbreak of the First World War. Eight out of ten of the new arrivals came from central Europe, the Pale of Settlement, or Poland. Youthful immigrants arrived in numbers that overwhelmed the established middle-class trading area around the Marais. Like the poor everywhere, newcomers placed a premium on gaining access to the inner city's semi- and unskilled labour markets. Most took up residence on the north bank of the Seine, around Montmartre, in the 18th *arrondissement*. Others settled in the 4th, closer to the Marais, where the ethnic quarter of the *Pletzl* bordered on that ancient redoubt of those unable to pay tax, the Place des Vosges and the street names – such as the rue des Mauvais Garçons – carried warnings. The better-resourced hired small *ateliers* where they plied their trades as buttonhole-makers, cap- and hat- makers, leather-workers, shoemakers or tailors. Many were *façonniers*, 'home-labourers', locked into the putting-out system that dominated the city's clothing trade. Others who needed space to store raw material included bakers, costermongers, locksmiths, painters, tinkers and the ubiquitous East European pedlars – *colporteurs*. Those with fewer skills or only their labour to sell, like bottlemakers, cart drivers, manual labourers, printer's assistants or waiters, hired bolt-holes in cheap and dirty hotels where filth encrusted torn and yellowing wall-paper.[6]

Hard pressed to provide urban employment for the thousands of native French abandoning the countryside each year, Paris was no better placed than Lyons, Marseilles or Rouen to absorb an influx of East European immigrants. Unemployment in the clothing industry deepened the misery of inner-city dwellers. Capital-intensive production techniques and mechanisation limited opportunities in the textiles industries – one of the few sectors in which refugees might expect to find employment.[7] Begging, delinquency and petty theft became an integral part of immigrant communities.[8] But, for the most desperate, there was only one thing left to sell: youth and sexuality. The formal, legally regulated world of work, ostensibly guarded by the legislature, gave way to the far greater exploitation of the informal economy, and beyond both lay the black economy of the *demi-monde* where the state claimed to rule but which in reality remained unpoliced, operating with its own codes.

Heightened competition for jobs, unhygienic conditions and increases in petty crime and immorality driven by urban poverty kept the lamps of anti-Semitism flickering. French socialism had long been tainted by racist tendencies and xenophobia and, outside the ranks of organised labour there were others even less subtle. In 1907, the fourth *arrondissement* elected to office a candidate supported by Eduard Drumont's notoriously anti-Jewish *Libre Parole* and two years later another journal in the same quarter, *La Cité*, carried a 'scurrilously anti-Semitic article'. For Drumont, ethnicity and immorality were linked to the issue of 'patriotism'.[9]

Fin-de-siècle Paris, famously tolerant and reluctant to prescribe sexual morality, was the commercial sex capital of the world and remained so until the First World War. By 1909, it was claimed that there were 100,000 prostitutes of every age in the capital drawn mainly from France, but also from other European countries. The city was also the premier entrepôt for organised trafficking in prostitutes that embraced virtually every Atlantic port city and often beyond. By the early twentieth century, however, the 'naughty nineties' were giving way to international agreements which sought to combat the grossest excesses of the commercial sex industry in the west. In 1904, thirteen European countries pledged their co-operation in the fight against organised prostitution and white slavery and, in 1908, Theodore Roosevelt ratified the agreement on behalf of the United States.[10]

Yet in that same year Marcus Braun, an American immigration officer visiting Paris, found the trade in flesh undiminished in the rue des Abbesses of the 18th *arrondissement*. Pimps and white slavers gathered in the Marché de Viande café each day to transact imports and exports and monitor the state of the trade. Close by, in rue Caulaincourt, Georges Hayum's mother, *la mère Dacheux*, ran a *maison de rendezvous* from which women were sent to destinations as far apart as Buenos Aires and Vladivostok. A police officer told Braun that the city was being 'terrorised by the worst band of brigands and cut-throats known as "Apaches" who were the worst "*maquereaus*", procurers, exploiters and debauchers of women in the world'.[11]

Apaches? Ever since James Fenimore Cooper whetted the appetites of readers with tales of North American natives' bravery in the 1820s, Europeans had been intrigued by Red Indians and 'Mohocs'. The symbolism, however, had little appeal for young Frenchmen until 1902 when a Parisian journalist, Emile Darsy, noting an upsurge in violent crime, characterised it as the work of 'Apaches'. The Apaches, drawing heavily on youngsters from the Auverne, pre-dated the influx of East Europeans into the capital. Individual gangs operated in several of the

Thomas Byrnes,
Chief of New York Police
Department, *c.* 1889.

Rev. Charles Parkhurst,
Society for the Prevention of Crime,
New York City, 1895.

The Old Bailey, London, *c.* 1910.

SS. Ionic, New Zealand-bound, on which Joseph Silver and Rachel Laskin travelled to Cape Town in 1898.

David Krakower,
court exhibit,
Johannesburg, 1898.

Pimps outside the American Club, Sauer Street, Johannesburg, 1898. Included,
but unidentified, is Constable H.E. Cuyler of the Morality Police.

Constable Manie Maritz, *c.* 1897.

Jan Smuts,
State Attorney, 1898.

Mostyn Cleaver,
Second Public Prosecutor, 1898.

Dr F.E.T. Krause, *c.* 1910.

Andrew Trimble and the men of the Johannesburg Detective Department, 1894.

Johannesburg Fort, *c.* 1900.

Officers of the Special Police, Johannesburg, 1884.

Potchefstroom Prison, 1899.

Railway station, Kimberley, *c.* 1900.

George Street, Kimberley – synagogue with pitched roof in background, *c.*1900.

Female Block, Valkenberg Mental Hospital, Cape Town, 1913.

Wale Street police station, Cape Town, 1900.

poorer *arrondissements*; because they shared a criminal argot as well as distinctive dance and dress styles, they tended to be seen collectively as 'Apaches'. With Paris setting the trend in an Atlantic world ever more integrated by the telegraph, telephone and steamship, it was not long before criminal or other subcultures in 'western' cities – including Buenos Aires, Cape Town and New York – were being characterised as Apache.[12]

Some felt that that it was the ready use of guns, knives and razors by Parisian Apaches that prompted the reintroduction of the death penalty in France. Braun noted that, in many instances, young Apaches in bars, cafés and dancing halls came to share the interests of pimps, procurers and prostitutes. In this, too, Paris appears to have given the world something new because its Apaches, unlike those elsewhere in the Atlantic world where women were at a premium, incorporated *gigolettes* into small-scale activities such as blackmail, gambling scams, street robberies and petty theft.

But since most typical Apache crimes were age related, requiring agility, speed and a willingness to use violence, not everybody could be drawn directly into this subculture of youth. Paris had its share of middle-aged pimps who had moved up the ladder to become burglars, jewel thieves and safe-crackers. Experienced criminals posed a far greater threat to the property of the local bourgeoisie than did the youngsters but got tarred with the same brush when sections of the Parisian press, such as *Le Matin*, ran campaigns against Apaches after 1907. The most skilled thieves of all did not confine their activities to the capital and the master craftsmen had long since become increasingly wide-ranging in their operations. The best of them employed the latest technology and techniques and saw the entire western hemisphere as their oyster.

Adam Worth was amongst the pioneers of transatlantic theft. The talented American-born son of a German-Jewish family raised in poverty in Boston, Worth was the Napoleon of nineteenth-century crime and the real-life inspiration for Moriarty, the fictional adversary of Sherlock Holmes. A brilliant operator who had stolen Gainsborough's portrait of Georgiana, Duchess of Devonshire, Worth was a bandit, bank robber and jewel thief with a special interest in diamonds. Business interests took him to places and prisons as far apart as Belgium and South Africa but, in 1870–74, he had been based in Paris where the American Bar, at 2 rue Scribe, was a regular meeting place for trans-atlantic robbers spending periods of self-imposed exile in Europe. A criminal genius with a taste for the high life, Worth was exceptional. Most journeymen thieves led far more prosaic lives.[13]

By the end of the nineteenth century, however, a reduction in passenger fares, along with the ease and convenience of steamship travel, had placed transatlantic criminal ventures within the reach of lesser craftsmen. Although the history of international burglaries and robberies linked to notorious specialist outlets in Antwerp, London and New York has yet to be written, it is clear that by the first decade of the twentieth century mobile thieves with craft skills were surfacing in distant outposts such as Buenos Aires, Cape Town and Rio de Janeiro.[14] In 1905, for example, it was noted that Jack Friedlich, an associate of one of Silver's partners in Kimberley, had, four years earlier, been involved in a large diamond robbery in the United States and that the proceeds of the heist had been conveyed from 'America to Europe' for disposal.[15]

The arrival of Jack Lis in Paris, in 1906, at age thirty-three, came at a propitious moment. Seldom were man and moment, personality and place, skills and support structures, better matched. With a strong frame, a liking for weapons and a murderous temperament, he could still joust with most pimps. The vibrant subculture of the Apaches, reinforced by East European criminals including some from Kielce, was ideally suited to his changing needs. The 4th and especially the 18th *arrondissement*, with its proliferation of railway stations and seedy hotels, gave him ample scope for a bread-and butter interest in pimping.[16] Paris between 1906 and 1909 offered the ideal environment in which to make the transition from pimp to criminal-craftsman. This shift in emphasis, which commenced while his brother was still in prison in Germany, complemented the personality changes that marked Silver's own career on his release from Neumünster.

The man who most influenced the two Lis brothers on their return to Europe was a brash youngster in his twenties who had grown up in a village less than twenty miles from them. Leibus Brjiski, son of a shoemaker-tailor father and a seamstress mother, was born in Pinczów, just south of Kielce, in 1885. Later in life Brjiski suggested, quite plausibly, that it was fear of conscription that prompted his emigration to New York where his common-law wife was another teenager, Paulina Neinstein of Biala. By 1902, Brjiski, then still only seventeen, was back in London. In the East End family connections got him a position in the rag trade where he worked for five years. Pushed early into adulthood, it was not long before he was consorting with gangsters and prostitutes. In 1907, aged twenty-one and an accomplished pimp and white slaver, he moved to the south coast and opened a brothel in the naval centre of Portsmouth.[17]

Moving freely between London, where female 'imports' entered the country, and the channel ports of Southampton and Portsmouth where prostitutes sometimes did a tour of duty prior to being 'exported', Brjiski became a successful criminal entrepreneur. At about this time, just weeks before he was deported to Poland as an 'undesirable alien', Brjiski met Jack Lis and 'Joan Goldburn', whose business had brought them to Southampton in June 1907. Jack and his 'French' *gigolette* 'wife' were on their way to South America to exploit Apache techniques in more provincial settings. Although Brjiski himself had no interest in international jewel theft at the time, he introduced them to others who did, including the brothers Cohen – Leibus and Mendel – as well as Sarah Haberberg and Moritz Kleinberg. They formed the core of the gang that the two Silver brothers joined after Joseph's release from prison.

The Cohens – like the Lis boys, half-brothers rather than siblings – hailed from the province of Piotrków, north of Kielce. The older of the two, Leibus, born in 1870, was from almost the same cohort as Silver. When exactly he left the Old Country is unknown but by the turn of the century he was living in London's East End and, in 1903, had married Sarah Haberberg, a seamstress twelve years his junior. Haberberg was an enterprising and spirited young woman from a tailor's family in Warsaw who, some time after 1906, had given birth to a daughter.[18] Mendel, four years younger than Leibus, was a 'tailor' who, like his half-brother, had emigrated to the United Kingdom at an early age. At some point his work in the rag trade, too, had given way to an interest in gangsters and prostitutes. Perhaps it was he who had coaxed Brjiski to the south coast since it was at about the time that Mendel took prostitutes to Southampton that Brjiski moved to Portsmouth. In Southampton, Mendel took up with an unnamed prostitute who, for many years and long after his move to the continent, kept him supplied with cash.[19]

The other member of this group who later worked with Silver was yet another 'tailor'. Moritz Kleinberg, born in Warsaw, in 1875, had like the others gone to London to work in the clothing trade in the East End. For several years he had also been an active burglar and

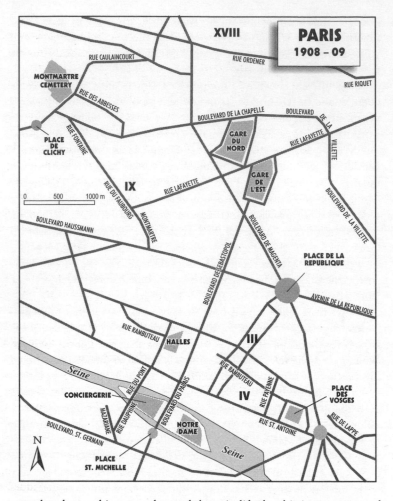

store-breaker and it was only much later in life that his interests turned to illegal emigration, prostitution and the more lucrative white slave trade.[20]

When Jack first met the Cohens and their friends in mid-1907, Silver was still in prison and it was only a year later that the group gelled into something approaching a gang. At the time of their first meeting, however, Jack was preoccupied with the project that had taken him to Southampton. On 14 June, he and his 'wife', twenty-one-year-old Goldburn turned 'Jenny de Liss', boarded the SS *Araguaya*. Despite travelling steerage, it was a pleasant voyage, with the ship calling at Rio de Janeiro, Santos and Montevideo. Three weeks later he told immigration authorities in Buenos Aires that he was a twenty-five-year-old Russian 'tailor' and Protestant, while Mrs Liss said that she was an 'artist'.[21]

Argentina, in the midst of an agricultural revolution dating back to the 1880s, was drawing in tens of thousands of immigrants a year despite being twice as far from Europe as the United States. Buenos Aires was a large commercial centre with rapidly developing construction, clothing, food and furniture manufacturing industries served by a militant, unionised labour force. The stylish 'Paris of the South', the capital also had an increasingly well-organised Italian and Jewish underworld which attracted adherents from the millions of immigrants from southern Europe and the 20,000 Russo-Poles who were funnelled through it between 1905 and 1914. Like many locals, *portenos*, before them, the Lises made their way to the immigrant precincts.[22]

The third precinct, later recast as an Apache stronghold by journalists wanting to evoke memories of Jack Lis during one of the city's moral panics, undoubtedly was a troublesome quarter. In a city where East Europeans were routinely referred to as 'Rusos', pimps as 'Caftans' and prostitutes as 'Polacas', the *barrio* bristled with rowdy immigrant meeting places. The marginalised and the poor, turning in unison like shoals of fish, moved constantly among its reefs searching for economic scraps while smooth-bodied predators lurked nearby, ready to glide in and feed on the feeders.[23] Bars abounded, while whole areas close to the dockside, such as that around the Paseo de Julio, were devoted to brothels. A few blocks away at the Place Lavalle, scores of 'Caftans' lounged about or sat in smoke-filled cafés and restaurants like the Victor Hugo on Corrientes. Several theatres, heavily, sometimes exclusively patronised by flashily dressed East European gangsters linked to the criminal Zwi Migdal organisation brought a nostalgic Yiddish repertoire to immigrants whose formative images and sounds were drawn from the Old World. Things were, however, not always as they seemed. Just beyond the visible retail prostitution sector was a sinister 'wholesale' dimension to the business; a world in which women were paraded in houses or theatres and auctioned off to the highest-bidding brothel-owners. Not surprisingly, the same nexus yielded a good number of assaults, murders and suicides each year.[24]

The neighbouring fourth precinct, replete with Frenchified argot, provided Jack with conditions in which he could bloom.[25] For a while he and his French 'wife' lived at 771 Lavalle, a house the police knew to be a brothel. Later they moved to 976, a few blocks away, which hardly housed a sewing circle for widows. Throughout late 1907 and early 1908 Jack, nominally a 'waiter', was seen by the police as just another 'Caftan' while his wife did what she had to. Still given to violence, Jack once spent several weeks in prison for a serious assault. The couple made a point of expanding their network of friends. Jack, who even in race-conscious Cape Town had worked with an American 'Negro', was never bound by ethnic or religious considerations, while Jenny was in a trade that was inherently friendly and outgoing. Their associates included half a dozen Russians, Spaniards and Italians who, in the mode said later to be quintessentially Apache, were ever ready to deploy women in specialist projects.[26]

While Silver was counting down his remaining months in prison, Jack and other Apaches who had arrived in Buenos Aires weeks earlier were involved in a series of minor, unsolved burglaries around the third and fourth precincts.[27] The gang's two most notable robberies, in which female accomplices either posed as, or interacted with, servants took place in the second quarter of 1908. In March, knock-out drops of the sort familiar to white slavers were used in a Viamonte Street apartment to overcome Dora Pikosch, an actress-singer in Yiddish theatre, along with her maidservant, before she was relieved of her jewellery valued at 12,000 pesos.[28] Eight weeks later the Apaches staged a second robbery, so spectacular that it is now part of local folklore. On 2 May, four men invaded the home of the opera diva, Josefina Cellini, in Lima Street, over-powered her faithful manservant and made off with 60,000 pesos' worth of jewellery. The jewels were instantly and expertly removed from their settings and parcelled out amongst the thieves for international sale.[29]

By the time police eventually arrested members of the Italian-Russian-Spanish gang, who retained Luis Varela, a lawyer with close ties to the Zwi Migda to defend them, there was no sign of the jewels. Investigations into the Cellini robbery dragged on interminably and the final, appeal court, rulings were not made until four years later. When a writ of habeas corpus secured his release, in mid-June 1908, Jack Lis seized his chance. With his 'wife' still languishing in prison for her role in the affair and his brother due for release, he slipped aboard a steamer under an assumed name.[30]

Back in England, Jack knew he could not rely on Brjiski to dispose of his share of the Argentinian loot. Earlier deported from Southampton to Warsaw via Ostend, Brjiski had doubled back and re-inserted himself into the white slave supply lines and was already back in Buenos Aires. But the Cohen brothers and Kleinberg were helpful. Mendel Cohen, familiar with the Low Countries, knew Russo-Polish workers in the diamond cutting industry in Antwerp, as well as an uncle of Brjiski's who was a fence. Jack may or may not have returned to France via Belgium but, either way, by early August 1908 he was back in Paris for the reunion with his stepbrother and niece, Bertha.[31]

In the Pale of Settlement, where Tsarist oppression during the nineteenth century had restricted Jewish mobility, the marriage of uncles to nieces was neither prohibited by civil or religious law, nor unheard of. Strictly speaking, twenty-year-old Bertha was not Jack's 'niece' and, after the family's problems in South West Africa, his brother had asked him to act as the girl's guardian, which he had done to the extent of telling the authorities that he would arrange for her education and training. Jack, however, took his brief lightly and, even in Swakopmund, it was evident that he had a sexual interest in Bertha, who was rumoured to be sleeping with Mande and others. He had never been a conscientious custodian, and by the time the family was reunited in 1908 Bertha had long been a prostitute and was certainly sleeping with him. It was a relationship that bordered on the incestuous; one that originated in a family where her uncle and father both believed that all women were, or could be turned into, whores.[32]

The relationship appears not to have troubled Silver. Lacking funds, all he wanted to do was pick up the pieces of his career. Never imaginative when it came to aliases, he looked around for a German moniker and settled on 'Abraham Ramer/Reimer' – the name of his colleague in Pittsburgh. He found himself a room at the top of the stairs at 17 rue Pavée, near the Place des Vosges in the 4th *arrondissement*. It was not a particularly East European neighbourhood and was better known for a troublesome colony of Auvergnats centred on the nearby rue de Lappe. He was within easy walking distance of rue Rambuteau, beyond which lay the fashionable Boulevard Haussman. Civilian life and a new language were difficult to adjust to and for a time he relied on Bertha to guide him around the 4th and 18th *arrondissements*. Most of her friends were petty criminals in their early twenties or thirties who passed as pedlars or tailors. Almost all were unemployed, slept wherever they could find a bed and were classified as 'vagrants' by a *gendarmerie* steeped in anti-Semitism. Her female friends, fewer in number, earned their income in predictable ways. Apache in aspiration and style, just below the surface they retained some of the trappings of the Old Country. Yiddish love of punning was much in evidence. The old Place des Vosges became the 'Place des Vurst' – Sausage Square – while Boulevard Sebastopol was reduced to 'Boulevard de Shabbes-tepl' or Street of a Sabbath Pot.[33]

Foremost amongst Bertha's friends, and close enough in age and intimacy to her for some to view him – erroneously – as her 'husband', was Benjamin Alverger, 'tailor' of no fixed abode. Other young bucks around her included Henri Berlinski and the adolescent Isadore Schlachter. Harry Guervich and Jules Rozendant, a small-time fence, were both slightly older men. The only married couple in their new circle were Jules and Marie Reitzon. A loosely knit association of thieves, the members constantly formed themselves into smaller groupings for various projects. Cunning small-time operators, they were active towards the end of 1908 and in the first part of 1909.

Early in 1909 Silver eased himself back into professional life, Apachestyle. He, Jack and Bertha teamed up with Berlinski and a fellow named Kasiary to relieve Mottel Seidenberg of goods of an unknown nature and unrecorded value. The burglary must have been conducted with some care. When the group was arraigned before investigating magistrates, on 18 January, the officials found insufficient evidence to prosecute and the state dropped all charges. Two weeks later, Bertha, playing *gigolette* to mutating bands of Apaches, was once again in trouble.[34]

On 2 February she was hauled before the Prefecture of Police for a grilling about various thefts. No charges were preferred but the police were remarkably methodical, confirming for her, and indirectly for Silver, how far routine scientific policing in Europe had progressed during his time in Africa. Bertha's fingerprints were taken using the method pioneered a few years earlier by Alphonse Bertillon in the very building in which she found herself.[35] A description of distinguishing marks was added to the record and, most distressingly of all, her photograph was taken: a quality reproduction which, to this day, resides in the archives of the Paris police.[36]

The interrogation was unpleasant but she held her nerve. She gave the name Silver rather than Lis, which could be traced via Berlin, and claimed to be a milliner. And whereas months earlier she had told the authorities in South West Africa that she was born in New York City on 26 March 1888, she now claimed to have been born in Kielce, on

26 March 1891 – yet another claim that cannot be verified at source. There may, of course, have been other reasons for shaving three years off her age. In Swakopmund, where she had been a seventeen-year-old prostitute, she may have wanted to appear older than she was. In Paris, implicated in theft, she may well have wanted a court to think she was younger.

But there was another problem contained within the misleading information she provided the police. Asked her father's first name, she gave it correctly as Joseph. By insisting that the family name was Silver rather than Lis, however, she made it impossible to place her father in London in 1888, the year of her birth. His presence there could nevertheless be verified from his application for a passport in Poland in 1884, and from evidence given by him and Adolph Goldberg, in court, in New York in 1889. But, if she had been born in Kielce in 1888 – which she could not possibly have been, since her father had left Poland in either late 1884 or early 1885 – what was her mother's first and maiden name? She had to come up with yet another name that could not be placed in Kielce or in London in 1888. It was a bridge too far. Uncertain how to respond in a way that would not compromise her father, she claimed not to know her mother's name! The response was so unconvincing that the investigating officer placed a question mark after the mother's supposed name. The net effect, however, remained the same – Bertha's age, place of birth and the real names of her parents were all concealed. Most importantly, there was no way her father, who had spent a life making parallel concealments, could be placed in London's East End in 1888.

The French, concerned only with cases of theft, had no reason to probe further. But Silver, inherently duplicitous and suspicious, had taken note of the new police methods and having his photograph taken particularly distressed him. Already he had had one unpleasant experience when a photograph of him in the company of prostitutes was produced in court. It was a fear which assumed growing proportions during the months that followed and he always worried that a mugshot would find its way to Scotland Yard. On 4 June 1909, he again appeared before examining magistrates charged with theft, complicity in an act of theft and vagrancy. The last charge, a hold-all allegation of the sort loved by police around the world, pointed to frustration on the part of the *gendarmerie* and they must have been dismayed when the state, again short of evidence, withdrew all charges a month later.

If, however, the police were disappointed they would hardly have been distraught; by then, they were pursuing another, more promising line of inquiry.[37]

In late February 1909, the Cohen brothers had tired of living in London and moved to Paris. The first indication of an impending move had taken place weeks earlier when Sarah Haberberg, 'Mrs Leibus Cohen', possibly directed by Jack Lis, had appeared, taken a brief look around then left.[38] Shortly thereafter, the 'tailors', Leibus and Mendel, took rooms at 67 rue du Faubourg Saint-Antoine, near the Place de la Bastille and close to Silver. Ambitious, with excellent underworld contacts throughout Europe, the Cohens scorned amateurish petty theft. Their interest lay in sophisticated approaches to well-researched projects using highly professional techniques to acquire goods of great value. Stolen items were moved through the hands of intermediaries as swiftly as possible before being sent abroad for rapid disposal. In short, they advocated an approach in keeping with that employed in the Cellini robbery. Silver, growing in confidence, was ready to take on bigger jobs since Jack, using the spoils of his Argentine adventure, had retreated to London where, under assumed names, he steered clear of the metropolitan police for three years. The Cohens agreed to take on Silver, Bertha and Alverger for a trial project.

Outwardly, there was not much to distinguish the building from others on the rue du Faubourg Montmartre in the 9th *arrondissement*. It was a grey four-storey tenement with a prominent garret of the sort that gives Parisian rooftops their distinctive eyebrows. The front was broken by pairs of symmetrically set windows underscored with black metal railings. What made number 24 interesting, however, was an attractive jewellery store at street level. Its proprietor, Jean Chauvet, lived in an apartment a little way down, at number 38. Inside was a display of the usual items and, in a small room behind the counter, a safe containing more valuable items.

Several days in late March were spent observing Chauvet's routine and that of residents in the rooms above the store. It was not long before somebody noticed that Chauvet tended to push closed the door of his safe – but not lock it – before taking lunch. In a way that was to become a trademark in the months that followed, someone – possibly Bertha – acting the *gigolette* won Chauvet's confidence, causing him to relax his vigilance, and the gang got the chance to make an impression of the keys to the front door. With any number of East European locksmiths in the 18th, it was easy to get copies made. The false keys were tested one night, the rough edges smoothed and a moment for the break-in decided on.

At midday on Saturday, 3 April, Chauvet locked up and set off to his apartment for lunch. Minutes later two, or three, people entered the store, opened the safe and removed bracelets, jewels and watches worth 20,000 francs. They left, not bothering to lock the door, and a woman who came to collect a watch left for repairs was surprised to find the store open and unattended. A policeman was summoned and Chauvet, who was rushed to the premises, confirmed he had been the victim of well-planned theft.[39] On this occasion the press, unusually, sat up and took notice. The following morning *Le Petit Parisien* and *Le Petit Journal* both reported the break-in on the rue du Faubourg Montmartre.

The thieves spent the rest of the day, and most of the week that followed, destroying incriminating evidence and disposing of the less valuable items through a network of pedlar-fences led by Rozendant and his friend, Segalowicz.[40] The *gendarmerie*, however, were not far behind. It is no longer possible to determine how the police picked up the trail since the court records have been destroyed, but it may have been an indiscretion on the part of Bertha that gave them their first clue. Some months later the Belgian police noted that she had a penchant for wearing stolen jewellery.[41] Five days after the burglary, the investigating magistrates were ready to act. Warrants were issued for the arrest of Alverger, the Cohens and the two Silvers. The whole lot were picked up later the same day and, the following morning, *Le Petit Parisien* reported the police progress.[42] 'Joseph Silver', a name known to readers of the *Cape*, *London* and *New York Times* and a host of lesser journals, had found its way into 'The newspaper with the largest circulation in the world'. He would not have enjoyed the publicity any more than did his accomplices. They were questioned and placed in the holding cells for the night. The following morning young Alverger and Bertha were released, but Silver and the Cohens were driven across town, down the Boulevard Saint-Michel to a prison that lay beyond the Jardin du Luxembourg.[43]

La Santé was used to house prisoners awaiting trial.[44] Built on 'Philadelphian' lines, with a separate cell for each inmate, if anything, it was more forbidding in appearance than Neumünster. Silver might as well have been back in Germany. In Sing Sing, claiming to be

Protestant had been a way of concealing his exit from Whitechapel and disguising his contempt for Jews. In La Santé he again claimed to be Protestant but was ready to engage in another private joke at the expense of the police and prison authorities. The use of the hated camera and his hair loss made him think about changing his appearance for personal as well as professional reasons. He was, he now claimed, a barber and 'wigmaker'. The Cohens, less familiar with the small privileges that might accrue to such statements in state-run institutions failed to have their religion recorded. La Santé did nothing for their mental or physical health, and they stayed there from 9 April to 27 May.

It was depressing. During the eight weeks spent there, arguably, only one thing was achieved. Silver knew from bitter experience that 'a man who is his own lawyer has a fool for a client'. Acting independently, he and the Cohens used the proceeds of the robbery to retain the services of some of the city's most prominent advocates. But, in that early bifurcated action, there was perhaps a warning that all was not well within the gang. He was defended by J. Erlich while the Cohens were represented by A. Cremieux. When they appeared on 22 and 27 May, they were defended with great skill. The four judges had to perform the oldest balancing trick in the world and weigh what they suspected might have happened against what had been proved: '. . . although grave presumption of the guilt of the accused exists in this case, a slight doubt nevertheless remains, from which they must be allowed to benefit'. The prisoners were freed and an unhappy Chauvet ordered to pay costs.[45]

Eight days later Silver and some Apaches were again in court, on another charge of theft, and yet again wriggled free for want of sufficient evidence. Two setbacks in the space of a week settled the matter in the minds of Chauvet, the police and the ministry. Chauvet hired senior counsel, the police squeezed the fence Rozendant, and the Ministry of Justice gave notice of appeal. The appeal was heard on 15 November 1909, with Messrs Monnot and Peysonnie appearing for Chauvet and the ministry. Confronted by learned peers and senior judges, Cremieux and Erlich found the going much harder and the turning point came when Rozendant was put on the stand. The pedlar put it beyond doubt that Silver and the Cohen brothers had 'received knowingly all or part of the stolen objects, consisting of tie-pins, rings and other objects decorated with gems and pearls'. This was a less impressive list than carried originally in *Le Petit Parisien*. Nevertheless, the judges were not disposed to treat the matter leniently. The accused were each sentenced to three years' imprisonment and instructed 'to pay jointly' damages of 2,000 francs to Chauvet and to meet costs of the prosecution.[46]

But it was all clever argument, legal procedure and talking heads. Chauvet, the *gendarmerie* and the ministry had won a Pyrrhic victory. Silver, having learned to take appeals by the state very seriously, had skipped the country. Years later, in Chile, it was said that he had escaped from prison in Paris. Shortly before judgment was handed down he and Bertha, like the Cohens, fled Paris, for Belgium. There they were to regroup under the leadership of Leibus Brjiski.

ANTWERP, BRUSSELS, LIÈGE
AND AACHEN
1909–1910

'What is robbing a bank compared with founding a bank?'

Bertolt Brecht, *The Threepenny Opera*

By late 1909 the brothers Lis, about forty years old, were fugitives from
justice at opposite ends of the Atlantic world. Jack was being sought by
Argentine authorities for his part in the Cellini heist, while Joseph was
wanted by the French police for his part in the Chauvet burglary. This was
no mere legal irritant; it was symptomatic of a more serious developing
problem. Like the Belgians then plundering rubber in the Congo, the brothers
had treated the ocean periphery as a 'robber economy' in which any one
part could be exploited to the death in the belief that there would always
be another patch of virgin territory left to work. Life was a race between
the declining resource of age and the need for new frontiers.

Silver's problems were more serious than his brother's. Large tracts
of England, France, Germany, the north-eastern United States and
southern Africa were no longer accessible to him and he was about to
invade the Low Countries, which would add to the list. In theory, the
American South, Midwest and west, along with sizeable portions of
central America, Cuba and all of South America remained untapped.
In practice, things were more complicated. He was getting older; constant
movement and syphilis were adding to his physical and mental burdens.
Acquiring new languages was easier said than done, and it was difficult to penetrate unfamiliar networks. In the circumstances, his adapt-
ability and stamina were remarkable.

There were other, professional, challenges. At the time he left Poland neither the Old nor the New World had been prepared for the transcontinental migration that followed the Tsar's assassination in 1881. In the two decades that followed, millions of Jews used the railway and the steamship to get to the nearest exit points leading to the Atlantic world. During that exodus, some God-fearing and a small number of anti-social elements had evaded the emigration, health or transport authorities, as well as the police of countries they had passed through. Several Old World administrations, preoccupied with the sheer mass of humanity making its way to the continental shoreline, failed to understand that not all East Europeans either could, or wanted to, be propelled into the main streams of assimilation at their destinations of choice.

Out on the Atlantic periphery, authorities accustomed to the measured migration of partly assimilated middle-class Anglo and German Jews were surprised by the emergence of pockets of East European crime in the 1880s and 1890s. The Jews were not alone; urban poverty pushed marginals from other ethnic groups, including Italians, into organised crime in the great port cities of the New World. Old World states, however, were equally unprepared for a counter-flow of bank robbers, burglars, fraudsters, pimps, prostitutes and white slavers – men and women from the margins seeking to profit from the illicit trade in property or people back at the centre. Not surprisingly, the idea of an international organisation to counter transnational crime had its origins in the era of the great migrations. Such a project was first mooted by Professor von Liszt, in Berlin, in 1893. A decade later the argument was taken further by the Argentine criminologist, Jean Vucetich, who urged greater regional and international co-operation in policing. But it was only in 1914, on the eve of the First World War, that the seed of the future Interpol was planted at an international criminal police conference convened by Prince Albert I, in Monaco.[1]

Silver and his Polish gangster friends' 1909–10 excursion into Belgium, Germany and Holland came at a moment when, possibly for the first time, he had a sense of the Atlantic world shrinking. He was running out of space not only because he had already exploited the most desirable urban locations, but, more disturbingly, because law enforcement agencies were starting to co-operate meaningfully in an effort to eradicate transnational crimes against people and property. The trend towards policing beyond national frontiers was most developed in western Europe, but also had transatlantic dimensions. Inter-state co-operation was predicated on new legislation, the utilisation of modern modes of communication, and techniques of mass surveillance.

By the end of the nineteenth century several countries, including Belgium and France, had systems of alien registration that made it easier to track law-abiding as well as law-breaking immigrants. By 1900, the demand for valid documents for inter-state travel was growing and, by the end of the First World War the presentation of passports on entry to or exit from a country was widespread. The first decade of the new century saw ratification of a slew of extradition treaties to facilitate the repatriation of fugitives not only between Old World countries, but between Europe and the United States of America as well as between America and South American states. America entered into extradition treaties with Argentina in 1896, Brazil in 1897, Chile in 1900 and Belgium in 1901 – all of which received presidential approval by 1903. Britain, too, signed extradition treaties: with the Argentine, Chile and Cuba in 1894, 1898 and 1905.

Legal instruments limiting the immunity and mobility of criminal or 'undesirable' elements complicated the lives of Brjiski, the Cohens and Silver, but hardly rendered them inert. Bureaucracy, documentation and extradition laws were not everyday hazards and could, with effort and forethought, be circumvented. Fingerprinting and photography, however, constituted a real hazard. These advances gave rise to the routinised exchange of information about the identity and movements of professional criminals. Continuous improvements in the speed and quality of postal services, the telegraph and the telephone helped with law enforcement. In western Europe, where France, Belgium, Holland and Germany formed a corridor carrying heavy criminal traffic, co-operation extended to allowing easy cross-frontier movement by detectives pursuing fugitives.

Silver's naturalisation papers – obtained via an incomplete application in 1893 – along with an American passport, obtained in 1895 by supplying false information, enabled him to follow his calling in most parts of the world. But his authorisation to travel was becoming dated and the day was not far distant when he would need a new document. He had already attempted, unsuccessfully, to become a naturalised citizen of the Cape Colony in 1905. Beyond this tissue of paper lies other, more disturbing, problems were emerging. After the rape of Laskin, in 1897, his photograph had been taken by the London Metropolitan Police and had been spotted on a file by a Cape detective visiting Scotland

Yard some years later. In 1899, William Coote, acting as informal British emissary to St Petersburg, had drawn the exploits of 'Joseph Schmidt', rapist and white slaver, to the attention of the Russians, with the result that he was a prohibited immigrant in the Tsarist empire. In 1899, he had been banished from the South African Republic and, in 1905, from German South West Africa. The following year, his photograph had been taken at Neumünster Central and a copy lodged in Hamburg and Berlin. In 1908, the Paris *gendarmerie*, too, had taken a mugshot of him along with his fingerprints. The latter picture, a singularly unflattering image, had been supplemented by another, altogether more pleasing semi-formal picture of him as a young man that the Paris police had acquired during the same raid. The latter images were later passed on to the Belgium authorities by helpful French police.[2]

Bureaucratic barbs were beginning to restrict his movement and erode his business. Circumventing them required patience, and careful planning had never been his forte. A string of failures on three continents attested to past deficiencies. The improvement in performance during his stay in Belgium and Germany was largely attributable to the professionalism of his new associates. Brjiski's Russo-Poles used aliases, disguises and forged identity documents, but they also cultivated other habits and practices to offset the advances in modern policing. The entire set-up he encountered in Belgium was on a level, and a scale, he had never previously experienced.

About twenty men and women would base themselves in a preselected city where they shunned involvement in petty crime; confining themselves to out-of-town operations, they used false keys to effect entry into selected business premises from which they removed huge quantities of cash, jewellery or negotiable instruments. Their low profile in the host city precluded amateurish mixing of burglary, pimping and prostitution. These precautions obviated the need to bribe policemen or interact with court officials working with the *gendarmerie*. All projects were meticulously researched and the largest undertaken on an out-of-country basis. Proper positioning prior to a heist demanded discipline, patience and secrecy, to be balanced by a mixture of cheek and opportunism when the moment presented itself. Mastery of the latest safe-cracking techniques was a prerequisite and, once the loot had been secured, mobility and speed were of the essence. Easily identifiable and especially valuable items were offloaded in neighbouring countries. It was a far cry from Silver's amateurish, youthful experiences.

Belgium was ideally situated for forays into adjacent states. A low-lying political creation of the post-Napoleonic era it was, thanks to the Rhine and its tributaries, linked to four neighbours renowned for their banking, commercial, financial or industrial strengths. Historic Antwerp, a port almost within sight of Britain, had a well developed *demi-monde*. Notable for its banks, commerce and diamond-cutting, the city was connected by canal, rail and river to Amsterdam, Paris and other west European centres. It was also within easy reach of Liège at the eastern end of the country, which was linked to Aachen and Cologne and, beyond that, to the industrialised Ruhr. Far beyond that, lay Poland.[3]

Kielce was the last thing on Silver or Bertha's mind when they got off the train at Antwerp in November 1909. They hoisted their bags and moved purposefully towards the exit of the station. Joseph Silver – a bird who had flown prison, and the wigmaker of Paris – had dyed his brown hair blond, acquired a new word-game identity as a 'dove', and got himself a forged American passport in the name of 'Abraham Taubentracht'. She was content to remain Bertha Silver. Outside the station, a few timid souls headed for the police station to sign the aliens' register but, Mr Taubentracht and Miss Silver turned left and marched south. Neither of them ever signed the register, intentionally compli-cating a police search six months later.[4]

Five minutes later they heard Yiddish words and phrases floating by on crowded sidewalks. Craftsmen, and merchants with hats perched at socially regulated angles, squeezed in and out of narrow doorways. Workers with cloth caps pulled down firmly to deflect the chill, scur-ried into cafés. With the old diamond-cutting quarter behind them, they stopped to ask the way. He, German-looking and pronouncing esses in the manner peculiar to Schleswig-Holstein, tried his French, asking after Longue Rue des Vanneux, also known by its Flemish name of Lange Kievitstraat. They readily found their way to number 140 where they asked for 'Scala' who, they had been told, was a Russian.[5]

Scala was not his real name, though many knew him by that alias. Nor, for that matter, was he Russian, although some of his best friends were. Depending on the day of the week he was an auctioneer, a dealer in job lots, or a salesman in one of Antwerp's street markets. Originally from Austro-Hungary or Poland, nobody, including the police, had ever got round to asking where he obtained his 'job lots' from. Perhaps they knew. His house was said to be the meeting place for figures from the Polish and Russian underworld who had friends and acquaintances

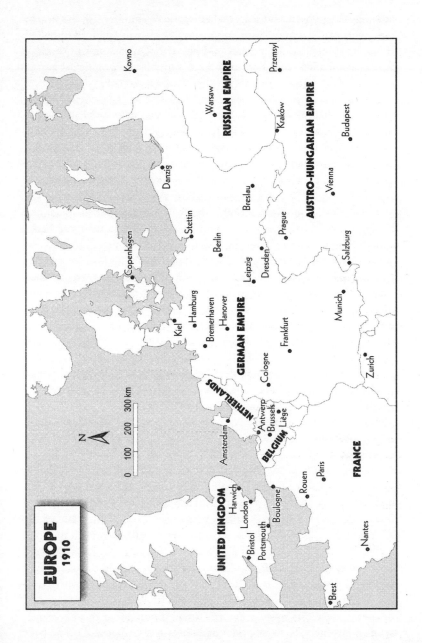

EUROPE
1910

UNITED KINGDOM
Bristol
Portsmouth
London
Harwich

FRANCE
Brest
Nantes
Rouen
Paris
Boulogne

BELGIUM
Antwerp
Brussels
Liège

NETHERLANDS
Amsterdam

GERMAN EMPIRE
Cologne
Frankfurt
Munich
Kiel
Bremerhaven
Hanover
Hamburg
Berlin
Leipzig
Dresden
Copenhagen
Stettin
Danzig
Breslau

RUSSIAN EMPIRE
Kovno
Warsaw

AUSTRO-HUNGARIAN EMPIRE
Przemysl
Kraków
Budapest
Vienna
Prague
Salzburg
Zurich

N

0 100 200 300 km

amongst the poorest and least skilled workers employed in the nearby diamond-cutting works. More pertinently, Scala was landlord to Leibus Brjiski's uncle, Wolf Sametband and his wife, Duina Kamisky, both of whom also hailed from Poland.[6]

Brjiski had hired a room two doors away. Sametband took them across and, on the basis of what he had been told by the Cohen brothers, introduced them to his nephew. Brjiski, exuding halitosis that clung to him tighter than his moustache, was pleased to meet somebody who, like him, had been trained on the Lower East Side. Since his deportation from Portsmouth to Warsaw two years earlier, he had been a white slaver escorting Polish women to ports such as Antwerp, from where they were sent on to the American seaboard or cities in South America.

It was during journeys through the Ruhr that Brjiski had acquired his knowledge of German cities, and found a mistress who had had a child by him. He had frequently visited large rail junctions, such as Aachen, where Polish women changed trains for the onward journey to Paris. In 1908, business had taken him to Argentina where he spent several months in Buenos Aires moving in Apache circles before changing direction. On his return to Antwerp in March 1909, he became more interested in sophisticated robberies than prostitution. He abandoned the working-class apparel of a gaunt, narrow-eyed, younger man. The old cloth cap was replaced by the fashionable straw boater of a *señhor* from the pampas and a plain neck-tie gave way to a bow-tie that had a dash of the tropics about it. No longer lean and clean-shaven, he sported a boldly twirled moustache.[7]

Brjiski, already planning his next excursion into Germany, was a model professional. Through him the Silvers renewed their acquaintance with the Cohen brothers and, via them, met 'Booter' – Moritz Kleinberg, an ex-Warsaw store-breaker, recently from London. Kleinberg knew the Cohens from the East End, where they and Sarah Haberberg had spent most of their time with Russian underworld elements drawn from Odessa. In Antwerp this Black Sea connection, which later drew Kleinberg back into Russia to organise the illegal emigration of white slaves, was consolidated when they were introduced to Stoermak Mottel, yet another of the gang from Odessa. Other notables in the circle were another married couple from Russian-Poland, Jacob Herlich who hailed from Salossyez and his wife, Marie, from Bedzin.[8]

During the closing weeks of 1909 small groups from this circle met, at irregular intervals, in low-class bars, beer halls, cafés and music halls around the harbour area. Many of their preliminary discussions, and most sensitive debriefings after operations, took place in Hoffman's saloon. The proprietor was trusted; everybody spoke fully and freely in his presence. Other, more routine intelligence-gathering activities took place in working men's clubs in the diamond-cutting quarter where employees occasionally let slip information about the business of the country's largest jewellers, or had it coaxed out of them by the Cohen brothers.[9]

The gang gave the appearance of operating in total secrecy. But within it, like an apple doomed to rottenness, a small spot could already be detected. Somewhere within Brjiski's inner circle, or just beyond it, was a person who bore a grudge. In October 1909 a letter had been posted in London, to the police in Antwerp, alerting them to Brjiski's record as a white slave trafficker. The Belgian police had done nothing about it; denunciations were common in the sex trade. Moreover, the spy's information was dated: Brjiski had acquired new interests. But the matter did not rest there. The unknown betrayer had moved closer and was listening, watching, waiting to see whether he or she could not get a better opportunity to strike. The informer had already resolved that the next time a communication was sent to the police it would outline forthcoming operations and future robberies.[10]

Brjiski's business and mistress took him out of town for two weeks in late November 1909. On the night of the 30th he slipped into a store in Munich and removed jewellery valued at 6,000 marks. So professionally was the snatch executed that it took fourteen months for German police to connect his prints to the theft. Back in Antwerp Scala, or somebody else, used guild alchemy to convert gemstones into banknotes. Like an old wolf willing to go out at night only when absolutely necessary, Brjiski settled down to rest. But the cubs in his expanding pack, especially the demanding males, had not been fed for some time. They became increasingly restless.[11]

Fourteen days after Munich, he took them on a hunt. In mid-December they set out for the Ardennes and the medieval bishopric of Liège, Belgium's third most important city, a regional educational centre grown plump on metal and mining profits. East European students and workers were a familiar sight in its streets and low-class haunts. The university, renowned for French instruction and low fees, had attracted Jewish students from Poland and Russia, while anarchists and socialists, admiring the strength of the trade union movement, found it equally amenable.[12]

Brjiski, Mendel Cohen, Kleinberg and an unnamed accomplice – almost certainly Silver – split up to find cheap accommodation. Most of the party stayed at the Hotel Moderne, spending hours lounging around nearby watering holes such as the Ober Boiern music hall and the Taverne Jean. Brjiski, during one of his forays into Prussia, had already settled on the target – the stockbroking brothers, Emile and François Marck in the rue du Pont d'Avroy. The Polish invasion, mounted from Antwerp and the Atlantic, lasted for a month. A near state-of-the-art operation was conducted with considerable skill.[13] Only while out drinking did the raiders draw unnecessary attention to themselves through brash behaviour. Unable to put his past behind him, Brjiski tried to persuade a married female employee at the bar of the music hall bar to accompany him to London while, in the tavern, equally bullish colleagues left a waiter puzzled by an inappropriately large tip for a few drinks. But apart from this frivolity Brjiski behaved utterly correctly and applied himself to the serious business of how to gain access to the Marck brothers' safe with clinical care.[14]

On 17 December, while Belgians were mourning the death of King Leopold, Brjiski had cause to celebrate. He had noted that the third floor of the house from which the Marck brothers conducted their business was vacant, and asked Emile Marck whether he could hire the apartment. Marck was not enthusiastic. He did not warm to this non-French-speaker who insisted on using English or Russian. Nor did he want to let a room to a single man in a building devoted to commerce. The brothers' business was located on the ground floor, while the second floor was divided between a company that marketed tyres and an apartment occupied by a respectable single woman. Brjiski simply did not fit the surroundings. A few days later, François Marck took the trouble to write a letter to the Antwerp police enquiring about the house in Lange Kievitstraat which Brjiski had given as his previous address. The response was not cheering: the place was apparently frequented by gangsters. But it was too late. Brjiski, insistent and willing to pay a term's rental in advance, had already signed a lease for the apartment.[15]

Worse followed. A few days after moving in Brjiski, never to be seen by day, returned late one night and asked Emile Marck for a key to a side entrance. In his haste Emile handed Brjiski a key to the door of the lobby leading to their offices. Two days later Brjiski returned the key, pointing out that he had been given the wrong one. Brjiski and friends could not believe their luck. With the most important logistical aspects in place, they retreated to make final preparations. On 21 December, the day of King Leopold's funeral, the Poles, even less over-come by the passing of the seventy-four-year-old monarch than the Congolese natives, made their way to Brussels. That evening Brjiski, passionate about Jewish cuisine, dined in rue de Baviere along with Mendel Cohen, Kleinberg and Silver; they were all spotted there by the Antwerp saloon-keeper, Hoffman.[16]

A great time was had by all. The late King was a man pimps and thieves could relate to. Leopold had achieved what almost no one, other than perhaps Cecil Rhodes, had done – he had stolen an entire country. In the King's case he had stripped the colony of its finest assets to make a personal fortune. Unlike the sexually ambivalent Rhodes, Leopold's private diversions were clear. Scorning bourgeois sensibilities, the King had taken a former prostitute as a mistress and consciously turned his back on public popularity. In short, the Belgian monarchy had propped up the greatest burglar-pimp of all time. And yet there was a differ-ence. Whereas the ruling classes upheld Leopold and those of high rank before a cowed church and state, Polish burglar-pimps were hounded and persecuted, marginalised by the middle classes and buried in sealed-off sections of cemeteries spread around a dozen of the Atlantic's great port cities. It was not so much immorality or theft *per se* that mattered, as the class, money and scale that underpinned it. Was that not the lesson of the master thief, Adam Worth?[17]

The would-be Adam Worths made their way back to Liège. Brjiski went to his room on the rue de Pont d'Avroy and, in the days that followed, kept an even lower profile than usual. At night he studied the interior of the building, determined where the electric alarm was located, established the movements of those who slept on the premises and plotted the way in which sound travelled through the converted house. The woman on the floor below almost never encountered him although, on several occasions, she heard stockinged feet along creaking stairways in the early hours of the morning. Only once did she have cause for complaint and that was when there was the noise of some-thing that sounded like metal being filed in the apartment above her. On New Year's Eve, 1910, the sound of male voices could be heard filtering down but it was to be expected at that time of year. The cleaning woman, too, rarely saw him since Brjiski had told her that she need clean his room only once a week. On the one occasion she did encounter him she was struck by the fetid smell of his breath.[18]

They struck in the early hours of 7 January 1910. Brjiski and his three accomplices took turns, over several hours, to open the safe so expertly and silently that not one of three women sleeping in the building that night heard a sound. A cascade of sand was released from between the safe's metal skins to litter the floor and cling to the hands and tools of the burglars. The locks were then picked. The door swung open to reveal a mountain of banknotes, coins and negotiable securities. The safe's contents were placed in a bag and stacked near the door while tell-tale surfaces were wiped clean of fingerprints. Brjiski crept back upstairs to wash his hands, leaving traces of sand on the soap before collecting his most portable personal belongings. Back downstairs the four hoisted their spoils and without even bothering to close the office door behind them, the gang slipped out of the side entrance and into the still dark street where they split up, each going his own way only to join up again, hours later, in Antwerp.[19]

At 7 a.m. Emile Marck entered the offices and discovered that the door between the lobby and the room behind it was ajar. The door of the safe was open and, on the floor before it, lay a small heap of sand. He rushed over to the rue du Parc to tell his brother what had happened. On his return he informed the police, who were quick to appear. Without careful verification it was impossible to tell the extent of the loss, but it had clearly been a very substantial robbery. The brothers informed their insurance company, La Francfortoise, while the authorities, alarmed at the magnitude of the robbery, appointed J.A. Bonjean as their examining magistrate

In Antwerp, the Brjiski gang counted the night's takings. Banknotes and coins worth 20,000 francs, never recovered, were shared amongst the four men. But even King Leopold might have blinked at the near money netted – negotiable instruments to the value of 150,000 francs, about US $25,000, in the form of bonds, debentures and share certificates. Many of these securities were direct, or indirect, derivatives from the murderously interconnected economy that Leopold presided over at home and abroad. Indeed, so steeped in blood were the Belgian Treasury, Congo and Katanga bonds that it was almost impossible to determine who the legitimate owners might have been. Other certificates had been issued by more orthodox Belgian enterprises, including shares in mining and metal firms to be found around Liège.[20]

They debated how, where and when the certificates should be marketed. England was an obvious possibility, accessible to all except Silver, who was known to Scotland Yard. But a quirk of fate had determined that in London, as in New York, the principal exchange for financial instruments was within walking distance of camouflage provided by sizeable East European communities. The City of London was joined to Whitechapel just as surely as Wall Street was linked to the Lower East Side. Hours later three men, in overcoats that would have done justice to a Polish winter, slipped aboard a ferry for the trip across the North Sea.

Despite Whitechapel's warm embrace, the three remained wary as they negotiated the fog on Commercial Road. It was not only the officers of the Met that concerned them. Violent ethnic clashes were not unknown in the East End and a bloody feud between the 'Bessarabians' and the 'Odessians' had barely ended.[21] They found the Odessa restaurant and introduced themselves to the man behind the bar counter using aliases that did not matter. Fosel Codet had been expecting them: he knew who they were. Unfortunately, so too did others and it was not long before their names and aliases were frothing up amidst the pilsner in Hoffman's saloon in Antwerp. The most readily negotiable of the securities – those issued simply to bearers without names – were passed to one 'Stern', a trustworthy middleman, who knew how to dispose of them amongst friends in the City. Brjiski and the others each took their cut, setting aside a further portion for the fourth man waiting for his share in Belgium.[22]

Mendel Cohen and Kleinberg remained relatively unobtrusive for some weeks. Brjiski was less disciplined and during two, perhaps three, stays in London in early 1910, he was often spotted dining at the Odessa, Zuckerman's or other Jewish restaurants. This unsettled his partners, who were distressed and then openly suspicious when, some weeks into his second stay, he started playing the gentleman. He abandoned the ordinary Jews of Whitechapel – and was said to be living in the suburbs and driving into town in an automobile each day. Self-indulgent behaviour attracted attention and the police, prompted from the Belgian end, started to monitor his movements, eventually forcing him to abandon his love of ethnic cuisine. Perhaps it was the same profligate behaviour and the police interest that caused the gang to retrieve the remaining securities from Stern and hand them to Mendel Cohen's sister-in-law, Sarah Haberberg, for safe keeping. She put them in a suitcase and deposited them in the left luggage facility at Charing Cross.[23]

Brjiski, however, had no intention of defrauding his partners. On the contrary, so conscious was he of his obligations that he risked communicating directly with his uncle. Writing in *mauscheln*, Hebrew-Yiddish, on 27 January 1910, he informed Sametband: 'I want to let you know that I will be in Belgium within ten days but not in Antwerp'. 'I will come to Antwerp for one night and pay all I owe, and I will then return [to England] and sail for America'. True to his word, he returned not only to pay outstanding debts but to plan more robberies with his Russo-Polish compatriots. The letter to his uncle, who knew about the Marck brothers robbery, however, had not been a good idea. It was intercepted by the Belgian police who got Rabbi Bemberger in Brussels to translate it. Brjiski was more vulnerable than he thought.[24]

His adversary was the young, ambitious acting examining magistrate in Liège, Bonjean. At the time of the robbery in the rue de Pont d'Avroy, the city was also home to six-year-old Georges Simenon, the author who, through his portrayal of Commissaire Maigret, was destined to give the Francophone world its most famous fictional detective and Liège its most honoured son. Bonjean, whose achievements in the Marck brothers case were recounted in the *Gazette de Liège* where Simenon later commenced his career as a reporter, would have been the envy of Maigret. By the time Brjiski got back to Whitechapel, Bonjean had made significant progress in the case.[25]

He interviewed dozens of witnesses and sought specialist evidence from expert witnesses including a chemist, handwriting analyst and a locksmith. He managed to reconstruct the movements of the gang prior to the burglary, and most impressively of all, got a policeman to persuade Hoffman to recount all he knew about his three principal suspects – Brjiski, Cohen and Kleinberg. Although aware that a certain 'Lys' was close to the gang, Bonjean did not consider him a prime suspect. His principal foe remained Brjiski and he had already constructed a watertight case against him. The only thing that hampered investigations was the inability of the police and immigration authorities to liaise closely – a common enough problem in Europe before the First World War. Even that, however, did not concern him unduly; he knew where Brjiski was. But while he was approaching the Foreign Ministry to approve an application for the extradition of Brjiski and the others, the rest of the gang in Belgium was finalising plans for a second robbery. The new, Apache-like venture would include two women and a girl – a novel departure for at least one notoriously misogynistic member of the gang. The target would be Roseels brothers' jewellery store at 40 rue Neuve, Brussels.[26]

In late January, with Brjiski and two former gang members in Whitechapel, a certain 'Charles Grunbaum' – described by the police as the mastermind behind the Roseels burglary – and Leibus Cohen arrived in Brussels and hired an apartment in the rue de la Blanchisserie. Who Grunbaum was, was never established. What is clear, however, is that despite his partially anglicised name, like that of 'Charlie' Silver back in Kimberley, he spoke German and that after the burglary he fled into Germany. It may also be worth recalling that Silver loved word-games, that Jewish newcomers in western society were often referred to as 'greeners', and that the suffix 'baum' lent itself to low-order punning. More importantly, Silver and his daughter were both held briefly for questioning after the Roseels burglary. Later still, it was asserted that Bertha liked wearing stolen jewellery and that although Silver claimed to be American, the Belgian police thought he was a 'German Jew'.[27]

In London, 'attic' or 'garret thieves' would seek out unoccupied houses, make their way to the top of the building, and then clamber along adjacent parapets and roofs. A variation on this *modus operandi* was used in rue Neuve.[28] The gang located unoccupied premises next to the jewellery store and then, pretending to hire it, used the opportunity to make wax imprints of locks in the building. But regaining entry to the empty building was not their only problem; it had unusually large windows and the interior was easily visible from a nearby hotel. So to conceal their presence the thieves entered the premises in mid-morning, concealed themselves in the loft for the remainder of the day and then, having been given the all-clear, used cover of darkness to climb on the roof.

It all took careful planning and preparation and, according to Leibus Cohen it was Grunbaum, the lone 'German' amongst the Russo-Poles, who played the leading role. At about that time, too, Silver and Bertha familiarised themselves with the capital and it is significant that when the police later sought them – two months after the burglary – the search concentrated on Brussels rather than Antwerp. By mid-March 1910, the gang was at last ready to put its plan into action.

A few days before the burglary Mr and Mrs Jacob Herlich, accompanied by Cohen – posing as 'Mr Köhler' – entered the jewellery store

intent on making what seemed like a substantial purchase. The real
purpose of the visit was for Marie Herlich to familiarise herself with
the proprietor while the men got an idea of the layout of the shop interior and security arrangements. Satisfied that everything was set,
Grunbaum and Cohen used false keys to let themselves into the unoccupied premises on 9 March and hauled equipment, food and drink up
into the loft of the building for a long wait.[29]

Shortly after 9 p.m. that evening Sarah Haberberg, her seven-year-
old daughter, and Marie Herlich took a stroll down the rue Neuve
keeping a close watch on the jewellery store. About an hour later the
proprietor left the shop for the day, locking the door behind him, and
walked off in the direction of his home, a few blocks away. As soon
as the door was locked Haberberg produced a whistle which she gave
to the child who – doing what children do – blew it as loudly as possible
for several minutes. The two women and the girl then followed Roseels,
making certain that he did not, for one reason or another, turn around
and return unexpectedly to the shop. He did not.

In the loft, having got the all-clear, Grunbaum, or more probably
Leibus Cohen, took the equipment, including a rope ladder and climbed
out on to the roof and, from there, on to the roof of the adjoining
shop. According to Cohen, he and Grunbaum spent five full hours
looting the store. Shortly after 4 a.m. they emerged, pockets stuffed,
carrying a hat-box and two suitcases bursting with gems, jewellery and
watches worth, the police later claimed, a breathtaking 250,000 francs.
Two hours later, with the help of the Herlichs, the two leather suitcases were deposited in the left luggage facility at the Gare du Midi.[30]

With the weak spring sun just threatening to breach the horizon,
Grunbaum, the Cohens and the Herlichs boarded the train for
Amsterdam. Hours later, they negotiated the sale of the contents of
their hat-box and pockets, sharing the cash amongst themselves. They
then split up, agreeing that the bulk of the goods would be entrusted
to the women and sent to the thieves' exchange in Whitechapel for
disposal. Marie Herlich returned to Brussels, changed addresses but not
her name, and revisited the Gare du Midi where she dipped into the
contents of the cases on her own account. She forwarded the cases to
a false name, at a *poste restante* address in Germany, to which her
husband, Grunbaum and the Cohens had already proceeded. In Cologne,
the cases were picked up by Sarah Haberberg who took them to
London, but not before the men, including Grunbaum, had again fished

around removing yet more items of value. Unlike negotiable instruments – mere paper until they were converted – gems, jewellery and watches were an immediate temptation for cash-strapped thieves. Within days of the robbery several gang members were stealing from one another and, if Leibus Cohen was to be believed, the most valuable items went to Grunbaum.[31]

In matters criminal, large developments are sometimes less important than seemingly insignificant ones. In Brussels the police, with nothing much to go on, had taken the abandoned ladder and checked at local shops until they discovered where the rope had been purchased. The storekeeper provided them with a reasonable description of the men. Detective Verhulst used this to trace them to the hired apartment and obtained their names. Extending his net, Verhulst established that Mrs Herlich was still in the city, although living at a new address, and arranged for her incoming letters and telegrams to be intercepted. He then communicated by telegraph with the gang in Cologne, using Marie Herlich's name, confirming their address and presence in Germany.[32]

Verhulst's patience was rewarded when, ten days after the burglary, Mrs Herlich revisited Amsterdam to sell loot that she had purloined for herself. He tailed her across the border and, with the help of Dutch police who succeeded in distracting her, discovered that she was in possession of forty gold watches that could all be traced back to rue Neuve. But when she experienced trouble in disposing of a second lot of watches through the same sources, she suddenly changed plans and darted off. Instead of rejoining the gang in Cologne, as originally agreed, she made her way to Breslau-Wroclow on the Polish border, which was close to her family home in Bedzin.

Breslau, on the banks of the Oder, was a well-known point of entry for poor *Ostjuden* as well as a commercial and industrial hub boasting superb transport links to most other major cities in Germany and onward, via sea links, to London.[33] Herlich went to Breslau, followed by the relentless Verhulst, and may have seen her family but again failed to dispose of any more of the stolen watches. She then boarded a train for the Schlesischer Bahnhof, hoping to sell some of the watches in Berlin before rejoining the gang in Cologne in what was becoming an extraordinarily fruitless journey.[34]

In Berlin, in unfamiliar surroundings and increasingly anxious to dispose of more loot before the gang reconvened, Mrs Herlich was reduced to touting watches on the street. Verhulst approached her and offered to introduce her to a contact who could sell all the watches: he then directed her into a police station where he had her arrested. Having applied for her extradition, he went on to Cologne where, with the assistance of the Germans, Cohen and Jacob Herlich were arrested and money they had in their possession confiscated. After initially hesitating, Cohen and Herlich became more co-operative and, by 5 April, Verhulst had returned to Brussels before setting out once again to try to trap the elusive 'fourth man', Herr Charles Grunbaum. He never did.[35]

While events relating to the Roseels break-in were playing themselves out in mid-March 1910, the cycle set in motion at the Marck brothers' that January was quickening as a result of investigations by the indefatigable Bonjean. Although Bonjean and Verhulst worked separately, never picking up on the underlying links, their cases were bound together in fascinating ways. Both crimes had been conceived of in Antwerp, and both had involved Brjiski, the Cohen brothers, the Herlichs and Silvers. In both crimes Sarah Haberberg – Mrs Leibus Cohen – had safeguarded and disposed of loot in Whitechapel. In both instances, too, accomplices remained unaccounted for: Brjiski's unnamed collaborators, and Cohen's 'missing' man, Charles Grunbaum.

Most intriguingly of all, however, both cases were being closely followed by an unknown male or female informer with an intense dislike of misogynistic pimps. The mystery source, it will be recalled, had earlier written to the Antwerp police about Brjiski's past as a white slaver and – as will become evident – also disliked Silver sufficiently to inform on him. Had the police in Brussels followed up on these unsourced clues they might have prevented yet another robbery by the Russo-Poles. But, at the time, the best Belgian authorities could do was to wait for the extradition of the fugitives they sought in connection with the safe-cracking in Liège.

In March, about the time of the Roseels break-in, Bonjean had persuaded the Metropolitan Police to arrest Brjiski, Mendel Cohen and Booter Kleinberg. Cohen and Kleinberg were picked up but Brjiski, having sensed that his presence in Jewish restaurants was being monitored, had already fled. In New York City he took on a bewildering array of new aliases, moving constantly between the Lower East Side and Paterson, New Jersey. Shortly after the arrests in Cologne, Mendel Cohen and Kleinberg appeared before a Bow Street court. The English judges were, however, of the opinion that there were insufficient grounds to warrant their extradition to Belgium.[36]

The examining magistrate in the Roseels case – De Laruwière – working with Verhulst, had more luck. Although Sarah Haberberg had been tipped off by telegram about her husband's arrest in Cologne and warned that she needed to 'be careful', she was arrested in Whitechapel in mid-April, along with Leibus's cousin, Max Cohen, and an associate named Bronovitch. The Metropolitan Police recovered half the securities stolen in Liège but, of the suitcases containing gems, jewellery and watches from Brussels, there was no sign. Haberberg's arrest brought home to the Belgian public, for the first time, the fact that there were important links between the burglaries. This interest in the Russo-Polish raiders was extended when it became known that the Germans suddenly wanted to pursue a jewellery-store theft that had taken place in Breslau-Wroclow some days after the burglary at Roseels, and which bore an uncanny resemblance to that perpetrated earlier in the rue Neuve.[37]

The arrest of Haberberg and her extradition to Belgium in June 1910 alerted the French to the continental marauders. In Paris, where the *gendarmerie* had been less than professional in dealing with the theft in the rue du Faubourg Montmartre, the police suddenly took renewed interest in the Cohen brothers and Silver. Their efforts met with mixed success. Mendel Cohen, on the far side of *La Manche*, remained maddeningly close yet safely tucked away behind the skirts of Mother Whitechapel. Of Joseph Silver there was no sign. In July 1910, Paris persuaded Berlin to give its request for the extradition of Leibus Cohen from Cologne priority over that of Brussels. Leibus Cohen was the only person to serve a sentence for the Chauvet burglary.[38]

In Liège, Bonjean turned his attention further afield. In March 1910, he wrote to the Chief of Police in New York City, giving him a detailed description and photograph of Brjiski as well as an account of the theft at the stockbrokers' in the rue du Pont d'Avroy. But the NYPD, an ocean rather than a channel away from Europe, were even less interested in the burglary at the Marck brothers' than the police in London had been. Like a fox terrier battling a slipper twice its size, Bonjean clung on, shaking underworld sources in Antwerp's diamond district for news of his quarry. He learned that Brjiski, still hankering after the food and drink of the Old Country, was frequenting Lazarus's Saloon on Second Avenue in New York. His man was living on the Lower East Side, and Bonjean knew it was only a matter of time. As he later recorded triumphantly, 'Finally, on May 13th, I knew that he was in

New York under the name of Luc Cohen, at 82 East Second Street.'
On 18 July, the NYPD arrested Brjiski.[39]

Brjiski, however, was equally resourceful. He and his attorney Henry
Rosenberg thought that the ocean, friend to so many Polish and Russian
refugees, would come to their rescue. Throughout a sapping Manhattan
summer Rosenberg and the distant Bonjean tore away at the legal niceties
of the extradition treaty binding the United States and Belgium. By the
autumn it was clear that the fox terrier had won: in mid-November,
Brjiski was put aboard the *Finland* and sent back across the Atlantic.
Bonjean had his day in court in Liège, on 8 April 1911, when Brjiski
was sentenced to five years in the Prison de Saint Gilles, in Brussels,
and banishment from the kingdom for a further ten years. Little more
than two and a half years later, he was unexpectedly granted parole.
Having been given two days to take leave of his uncle and friends in
Lange Kievitstraat, he was escorted back across the country and, on
Christmas Day 1913, put across the border to Germany.[40]

In Brussels, De Laruwière and Verhulst did not have to wait as long
as Bonjean to see the back of the Russo-Poles arrested in London and
Cologne. By late 1910 all except Leibus Cohen, still languishing in Le
Santé for his part in the Chauvet break-in, had been extradited and
appeared before a tribunal for their role in the Roseels burglary. Jacob
Herlich was sentenced to five years, and the women, Marie Herlich
and Sarah Haberberg, four years each. On 16 July 1913, Leibus Cohen
was extradited from France to Belgium and sentenced to five years in
Brussels. By the eve of the war, the police in continental Europe were
moving closer together just as surely as their armies were moving ever
further apart.[41]

Amidst the developments round the Marck and Roseels robberies,
in mid-1910, there was one notable omission – perhaps two. Joseph
Silver and his daughter, in the Low Countries since late 1909, had
avoided arrest despite having been seen with Polish compatriots on
several occasions and being questioned about the rue Neuve break-in.
With the exception of Verhulst, who pursued 'Grunbaum', the Belgian
police had never considered the Silvers to be centrally involved in
burglaries in Brussels and Liège. This indifference was not shared by
the unknown informant in Whitechapel. By mid-1910, that person –
Mendel Cohen or Moritz Kleinberg or, more likely, Sarah Haberberg
– was sufficiently angered by Silver's charmed life to want to inform
the police about yet another burglary being planned.

On 9 May 1910, New Scotland Yard sent a message to police in Aachen, warning them that 'Joseph Silver, alias Joseph Lys, alias Abraham Ramer travelling through Europe on an American passport under the name of Taubentracht' was intent on robbing a bank situated diagonally across the way from the Hotel Kaiser. The Metropolitan Police must have had a good idea of his previous movements and *modus operandi*, for they also told the German authorities that, once the theft had been executed, Silver would probably seek refuge in Belgium.[42]

Located in a wooded Prussian valley, Aachen nestles in a corridor linking Liège in eastern Belgium to Cologne. An ancient Christian settlement and once the favoured residence of Charlemagne, the city had long been a site for pilgrims making their way to its cathedral, or for visitors seeking to benefit from its hot-water spa. By the late nineteenth century, however, Aachen's religious significance, like Liège's, had been eclipsed by a vigorous mining industry that endowed the city with added commercial, financial and industrial importance.

By 1910 the expanding German rail network included Aachen as an important trans-shipment point for East Europeans making their way to Brussels, Paris or beyond. Its citizens and the police were accustomed to the sounds of Polish and Russian but were less comfortable with Yiddish, bastardised German, the 'secret language' of the Jews. For Silver, ostensibly a 'German Jew' rather than a *Polnische Schnorrer*, language was not a problem.[43] Nor was a city with the usual array of bars, cafés, run-down hotels and music halls. They, along with the pimps and prostitutes that went with them, were part and parcel of most industrialising cities in the Ruhr. In Aachen, everyone, including the Mayor who had recently complained about it, knew that lower-class, lumpen elements crowded into the downtown area around Steinstrasse.[44]

Given his class and cultural camouflage, the police had some difficulty in tracing him. Perhaps his liking for baths and spas drew him away from his usual haunts to slightly more salubrious quarters. A day or two after receiving the warning they made a few inquiries which yielded little. A civil servant thought he might have seen someone answering to Silver's description in a street about a week earlier, on 3 May, but further inquiries produced nothing. There were other problems. The letter had mentioned the 'Hotel Kaiser' but there was no Hotel Kaiser in the city. Two establishments bearing similar names – the Kaiserbad and Kaiserhof – were checked but neither had a bank opposite it although, in one case, there had been a branch that had closed some months earlier. On 11 May, the police, feeling more comfortable, reported that, 'it's not impossible that Silver has left Aachen for the time being, or perhaps for good and that, after looking around here, he has moved off to another town and planned a burglary there'. Within a week they knew better.[45]

Between 2 p.m. on Saturday 14 May and 8.30 a.m. on Tuesday the 17th, one or more persons using false keys let themselves into the Aachen and Munich Fire Insurance Company in the city centre and, after several hours of labour left, taking care to lock the doors behind them. In the interim ghostly intruders, as determined as they were invisible, prised open the safe door using a chisel-like instrument and removed close on 50,000 German marks in notes and gold coin – close on US $12,000 in value. The theft was notable not only for the amount of cash removed but for the meticulous planning that preceded it as well as its superb execution. Gaining access to the outer office itself required keys to two separate sets of metal and wooden doors. Beyond that lay the vault guarded by a metal door that operated with a special lock that required the simultaneous turning of two keys which, for security reasons, were kept by two different employees. Beyond that, stood the safe. It would have taken a daring, menacing and knowledgeable man, or perhaps an enticing, friendly and persuasive woman, or both, considerable effort to obtain impressions of all the keys.[46]

By the time the crime was discovered on the Tuesday morning Silver was safely across the border and hastening towards his most constant companion – the Atlantic. That afternoon, the *Echo der Gegenwart* carried an item noting that not a single door or lock had been damaged during the burglary. It pointed, the newspaper suggested, to an inside job. The police thought so too. Within hours all the employees, including those who held the keys to the special lock, had been questioned. But this yielded nothing. Showing new urgency, the police informed their counterparts in Brussels but it took four days for the communication to find its way to Verhulst who, by then, could only draw the circular to the attention of the relevant police division. Back in Aachen, the police made no progress and, by Wednesday, the *Echo der Gegerwart* was just that, an echo. It was reduced to reporting that there was not so much as a fingerprint to go on, and that the fire company would have to look to its own insurers to recover its loss.[47]

In Paris, the *gendarmerie* picked up on exchanges between Aachen and Brussels and asked for Silver to be extradited for the Chauvet break-in should he be arrested. They followed this up with a request to the Dutch police to be on the lookout for him. By mid-May 1910, immigration authorities and police forces in four countries bordering the North Sea were alert to the fire insurance burglary and taking renewed interest in the movements of the last of the Russo-Polish raiders. It had been a very professional operation leaving police with almost nothing to pass on to continental collaborators.

The authorities in Aachen obtained two photographs of Silver from Brussels but it was not until days later that they made something approaching a breakthrough. On 3 June the police found two women who had been out on the night of the burglary searching for an errant spouse and remembered encountering 'two men' outside the company's premises. A bearded individual, who the police felt had probably shaved off his beard after the burglary, was unrecognisable from the descriptions they had but the second, seen leaving the building carrying a leather bag, could well have been their man. On 6 June, the company, clutching at straws, offered 5,000 marks for information leading to the arrest and conviction of the thieves.[48]

The police in Aachen managed to establish, via a series of cross-border police circulars and telephone calls, that their suspect was part of a gang originally based in Antwerp. They pursued their inquiries in Brussels and Liège, where the full extent of the linkages between the burglaries in the rue Neuve and the rue du Pont d'Avroy were slowly surfacing. In Liège they were hampered by the fact that Bonjean had been promoted to Vice-President of the court in the wake of Brjiski's extradition. Queries directed at counterparts in Brussels brought more disappointment.

He was on the run and, though the police in various countries were noticeably more co-operative, untraceable. For Silver, it was an all too familiar position. Moving on, in haste, was the way in which the great robber economy functioned. Despised and marginalised in Russian-Poland, many Jews had welcomed the advent of the great migrations only to find that the contagion of anti-Semitism had found its way into their baggage and accompanied them to the farthest corners of the Atlantic. The New World had taken in many of the outcasts of the Old, but hardly embraced them or fully opened new labour markets to them. In many places the words for Russian or Polish Jew, or synthesised variations thereon, had become synonymous with the words for boor or crook or, worse still, for pimp or prostitute.

Yet this time, there was something different. At the age of forty-two, for the first time in his life, this deeply disturbed, poverty-stricken, woman-hating nothing from Kielce was loose in the world with $10,000 or more in his pocket. The question was: where to hide? Where was he to make the fresh start that a small part of him was always in search of? In truth, only the south-western corner of the Atlantic remained open to him. In some ways the Tsar's stepsons had already made the choice for him and, if not they, then Jack, or Brjiski. He was on his way to Argentina where the world's largest, best organised community of East European criminals awaited his arrival with mixed feelings. Buenos Aires and its amazing underworld beckoned.

XX

BUENOS AIRES
1910

The most terrifying reflection is that all these [Russians] are
not the product of the exceptional but of the general – of
the normality of their place, and time and race.

Joseph Conrad, *Under Western Eyes*

OTHERWISE full, the Argentine records refuse to yield the date or name
under which Silver slipped into the city in the winter of 1910. Neatly
attired whenever funds permitted, in his dark suit, starched collar and
felt hat he had all the cover that a man no longer forced to travel third
class needed. The turbulence of the Atlantic, like the Red Sea aeons before
it, had calmed as the harbour's dock opened to take in the silky smooth-
ness of the River Plate. Ashore, he walked through a gateway into the
Paseo de Julio and every one of his senses, prompted by the vibrancy of
the place, was sparked into life. To a remarkable degree Buenos Aires
was the Argentine, and Argentina, in turn, was Buenos Aires.

By 1910 Argentina had, with the exception of a depression in the
1890s and shorter periods of recession in recent times, experienced an
economic boom that stretched back three decades. From the turn of
the century exports grew by 5 per cent per annum. Along with its
southern cousin, South Africa, Argentina produced the lubricants that
kept the northern motors of global economic expansion running
smoothly. While the British colony in Africa supplied London with the
gold that underwrote international trade, the Argentine provided the
cities of Europe with an inexhaustible supply of cereals, chilled meat
and other animal products. Large-scale export of primary commodities

characterised the southern economies just as surely as a modest counter-flow of foreign investment contributed to the emergence of small, vulnerable, manufacturing industries. In Argentina, about five hundred families formed a governing commercial and landed elite, while on the Witwatersrand just two dozen deracinated Randlords determined the economic future of the entire country.[1]

Skewed so as to benefit the long-term interests of the industrialised nations, the long southern boom nevertheless attracted money and men in prodigious quantities. Argentina became the darling of the City, and by the First World War had eclipsed all other competitors to become the largest site of British investment abroad.[2] Impressive sums of French and German capital followed. Leading commentators saw Argentina as an emerging rival for the United States and the country's population increased from under 2 million in 1870, to over 8 million by 1914. Amongst millions of new immigrants, most of them from the sunny reaches of southern Europe, there was a growing number who came from the shadowy domains of the Tsar in eastern and central Europe. In the decade before the war over 20,000 Russians and Poles made their way south, and by 1910 – the high point in the inflow – an estim-ated 5 per cent of immigrants each year were Jewish. Tucked away within this minority was the even smaller minority of pimps, prosti-tutes and some of the world's most notorious white slave traffickers.[3]

In Argentina, arable land stretched all the way to the coast, blurring the distinction between city and countryside. Buenos Aires thrived, dominating its entire hinterland. By the mid-1890s the capital housed 5 per cent of the nation's population and by 1914 half of its 1.5 million inhabitants were foreign-born. In the very year Silver arrived, 1910, a newly opened railway reached out across the Andes to link Buenos Aires to Santiago in Chile and within the capital itself a modern tramway system was unveiled to serve its citizens. By the outbreak of war, Buenos Aires was second only to New York City in size on the Atlantic seaboard and the largest city in Latin America.[4]

Muscular capitalism such as occurs when an adolescent spends too much time in the gym gives rise to an unnatural physique. Argentina's bulk outstripped the state's slender frame, causing its indigenous commercial and landed elite to lean too heavily on an unskilled prol-etariat of Italians and Spaniards, and 100,000 Jews sucked in from the Tsarist empire. After the turn of the century this unbalanced contest – between a small nativist ruling class seeking to protect its profit margins and political hold, and a huge immigrant working class struggling to contain rents, working hours and grow wages in an inflationary climate – became increasingly fraught and volatile. The government, alarmed by radical ideologies and immigrant workers who threatened to make Argentina *the* centre for revolutionary politics in the western world, armed itself with repressive legislation. The Residence Law of 1902, the Ley de Residencia; allowed the state the right to deny entry to the country to any person who posed a threat to public safety, or who had been convicted of a criminal or political offence in his or her home country. But, for several years, the law was observed mainly in the breach since the economics of mass immigration easily trumped the state's ability to enforce the will of a tiny elite.[5]

The middle-class Union Civica Radical, infused with cultural nationalism, was undercut at street level where the sharply focused ideologies of labouring folk held great sway. Immigrants versed in anarchist, anarcho-syndicalist or socialist rhetoric and traditions posed awkward questions about the deteriorating economic, political and social conditions. To this swelling chorus of working-class protest, Jewish workers added a voice conveying their own versions of anarchism, *Bundism* and socialism built on the experiences of eastern and central Europe. And, as always when nationalists battle with socialists, there was no shortage of anti-Semites suggesting that the voices of the left were orchestrated by 'the Jews'.[6]

The ensuing clash between conservative 'natives' and revolutionary 'foreigners' was felt most keenly in Buenos Aires which housed four of every ten of the nation's factories and workshops. After 1900, almost every year saw a greater number of strikes; by mid-decade, there were never less than a hundred a year. During the recession of 1906–7 the number jumped from 170 to 231 and in the latter year working-class action culminated in a general strike prompted by unaffordable rents that was supported by more than a quarter of a million *portenos*. Each year after 1900 saw tens of thousands of workers participating in May Day demonstrations and parades, and in 1909 and 1910 further, well-supported general strikes undermined the confidence of an already stretched ruling class.[7]

With the political fabric of the country unravelling and the state hard pressed to control workers during strikes and May Day protests, Argentina manifested many classic pre-revolutionary symptoms. The police, under pressure to improve intelligence-gathering and show they could counter the growth of radical movements, expanded their network of agents and collaborators amongst the criminal as well as the working class. The results were predictable. An increase in denunciations, informing and treachery fostered a climate of fear and suspicion and did little to build confidence in the system as a whole. The resulting insecurity was not confined to the labouring or dangerous classes. Smaller middle-class communities, too, became unhinged as the more assimilated members of society sought to increase the distance between themselves and less acculturated kinsmen.

Tremors in the political bedrock threatened to split the edifice of urban society, with potentially damaging consequences for the countryside too. In 1909, confronted by yet another general strike, the Figueroa Alcorta administration (1904–10) and the Chief of Police in Buenos Aires, Colonel Ramón Falcón, agreed on new measures to counter mid-year demonstrations. By dusk on May Day, eight anarchists were dead and two score lay wounded. Heavy-handed action from above invited counter-terror. On 14 November, a young anarchist, taking his cue from *Narodnaia Volia*, the People's Will of his Mother Russia, rolled a bomb beneath Falcón's carriage, killing the Chief of Police and his assistant. The fact that Simón Radovizky was nominally Jewish did not escape the notice of the insecure or the vicious, and the vapour of anti-Semitism clung to the banks of the River Plate.[8]

Retribution against anarchists and Jews – for some, hardly separate categories anyhow – followed. A 'state of siege', the modern day state of emergency, was declared and the Law of Residence used to round up non-naturalised union leaders and their followers, who were placed aboard ships and sent into banishment. The new year of 1910 saw more repressive legislation and the Law of Social Defence empowered the police to deport or imprison those suspected of having anarchist connections. In these circumstances Silver's slipping into the country unnoticed becomes more impressive and his desire to seem older rather than younger, German rather than Russian, and middle- rather than working-class easier to understand.[9]

The stench of anti-Semitism refused to lift. It lingered and troubled a domesticated middle-class element that did not want its hard-won urban security polluted by either *landsleit* crowding into the *barrios* or by pimps, prostitutes and white slavers occupying fortress Lavalle. It seemed that anarchists, socialists and gangsters were intent on behaving in ways that would see the flames of anti-Semitism set the pampas alight. But since anti-Semitism is, by nature, less sensitive to differences of class than to ethnicity and religion, Jews of *all* classes, including the Russo-Polish gangsters, were becoming apprehensive as mid-year, 1910 approached.

May Day passed peacefully, but anarchist and socialist unions used the occasion to announce a general strike that would commence on 18 May, to coincide with the centennial celebration of the nation's independence. It was a proclamation calculated to unsettle the elite and its administration, and the militia chose to take pre-emptive action. On 13 May the offices of *La Protesta*, the anarchist mouthpiece, along with the socialist *La Vanguardia*, were closed, sacked and burnt. The protests that followed precipitated yet another state of siege and 'patriotic groups' invaded Jewish neighbourhoods, burning a tailor's premises, stoning an anarchist bookshop and looting stores. Anarchists, in a spasm of retaliation, planted a bomb in the theatre of the bourgeois, the Colón, which, in turn, triggered more action that effectively halted their challenge. More repression, a change of government and the electoral reform of the *Sáenz Pena* law two years later, choked off working-class ambitions and, by the start of the First World War, a measure of stability had returned to class politics in Buenos Aires.[10]

When Silver crept into the capital, in mid-1910, the air in the Plazo de Mayo was still crackling with talk of crises, conflict and constitutions. He, like his gangster friends in the city, had little formal interest in the links between Jews and politics. The only person that he had known to follow such matters was the policeman, Charles Jacobs, who had dogged the footsteps of Emma Goldman and other anarchists on the Lower East Side. And the only time he ever witnessed an anarchist outrage – when Norcross attempted to blow up the millionaire Russell Sage – he and Jacobs had been more interested in the pickpockets working the crowd than the pedigree of the bomber. In Buenos Aires twenty years later, that neat distinction between crime and politics seemed harder to sustain. And, as he was about to learn, when the ruling class and proletariat jostled for turf, it was often those with the greatest propensity for treachery – the police and the gangsters – who got to rub shoulders.

Argentina's economic structure, its changing religious contours and the clash of class interests to which they gave rise shaped the organisation, subculture and tactics of the Buenos Aires underworld in at least three major ways. First, a labour-hungry economy ingesting millions of

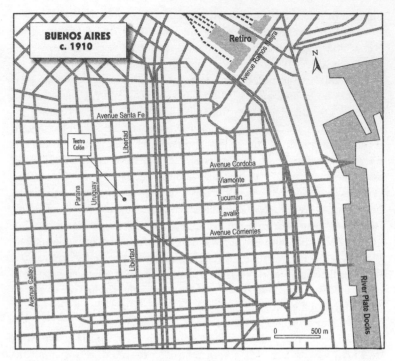

male immigrant workers each year fed directly into an alienated, feckless, urban culture characterised by serious drinking and frivolous sex. Commercial sex, which flourished in a tolerant Catholic environment, grew at almost the same pace as the economy and East European immigration. By 1910, 22 per cent of the registered prostitutes in the city were of Russian or Polish origin.[11]

Secondly, as the elite took fright at the influx of workers with radical ideologies and the entrenchment of organised ethnic crime, so the middle classes were at greater pains to distance themselves from coreligionists who, they felt, jeopardised their own chances of assimilation. For middle-class Jews and Russo-Polish gangsters this ended in the logic of double jeopardy – the devout were guilty if they distanced themselves from their kin – 'Jews are the worst anti-Semites of all' – or if they failed to do so – 'All Jews are the same'.[12] In the event, a good number of Jews took the first option and made strenuous efforts to distance themselves from those they deemed to be *tmeyim* – the unclean. The double marginalisation of 'foreign' pimps, prostitutes and white slavers – from their own community and the Catholic mainstream – increased the predatory disposition of a corrupt police force infused with cultural nationalism. Russo-Polish gangsters were a loathed subset within an unevenly tolerated Jewish minority.[13]

Thirdly, as radical political change threatened in mid-decade, the police used time-honoured methods including blackmail, bribes and threats to get criminals to inform on workers and the trade union movement. Russo-Polish gangsters in working-class neighbourhoods, such as Lavalle, were approached to inform on Jewish anarchists and socialists.[14] Some, including no doubt a number who had collaborated with the Okhrana, the Russian secret police in the months after the assassination of Alexander II, were happy to oblige.[15] Most gangsters, however, were less concerned about the threat the working poor posed to the state than about the threatening behaviour of middle-class Jews. So, while some *tmeyim* turned their attention to the doings of the *gente de pueblo*, the working masses, others used the same technique – infiltration – to penetrate and disrupt middle-class Jewish civic organisations bent on ridding the city of the 'unclean'.[16] This noisy, internecine conflict – between Russo-Polish gangsters with interests in drugs, gambling and prostitution and law-abiding Jews – could be traced back at least to the 1890s and persisted, in various forms, until the mid-1920s.

Cast adrift from moorings by a storm of bad press in Rio de Janeiro, a small group of Galician and Russian pimps, prostitutes and white slavers washed up on the banks of the River Plate in 1879, where they were soon joined by Polish and Romanian professionals of the same ilk.[17] Within five years, this motley crew held sway at a restaurant in an inner-city Jewish neighbourhood and, in 1885, constituted themselves more formally. The Club of Forty, *El Club de los Cuarenta*, like many immigrant organisations was, in the first instance, a mutual aid association seeking to protect its members' interests in the face of life's vicissitudes. In addition, however, El Club imported, allocated and distributed prostitutes within the city and fast-growing provincial centres including Bahia Blanca, Cordoba and Rosario.[18]

Crime, risk and secrecy spurred the formation of El Club, which soon earned pariah status. But law-abiding merchants and workers had no less need of a mutual aid society so, in 1894, European Jews formed a burial society which later broadened its functions to become the Chevra Keduscha Aschkenasi. Despite vast differences, the two organisations existed side by side for several months. But, whereas the Chevra readily got the support of religious office-bearers when burying its dead, El Club had great difficulty in getting rabbis to sanction the burial of the 'unclean'. Pimps and prostitutes, who admitted leading imperfect lives, felt that, whatever their moral transgressions, they remained Jews and that they were entitled to a religious burial. These differences were the source of ongoing resentment on both sides.

In 1898, the gangsters, ever pragmatic, offered the Chevra a large donation on the clear understanding that *tmeyim* would henceforth be granted religious burials, presided over by rabbis. When their offer was rejected, the gangsters created institutions and structures to ensure that their members left the world in recognisably Jewish fashion. Two years later the Sociedad Israelita de Soccoros Mutuos Aschkenazi acquired its own cemetery in the working-class suburb of Avellaneda, and a synagogue in centrally located Libertad Street. Thus, by 1900, the very idea of 'community', and what it was to be a 'Jew', was being contested.[19]

By the turn of the century the *tmeyim* had become separated in life, and death, from law-abiding *landsleit*. More disputes over cultural terrain and physical space followed as the 'unclean' of Russian and Polish descent, in keeping with immigration patterns, started outnumbering Jews of Galician and Romanian origin. This continual struggle for 'ownership' of the community soon spilt over into theatres presenting a growing repertoire of Yiddish drama. East European traders, pedlars and workers in search of cheap entertainment that voiced aspects of their lives, in the mother tongue, jostled with pimps and prostitutes to see popular productions that were recognisably Jewish. In the short run, this competition for space was won by Russo-Polish gangsters and their women.[20] Flashily dressed *chevreleit* and their *nekeives*, behaving in ways the middle classes found loud and objectionable, dominated audiences in the Alcázar, Doria, Mayo and the Olympia theatres. Not all such arrogance and flouting of cultural norms was confined to official performances. White slavers made regular use of the Alcázar to stage auctions where newly imported prostitutes from Europe were paraded and then passed on to the highest-bidding pimps from Buenos Aires or farther afield.[21]

Space in other fora that allowed for the mixing of the sexes, such as the racecourse, was equally vigorously contested by the pimps and prostitutes.[22] Such instances of anti-social behaviour brought opprobrium on *all* Jews. Tension between the *tmeyim* and more righteous and/or political Jews mounted throughout the first decade of the twentieth century as immigration accelerated, the cost of living increased, and labour unrest became ever more manifest and explosive. Perhaps significantly, this intra-communal conflict became more pronounced and physical after the recession and rent strike of 1907.

In 1908, Juvented, a Jewish working-class organisation, campaigned against landlords renting properties to pimps and white slavers. At the same time Yugent, an offshoot of radical Paole Zionists, boycotted Jews doing business with *tmeyim* in an attempt to eradicate the embarrassing elements from Yiddish theatre. Yet another group, the Club Israelita, petitioned the administration to deport those who trafficked in women while the Argentine Comité de Moralidad Pública y Contra la Trata de Blancas, helped orchestrate the arrest of a hundred Russo-Polish white slavers in 1909.[23]

Organised campaigns against the *tmeyim*, embedded within the context of already fraught annual Labour Day eruptions resulted in a lot more pushing and shouting. Not all gangsters, *tenebrosos*, got away with mere isolation or obloquy.

Burak and Frankel, traffickers who had gone to Russia and returned with women they sold as white slaves, had acquired a café on Tucumán Street frequented by the 'unclean'. Unknown to them, however, the brothers of one of their victims had followed them to Argentina and obtained positions in the café. On 12 May 1909 – two weeks after the police had shot eight anarchists in the general strike – the irate brothers gunned down the white slavers, killing Burak, and seriously wounding Frankel.[24]

In an antagonistic and fractious setting the pimps and white slavers had trouble holding their lines. In 1906 the numerically preponderant Russo-Poles decided to part company with Galician and Romanian *tenebrosos* and form their own mutual aid society. On 7 May, a delegation led by Noé Trauman filed the documents giving the Sociedad Israelita de Soccoros Mutuos Varsovia, the Warsaw Society, a legal persona. Although the societies continued to co-operate and combined to purchase land for a cemetery in Avellenda, the Warsaw Society became the more important. Until 1927, when it came under pressure from the Polish ambassador to change its name and it became the *Zwi Migdal*, the Warsaw Society dominated the Buenos Aires underworld.[25]

With a membership well in excess of a hundred, the Warsaw Society had headquarters in an elegant mansion in the inner city as well as a synagogue of its own. While the mere existence of such an immoral society dismayed the Jewish community, the police, as corrupt as they were hard pressed, had a more ambiguous relationship with its members. Not only were they a source of bribes and information about anarchists and socialists, but they provided a useful distraction in times of civil turmoil. It was presumably no coincidence that, within forty-eight hours of Simón Radovizky having assassinated Ramón Falcón, the police in the third precinct had picked up and held ninety-eight Russo-Polish pimps and white slave traffickers for questioning.[26]

Silver, who arrived in the capital just months after the swoop on the *tenebrosos*, in November 1909, could no more avoid Warsaw Society pimps than an Irishman could avoid drunks in a public house on St Patrick's Day. Place and time, personality and purpose, drew him towards kith and kin. His Neumünster resolve – to eschew the low life of working with whores – was lost within days, if not hours, of his arrival. He was at home amongst pimps and prostitutes and the country was experiencing strong, if turbulent, growth.

There was a familiar, if not a friendly, face on every street corner and in every second café. He bumped into Moritz Sztunke, boyhood acquaintance from Kielce, who had last been heard of hanging around the wholesale 'meat market' in Paris. Sztunke was on his way to Bahia Blanca. Another figure from the past was Simon Kumcher. 'Monkey Jack' had been one of his bachelor front men at the American Hotel in London. Another figure from the golden era, who had stood trial with him in Pretoria, was Sam Stein. Yet another of Silver's business and gambling partners was Solomon Goldstein. Once the largest supplier of furniture to bordellos in Buenos Aires, he had abandoned Cape Town after the police corruption trials. Silver's interactions with all these men were problematic – he knew them and they him – and all information was valuable. Kumcher and Stein had ended up being accused of serious crimes and only narrowly avoided lengthy sentences. Stein and Goldstein knew he had a record of informing, betraying and helping stitch up rivals – practices severely at odds with the unwritten code of the Warsaw Society. It was only the fact that he was flush with cash, paying for his own drinks and finding his way through the new maze so gingerly that allowed him to interact with pimps in a manner approaching normality. For the time being, he was allowed to circulate fairly freely.

Goldstein was well connected and it was probably through him that

Silver got to meet some rank and file members. The Zwi Migdal was an extraordinary wholesale importing agency with supply lines, routed through Paris or Marseilles, stretching back into distant corners of the Old Country. Its auctions enabled prostitutes to be circulated through the brothels of Buenos Aires and provincial capitals while an allegedly 'secret wireless code' underscored its logistical capacity. Its legal affairs were handled by a small number of well-placed attorneys who dealt openly with local political notables. These included the strikingly named Ponce de Leon, who had acted for Jack Lis and others in the Cellini robbery in Buenos Aires in 1907, and the pushy Luis V. Varela whose conduits of influence were said to extend all the way into the office of the Mayor.[27]

Amongst lesser figures he met were José Finn and the altogether more formidable Moritz Hendler. Born in Pińczów just south of Kielce, Hendler had links with white slave traffickers so strong that even the normally uncaring Russians had packed him off to Siberia. At a time when it was not as difficult as it was to become later, Hendler had escaped and made his way to Buenos Aires where he became the business associate of the resourceful Gil 'Top' Steiman.[28]

Steiman was the real thing. A short, stocky Pole with a prominent head, he had eyes that stripped flesh from bones. Dressed in a tailored suit that distinguished him from the lesser men and sporting a light cane useful for dealing with wilful women, Steiman was short-tempered and seldom far from violence. In 1897 he had served a month for 'serious assault' and twelve months later had been involved in another violent fracas. Cunning as well as enterprising, he had spotted the hidden menace in the Residence Law and, in 1902, had become a naturalised Argentine, rendering himself eligible for national service. Steiman, like some who followed in the Mafia, was a patriotic gangster – a man willing to defend the state in return for the right to plunder its citizens. It was a position akin to that of many nationalist politicians.[29]

By 1905, Steiman was often the officer of choice for the Warsaw Society when experienced prostitutes, or tyro white slaves were put up for auction in houses or theatres. As chief auctioneer he was in constant contact with European traffickers including some in Odessa, which enabled him to acquire 'remounts' and 'fresh goods' at competitive prices. His knowledge of the city's retail sex trade was unrivalled and in 1905 he published *A Guide to the Joys of Buenos Aires*. His talents did not go unnoticed and when the Warsaw Society was registered a few months later he became a signatory to the founding document. By 1910, the Auctioneer was the owner of one of the city's largest gambling dens, in Tucumán Street, but his core business was a brothel, at 1987 Lavalle Street. A mansion with two courtyards surrounded by many rooms, the Hotel Robinson obviously had some appeal for Anglophones familiar with Defoe's Crusoe, marooned on an island off Chile. Castaways and sailors who ended up at the Robinson, however, did not always leave fully satisfied. It was, arguably, the most notorious brothel in the city. From 1908 onwards it was under police surveillance, until the assassination of the Chief of Police.[30]

After Falcón's murder, in November 1909, Steiman, Finn, Goldstein and scores of other 'Caftans' were picked up and held for questioning. The police, more concerned about the departed chief than pimps and prostitutes, scoured the Russo-Polish underworld for information that might produce leads on Jewish anarchists. Steiman, a patriotic *tenebroso*, was either encouraged to, or volunteered to, become a police spy. He was well placed; the anarchists' Biblioteca Rusa at 2000 Lavalle was just a few doors away from the Robinson. Radovizky, the assassin, had often used the library and once complained that police spies were frequenting the place. Whether Steiman informed on Radovizky even before the murder is unclear, but what is not in doubt is the fact that, from about that time he – by his own admission – started paying rent to the police for his operations on Lavalle and Tucumán not only in cash but by way of information. Self-proclaimed patriotism always attracts more scoundrels than saints.[31]

Steiman and Silver, one a police spy and the other an ex-policeman and consummate informer, were so alike that it is not worth pausing to explore differences. Ambitious, treacherous misogynists they shared an interest in applying techniques of mass marketing to commercial sex. They sensed intuitively that they could do business. Silver, already acquiring his first phrases in Spanish, and anxious to explore productive outlets for capital raised in Europe, found in Steiman the perfect guide. In the latter half of 1910 he moved so consistently in the wake of the Auctioneer that he came to the attention of the Buenos Aires police, although they never arrested him.[32]

By the end of 1910, however, he was no closer to investing in a new business than he had been when he first arrived. The curiosity of the police alone is unlikely to have deterred him; there were other reasons. He remained wary of Steiman and had no family members to draw on.

The times were also troubling. From his travels in southern Africa he knew how damaging civic action, moral panic, press campaigns and new legislation could be. But, most of all, he was concerned about what his former partners, Goldstein and Stein, were revealing about his troubled past. The leadership of the Warsaw Society was not to be trifled with, and from his later, embellished accounts of its willingness to execute police informers we know that he was genuinely mindful of its sometimes harsh discipline.

The solution to his problems may have come to him spontaneously but is more likely to have arisen in discussions with the Auctioneer, who was experiencing difficulties of his own in managing the role of double agent. When it did come, the answer was blindingly obvious; it had been on everyone's lips for months and in the newspapers on an almost daily basis. The trans-Andean railway, opened in May 1910, meant that Buenos Aires and Santiago were, for the first time, within easy reach of each other via a service that operated three times a week. The wonder of steam placed distant Chile in the penumbra of the Argentine economy and, beyond that, the Atlantic world. For traffickers transport and mobility were all, and supply lines that already spanned half the world had just been extended into a previously untapped market.[33]

With 1910 drawing to a close and the resolve of Neumünster eighteen months and half a world away, he made his way through the construction works at the Retiro station and boarded a train for Santiago. He was going to renew his interest in the business he knew best. It did not trouble him that he was once again in a pioneering role. Had he not introduced isolated South West Africa to a more modern version of the commercial sex trade? True, it had not worked out, but how was he to have foreseen the petty jealousies and vested interests of German officialdom? This time it would be different. Behind him lay a financial backer and partner, the Auctioneer, with access to all the resources of the Warsaw Society. Indeed, all Silver was doing was helping to extend the orbit of a society – one that already had thriving branches in most provincial capitals of the Argentine and Rio de Janeiro – into the realm of the Pacific.

SANTIAGO–VALPARAISO
1910–1912

> All the physicians and authors in the world could not give
> a clear account of his madness. He is mad in patches, full
> of lucid intervals.
>
> Cervantes, *Don Quixote*

CHILE was the strangest-looking country on the continent. The elongated strip of coastal land history accorded it lay pressed against the north–south extent of the Andes. The country was squeezed into the space between the mountains and the Pacific. The north was roasted by the Atacama while, 2,000 miles to the south, Terra del Fuego – gouged by coastal inlets and rugged fjords – was caked in ice. Only the temperate Central Valley escaped the extremes while the whole country was occasionally racked by violent earthquakes.

When the Incas sought to conquer native Aracuanians in the fifteenth century, they were resisted and confined to a few outposts in the Central Valley. But once the Inca heartland itself had been overrun by conquistadores, it was only a matter of time until Spain, hoping for another Peru, colonised the south and west. After 1810, however, *criollos* – the native-born sons and daughters of the original European immigrants – mounted ever more serious political and military challenges to Spanish rule. Over an eight-year period, under the leadership of the Irish-born Bernardo O'Higgins, Chile attained, then lost, and eventually regained its independence in 1818.

Chile, dominated by a vast coastline, had a special relationship with the sea. In 1818, with the Napoleonic wars at an end, O'Higgins recruited a retired British captain, Thomas Alexander Cochrane, made him an admiral and told him to organise the navy. The country's sea power stood it in good stead as the repercussions of a new order in the Old World produced ripples in South America. In 1836–39 Chile broke up a menacing confederation between Bolivia and Peru and, when the two again combined to challenge Chile's hold over its northern reaches, in 1879, the Chilean navy played a decisive role in defeating Peru. The five-year-long War of the Pacific saw Chile make substantial territorial gains which contributed indirectly to a budgetary crisis and civil war that eventually rendered its presidents more subservient to congress. Between 1891 and 1924, Chile benefited from political and economic liberalism overseen by a parliamentary, rather than a presidential-style, republic.

Chile's new-found confidence and mobility derived, in part, from the exercise of neglected economic muscle. In the south the export of wool prompted an expansion in pastoral activity. From 1890 to 1914, the huge haciendas of the landed elite in the Central Valley concentrated on beef, cereal, dairy products, fruit, wheat and wine production to supply burgeoning domestic and export markets. But the real power in the modern economy lay in the expanded north, the *Norte Grande*, where the important copper mining industry was being supplanted by a new source of wealth: massive nitrate deposits, much sought after by manufacturers of explosives and fertilisers, drew significant foreign investment from Britain and Germany.

Nitrates, subject to fluctuating prices that became positively erratic in times of uncertainty, became the principal driver of the economy. The number of workers in the industry rose from 13,000, in 1890, to 45,000 by 1914, while, in the same period, production doubled from one to two million tons per annum. The population of Norte Grande grew from 2,000 in 1875, to close on 750,000 by 1914. Increased foreign earnings and an expansion in commercial agriculture promoted growth in manufacturing. Predictably, most enterprises were devoted to the processing or production of basic items of food or clothing in the Central Valley and by the First World War Chile boasted 7,500 factories employing a labour force of close on 80,000 workers.[1]

With the first twinges of industrialisation and proletarianisation becoming apparent by the turn of the century, agricultural labourers, peasants and the unemployed abandoned the countryside in growing numbers and made their way to urban centres or the mining towns of the north in the belief that unskilled wage labour offered a more secure

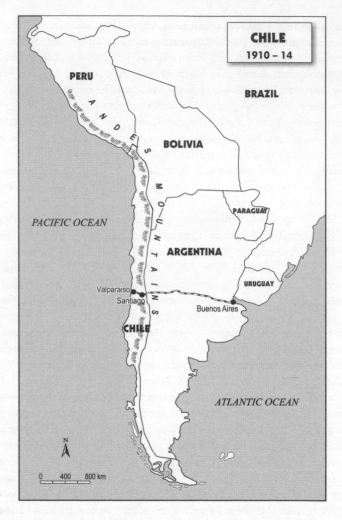

future. They were joined by about 50,000 Spanish-speaking immigrants, between 1890 and 1914. In a country where the population at the outbreak of the First World War still numbered barely 3.5 million, progressive urbanisation was most visible in the Norte Grande and in the three principal cities of the attractive Central Valley: Concepción, Santiago and Valparaiso.

Even then, Chile's urban centres were dwarfed in comparison with Argentinian or Brazilian equivalents. By 1914, Santiago still mustered fewer than half a million inhabitants while, less than a hundred miles away, the principal port, Valparaiso, housed barely 200,000 souls. Restricted commercial possibilities in a Pacific-facing nation, and a landed elite embedded in a Catholic majority with a reputation for harbouring anti-Semitic sentiments, combined to make Chile a singularly unattractive destination for East European Jews. Santiago hosted a minuscule Jewish community which, after the First World War, was served by just one synagogue while cosmopolitan Valparaiso never had enough resident Jews to warrant the construction of a *shul*.[2]

Neither Santiago nor Valparaiso escaped the challenges of an industrialising order. Thousands of single migrants lived in low-slung mud-and-wood adobe houses while working-class families crowded into *coventillos*. Crime, drunkenness and disease, along with prostitution and poverty, painted in Dickensian colours, were everywhere to be seen. In 1905, Valparaiso, where the hospital struggled to accommodate the number of patients admitted with stab wounds, was described as 'infected, foetid, pestilent, with its streets covered with a thin layer of fermenting filth'. Each year, 100,000 Chileans died from preventable diseases. In Santiago, where cheap liquor was more readily obtainable than reliable drinking water, over 500 legal brothels and thousands of illegal *casas de tolerancia* catered for the sexual needs of middle- and working-class males outside of marriage.[3]

Workers found it hard to meet the cost of food and rent amidst appalling social conditions. From the turn of the century *mancomunales*, labour brotherhoods, sprouted in urban areas, some mutating into fully fledged trade unions. Influenced by the anarcho-syndicalist and socialist ideas circulating in Argentina and Spain, the usual suspects – metalworkers, printers, railwaymen and tramcar drivers – mounted resistance, culminating in a general strike in Santiago and Valparaiso in 1907. Although unsuccessful, the strike prompted anxieties in the landed elite and urban middle class who responded with the age-old chant of 'foreign agitators'.[4]

Uncertain of its role in a society where small tremors could presage deep-seated shifts, the elite – the *gente decente* – led a hedonistic social existence. Much taken with things French, the affluent spent lengthy periods abroad. When a navy Captain, Jorge Montt, overthrew President Balcemeda during the civil war of 1891, it was reported that there was not a ballroom in Paris large enough to accommodate celebrating Chileans. Back in Santiago, the elite dominated coastal venues in summer as they dined and drank in time-honoured fashion. In winter they adopted Parisian customs, clothes and manners for a circuit that embraced concerts, dance, drama, opera and the racetrack.

In 1910 – the year of the centennial celebration of Chilean independence – the aspirations, cultural achievements and successes of the elite were everywhere to be seen. In Santiago, overlooked by snow-capped peaks, the 350-year-old city's newly cobbled streets and improved street lighting paved the way for the opening of the Palacio de Bellas Artes. Two large and elegant *parques* evoked civic pride as did the view from the *Cerro San Cristobel* that peered down over the city. But even the fireworks seemed duller when viewed from afar, through a mist of sadness that refused to lift from the valleys. During the festivities Jorge Montt suddenly passed away, and was replaced by Emiliano Figueroa Larrain.

Silver disembarked beneath the canopy of the Estacion Central in the closing months of 1910 and entered a capital that was making steady economic progress. The presence of large numbers of males around the station was cheering, while a glance down the nearby streets revealed new tramlines and any number of cantinas and places offering cheap accommodation to working-class men and their women. In the city centre a few miles away, where faded signs of celebration clung to lamp-posts like autumn leaves, there were a number of middle-class hotels, restaurants and saloons. Despite these outwardly reassuring signs there were other, elusive, things about the society.[5] Behind the buildings and *palacios* and usual signs of material progress – far beyond the bunting, and the hollow sound of brass bands attending military parades – there was a haunting emptiness at the heart of the Chilean soul. It was as if the roots of its national structures had failed to penetrate fully the realities of people's lives to produce a living unity. It was a feature the country shared with Argentina, where the tango, like Portuguese *fado*, seemed capable of stirring only sadness. Viewed from afar the foundations of Chilean life appeared solid but, seen from closer up, surfaces were brittle and fragile, exuding a sense of impermanence.

If Chileans sensed this, perhaps most outsiders also detected it. Not so Silver. No longer as subject to impulsive behaviour, he had mellowed somewhat even though the emotions of caring or compassion eluded him. Rational, if a trifle unstable, he realised that he was a criminal on the run, a foreigner who spoke little Spanish and a 'Jew' in a place largely without Jews. Beyond the novelty of another frontier experience there was not much to commend Santiago. He also knew that his ambivalence about dealing with prostitutes had to be controlled if he was to avoid a repeat of his experiences in South West Africa.

In late 1910, using capital raised via the Aachen and Munich Fire Insurance Company, he bought the run-down Hotel Venecia. At 284 Merced Street, it was on the northern perimeter of the inner city, opposite the Parque Forestal. Janus-faced, it looked up and down market. On the one hand it was close by the Mapocho River and a working-class neighbourhood which, amongst others, housed Italians who, at the time, were considered second only to Jews in terms of untrustworthiness. But it was also just three blocks away from two prestigious institutions frequented by the elite and the middle class – the National University and the Palacio de Bellas Artes.[6] Besides the Venecia, which had a bad reputation, he hired a few houses nearby to serve as reception and recycling depots for French and Russo-Polish prostitutes forwarded by Steiman in Buenos Aires. The houses were later integrated into a supply chain that ran as far as Valparaiso where the same model – base hotel linked to 'safe houses' – was employed by the partners.

Most of the older women in the Venecia were prostitutes reaching the ends of their working lives. Recruited in France, they had been fed into Atlantic routes supplying the global trade. Experienced continental women were forwarded to Santiago where they catered for the Francophile tastes of the local elite and their sons. Others who knew their way around, including some Russo-Polish women, served the lower end of the market. Amongst these groups was a small number of young women who had been recruited into the trade through deceit and violence; women who, to all intents and purposes, were white slaves. At least one of these unfortunates spent close on six months in the Venecia.

Rosa Kantor, a Polish Jewess who had been relegated by misfortune and poverty to playing the role of housekeeper for her brothers after her parents' death, was a classic target for white slavers. Although literate and 'devoted to domestic activities', she failed to attract a suitor in a community where early marriage was the norm. In danger of becoming a burden, she was twenty-five years old when, out in the village one day in 1911, she was approached by a 'Russian' bachelor. Using 'flattering and persuasive' words, he became a visitor. He promised her 'money, comfort and more than a thousand hopes of improving my condition', she said; and that she could avoid a 'poor and wretched life'. Her brothers through ignorance, naivety or relief – perhaps all three – agreed to the marriage that preceded the couple's departure for Argentina. The high seas honeymoon, the middle passage that led to 'slavery', was uneventful. The 'husband', anxious to avoid complications, was in affectionate and attentive mood. How was she to know that she was already in the grip of a Zwi Migdal operative? He was an agent of Steiman's and, a year later, was arrested and imprisoned in Germany when a similar ploy went wrong. It was no consolation. On her arrival in Buenos Aires, Kantor was taken to 1987 Lavalle, where 'the Russian who brought me from my country with false promises sold me to Steiman for two thousand pesos, as if I were an object'. In the clutches of the Auctioneer her options, she later claimed, were reduced to escape, or early death.⁷

When Steiman fell into disfavour with the courts and police in Buenos Aires, Rosa and six others were sent, under escort, to Santiago where they worked in the Venecia. She was supervised by Silver who, in charge of a brothel and bent on control and humiliation, answered only to the demons of his mind. Discipline and surveillance, Kantor said, were like that of a 'prison' and every day she and others faced the choice of life or death. That may, of course, have been overstatement, but Hannah Opticer and Hannah Vygenbaum before her had disappeared, and who knew what had once happened in Whitechapel? In Santiago, no prostitutes went missing on Silver's watch.⁸

When he was eventually joined by Steiman, whose abnormality was more manifest than his own, the regime in the brothel deteriorated further. The Auctioneer, self-proclaimed 'Master', enforced discipline with punches, kicks and use of his walking stick. The women, openly referred to as slaves, were flogged, forced to beg forgiveness and to thank him for favours by assuming the prone position and kissing his boots. Perhaps it was the misogynistic megalomania that led the Master to believe that no woman would dare escape his domain that made him less watchful than his partner. It was on his watch in Valparaiso that two women and, at last, Rosa Kantor herself, escaped from another 'prison'. It was Kantor, too, who told the police that she had suffered so much heartache and humiliation that, if she was made to suffer any more her eyes, incapable of shedding any more tears, would ooze blood.⁹

For most of 1911, with nitrates underpinning the economy, Silver 'imported' French and Russo-Polish women to staff the business in

Merced Street. As always, however, success did not depend exclusively on entrepreneurial skills. He and the Auctioneer obtained protection for the business from low-ranking police officers. Although the Venecia and later its successor, which differed only in name, the Hotel Robinson, became ever more notorious, the owners avoided direct collision with the law for close on two years. At different times, he and Steiman obtained advance warning of impending moves against them and in Valparaiso the Auctioneer once went so far as to invite the police to the opening of one of the partners' new 'hotels'.[10]

A trans-Andean success story did not go unnoticed in Argentina. In the aftermath of the assassination of Falcón and the clamp-down on anarchists and 'Jewish' fellow travellers, several burglars, thieves and a few Zwi Migdal members moved to Chile. By late 1910, changes were becoming noticeable. It was said that there was a deterioration in the moral climate and a growing number of French and Polish women were reported to be working in Santiago's brothels and cheap 'hotels'. The retail trade in commercial sex followed the stock market.[11] For the proprietors of the Venecia the influx was a mixed blessing. On the one hand it brought familiar figures to town, including Daniel Lewin, a professional jewel thief implicated in the never-ending Cellini case and the pimp brothers Jorge and José Finn, one of whom had long owned a brothel in Valparaiso. In Buenos Aires, the Auctioneer welcomed commission on orders for women forwarded to expanding outlets across the Andes.

On the other hand, this expansion undermined the competitive edge the partners had enjoyed during the earliest months of trade in Merced Street. By September 1912, fifty French and Russo-Polish prostitutes were working in Santiago. Competition manifested itself in falling revenue, which had to be offset by new and more aggressive forms of advertising. Silver got the pimps to hand out cards telling clients how to find the house on Merced. This campaign, around the Parque Forestal and Palacio de Bellas Artes where the middle classes and students mingled, caused a minor outcry. More importantly, it soured relations between rival, foreign brothel-owners already struggling to protect turf in a market that was becoming over-traded.[12]

The year 1912 was not an especially good one although it started out well enough. In March, Silver learned that the appeal court in Buenos Aires, citing purely technical reasons, had at last found his brother Jack and Daniel Lewin formally not guilty for their part in the

Cellini robbery. It opened the way for Jack and Bertha to join him but Silver did not receive this news as uncritically as he once might have. He was reasonably settled in Chile and wary of Jack getting involved in an undertaking that might compromise his own position. Moreover, it was clear that to all intents and purposes Jack had become his daughter's common-law husband. Having his stepbrother as a son-in-law appears not to have raised any moral qualms although it did prompt strategic questions. The couple boarded the *Amazon* in Southampton in early September 1912, but when they disembarked Bertha remained in Buenos Aires while Jack proceeded to Santiago. Before too long, he was spotted hanging around the Hotel Venecia.[13]

For Steiman the year got worse as it wore on. The Buenos Aires CID which had been so keen to receive information about anarchists after the commissioner's assassination soon tired of what they saw as just another Jewish pimp-informer and removed Steiman's CID protection. Uniformed policemen started demanding protection money for the brothel in Lavalle. At the same time, the Jewish community and state extended the drives to marginalise the Zwi Migdal. By the end of the first quarter, the Auctioneer's protection payments were in arrears and the police becoming impatient. These escalating demands, coinciding with a dip in profits at the Venecia, could not have come at a worse moment – Silver, too, was coming under growing pressure from the police for protection payments. In April, Steiman, feeling the pinch, sold a share of the Lavalle business to an unknown partner and fled Argentina leaving a number of angry policemen to keep an eye on what remained a notorious brothel.[14]

At the Venecia, the cash-strapped Steiman put the women under intense pressure. The place, cursed with omnipresent proprietors in need of every stray peso wedged beneath a bed, was noisy and violent. Clients started complaining about being robbed. This resulted in escalating protection fees directed almost entirely at the senior partner, Silver. All of this came at a time when he was already the object of resentment by the owners of rival establishments employing French and Russo-Polish prostitutes. And unavoidable professional resentment took on an ugly public dimension. One morning, in May 1912, an anonymously printed pamphlet was placed in every postbox of the Central Post Office on the Plaza de Armas recounting parts of his colourful criminal history and reproducing, in full, an incriminating letter from Jack. It was a tactic usually associated with radical, underground political movements. In Russia, anti-Semitism had helped render political behaviour 'criminal' with the result that anti-social behaviour too sometimes acquired a 'political' tinge. In Argentina, Chile and South Africa, too, Jewish criminals sometimes drew on the tactics of politically minded co-religionists while conducting purely professional – criminal – vendettas.[15]

The authorities, having got wind of a scheme involving the brothers, increased the number of police on Merced Street. Heightened police surveillance, bad for business and planned projects alike, was at once detected by the ex-policeman proprietor. Silver responded by claiming to have sold the Venecia to Steiman, who then renamed it the Hotel Robinson after his faltering establishment in Buenos Aires. In practice, Steiman merely took a larger share of the business while Silver continued to own the majority stake. Later that year, the Commissioner of Police was still convinced that the Lis brothers were the real owners of the new, supposedly more salubrious, Robinson.[16]

Alarmed by these developments, Detective Eugenio Castro interviewed Silver and Steiman, who confirmed transfer of ownership and the intention of the 'new' owner to turn the hotel into an 'honest place'.[17] Steiman used the occasion to tell the CID that he had, until recently, been assisting Buenos Aires police in identifying anarchists. Castro found the lure irresistible. By the end of May 1912, Steiman was using his Russian and Yiddish to help the Chilean authorities keep abreast of developments amongst anarchists and syndicalists. The Robinson, still operating as a brothel with imported prostitutes, had got itself a new, political lease.[18]

A few weeks later Steiman sensed the need to return to Buenos Aires and attend to his ailing business in Lavalle Street. In mid July, he called on the Argentine Vice Consul in Santiago to obtain a travel document. He told Salvador Nicosia about his work with the Argentine police and left him with the impression that it was his role as an informer for the Chilean police that ensured the survival of the business in Merced Street.[19] His stay of ten weeks in Argentina was not an unqualified success. Having been prosecuted unsuccessfully for placing a woman under the age of eighteen in a brothel the previous year, and having failed to settle his protection debts, he suddenly found himself confronting a new charge, for the same offence, in October 1912. A second court appearance within months was sufficient to convince him that his future did indeed lay west of the Andes.

But when he got back to Santiago in late 1912, Steiman found that Silver had been joined by his stepbrother and that during his absence the place had been so rowdy that the uniformed police had again attempted to shut it down. Pleased to have Steiman back in town and his flow of political intelligence restored, Castro eased back on the levels of surveillance around the Robinson Hotel. It was probably an error; Jack Lis, separated from his niece-wife in Buenos Aires, was bent on a new venture.[20]

In May 1912, a popular Buenos Aires magazine, *Fray Mocho*, had run an article on the 'Apaches' involved in the Cellini case in which Jack was still referred to as a 'fugitive from justice'. Undeterred by adverse publicity, he had re-entered Argentina under his own name and boarded the train for Santiago. His brother must have known that he was bent on staging a heist, linking up with Bertha and making a quick getaway to London which had, in effect, become the couple's home. But Jack's obsessive focus on a new job had potentially serious consequences for the core of a dysfunctional family. Silver realised that after the robbery – in which he wished to have no direct part – he, too, might have to abandon the Pacific and use his white slave contacts to re-establish himself as a 'trader' in the old Atlantic world.

The details of the robbery that followed several weeks later remain sketchy. It would appear that Jack retained a preference for an Apache-style operation and it was presumably his brother who suggested that Rosa Lieberona Marin, a young white slave from the Robinson, play the role of *gigolette*. He was also assisted by a few low-ranking police officers whose names were given to him by the proprietors of the Robinson. Jack spent several days in late October refining the plan, studying the target and fixing on a date that would benefit from the heightened Christmas cash flow. There was a minor scare in November when Eugenio Castro, frustrated by Steiman's inadequacies as informer, got the Mayor to have the Robinson closed down. With guards outside the front doors, Silver and Steiman decided to move the business, lock, stock and barrel. Jack and other pimps were told to take the prostitutes and 'slaves' to the station for the train ride to Valparaiso where they would be met by the Master.[21]

Jack spent several days in the port taking care of the partners' interests as French and Russo-Polish women were shuffled between outlying Zwi Migdal reception depots and a brothel in the downtown area. The new business was within easy walking distance of the harbour which, with the Panama Canal still under construction, attracted hundreds of ships and thousands of sailors each year. But even in Valparaiso, where whores were outnumbered only by feral cats and dogs, an influx of women from Santiago could not remain hidden. Before long, the Chief of the local CID, Carlos Alamos, was taking an interest in business of the Lis brothers and Steiman.[22]

Underworld informers brought in fascinating, not always truthful, snippets about Silver's career and Jack's role in the Cellini robbery. Alamos remained unmoved. The Lis brothers were small fry compared with other fish in the local market. Six years earlier he had witnessed the execution, by firing squad, of Emilio Dubois a notorious Don Juan and serial killer who had murdered at least four prominent businessmen. One thing, however, did cause the detective to sit up and take notice: Jack, with the help of unnamed policemen, was planning a 'big job' in Santiago. Murderers, pimps, rapists and white slavers were one thing; crimes against property another. Eventually he decided to pass on the information to his opposite number, but Alamos was slow putting pen to paper and, by the time he got round to doing so, Jack had left Valparaiso for Santiago.[23]

Back at the Robinson now reduced to empty rooms with hard-ridden beds standing around like hollow-backed mules outside a roadside canteen, Silver was finalising the sale of the property, his task complicated by the Mayor's men and police. By the time Jack got there he was becoming uncomfortable with the attention he was attracting while Jack, entering the run-up to the big job was equally keen to avoid observation. The police noted that, on 26 November, Jack got a cab to 'Pedro the Gringo's' house, in Lira Street and then kept changing addresses. Silver stayed on in Merced Street.[24]

Castro was still considering what to make of this when he received the letter from Alamos. The contents passed through his mind like the current in a newfangled street lamp, lighting up dim understandings. It was less the news that Silver was a man with a record for rape and white slaving that surprised him than the realisation that Jack was bent on staging a project in Santiago.[25] He was unsure of his next move. He felt vulnerable and sensed that, if not handled properly, the situation might cost him his job. He needed to come up with an appropriate professional response that would leave the public in no doubt what they were up against. He would have an off-the-record discussion with the editor of the city's oldest and most respected newspaper.

And what of Steiman? His role was unclear, so there was probably not much point in pursuing him. He had, in any case, moved to Valparaiso. It was safe, he thought, to assume that only the Lis brothers were involved in the envisaged 'big job'. Castro decided to move against both of them, not realising that, while the one was an Apache bent on robbery, the other was no more than an ageing, neurosyphilitic, brothel-owner.

On 5 December, former 'special agent' Silver left the house in Merced aware that he was being followed. This was confirmed when, shortly after lunch, he was approached by a member of the CID and told that Castro wanted a word with him. They went to police headquarters only to be told that Castro was not available. Silver told the duty officer he was about to leave for Valparaiso where he had business to attend to, and was reassured when told that he was free to leave but that he should speak to Castro on his return. He was gone for several days attending to business but, on his return to Santiago, did nothing to contact the police.[26]

Castro had him fetched. What transpired next was recorded in Silver's own words three days later. On 10 December, police officers

> came to my house and forced me to accompany them. I asked them whether they had a warrant to arrest me and they informed me that Eugenio Castro was waiting for me, and showed me an order issued by the Third Criminal Court. I, along with ... Jack Lis, accompanied them to police head-quarters. Once inside the section they took [the two of] us up to the second floor, [they] insulted me, and *forced* us to have our photographs taken.[27]

The brothers were subjected to further interrogation and, from questions put to them, they knew that Castro was simply on a fishing expedition. At the end of a very unpleasant afternoon they were taken back downstairs and locked up.

Silver was livid; angry with Castro, but furious, too, with his brother. Quick to foreground personal interests, he felt Jack's indiscretions left him vulnerable in Chile and the few destinations that remained open to him. Again he was aware that the world was closing in on him and this fed into mounting concerns about the retrospective reach of co-ordinated scientific policing. His American passport was about to expire and the continental police had his fingerprints as well as photo-

graphs of him as a young and older man. Could a combination of
fingerprints and mugshots place him at earlier, unsolved crimes? He
had kept himself informed about the outcomes of important trials
which revolved around issues of identity and, in South West Africa,
had pointedly referred the judge to the case of Adolph Beck. It may,
however, have been that another, more pertinent example crouched in
his consciousness. In 1903, Severin Klosowski, a Pole and former East
End barber, was hanged for poisoning unwanted wives lured into biga-
mous marriages. During the trial of 'George Chapman', as he then
was, the prosecution had made liberal use of photographs to identify
the accused who had been a hairdresser in Whitechapel, in 1888, and
was once suspected of being 'Jack the Ripper'.[28] Perhaps Castro's
mugshot – which could be added to the gallery of police photographs
of Silver in Brussels, Cape Town, Hamburg, London, Paris and New
York – might imperil the security of his greatest secret? The more he
thought about it, the more disturbing he found it. It offended his sensibilities as an American citizen and he resolved to challenge it.

He bombarded Castro with quasi-legal arguments until, on 13
December, he was granted an audience with the judge in Third Criminal
Court, Juan Tupper, and sought an urgent interdict. He recounted the
circumstances of his arrest, alleging that the police had been spying on
him for days without just cause. He had not, he said, 'stolen anything,
or committed any other sort of crime'. He questioned the legality of the
warrant issued for his arrest and, in an act of betrayal without precedent, admitted that 'Jack Lis' was not his blood brother, but a *hermanastro*
– a maternal half-brother. It was a gratuitous disclosure designed to create
distance between him and Jack. 'Taking a photograph of an honest man',
he argued, 'and placing it in a gallery amongst those of known criminals was an outrageous violation of [a man's] rights'. Such an image, he
submitted, 'could be circulated around the country and abroad, like those
of a common criminal'. 'I beg your Honour', he continued, 'to order the
chief of the CID section to hand over the photograph, along with any
other impressions made by the anthropometrics section to the court', and
to 'forbid their circulation beyond Santiago'. In short, he tried to ensure
that police in Brussels, Buenos Aires and London remained unaware of
his whereabouts and that he be allowed to return to western Europe
without having to face an incontrovertible form of identification.[29]

Tupper denied his request but the action may not have been entirely
in vain since, shortly thereafter, he and Jack were released without

charges being preferred. Still concerned about the fingerprints and photograph, Silver threatened to take the matter to the American consul, Henry P. Fletcher. But it was bluster; nothing came of it and the police were emboldened. With intelligence still dribbling in, Castro contacted the CID in Buenos Aires, for more information about the brothers Lis and Steiman.

Castro was dumbstruck by what his Argentinian counterpart, José Rossi told him. The brothers were considered to be dangerous criminals and were well known in Buenos Aires. Jack had recently been highlighted in an edition of *Fray Mocho*, while Silver had come to their attention because of his association with Steiman. Steiman, in turn, had been the subject of an article in the house journal of the Buenos Aires police, *Sherlock Holmes*. Sleepy Santiago, accustomed to far less menacing low-life types, had suddenly been invaded by experienced international criminals. Keen to position himself publicly, Castro sought out his journalist contacts. On 19 December 1912, *El Mercurio*, the most measured of the local journals, ran a fairly innocuous but well-informed piece, '"Apaches" in Santiago de Chile?' The article alerted readers to Jack Lis, Silver and Steiman who, it claimed, had already 'quarrelled' amongst themselves before leaving for the coast.[30]

Unwittingly, Castro had flicked an ideological match into a kerosene spill in a deserted alley. At the time, it hardly mattered. There was no breeze, the flame was small and the liquid appeared to be dribbling away. But in the distance could be heard the rustling of wind. Slowly, the fuel collected into a more sizeable pool. Press, police and public opinion made for a flammable mixture and, some months later, the detective had reason to ponder the dangers of his smoking habits.

By the second week of December Silver, Lis and Steiman were back in Valparaiso. Castro, happy to have avoided further complications, thought no more of it as his would-be adversaries re-inserted themselves in the old part of the port. They were back on Alamos's patch, and he could relax. From that point onward, just about everything connected to the events that followed in Santiago remains unclear. We do not know when exactly the robbery took place, how many men or women were involved, whether corrupt police were implicated, or how much money was removed although, from short press reports, it appears to have been a substantial amount.

On 24 December, the tills awash with Christmas cash, one or more people muscled into the hallway of the bank and exchange agency run

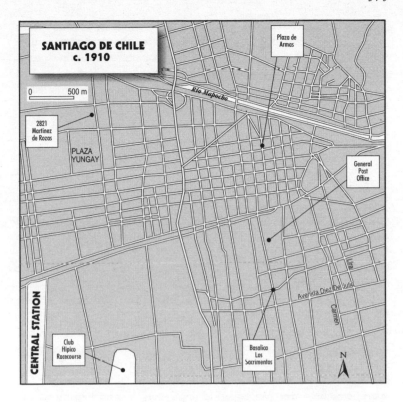

by Munóz-Arce Brothers on Estado Street in downtown Santiago, and committed an 'audacious robbery'. On the same day, news of the robbery was conveyed, in two sentences, to the readers of *El Mercurio*. The following morning the newspaper provided a splash of additional, factual, information. The 'principal thief', who had already fled the city, was a certain Cosman who had until very recently been staying at the Pensión Imperial. The police, already on the track of the 'young foreigner', were confident of an early arrest.[31] But he disappeared. As far as can be told, the mysterious 'Cosman' was never again seen or heard of in Chile. Nor did Jack ever seem to pull off the 'big job' he had once talked about so indiscreetly in Valparaiso. What we do know for certain is that at about the time of the Munóz-Arce robbery Jack Lis hared off back to Bertha in Buenos Aires because, by the end of that month, December 1912, she was carrying the couple's first child, Monty, who was born back in London's East End in August 1913.[32]

There are clues indicating what the police were thinking and actively investigating in the first quarter of 1913. In late January, with the unfortunate Castro still making little progress, his Prefect of Police, Colonel Nicolás Yavar, approached the British ambassador, Sir Henry Lowther, for assistance. One of Silver's nightmares was about to come true. Yavar gave Lowther photographs of 'Joseph and Jacob Silver' and asked Scotland Yard to share any information they might have on the brothers. Since brothel-keeping was not illegal, this request was probably triggered by inquiries relating to the Estado Street robbery.[33] On 3 February, Lowther forwarded the request to the Secretary of State for Foreign Affairs. By late March, Sir Edward Grey, like many before him, was contemplating the name 'Silver'. But the circuits in the British civil service were no better greased than those in supposedly creaking Latin American administrations and Scotland Yard's records were worse than Rossi's. By the time Grey replied to Lowther it was mid-April and such sparse information as the letter did contain was of no great assistance to Yavar or Castro.

Scotland Yard knew that 'Joseph Silver' was the name of one 'Abraham Ramer' for whom they had a set of fingerprints. But that, apparently, was all they knew. The name was not linked to either 'Ramer' or 'Taubentracht's' recent exploits in Belgium or Germany. Neither was the name 'Silver' connected to a spate of petty thefts under other aliases, in London, in the mid-1890s. Most alarming of all, the Yard failed to link the name to the psychopathic 'James Smith' who had raped and held Rachel Laskin hostage for several weeks in the American Hotel in 1897. Aliases adopted in London more than a decade earlier, including James Smith, had yielded Silver an unexpected dividend.[34] 'Jacob Silver' was equally fortunate. Scotland Yard failed to link the name to 'Maurice Silvermann', a sidekick of James Smith's, or to other aliases linked to burglaries and thefts committed at later dates. Sloppy police work and poor record-keeping helped keep the Lis brothers off the hook in Chile in 1913.[35]

Castro, convinced the Munóz robbery was a classic Apache operation, picked away at what he had. His evidence pointed to Jack Lis and a female accomplice rather than the elusive Cosman. Lis, assisting his brother and Steiman in Valparaiso, was a frequent visitor in the capital where he and other pimps collected 'fresh goods' forwarded by Zwi Migdal 'exporters'. Castro convinced Tupper that he had a case and persuaded him to issue warrants for the arrest of Lis and Rosa

Lieberona Marin when next they appeared in Santiago. He did not have long to wait. On 11 April, he had them picked up and arraigned before the Third Criminal Court where, in view of the lateness of the hour, they were ordered to be kept in the holding cells. And there they remained until the end of the month when Jack was released on bail of 2,000 pesos. But Castro could not make the charges stick. Lis was never re-arrested, let alone charged with the Munóz robbery. As late as November 1913, Jack, with Bertha and baby already back in London, was said to be a shop assistant in Valparaiso and still under surveillance. Castro was wasting his time. By then the proceeds of the robbery – never recovered – had, it seems, long since left the country.[36]

Frustration seldom travels alone. In 1913, amidst growing economic uncertainty and political tension, the price of nitrates began to wobble like a jelly in the Atacama sun, and then simply collapsed. With the price and volume of its leading export commodity at a new low, the citizenry became nervous and unsettled. Unease was not confined to Chile. The economies of neighbouring states, too, faltered and the authorities made new efforts to curtail organised crime. With disquiet in the air everywhere, Castro's discarded match suddenly ignited the kerosene, causing an ideological blaze that threatened to engulf urban Chile in a bizarre moral panic. If the spark for the conflagration came from the police, then tinder was provided by a cunning old police informer who, for some months, had been residing in Valparaiso.[37]

XXII

VALPARAISO–SANTIAGO
1913

I stand alone here upon an open sea with two oceans and
a whole continent between me and the law.

Herman Melville, *Moby Dick*

SILVER, Jack and Steiman regrouped in venerable Valparaiso, a city
Francis Drake paid a passing compliment by sacking it in the sixteenth
century. A bustling harbour losing confidence at the same rate that its
nemesis, the Panama Canal, was being constructed in the north, the
port boasted a thriving colony of British, German and other merchants.
La Matriz, the mother church, stood at the foot of one of the rounded
hills looking out over the brooding blue bay. Just below 'the foundation' and Serrano Street, which struggled to separate the sacred from
the profane, lay a mess of angled roads separated by ancient squares
containing a few benches and fountains that spoke of better times.
Between all of this sprouted cafés, bars, saloons, brothels, boarding-
houses and hotels dominated by a cosmopolitan *demi-monde* that threatened to overwhelm shops, markets and houses commanded by the street
vendors and businessmen who felt themselves to be the rightful owners
of the old quarter.

Like most of Chile, Valparaiso lived in constant fear of nature. Every
now and then, the gods gave the Pacific coast, with its dissolute jumble
of humanity, a thorough shaking. In 1906, an earthquake caused the
city's shoreline to drop by six metres. In nearby Cochrane Street, on
the Antigua Plaza Municipal, the same rumblings caused major damage
and disrupted the building of an ornate, three-storey building in the

classic style designed by the architect Dazorola. Undeterred, Dazorola had construction resumed and by 1907 the completed structure was ready for occupation. But good tenants were hard to come by in the wake of the disaster, and if they were to recover their costs, the owners of the new building could not afford to be too fussy.

If completion of the Dazorola building was ordained on high, its occupation was commanded from below. In 1911 a Spanish-speaking 'Russian' couple hired a portion of the building which, they said, would be transformed into a hotel. Jorge and Lilly Finn, Zwi Migdal pioneers, turned 309 and 311 Cochrane Street into the short-lived Alfani Hotel, soon to be followed by the more successful El Globo Hotel occupied by a dozen or more friendly French and Russo-Polish women looking after the needs of cardsharps, gamblers and hard-drinking men. Instant notoriety followed when clients found wallets missing from trousers hung over straight backed chairs. With customers and other insalubrious establishments unhappy, the El Globo was twice within twelve months the subject of complaints to city and provincial authorities.[1]

In the harbour area the dominance of the Finns' establishment forced Silver and Steiman to locate their business farther afield than they might have liked. It could only have been Silver, with his twin interests of personal pollution and ritual purification, who decided on a house opposite the Almendro Baths in Urriola Street, on the fringe of the dockland area. The new Robinson Hotel, named after its troubled predecessors but now at least closer to the island of Crusoe fame, lasted only weeks. Like the El Globo and possibly without police protection, this Robinson, too, was soon raided and closed after complaints of robbery and violence.[2]

Knowing they were being watched by Alamos's spies, he and Steiman bribed a few low-ranking CID officers and, even before the Munóz Brothers robbery in December 1912, had relocated their businesses, avoiding the heavily traded downtown area. Steiman, arrogant to the point of stupidity, boasted about his police contacts and hired premises at 64–66 Calle San Ignacio. Unable to resist his marketing instincts, he sent out printed invitations – including some to detectives – requesting the pleasure of their company at the opening of the Hotel Olimpio. But not everybody was pleased, for the brothel was close by the girls' high school.[3]

Silver was aware of his partner's history as a police spy so was a bit more cautious. A partnership between informers was inherently fraught and unstable. He hired lower-profile premises from the widow Amalia Rodríguez, in nearby Olivar Street, to cater for the overflow from the Olimpio. In this more discreet setting he installed the young Polish white slave, Rosa Kantor, renaming her 'Rosa Smith' – a composite name which may have derived from his first 'wife's' name, Rose, and Smith of Stamford Street. Silver and Steiman also hired an even more innocuous house, again conveniently close to the Olimpio, at 528 Chacabuco. A reception depot for recent Zwi Migdal 'imports', the latter served as a safe house for any pimps or prostitutes in need of a bolt-hole.[4]

Carlos Alamos was not taken with the new developments. Only a few months earlier he had been called in to deal with the French consul about a nineteen-year-old white slave, Juliete Rabout, held in the El Globo.[5] Back in the capital, *El Mercurio* spread the story that there were thirty-eight white slavers and 200 foreign prostitutes working in Valparaiso.[6] The Rabout case, reports of assault on clients, the beating of prostitutes and robberies in the Silver–Steiman houses were cause for added concern. Police spies brought in snippets of information about the extent and nature of white slave trafficking in an Atlantic world that had suddenly reached out to embrace the distant Pacific coast and Alamos decided to go public with his findings.

In March 1913, the Valparaiso *Police Review* ran a four-page article on the 'White Slave Trade in Chile' crafted by the secretary to its Criminal Investigation Department, Hugo de la Fuente Silva. It was a strange piece which, in retrospect, suggests that the Jew-hating Silver, excluded from Buenos Aires by former underworld associates, unhinged by the recent police search for his antecedents, and keen to take insurance against Steiman, had been first to break ranks and develop his own line of access as police informer. How else does one account for an article which, given the stronger north–south trade routes of Atlantic world white slavery, chose instead to focus on the comparatively weakly developed links between the Argentine and South African underworlds? And, in an essay which did not hesitate to name names, why was there such a palpable silence about the role of Silver? As with the great Holmes, it was another puzzling case of the dog that failed to bark.

The article conflated several terms. The white slave traffick, it suggested, was dominated by an unnamed criminal organisation in Argentina presided over by Apaches, or *tenebrosos*. The real business of acquiring slaves was in the hands of 'Caftans' – Russian and Polish

Jews – who, through their mastery of the techniques of deception and the manipulation of kinship ties, preyed on innocent or naïve women in the poorest villages of the Old World, by promising them marriage and a better life in the New. Moscow and Warsaw were the most important export centres in the northern hemisphere, while the biggest markets were in the far south, in Buenos Aires and Cape Town, where women might be sold to the likes of 'a Steiman or a Finn'.[7]

In Fuente Silva's version of the trade, as in Silver's, the links between Buenos Aires and Cape Town loomed disproportionately large.[8] It was presumably Silver's fear of being fingered by former associates who knew of his propensity to inform and the street justice that might follow that caused Fuente Silva not to name Zwi Migdal. The Caftans' organisation, he suggested, operated with codes of honour and silence, was better organised than the Italian Black Hand and Camorra, and enjoyed secret, coded, postal communication world-wide. To illustrate the hold and reach of the Jewish underworld, Fuente Silva – more likely Silver – offered an illustration:

> Not long ago two caftan brothers who had betrayed their fraternity back in South Africa arrived in Buenos Aires. Those betrayed had sent word ahead to Buenos Aires and, on the day of their arrival in the Argentine capital, the brothers were found drowned in the working class quarter of La Boca; both had had their arms broken. The avengers had taken them to a remote part of that working class *faubourg* and, after breaking their arms to ensure that they were unable to save themselves by swimming, had thrown them into the river where the brothers had met a horrifying death.

Unfortunately, this tale – an ex-Cape Town informer's nightmare – was, in large measure, the product of an overheated imagination. Difficult to verify from Argentinian sources, the account is loosely based on the exploits of 'Mateo' Vasalenko aka 'The Russian'. Vasalenko was the principal suspect in a gang of 'Caftans' said to have stripped, mutilated and then strangled two rivals at the Isla Maciel in La Boca, in December 1912.[9]

Fuente Silva, however, was more intent on capturing the attention of politicians. He urged the government to study the white slave trade,

take note of inadequate existing legislation and consider introducing a
ley de residencia which would give Chile the right to refuse criminals
entry. Although he failed to capture the imagination of members of
parliament, or secure the outcome the police desired, the article, by
linking Apaches and Caftans, weakened resistance to a developing bout
of xenophobia.[10] With the public more informed about the 'likes of a
Steiman or a Finn', Alamos was better positioned to take action when
a new round of complaints surfaced about the El Globo and Olimpio
hotels. In the third week of March the police raided the Olimpio, signalling
the end of Steiman's publicly proclaimed CID protection. The raid
prompted an unprecedented response from his partner. Silver gave notice
of his intention to close the brothel in Olivar Street. Widow Rodríguez,
at first merely distressed at losing a rent-paying tenant, became more
vocal and then furious when she discovered that, as part of his exit
strategy, Silver was also intent on selling off the furniture in her house.
She told the police that the place had been used as a brothel and made
other, very serious allegations that were impossible to ignore.[11]

In a new article that first surfaced in Santiago, it was claimed that
Silver had a record of abduction and 'corrupting the morals of minors'
and that he had previously been sentenced for similar offences in Paris,
Africa and Buenos Aires. *El Mercurio* told readers that 'In the French
capital he had been sentenced to four-and-a-half-years' imprisonment',
but 'had managed to escape to America'. With the press and Santiago
police making the running, he and 'Rosa Smith' made a brief court
appearance while investigations into other 'serious' crimes at the house
in Olivar Street continued. But he was a past master at intimidating
witnesses and playing the police off against one another. Nothing more
was heard of the charges.[12]

It was Silver's last public appearance in Chile. After his arraignment
in March 1913, he retreated into his role as silent partner in the
Olimpio. He avoided the Chacabuco Street depot linked, via a cellar,
to the Olimpio.[13] What exactly his secret deal with the Valparaiso CID
was, is difficult to know. Strategic absences, more complaints and a
new cycle of police raids were accompanied by a reduction in the discipline and internal surveillance of women in the brothel. He may have
learned from his experience in Cape Town and have been staging a
planned disengagement.

Alamos used everything at his disposal, including ineffectual public
health regulations, to continue the war of attrition against the El Globo

and Olimpio. By mid-year business at the Olimpio, staffed by ten to twelve women, had slumped to a new low and was exciting an unprecedented number of complaints from weary neighbours and journalists. In early August, Steiman appeared before Judge de la Barra, in Santiago, who was investigating charges ranging from theft to abduction. The public got to hear of the Master's deranged in-house practices despite women in the Olimpio having endured 'terrible threats' from unnamed partners trying to prevent them from giving evidence. Fuente Silva, on cue, penned a second, even less focused article on the 'White Slave Trade', for the Valparaiso *Police Review*.[14]

Steiman's enforced stay in Santiago and the gravity of the charges he faced if the state decided to prosecute, marked the final stages of his partnership with Silver, whose secret co-operation with the CID enabled him to retreat from Chile unscathed. In the Olimpio, prostitutes, sensing Steiman's vulnerability, staged a rebellion – an event as rare in a brothel as on a slave plantation. The first to go was, in fact, not a 'slave' at all, but an independent-minded French woman, 'Margarita' who, having been withdrawn to give evidence, 'took advantage of the circumstances and escaped'. She was next heard of in France. Her success emboldened others. By the time the Master got back, two other women had 'escaped from the prison that he kept us in'.[15]

Amazingly, the edifice of the Olimpio complex held. Steiman was released from prison because, as Rosa Kantor-Smith later recalled, 'when we were called [to give evidence] we told the Judge that we were unwilling to prefer charges'. But when the Master was re-arrested and taken back to Santiago for yet more questioning some weeks later, even the most terrified slaves needed no further prompting. 'Encouraged by the example of my friends,' Kantor explained, 'and wanting to regain my freedom so that I could live without blows and threats, I decided to escape from the house that, to me, was a prison . . . So one morning at eight o'clock I put on my clothes, packed my case and went into the street. I found a nearby policeman and begged him to find me a carriage. He did as I asked and I escaped, nervous and sad, from Chacabuco Street where I had suffered so much.'[16]

In September 1913, Fuente Silva, still building the campaign against those linked to the Zwi Migdal – an organisation he never once referred to by name – again chose to foreground Finn and Steiman in the third article on the 'White Slave Trade' to appear in the Valparaiso *Police Review*.[17] Its content and timing were again chosen with half an eye on the local legislature: it appeared in the same month that Argentina passed its new anti-pimping legislation, the Ley Palacios. With the public already unnerved by the deteriorating economic situation, much alarming talk about Apaches and Caftans, and an invasion of gangsters from Argentina expected at any moment, the nation's ideological floodgates were opened. Full-scale public madness followed.

The charge against the windmills was led by the newspapers most influential in Catholic circles, *La Unión* and *Las Ultimas Noticias*, rather than the liberal *El Mercurio*. Throughout October, in the face of a modest increase in the numbers of pimps and prostitutes in the capital, the two ran thinly disguised anti-Semitic campaigns. Santiago was 'full' of men with 'curved noses, thick lips, long ears and dark curly hair'. Ancient Pompeii had been overrun by 'Caftans' and 'professional beauties'. Was 'the capital going to be another Pompeii'? Montevideo was under attack from sinister forces unleashed in cynical Buenos Aires. Chile should never allow itself to 'be colonised in such a revolting way'. What was needed was the cat-o'-nine-tails which had been introduced to good effect in Cape Town and London. A call to arms in Chile was clearly in order; '*By fire and by sword, away with the caftans!*'[18]

High up in the mountains, it seemed, hundreds – nay, thousands – of armed Apaches, Caftans and *tenebrosos* were massing unseen, waiting to sweep down into the rural idyll of Chile and abduct local women before imposing a reign of terror. *Las Ultimas Noticias* had it on good authority from 'a distinguished Argentine gentleman who has just arrived from Buenos Aires', that the Santiago police had no idea of the size of the invasion and that 'more than five hundred people have crossed the Andes' to do 'business here'. *La Unión*, the most noxious tocsin in town by far, estimated that some 4,000 representatives of 'Babylonic vice' were girding their loins.[19]

With real Apaches and Caftans in short supply, it was left to the press to reveal what levels outlandish *tenebrosos* would sink to in order to get their filthy way. The Caftans, accustomed to the long, flowing, feminine garments of ungodly East European and Middle Eastern cultures, had taken to disguising themselves as women! On 24 October, in the Alameda, near the Del Carmen church, a doctor caught sight of an unusually tall woman, dressed in black and wearing a veil as if she were a widow. Unconvinced that the dress and figure were feminine, Doctor Lay challenged the person to identify him/herself. A scuffle ensued, and when it was discovered that the person was indeed a man dressed as a woman, the cry went up that it was a 'Caftan'. Youths attacked the man, beating and kicking him until he was rescued by two policemen who marched him off to the police station.[20]

La Unión endorsed the actions of the 'sporting' youth who had shown themselves to be fine 'boxers' and 'footballers'. The fact that the 'Caftan' appeared to be a local blacksmith interested in cross-dressing for 'personal reasons' seems to have been lost on a frothed-up editor. Transvestite terror lurked everywhere; women seeking to ward off the attentions of Apaches and Caftans intent on abducting them and turning them into white slaves were advised to defend themselves with hatpins. With men dressing as women and the signs and symbols of gender cloaked in Satan's robes, Chile's moral universe was at risk. Was the fate of Pompeii only hours away?[21]

Who knew what was in the air? There was a lot of it about; and it was catching. In the offices of *Las Ultimas Noticias*, the editor was not surprised by these developments. His reporters told of the abduction of young women by Apaches who, being of a more chauvinist stripe, were unwilling to don dresses.[22] Indeed, on the morning of the transvestite terror, the paper carried stories of two Apache atrocities. In Cathedral Street a 'kindergarten teacher' had a cloak thrown over her head by an Apache bent on robbing her but she had warded him off with a 'rapier-sized pin'. In Marcoleta Street, an eighteen-year-old girl from a poor family, 'all youth and beauty', was called to a cab by two men. As she got near an Apache leapt down and placed a handkerchief over her nose and bundled her into the cab that then sped off. The police, who as usual were nowhere to be seen when needed, only found out about this appalling occurrence when a boy who had witnessed it all drew it to their attention. It was most alarming.[23]

Once the blacksmith had been mobbed, it was only a matter of time before *Las Ultimas* came up with tales of cross-dressing and skulduggery. Some men had led seemingly decent lives but, under changed circumstances, stood revealed as Apache agents. In San Pablo Street, 'an honest manufacturer of mouse traps', an 'ideal husband', dressed up as a woman, stalked a chemist's daughter, stuffed a silk scarf into her mouth and applied an unnamed drug to her nostrils before trying to rob her. It got so bad that working folk armed themselves with sticks and stones as they went about their business. It was not difficult to understand why. Two cunning Apaches, 'dressed as prostitutes', reportedly overwhelmed a tipsy liquor inspector with 'powerful drugs' before dragging him into a motor car. 'The city of Santiago,' it was announced, 'was living in terror.'[24]

It would have been laughable had the underlying situation not been serious. Somewhere within this struggle to cope with fears, real and imagined, in a modernising urban setting where gender and sex were cloaked in misleading apparel lurked genuine evil in the shape of Silver and Steiman. The near classic 'moral panic' peaked at precisely the moment when details of Rosa Kantor's shocking journey into white slavery were made public. The resulting, bewildering concoction of ideas – five parts fiction to one part fact – was an unpalatable and threatening mixture. The authorities struggled to find an ideological antidote.

Mayor Pablo Urzúa did as mayors do: he donned his harlequin suit and stepped out to do the balancing act demanded by audiences. On 8 October, he wrote to the Prefect of Police, Colonel Yavar, stating that he, too, had noticed the influx of Caftans, a 'filthy gangrenous' lot who in the absence of a residence law, would infect public morals. He instructed the Prefect to use the existing, inadequate legislation, to curb the onslaught and followed it up with a request for a report on the names and numbers of foreign invaders; male and female. *La Unión* was only partly reassured. 'The Mayor', its readers were told, could have been 'more explicit' and 'more energetic'.[25]

In the *barrios*, where the written word penetrated less deeply than the spoken, news of the Mayor's moves did nothing to curb sightings of Apaches and Caftans bent on abducting the beautiful and the innocent. It was left to *El Mercurio*, which a year earlier had used a briefing on the Lis brothers to start all the talk of Apaches, to restore some balance. Its journalists neither saw nor heard of a single Apache or Caftan abduction or, if they did, they failed to report it. The editor, chastened by earlier reports to which he and Castro had contributed, ran a set of sober leaders commending the police and endorsing calls for a residence law.[26] Fires fuelled by newspapers are sometimes best doused by printer's ink and, after the assault on the blacksmith, the paper came into its own. On 28 October, *El Mercurio* brought out the extinguisher.

Newspapers highly regarded in church circles, it suggested, were guilty of sensationalism, circulating 'exaggerated accounts' based on the tales of men who had been robbed or tricked by 'professional adventuresses'.

All immigrants from Argentina were in danger of being categorised as Apaches or Caftans, and it was unnecessary for 'intelligent reporters to prostitute themselves for the satisfaction of the mob'. *El Mercurio* returned to the attack the following day, focusing on 'real or invented' accounts of abduction.[27] Its middle-class readership carried the day. By 4 November, when the Prefect of Police made public his report with names and numbers of Apaches and Caftans, the editorial mouth of La Unión was so filled with humble pie its voice was barely audible. There were, at best, about fifty foreign pimps in the entire country. Most were 'French' while one or two had 'German' connections but many were away, travelling abroad. The Caftans were in a minority and Silver and Steiman were no longer based in Santiago. At very most, there were 'about twenty French or Polish' women in town.[28]

Cooler breezes dissipated the accumulation of ash and hot air. Down on the coast the haze was slower to lift. In October, at the height of the populist eruptions, Fuente Silva for the first time found the time and space to devote a few lines to Joseph Silver. But this short, bland article in the *Police Review*, illustrated with a photograph supplied by the Santiago CID and marked 'to be continued', was again more notable for its silences than its content. It made no mention of his record as a white slaver, something even *El Mercurio* had picked up on. Nor was there a whisper about the inability of the state to follow through on the charges of theft made by Amalia Rodríguez, or her revelations about the true nature of the business in Olivar Street. It was only several weeks later, in December 1913, that the Valparaiso *Police Review* got round to carrying a slightly fuller account of the brothers Silver.

By then, Argentine officials were attempting to have Steiman and others extradited on yet another charge of having 'corrupted' a minor.[29] But the Auctioneer, the Master, bestrode the southern continent for three decades more and remained an active member of the Zwi Migdal, based in Buenos Aires, for another decade.[30] Jack Lis, too, amongst the first of the Apaches to invade Buenos Aires, remained in Valparaiso overseeing the winding down of his absent brother's business interests.

Of Silver himself there had been no sign for months. Fuente Silva was willing to make public disclosures about him only *after* he left town; again affirming his ability to control police handlers. He had fed them information on rival underworld figures, including his own partner, in order to avoid prosecution. A connoisseur of moral panics, he relished the control and notoriety that came from behind-the-scenes manipulation of public events. The fact that such campaigns were on the moral margins of society and ostensibly conducted in the public interest, inflated his sense of self-worth and helped settle scores with the Jews he loathed. In the latter half of 1913 he slipped aboard a trans-Andean train and made his way to Buenos Aires, ready to re-engage with London, city of his darkest deeds, and other centres in the northern hemisphere. For a man living in a perpetual moral fog, with an uncontrollable yearning for secretiveness, subterfuge and spying, it was certainly a move in the right direction.

XXIII

LONDON, NEW YORK AND
RIO DE JANEIRO
1914–1916

> Never less idle than when unoccupied, nor less alone than
> when without company.
>
> Scipio Africanus, 200 BC

SILVER'S outline, even when picked out by the light of officialdom
peering into dark places, was seldom clearly defined. Charming and
persuasive when the occasion demanded, or when trading information,
he was an acquaintance rather than a friend, feared rather than trusted.
The air of mystery surrounding him was eclipsed by a glibness and
plausibility that made him a credible partner for any project on either
side of the law. Beneath a mask of rationality, however, there were inner
struggles that he was only partly conscious of, and that will remain
forever hidden from us. The civil war within him saw cunning pragmatism and entrepreneurial energy ranged against limited foresight and
instinctive duplicity. His enemies now were ageing and illness.

Virtually nothing is clear about his life between the time of his leaving
Chile, in late 1913, and the end of 1916. Some of his movements in
an unsettled Atlantic world, where peace was giving way to war, can
be traced. No more than a pencilled outline, the etching is devoid of
shading. With the external universe so poorly charted, it is unsurprising
that his inner turbulence is even more difficult to capture. Perhaps if
we reconsider the journey thus far, by looking back down the road
travelled it may be possible to anticipate turns to come and follow the
outline of a slow moving, furtive figure, to its all too mysterious end.

By the outbreak of the First World War, Silver was in the fifth decade of a tortured existence. From the moment he obtained a passport as a sixteen-year-old, in 1884 – perhaps before – until 1913, when he was forty-five, he was seldom out of trouble with the police of four continents. Of the three decades separating these dates, a minimum of eight and a half years had been spent in prison; for one in every four years of his adult life he had been behind bars. Somewhat surprisingly, given his impulsive behaviour and sexual proclivities, very little of this imprisonment could be attributed directly to his primary pursuits of brothelkeeper or white slaver and therein lies another paradox.

Until he was thirty-five, most of the time in prison came from sentences for petty larceny, for crimes against property. The theft of a few dollars earned him two years in Sing Sing, a roll of satin nine months in Pentonville, and an umbrella three months in Wormwood Scrubs. Many of these crimes were born of compulsive behaviour, of rash actions undertaken on the spur of the moment. By comparison, sex crimes, including aggravated assault, rape and sodomy – which became less frequent after he turned thirty – cost less by way of imprisonment. Luck, good legal counsel and systematic intimidation of witnesses contributed to the latter 'success'. In London the finest barristers saw him acquitted of raping Rachel Laskin. In Johannesburg and Potchefstroom, release from prison occasioned by the outbreak of war saved him from serving most of a two-and-a-quarter year sentence for living off the proceeds of prostitution and sodomy. Only in Windhoek where the colonial administration may have been more concerned about alleged gun running and safe-cracking exploits than a conspiracy to place acid in a woman's vagina, or his living off the proceeds of prostitution, had he earned a three-year sentence with hard labour. In consequence, he had an intense hatred of Germans.

If his propensity for impulsive behaviour and outbursts of violence directed against men, and especially against women, had abated by the time he reached forty then so, too, had the tendency to tell pointless lies, the need to get involved in conspiracies or to engage in the grossest betrayals. The worst acts of violence probably occurred between the ages of sixteen and thirty, when his mind was most agitated and his body strongest. If he did murder anyone before he was twenty, it remained undetected but by 1897 he was still capable of using a knife to stab a rival pimp. Small facial scars, recorded in prison registers, speak of unknown incidents in which fists or knives were used. After the age of thirty, open violence seems to have been supplanted by a willingness to resort to more psychological terror.

What Silver did during late adolescence in Kielce and early manhood in London's East End remained subject to his most determined efforts at concealment. From his early twenties, when he was embroiled in police and criminal subterfuges in New York and Pittsburgh, until his late thirties – in Cape Town – he remained vulnerable to charges of conspiracy or perjury. After fleeing Paris in 1909, he avoided those charges. Although old fault lines of treachery re-emerged in Santiago, where he informed on professional colleagues, he fell short of making such specific allegations against them that they culminated in successful prosecutions.

Fixing tendencies in Silver's psyche, however, is like trying to capture images on the surface of a wind-ruffled pond. No sooner does a picture suggest itself than clear lines are transformed into meaningless swirls. Using this flawed, liquid looking-glass, one can peer at the changing patterns of occupation he offered police as his career unfolded. In his youth he claimed to be a barber, and probably was. In his twenties, when theft of property formed an important, if secondary, part of his repertoire, he was a 'draper', 'jeweller' or 'watchmaker'. At the height of his conspiratorial adventures he was a 'detective's agent', a 'policeman' or a 'special agent'; none of which claims was entirely devoid of truth. In his thirties, imperfectly tethered to hired or bought properties as brothel-keeper, he was a 'hotelier', 'restaurateur' or 'storekeeper'. And, in his forties as he became more heavily involved in the circulation and recycling of white slaves he was a 'livestock speculator', 'merchant' or 'trader'. He appears to have acquired the ability to cultivate an air of concern and to present a demeanour capable of taking in peers as well as police. It may or may not have been co-incidence that his earliest, closest professional association, if not a proper friendship, was with the actor Haskel Brietstein who took the stage name 'Goldberg'.

At his core there was an emotional emptiness. Even the relationships with Jack, or the cousins, Anker and Fierstein, were hollow. In mid-career, when in need of their muscle power, he used the glue of kinship to mould them into a gang. But, as his exploits became less dependent on strength and more on craft and cunning, these relationships and those with other male friends, like Goldstein, withered. In Chile, endangered by Jack's Apache exploits, he deliberately distanced himself from his 'brother' by referring to him, more correctly, as my 'maternal half-

brother'. His relationship with his daughter was thoroughly opportunistic. He ignored Bertha as an infant, as an adolescent he used her
as an adjunct to his pimping enterprises and, by the time she was a
mature women sleeping with his 'brother', treated her as no more than
a trading partner.

His, early, dissolute years were replete with the drinking, smoking
and whoring characteristic of a pimp's life, but there is no surviving
record of his ever having been arrested for public drunkenness. Syphilis
never incapacitated him to the point where it warranted special mention
in his prison records. Yet we know, from several studies of the progressive, uneven temporal development of neurosyphilis that, by the time
he left Chile it must have been manifest in changes in his personality
and well-being. For all that, he continued to take pride in dressing as
neatly as possible and was seldom seen without suit, collar, tie and felt
hat. The handsome features of a twenty-year-old had, especially after
his stay in Neumünster, made way for a slightly more haggard appearance. By the time he reached Chile, his hair had thinned and retreated
and the scar beneath his left eye had become more prominent; his jowls
were heavier, and he was more round-shouldered. His eyes had taken
on the glassy look of a taxidermist's fox. Yet, when next he commissioned a portrait, in New York in 1914, his tonsured appearance offset
by a fashionable suit lent credibility to his presentation as a well-
travelled merchant.

From Chile he went to Buenos Aires, where the ranks of the Zwi
Migdal had been decimated, but hardly obliterated, by the promulga-
tion of the Ley Palacios in October 1913. For a 'trader' with some
capital, New York City was – for reasons we will explore later – no
longer as attractive a venue for his purposes as it had been when he
was younger. Like many Argentine pimps and white slavers of East
European origin, he was of the view that, amidst deteriorating circumstances in the Atlantic world it was best to try to re-establish himself
in the new, European frontiers of turbulence. Not surprisingly, he settled
on London, where Jack and Bertha had set up home and which was
the site of his earliest, life-shaping experiences. The East End,
Whitechapel in particular, was a place of magnetic interest and importance to him. Bertha's roots there were equally deep. Born and raised
in the East End, when she emigrated in 1915, she claimed that the person
closest to her was a Mrs M. Dorfin (Dorfman) of 82 Hessel Street,
Whitechapel. This may well have been the woman to whom Silver, or

his 'wife', had handed Bertha for adoption at some point in her infancy.[1] Bertha's claim may hint at progressive estrangement from her father.

In London, he was struck anew by Europe's material, scientific and technological progress. The signs were everywhere; some had been apparent in Buenos Aires and Valparaiso too. In major centres cars, buses, trams and trucks had displaced the old horse-drawn vehicles. Gas lamps emitting tiny coins of illumination at regular intervals along dark thoroughfares had given way to swathes of electrified light in public places. Old-fashioned steam power had retreated before the rise of the electric motor and, in the most advanced circles, it was said that the fuel of the future was oil rather than coal. The telegraph remained a wonderfully efficient instrument for business but the telephone now seemed to cover much of the country.

Britain's decline as a manufacturing power was offset by its increasing reliance on commerce, finance and trade to sustain growth. A nation of urbanised islanders, it depended heavily on its merchant fleet for imported food and raw materials, and the navy to ensure mastery of the seas. Germany, too, was surging ahead. The old Prussian military elite had been reconciled to new industrial pioneers in chemicals and electricity in the west of the country who had helped to create an enlarged, unified nation linked by a growing and well integrated rail network.

The pace set by Britain and Germany was not easily matched. Austro-Hungary, France and Russia had taken belated strides to industrialise but remained confronted by problems limiting growth of the sort that allowed for tightly integrated political and military muscle. In Vienna, Austria struggled to keep intact a sprawling domain in which there was always the danger of its southern Slavic elements shearing off – a prospect that appealed to its Tsarist neighbour. In Paris, the loss of Alsace-Lorraine during the Franco-Prussian war kept anti-German sentiments alive. France, still recovering its demographic strength after the Napoleonic wars, relied heavily on agriculture and was hampered by the slow emergence of larger urban markets. In St Petersburg, French finance struggled to assuage the enormous hunger for industrial capital in a largely agrarian society where an unfocused monarchy, supported by a feeble political elite and archaic bureaucracy, battled to co-ordinate the sale of grain in a largely vain attempt to procure funds for the development of a modern infrastructure. Neither the residual strengths of the weaker nations, nor the limitations of the two strongest powers, however, did much to curb their ambitions on the world stage, or help drain them of an excess of nationalism acquired in the late nineteenth century.[2]

By 1911, Germany had signalled its intentions of re-arming and preparing for a short, sharp, continental campaign that would, with the help of the Austro-Hungarians, ensure its place as a world power. France and Russia, sensing this, slowly started their own preparations for war while Britain, banking on its naval supremacy, became an increasingly concerned observer. Scientific and technological innovation now found profitable outlets in the development and manufacture of machinery for war. Aircraft, heavier mobile artillery, new battleships, modern machine-guns, rifles and submarines in substantial numbers all became part of the new arsenal of war. Joseph Silver was easing himself back into a world on the brink of catastrophic changes. But while many saw a conflagration backed by such awesome weaponry as being quick, if not painless, a few far-sighted analysts, including a Pole, Ivan Bloch, saw all too clearly that the war would result in a protracted slaughter often bogged down in stalemate.[3]

Not even insular England could escape the tension accompanying preparations for continent-wide conflict. Months after the passing of the Aliens Act in 1905, a supposed influx of foreign spies orchestrated by the Kaiser occasioned some public concern and twitchiness in Whitehall.[4] In London's East End fear of East European Jews rose to new heights when, in December 1910, four armed burglars in a jewellery store in Houndsditch made good their escape by killing three policemen. Russian and Yiddish literature discovered on the premises the burglars had occupied strengthened the supposed links between anarchism, crime and Jews in the public and official mind.[5] A few weeks later, Winston Churchill drafted new legislation which, he conceded, contained 'two naughty principles; first, a deliberate differentiation between the alien, and especially the unassimilated alien, and a British subject, and second that any alien may, in certain circumstances, be deported before he has committed an offence'.[6] These startling provisions never passed into law largely because the panic subsided, but must nevertheless have been fresh in the minds of the 'alien' underworld.[7]

With this pervasive racist ideology, 'merchants' and 'traders' had to give careful thought to their movements. This was particularly important for Silver, whose American documentation – both genuine and fraudulent – was expiring, and whose criminal record made him an unlikely candidate for British citizenship. The prospect of being marooned in a grey and wet England while armies of men and platoons of prostitutes opened up new opportunities on the continent was a gloomy one. He knew he had to return to the United States to acquire a new passport. But unknown business in London, and perhaps in Hamburg, detained him. Summer 1914 was almost upon him by the time he managed to get to Liverpool.

His choice of a ship was interesting. The *Mauretania* – sister to the *Lusitania* and the spanking new *Aquitania* – belonged to Cunard and had been constructed from money lent to the company by the British government in 1903, in an attempt to wrest the Blue Riband from German hands. In a decade of ever larger and more luxurious liners, the *Mauretania* was expected to do the North Atlantic westbound run in record time – something she succeeded in doing in 1909 – and to keep the company flag fluttering above that of the White Star Line, owner of the *Olympic* and *Titanic*.[8]

Using the last of the funds raised from the Low Countries campaign four years earlier, Silver revealed himself as a forty-four-year-old merchant of undisclosed nationality who wished to travel in reasonable comfort. He bought a second-class berth in one of the most prestigious vessels afloat and was issued with ticket number 92569. In itself, the number would be of no interest were it not for the purchaser of the very next ticket, number 92570. 'Jacob Roland', also a 'merchant', but 'British', was thirty-nine years old and going to settle permanently in the United States. The chances are that Mr Roland was Jack Lis – he bore Jack's authentic name, Jacob and was separated from Silver by exactly the same number of years that distinguished the brothers Lis. Silver and Roland were aboard a vessel carrying numerous young Russian women travelling steerage. It seems they were escorting prostitutes to New York.[9]

The *Mauretania* eased out of Merseyside on 16 May 1914 and a little under a week later nuzzled up to the docks on the Lower East Side. The two 'merchants' expected a relatively easy passage through immigration. But they and their charges had to remain vigilant. The Immigration Acts of 1903, 1907, 1910, and the even more specific Mann Act of 1910, made entry into America progressively more difficult for those engaged in the commercial sex trade. In 1908, after initially hesitating, Theodore Roosevelt had ratified an international treaty designed to suppress the international white slave traffic. In New York,

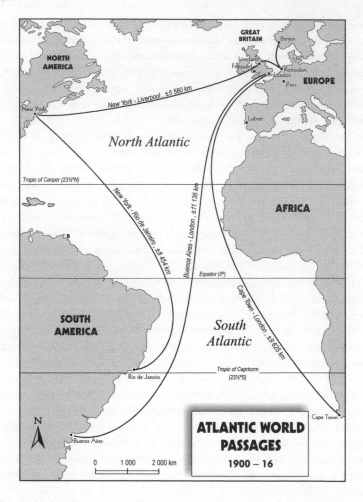

ATLANTIC WORLD
PASSAGES
1900 – 16

the state legislature in Albany was moving to outlaw all forms of commercial prostitution – an objective which was achieved just months later, in 1915.[10]

This hardening of the state's attitude to pimps and prostitutes was not all that distinguished New York in 1914 from the city Silver had known twenty-five years earlier. As in Buenos Aires, where the passage of the Ley Palacios of 1913 was a triumph for law-abiding Jews over the Zwi Migdal, respectable New York Jewry was set on rooting out anti-social elements. In 1912, a communal ethnic structure, the New

York *Kehillah* had established a Bureau for Social Morals which was in effect a Jewish detective agency and police station. It monitored the activities of Jewish criminals and, when it did not take vigilante-style action itself, reported offenders to the police.[11] This, too, was a far cry from the 1890s when the only ethnic organisation that packed a stiff communal punch was the Max Hochstim Association which later mutated into the shady New York Independent Benevolent Association.[12] With federal and state legislatures leading a charge supported by a militant Jewish communal organisation, law enforcement agencies were in the ascendant. This change in the balance of power had profound implications for criminal organisation on the turbulent Lower East Side. Cracks started appearing in a few of the largest gangs.

In July 1912, 'Big Tim' Sullivan, whom Silver probably knew from the 1890s, was shot shortly before he was due to appear before a Grand Jury and give evidence about police–underworld links. The elimination of Herman 'Beansy' Rosenthal, a small-time gangster, shocked the community and contributed to a debate on Apaches and lawlessness. All this spurred the *Kehillah's* efforts to establish a Bureau for Social Morals. For anyone branded an 'Apache' in Buenos Aires, Paris or Santiago this was unsettling talk. New York was less welcoming towards 'merchants'.[13]

Silver went to the Lower East Side, where he stayed with a Moritz Rentkoff, at 162 East 4th Street. It took him a month to get his bearings and strike the deal that was to give momentum to his life in the twenty-four months that followed. The precise nature of his business can only be speculated on, but presumably it did not revolve around the importing of brooms or selling of brushes. The only clues we have lie in the application for a passport which he submitted, along with a photograph, on 29 June 1914.[14]

The new application, filled with lies, claimed that he was born in Myslowitz, close to Kraków. The application was prompted, he said, by the need to go abroad, but he planned on returning to the United States 'within two or three months'. That much at least was probably true and he was given a passport to proceed to the United Kingdom that was valid until 30 December 1914. But what the purpose of his trip could have been other than to recruit and direct prostitutes is impossible to tell. We can reasonably infer from the 1914 application that he was intent on returning to England and then pushing on towards his newly invented place of birth, in Myslowitz, before returning to New York City after a round trip on business.

Myslowitz was a focal point for the white slave traffick. After a cholera outbreak in Hamburg in 1894, it was illegal for emigrants travelling to Baltic ports to pass through Prussian territory without prior inspection and disinfection at remotely sited control points. In 1906, Myslowitz, located at a rail junction, became one such disinfection station. This enforced halt created a new business opportunity for the Cunard and White Star Lines. The Hamburg-America Steamship Company, too, opened a hugely successful agency in Myslowitz under the direction of Max Weichmann. Weichmann became an enormously wealthy man who not only 'contributed to charity' but maintained an 'open charge account at the bar of the Hotel International for his police friends'. Myslowitz held other attractions for the neurosyphilitic Silver: it was less than a 100 miles from Kielce.[15]

Myslowitz's grand emigration hall, a filter through which thousands of women passed each year, was a slaver's dream – a trading outpost on the frontier of female poverty, oppression and vulnerability. While civil servants attended to the state's legitimate business inside the hall, outside Weichmann's employees and associates routed pimps and prostitutes, or potential 'fresh goods', to distant corners of the Atlantic world. Amongst the most helpful of his personnel was 'The King of the Agents', 'The King of the Border' and 'The King of the White Slave Traffickers', Samuel Lubelski, brother of Mozek Lubelski, a senior member of the Zwi Migdal. What Silver would have been only partially aware of, however, was that at precisely the moment he was applying for a document that would allow him to travel to his 'place of birth', Samuel Lubelski was being prosecuted and sentenced to nine years' imprisonment for his role in extensive cross-border white slavery operations. But perhaps not even that would have been too discouraging since only four of eighty cases of white slavery in Myslowitz between 1894 and 1914 produced convictions.[16]

Within hours of taking delivery of his passport at Rentkoff's apartment, Silver was back up-town at the Cunard agency securing a ticket for his return to the United Kingdom. Unusually, haste and taste combined well. The *Aquitania* was preparing for only its second passage east and Silver secured himself a second-class berth. It was the vessel's penultimate round trip before being commandeered by the Admiralty and refitted as an armed merchant cruiser. So keen was he to get back to England that, instead of proceeding to Liverpool, he opted to disembark in Wales and travel by rail to London. The ship docked in Fishguard on 7 July 1914; hours later, the Great Western disgorged Silver at Paddington. He sensed the almost physical attraction Whitechapel still held for him and disappeared into it. He was not to emerge for six months.[17]

In truth, the Kaiser and the Austro-Hungarians were at least partly to blame for his prolonged stay. When a teenage terrorist trained by the Serb-sponsored Black Hand assassinated the heir to the Habsburg throne, Archduke Ferdinand, on 28 July 1914, the Austrians replied with an ultimatum which, if accepted, would have made Serbia a client state. Within days the Central Powers mobilised their forces; a move that was responded to in kind by France and Russia who were joined by Britain when Germany dictated further, equally unacceptable, terms to Belgium. German troops crossed the Belgian frontier on 3 August, Britain then declared war on Germany.

Crudely sketched, German plans were predicated on co-ordinated warfare in two theatres. The major force would strike a pre-emptive blow, opening a western front by punching a hole through Belgium as it moved south to secure the principal objective, France. The latter was to be achieved before an effective counter-thrust could be launched by Allied forces, who would have to wait on the arrival of the British. At the same time, Austria-Hungary would assume responsibility for the eastern front, holding Russian forces to the north and east, and then pushing south into Serbia as well as engaging the Italians across the Alps. In theory, once the Central Powers had achieved their objectives on the western front, German forces would be switched to the eastern front and assist in defeating the Russians. In practice, the war took a different course. Early German gains on the western front gave way to the stalemate of trench warfare while, on the eastern front, Austro-Hungarian forces performed so poorly that they had to be assisted by German troops that were required elsewhere.[18]

By December 1914, predictions about a lengthy war on a scale hitherto unthought of, a war so consuming of human life that it would forever be known as the Great War, were becoming a reality. The light-headed feeling that came with nationalism was making way for the inhalation of mustard gas in muddied trenches on distant battlefields. In London, Paris and St Petersburg the mood was increasingly sombre, while in Berlin and Vienna the cheaper scent of hope still lingered in the air.

Any thought of a swift foray into Myslowitz was abandoned. Silver moved in with Jack and Bertha at 8 Gunton Road, Upper Clapton, where his daughter was expecting the couple's second child, Bernard, born on 18 March 1915.[19] Jack, a 'drapery job buyer', was almost certainly dealing in stolen goods, while his wife, under her professional name, Miss Bertha Silver, was running prostitutes, from Charing Cross Road, in the sleazier part of the West End.[20] Her father is unlikely to have profited from either enterprise. Indeed, his indirect dependence on the couple during this period may have contributed to a further cooling off in the relationship. Without an income, and with his passport expiring at the end of the year, he gave thought to his next move. Europe was, for the moment, impassable and the old Atlantic world beckoned.

By the closing weeks of 1914 he was back in Liverpool, clutching a hastily extended passport allowing him to return to New York. But the North Atlantic was no longer a playground for Blue Riband honours. Although primarily a land war, the English Channel, the Irish Sea and the high seas had all become dangerous to negotiate. Britain, claiming mastery of the oceans, sought to enforce a blockade of German ports. Yet a German submarine had sunk three cruisers in the North Sea in September and, weeks later, a second British detachment had been destroyed off the coast of Chile by a squadron under the command of Admiral Graf von Spee. If one was to venture abroad, it was best to be an American, sailing in a vessel flying the American flag. Silver was comfortable aboard the American Line's *Philadelphia* which, under its former name, the *City of Paris*, was the very ship that Charles Jacobs had been so keen to get him aboard during their epic conflict back in 1895.[21]

The *Philadelphia*, having left on 2 January 1915, made New York safely. The ship's manifest leaves no clues to who his travelling companions may have been. From what transpired later that year, however, it may have been part of a reconnaissance trip leading to the relocation of all those based in Gunton Road. He did not linger on the Lower East Side. A month later he boarded a British vessel, the *Voltaire*, and made his way south to an unfamiliar setting that fell within the Zwi Migdal's zone of influence. On board, too, was one 'Annie Rosenberg', an unaccompanied, twenty-eight-year-old 'Russian hairdresser', travelling steerage. Given Silver's fondness for the name Hannah/Anna and his historic ties to the hairdressing trade, she may have been a woman under his control. The voyage came after extensive raids on brothels and gaming houses in New York led to increased traffic up and down the eastern coastline of the Americas.[22]

Brazil was a novelty, Brazilian prostitutes not so. Indirectly, it was the German army that had first introduced Silver to Latin-American-based prostitutes in South West Africa, in 1905–6. 'Katia' Abrahams, Fanny Bernstein and others had contributed to his subsequent stay in prison in Neumünster. Bertha, too, had been impressed by the women's tales of life in Brazil where prostitutes were unusually successful in protecting elements of their personal and religious lives. Years later she found her way to Rio de Janeiro where she and a few of the veterans from Swakopmund and Windhoek could reminisce about their days in Africa during the Herero rebellion.[23]

On 12 February 1915, the first thing he noticed as the *Voltaire* entered Rio de Janeiro was the presence of another British steamer, the *Alcantara*, on its way from Buenos Aires, bound for Liverpool. He disembarked swiftly, informing immigration authorities that he was an American national, a widower and merchant based in New York. At least some of it was true, but which of his 'wives' had died, and under what circumstances, only he knew.[24] Nor do we know what happened to Hannah/Anna Rosenberg. He hurried ashore because he needed to talk to somebody intent on leaving on the *Alcantara*, which was scheduled to sail within days. Cheynele Roubinsky was a twenty-six-year-old unaccompanied Russian 'dressmaker'. What made her interesting was her destination. She told the Brazilian authorities that she was going to London, where she could be found 'c/o Miss Silver, Flat No. 2, 162 Charing Cross Road' – an address dominated by people on the fringes of theatre life.[25] Father and daughter were both engaged in the international traffick in women.

Perhaps it was inevitable that he found his way to Rio de Janeiro even though he did arrive there late in life. The first East European pimps, prostitutes and white slavers had turned up there by the late 1860s; years before the assassination of the Tsar prompted a mass exodus in the 1880s. By the late 1870s, several pimps and white slavers had established a loosely knit organisation in Rio de Janeiro that was to become the precursor and progenitor of the Zwi Migdal. Although the local trade in commercial sex, especially its upmarket dimension, was dominated by the trend-setting French as it was everywhere else along east coast Latin America, the prominence of an East European element reputed to have pioneered anal sex and sado-masochism in the city offended law-abiding Jews.[26] In 1896 and 1910, pimps and 'Polacas' – low-class Jewesses catering for the cheaper end of the market – along with white slavers were publicly vilified and physically attacked by more religious Jews.[27]

Catholic tolerance and understanding of the weaknesses of the flesh meant that by 1915 Rio de Janeiro had over 400 official brothels and countless *casas de tolerancia*. Of the former, a hundred or more were 'Russian' or 'Polish', with links to Buenos Aires and the Old World.[28] As in most cities, municipal authorities and police attempted to confine the sex trade to a designated quarter, a *zona* also known as *Mangue*, 'the swamp'. In the old days Silver would have taken to the mangue like a pimp to a poolroom but now even the slow-moving Brazilian legislature was getting into line with other countries around the western rim of the Atlantic world. In 1904, the Congress 'ratified an international anti-white slave treaty' and, in 1915, passed new legislation to deport foreign pimps and made it illegal to operate brothels, or rent out rooms, that would facilitate commercial sex.[29]

With civic-minded officials around many parts of the western Atlantic becoming less tolerant of the trade, Silver had no intention of settling. Rio was a convenient wartime port which, although beyond reach of real or imagined enemies in Argentina, still allowed him to do business with the Zwi Migdal. Eight weeks later he was ready to board the British-owned vessel, *Amazon*, for Liverpool. He was not alone in undertaking the risky ocean voyage to the United Kingdom and it was presumably not by chance that some of his fellow travellers were white slavers.

Harris Schwartz, a Russian 'merchant' and David 'Moises' Branstein/ Bronstein, a Polish *porteno* had boarded in Buenos Aires. Branstein, an early member of the Warsaw Burial Society who later donated a fine oak altar to the Zwi Migdal *shul* in Cordoba Street, had emigrated to Argentina in 1908. A jeweller by trade, he had never opened a store, separated from his wife for 'personal reasons', and formally joined the Zwi Migdal in 1910. A close confidant of its president, he was well known in 'slaving' circles although he always claimed to have no knowledge of the Zwi Migdal's activities beyond its function as a burial society. Branstein, Schwartz and Silver were like peas in a pod and lent new meaning to the term 'merchant navy' as the steamer slid out of Guanabara Bay. All three were bound for addresses in London's

East End that were within walking distance of one other.[30]

The *Amazon* docked in Liverpool on 3 April, but the German challenge, thwarted on the western front, was assuming alarming proportions on the Atlantic. The three men made their way to London. Just four weeks later, the Germans reminded them how fortunate they had been. On 6 May 1915, a U-boat sank the *Lusitania* off the south coast of Ireland with the loss of over a thousand lives including those of 128 Americans. The loss of the vessel caused outrage in Allied circles: it paved the way for America's entry into the war and proved a setback for Germany in its efforts to get support in unaligned quarters. A temporary withdrawal of U-boats from the North Atlantic and English Channel followed, but by then the ideological damage had been done.

The sinking of a liner on the Liverpool – New York run had serious implications for Silver and the family business. American and British steamships had to be avoided and, where possible, travel had to be restricted to vessels belonging to neutrals. He was marooned in England but determined to rejoin Jack in the United States along with Bertha and her two children. The problem was compounded by their need to move two new recruits to New York. His solution was as simple as it was selfish. On 8 December 1915, Bertha Lis, a wife without her husband, Jack Lis of 43 Lexington Avenue New York City, but accompanied by her two small British-born boys, Monty and Bernard, appeared in Liverpool. They were accompanied – indeed the contract numbers reveal that the tickets had been purchased, in sequence, from the same outlet – by a seventeen- and eighteen-year-old who had been permanently resident in England. The younger, a 'tailoress', Getel Yonasnowitz, was Russian, while the older, Jenna Borgeand, was from Finland. The party boarded the *Philadelphia* and, six days later were safely in New York where they would have been met by Jack.[31]

Mindful of self, Silver took a more circuitous, but safer, route back. He made his way to an east coast port, probably Newcastle. Using his American passport he crossed the North Sea and then either slipped into the Netherlands or made his way directly to neutral Norway. On 13 January 1916, in Bergen, he boarded the pride of the Norwegian-American Line, the *Kristianiafjord*. Launched just two years earlier, carrying over a thousand passengers in three different classes, it was the vessel of choice for arms dealers, revolutionaries and spies after the outbreak of war.[32] The chilly northern loop to New York took ten days. There, he had more interesting things to tell immigration authorities.

He was once again 'married'. Who the lucky lady was, we know not. But, given that he had been a 'widower' only months earlier, perhaps London had offered up one more bride-victim. Like earlier wives, this one was never again heard of. Perhaps she languished back in the East End, waiting to join him in Manhattan. More puzzling was why he told the authorities that he was going to 1883 Main Street, Waltham, Massachusetts. There was no such number in that street at the time. Was it a tell-tale slip of memory, an inability to recall accurately Jack's address or was there more to it? By 1916, there were few white slavers in Boston.[33]

By chance, his arrival in New York coincided with a public commotion that may have influenced the way he perceived the war and his future. Forty-eight hours before disembarking, Ignácz Trebitsch, author of a set of newspaper articles notable for their stridently anti-British propaganda, had published a rehashed version of his life entitled *Revelations of an International Spy*. Better known as Trebitsch Lincoln, he and this self-made pseudo-Englishman shared remarkably similar traits. Trebitsch, a central European, turned his back on Judaism and for a time became a nominal Christian. Young and self-centred, he was prone to petty theft, led a promiscuous life, was indifferent to the feelings of others and deceitful enough to become an informer and spy. But, whereas Silver had started life on the low road with a ghetto-criminal as father, Trebitsch, the son of a prosperous merchant south of Budapest, had taken the high road. While Silver's afflictions led to Pentonville, Trebitsch's took him to parliament. In 1910, Trebitsch became Liberal MP for Darlington. When this role ended his love affair with England soured and, on the outbreak of war, he crossed the Channel to become a German spy before fleeing to the United States.[34]

By January 1916 Trebitsch's antics had stretched British tolerance to breaking point. After a set of alarums and excursions, replete with disguises and orchestrated press interviews while supposedly on the run, he was eventually arrested, extradited and made to do time in Pentonville until July 1919. What Silver made of these gyrations at a time when the world's most successful spy, Salomon Rosenblum, alias Sidney Reilly, was also in New York, can only be speculated upon. It is possible that Reilly and Silver had met in the underworld of Brussels, in 1910, when Russian and Polish safe-crackers and bomb-making anarchists alike had an interest in manufacturing and using explosives.[35] Trebitsch, if not the more classy Reilly, would have alerted him to new possibilities for wartime excitement.

Silver did nothing unusual. He slithered back into his old haunts on the Lower East Side and hired an apartment in the street where, a quarter of a century earlier, he had undertaken the botched burglary that sent him to Sing Sing. The street directories record that in 1916 and the first part of 1917 'Joseph Silver' resided at 87 Clinton Street. He was within walking distance of dozens of barbershops, brothels, cafés, cigar stores, dancing academies, gambling dens, hotels, restaurants and poolrooms. True, most of the places were frequented by youngsters, including several peddling cocaine, but here and there one could still encounter occasional 'craft' practitioners – such as the horse-poisoners – though they, too, were being forced to bend the knee before change. The names of burglars, cadets, fences, gamblers, gangsters, pickpockets, pimps, prostitutes, strike-breakers and thieves were recorded by Abe Schoenfeld, the chief 'detective' of the Bureau for Social Morals. Their monikers remained as colourful as ever but few would have meant anything to him. 'Benny the Hunchback', 'Crazy Wolf', 'Cockeye London', 'Hymie Rubbernose', 'Joe the Greaser', 'Little Nigger', 'Three-Fingers Jerry' and 'Whitey the Ox' all belonged to the wartime generation, but tucked away in the Bureau's list were the names of one or two genuine old crooks that Silver would have had no difficulty at all in recognising including one, an elderly 'burglar and fence', with the familiar name of Goldberg.[36]

He spent twelve or more months on the Lower East Side, seemingly uninvolved with Jack or Bertha while, on the far side of the Atlantic, the war without end deepened. By 1916 it was a war of attrition in Europe, where shortages of food, clothing and rationing were becoming a way of life, and in the trenches along the western front Verdun and the Battle of the Somme saw the butchery of mankind on a scale previously unimagined. On the eastern front, too, the Germans held their positions. It was only further south, in Galicia that there were any signs of an Allied advance.

In the war on crime Silver had often found himself operating on both sides simultaneously. Lacking a moral compass and incapable of passivity, he had spent his life travelling to find the frontiers where good and evil were confronting one another. A settled social order was, for him, inimical to the sense of well-being that was always elusive. The sights and sounds of conflict and disorder were irresistible. Once

the thunder of battle commenced, like a soldier under fire, moral insou-
ciance carried him through any amount of betrayal and treachery. Far
from the Old World white slave supply lines he craved, and artificially
confined to a New York where the demand for prostitutes had been
curbed by mid-town moralists, he was deeply frustrated. But, in the
world inhabited by the disturbed and the insane, chaos, destruction
and war are the very hothouses of hope.

By 1917, when millions saw only gloom and despair, Silver detected
a glimmer of light and opportunity in two discrete political developments. Although initially difficult to reconcile, they were seen as united
in the mind of a man who, amongst many other things, was also a
'Polish-American'. First, in April 1917, after a delay of some months,
America decided to enter the war having debated the import of the
Zimmerman telegram in which Germany invited Mexico to embark on
a military adventure to conquer territories lost to the United States
decades earlier. In Europe, the arrival of American troops on the ground
gave Allied forces new impetus on the western front and changed the
course of the war. At sea, America replaced ships faster than German
U-boats could sink them. This enabled the British Navy to redeploy
stretched resources and to reassert mastery of the North Atlantic.

Secondly, Germany, anxious to deepen tensions within a desperate
and divided Russia, decided to set up a provisional government in
Warsaw with a view to Poland's regaining independence. For Silver,
who as the 'American', Joseph Schmidt, had been a prohibited immigrant in Russian-Poland since 1899, this paved the way for a return to
Kielce.[37] By 1917, the United States, ever helpful, had reopened the
North Atlantic and the way to Europe while Germany had secured the
road to Poland. What more could a Polish-American want? And, as if
that were not enough, he travelled on an American passport which
showed that he had been born in Myslowitz and thus had legitimate
grounds to be in German Silesia. The world was once again alive with
possibilities.

Silver made his final crossing of the Atlantic in an unknown vessel
in the first or second quarter of 1917. In the three decades that had
elapsed since leaving Kielce, he had done the equivalent of circum-
navigating the globe three times; he knew the Atlantic world back-
wards. There were few major cities he had not visited, nor an East
European underworld within them he had not explored. Starting as
cadet and sneak-thief he had risen through the ranks of burglars, pimps

and white slavers to become, in Johannesburg, the boss of a crime syndicate capable of holding its own with the best that Buenos Aires, Cape Town, London, New York or Paris could offer. His name had crossed the desk of some of the most famous and senior government figures of the day, and yet he, and his greatest, secret, remained unknown. The western hemisphere had long been his playground, but it had lost its appeal. Everything was topsy-turvy; the Old World suddenly seemed more exciting than the New. Oh what a lovely war!

XXIV

JAROSLAW
1917–1918

For a thousand years the Russians and their Church have done their best to exterminate the Jews and their religion. With what success? Here in Rovno were thousands of Jews shut in an impregnable world of their own, scrupulously observing a religion incessantly purified, practising their own customs, speaking their own language, with two codes of morals – one for each other and the other for the Gentiles. Persecution has only engendered a poison and a running sore in the body of the Russian people. It is true what Miroshnikov said, as we drank *kvass* in a little Jewish bar – that all Jews were traitors to Russia. Of course they are.

John Reed
War in Eastern Europe: Travels through the Balkans in 1915

WHAT swirled through Silver's mind as he disembarked in the neutral Netherlands and re-entered Germany in late 1916 or early 1917? To what extent was it part of a homing instinct underpinned by a warped boyhood relationship with his mother, or was it just another commercial excursion with the possibility of settling scores with the Germans? He had always had a poorly developed sense of danger but, like a fly in range of a chameleon's tongue, was now at greater risk than ever before.

After leaving the Old World Joseph Lis had – over three decades – mutated into the layered personality of Joseph Silver. Rational and intelligent but less capable of dealing with stress than he had been as a young man, he was aware of problems of identity and documentation.

Back in a setting where it was difficult to hide Jewish origins the triple persona embodied in an American, Protestant Silver would be unhelpful in Germany or Poland. The Silver–Lis–Jew layers needed to be reversed and become more Jew–Lis–Silver-like in emphasis. In a way it was a regression. After the United States joined the Allies in the struggle against the Central Powers, in April 1917, his American passport was more a hindrance than help. So, at some point along the road to Warsaw in the opening weeks of 1917, he re-emerged as 'Filip Skrzat', a Polish Jew.

Skrzat was a Jew on a continent which, when war broke out, was still home to one of every two Jews in the world. In the western part, half a million fairly well acculturated Jews had made Germany their home; after the 1880s, they had been joined by 50,000 partially assimilated *Ostjuden* in the cities of Bavaria, Prussia and Saxony. Even taken together, the number of 'western' Jews was dwarfed by the numbers in central and eastern Europe. Most politically oppressed and poverty-stricken Jews huddled in the villages, small towns and a few large cities of Austria-Hungary, Poland and Russia. The Pale of Settlement confined four million Jews to western Russia while a further two million squeezed into adjoining 'Russian Poland'. In the south, Galicia, a frontier province of Austria, was home to a million and, beyond that, were yet more. It was the misfortune of half the world's Jews to be trapped amidst the greatest armed conflict of all time. Surrounded by poorly disposed belligerent forces, they were without easy access to neutral territories or the sea.[1]

Vulnerable to snowstorms of prejudice drifting in from every angle, the plight of the Jews was perhaps worst on the Polish plains, Europe's favourite battleground. There, even the firmest institutional structures were racked by the swirling aspirations and opportunism of nationalists wishing to free themselves of the Tsarist yoke. Sensing their strategic importance on the eastern front, many Poles told Jewish 'spy' stories to whatever occupying force they faced: east-bound armies swallowed tales of Jewish 'treachery' as readily as did west-bound ones. One day it was Germans being told of Jews spying for the Russians; the next, it was Russians hearing how the Jews had all along spied for the Germans.[2]

Raped, plundered and executed, Jews in the eastern zone nevertheless tried to do their patriotic duty as well as protect families and livelihoods. In Germany, prominent Jews were called to help organise the national food supply and mobilise industry for the war effort. In Austria, where Jews had once enjoyed more civil rights than in Russia, all Jewish immigrants were banned from entering Galicia after 1915 and those already domiciled were prevented from moving between districts. Despite these and other restrictions, over 50,000 Jews chose to serve in the Austro-Hungarian forces. In Russia, where the Pale of Settlement had nominally been disbanded, hundreds of thousands of Jews were expelled from the cities and their homes. Yet, despite ongoing persecution, over a quarter of a million Jews served in Russian armies that confined any Jew's military ambitions to the rank of corporal.[3]

By the time he reached Germany, in January 1917, Silver must have known that on the eastern front, civilian and military Jews alike faced death at every turn. He would also have learned that the area around Myslowitz–Kraków had been disrupted by a ten-month Russian occupation during which thousands of Jews were dislocated and expelled, and that virtually all organised white slave traffick in Germany had ground to a halt. Undeterred, he hovered around Hamburg and other northern and western cities familiar to him from his 1910 exploits. He met Jakob Pilat, a thirty-three-year-old native of Wolin, in northern Poland, who did not share his interests in the commercial sex trade but was a thief. For Lis, however, the real magnet remained in the southeast and the utterly bizarre nest he had come from.

As first the German and then, somewhat belatedly and ineffectually, the Austro-Hungarian armies consolidated their hold on Poland in 1916–17, the Central Powers extended sexual services to troops on the eastern front. In Lódz, Vilna and Warsaw mobile brothels soon arrived to supplement existing establishments that expanded as the war dragged on. With deepening poverty and social dislocation, the southern and eastern zones saw massive increases in Jewish prostitution. In Russia, where war-weariness and political fragility went hand in hand, Jewish prostitutes were automatically exempted from normal residential restrictions.[4] But if Lis and Pilat were cheered by what they saw in Brietstein's birthplace, Lódz, they must have been delighted by Warsaw. The Germans got on extremely well with Zwi Migdal brothel-owners who had fled Buenos Aires after the passage of the Ley Palacios in 1913. In a curious reversal made possible by global turbulence, New World criminals had returned to the Old as wartime profiteers. After the war, many returned to Argentina to reclaim a place in the southern sun. Zachariah Zytnitsky, at home in wartime

Warsaw, later returned to South America to become president of the Zwi Migdal.[5]

Pushed along by freak counter-currents, Lis steered himself towards Kielce after an absence of more than three decades. By then under the control of an Austro-Hungarian army that had failed to distinguish itself, the town and southern surrounds had seen considerable conflict. Here, too, however, organised prostitution thrived amidst physical destruction and the palpable demoralisation of law-abiding Jews. Wolf Berkowitz's brothel flourished throughout the war, servicing Austro-Hungarian troops, the German army, Polish militia or Russian Cossacks with the lack of discrimination that marks true professionalism.[6] For hundreds of Jewish artisans, shopkeepers and merchants, however, the Great War was nothing short of a disaster. From the outbreak of hostilities in 1914, until the restoration of Polish independence in 1918 – which was promptly marked by a pogrom in the city – the community was tormented by a succession of occupying forces. During the early stages of the war the epaulettes of the advancing victors and retreating vanquished changed with bewildering rapidity but the barely concealed hatred of the Jews remained constant.[7]

In August 1914, Jozef Pilsudski's legionnaires, siding with Austria-Hungary in the hope of snatching Polish independence from the spoils of war, entered Kielce. The town's patriotic Russian-born rabbi, Moses Jeruzalimski, observed with alarm how Pilsudski elicited an enthusiastic response from Poles and a cautious endorsement from his congregants who had little reason to love the Tsar. The Russians, encamped to the north of the town were slow to mobilise but eventually dispatched a regiment of Cossacks to flush out the legionnaires. Pilsudski's expulsion left the local Polish nationalists almost as angry as it did the commander of the Tsarist forces, who took the view that citizens had afforded him an inappropriately generous reception. As punishment, the Russian military gave inhabitants twenty-four hours to pay a fine of over 100,000 roubles, or face the prospect of having their homes bombed. Jeruzalimski, a Russian-speaker, made great demands of his congregants who came up with the money 'down to the last groszy'. Doubly aggrieved, Polish nationalists then spread the rumour that 'the Jews' were responsible for the legionnaires' reception and that it was they who had acted as spies for the Austro-Hungarians. These tales further inflamed the Cossacks who, directed by local hotheads, were encouraged to loot Jewish stores. In the midst of this Jeruzalimski

rendered further service to the community when he intervened with
Kielce's Catholic Bishop, Lusinski, to help soothe tempers and uncouple
a potentially murderous Cossack–Polish alliance and pogrom.[8]

These events, which took place within days of the commencement of
hostilities, set the tone for the remainder of the war. The last quarter of
1914 saw the front line first to the south-west, then through, and finally
north-east of the town as the battles for Warsaw and Lódz unfolded.
Kielce was occupied, in turn, by Austro-Hungarians, Germans and
Russians. Each change brought its own terrors for Jews, whose divided
loyalties were exploited mercilessly by angry Poles. Jeruzalimski collapsed
beneath the strain placed on him by military commanders and retreated
to his native Ukraine, where he died, in mid-1915. In addition to having
to provision the army of the day, Jews were assaulted, banished, executed,
fined, hanged, imprisoned, raped or stolen from with impunity. A further
burden was placed on the community when thousands of terrified Jews
fled adjacent hamlets and surrounding villages to seek refuge in Kielce.[9]

By the time Lis and Pilat got there, in 1917, Kielce was controlled
by the Central Powers and the military situation in the province was
more stable. The front line was farther east towards the rather porous
Ukrainian border and the Austro-Hungarian fortress town of Przemysl
which the Russians had besieged during 1914–15.[10] The plight of the
citizens and Jewish refugees had, however, deteriorated further. Hunger

and poverty were endemic. Amidst these dismal circumstances Silver found a father who had humiliated him as a boy to the point where, in the hope that the deed might follow the wish, he had once pronounced him 'dead', and a mother whose uncontrolled sexuality had done much to inform his lifelong quest to conquer, control and humiliate women.

His parents, reunited in 1912 after a separation of twenty years, were living near the market. The house, at 7 Hipoteczna, was more substantial than the rooms the family occupied when he had left home as a sixteen-year-old. It had taken a lifetime to rise from below the breadline to rudimentary comfort. His father, now seventy, and mother, sixty-five, had survived the bankruptcy and litigation that accompanied his departure in 1885, and had been largely rehabilitated in the tolerant Hasidic community and in the eyes of the civil authorities. Ansel and Hannah Lis's names were on the municipal electoral roll when Polish independence was regained in 1918. Many years later, when survivors of the Holocaust gathered in Israel to put together a book of remembrance, Ansel was remembered as a 'respected home-owner'.[11] But, perhaps significantly, the names of the older Lises are conspicuously absent from the lists of those who held office, or supported a host of communal associations. Nevertheless, and crucially during the First World War, they had access to Rabbi Abraham Abele, who, like his predecessor, Jeruzalimski, was called upon to mediate between army officers, city authorities and local Jewry.[12]

Silver's slender connection to the town of his birth – a link later deliberately obscured after his emigration and by his troubled time in Whitechapel – assumed renewed significance in the closing months of the war when he was forced to reactivate it. At the time, however, the reunion with his parents, more especially with his mother, must have had a meaning we can never know. Were any ghosts laid to rest or, as one suspects, did the mazurka of madness continue unabated? Within days he and Pilat left, heading towards the eastern front and the garrison town of Przemysl which had been reoccupied by the Austrians and Germans, after its loss in 1914–15. There, a hundred or so miles south-east of Kielce and on the leaking Russian border, the pair joined four other drifters.[13]

It is difficult to know what to make of this band. They moved around the fortified village of Jaroslaw, some way from the front but sufficiently close to it to exploit the turbulence behind the line on both sides. If procurement had been Silver's objective on leaving New York, the idea had long since been abandoned. It seems more likely that the gang was part of a ring of cross-border black-marketeers moving alcohol, cigarettes, grain, fodder or remounts across a frontier where the Russians, in particular, remained desperately dependent on horses. For Lis, whose eye for the main chance had once seen him moving fodder, horses and possibly even guns along German lines in South West Africa, this would not have been a novel experience.[14]

Smuggling, by its nature, depends on intelligence and, to the extent that smugglers need to know how and where the state has deployed its forces, all smugglers are 'spies'. A smuggler of women by profession, Silver had spent his life anticipating, dealing with, and circumventing vigilance organisations, border guards, immigration officials and policemen. But spying on border guards in peacetime and spying on an army at war are different propositions and he did not manage them any more successfully than he had negotiated similar problems in German South West Africa. If anything, it was the prospect of booty, not politics, that drew him in.

On 1 March 1917, Austro-Hungarian officials attached to the military court in Jaroslaw sent a letter to Schleswig-Holstein asking police in Hamburg to arrest Josef Lis/Skrzat and Jakob Pilat, wanted on unspecified charges of theft and espionage. Routing the request through Hamburg was significant. The Austrians presumably already had an inkling as to where and when Lis had re-entered Germany or knew about his imprisonment at Neumünster. The police spent the better part of a week searching for the suspects and then forwarded the request to Gelsenkirchen, closer to the banks and insurance companies Lis had plundered in 1910. But, despite police headquarters in Berlin having come up with a photograph of Lis, the trawl through the Ruhr was equally unsuccessful. By 20 March the Germans had shelved the case.[15]

The search came at the end of six months during which the eastern front had been virtually static and conditions for cross-border criminal operations favourable. It also coincided with momentous changes in Russia that were to re-energise the Central Powers. In March the garrison in Petrograd mutinied, a soviet was formed, and Tsar Nicholas abdicated. The Germans, fomenting disorganisation for the provisional government, facilitated Lenin's return, allowing the 'Sealed Train' safe passage to Sweden a month later. With the Bolsheviks on the ascendant in Russian cities and Tsarist front-line troops demoralised, the Central Powers reasserted themselves on the eastern front – a move given additional momentum when Lenin's October revolution triumphed. With Red Russians unwilling to take up the fight while their revolution was threatened by conservative White forces, the Central Powers consolidated their push east until the Treaty of Brest-Litovsk, in March 1918, halted armed conflict.

The collapse of Tsarist Russia and renewal of conflict along the eastern front in the latter half of 1917 underscored the importance of Jaroslaw and the bitterly contested fortress of Przemysl east of it. Thus, while the Germans soon lost interest in the whereabouts of Lis and Pilat, the Austrians kept up the pressure on the gang. The fact that they continued to do so until the end of the war suggests that the army's provisions and supplies had been targeted by Lis and his associates. By late 1917, he and four others in the band, but not Pilat who had disappeared, were in the military prison in Jaroslaw. Their plight deepened when they were told they would be prosecuted in the superior court, in Przemysl.

The Austrians, who had been pushing the Germans to find him, now devoted themselves to more urgent matters on the eastern front. The army was never in a hurry. Military prisons were all the same; it was Kimberley and Windhoek all over again. The Central Powers made their last great push against disintegrating Tsarist armies, but in Jaroslaw not a soul stirred, nothing happened. It was an insane situation; he was an American Jew held on Polish soil, by the Austrian army, on the grounds of being a Russian spy. Divisional headquarters' files covering counter-intelligence around Lublin and L'vov reveal no trace of any Lis or Skrzat in 1917. Amidst so many confusing ethnic identities and quests, only the thick ice inside his cell and a wind that bit to the quick had unmistakable origins – both were Siberian.

Jaroslaw, in January 1918, compared poorly with Ossining in 1890. Back then and not yet twenty-two in 'The House of Fear', lock-step marches, striped prison garb and a two-and-a-half-year sentence had all seemed insurmountable and yet, somehow, he had survived on the banks of the frozen Hudson. In Sing Sing, due process had been his implacable enemy; in Jaroslaw he longed for a mere glimpse of that old foe. His birthday came and went. Only in March, when news of the signing of the Treaty of Brest-Litovsk warmed the attitude of Austrian officers, did the chill in his soul start to thaw. With the Bolsheviks preoccupied with domestic problems and the Russian army in tatters, the Central Powers hastened Polish 'independence' and turned their attention to the western front for a push which, they believed, might yet win the war.

New developments on the eastern front were encouraging and, even in the old Fox, were capable of rousing the instinct for opportunism. Wars were unpredictable: military reverses could rescue a man. Had not the Boers opened the prison in Potchefstroom in an attempt to confound the British? Maybe the Poles, who were putting on political weight for the first time in a hundred years, could be persuaded to intervene on his behalf? Perhaps that indefinable homing instinct that lies buried deep within all of us, and had taken him back briefly to Kielce, might yet save him? His father – no, his mother – might get Rabbi Abele to intervene with the Austrians.

Communication was difficult and it took weeks to get messages to and from Kielce. So slow were the exchanges that they were overtaken by events. One day, without warning, he was taken suddenly from the prison and placed before the court. Only a single-line entry in the court register records that case number 2605 against Joseph Lis was heard before the Divisional Court of Przemysl on an unknown date in mid-1918. Neither the record of the proceedings of the military court, nor the sentence it imposed have survived. But, given the appeal that followed, it is reasonable to infer that the court imposed the maximum sentence at its disposal on a 'spy' who was, almost certainly, also a thief.[16]

Time – meant to unwind at the lazy pace remembered from child-hood excursions to the river at Sandomierz – now worked against him. Hours sprinted into days, days into weeks and months ran off with what was left of his life. Confused ideas about the right of appeal, conspiracies and denial raced through his mind. Amidst so much haste it nevertheless took for ever to establish that someone of standing had brought his plight to the attention of the Austrian authorities in Kielce. Major-General Zechbauer, officer commanding the Kommando der Besetzungstruppe charged with maintaining the peace in the city, called for Lis's papers from Jaroslaw. An entry in an Austrian register, held in Vienna, records that the files on the case were forwarded to Kielce.[17]

In the past, bluster and legal objections had delayed the implemen-tation of sentences. Now, against the odds, he had secured a stay in execution. Did he sense that, after four years, the conflict without end had only months to run? If his intermediaries had factored in this possi-bility, then the plea for clemency orchestrated through the Kommando der Besetzungstruppe assumed vital importance. A recommendation for mercy on the eve of Polish independence might well be favourably received but, if the war dragged on, his chances of avoiding the firing squad were slightly reduced.

He sweated through high summer. There was time aplenty for him to retrace the paths that had brought him back to Poland. The hounds of curiosity had tracked him to the farthest corners of the earth and uncovered most of his burrows but never retrieved the story which only he knew and kept hidden. Many of those who knew of his physical and psychological assaults on prostitutes, about the unaccounted-for disappearance of women central to his life, or about the systematic rape and torture of women destined for the white slave trade had, like his cousin, Joe Anker, since died or, like Rachel Laskin, were confined to a distant asylum. His darkest secret was safe. The great Cimmerian pondered his crimes as the Allies counter-attacked in the west and the Austro-Hungarians and Germans slowly realised the war could not be won. His appeal for leniency and case notes by Zechbauer were sent back to Przemysl at almost exactly the same time that Berlin and Vienna directed their first serious overtures for peace to the United States.

The files remained in Kielce, but the appeal for clemency clamoured for a decision. The Austrians did nothing, until one morning he was taken from Jaroslaw on the short journey to Przemysl. What happened next is, as with so much in the life of the Fox, unclear but it is almost certain that he was executed. On 1 October 1918, an officer in Jaroslaw noted that the case had been brought to a conclusion in keeping with the – now missing – notes relating to the matter. It was an appropriate, yet infuriatingly vague endorsement. Old Volpone and his faithful Mosca denied the hounds the satisfaction of a final glimpse of his fate as he disappeared down the archival burrows for the last time.[18] Joseph Lis never reappeared. The Great War ended a week later – at the eleventh hour of the eleventh day, of the eleventh month.

Somewhere in a field in Poland, beneath a blanket of snow, lies a neglected mound. Perhaps that grave, like another roasting beneath an African sun, is marked by a number only. Silence embraces them, but those who listen carefully can hear the murmurings of tragedy. Say Kaddish; they were born in the first vexing times.

XXV

SILVER'S SECRETS:
WHITECHAPEL, 1888[*]

In high art and pure science, detail is everything.

Vladimir Nabokov

Suppose we catch the Whitechapel murderer, can we not, before handing him over to the executioner or the authorities at Broadmoor, make a really decent effort to discover his antecedents, and his parentage, to trace back every step of his career, every hereditary instinct, every acquired taste, every moral slip, every mental idiosyncrasy? Surely the time has come for such an effort as this. We are face to face with some mysterious and awful product of modern civilization.

Southern Guardian, 5 January 1889

A Problem

PERHAPS the only uncontested statement to be made about events in the East End, in 1888, is that, during that year, Whitechapel was the location of a set of unprecedented, interlocking assaults and murders that left a lasting impression on the western imagination. The original interest, fanned by the first newspapers enjoying mass circulation, never waned

---

[*]My early diagnosis of Joseph Lis as a classic psychopath was first confirmed in discussions with Professor L. Roos of the Department of Psychiatry, at the University of Pretoria. The systematic development and extension of my understanding of Lis's behaviour as psychopath and neurosyphilitic, however, owes most to the generous advice and expert guidance of Professor Robert Kaplan, Forensic Psychiatrist at the Liaison Clinic, Wollongong, Australia. Any remaining errors of fact or interpretation are, alas, all my own.

Joseph Silver as a young man, a picture used by continental police during the
Low Countries campaign, 1909–1910.

and has, in the twentieth century, been supplemented by new insights into the motives of serial killers derived from Freudian psychology and modern psychiatry. Beyond those observations, however, just about everything crumbles beneath the weight of competing analyses and interpretations. True, an uneasy consensus has developed around the idea that the slayings of Mary Ann Nichols, Annie Chapman, Elizabeth Stride, Catherine Eddowes and Mary Jane Kelly constitute an irreducible core once all extraneous matter has been drained from the bloodbath and form the so-called 'canonical five' murders. But even that is questioned. The number of murders attributable to one or more hands is contested, the possibility of there being other victims before and after the canonical five is debated, and some even doubt that the slayings were confined to London. The enduring interest in this, the greatest whodunit of all time, comes from the deep-felt need to establish the real identity of the killer, the almost mythological 'Jack the Ripper'.[1]

Part of the problem in establishing the killer's identity stems from the need assumed by some analysts to explain why the murders ceased after the slaughter of the final victim, Mary Jane Kelly. Some candidates have appealed to sleuths, in part because there were such clear-cut ends or terminal points of their suspects' careers once the murders ceased. Montague Druitt, barrister, committed suicide in 1888. Aaron Kosminski, a barber, was committed to Colney Hatch Lunatic Asylum in 1891. Severin Klosowski, a barber-turned-publican, emigrated to the United States, in 1891, and later returned to London where, in 1903, he was hanged as 'George Chapman' for poisoning three of his wives.[2] As we shall have occasion to note, however, while there is reason to ask why the murders ceased, there is no need to accept the attendant notion that serial killers, having embarked on a murder spree, have a need to continue killing until they are apprehended.

In recent times a certain weariness has set in amongst those searching for suspects. Aware that false lights have sometimes been set upon cliff tops, the best researchers insist on keeping their eyes firmly on the narrow, but safe, path of primary sources. It is precisely *because* good scholars understand the limitations of the surviving documents that they are frustrated by the absence of material that has been lost or misplaced. No wonder a note of resignation has crept into the writings of some analysts. It is almost as if they now accept that existing evidence may never yield a definitive answer and that it will be impossible to show, 'beyond reasonable doubt', who 'the Ripper' was.[3]

The conclusion is perhaps unduly pessimistic and rigorous investigators need to be careful not to overstate problems to the point where
they discourage those wanting to do the research that waits to be
done. The suggestion that 'the identity of Jack the Ripper isn't really
very important. It's the story of those crimes, of the women who died,
and of the society and the time in which they lived that matters' is
a touch disingenuous.[4] Social history is an adjunct to, not a substi-
tute for, rigorous enquiry. Nor does it help to be told that the killer
perhaps had 'no discernible motive beyond the desire to kill and mutilate'.[5] We must never lose sight of the mutilation of the reproductive
organs and harvesting of the body parts of the victims and the need
to link these facts to the advances made by forensic psychiatrists in
the study of the personalities of serial killers. Difficult as it might be,
we need to acknowledge that two principal questions endure: *who*
perpetrated the murders and *what* could the motive be for such gruesome slaughter?

If, for understandable reasons, these two fundamental questions are
skirted, it leads to related observations equally lacking in conviction.
Thus, one usually cautious analyst is tempted into suggesting that, 'like
most serial killers, Jack the Ripper was a sordid man, empty in soul
and spirit, of no particular merit or distinction', and that he died 'name
unknown, his secret unsuspected'.[6] A second, equally judicious, historian is driven in the same direction: 'there is every possibility that the
man the Victorians called "the master murderer of the age" was in
reality a complete nobody whose name never found its way into the
police file . . . some sad social cripple who lived out his days in obscur-
ity, his true identity a secret now known only to the dead'.[7]
Uncharacteristically rash speculations from otherwise careful analysts
are born of a frustration we all share; of an inability to rise above the
limitations of our fragmentary primary sources. 'History,' one analyst
concludes somewhat reluctantly, 'can take us no further. Perhaps
psychology can.'[8]

Indeed it may, but a search that relies on a blend of history, psychology
and silence is not promising, smacking, as it undoubtedly does, of scholarly alchemy. But, given where we find ourselves, we have to experiment, hoping to stumble upon the truth. Joseph Lis, to saddle him with
his real name, in 1888, went to his death thirty years later, in 1918,
shrouded in mystery, clutching a vital secret – where he was and what
he was doing, between 1885 and 1889. Once we have discounted his

dissembling and placed Lis in London, we can use modern psychiatric findings to assemble a profile of the East End killer and then re-examine his mind and motives before and after the Whitechapel murders, before trying to establish whether or not he was indeed 'Jack the Ripper'.

Perfidy in Albion: A Man, a Place and a Time

Throughout his adult life, Lis made conscious and consistent efforts to keep hidden his birthplace and earliest travels. He took pains to conceal what should have been the most innocent period of his life – from the time he applied for a passport to proceed to England as a sixteen-year-old, in Russian-Poland, in 1884, to the moment he entered Sing Sing, in October 1889. For him, the need to keep moving and search out new stimuli was part professional necessity, part illness; he cloaked them in deceit and lies. Yet amidst all the routine dissembling and obfuscation, lies of commission and omission, the thing he wanted most to hide was his presence in London, the East End and Whitechapel, in 1888.

The first omission, which later had to bear a load of other, commissioned, lies, came in his application to become a naturalised American, in 1891. In retrospect, it was an application so lacking in detail that it may have been processed corruptly. He failed to disclose his date of birth, in 1868, or to indicate when or where he had first entered the United States. In 1895, when first applying for an American passport, he trimmed a year off his age, claiming to have been born in Warsaw in 1869, thereby bedevilling attempts to establish his date and place of birth or to trace the document he left Russian-Poland with in 1884–85. He then claimed, falsely, to have entered the United States on the *Bothnia*, at New York, in February 1885, and to have lived there continuously for ten years.

Dissembling on this scale, about fundamental facts relating to birth, place of origin and emigration paths is unlikely to have been prompted by the desire merely to conceal the petty thefts of a youthful offender. It hints at more serious, perhaps even truly heinous, crimes being hidden in the period so deliberately concealed.

In 1914, he reapplied for an American passport. Still untruthful as to his date of birth, he now changed his place of birth to Myslowitz, Silesia, leaving him without a direct link to Kielce, Poland, or the Russian administration that had sanctioned his original journey to England. He also stated that, with the exception of the period 1901–2, during which he was in Cape Town, he had lived in the United States continuously since 1885. This concealed not only his first stay in the East End, in 1885–89, but time spent on the South Bank and in Whitechapel, in 1895–98, when he was prosecuted for very serious sex offences.[9] All these lies are at odds with his and Adolph Goldberg's admissions in open court, when there was nothing to be gained from it, to have met, in London, during the first quarter of 1889. Nor do they tally with information provided by Lis, during an interview with the tough-minded lawyer, Frank Moss, in 1895. While seeking employment as a detective/special agent, Lis told Moss who was looking into his background that he had first entered New York City in 1889.[10] That, too, was commensurate with his having already acquired a command of English before 1889, during a stay in London between 1885 and 1889.

These crucial deceptions are also at odds with other facts pertaining to the period 1887–89. It can be proved that, in late 1887, Lis's closest friend, the actor Adolph Goldberg, lived at 3 Vine Court, and that a Lewis Lis, 'general dealer', resided at nearby 35 Plumber's Row, in the heart of Whitechapel. It is an established fact that, in December 1887, Goldberg was party to a burglary at Spiegel's warehouse, opposite the general dealer's store, and that shortly thereafter Lewis Lis and his family abandoned their home and appear to have emigrated. From what is known of Goldberg and Lis's subsequent close collaboration it would have been an extraordinary coincidence for the burglary at Spiegel's to have taken place without Joseph Lis's prior knowledge, at an address that just happened to be opposite a business owned by somebody whose surname also happened to be Lis. What is far more likely – but cannot be proved conclusively – is that Joseph Lis was well known to Adolph Goldberg before late 1887, that he enjoyed some access to Lewis Lis's premises at 35 Plumber's Row – until 30 September 1888 – and that he was implicated in the burglary.

Joseph Lis's documented falsehoods were also mocked by a living reality that placed him in the East End between 1885 and 1889: his illegitimate daughter, Bertha. While she was an infant and farmed out to an unknown woman for raising, her date and place of birth were of little consequence to her father whose earliest East End exploits were being concealed by a set of lies accumulating in the offices of the American administration. Once Bertha linked up with her father and his stepbrother, Jack, in various underworld activities, in 1905, however, the situation changed. She came under pressure not only to conceal *her* date and place of birth so as to mask her own crimes, but to help safeguard *his* secret – that she had been conceived in 1887, and born in the East End, in 1888. Throughout her adolescence and well into her late twenties, as long as she circulated within the wider orbit of her terrifying father, Bertha Lis buttressed her father's lies.

Joseph Lis's claim, in 1905, that she was laid up in a hospital in the East End, Bertha's subsequent journey to Hamburg to join her aunt, the family's onward journey to German South West Africa, and her frequent returns to England in later life all spoke of a Jewish upbringing in London. So, too, did the fact that it was the place where she lived with her uncle/husband, Jack, registered the births of their two sons and that, when asked for the name of a close contact, in 1915, gave the name D. Dorfin (Dorfman), of Hessel Street, Whitechapel – a woman whose husband was a music hall artist living at an address only a few minutes' walk away from Vine Court, where Goldberg lived, and Plumber's Row.[11]

What we know of Joseph Lis's movements after obtaining a passport, in Poland in 1884, and his later travels, as well as the flanking movements of his cousin, Joseph Anker, his 'brother', Jack, and daughter Bertha, all point to him having spent 1887–88 in London. But, even if Lis were in Whitechapel at the time of the murders there is no incontrovertible evidence linking him to the killings. The knife covered in blood – 'the smoking gun' – was not to be found in 1888, and it may now never be retrieved.

In the absence of conclusive material evidence, the best we can do is to try and understand what might have shaped the mind and motives of the killer and then explore to what extent they were consonant with what we know of Joseph Lis. But since most of what we know of Lis is drawn from his later life, we have to explore the archaeology of Joseph Silver's thinking and behaviour in the hope of discovering there fragments that point to the killing fields in Whitechapel. It is an arduous, difficult journey that takes us down through various layers of the mind, including those of the anti-social personality, the psychopath, the serial killer and then, of necessity, the world of the neurosyphilitic.

An Articulation of Insanities

'Serial killers' are defined as persons who have murdered at least three people. Studied as a group, a disproportionate number appear to come from families characterised by absent or distant fathers who were often physically, and sometimes sexually, abusive. Ambivalent relationships with their mothers are considered critical to the shaping of their personality disorders. Young boys who go on to become serial killers appear to have been troubled by the real or imagined promiscuity, or strong sexual proclivities, of their mothers. In a significant number of cases these problems were compounded by inappropriate intimate, physical contact between mothers and sons, provocative displays of nudity, or the witnessing of parental, or other, couplings.[12]

The earliest signs of an emerging disorder might include abnormal or deviant sexual behaviour, an inability to concentrate and chronic inattentiveness, lying, thieving, fire-setting, torture of animals, truancy or bed-wetting. In young adults, other symptoms might include abuse of alcohol or other substances, callousness, sadistic sexual fantasies and homosexual as well as heterosexual experiences. Most *acts* of serial killing appear to come in the wake of the abuse of alcohol or other substances, and sexual fantasies of a sadistic nature. Many serial killers seem to have predisposing genetic factors, or to have suffered some form of head trauma, including blows to the head.[13]

Serial killers, including sexually sadistic killers, tend to suffer from low self-esteem and display their desire to exercise total control over and/or humiliate victims who are often unknown to them prior to the fatal encounter. In short, biological, genetic, psychological and sociological factors all contribute to the make-up of serial killers who are overwhelmingly, but not exclusively, male. What is striking about sex killers who need not necessarily be serial killers, but who are often psychopaths, is the youthful age at which many claim their first victim. In a recent study of sex killers, in America, it was found that in a sample of thirty-three, 39 per cent had claimed their first victim by the age of twenty.[14]

Given that most serial killers are what, since Cleckley's studies in the 1940s, is termed 'psychopaths', it is important to understand the nature of psychopathy. Psychopaths manifest a cluster of five core features which can be distilled from a longer list of traits developed and refined by Cleckley's distinguished successor, Hare, in 1991. First, psychopaths, who have normal, sometimes even above-average, intelligence, are non-delusionary persons and do not display significant intellectual or psychiatric problems in clinical settings. Secondly, they manifest a general lack of empathy, have 'shallow emotions', disregard the feelings and rights of others, are highly manipulative and are unable to develop genuine or lasting relationships with others. Thirdly, psychopaths, characterised by their anti-social behaviour, are unable to accept responsibility for their actions or to show remorse. Fourthly, they manifest an inability to control their behaviour effectively and have a propensity to act impulsively. Fifthly, psychopaths often have a highly transient lifestyle and, constantly seeking new or novel experiences, seldom undertake long-term planning or enter into long-term personal commitments.[15]

If small numbers of serial killers are seen – like acrobats – to be standing on the shoulders of more numerous psychopaths, then psychopaths, in turn, stand squarely on the shoulders of an even larger number of deviants whom psychiatrists see as suffering from Anti-Social Personality Disorders (ASPD). In order to understand more fully the origins, nature and manifestations of psychopathy then, it is necessary to devote some attention to ASPD. In doing so, however, we should note that while the pyramidical structure outlined here can be safely viewed from top-down in attempting to understand its load-bearing human platforms, it cannot be inverted and seen from the bottom up without diminishing its explanatory power. Put simply, while almost all serial killers are psychopaths, and all psychopaths display elements of Anti-Social Personality Disorder, not all ASPD sufferers are destined to become psychopaths, or all psychopaths serial killers. Overlaps between categories do not make for inevitability.[16]

ASPD, in which genetic factors play a minor but important part, occur in about 3 per cent of the male, and 1 per cent of the female, population. The disorder is five times more likely to occur in cases where first-degree male relatives, such as the father, also suffer from the disorder than in cases where they do not. Inconsistent maternal care is a contributory factor and there is general agreement that 'parental deprivation or deviance' during the formative period of separation-individuation of the child is critical to the development of the disorder. ASPD is more common among young adults, especially those who are mobile, living in urban areas and drawn from lower socio-economic groupings. Biochemical studies suggest that low serotonin output reduces glucose regulation and increases the propensity in many sufferers to consume alcohol; while psycho-analysts also point to homosexual tendencies, misogyny and the presence of an Oedipal complex.[17]

Superficially charming and with good verbal abilities, those ASPD sufferers who go on to become psychopaths are capable of initiating but not maintaining relationships. Aggressive, fearless and impulsive behaviour leads to fights or bouts of rage in which a reckless disregard for their own, or others', safety is manifested. Deceitful, manipulative, parasitic, prone to using aliases, lying and unreliable, psychopaths are not inherently disposed to criminal behaviour. But, exposed to an abnormal social environment, or having sought it out, they will readily adapt to it as if it were the norm. Perpetrators of anti-social or criminal acts, they are frequently arrested and given to argumentation, conspiracy theories, paranoid views and elaborate rationalisations. 'Splitting', notes one analyst, 'remains [their] main defence'. This means that people about whom psychopaths have ambivalent feelings are often divided into inner, inchoate, categories of 'good' or 'bad' which, in turn, further shapes the deviant's own, often amoral, behaviour. Early observers saw psychopaths as 'morally insane' but, lacking delusions, they present, in a telling phrase, a 'Mask of Sanity'.[18]

The interconnections between ASPD, psychopathy and serial killing make for striking similarities in the manifestation and denouement of the disorders over time. The importance of this in the case of Lis and the Whitechapel murders is difficult to overstate. The onset of ASPD, one set of psychiatrists observes, occurs most frequently at the age of fifteen and, 'once an antisocial personality disorder develops, it runs an unremitting course ... with the height of antisocial behaviour usually occuring in late adolescence', although 'symptoms decrease as persons grow older'. Others specialists agree: 'Antisocial behaviour is most pronounced in early adult years and gradually decreases with age' although some 'maturation of the personality might also take place' later.[19]

Some Symptoms Manifest

A review of Lis's childhood (age 0–16), the inferred 'missing' part of his life, in London, 1885–89 (16–21), and what we know of his early manhood in New York City and Pittsburgh (22–27) is commensurate with his having suffered from ASPD from the time that he collected his passport in Kielce and left for England. What is incontestable is that, from the moment he entered the United States, in 1889, until the end of his life in 1918 (aged fifty), he manifested the symptoms of a fully developed psychopath. Hare's 'revised check-list for psychopathy' (PCL–R), reads like a profile of Lis's inner life: glibness and superficial charm, grandiose sense of self-worth, need for stimulation, pathological lying, deceitfulness and manipulativeness, lack of guilt or remorse, shallow affect, callousness and absence of empathy, parasitic lifestyle, poor behaviour controls, promiscuous sexual behaviour, early behavioural problems, lack of realistic long-term goals, impulsivity, failure to accept responsibility for own actions, many short-term marital relationships, juvenile delinquency, revocation of conditional release, and criminal versatility.[20] None of this, of course, makes Lis a serial killer. But we know, with certainty, that, in addition to his mental afflictions, Lis suffered from neurosyphilis.

Syphilis manifests itself in four successive, but unequal, phases. The primary stage is marked by a lesion on the penis, 'the pox' of yore, which soon clears but, four to eight weeks later, is followed by the secondary stage which gives rise to eruptions and skin rashes on the face or back. In the tertiary stage, spirochetes embed themselves in the soft tissues of the body and brain, and can take from one to five years to manifest themselves as sub-acute, chronic symptoms including headaches, lethargy, malaise, a loss of concentration, emotional instability and irritability. The quaternary stage usually presents about ten to twelve years after the primary infection but can take as little as three or as many as twenty years to manifest itself. Abnormalities in pupil size and responses to light are accompanied by shooting pains in the lower limbs, difficulty in controlling handwriting, and the development of a high-stepping gait. In its final phase, the disease affects the central nervous system, resulting in insanity and, in its terminal stages, a general paralysis. The onset and development of insanity, which varies from patient to patient, can manifest itself in bombastic behaviour during which the victim may have delusions of power.[21]

The impact these stages had on the life of the young Lis and, more especially, on the middle-aged Silver, need not detain us here since they take us beyond the Whitechapel murders. Three linked points do, however, need to be made. First, working back from the admissions register in Sing Sing, when the lesions on his face were visible and note-worthy (1889), the onset of a pattern of expansive behaviour (1895) and the tell-tale handwriting of the syphilitic (1903) it would seem that Lis's primary infection dated back to late 1887, or early 1888. Regardless of the exact date, however, Lis could not have failed to notice the appearance of a chancre on his penis or understood its significance. With the possible exception of a brief spell in his early forties, Lis had a lifetime's involvement with prostitutes of all ages and the most likely source of his primary infection was one of the thousands of unregulated streetwalkers in Whitechapel.

For Lis, there was a world of difference between streetwalkers and brothel-based prostitutes. Both sets of women were dangerous and redolent with the potential for pollution, but streetwalkers were relatively independent women who retained a measure of initiative, no matter how small, as they set out to hawk their sexual temptations, in public, amongst men *they* ultimately chose. In brothels, women working within controlled, private spaces were approached by men who sought them out for sexual connection. Disease proffered randomly by street-walking females *to* men differed radically from the danger of pollution sought *by* men who chose to seek out and sleep with prostitutes.[22] It took two to copulate but, in the two cases, the initiative and locus of control differed. Streetwalkers – like dirt, 'matter out of place' – were a source of danger to men, combining a potentially fatal mixture of sexual temptation and infection. As a source of defiling menstrual fluids and vectors of infection all women, but especially prostitutes, were an abomination. Whores, who sometimes even sacrificed their children in their unbridled pursuit of sexual pleasure, had 'blood [on] their hands'.[23]

Secondly, Lis's more expansive behaviour ran from around 1895 to 1906 (ages 27–36), and coincided with the high-energy consumption required for mid-career achievement. To an extent, his self-importance was rooted in real, official duties: first, as a special agent in New York (1895) and later as detective in Kimberley (1902). Thirdly, just as Lis–Silver was approaching a stage in his life where it might be reasonable to expect a gradual amelioration in his psychopathic condition, neurosyphilis prolonged his changing notions of grandeur. For most of his life Silver was psychopathic *and* neurosyphilitic.[24] It is only against this broad backdrop that one can develop a deeper understanding of the psychological underpinnings of Lis's behaviour from the moment that he left Kielce, in 1885, through to the moment that the murders in Whitechapel commenced, in 1888.

There is no point in rehearsing here all the details of Lis's childhood. The first-born child in a family comprising six children by the time he left home and eventually nine, he was packed off to *cheder* just before his mother had an illegitimate child by an unknown lover.[25] 'Parental deprivation and deviation' during his formative period and a father who, if not sexually abusive, was known to have questionable morals, could not have assisted in the boy's development.[26] Public humiliation, in the form of newspaper reports about his father's involvement in a burglary, at a sensitive time in the twenty-four months leading up to his bar mitzvah, may have alienated him not only from his wayward father but from the elders in the community and the overtly religious dimensions of Judaism in the synagogue.[27] As we shall see, however, there is also reason to believe that a Jewish boyhood left him with vivid images of a vengeful God, derived from the Bible and *aggadah*, folklore, in which gross female immorality was especially harshly dealt with.[28]

Lis's most ambivalent feelings were reserved for his sexually charged, unfaithful mother, Hannah. Whilst the dead cannot be interviewed, their deeds can be interrogated and therein lie the clues to the depth of his love for his mother. The most obvious example of his affection is evident in the way in which, on his release from Sing Sing, and seeking to make a clean start, he used her maiden name, Kwekzylber, to fashion himself a new family name, 'Silver'. But his love of Hannah was not confined to that single, symbolic instance: it spilled over into more intimate manifestations in his life.

In violation of Jewish custom Silver not once, but twice, married women with the name Hannah/Anna. Taking brides who bore the same name as his mother set him apart from the codes supposedly governing him, just as surely as did the fact that, by marrying the women in civil ceremonies, he consciously distanced them from their religious roots. The symbolic significance of this may lie in the realm of psychoanalysis, but is not difficult to speculate about. In the same way it needs to be noted that, within weeks of his leaving Whitechapel and entering New York, in 1889, he took up with a woman whose real name was Esther Heller but who, for purposes of prostitution, either took on or, more likely, was given the name 'Annie'. Part of Joseph Lis loved his mother, and perhaps it was that same, largely unfulfilled longing for her which towards the end of his strange life spurred him on to return to her, to Kielce and the eastern front.[29]

Silver's two recorded marriages were both to brothel-based prostitutes rather than streetwalkers and their subsequent fate remains unknown. Hannah Opticer (1895) and Hannah Vygenbaum (1902) disappeared at awkward junctures in Silver's life, never to be heard of again. No mention of the marriage to Opticer was made at his rape trial, in 1898, when his wife might have been able to give evidence of character for either the prosecution or the defence. Vygenbaum disappeared when she was due to give potentially incriminating evidence against him at a trial in Cape Town, in 1905.[30] After each of these marriages he reverted to referring to himself as a bachelor and, later in life, described himself as a widower at moments when it was impossible to tell either who his most recent wife might have been, or what unfortunate fate might have overtaken her. Hannah Opticer and Hannah Vygenbaum, like 'Rose', the mother of his illegitimate daughter, Bertha, were never again openly spoken about by him, by his daughter, by his loyal stepbrother Jack, or by any of the cousins who were in his thrall. It was as if they were all long dead.

In the Whitechapel murders, however, it was not affection for a mother that drew the killer to most of his victims, but an intense hatred of women with loose sexual morals, of prostitutes in general and streetwalkers in particular. The earliest victims in the sexually motivated, sometimes fatal, knifings which preceded the murder and mutilation of the canonical five, were all middle-aged. Annie Millwood (25 February) was thirty-eight, Ada Wilson (28 March) was thirty-nine, Emma Smith (3 April) was forty-five and Martha Tabram (7 August) was thirty-nine. With the exception of Mary Jane Kelly (9 November) who was twenty-five and an exceptional case, the canonical five were also middle-aged. Mary Ann Nichols (31 August) was forty-three, Annie Chapman (8 September) was forty-seven, and Catherine Eddowes (30 September) was forty-six. Elizabeth Stride (30 September), whose body was not mutilated – because her killer was interrupted – was forty-four.

In itself, the age of each victim is not especially important. Viewed collectively and placed within the broader context of modern findings about the emergence of serial killers, they assume greater significance. Some authorities argue: 'The victim, in the majority of cases, a woman, became the target of the "badness" from the mother'.[31] Another analyst suggests that, 'the impulse to sexual homicide might be set in motion primarily as a mechanism for exacting revenge against persons symbolically representative of the hatred-inspiring parent. Where the mother was the offending parent, one might speak of the future serial homicides as symbolic matricide.'[32] In Lis's case, aged twenty at the time of the murders with a mother then thirty-eight, it is difficult to attribute his motives exclusively to Hannah Kwekzylber's real or perceived inadequacies.[33] As noted, Lis's feelings for his mother appear to have been ambivalent rather than uniformly hostile and his father, too, led a life that was hardly unblemished. That noted, observations about the propensity to transfer the mother's 'badness' ring true.

But if we lack total insight into parental influences on Lis's earliest experiences so, too, does a full understanding of his adolescent sexuality and the accompanying fantasy life to which modern-day analysts attribute so much significance elude us. We cannot know exactly what accounts or experiences excited or inflamed his imagination. One tale, however, may have been unavoidable. The claim that 'the uterus and other organs were extracted from female corpses for the purposes of making thieves' candles which, according to superstition, caused those on whom the light fell to go to sleep', could not have been lost on an adolescent with a burglar father.[34] In 1884, shortly before Lis left home, a Galician Jew, Moses Ritter, was tried for raping a Christian girl in a village near Kraków and then hiring a Christian Pole to murder and mutilate her in order, so rumour had it, to make a thieves' candle. It is difficult to imagine this tale not reaching Kielce.[35]

Lis's earliest homosexual experiences, too, can only be the subject of conjecture but his later behaviour is consistent with possible sexual abuse at the hand of his father or his mother's lover.[36] We also know that, between the ages of sixteen and twenty (1885–88), he sought the company of men in barbershops, boxing booths and gambling dens – settings that excluded females and boasted talk that tended to objectify and sexually demean women. Whether his preference for male company gave rise to homosexual acts of affection and/or physical release in unknown, but it is notable that his closest friendships during early manhood (1885–95) were with two men who were fifteen and seven years older than he was – Adolph Goldberg and Charles Jacobs. It seems reasonable to suggest that his homosexual experiences probably gained their fullest and most sustained expression during the two-year spell in Sing Sing between the ages of twenty-two and twenty-three (1890–91). By the time he was thirty-one, he had been convicted of sodomy, for a non-consensual sexual act, in Johannesburg. The latter offence, however, came at a time when he was entering into a phase of more expansive behaviour and is as likely to have been induced by neurosyphilis as psychopathy. Like most psychopaths, once confined, Lis tended to be a model prisoner.[37]

His attitude towards, and sexual experiences with, women after puberty are also unclear although, perhaps not unusually, he had fathered a child by the age of twenty. If, however, his actions and attitudes towards women after the age of twenty-five offer clues to what his behaviour might have been like during adolescence, then it demonstrates a profound hatred of women and their sexual organs, a willingness to live off them in parasitic form as a pimp, and to buy and sell them as a white slave trafficker. To understand this misogyny fully it is necessary to digress briefly, and reflect on aliases he used during his career. He often took on the names of acquaintances like Abraham Ramer or James Smith (an important issue that we shall return to in the context of the Whitechapel murders). When his identity as 'Lis' imploded at the age of twenty-three, in Sing Sing, he emerged as Silver. When he linked up with his younger stepbrother Jacob/Jack shortly thereafter, the latter became his henchman as 'Maurice Silvermann'. But Lis also adopted names designed to mock law enforcers, or to signal his private hatred of women.

As Silver, 'president' of the 'pimps' union', in Johannesburg, Lis gave the 'secretary' of the organisation, a relative of Goldberg's, the alias 'Joe Gold'. Silver and Gold thus controlled the underworld in the mining capital of the world at a time when the virtues of bimetallism were being debated. Love of punning, a Yiddish trait, seldom deserted him. When Lis joined an experienced gang of safe-crackers in a round of robberies at financial institutions in the Low Countries in 1909–10, he took the self-mocking name Greenbaum – a name suited to a 'greener', a rookie. When an immigrant, English-speaking detective in Cape Town enquired as to whom he had sold a house used as a brothel, Lis gave himself the mocking Afrikaans-Dutch name 'Nieman' – 'no one'. He also made it his business to keep abreast of the most notorious case of mistaken identity in his lifetime, that of Adolf Beck, also no stranger to London's low-life. In 1906, Silver, in a tight spot in German South West Africa, urged the judge in his trial to familiarise himself with the recent Beck case. Spreading confusion about names and identities was central to Lis's extraordinary peripatetic career.[38]

But there was a more sinister dimension to Lis's aliases. Whilst extorting money from prostitutes in Johannesburg, in 1898, at the apex of his criminal career, he suddenly took on the name 'Ludwig'. Charles Ludwig, it will be recalled, was a barber and knife-wielding Jack the Ripper suspect working in the Minories who had menaced a woman with a large knife and was later prosecuted for threatening to stab a young man at a coffee stall in Whitechapel High Street. There was, of course, another barber, who may have been an equally chilling, and proximate, model for Lis.[39]

Severin Antoniovich Klosowski, a former *feldscher* and later as 'George Chapman' a notorious wife-poisoner, used the name 'Ludwig Zagowski' while employed in barbershops in Whitechapel in 1890, perhaps even earlier. A compatriot, three years older than Lis, who hailed from Nagornak 125 miles north-west of Kielce and had served an apprenticeship in the adjacent province of Radom, Klosowski spoke Yiddish and sometimes passed himself off as a Jew. A hairdresser with a liking for late nights and perhaps prostitutes, Klosowski emigrated to the United States in 1891 and, a man after Lis's heart, admired things American. Both were given to adopting aliases, consummate liars, fascinated by pharmaceutical products and the criminal law, ruthless misogynists and snappy dressers. Lis had a lifelong liking for men like his stepbrother who, if they were not out-and-out psychopaths were dangerously anti-social. In Kimberley one of Lis's closest confidants was the treacherous pimp and jewel thief Sam Rabinowitz, and in Santiago his partner was the clearly demented white slave trafficker Gil Steiman. It seems eminently plausible to suggest that Lis and 'Ludwig Zagowski', young Polish barbers, men with well-developed sexual appetites and given to experimenting with their ethnic and religious identities, became acquainted in London's East End in 1887–88.[40]

In Johannesburg, thousands of miles away and a decade after Lis's unhappy time in England, the name 'Ludwig' was subtle and indirect enough for its significance to be lost on police and prostitutes alike. But Lis's hatred of prostitutes was not confined to verbal games and, on half a dozen occasions, he recorded his contempt for them in his contorted, syphilitic handwriting.[41] Argumentative and legalistic after exposure to the American constitution in courts and legal processes Lis – manifesting a touch of paranoia – never hesitated to address letters to judges or senior state officials, pointing out what he believed to be 'conspiracies' against him by prostitutes.[42] Nor did he hesitate to threaten them with assault or worse. These were not idle threats. The hapless Rachel Laskin was so badly battered by him in the American Hotel in London, in 1897, and again a year later, in Johannesburg, that it may have contributed to brain damage and the insanity that ensued. Disturbed by a woman during a burglary in Manhattan only months after fleeing the East End, he told her that he would kill her if she screamed and then, quite gratuitously, spat in her face on his way out. When a prostitute lured into one of his brothels, in 1903, told him she would leave he told her, *'My Dear Girl, if you do not remain here I will kill you, I will murder you'*. Then, in a phrase, the full import of which only he could know, he said: *'You do not know who I am. I am Joe Silver'*.[43] Indeed, she may well not have known who Silver was. Nor would she have known that 'Joseph Silver' itself was a construct that dated back only to New York in 1893, and that beyond that, in times past, lay Whitechapel, Lis and heaven knew what other identities.

But it is not just that he continued to menace prostitutes until he was into his forties that is of interest to those trying to make sense of the Ripper murders, but the forms that his conspiracies and threats against them assumed. As with many sexually sadistic killers who are psychopaths, and like the East End murderer, Lis not only hated women but had a particular loathing of sex organs with the potential for infection and pollution. Here, again, there is circumstantial evidence pointing to biblical readings influencing the way in which he sought to manage this problem amongst the Jewish prostitutes confined to his brothels.[44]

After menstruation, married Jewish women are under *halakhahic* injunction to undergo ritual purification by stripping and immersing themselves in a *mikveh* or other, designated, baths before resuming sexual relations with their husbands.[45] For the young Lis, who grew up within a few blocks of a *mikveh* and developed a prurient curiosity in monitoring the movements of female innocents and the worldly-wise alike, public baths were places of enduring interest. As a pimp, in his thirties and forties, with his sex drive waning beneath advancing neurosyphilis, ritual cleansing demanded his attention. In Cape Town, he acquired a half-share in the Caledon Street Baths in District Six, in the street housing the largest number of Jewish prostitutes in the city. In Swakopmund, where the baths were notorious as a site of sexual danger, he cycled prostitutes under his control through the premises. In Valparaiso, kept away from the city centre, he opened a brothel in Urriola Street, opposite the Almendro Baths. In Leviticus it is written that: 'The woman also with whom man shall lie with seed of copula-tion, they shall both bathe themselves in water, and be unclean until the even.'[46] For Lis there was a need for prostitutes in brothels to undergo ritual cleansing and, if *their* vaginas were menacing, how much more so those of the uncontrolled streetwalkers?[47]

A focus on the female sex organs by a misogynist who was carrying a clasp knife at the time of his first recorded arrest, for burglary in 1889, and who continued to carry one until he severely stabbed a fellow pimp, in London in 1898, hints at possibilities but, in itself, proves nothing. Nor does it help to know that his exposure to the barbering and tailoring trades familiarised him with the scissors and razor. But how many such trifles can one lay at the feet of the Goddess Coincidence before faith itself is questioned? The evidence against Lis – seemingly so slight in its individual components – needs to be viewed collectively, not singly. Cumulatively, it points not only to his expressed willingness to murder, but to murder prostitutes and mutilate their sexual organs. In Johannesburg in 1899, at the very moment he was presenting himself as 'Ludwig', five prostitutes testified, under oath, that he had threat-ened them with unspecified 'bodily harm'. A sixth woman was more specific. He told her that if she give evidence against him, he 'would open up her belly'.[48] Was this a madman's poetic licence, or was it born of personal experience?

Like the barber-poisoner Klosowski, Lis appears to have developed an interest in 'knock-out' drops and other stupefacients used in the white slave traffick during his early twenties, while in New York; perhaps earlier. In London in 1897–98, members of his gang added a chemical 'smelling of cloves' to alcoholic drinks in order to drug women prior to raping them. A few months later, in Johannesburg, Lis befriended a medical doctor and a pharmacist whose outlets supplied abortifacients and medicines for sexually transmitted diseases to pimps and prosti-tutes. Seven years later, in German South West Africa, he was in the inner circle of a group plotting to insert 'blue vitriol' into the vagina of a recalcitrant prostitute. This diabolical thought was the product of a mind obsessed with cleansing and curing, or destroying and muti-lating, the sexual organs of 'whores'.[49]

In retrospect then, we know that Lis, a man at the apex of a psycho-pathic condition at the time of the East End murders, later harboured the most destructive thoughts imaginable about the reproductive organs of prostitutes. Yet, without the bloodied knife, a deathbed confession, or some hitherto undiscovered eyewitness placing him at the scene of the murders, many will remain sceptical that he could possibly have been, let alone was, the elusive Ripper. The latter are extreme tests which, given police efforts at the time and some poor archival work thereafter, can never be met by historians. That, however, is insufficient reason for accepting the psychological profile of a killer, without adducing circumstantial evidence to back the claim that a new suspect has been identified.

This brings us to a question that is unavoidable. If Lis, who threatened prostitutes for two decades after the East End slayings, was the Whitechapel murderer, then what stopped him from committing more such murders in later years? This is a persistent question and one which, in the popular mind, provides the rhetorical flourish with which all known suspects are now routinely dismissed. It prompts two answers. First there is nothing inherent in psychopathy or serial killing to suggest that, once started, murderers have to continue their slaughter until they are successfully apprehended. London, in the mid-1960s, witnessed the murder of between three and six prostitutes at the hands of an unknown serial killer. But then, after three murders in eight months, 'they stopped altogether and the mysteries were never solved'.[50]

A second response is to suggest that we simply do not know that Lis did not kill again and that, as in the East End in 1888, he remained unidentified and undetected. He was certainly never questioned about the murder of a prostitute, let alone about one involving the systematic mutilation of the female sex organs. That, in itself, does not prove or disprove anything. Prostitutes, often rootless women without strong family ties, are favourite targets of psychopaths and notoriously difficult to trace or identify once they disappear.[51]

But here again, we need to digress and reflect on Lis's ever-changing 'bachelor'/'widower'/'married' status as he moved about the Atlantic world. On his return to London in 1895, seven years after the Whitechapel slayings and on his marriage to Hannah Opticer, he described himself as a 'detective's agent' and 'widower'. Was this some sort of sick joke? Having just completed a tour of duty as 'special agent' for the Society for the Prevention of Crime, his willingness to cast himself, rather grandiosely, as a detective is perhaps understandable. But who, pray, was the 'wife' he had lost? Could it have been that, in his disturbed state, he had symbolically 'lost' his lover-mother-wife back in Kielce? Or was the departed one perhaps his daughter Bertha's mother, who, like many others in the mid-1880s, might have died in childbirth? Or, had he unexpectedly taken leave of some other, equally real but unknown, woman back in New York or Pittsburgh – like Rosa Schmidt – for whom there is no death certificate? Or, most disturbingly of all, had he, during his earlier visit, in a way that only he knew, symbolically or really 'lost' another Hannah-like 'lover-wife' in Whitechapel, in 1888; someone like, say, the gruesomely butchered Mary Jane Kelly?

On entering Brazil, in early 1915, he told the authorities in Rio de Janeiro he was a widower. Which of his common law or legal wives had passed away in the interim we again do not know. Just a year later, upon re-entering the United States, after another intervening stay in the East End, which he returned to again and again, he informed US officials that he was married but provided no details about his new wife. Whereas certificates for two of his official marriages can be retrieved, there seem to be no death certificates for any of the missing 'Mrs Silvers'. In Lis's mind the word 'widower' obviously had meaning but what that may have been, and to whom it may have referred is unknown. He was either a man with extraordinary bad luck – twice made a widower from undocumented, presumably natural causes before he reached the age of fifty – or he was a man who, when placed under pressure, was capable of losing a wife.[52]

If Lis was unlucky enough to have lost an unknown number of wives, then there is no record of sadness, of ceremonies, of graves, of farewells, of letters, or mention of how, where or when even 'legally' acquired wives were lost. The haunting silences around the one, traumatised common law partner that can be traced could fill a universe. His systematic physical and psychological dismantling of Rachel Laskin was a matter of complete indifference to him. There was no sign of contrition for having assaulted her, for driving her insane, for having had her committed to a 'madhouse', for refusing to pay for her upkeep, or for having left her to die in a colony thousands of miles from her kin. His daughter and stepbrother, too, never once spoke or wrote of his deceased wives.

Lis's closest flesh and blood fared no better than the lost wives. He abandoned Bertha almost at birth, and certainly before her first birthday. He did not see her again until he reappeared in the East End in 1895, when she was seven years old. He then left and only re-engaged with her when she was seventeen. Her moral development concerned him no more than did her prostitution. Nor did it trouble him that she married his half-brother, Jack, or that she had children by him at a time when the boundaries of incest were being renegotiated. Not once did he even glimpse the sometimes hazy line that divides vice from virtue. Like a short-sighted man, he sensed from what others said that there was something out there, but all he experienced was a puzzling blur. He responded, as do most psychopaths, by attempting, as best possible, to split what he could not sense into 'good' and 'bad' but was then utterly incapable of keeping the categories sufficiently far apart to be able to act on them in a manner that allowed for deeper coherence, consistency or even stability.

His persistently anti-social behaviour, most evident before the age of forty, was marked by a readiness to betray underworld accomplices to the police and in that sense he was a 'criminal-policeman'. That drew him even further into the moral twilight, into poorly lit recesses where criminal intelligence was traded for short-term advantage or profit and it was impossible to tell where 'justice' lay. So plausibly could he trade at the stalls of deception, half-truths and lies that he became a 'special agent' for the Society for the Prevention of Crime in New York in 1895, and, in 1902, a plainclothes detective for the Cape police in Kimberley. But the line remained fuzzy. While attempting to enforce the law he could never resist breaking it; he was always a 'policeman-criminal'. A confused pseudo-morality allowed him to create or destroy prostitutes with almost equal alacrity.

What possible light might such a non-cohering process of 'splitting' throw on the East End murders? Are there remaining psychological or other clues that might point to Lis?

Experiments with Death:
The Good Fortune of an Apprentice Murderer

Psychiatrists who have studied the mindsets of murderers point to cumulative pressures resulting in a crisis which can be the prelude to killing. A 'catathymic crisis', they suggest, 'is characterised by a seem-ingly insoluble psychic state of chronic and aversive tension (called an incubation period), projection of responsibility for the internal tension state onto the external situation (the marriage or the spouse) with the perception arising that violence is the only way out of the situation'.[53] Those studying serial killers also point to sadistic fantasies which may be followed by preliminary behavioural 'tryouts' which, if undetected, could be followed by a series of core, incrementally violent, homicides. What can these modern findings tell us about the assaults on Annie Millwood, Ada Wilson and Emma Smith that took place between 25 February and 3 April 1888? And what, if anything, can they tell us about the mindset of Joseph Lis in 1888?

It is impossible to know what exactly Lis was thinking during the earliest part of his stay in the East End (1885–86). What we do know is that he felt that he had been betrayed by his morally lax mother, that he had powerfully misogynistic tendencies and that he had a deep-seated hatred of prostitutes whose reproductive organs were, simultaneously, a site of sexual temptation as well as a source of venereal infection and pollution. He may also have tried to distance himself from his Jewish roots, toyed briefly with Protestantism and, almost certainly, re-read the works of the later biblical prophets.

What *is* certain is that he found himself in an environment highly charged by covert and overt debates relating to the dangers of female sexuality including the raising of the age of consent to sixteen in 1885, the publication of Stevenson's Jekyll and Hyde in 1886, and an attempt to rid the East End of brothels by F.N. Charrington in 1887.[54] The latter year must have been particularly stressful, perhaps even an 'incubation period', since it coincided with a heightened sex drive, contracting syphilis and impregnating 'Rose', a woman whom he never again chose to identify or support. February to March 1888 coincided with the final trimester of the pregnancy which culminated in the birth of Bertha, whose most likely date of birth, we have noted, was 25 April 1888. If Rose was but a streetwalker, it would have been a period of escalating tension for Lis as he contemplated what becoming a father might entail. If Lis did briefly assume responsibility for the confined mother of an unwanted child, then it may just have spurred him into being more active than usual in extracting cash from streetwalkers in Whitechapel.

The approaching birth would also have unleashed within him other deep-seated anxieties rooted in moral dilemmas he could never fully escape. Like Hannah, the sexually active mother whom he loved and loathed, a woman who had given birth to a *mamzer* – a child born of a man other than her husband – he was about to sire a child out of wedlock.[55] His mother, who had abandoned and betrayed him, was a woman he had turned his back on as an adulteress, if not a harlot, and now he was trapped in a similar situation. Women everywhere were vectors of pollution and most, if not all, were whores. What store of knowledge about moral matters did he have to draw on other than the lurid biblical tales of vengeance he had been exposed to as an adolescent, or the sometimes brutal medieval folklore of the Jews he despised? If as seems likely this was happening, then a fatal convergence was taking place – a 'catathymic crisis' if ever there was one.

Two of the 'tryout' assaults – on Ada Wilson and Emma Smith – are of interest since, unlike in the Millwood case, they yielded potential clues to the identity of the assailant/s. Ada Wilson lived in Maidman Street, Bow, well beyond the customary haunts of the 'Ripper'. She escaped death, on 28 March, when 'a strange man of about thirty with a sunburnt face and fair moustache' came to her house, 'demanded money and, drawing a knife from his pocket, stabbed her twice in the throat. He was five foot six inches tall and dressed in a dark coat, light trousers and wideawake (broad-brimmed soft felt) hat'. Several researchers, it should be said, find her tale implausible.[56]

The assault on Emma Smith by three men, on 3 April, is, any case, more important for anyone wanting to establish the identity of the moving force behind that and the murders that followed. Indeed, the very fact that Smith was attacked by a gang, a small 'mob', may, in retrospect, prove to be a first, significant, clue.[57] She was raped by her assailants and a blunt object then rammed into her vagina, causing the rupture that induced the infection from which she died within thirty-six hours. She had an ear badly torn during her ordeal; a second, small, biblical clue pointing to one of the assailants.[58] On this occasion, the information forthcoming was more interesting and reliable than that supplied by Ada Wilson. Before expiring, Smith recounted how she had seen three men approaching her in the Whitechapel Road but, seeking to avoid them, had crossed the road, been followed and attacked opposite 10 Brick Lane. One of her attackers, she alleged, was a youth, of about 'nineteen years' old.[59] It may well have been a third clue.

Emma Smith's account is consistent with her having known one or more of her assailants and, if there was one whom she recognised, then it was probably the young man about whose age she was so precise. Given the circumstances, it would not have been unreasonable for her to have estimated her assailant's age as 'about twenty', or say, under 'twenty-five'. What, other than knowledge based on prior experience, caused her to settle on the age *nineteen* at a time when, just weeks before, Joseph Lis had turned twenty? Could it not be precisely *because* she had previously been a victim of Lis's predatory and/or violent behaviour that she was reluctant to get the police involved after her assault? Walter Dew, a policeman who was later to help verify the murder of Mary Jane Kelly, left memoirs which were sometimes confused, or just plain wrong in regard to some of the details of the Whitechapel murders. But, for him, one thing always stood out clearly: 'I have always held that Emma Smith was the first to meet her death at the hands of Jack the Ripper'. Dew must have had *one* of Smith's three assailants in mind when he recorded that observation, but which one?[60] Could it have been the youngest?

If Lis was one of Smith's assailants, and in retrospect this seems a distinct possibility, it raises further, unavoidable questions for those seeking to establish the Ripper's identity. Who were the other two assailants? Why, after the unintended death of Smith, and the deliberate slaying of the prostitutes that followed, did they not reveal their misgivings or suspicions to police investigators? Again, the harsh truth is that we do not know who they were, nor are we likely ever to establish their identities beyond doubt. What we can do, however, is speculate as to who they may have been on the basis of three common-sense assumptions. First, it is reasonable to assume that the two older assailants shared Lis's misogynistic disposition. Secondly, Lis, possessed of charismatic qualities, may have had them in thrall through a combination of charm or terror aided by underlying ethnic or linguistic affinities. Thirdly, Lis's links to them may have been cemented by kinship or friendship arising from professional associations.

The category, stretched but slightly, could be made to include several familiar suspects to be found in the best of the literature dealing with the East End murders. Charles Ludwig, the knife-wielding German barber from the Minories, or Severin Klosowski, the unstable Polish hairdresser who had so much in common with Lis, present themselves as obvious candidates. It could also have included another knife-wielding threatener of prostitutes, the notorious John 'Leather Apron' Pizer sometimes to be found in Mulberry Street, just a block away from Lewis Lis's general dealer's store in Plumber's Row. We just do not know but, again with the benefit of hindsight, some of these suspects appear to have been more of the 'loner' type and are unlikely to have formed part of what would, in essence, have constituted a 'gang'. If so, there are two other, plausible, candidates that we need to interrogate.

In mid-December 1888, shortly after the fifth of the canonical murders, a statement made abroad by an American German, J.I. Lowenheim, was forwarded to the Home Office for consideration. Lowenheim recalled that, shortly before 'the first crime', while staying at a house in Finsbury Square, close by Moorgate, he had counseled one 'Julius Wirtkofsky' about a 'special pathological condition'; probably syphilis. Wirtkofsky, a 'Polish Jew', had told Lowenheim that 'he was determined to kill the person concerned' (for the infection) and 'all the rest of her class'.[61] No more was heard of Wirtkofsky but it is interesting, perhaps important, to note that from 1898 to 1905 the name-stealing Lis's most reliable, trustworthy and violent lieutenant was a Polish Jew with American connections, Wilf/Wulf Witkofsky. It is not known where or when Lis first met Witkofsky, but it could well have been in London in the mid-1880s. Be that as it may, Lis later used Witkofsky as an enforcer in pimping and white-slaving operations. While Lis was in prison in Johannesburg, in 1899, Witkofsky and others assaulted state witnesses, including prostitutes, to ensure that they would not give evidence against Silver.[62]

Another likely candidate for the assault on Emma Smith was Lis's older cousin, Joseph Anker. Again, we do not know when Anker first entered the East End but the most probable date is in the mid-1880s. Like Witkofsky a full-time pimp, Anker was a predatory creature willing to engage in violent sexual assaults to acquire white slaves. Indeed, it was Anker who first introduced the tragic Rachel Laskin to his cousin back in Whitechapel, in 1898, and he remained Lis's loyal henchman right from then to 1903.[63]

Regardless of the identity of the nineteen-year-old's accomplices, they were complicit in Smith's murder and had reason to remain silent about the attack and to keep any suspicions to themselves that may have arisen during the slaughter that followed. The nineteen-year-old was fortunate that Smith had died before he could be positively identified. It was not his first stroke of luck. Annie Millwood, who had been attacked during another 'tryout', on 25 February, had collapsed and died from natural causes in the South Grove workhouse just weeks after recovering from her stab wounds. Neither she nor Smith were around to assist police with their inquiries later that year when the main killing spree commenced in autumn. The good fortune of an apprentice killer emboldened a man increasingly bent on butchery. He had learned that dead women told no tales.

The Whitechapel murderer's luck held throughout the killings that followed, but the killer also manufactured his good fortune. 'The

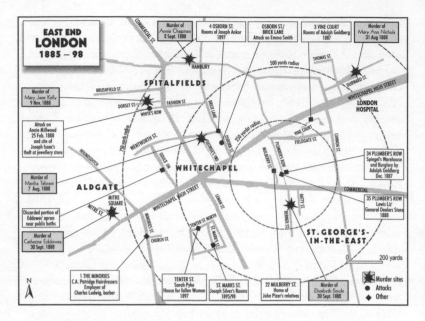

EAST END
LONDON
1885 – 98

Murder of
Annie Chapman
8 Sept. 1888

4 OSBORN ST.
Rooms of Joseph Ankor
1897

OSBORN ST./
BRICK LANE
Attack on Emma Smith

3 VINE COURT
Rooms of Adolph Goldberg
1887

Murder of
Mary Ann Nichols
31 Aug 1888

Murder of
Mary Jane Kelly
9 Nov. 1888

Attack on
Annie Millwood
25 Feb. 1888
and site of
Joseph Isaac's
theft at jewellery store

Murder of
Martha Tabram
7 Aug. 1888

Discarded portion of
Eddowes' apron
near public baths

Murder of
Catherine Eddowes
30 Sept. 1888

34 PLUMBER'S ROW
Spiegel's Warehouse
and Burglary by
Adolph Goldberg
Dec. 1887

35 PLUMBER'S ROW
Lewis Lis'
General Dealers Store
1888

1 THE MINORIES
C.A. Partridge Hairdressers
Employer of
Charles Ludwig, barber

TENTER ST.
Sarah Pyke
House for fallen Women
1897

ST. MARKS ST.
Joseph Silver's Rooms
1895/98

22 MULBERRY ST.
Home of
John Pizer's relatives

Murder of
Elizabeth Stride
30 Sept. 1888

Murder sites
Attacks
Other

0   200 yards

victims', our best guide notes, 'were comparatively few. They were drawn from one small class of the population. And they were slain within an area less than a single square mile in extent.'[64] It is what is unstated in that observation that is important – the murderer probably knew some of the victims by sight or, in the case of Kelly, even better. He also possessed extraordinary knowledge of the local, almost labyrinthine geography.

Unless we wish to believe – as Lis would have Attorney Frank Moss believe seven years after the East End killings – that, prior to 1889, he was beyond reproach and that he had embarked on his first burglary aged twenty-one, we have to accept the far more likely proposition that he was an adolescent miscreant who had been breaking and entering premises long before that, including the four years spent in Whitechapel. This is an important subject to which we shall return but, for the moment, it is necessary to note only that, until he was forty years old, Lis found burglary and store-breaking irresistible. Reconnaissance work – plotting alternating patterns of light and dark by day, night or season, establishing the safest lines of access and egress, or knowing where doors or windows were situated – was part of a routine, the quotidian habit of a consummate thief.

In the East End a serial killer would need to know the main arterial roads and streets and the human traffic they carried, as well as have an intimate knowledge of its bewildering alleys, courts, lanes, rows and yards. Jack the Ripper clearly enjoyed a measure of luck but, to the extent that he was capable of quick, brutal murder and mutilation before escaping unobserved, he made his 'luck'. Seen from this perspective the five core murders were hardly predicated on chance.[65] It also makes the perpetrator less likely to have been an artist on an occasional visit, a day-tripper down from Liverpool, a physician more at home in the West End, or some royal 'slumming it' in an unknown East End.

The Evolution of a *Modus Operandi* and Three Quick Successes

The death of Emma Smith that April was presumably a cause for serious introspection on the part of the nineteen-year-old. Whatever *frisson* of satisfaction the death of the whore unleashed in his mind would have been tempered by the realisation that the police would investigate the murder and that there was a chance that he might yet be betrayed. New to the delights of death, his desire to wreak yet more mayhem was temporarily curtailed. Perhaps he encouraged his accomplices to leave town or emigrate.

The summer of 1888 was an equally thoughtful time for Lis. The return of the sun brought people out into the streets and warmed the sluggish seasonal economy. He may have found intermittent work as a barber. But the net of normality must have struggled to contain the personality of the beast that thrashed about within him. By summer's end, the baby, born just days after Smith had died, was developing apace. No longer a small inert body that slept only to wake, cry and be fed before sleeping again, it now recognised faces, sat up, reached for objects and laughed.

The enormity of his predicament became clearer with the passing of each day; his brooding more intense. He was infected with syphilis and waited for the tell-tale rash to erupt on his face or back. Like most men with the pox he took an interest in chemical curatives and perhaps dosed himself with mercury, a treatment that produced its own, sometimes quite disturbing, side-effects. Even so he remained trapped in a distant city and, surrounded by the temptations of polluted prostitutes, was confronted by a situation which mirrored that outlined in the Book of Ezekiel where God, exasperated by the lewdness and neglect of Aholah and Aholibah, asked a mortal – a man like Lis himself – 'Son of man wilt thou judge [them]? yea declare unto them their abominations.'[66]

Summer spent, the days shortened and sharper autumn evenings trimmed the number of working people scurrying about the warrens of Whitechapel. The pressure built; never again would the tides of madness surge so high within him. As the evenings chilled, the profiles of whores on street corners stood out more clearly. Nor was he on his own in trying to wrestle with transforming impulses. His actor friend, Adolph Goldberg, could have told him how, each night somewhere on a West End stage, a doctor was experimenting with a concoction that turned Henry Jekyll into the raging William Hyde. It was precisely the sort of bizarre tale that would have impressed itself on Lis.

On an overcast bank holiday evening, Monday, 6 August, Martha Tabram was working the streets with a friend, Mary Ann Connelly, known to some as 'Pearly Poll'. They spent the letter part of the night drinking in the company of two soldiers before going their separate ways, presumably intent on attending to the needs of clients. In the early hours of Tuesday morning Tabram met someone in Whitechapel High Street, who persuaded her to accompany him through a covered archway leading to some courts and alleys. They went up an unlit staircase to the first-floor landing of George Yard Buildings. There, without sexual intercourse having taken place, he took out a large penknife and stabbed her repeatedly in the neck, abdomen and vagina. A long-bladed instrument, like a bayonet or a dagger, was probably used to inflict a deeper wound to her breast. All in all she was stabbed thirty-nine times. Her crazed assailant, amidst what today is characterised as a frenzy of 'picquerism' appears to have derived 'sexual pleasure' [by] stabbing, cutting or slicing another person'.[67]

The body was discovered in a pool of blood with legs splayed. It appeared that the victim had been attacked directly from the front and the assailant may therefore have been splattered with blood. It was a messy, risky way of wielding a knife. The killer presumably learned the lesson. In the four outdoor murders that followed, the method was apparently modified so that the knife was produced only after the victim had been subdued, often from behind and usually by strangulation. It was a method which had the benefit of limiting the victim's bleeding.[68] There were no witnesses and the police made little progress.

No similar murderous assaults took place for three weeks as the killer, pondering the path he had embarked upon, gave further thought to the pollution wrought by prostitutes and the best moment at which next to strike and clear the streets of them. It seems it was during this period that the assailant, dwelling on the biblical passages and Jewish folklore that barely outlined the earliest assaults and killings, focused more intently on the hours preceding, or following on, the Sabbath.

In Buck's Row, in the early hours of Friday morning, 31 August, the killer coaxed Mary Ann Nichols into accepting an initial approach to trade her sexual favours. From the investigations that followed it would appear that she may have been grabbed from behind and partially strangled prior to being laid on the ground where her throat was twice slit with such force by a knife that one of the cuts reached through to the vertebrae. It was a classic case of overkill. A jagged cut to the abdomen and two stab wounds to the genitalia were then inflicted. No viscera were removed but, as part of his developing 'signature' as a serial killer, the Ripper hoisted the woman's clothes 'almost to her stomach'. For the third time there was a small – still almost undetectable – sign of the biblical source that was shaping the pattern the murderer was intent on developing. One of Nichols's fingers *bore the impression of a ring*. 'There were no marks on the finger to suggest that it had been wrenched off and it's not known whether Nichols was wearing the ring on the night of her murder'. With the benefit of hindsight we can suggest that she probably was.[69] Had not Ezekiel warned the whores that: 'They shall also strip thee out of thy clothes, and take away thy fair jewels'?[70]

The police had nothing to go on but for some weeks sought, unsuccessfully, to find and interview a Polish Jew, John 'Leather Apron' Pizer. The murderer, having improved and refined his technique for the slaying of streetwalkers in semi-public places, was now growing impatient to continue his attacks on the female sites of sexual pollution and reproduction, and to extend his campaign of public purity in unmistakable fashion. On the eve of the very next Sabbath, Friday 7 September, he was back out on the streets.

Annie Chapman, second of the canonical five, was seen entering Little Paternoster Row, turning into Brushfield Street, and making her way towards Spitalfields church at about 1.50 a.m. on Saturday morning.

Some time after that a search for clients took her further east still and her body was later discovered in the yard of a house at 29 Hanbury Street. The murderer's evolving technique had worked perfectly and he left his most complete signature yet. The woman appeared to have been strangled, laid down and her throat severed with 'two cuts from left to right'.[71] 'Almost all the blood would have drained out of the divided vessels, accounting for the almost bloodless effect of the subsequent incisions in the abdomen and pelvis'.[72] It was ritualised overkill, almost like a *shochet* who, having cut the windpipe and gullet of an animal, would allow it to bleed to death before covering any spilt blood with earth. And, like the *shochet*, the killer had opened the abdomen and removed internal organs in a search for impurities or imperfections.[73] 'From the pelvis the uterus and its appendages, with the upper portion of the vagina and the posterior two-thirds of the bladder had been entirely removed.'[74]

As before, the body was discovered lying on its back with the legs drawn up as if to display the handiwork of the executioner.[75] Yet, amidst all the gruesome crudity there was again one puzzling, minor subtlety. On the third finger of her left hand Annie Chapman had worn *three brass rings* that she had bought from a black man. Despite all his exertions the butcher had made time to wrench these bits of cheap jewellery from the dead woman's fingers.[76] Whores, it seemed, were expected to eschew any adornment.

This time, however, there was a witness, Mrs Long. She had got a glimpse, in profile, of a man she thought was over forty years of age. 'He was dark and in her opinion looked like a foreigner (generally a euphemism for a Jew). He wore a brown deerstalker hat, she thought a dark coat, but was not quite certain of that, and overall had a shabby genteel appearance.'[77] Again, there was not much to go on; the murderer's 'luck' was holding.

Two days after the Chapman murder, the police arrested 'Leather Apron' Pizer at the home of relatives in Mulberry Street but he was soon exonerated. 'Pearly Poll' Connelly, Elizabeth Allen and Eliza Cooper, three prostitutes, some based in Crossingham's Lodging House on notorious Dorset Street, had made statements to the police indicating that they had reason to suspect a man living at some distance from them to the south-east of the district, *'not far from Buck's Row'*.[78] Pizer, who led a largely itinerant lifestyle and did not reside or work continuously in Mulberry Street, was clearly not the Ripper but the general direction in which the streetwalkers pointed the police is never-theless intriguing. Could the women's statements (now lost) have contained a more general clue, only partially understood or misinter-preted by police at the time? How will we ever know?[79]

Short even by Whitechapel standards, Mulberry Street debouches at its eastern end directly into Plumber's Row; the street on which Lewis Lis's general dealer's store was located. Go up Plumber's Row, turn first right into Fieldgate and, within a three-minute walk, on your left, you will find Vine Court – the address at which Joseph Lis's closest friend, Adolph Goldberg, was residing in late 1887 when he was arrested for theft from Spiegel's warehouse in Plumber's Row. The arc curving between Plumber's Row and Vine Court is significantly more proxi-mate in direction and distance to Buck's Row (now Durward Street) than is Mulberry Street. The very quarter identified by the streetwalkers – north and east of where Pizer was arrested on a visit to a relative's home – reeks of Joseph Lis.

The killer, admiring handiwork that was receiving growing public recognition, revelled in the panic it induced amongst the populace at large and streetwalkers in particular. Alongside his troubles and self-doubt it gave him a feeling of importance and transformed him from passive victim to active agent. He waited to see what progress the police made. 'None', was the answer. He did not want to be caught, but he did want people to understand that he was the offspring of a people he despised, the child of a mother whom he loathed and that he drew his inspiration from an ancient Masoretic text. Three weeks passed. The East End threatened to return to normal and the whores started moving about more freely, peddling their sex. He waited for the eve of the next Sabbath.

Confidence Unbound and Significant Signs Unheeded – Two Murders in One Night

Joseph Lis, a Jew almost only by virtue of his birth, must have moni-tored the murder of the prostitutes, the mutilations and the removal of a uterus – the source of the child that now trapped him – with approval and fascination. In much the same way he would have been delighted by the mounting terror that gripped sections of the East End. In later life, too, he was often the secret, and sometimes not-so-secret, instigator of great moral panics which, spurred on by sensationalist news-papers, swept through Bloemfontein, Cape Town, Johannesburg, Santiago and Valparaiso like sluiced water. The hidden influence he exercised while inducing mass fear and social disorder fed his narcis-sistic personality. Nor would it have distressed him that, after the Chapman murder, the attention of the penny press focused on the blameless John 'Leather Apron' Pizer, or that 'the indignation of the community quickly developed anti-Semitic overtones and on the day of the [Chapman] murder the crowds assembling in the streets began to threaten and abuse Jews'.[80] As we shall see, for all that he harboured within him grandiose biblical notions, Lis held organised Judaism in contempt and was very poorly disposed to religious Jews.

Indeed, in order to put distance between himself and the Jews he hated, he later passed himself off as a 'Protestant' on the basis of rudi-mentary knowledge of the Church that could only have been acquired during his stay in London. The most obvious conduit for this flirtation was the Church of England's mission in the East End, the London Society for Promoting Christianity amongst the Jews. The local branch, under guidance of a converted Jew, the Reverend J.M. Epstein, encour-aged Jews to convert and attended to the medical needs of poor Jewesses. But the society was also a magnet for manipulative or psychopathic personalities, such as Lis and Trebitsch Lincoln, in search of a bed, a meal or small sums in cash. In 1885, the year Epstein took control of the society's operation in Spitalfields, he recorded his disappointment at being exploited by Jewish 'hypocrites' and 'impostors'. Lis hated Jews almost as much as he did his parents and anti-Semitic sentiments, or an ethnic disturbance in the East End, would not have troubled him at all.[81]

The International Working Men's Association, popularly known as the Berner Street Club and linked to the socialist newspaper the *Worker's Friend* in the building behind it, was another venue frequented by East Europeans with little sympathy for organised Judaism. Shortly before the next murder, the canonical third, which took place in the yard adja-cent to it, the club hosted a gathering at which secular Jews publicly renounced their religion.[82] Berner Street, off Commercial Road, was virtually an extension of Plumber's Row, immediately north of it. The club premises offered good social cover for any irreligious Jew bent on mischief.

Elizabeth Stride's body was discovered behind the gate beside the club after the Sabbath, in the early hours of the morning of Sunday, 30 September 1888. Her assailant, it would appear, had been disturbed before he could complete his gory business because the corpse lacked the signature that was becoming associated with the killer. The doctor who arrived at the scene at 1.16 a.m., very shortly after the woman's death, reported that:

> The incision in the neck commenced on the left side, 2½ inches below the angle of the jaw, and almost in direct line with it, nearly severing the vessel on that side, cutting the windpipe completely in two, and terminating on the opposite side 1½ inches below the angle of the right jaw, but without severing the vessels on that side . . . The blood was running down the gutter into the drain in the opposite direction from the feet. There was about 1 lb. of clotted blood close by the body, and a stream all the way to the back door of the club.[83]

Although the woman's legs were drawn up, they were not splayed and, given that the killer had not had the opportunity to engage in the mutilation of the lower abdomen, the victim's clothing had been left alone. As in other cases, it seemed that Stride's body had been laid down after she had somehow been subdued. There were no ring marks on the victim's fingers. The murderer, disturbed before he could complete his mission, had fled.

This time there were two witnesses able to offer descriptions of the suspected killer – a policeman and one Israel Schwartz who had earlier seen a man manhandling Stride on the pavement opposite the spot where the body was discovered.[84] PC William Smith, who had passed through Berner Street on his beat, recalled seeing a man with a woman he later identified as Stride. 'The man was about five foot seven and wore a dark overcoat and dark trousers and was wearing a hard felt deerstalker hat. He was clean-shaven and appeared respectable, and Smith guessed his age to be about 28.' Schwartz saw a man; 'age about 30. 5 ft 5 in. comp[plexion] fair hair dark, small brown moustache, full face, broad shouldered, dress dark jacket & trousers, black cap with peak, had nothing in hands'.[85] None of this seemed to matter much since the murderer had hurried off into the night.

Minutes later, at 1.44 a.m. that same morning – the night of the so-called 'double event' – the body of Catherine Eddowes, the canonical fourth victim, was found nearby in the semi-enclosed confines of Mitre Square, an area that fell within the jurisdiction of the City. 'The throat was cut, the wound extending about six or seven inches from the left ear to about three inches below the lobe of the right ear.'[86] 'There was a quantity of clotted blood on the pavement on the left side of the neck, round the shoulder and upper part of the arm, and fluid blood coloured serum which had flowed under the neck to the right shoulder – the pavement sloping in that direction.'[87] The scene presented could have come from an abattoir.

'The abdomen was all exposed; the intestines were drawn out to a large extent and placed over the right shoulder; they were smeared with some feculent matter; a piece of about two feet was quite detached from the body and placed between the body and the left arm.'[88] The killer '. . . had removed the left kidney and the uterus was cut away with the exception of a small portion, both organs being absent, presumably taken away by the murderer'.[89] In addition, unusually, there had been 'great disfigurement of the face'.[90]

In the confines of the square, the murderer had greater opportunity to express his rage – in that sense, it was a portent of worse to come. His signature, boldly written, was there for all to see. The body lay on its back, thighs naked, 'the right leg bent at the thigh and the knee' to emphasise the lewdness of the whore, and 'the clothes drawn up above the abdomen'. Near her right hand lay a thimble but there was again no sign of a ring, or marks on her fingers to indicate that she had worn one. The killer had, however, embellished his work and that, too, was a sign of things to come. He had taken a moment to slice off 'the tip of the nose'; and see to it that 'the lobe and auricle of right ear was cut obliquely through'.[91] The ear later fell off in the mortuary.

God's work amongst the whores, as outlined by Ezekiel, had been done: 'And I will set my jealousy against thee, and they shall deal furiously with thee; they shall take away thy nose and thine ears; and thy remnant shall fall by the sword; they shall take thy sons and thy daughters; and *thy residue shall be devoured by the fire'.*[92] The destination of the missing uterus was probably clear, but if there were lingering doubts they were soon to be dispelled by the scene that would be encountered at the site of the fifth, and final, murder. The significance of these new clues seems to have been as lost on observers at the time as it has been on scores of analysts who have pored over them for a hundred years since. They were signs which only a concerned rabbi or distressed Old Testament scholar dreading the pogrom that the perpetrator secretly yearned for, could have kept silent about. But the killer, anxious to avoid another silence about the source of his inspiration, moved off into the blackest night bent on leaving an even more blunt directive elsewhere.

Yet again there was a credible witness who may have caught a glimpse of the murderer not long before the slaughter on Mitre Square commenced. According to that informant, who seems to have been under-utilised, 'He was aged thirty, five foot seven or eight, of fair complexion, with a fair moustache, of medium build, wearing a pepper-and-salt coloured loose jacket, a grey cloth cap with peak of the same colour, and a reddish handkerchief tied in a knot round the neck and having the appearance of a sailor.'[93]

At this point we have to pause and note that, of all the victims, Eddowes and Stride were the two most at ease in the company of Jews. When not prostituting herself, Eddowes 'got her living by hawking about the streets and cleaning amongst the Jews', or doing 'charring' as a 'shabbos goi'.[94] It seems that from her street-walking experiences Eddowes, like Emma Smith before her, had an idea of who the murderer was. Returning to London after hop-picking and warned about the new danger, she is said to have replied: 'I have come back to earn the reward offered for the apprehension of the Whitechapel murderer. I think I know him.'[95] If she did know him, and if he knew that she suspected him, it may help account for her brutal ending since psychological profilers claim that 'facial mutilations are evidence that the killer and the victim are known to each other'. Again, in hindsight, we can see that that, too, may have been a portent of the even greater horror to come, since the closer the relationship, 'the more extreme the mutilations'.[96]

Stride's connection with East European Jewish immigrants may have been at least as close since, unusually, she spoke some Yiddish. This fact may have acquired additional importance at a time when anti-Semitic sentiment was becoming a cause for official concern. If the killer knew his victims, or they half knew him, might it not have facilitated an initial seemingly friendly approach in such fraught times?[97]

But let us return to the chase on that Night of the Signs; the only occasion on which the killer left a material clue hinting at identity and motive. *Where* did he go upon leaving Mitre Square? What underlying considerations, consciously or subconsciously, dictated his exit path on a night when he seems to have *wanted* his pursuers to understand the symbolic significance of the route he chose to retreat along? After butchering Eddowes, the killer cut some cloth from her apron and used it to mop himself and wipe clean the blade of the knife. Then, still clutching the rag, he moved in an easterly direction keeping off, but parallel to, the busy Aldgate High Street which a few blocks further east became Whitechapel High Street.[98] His final destination could well have been Plumber's Row, but he suddenly looped north, into Goulston Street. *Why?*

The killer, who came across as 'shabby genteel' in appearance and took some interest in his apparel, would have been familiar with, and comfortable in the area – the 'commercial nucleus' of the Jewish East End. 'This was the Lane: not the Petticoat Lane of the Sunday morning tourist but the six-day street market in Wentworth St. and the narrow turnings off it – mainly Old Castle St., Bell Lane and Goulston St. as well as parts of Middlesex St.'[99] Goulston Street housed a new and second-hand clothing market that was supplied with legal and illegally accquired goods that appealed to a man with a meagre income seeking to keep up appearances or, for that matter to thieves, such as those from Spiegel's warehouse, disposing of 'hot' property.

On the night of the 'double event', however, the murderer was not interested in acquiring new garb, but in using a bit of Catherine Eddowes's apron to cleanse himself; to rid his clothing, knife and person of unwanted blood. It was unlikely to have been a conscious, fully thought through act but it is nevertheless noteworthy that he chose to drop the bloodied, polluted rag on the stairs to the entrance of the building at number 108–119 Goulston Street. It was a spot only yards from the local *mikveh* where women cleansed themselves after menstruation.[100] Had not the prophet Ezekiel also recorded: 'Then will I sprinkle clean water upon you, and ye shall be clean: from all your filthiness, and from all your idols, will I cleanse you'?[101] Goulston Street was a mandatory port of call for all polluted women, including many of the filthy whores that infested Whitechapel.

There was nothing unconscious about his next action. Directly above the discarded apron fragment, in what Detective Daniel Halse later described as 'a good schoolboy hand' – the hand of a young person – he chalked the words: 'The Jewes [*sic*] are the men that will not be blamed for nothing'. Later still that morning senior police officers,

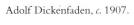
Adolf Dickenfaden, *c.* 1907.

Market Square, Bloemfontein,
c. 1903 with offices of
The Friend newspaper
front left and Post Office
in the background.

Bloemfontein Station,
c. 1903.

Court building and
advocate's chambers (front
right), Maitland Street,
Bloemfontein, *c.* 1903.

George Dacheux (alias Le Cuirassier, alias Bach), business confidant of Joseph Silver in Cape Town, *c.* 1904.

Koskes Boarding House (left), St George's Street, Cape Town, *c.* 1890.

Bertha Silver, Paris, 1909.

Swakopmund, German South West Africa, 1909.

Neumünster Prison,
Schleswig-Holstein.

S.S. Bürgermeister, the ship on which Silver was transported from German South West Africa to Neumünster Prison in 1906.

Jack Lis (Jacobo Jack Lyss),
Santiago, Chile, 1912.

Joseph Silver
(Paris Police), 1909.

Mendel Cohen,
Portsmouth, 1907.

Leibus Brjiski,
Antwerp, 1909.

Noe Traumann,
Chairman, Zwi Migdal,
Buenos Aires, 1907.

S.S. Amazon.

Joseph Silver as Josè Silva,
Santiago, Chile, 1912.

Joseph Silver,
passport photograph,
New York City, 1914.

344, 4th Street East, New York, Silver's residence, *c.* 1915.

S.S. Mauretania.

sensing the approach of daylight, and fearing that the graffito might well incite untold violence against the Jews once it became visible to members of an already over-excited public, eventually instructed that it be removed. A sponge was used to wash it down.[102]

Again, as with the *mikveh*, it may have been by chance that, of all the streets available to him on that Night of the Signs, the killer just happened to leave a chalked message on a building in Goulston Street. But how many coincidences can we stack upon one another before they collapse into meaning and pattern, albeit unintentionally? The street was the site of the Society for Promoting Christianity amongst the Jews' Goulston Street Mission Hall.[103] If there was any street in Whitechapel in which Jews were routinely confronted by the challenge to repent their sins and reflect on the correct approach to God, then it was Goulston. In Goulston Street, where the Jews were publicly warned about the error of their ways, they were constantly exhorted to become Protestants. What better place to warn all and sundry that the Jews were blameworthy?

Here, we again need to pause and reflect on the nature of Lis's rela-tion-ship with Jews and Judaism. Born a Jew, he was raised as a Jew, and the two wives he married in formal civil ceremonies were both Jewesses. Almost without exception his friends and business partners in a lifetime of crime were deracinated, secular Jews. With few excep-tions, he showed a lifelong preference for recruiting, exploiting and working with Jewish prostitutes. He was aware that many saw him as a 'Jew' and once while in prison, in Bloemfontein, asked to be released in order to be able to observe the Jewish holy days.

But if ever there was a classic case of Jewish self-hatred and psycho-pathic 'splitting' then it was Joseph Lis–Silver. In everyday life he befriended, tolerated and worked only with those 'Jews' who, with defi-cient or lax moral codes, showed contempt for Judaism and its values. For him, the only good Jew was a bad Jew; one whose anti-social behaviour and practices might bring shame on the community and ignite the embers of anti-Semitism. Lis wished destruction on decent law-abiding Jews. He lived a predatory existence, seeking to exploit or plunder their persons and property. In his quest to control and domin-ate women he assaulted, raped or seduced young Jewesses while Jewish males, especially jewellers, were a favourite target for theft.

Likewise, his most cynical betrayals were reserved for vulnerable, criminal Jews, while vendettas, revolving around personalised notions of 'justice' and 'law enforcement', were aimed at slightly better-off, professional Jews. Gil Steiman, David Krakower, Leon Alexander and Max Harris could all bear testimony to the former, while Detective Charles Jacobs and Attorney Louis Lezard were witnesses to the latter. If Lis's relationship with prostitutes said something about his relationship with his mother, Hannah, then perhaps his relationship with pimps said something about his father, Ansel.

So anxious was he to distance himself from Jews and Judaism that, after fleeing the East End, and being admitted to prison in the United States in late 1889, he took a calculated risk and told an unbelieving warder that he was a 'Protestant'. When perceived as being Jewish, or seen to be associating with Jews, he cast himself as a victim by distorting information in ways that reflected poorly on Jewish customs and practices. Sensing Frank Moss's underlying anti-Semitism, he portrayed himself as the dupe of an unscrupulous *shadchan*, a matchmaker, when, in fact, he was part of a gang of pimps, prostitutes and white slavers. If ever there was a man who would revel in the gathering discomfort and fear of the Jewish community in Whitechapel; a person who would welcome the social anarchy that might follow upon widespread looting and rioting in the Jewish East End, it was Lis. Would not a twenty-year-old psychopath be capable of chalking up on a wall, in 'a good schoolboy hand', 'The Jewes are the men that will not be blamed for nothing'?[104]

If then in some perverse way Lis saw himself as a failed Jew, a latter-day Hyde-like mutant, the offspring of an abusive father and harlot mother, of supposedly Jewish parents, were there other clues pointing to his 'Jewishness' and a special hatred of the prostitutes who moved freely amongst the Jews around the Sabbath hours? In order to establish this we need to go back and probe some of his other ideas and experiences.

We will never know the full extent of biblical ideas, folklore or superstitions about sexual behaviour and mores that lodged in Lis's consciousness from the time that he could store information and images, read and write. What we do know, however, is that 'the golden age of hasidic anthology, beginning in the 1860s, was overtly and covertly influenced by the folklore renaissance sweeping through Europe at the time'.[105] The younger Lis's mind was – in part – shaped at precisely the historical moment when the fanciful, strange and weird had an exciting new purchase on the popular imagination.

Only a handful of his letters survive but, even from those, it is evident that he retained bizarre, violent images of biblical or medieval provenance that revolved around issues of retribution and vengeance. When he realised that Lorimer, his detective-handler in Cape Town was about to betray him, he pleaded, 'Do not give me up to the fury of an angry mob who would like to see me burned at the stake.' A few months later, in Windhoek, in a letter of appeal to the Governor, he conjured up an image of biblical Sodom and cast von Lindequist as the 'Angel of the Lord' – a thinly disguised, version of the Hebrew 'Angel of Death' (malakh ha-mavet) – who would 'find out and destroy the court' that had sentenced him.[106] From the Middle Ages until at least the 1870s East European Jews, eschewing blood-letting but seeking simultaneously to cleanse their communities of anti-social elements, drowned their informers in mikvot or rivers. In one instance, the body of a collaborator was incinerated in the bathhouse's furnace.[107] Hardly surprising then that Lis, the consummate police spy, regaled his handler in Valparaiso with a partly fictionalised account of the fate of two gangsters who had betrayed the Zwi Migdal. The informers, he said, had had their arms broken before being thrown into a river to drown.[108] The violent nexus of folkloric and religious ideas loosely linking blood, cleansing, death, fire, mikvot, purification and pollution was firmly established in Lis's tortured mind.

In the same way, it might be asked whether the Bible was the direct, or even the sole, source of inspiration for the murders in Whitechapel. Medieval rabbinical writings recorded that communal reactions to 'serious sex offences' had assumed forms 'foreign to Jewish tradition' to include banning, '. . . flagellation, monetary fines, public disgrace, branding, shaving of the head, or cutting off the nose'.[109] Is it possible that somewhere Lis had heard echoes of writings that drew on Ezekiel, rather than Ezekiel itself? If so, Catherine Eddowes was possibly the first victim to have her nose removed since the last recorded case in fourteenth-century Spain. Not surprisingly, this important clue was lost on a world that focused more eagerly on sexual organs than appendages like noses and ears.

Signs unheeded deeply irritated a man intent on implicating the Jews he hated. But obscure clues pointing to medieval Jews were lost on biblical scholars, fearful rabbis and the hard-pressed police alike. They were certainly beyond a public utterly enthralled by tales of prostitution, sex and mutilation. The next murder – and the unfortunate victim's history – could have been taken almost directly from the pages of the book which everybody professed to know.

The October Sabbatical: Preparing for the Personal

The targets and technique of the East End murderer, fuelled by a hatred of prostitutes and perhaps compounded by personal misfortune triggered by a venereal infection, had mutated steadily during 1888, and the attacks may even have dated back to late 1887.[110] Exploratory physical assaults, imperfectly conceived, had commenced in spring 1888, with seemingly random attacks on women on their doorsteps, or in the case of Emma Smith, by a gang working the streets, and then, for whatever reason, had ceased during high summer. When the slaughter proper commenced, in autumn, it focused on streetwalkers who were coaxed into contemplating copulation in semi-public places before being murdered and having their uteri harvested. A chance encounter in Mitre Square with a woman he may have known allowed the murderer to express his loathing of streetwalkers more fully. When that butchering, too, went undetected the groundwork was laid for a personalised attack on a victim well known to the murderer. Increasingly convinced of his invincibility, the killer moved sweetly from the unknown to the known.

After the 'double event' of September/October Lis, going about his business under an assumed name, may have shifted his activities away from lines running close to Whitechapel High Street, to a point further north. With the notable exception of the Chapman murder, in Hanbury Street, all the murders had taken place in a belt lying on either side of the High, with Plumber's Row off to the right, close to the centre of the zone of death. If all this did indeed happen – and these probabilities will be explored fully below – we can only speculate as to why it might have been so. Perhaps the murder of Elizabeth Stride, in Berner Street, just a stone's throw away from Lewis Lis's general dealer's store at 35 Plumber's Row, had prompted a rift amongst the Lis clan?

In retrospect, there may have been something to the gloomy memoirs of the head of the Criminal Investigation Department written in 1910. Sir Robert Anderson noted:

> One did not need to be a Sherlock Holmes to discover that the criminal was a sexual maniac of a virulent type; that he was living in the immediate vicinity of the scene of the murders; and that, if he was not living absolutely alone, his people knew of his guilt, and refused to give him up to justice. During my absence abroad the Police had made a

house-to-house search for him, investigating the case of every
man in the district whose circumstances were such that he
could go and come and get rid of his blood stains in secret.
And the conclusion we came to was that he and his people
were low-class Jews, for it is a remarkable fact that people
of that class in the East End will not give up one of their
number to gentile justice.[111]

If Lis, under an assumed name did abandon the Plumber's Row
vicinity, then it seems that he moved north, nearer to Dorset Street
where the woman he by now loathed more than any other in the East
End lived. Throughout October he observed her movements, monitoring the pattern and volume of traffic in the courtyard in which she
lived. Gaining untrammelled access to her would be difficult since she
was also the common law wife of a porter working in the Billingsgate
Market. It was frustrating, but he was patient. Then, on the second-
last day of the month, the man who shared her small room in Miller's
Court suddenly moved out. It was the moment the killer had been
waiting for. He found a room for a short-term stay around the corner
from Dorset Street. He was in Little Paternoster Row.

The Perfect Execution of a Whore:
The Hand of Man and the Voice of Ezekiel

Mary Jane Kelly was different. She was young, just twenty-five, physically attractive and sufficiently clean and well dressed to attract the
attention of men, including, presumably, off-duty sailors and soldiers
frequenting the area. Detective Walter Dew remembered encountering
her on the streets where she was 'invariably wearing a clean white
apron' and Melville Macnaghten, who never saw her but was later to
become the assistant commissioner CID, had heard it said that she was
'possessed of considerable personal attractions'.[112] Mary Kelly may
have thought so herself. Others certainly did.

She was born in Ireland but, as a child, had moved to Wales where
her father held a position in an ironworks. At about the age of sixteen
she had married a collier named Davis, or Davies, but was widowed
two or three years later when he was killed in an explosion. At some
point before, or as likely after his death, a cousin in Cardiff introduced

her to a life of prostitution and, possibly as a result of her new lifestyle, she spent some months in an infirmary. Around 1884, she moved on to London and found herself a position in a West End brothel where a client was so taken with her services that he persuaded her to leave the country and accompany him to Paris.

But France was not to her liking and she returned to England where, for whatever reason, she was unable to reclaim her former status and took to street-walking in the East End. The loss of caste was difficult to accept and she retained some affectations, sometimes calling herself Marie Jeanette Kelly. She clung to the few items of finery she still possessed, including a few expensive dresses. Given the advantages that age, class, dress and experience had bestowed upon her, she retained the ability to attract men interested in more than casual, commercial sex. At different times she had taken up with favoured suitors and intermittently led the life of a common law wife. The first of these live-in lovers was a man by the name of Morganstone who lived near the Gas Works in Stepney but, after leaving him, her life was beset by three different men, all named 'Joe'.

The first Joe was Joseph Flemming, a plasterer, who lived in Bethnal Green. Part of Kelly's problems stemmed from her ability to develop genuine feelings for her lovers and care about their well-being. She remained on good terms with Flemming even after they had separated. In April 1887, after having lived for a time on her own in Cooley's Lodging House, Thrawl Street, Spitalfields, she met a second Joe, Joseph Barnett, an Irish cockney, a hawker and later a porter. The couple got on well but shared a penchant for liquor which did not help pay the rent and they moved through a succession of lodgings in George Street, Little Paternoster Row and Brick Lane. At the beginning of 1888, they rented 13 Miller's Court, in Dorset Street, from John McCarthy, owner of a chandler's shop.

They lived without apparent rancour or mistrust until Barnett's income started to falter. Possibly at about the same time Mary Jane took to supplementing their income by street-walking. Her prostitution displeased Barnett, who left her, though on the usual amicable terms that spoke well of her. It was presumably during one of these forays into the streets of Whitechapel – before she and Barnett parted – that she met a third 'Joe'.

It is clear from the existing evidence that this Joe – Joe III – was *not* Joseph Flemming the plasterer, Kelly's former lover, with whom she remained friendly and perhaps continued to see even after she and Barnett had moved in together. According to Julia Venturney, the German charwoman who lived opposite the couple, Kelly had told her that she was 'very fond of another man named Joe' who, although he occasionally gave her money, 'had often ill-used her because she lived with Joe (Barnett)'.[113] Venturney, in a revealing statement, had no recollection of that Joe being a mason's plasterer or anything like it but thought that he might have been 'a costermonger' – an occupation more easily aligned to a general dealer's outlet, such as that in Plumber's Row, than to the building trade Flemming was associated with by the sensitive and vigilant Barnett.[114]

There are, however, two other linked reasons – the one a significant silence, the other a public acclamation – which endorse the view that Joe III was not Flemming. If Flemming had been the only other Joe in Kelly's life, and if he 'often ill-used her' for living with Barnett, he would have been an obvious suspect in the murder that followed. Yet there is not a single account or document emanating from investigators or the press at the time, that points to them seeking to establish the presence or whereabouts of Flemming for questioning. If Flemming *was* Kelly's occasionally violent client or lover why did he attract so little attention, why were the authorities so utterly indifferent? It could only be because they had discounted the possibility of his having been the abusive Joe noted by Venturney. Even more significantly – and as we shall shortly see – immediately after the murder of Kelly the police *did* actively seek and then arrest another man by the name of Joe to help them with their inquiries and it most certainly was not Flemming or Barnett. It was another Joe entirely, a third Joe. The existence of this mysterious Joe III who, unlike Flemming, Barnett was clearly unaware of, may also help account for Barnett's observation that Kelly 'seemed afraid of some one' who remained unknown to him.[115]

Mary Jane's relationship with Joe III remained clandestine throughout the period she and Barnett shared the room in Miller's Court. Even after her murder, nobody came forward with Joe III's full name. She frequently asked Barnett to read to her about the murders from the newspapers and Walter Dew was of the opinion that, 'There was no woman in the whole of Whitechapel more frightened of Jack the Ripper than Marie Kelly', and it is at this crucial juncture that one careful chronicler of the murders quite correctly poses the question – could it have been 'the other "Joe" [III] in her life?'[116] It almost certainly was the person she secretly feared and therein lay the key to Kelly and Joe III's relationship. He wanted exclusive access to a prostitute he was attracted to and wished to exploit but she – out of loyalty – was unwilling to abandon Barnett.

Once we have seen how Kelly was butchered, and exposed her killer's biblical template, it is possible to retrieve at least part of his thinking. In his mind, she was a woman of uncertain origin, a person difficult to categorise. She had started out as a girl-bride aged sixteen, lost her husband, become a prostitute in an upmarket brothel and obtained exotic sexual experiences abroad before returning to become an adulterous common law wife and streetwalker. Kelly was an elusive, pretentious, temptation; a whore whose foreign fornicating had allowed her to assume airs and dress above her station. She was a vendor of sexual pollution. She was also a woman who, despite his kindnesses to her, considered herself to be too good for him and – crucially – had rejected his offers either to move in with her, or to take control of her career as a prostitute. She had acted hatefully towards him and because of her disdain, life trajectory and suspicions deserved the maximum penalty and public exposure as a whore, just like the others.

On Thursday evening, 8 November, Barnett called in to see Kelly and spent less than half an hour chatting amiably before leaving. She, as ever, was short of money, as was he; he had none to give or lend her. Between Barnett's departure and the hour approaching midnight Kelly commenced a night's work which apparently included some drinking. At about 11.45 p.m. Mary Ann Cox, a prostitute in Miller's Court, encountered Kelly, very drunk, escorting a rather 'stout' client into her apartment and, at about 12.30 a.m. Catherine Picket, an irritated flower-seller, heard Kelly singing. Presumably Kelly recovered her composure and again ventured out in the wee hours of the morning.

Several days after her murder, George Hutchinson, an acquaintance who took a very active interest in Kelly, her clients and her work, went to the police to explain that, at about 2 a.m. that Friday morning, he had encountered Kelly on Commercial Street. She asked him to lend her sixpence but he was unable to do so. He then watched as she was approached by a man he had seen earlier and who then struck up a conversation with Kelly before they moved off. Hutchinson, for reasons of his own, had taken particularly careful note of the man, followed them, and watched as they entered Miller's Court where he waited to see if they re-emerged. The description of the engaging, superficially agreeable man Hutchinson had seen Kelly pick up was as follows:

> Age about 34 or 35, height 5 ft. 6, complexion pale, dark eyes and eye lashes, slight moustache curled up each end and hair dark, very surly looking: dress, long dark coat, collar and cuffs trimmed astracan and dark jacket under, light waistcoat, dark trousers, dark felt hat turned down in the middle, button boots and gaiters with white buttons, wore a very thick gold chain, white linen collar, black tie with horseshoe pin, respectable appearance, walked very sharp. Jewish appearance. Can be identified.[117]

The couple did not re-emerge and after lingering for three-quarters of an hour the frustrated Hutchinson left. Two women in Miller's Court later claimed that, between about 3.30 and 4 a.m. that morning, they had heard a brief cry of 'murder'. Mrs Cox thought that she had heard the footsteps of a man leaving the court, at about 5.45 a.m.[118]

That morning, McCarthy, owner of the property, sent an assistant to try to collect some of the arrears in rent Kelly owed him. When the man failed to gain entry and pulled aside the muslin curtain in the room he got a glimpse of the Angel of Death's laboratory. The face was mutilated extensively, 'gashed in all directions, *the nose, cheeks, eyebrows and ears partly removed*'.[119] Dr Thomas Bond, called to the scene by the police, noted:

> The body was lying naked in the middle of the bed, the shoulders flat but the axis of the body inclined to the left side of the bed. The head was turned on the left cheek. The left arm was close to the body with the forearm flexed at a right angle & lying across the abdomen, the right arm was slightly abducted from the body & rested on the mattress, the elbow bent & the forearm supine with the fingers clenched. The legs were wide apart, the left thigh at right angles to the trunk & the right forming an obtuse angle with the pubes.
>
> The whole of the surface of the abdomen & thighs was removed & the abdominal cavity emptied of its viscera. The breasts were cut off, the arms mutilated by several jagged

wounds & the face hacked beyond recognition of the features & the tissues of the neck were severed all round down to the bone. The viscera were found in various parts viz: the uterus & kidneys with one breast under the head, the other breast by the right foot, the liver between the feet, the intestines by the right side & the spleen by the left side of the body.[120]

In his official report, Bond stated: 'The pericardium was open below & the heart absent', and the *Daily Telegraph* seems later to have confirmed this, stating, 'on good authority', that 'a portion of the body organs was missing'.[121] Where could the heart have gone? We will never know, but Inspector Frederick G. Abberline, Scotland Yard, in charge of the case was reported as stating at the inquest: '. . . *there had been a large fire so large as to melt the spout off the kettle*. I have since gone through the ashes in the grate & found nothing of consequence except that articles of woman's clothing had been burnt.'[122]

Ezekiel had again lit the way:

Heap on wood, kindle the fire, consume the flesh, and spice it well, and let the bones be burned.

Then set it empty upon the coals thereof, that the brass of it may be hot, and may burn, and that the filthiness of it may be molten in it, that the scum of it may be consumed.

She hath wearied herself with lies, and her great scum went not forth out of her: her scum shall be in the fire.

In thy filthiness is lewdness: because I have purged thee, and thou was not purged, thou shalt not be purged from thy filthiness any more, till I have caused my fury to rest upon thee.[123]

The 'Son of man' had helped cleanse the city of whores. The prophet himself had drafted the psychopath's charter and exempted the murderer from emotion and remorse alike; 'Son of man, behold, I take away from thee the desire of thine eyes with a stroke; yet neither shalt thou mourn or weep, neither shall thy tears run down.'[124] Previously he had removed their rings, cut off their noses and ears, displayed their lewdness, hacked their filthy genitalia and harvested their uteri so that they would never again have offspring. A sullied heart, almost certainly consigned to the flames for purification, was missing. Surely this time everybody who could read would understand the message in full? It was there for all to see:

Ezekiel 23

3. And they committed whoredoms in Egypt; they committed whoredoms in their youth: there were their breasts pressed, and there they bruised the teats of their virginity.

8. Neither left she [Aholah] her whoredoms brought from Egypt; for in her youth they lay with her; and they bruised the breasts of her virginity, and poured their whoredom upon her.

9. Wherefore I have delivered her into the hand of her lovers, into the hand of the Assyrians upon whom she doted.

17. And the Babylonians came to her [Aholah] into the bed of love, and they defiled her with their whoredom; and she was polluted with them, and her mind was alienated from them.

21. Thus thou calledst to remembrance the lewdness of thy youth, in bruising thy teats by the Egyptians for the paps of thy youth.

22. Therefore, O Aholibah, thus saith the Lord God: Behold, I will raise up thy lovers against thee, from whom thy mind is alienated, and I will bring them against thee on every side;

23. The Babylonians, and all the Chaldeans, Pekod, and Shoa, and Koa and all the Assyrians with them; all of them desirable young men, captains and rulers, great lords and renowned, all of them riding upon horses.

24. And they shall come against thee with chariots, wagons and wheels, and with an assembly of people, which shall set against thee buckler and shield and helmet round about: and I will set judgment before them, and they shall judge thee according to their judgments.

25. And I will set my jealousy against thee, and they shall deal furiously with thee: they shall take away thy nose and thine ears; and thy remnant shall fall by the sword; they shall take thy sons and thy daughters; and thy residue shall be devoured by the fire.

26. They shall also strip thee out of thy clothes, and take away thy fair jewels.

27. Thus will I make thy lewdness to cease from thee, and thy whoredom brought from the land of Egypt; so that thou shalt not lift up thine eyes unto them, nor remember Egypt any more.

28. For thus saith the Lord God; Behold, I will deliver thee into the hand of them whom thou hatest, into the hand of them from whom thy mind is alienated.

29. And they shall deal with thee hatefully, and shall take away all thy labour, and shall leave thee naked and bare: and the nakedness of thy whoredoms shall be discovered, both thy lewdness and thy whoredoms.

36. The Lord said moreover unto me: Son of man, wilt thou judge Aholah and Aholibah? yea, declare unto them their abominations.

37. That they have committed adultery, and blood is in their hands, and with their idols have they committed adultery, and have also caused their sons, whom they bare unto me, to pass for them through the fire, to devour them.

45. And the righteous men, they shall judge them after the manner of adulteresses, and after the manner of women that shed blood; because they are adulteresses, and blood is in their hands.

48. Thus will I cause lewdness to cease out of the land, that all women may be taught not to do after your lewdness.

The only person of note who seems to have given thought to the possibility of the Bible having had a role in the slayings was Thomas Bond. After the Kelly murder the police asked him to review the medical evidence and 'profile' the killer. But not even Bond was convinced: 'It is of course possible that the Homicidal impulse may have developed from a revengeful or brooding condition of the mind, or that Religious Mania may have been the original disease, but I do not think that either hypothesis is likely.'[125] In truth, there probably *was* no easy, mono-causal, explanation for the murders. An extremely complex set of inter-twined factors informed the killer, including a fraught relationship with his mother, adolescent sexual socialisation, a loathing of streetwalkers as vectors of pollution and, in the personalised case of Kelly, a desire for revenge born of rejection.

After the 'double event', the police conducted an extensive but unsuccessful house-to-house search and distributed 80,000 notices seeking information that might lead to the killer. In the wake of the Kelly murder, a further house-to-house search was conducted in Dorset Street and the immediate neighbourhood. This time it yielded one, potentially interesting, clue. The deputy keeper of a lodging house in Little Paternoster Row, Mary Cusins, recalled that on the night of the murder she had heard an agitated lodger 'walk about his room'. The lodger's unusual behaviour and sentiments, including a threat to do 'violence to all women above 17 years of age', was confirmed by another lodger, Cornelius Oakes, who had noted that the man 'often changed his dress'. The man had left immediately after Kelly's murder, leaving behind a violin bow – part of several musical instruments he had in his possession but which he was either unable, or unwilling, to play. The police were sufficiently interested to ask Cusins to keep an eye open for him and, if he were to return, to let them know. His name, too, was 'Joe' – Joseph Isaacs.[126]

A Missing Man, and a Man Missed but not Forgotten

Hutchinson's description of the Dorset Street suspect who he may have seen as a rival for the attentions of Mary Kelly, along with that of others supplied by persons around Berner Street, Hanbury Street and Mitre Square at the time of the earlier murders, can be reduced to a composite picture. A modern analyst, who simply fails to mention that there was also widespread agreement that the killer was right-handed, offers the following:

> He was about 5 feet 6 inches tall at the most and quite muscular. He had a pale, almost certainly brown moustache, had a fairly stout or stocky build, and was aged in his late 20s to mid-30s. He lived in the area where the murders took place and knew it like the back of his hand. He was a loner, and if he was employed, he had an unskilled job that may have involved his working alone. He was not surgically skilled. He was probably unmarried and possibly impotent, although he may have had sexual encounters with prostitutes. He dressed fairly neatly, or tried to, in shabby-genteel clothing. He probably possessed a deerstalker hat. He would not have committed suicide, or moved away from the area, and the police may have interviewed him at some stage.[127]

How compatible is this sketched outline with our peripatetic young Polish psychopath?

In 1889, Lis, aged twenty-one, is described in the Sing Sing records as being five feet eight and a half inches in height and weighing 140 pounds. From later, photographic evidence, we know that he had a brown moustache which he wore with the ends curled. He came from a family with an interest in the clothing trade, took pride in his appearance and often wore dark suits, a waistcoat and felt hat. Like many others at the time he sported a pocket watch and chain and also possessed a horseshoe tiepin.

A powerful, muscular, man, Lis was right-handed; a fact confirmed by a forensic graphologist accredited by the American Association of Handwriting Analysts and World Association of Document Examiners.[128] We also know from his handwriting that it did not match that in the infamous letter addressed to George Lusk, chairman of the Whitechapel Vigilance Committee, after the night of the double event and which was accompanied by part of a human kidney. Nor does his handwriting appear to match that on any of the hundreds of other letters addressed to the police by cranks, mischief-makers, or the two newspapermen who may have coined the name 'Jack the Ripper'.[129]

Lacking the profile of a serial killer of the type now routinely used by forensic psychiatrists, and without the benefit of DNA testing, or the fingerprinting systems that came a few years later, the London Metropolitan Police had little more than physical descriptions of the murderer produced under difficult circumstances to go on. An inability to understand that a primary, non-delusionary mental illness was driving the killer was not confined to the officers of the Met since the concept of psychopathy itself belongs to the mid-twentieth century. Throughout Lis's life, capable administrators, civic activists, detectives, soldiers and hardened policemen on the beat realised that there was a menacing quality to him, and that he was a manipulative, treacherous man. But not even during an unevenly developed bout of syphilis-induced grandiosity from 1895 and 1906, did they act on the assumption that he was being manifestly 'mad'. In 1903, Detective Richard Ovendale noted of Lis that 'a more dangerous man would be hard to find throughout the length and breadth of South Africa', but by then he had already taken in several other Bloemfontein officers. Lis, involved with police throughout his life, compromised the careers of several professional officers.

Sir Charles Warren did not resign as Commissioner of the London Metropolitan Police, in 1888, because of his officers' inability to apprehend Jack the Ripper, but a lack of success in Whitechapel contributed to escalating problems. In 1895, Lis embarrassed Warren's counterpart in Manhattan, Superintendent Thomas Byrnes, and dragged the names of officers McManus and Jacobs across the pages of the *New York Times* until, after the elapse of a decent interval, both detectives left the police department. In Johannesburg, in 1898, Constable Manie Maritz, who went on to become a general and Boer War hero, temporarily lost his position as a policeman as a result of Lis's machinations – a setback that ignited anti-Semitic sentiments which later turned Maritz into a leading Nazi sympathiser. In Bloemfontein, Cape Town and Kimberley too, Lis sullied the reputations of several detectives who, erroneously, believed that he could be controlled. Indeed, as late as 1914, in Valparaiso, he was still making fools of policemen.

Seen as bad and suspected of being mad in some indefinable manner, Lis, under another name, was prevented from re-entering the Russian empire in 1899. He was banished from two countries – the Zuid Afrikaansche Republiek, in 1899, and German South West Africa, in 1906. On two occasions between 1900 and 1903 he was deported, under armed military escort, from inland cities to Cape Town and once, in 1906, was transported to Germany to serve out a prison sentence. A witness of his earliest exploits in New York and Pittsburgh, a woman whom he had often threatened and usually a very reliable informant, also recalled his being investigated on a charge of arson but, unfortunately, provided insufficient detail for the case now to be traced. He was widely regarded by pimps, prostitutes and policemen as being a dangerous and menacing man.

In 1888 Lis, who secretly craved public recognition, would have revelled in the coverage Jack the Ripper's exploits elicited in the penny press as well as in the fear that his actions engendered amongst the populace at large or within the ranks of streetwalkers. In later years, seldom far from organised prostitution, or its most extreme controlled and disciplined form, white slavery, his name featured in every major newspaper in America, Belgium, Chile, England, France, German South West Africa and every one of the colonies of southern Africa. In various forms, sometimes only after he had left the country, his name crossed the desks of President Paul Kruger, Tsar Nicholas, Sir Edward Grey, Police Commissioner Theodore Roosevelt and State Attorney, J.C. Smuts.

If Lis was the East End murderer, it is understandable that the secret he took to the grave with him under that name failed to echo easily in the ears of pressmen, policemen or presidents at the time. But, given his underlying neurosyphilis and occasional behavioural excesses after 1895, did not others – criminals, or the prostitutes who lived in constant terror of him – ever suspect him of having been the Whitechapel killer? Alas, as with so much about Lis, we will probably never know. The fears and suspicions that those drawn from his own world might have held about him remained unrecorded – his greatest secret remained intact.

Or did it? In 1906, the disgraced former Member of Parliament at Westminster and convicted swindler turned journalist, Jabez Spencer Balfour, claimed that while serving a lengthy prison sentence that commenced in 1895 he had twice seen the man rumoured to be the East End murderer. At first glance it is an interesting claim given that Balfour and Lis's paths had crossed twice in the mid-1890s when they were doing hard labour in Pentonville and Wormwood Scrubs. Upon closer examination, however, Balfour's claims dim. He provided a physical description of the supposed Whitechapel murderer that could not remotely be reconciled with that of Lis and, even more diconcertingly, his observations were said to have taken place in two prisons that Lis never set foot in – Parkhurst and Portland on the Isle of Wight. Balfour's deliberately personalised and sensationalised views can perhaps be disregarded.

But was that all there was to prison scuttlebutt? Can the rest of what Balfour reported be as easily dismissed? He claimed to have conversed 'with a man who was living in Johannesburg in the year 1900, who was there intimately connected with two well known men [Cleaver and Skirving?], who declared they knew Jack the Ripper personally'. As startling was his claim to have spoken to yet another informant who was alleged to have met the East End killer on the night train between the Transvaal and the Orange River Colony in about 1903 when we know that Silver was based in Bloemfontein in 1902–03, and that he undertook at least one clandestine rail journey to Johannesburg during that time? And what are we to make of Balfour's 1906 observation that the Whitechapel murderer was 'living still in some remote British colony' when we know that Lis had only just left the Cape Colony where he had been resident fully five years? The broad chronological accuracy and geographically specific nexus of this hearsay have an eerie correspondence with what is known about Joseph Silver's career. Could it not be that, within underworld circles

and the prison systems, there was some reasonably informed speculation about Lis's earlier life?[130]

A more important question, however, is whether, at the time of the
murders, the young Lis would have contented himself with indirect
embarrassment and manipulation of the police via a chalked notice above
a doorway, or whether he resented the Ripper getting all the attention
while he – the real hand behind the darkest of deeds – remained forgotten
and neglected? Would he not, like many other serial killers, return to the
scene of his crimes to savour success, taunt the police and perhaps,
without thinking, leave yet another clue to his identity? To answer this,
probably determinative, question, we need to pursue the man who went
missing from the lodging house in Little Paternoster Row.

God's Self-appointed Agent in Little Paternoster Row

The 1881 census, taken months *before* the assassination of Tsar
Alexander and pre-dating the mass influx of poor Polish and Russian
Jews that followed, records the presence of two cigar-makers, both
named Joseph Isaacs, living in the East End. One Joseph Isaacs
(JI-Boyd), then aged twenty, was part of an extended family including
two gainfully employed sisters living at 16 Boyd Street, in St George's-
in-the East. The other Joseph Isaacs (JI-Went), twenty-three, was born
in Whitechapel and lived with his father, in Wentworth Street.[131]

Both Isaacs, if still residing in the East End in 1888, would have
been about thirty years of age at the time of the Ripper murders.
JI-Went was an English-born Jew, while JI-Boyd, too, would, by 1888,
have been reasonably well assimilated. Neither of them, having lived
in the area for the better part of a decade, would have come across as
a recent East European immigrant. Both Isaacs had family ties, were
not of itinerant habits, appear to have had unremarkable temperaments,
were not professional musicians and neither had a criminal record
under that name, either before or after the Whitechapel murders. As
we shall see, they differ in crucial respects from the 'Joseph Isaacs' in
Little Paternoster Row.

That Joseph Isaacs, probably just 'Joe' to most East Enders, 'well
known in the locality', abandoned his usual haunts after the Kelly
murder, on the night of 8–9 November 1888.[132] It was a precaution
both necessary and wise since his 'appearance certainly answered the

published description of a man with an astrachan trimming on his coat'.[133] He then retreated to an unknown address, in north London, where he was prosecuted and convicted in the Barnet Police Court for an unspecified offence of petty larceny on 12 November and sentenced to twenty-one days in prison with hard labour.[134] Forty-eight hours after his release, on the afternoon of Wednesday, 5 December, and still short of cash, he suddenly reappeared at the lodging house at 6 Little Paternoster Row, and asked Mary Cusins for the violin bow which was returned to him. He then left.[135]

The lodging-house keeper, hoping to attract the attention of a constable, followed. Isaacs turned into Dorset Street, went past Kelly's apartment in Miller's Court, turned right into Commercial Street and right again into White's Row. He walked past the house where Annie Millwood had been attacked and went into a nearby jewellery store. He handed the bow to the proprietor, Julius Levensohn, asking that it be repaired and, while the owner was distracted, grabbed a gold watch valued at thirty shillings and 'bolted out of the shop'. Cusins, watching from afar, saw that he 'almost immediately ran out' of the store but, with no policeman in sight, there was nothing that either she, or Levensohn could do.[136] Isaacs then made his way to a pawnbroker, at 184 Bishopsgate Street, where he spoke to the assistant, Robert Jack, and pawned the watch for twelve shillings.[137]

The following afternoon, easily recognised in Drury Lane by Detective William Record who must have known him by sight, Isaacs was accused of having stolen the watch, and arrested. He allegedly replied with an almost personal apology, 'Yes, I am very sorry. I did it. I was hard up.'[138] He was taken to Bow Street station and a telegram sent to the Whitechapel division. Significantly, it was the man in charge of the murder investigations, Detective Inspector F.G. Abberline himself who hurried across to Bow Street and the prisoner, 'strongly escorted', was taken back to the Leman Street station. The following day, Friday, Isaacs appeared in the Worship Street Court, describing himself as a 'cigar maker' of no fixed abode and was charged with the theft of a watch.[139]

Abberline had little interest in what had transpired at the jewellery store beyond the opportunity it gave him for holding Isaacs. Since at least the time of the Nichols murder he and his colleagues had been interested in Jewish suspects and, after Cusins's and Venturney's statements he must have been particularly interested in anybody named

Joseph who also happened to be Jewish. He was reputed to have said, while collecting his prisoner in Bow Street, 'Keep this quiet; we have got the right man at last. This is a big thing.'[140] At the time it was, far and away, the most public enthusiasm Abberline evinced about making real progress in leading his inquiries to a satisfactory conclusion.

On Saturday, 8 December, the London Evening News followed up on this earlier account in the Northern Daily Telegraph, reporting that Joseph Isaacs was being questioned about 'a recent attempt to murder a woman in George Street, Spitalfields'. This referred to the assault on Annie Farmer, a streetwalker, in a lodging house in George Street, on 21 November. That same Saturday, the London Evening News reported that the suspect, Joseph Isaacs, was 'being connected with the Whitechapel murders'; including, presumably, that of Mary Jane Kelly.[141]

On Monday, 10 December, the Manchester Evening News carried a final report on Isaacs, stating that 'The police are continuing their enquiries into the antecedents of Joseph Isaacs, said to be a Polish Jew.'[142] Thereafter the press clearly lost interest as detectives failed to link their immigrant suspect more closely to either the attack on Farmer or the Whitechapel murders.

Could Isaacs have been Joseph Lis? First indications are not promising. Early reports described Isaacs as being of 'short stature' – yet Lis stood five feet eight inches tall. Later reports make no mention of Isaacs's height but make another claim never repeated – that he was thirty years old, which was way off Lis's twenty-plus. It is difficult to know what to make of hurried observations made under unknown circumstances. Did reporters actually get to see the suspect and, if so, for how long, and in what surroundings? How could the suspect simultaneously be reported as answering the published description supplied by George Hutchinson (five feet six inches) and be of 'short stature'? At the time, five feet six inches hardly qualified as 'short'. None of the surviving sources go on to mention the suspect's height, and court documents do not even record Isaacs's age, let alone his being thirty.

Diverging accounts of the 'facts' regarding age and height may make it difficult to state beyond all doubt that one Polish Jew, the mustachioed Joseph Isaacs wanted for questioning in connection with serial sexual killings, was in fact none other than another mustachioed Polish Jew with a predilection for sexual crimes, Joseph Lis. Beyond these two, supposedly hard, factual discrepancies, however, lies a hidden host of circumstantial and psychological clues that make it almost impossible to resist the conclusion that 'Joseph Isaacs' was Joseph Lis.

Sources of Laughter and Fathers who Sacrificed Sons

The choice of 'Joseph Isaacs' as an alias in itself points, in part, to Lis. Whatever reservations Lis had about his self-worth he was, for many years, unwilling to abandon his first name which, when speaking, he invariably rendered as Joe. There could have been any number of practical as well as psychological reasons for this reluctance. There is no recorded instance of Lis being found without his authentic first name before 1895. Even when he took the surname 'Silver' he clung steadfastly to his first name. After that, whenever he did assume an alias, it was usually the name of a person he had actually known, such as Abraham Ramer, or at least knew of, like the unlikely James Smith which allowed him to retain the initials J.S. It is possible – even probable – that, on first entering the East End, in 1885, he retained the name Joseph which he was always comfortable with, but reached out to borrow Isaacs from some real live individual whom he had either been impressed by or possibly even accompanied in some petty criminal adventures.

John Isaacs appeared in the Thames Police Court on 2 June 1887, and was sentenced to three months' hard labour, and then in the Marylebone Court, on 21 January 1888, where he was again convicted and sentenced to seven weeks' imprisonment. John Isaacs targeted Jews in his burglaries and showed a preference for stealing cloth or clothing. This was a pattern identical to that adopted not only by Lis's closest friend, Goldberg, in Plumber's Row, in late 1887, but by the young Lis himself in New York, in 1889, and again in London in 1895. Indeed, in the second of the John Isaacs burglaries, that of January 1888, he had been assisted by some unknown accomplice.[143]

The biblical name Isaac derives from the three-lettered Hebrew root, *tsachak*, meaning 'to laugh'. It was the sort of self-referential pun the older Lis enjoyed when presenting the police with names like Nieman or Greenbaum. Maybe, by late 1887, or even earlier, Joseph Isaacs who had been so easily recognised by Detective William Record, had been laughing at the police in Whitechapel for several months for reasons we can only guess at. If so, then by the time of his arrest, in late 1888, he stood on the very threshold of the greatest triumph ever in sick, sardonic humour. Maybe the killer of Mary Jane Kelly was enjoying a private joke at the expense of the police?

If, however, Lis was exploring the Bible in an effort to make greater sense of his life during a psychological implosion there were more complex reasons for embracing the alias Isaac. Abraham and Sarah had laughed when God suggested that, notwithstanding their advanced years, they would become parents to the son they would go on to name Isaac. Maybe Lis–Isaacs, too, had laughed out loud when told that he was to be the father of the child that was to be Bertha; another name that lent itself to punning? In more sombre circumstances, however, Abraham – who had himself once passed through a fiery furnace – had been willing to sacrifice his son, as a 'burnt offering', before Isaac was saved by God's intervention.[144] 'Do not give me up to the fury of an angry mob who would like to see me burned at the stake', Lis wrote to his startled police handler in Cape Town when he was already into his thirties and the twentieth century well under way. The Book of Ezekiel, too, is redolent with intimations that the prophet had been abandoned, if not sacrificed, by uncaring males, 'the elders of Israel'.[145] How will we ever know whether, by adopting the name of the one to be sacrificed by fire Joseph Lis was not trying to tell us something about his troubled relationship with his father, Ansel?

It is difficult to get an unrestricted view of Lis draped beneath a mantle of semantic evidence. What is more interesting and a trifle more revealing is to note that, when arrested, Isaacs claimed to be a 'cigar maker' – an occupation with special connotations for Lis. The fact that his mother, Hannah, had been a dealer in tobacco when she first met his father might be a coincidence. So, too, might be the fact that Lis, like many other brothel-keepers, later chose to disguise some of his bordellos as 'cigar shops' – that being commonplace. But could it be mere coincidence that, when looking for cover as a plainclothes police officer dealing with illicit diamond buyers in Kimberley, and while embroiled in a legal vendetta with Louis Lezard, he gave his profession as 'cigarette agent'?

In the same way we have to ask why it was that Oakes, the lodger in the house on Little Paternoster Row, remarked not only on the fact that Isaacs made misogynistic statements and threats filled with violence directed against women over the age of seventeen, but also that he 'often changed his dress'. As already noted, Lis took pride in his appearance and the butcher of Whitechapel had good reason for wanting to change his apparel. Oakes also saw that, although Isaacs owned various musical instruments, he never played them. Not surprisingly, there is no record of Lis ever having played a musical instrument. But, with some musicians seeking to profit from the increased flow of visitors to the East End there was greater traffic through the lodging houses and more opportunities for an opportunistic thief with poor self-control.[146]

For all that, Lis remains shrouded beneath a sheet of coincidences. All we can do is to tug away at the cloth of circumstantial evidence in the hope that it will fall away to reveal a more recognisable figure. After recovering the violin bow, Isaacs, a Jew, made his way to a jewellery store owned by a Jew. As we know, the Jew-hating Lis had a lifelong interest in jewellery stores and preferred Jews – male and female – as targets for his anti-social activities. It was what Isaacs did next, in Levensohn's shop, however, that is perhaps most revealing of all – he snatched a watch and ran away. It was an impulsive act of the sort associated with psychopaths which Lis was to repeat on two occasions in his twenties and thirties that we know of. In New York, he leapt over the counter of a laundry and 'grabbed a box from the Chinaman's drawer' and, in London in 1895, stole an umbrella when already living off the proceeds of prostitution.

The cloth of coincidence can no longer conceal the profile of Joseph Lis. On 2 January 1889, Joseph Isaacs appeared in the Worship Street court and, found guilty of theft, was sentenced to three months' hard labour in Pentonville. The sentence itself was entirely unexceptional, but it did give rise to three, otherwise puzzling features that are remarkable for the way in which they collectively mock supposed coincidence.

First, despite being 'well known in the locality' – presumably to the police rather than the public at large – and twice being prosecuted for minor offences in one month, there is no earlier criminal record for Joseph Isaacs; nor is there any *after* January 1889. November 1888 was an entirely aberrant month in the life of Isaacs. He had presumably been known to the police in some other capacity prior to 1888 and, after 1889, became an honest but untraceable man, changed his name, died or emigrated; or a combination of these factors may account for his disappearance from familiar haunts. Secondly, amongst the inmates Isaacs would have encountered almost immediately upon entering Pentonville was Adolph Goldberg, Lis's friend for nearly half a decade, a man who found himself in prison for having committed a burglary in a warehouse, in Plumber's Row, opposite a business owned by a man also named Lis. Thirdly, Isaacs's release date, like Lis's friend Goldberg's, was April 1889. Finally we have to note that, within months of Goldberg's release from Pentonville, he admitted to having met up with Lis in London, and was again in his company in New York. The logic of all this is inescapable: Joseph Isaacs *was* Joseph Lis.

Isaacs's Salvation

One of the most thorough analysts of the East End murders has noted: 'As far as is known Isaacs merely behaved oddly and was a petty thief, but the fact that Inspector Abberline was summoned and that Isaacs was taken to the Commercial Street Police Station under heavy escort suggest that he was suspected for far more than that, and one suspects that he was suspected, and perhaps *strongly* suspected of being Jack the Ripper.'[147] The question is irresistible: if Abberline and the Leman Street detectives had Isaacs in custody stemming from a line of inquiry arising from suspicious behaviour observed on the night of the Kelly murder, how did the young Joseph extricate himself? Lacking documentary evidence, we have to speculate and note how a rare combination of chance and design came to the rescue of the man suspected of the Whitechapel murders.

First, we need to remind ourselves of how Lis, throughout his life, cultivated formal and informal links with the police. Isaacs may have been a low-level informer known to the police. The 1887 burglary at Spiegel's warehouse in Plumber's Row was resolved when the police, acting on information received from unnamed informants, made several arrests. As *Reynold's Newspaper* records: 'The three prisoners [Goldberg, Cohen and Levy] were found offering the overcoats for sale to different clothiers, and as the news of the robbery had been communicated to the police, they *received* such information as enabled them to trace the prisoners, and they were taken into custody.'[148] Jewish dealers in the Lane and perhaps Goulston Street would have presented themselves as obvious outlets for stolen goods but that is not particularly relevant. Planning and executing break-ins as part of highly personalised plots to frame or set up underworld colleagues was part of Lis's stock in trade. He did so repeatedly in New York in the 1890s and once again, with spectacular cynicism, in Bloemfontein, in 1902. In December 1888, a detective had no difficulty whatsoever in picking out Joseph Isaacs in Drury Lane. Even though he was 'well known' to the police *before* 1888, Joseph Isaacs had no criminal record because the police probably knew, and had used, him as a nark.

Secondly, the police saw in Joseph Isaacs a man with a penchant for crimes against property rather than people. His November exploits in Barnet, where he had been imprisoned for twenty-one days, and the theft at Levensohn's appeared to have been of a piece – minor, impulsive acts, of a petty thief. Such offences were not easy to reconcile with the butchery of women by a young man who could also be plausible and persuasive.

Thirdly, Isaacs was able to provide a thoroughly overwhelmed police force with an uneven mix of true and false alibis.[149] The false alibis would have had to cover all the murders prior to and including that of Mary Jane Kelly. Without archival sources it is now impossible to know what precisely those false alibis consisted of but, in theory, there was more than one source that Lis/Isaacs could have drawn on. His co-assailants in the Smith murder, knowing what was at stake for them, might have been one. Another might have been Sir Robert Anderson's nightmare – the Lis family of 35 Plumber's Row who, for whatever reason, appear to have abandoned their business after the East End murders.

Fortunately for Isaacs, any false alibis would have nestled within the immediate context of more recent, cast-iron, truthful alibis for other, equally disturbing attacks that post-dated the Kelly murder and were, by then, preoccupying the police. Abberline was interested in Isaacs not only because of the Kelly murder, but for the attack on the prostitute, Annie Farmer on 21 November.[150] On that date, however, Isaacs had been in prison serving his sentence for a minor offence committed in Barnet. The police were still evaluating that evidence – it took them the better part of a month – when there was what may have been yet another murder of a streetwalker. Rose Mylett was found dead but 'the throat had not been cut and the body had not been mutilated, faint marking around her neck suggesting that she had been strangled'.[151] Her death had occurred during the early hours of 20 December – at a time when Joseph Isaacs was still in police custody being investigated for the earlier murders in Whitechapel.

Amidst mounting mayhem, Abberline seems eventually to have decided that Isaacs/Lis was little more than a petty thief, a youthful nark known to bobbies on the beat, and possessed of sufficient alibis for events both before and after the Kelly murder for him not to be Jack the Ripper. But, if Lis *was* indeed Jack the Ripper, then why did he not kill again?

Ezekiel Bound Over

Mary Jane Kelly was murdered in the early hours of 9 November 1888. For all but three days of the month that followed, Isaacs/Lis was in prison. Released on 3 December, he was back in police custody three days later, on the 6th, and was kept there until he appeared in court on 2 January 1889, when he was sentenced to three months' imprisonment. Upon his release in April 1889, in a move that at present cannot be traced, he and Goldberg emigrated to America under unknown names. In October 1889, Lis was sentenced to two and a half years' imprisonment in Sing Sing, from which he was not released until mid-October 1891. Isaacs/Lis spent thirty of the thirty-six months that followed the last of the East End murders in prison – the vast majority of them in the United States. Having passed through the most tempestuous period of his psychopathy, he emerged from Sing Sing aged twenty-three, depressed and reflective but hardly cured. He maintained a lifelong loathing of prostitutes and went on to threaten many with death – including threatening to open up the belly of one – but was never prosecuted for murder.

Jury Duty

What then are you, members of history's jury, to make of this case? How are you to deal with all that you have seen prior to this reading and to assess only that which you have learned afresh and seen conclusively demonstrated here? By what standards are you to test the evidence presented, contemporary and historical? How would you, if asked, find the accused, Joseph Isaacs, previously known as Joseph Lis, charged with the attack on Emma Smith and the five canonical murders in London's East End during the course of the spring and autumn of 1888? Would you find the accused guilty? Or not guilty?

The court, depending on the nature of the charges brought, would

insist on posing one of two tests before you could convict the accused.
In a civil matter, if, say, a descendant of the 'canonical five' were to sue
Lis/Isaacs for compensation arising from trauma, or for loss of earnings
sustained as a result of the death of a relative, you would be directed
to convict the accused only if, after considering all the relevant evidence,
you were persuaded that, on *the balance of probabilities*, he was guilty
as charged. In a criminal case which, historically, might include the imposition of the death penalty upon conviction for a capital offence, the
law would, quite rightly, pose a far more stringent test – that the evidence
prove, *beyond reasonable doubt*, that the accused is guilty.

Before proceeding with the lesser test, it is important that you try
to rid your mind of all pre-existing beliefs, images, perceptions and
prejudices that may have come to you from other factual or fictionalised accounts of the murders via books, films, folklore, drama or tele-
vision. It is a formidable task. The popular mind is filled with a pastiche
of factual and fictionalised evidence propping up unlikely suspects such
as the top-hatted figure, dressed in dark coat, carrying a black bag,
who was possessed of considerable anatomical knowledge and/or
surgical skills. The latter profile was rejected by Dr Thomas Bond who
was of the opinion that the killer 'had no scientific or anatomical
knowledge', perhaps not even 'the technical knowledge of a butcher or
a horse slaughterer or any person accustomed to cut up dead animals'.[152]
Bond's view, however, gravitated towards the far end of the spectrum.
At least three other medical men involved in post-mortem examinations
arising from the murders were of the opinion that the killer was possessed
of some, indeterminate, amount of anatomical knowledge and/or surgical
skill.[153] It could have derived from insights commensurate with that
acquired by a disturbed adolescent raised in a town known for its abat-
toirs and who, later in life, numbered two butchers amongst his close
gangland associates. Or, it could have come from the rudimentary
training that went with being a barber or *feldscher* – at the time, very
much the poor man's doctor.

Nor has the image of the bag-carrying medical student or trained
doctor been dealt with kindly by modern forensic experts. Here, for
example, are two profiles of recent vintage. The killer, suggests one
American Federal Bureau of Investigation analyst, was probably:

> A local, resident male in his late twenties. Since the murders
> generally occurred at weekends, he was probably employed.

Murders took place between midnight and 6 a.m., suggesting that he was single, with no familial ties. Of low class, since murders evinced marked unfastidiousness. Not surgically skilled or possessing anatomical knowledge. Probably known to the police. Seen by acquaintances as a loner. Probably abused/deserted as a child by mother.[154]

A clinical psychologist, having reviewed all the relevant material, suggests:

This kind of pathology usually starts around the age of 15. At or before this time he had begun to kill or mutilate animals, fantasizing about them as being people. At this time too he would have begun to have an unnatural fascination with fire . . .

I suspect that Jack was about 28 to 31 years old. I believe that Jack probably lived in the Whitechapel area. He was probably never more than a short distance from what he considered to be a safe place. He had a demeaning job, probably as a labourer, as I believe him to have been somewhat muscular. He lived alone . . .

By taking away these parts [the bodily organs harvested] he is showing the signature one would expect of a serial killer. Some believe that the way in which the dissection was done indicated that the killer had some surgical skill or knowledge. I believe that this is not necessarily the case. Jack was just cutting in a manner that felt good to him . . .

Jack was probably good at concealing that part of his behaviour that was pathological. He was able to do his job and even socialize in a general sort of way. He may even have been a regular customer at one of the pubs in Whitechapel.[155]

The doctor-killer's is not the only image you need to banish from your mind before reviewing the evidence more clinically. There are other, almost all unlikely, images of suspects arising from a cottage industry that has clamoured for your attention: an eccentric artist whose paintings are said to have revealed dark images; a cricket-playing, suicidal, barrister; a dirt-eating, feeble-minded, compulsive masturbator; an itin-

erant thief who favoured Eton college and other soft targets; a member
of the royal family and if not him, then either his physician or his tutor;
or, an out-of-town, fifty-year-old cotton merchant who kept a diary of
the murders; and, more reasonably, some other peripatetic psychopath,
who married his victims before administering poison to them.[156]

Of course fact and fiction have both played a part in providing a
context for your historical imagination and in shaping your image of
a suspect. We have to acknowledge that, but then move on and agree
with commentators who argue that:

> Stripped of his iconic veneer, Jack is just a murderer. Someone
> who found women who had no other option but to sell their
> bodies then strangled and mutilated them. Not a devil. Not
> a ghost. Not a black magician endowed with supernatural
> powers. An ordinary person, one of the crowd, like you or
> I. Someone who could pass without let or hindrance in the
> East End streets with no one noticing his presence as being
> out of the ordinary.[157]

This is not the place to rehearse the expert testimony of criminologists,
doctors, handwriting analysts, historians, policemen or psychiatrists.
Nor is it the moment to repeat the new, detailed, circumstantial evidence
about the context of the events leading up to, during, or immediately
after the murders. Suffice it to suggest that any doubts you may entertain about any one piece of the evidence will have been eclipsed by the
compelling coherence of the case as a whole. If that much is conceded
then, on the balance of probabilities alone, Joseph Isaacs/Lis, as he then
was, stands convicted in a civil court.

But since the matter extends beyond the bounds of civil law, you
need also to consider whether the evidence against the accused points,
beyond reasonable doubt, to him being guilty of murder. This is a more
serious charge and one on which you will, rightly, have to be reminded,
however briefly, of the pertinent issues. Before this it may help to know
that, in the two years preceding the slaying, not a single murder was
committed in Whitechapel. While scores of men or women met with
violent deaths as a result of accidents or suicide, nobody appears to
have been strangled and then mutilated.

It is within this context that you have to ask yourself two related
questions. What are the chances of there having been more than one

young, dark-haired, mustachioed, Polish, Jew-hating, right-handed, misogynistic, psychopathic and syphilitic male in the East End at the time? And, more importantly, what are the chances of there being in Whitechapel, at precisely the same historical moment, more than one male with a liking for aliases that retained his first name, who carried about a clasp knife while committing burglaries, who had an intense hatred of a promiscuous mother, who loathed prostitutes' reproductive organs and who held violent biblical and/or medieval notions including the linked issues of cleanliness, fire, pollution and vengeance as set out in the Book of Ezekiel? No, Joseph Isaacs/Lis was the right man, in the right place, with sufficient motive to commit murder.

But, even if Joseph Lis, living under the name Joseph Isaacs, was *that* man, what evidence is it that connects him *directly* to the attack on Emma Smith and the other murders? Even among the existing, paltry, documentary evidence, there is an unmistakable, sinister black thread of facts that runs through the core attacks and links the psychopathic Lis–Isaacs directly to the murders. Here are a dozen, clearly verifiable facts:

- Before her death, Emma Smith insisted that one of the men who had attacked her sexually and perhaps torn her ear was no more than nineteen years of age. That was within weeks of Joseph Lis having turned twenty. Significantly, it is an age which fits with no other suspect hitherto linked to the case. It is also one that, in keeping with the findings of modern medical research, suggests that the killer could well have been a man much younger than previously thought.
- It has been demonstrated, beyond reasonable doubt, that Joseph Lis contracted syphilis at about the time of the Whitechapel murders and that he was about to become the father of a child he did not want. Alone amongst the suspects hitherto identified he had reason to be preoccupied with the vagina and reproductive sexual organs of streetwalkers. That, in itself, gave him reason to attack and indulge in the harvesting of the organs of some of his victims.
- It has been shown that, in 1887, Adolph Goldberg, later Joseph Lis's closest friend, resided in Vine Court, off the Whitechapel Road and that in early 1888 Lewis Lis and family occupied number 35 Plumber's Row. It is also known that, in December 1887, Goldberg was one of a group of men who broke into Spiegel's warehouse at number 34 Plumber's Row opposite the general dealer's store. Given the spatial distribution of the murder sites it is eminently reasonable to

assume that, prior to the Kelly murder, the premises at 35 Plumber's Row provided Joseph Lis with a bolt hole which he utilised on some occasions.

- It has also been established, again beyond reasonable doubt, that Joseph Lis was a Jew with a profound hatred of Jews; a man who invariably chose other Jews as targets for assault (including one stabbing), or theft, or as victims in protracted vendettas. It is reasonable to assume that on the night of the double event it was his 'schoolboy hand' that wrote: 'The Jewes are the men that will not be blamed for nothing'. Both the age of the author of that infamous graffito and the appalling content of the message point directly to Joseph Lis, later Joseph Silver.

- From surviving letters, it can be demonstrated that Joseph Lis entertained dark thoughts about revenge of a biblical or medieval nature. Such thinking was clearly compatible with a reading of the Book of Ezekiel which, outlining the demise of two biblical prostitutes, formed the template for two, possibly three, of the murders. It is only if the reading of the Book of Ezekiel by the killer is accepted, that analysts can make sense of the cutting off of the noses and ears of two of the victims, and the possible incineration of the uterus of Catherine Eddowes and heart of Mary Jane Kelly.

- It is known that brass rings belonging to Annie Chapman were wrenched from her fingers. A ring was probably also removed from the hand of Mary Ann Nichols. Given that brass rings were intrinsically worthless, the deliberate removal of such jewellery is in line with the strictures to be found in Ezekiel 23.

- It was established at the time of the murders that Mary Jane Kelly was involved in an abusive and potentially violent relationship with a secret admirer whose name was 'Joe'. Given that this was not Joseph Flemming, an earlier lover, or Joseph Barnett with whom she had only just parted company on amicable terms, the chances have to be that this was the same 'Joseph Isaacs' who was so agitated on the very night of Kelly's murder that he attracted outside attention.

- The use of the name 'Joseph Isaacs' – in both its first and second components – and for which there is no surviving criminal record before or after the murders, was well in line with the psychological history and patterning of aliases adopted by Joseph Lis in his lifetime. When all the relevant facts are taken into consideration and analysed carefully the evidence is compelling that Joseph Isaacs was Joseph Lis and that he was known to the police prior to the murders.

- At the time of the murders, the arrest of no suspect occasioned more excitement or interest in the senior officer investigating the deaths, Inspector F.G. Abberline, than did Joseph Isaacs. This was in keeping with police preoccupation about a Jewish suspect who may also have been known as Joe, and who had probably had an abusive relationship with Mary Jane Kelly.

- The most detailed description we have of the likely murderer, that provided by the observant, voyeuristic George Hutchinson, tallies remarkably well with that of the younger Joseph Lis. It was also stated by the press at the time to match the description of 'Joseph Isaacs' who, we have good reason to believe, was Joseph Lis.

- The scientific and medical evidence presented at the time of the murders suggests, overwhelmingly, that the killer was right-handed. Joseph Lis, as we now know from an independent, accredited, expert witness, was right-handed.

- Like many serial killers, Joseph Isaacs–Lis returned to the scene of his most recent crime by going to Little Paternoster Row and then walking past Miller's Court on his way to White's Row (also the site of an earlier attack on Annie Millwood) where he sought to have the violin bow repaired. Moreover, as 'James Smith' he returned to exactly the same area of the East End, in 1897/98, after an absence in the United States, and was actively involved in matters relating to the assault, recruitment, rape and exploitation of prostitutes.

Again, the importance of any one of these indicators is open to questioning but, taken together, they point to a single, outstanding, suspect with motive and linked *modus operandi* and offer an unparalleled, powerful, integrated template for the East End murders of 1888. It requires courage and conviction to cross the frontier of coincidence and press on beyond plausibility to reach historical truth. Mary Jane Kelly undoubtedly already knew and continued to fear somebody capable of misogynistic violence; she even told a trusted female friend about her experiences at the hands of the mysterious 'Joe'. You now know – *beyond reasonable doubt* – that his name was indeed Joe, Joe Isaacs or, to give him his real name, Joseph Lis or, much later still, Joseph Silver. Condemn him, but grant the man-beast a final wish – that his remains be left undisturbed in some far-off grave and that he continue to be known, for all time, as 'Jack the Ripper'.

APPENDIX:

CLIO AND THE FOX:
THE HUNT FOR JOSEPH SILVER
AND HIS HIDDEN PASTS

... I have a terrible obligation and it is to know, to know
everything, day and night to know what you call yourself,
that is my job, that is my job, to know a life is not enough
nor is it necessary to know all lives ... I search until I find
the deep weave, thus I also find the unity of men ...

Pablo Neruda, *Hablando en la calle*

RUSSIAN, like many other languages, bulges at the belly with proverbs
about the cunning and elusiveness of the fox – 'Lis'. My first glimpse of
Joseph Lis almost failed to register, not least because he was using the
alias he was most comfortable with through most of his later life, 'Joseph
Silver'. Perhaps I could be excused the oversight, for he could not have
been farther away from his native habitat, the snowy woodlands of
Poland's Holy Cross mountains. I got a glimpse of him beneath the
pounding heat of an African summer, in Johannesburg's Public Library,
in the late 1970s. Out of the corner of an eye reluctant to focus on yet
another issue of the *Standard & Diggers' News*, I caught sight of what
looked like an interesting snippet. It was a report on a court case, quoting
minutes of a meeting of an 'American Club', held in 1898 and presided
over by Silver. A pimps' club devoted solely to organised prostitution and
white slavery was of interest at a time when I was researching ways in
which class, colour and commercial sex were reconciled in a racially
segregated mining community. More interested in processes than personalities, I was nevertheless sufficiently intrigued to jot down his name.

I thought no more of him for several weeks as I looked for ways in which Johannesburg's immigrant underworld reassembled and repositioned itself after the South African War of 1899–1902. Then, one morning, I got a second, tantalising glimpse of the Fox. In 1903 the *Star* reproduced an item from the *Bloemfontein Post*, which reported that Silver had appeared as a witness in connection with a break-in at a jewellery store. The case seemed unusual since the police appeared to have played a very strange role in events surrounding the break-in. It was intriguing because the first report I had read on Silver mentioned that, some years earlier, he had been a 'special agent' for the Society for the Prevention of Crime in New York City. Lis may have been a criminal, but his connections with the police were clearly complex. Not realising what exactly I was embarking on, I wondered what it was that had brought a 'special agent' with American experience to southern Africa.

I drove to the state archives in Pretoria to see what could be collected from that largely stagnant pool of official records of the old 'Transvaal', the Zuid Afrikaansche Republiek (ZAR). The answer, in terms of court and police records, was not much. Official correspondence was disappointingly thin and revealed little about the day-to-day operations of an underworld boss in the pre-war period. Somewhat belatedly, I realised I was probably dredging for evidence at far too superficial a level. Many junior and middle-level officials in the ZAR were corrupt and unlikely to have left traces of their dealings with him. The bucket would have to go down much deeper if I hoped to retrieve anything meaningful; perhaps more senior members of the administration would have shared my concerns? Seen that way, there was one obvious set of correspondence to interrogate – that of J.C. Smuts, the talented young State Attorney whom President Kruger had appointed to deal with precisely such matters in exactly the same year that Joseph Silver arrived in Johannesburg.

Hancock's biography of Smuts revealed nothing about Silver although it did point to the State Attorney's 'Secret Minutes' as an untapped source that historians might wish to explore. I returned to the archives, called for the minutes and, to my delight, uncovered the titanic struggle that had been waged for control of the Johannesburg Public Prosecutor's Office in the late 1890s. This tale of duplicity and double dealing was later published as 'The Modernisation of the Kruger State: F.E.T. Krause, J.C. Smuts and the Contest for Control of the Johannesburg Public Prosecutor's Office, 1898–1899' (*Law and History Review*, Vol. 21, No. 3, Fall 2003, pp. 483–525).

Encouraged by what I read in the 'Secret Minutes', I tracked down a copy of *A Young South African: A Memoir of Ferrar Reginald Mostyn Cleaver, Advocate and Veldkornet*, a work compiled by 'His Mother' – Marguerite de Fenton – and published in 1913. It was one of only four published sources which I managed to trace that had any reference to Silver. A second was *The American Metropolis: From Knickerbocker Days to the Present Time, New York City Life in its Various Phases* by Frank Moss, LL.D, 'of the New York Bar, Counsel to the Society for the Prevention of Crime, Trustee of the City Vigilance League, President of the New York Board of the Police, etc.', with 'an introduction by the Reverend Charles Parkhurst, D.D'. It contained an extract from an interview with a criminal referred to only by his initials and it took me the better part of a decade to verify that 'J.S.' was indeed Joseph Silver. A third source, uncovered after half a decade's fruitless searching of literature on the Argentinian underworld, was A.G. Escobedo's *La Prostitución en Santiago, 1813–1931* (Santiago 1994) in which he appears as 'Josè Silves'. The fourth, a Polish source, based in part on an interview conducted in Silver's birthplace, was K. Urbanski's *Leksykno Kielc, Driejow Ludnusci Zydowskief, 1789–1999* (Kraków 2000) which appeared much later. But I have already been side-tracked; let's pick up the trail and rejoin the hunt.

It so happened that, in 1978, my father, a former detective in the South African Police Force who had been eased out of his position for political reasons after Afrikaner nationalists assumed power in 1948, was being treated for cancer in Bloemfontein. Large doses of radiation left him debilitated and depressed. In an attempt to lift his spirits, I asked him to go to the Free State Archives and local public library to see what he could find out about Silver. Some weeks later he handed me a small sheaf of handwritten notes laying out what had happened to the Fox and friends in the Orange River Colony in 1902–3. From this new material it was clear that, after his departure from Johannesburg in 1899, Silver had been a criminal-policeman and policeman-criminal in Cape Town and Kimberley. My father recovered some of his health and, curious to know where the path had come from and led to, kept asking how my research into Silver's antecedents was progressing. In truth, it was going nowhere. In 1979, after a decade abroad in self-imposed exile, I had returned to South Africa and taken up a position in an institution which later made it clear that it had reservations about my research ability and then, on another matter that demanded due process and some moral courage, publicly distanced itself from me. At the time, however, still in idealistic vein, I was charting historical challenges Africans confronted under the apartheid order and working on the life of Kas Maine, a black South African sharecropper. Nothing could have been farther from the cosmopolitan, urban, criminal universe of Silver than the ethnic, law-abiding, rural domain of Maine.

As I pursued the extraordinary life trajectory of Maine, there was little time to think about Silver. But questions about his earlier career and fate just would not go away. After months of evasion I succumbed and took a short trip to the Cape archives. In most South African archives court records are the first ritual sacrifices before the managerial gods of 'Cost' and 'Space', making them an unpromising source. Not so in Cape Town. Picking away, I uncovered a bit more about Silver's life. Sometime criminal, sometime policeman, often both simultaneously, he had indeed been in Cape Town and Kimberley before Bloemfontein. Moreover, there were documents pointing to a 'wife' who, having gone insane, had been placed in care in the city's Valkenberg 'lunatic asylum'. A note at the very end of a file of police correspondence indicated that, in 1905, Silver had left by ship for Swakopmund in German South West Africa.

Even then, I was not to be fully deflected from seemingly more important projects. Working in the snail-mail era, I sent a query on an old-fashioned blue aerogramme to the South West African Archives – now Namibia – enquiring whether they held any material on Joseph Lis/Silver. Some weeks later I received a courteous, generous reply. There were several files, in Gothic script, recording the doings of Silver – and his brother 'Jack' – as they swept through the German colony in 1905–6. The documents, products of a bureaucracy that had once prompted a classic deliberation by the great Max Weber, were a revelation. In southern Africa, with the exception of the Cape Colony, journalists had more to say about Silver than state officials. In German South West Africa, official correspondence was fat with information while lean little newspapers with small readerships carried almost nothing on my subject.

Hail the Prussians! They had dragged their sense of history along with them as they took occupation of a desert colony. Even in distant 'South West' forms and procedures could not be avoided by those arrested on suspicion of having committed crimes. All suspects not only had to give their name, date, place of birth and religion, but the names, addresses and occupations of their parents! The Fox had been born of

Jewish parents, in Kielce in Russian-Poland, in 1868. In a fit of calculated candour, Silver had also provided a statement again mentioning
his role as a 'special agent' in New York, adding that he had once
owned the American Hotel in Waterloo, London. The files revealed
that he had been given a remarkably stiff three-year sentence for
pimping and that the administration, which appeared unusually fearful
of him, had had him transported to Schleswig-Holstein to serve his
time in a facility in Neumünster. On his release, in 1908, Silver had
said he was going to Paris.

The scents of the Fox – which led back in time to intimate small-
town Poland and the anonymity of London and New York City, and
then forward, to Paris – drove the hound mad. Restrained only by my
linguistic shortcomings, I pawed at the ground, whined and yelped in
frustration. In the end I forced a compromise upon my divided self: I
would continue to contribute as best I could to the African project I
was engaged in, but would collect material that might, one day, support
a life of Lis. But where to start? Of the history of London and New
York I knew nothing. I barely knew where Poland was, let alone Kielce,
a small centre some way south of Warsaw.

A graduate in psychology adrift in a post-Freudian world, it still
made sense for me to start at the beginning. If I could put together
fragments of Lis's childhood, it might provide a few clues for understanding the man. It is difficult to explain what happened next, to
understand how chance and obsession can produce craft-magic. In
1979, the Cold War was still sending chilly ideological breezes and
warm gunsmoke down the continent, and South Africa was in the grip
of white-minority nationalists. Communication with the Soviet Union
or Warsaw Pact allies was frowned upon and might attract the attention of the security police who, a decade earlier, had issued me with
an official warning under the notorious Suppression of Communism
Act. There was little chance a letter to an eastern-bloc country would
reach its destination, let alone a reply find its way back. With e-mail
still a world away, I wrote to various institutions enquiring about
archives; the Polish Cultural Institute, in London, came up with an
address in Kielce. I then sent a letter, in English, to the 'Director of the
Archives' in Kielce, asking for information about Joseph Lis. It was a
precocious message stuffed in a bottle by a schoolboy-historian and I
only half expected a reply.

The archives in Kielce, I later learned, were housed in a building that once had been the synagogue in which Joseph Lis's parents worshipped and it housed as fine a collection of documents as one could hope for. My optimistic query floated through postal currents that security forces liked to fish in, but nobody cared or noticed. The letter washed up on the desk of a director where it lay amongst many other papers. Written in English, emanating from an unloved part of southern Africa, it could have languished there, shimmering in the in-tray like a species of unknown fish caught in the net on a distant shore. Instead, Clio intervened and deputed one of her hundreds of helpers to assist me. The Goddess, bless her, could not have chosen more wisely.

The archivist, Jerzy Szczepánski, was twenty-nine years old, and about to complete a study of 'Civil Servants in the Polish Kingdom, 1815–1866' at the Warsaw Academy of Science. His skills were as amazing as his generosity. Within days he ferreted out records relating to Joseph Lis's birth and uncovered an application, in August 1884, for a passport to proceed to England. He also uncovered an application by Lis's father, in 1879, for an internal passport to proceed to Warsaw amidst objections from the police who considered him a primary suspect in a serious robbery. All these details, meticulously sourced, were put down in a wonderfully warm and lengthy letter to me. That letter, too, somehow swam past often pesky Polish and South African fishermen.

I was delighted by the response. There was an obvious interest in, and curiosity about, the research I was doing along with questions about where things Polish could possibly fit into the broader work I was engaged in. But there was something that left me uneasy about a letter, handwritten on plain paper, sent from an address that was obviously not that of the archive. It was several days before the full significance of this dawned on me – Szczepánski, seemingly disillusioned with life in Poland, was probably not in a position to reply to me officially and was, in the most careful way possible, sounding me out about the possibilities of obtaining employment in South Africa. No wonder he was writing from home! He was operating in a political environment far more difficult than my own, and thinking about abandoning Poland.

Here was an unusual situation – two men connected by a love of history, one locked into 'communist' Poland and the other, equally reluctantly, stuck in 'fascist' South Africa. It was the start of a ten-year-long exchange, punctuated on both sides by the desire for a face-to-face meeting. We attempted to meet, in 1988 in the docks at Hamburg, with my having flown there from Johannesburg and he having sneaked in on a day ferry from Gdansk, but mishaps denied us a rendezvous. When I did eventually meet him later that year, he took me on a fascinating tour of Kielce and the world that Lis and his extended family grew up in. What the low-level agent in the Polish police who followed us around made of that visit during the terminal phase of the Cold War only he would know. Hopefully, somewhere in a police archive there is a document recording that, more than a hundred years after his birth, Silver was still attracting the attention of officials in the Old Country, albeit in an unintended way.

For months the post brought a drizzle of facts about the unenviable life of the family Lis in the nineteenth century, while I built on the one clue I had – that he had been granted a passport to travel to England, where he would have arrived in early 1885. From material acquired from Windhoek I knew that he must have been in the UK between 1885 and 1889. Indeed, the information I had pointed to his illegitimate daughter, Bertha, having been born there in 1888. But ne'er was there a more futile search. There was no record of a departure from Hamburg, no record of an arrival in Britain and no unofficial record proving that he had been there, or that his daughter had been born there. With heavy heart I decided that I should, for the moment, concentrate on the New World. But if I could not find him in England, with its great passion for history, what chance was there of finding him among the millions of immigrants on New York City's Lower East Side in the early 1890s? I had, however, reckoned without the assistance of She-Who-Works-in-Mysterious Ways. If 'old' English sources failed me, then 'modern' American ones rescued me.

Street directories, the index to the *New York Times*, reports in other journals as well as Manhattan court documents and state prison registers provided a rich vein of data not only on Lis but on the actor, 'Adolph Goldberg', his close companion until 1895. An application by Lis to become a naturalised citizen in 1891, after a spell in Sing Sing, deepened the mystery about his earlier undocumented stay in England. So, too, did a passport application in 1895 when he was fleeing the wrath of the New York Police Department. Both applications acknowledged that he had entered the USA from England but, whenever probed about his pre-1889 stay in London, Lis *always* responded with lies. Why? The manifest of the ship that he supposedly arrived on did not carry his name, or that of anyone approximating his age or personal details: indeed, the vessel had not even been in New York on the date he nominated in March 1885. No immigrant was likely to forget both the date of his arrival in New York and the name of the ship that carried him to the United States. It was part of a constant, calculated effort, in travels around the Atlantic world over a period of thirty years, to conceal his stay in England in the late 1880s. What was he trying to hide? Further evidence of obfuscation came from a fragment of evidence offered by Goldberg, in a Manhattan court case, when he let slip that he had been in Lis's company in London in 1889 – something that also made me keen to track Goldberg's movements in the hope of discovering a paper trail. Moreover, in Frank Moss's account in the *American Metropolis*, the increasingly less mysterious 'J.S.' that I had been tracking stated that he had entered the United States not in 1885 – a convenient date for someone later trying to maximise the elapse of time in order to become a naturalised citizen and acquire a passport – but in 1889. Everything then, as now, points to Lis having been in London's East End during the mid- to late 1880s.

Unable to find evidence of the Fox in England in the period that interested me, I decided to concentrate on Goldberg. Goldberg never betrayed his friend but, indirectly, he eventually led me to an address in Plumber's Row in Whitechapel. I put together Goldberg's movements and criminal record, much of which chimed with the way he and Lis later operated in New York City, but was unable to find incontrovertible evidence proving that they had been together for most of the period 1885–89. Lis – as he then may have been known briefly – would have been sexually active and in the East End at the time when he may have been a barber. Indeed, in Silver's most truthful account of his early life, given to Frank Moss, he claimed to have been a barber and in possession of $1,000 when he entered the USA in 1889. Again, I could only ask – but never answer – the question: what was this violent, knife-carrying misogynist doing between 1885 and 1889? Why did he and those around him make it their project to conceal his presence in the East End of London at a time when some unknown woman gave birth to his daughter? Whoever that woman was, she, along with one other prostitute, perhaps two he had lived with, had later disappeared.

By contrast, the period between Lis's hurried return to London, from New York in 1895, and his departure for Johannesburg, in 1898, was fairly well documented. It was a short interlude but one in which there was abundant evidence of his pursuit of prostitutes, violent sex assaults, willingness to use a knife and an engagement with the international

white slave traffick. It was during the same short stay that he forged
the madness of Rachel Laskin, the first of several prostitute wife-slaves.
As 'Lizzie Josephs' she was later confined to the mental hospital in
Cape Town and to a miserable death decades later in an up-country
mental hospital, not knowing her real name. Depending on one's views
on the development of personality, patterns of mental illness and continuities in history, the period in London from 1895 to 1898 might, or
might not, throw light on what had happened in 1885–89. I thought
it did.

But where did such damning information come from? A trawl through
records in the Family Records Centre, London, uncovered one of at
least two sham marriages in different countries. Hannah Opticer married
Lis in a civil ceremony in Lambeth in October 1895, and was never
again heard of – a fate she shared with Hannah Vygenbaum who, like
her, got married before state officials in Simonstown in 1902 only to
disappear later. A register of cases heard in magistrates' courts in
London revealed other, less serious crimes against property. It was,
however, a short extract from the records of the Jewish Association for
the Protection of Girls, Women and Children (JAPGWC) for 1898 –
now housed in the Hartley Library at the University of Southampton
– forwarded to me by Ed Bristow, that alerted me to the extent of
Silver's operations in the East End and links to the wider world. An
entry in a street directory confirmed Silver's presence at the American
Hotel, and the index to the London *Times* pointed me to the court case
referred to in JAPGWC records. Unfortunately the *Times*, and more
especially so the records of the Old Bailey, proved to be disappointingly thin: both noted, in Victorian fashion, that details of cases in
which Silver, his kin and other gangsters had appeared 'were unfit for
publication'.

I was, I thought, making excellent progress. The picture for London
(1895–98), when placed back to back with reports about the 'King of
the Pimps' in Johannesburg (1898–99), gave me a far better idea of the
scope of the project I was working on; when the Fox heard baying he
was apt to put water between himself and the hounds. What could stop
me now? I was certain I would find him in Paris, in 1908, where he
would, almost certainly, be operating as a pimp or white slaver. The
dog bounded along. How foolish I was and how severely Clio punished
me for a lack of professionalism! She had showered me with contacts
and evidence and, instead of working carefully through the material I

had collected and pausing to pick out ambiguity, contradiction and paradox, I had grown impatient. I had so much more to learn about his personality, his *modus operandi* and the world in which he operated. A more careful study of the data gathered in the Cape and South West Africa should have alerted me to the fact that he was far more complicated than I initially thought – that he was a man, unequally divided, whose inner struggles, if not between good and evil, were between evil and less evil. Seen from that angle, the most horrifying behaviour lay in systematic attacks on the bodies, minds and personalities of women and the lesser evils in his crimes against property. When at last I tracked him down in Paris he was neither pimp nor white slaver. Perhaps I should have known this – had he not just completed three years in a prison in Neumünster, for pimping?

On entering France, Silver appears to have taken a decision to eschew contact with prostitutes and organised prostitution. It was a shift that may, in part have been facilitated by his violent brother, Jack, recently returned from Argentina after a major jewellery heist at the home of an opera diva. In Paris, Silver reverted to a pattern practised with Goldberg, but this time in more sophisticated fashion and at an elevated level. The casual burglary, petty theft and store-breaking of an adrenalin-charged muscular youth willing to settle for small, regular hauls gave way to cerebral exploits by a middle-aged jewel thief and safecracker in search of fewer, but far larger, rewards. He was not to be found in his usual low haunts and only deliberate sifting of registers in Parisian courts finally revealed his whereabouts. Clio knows that mule-like obstinacy and stamina can sometimes compensate for a lack of insight or wit. I had him traced in an account that was disappointingly terse and sought to supplement it with material drawn from newspapers and prison registers. Desiccated fruit yields no juice. He had indeed been in the City of Light, played a part in a jewellery store theft, been arrested and appeared in court but somehow managed to avoid serving a term of imprisonment.

What to do? He could have gone anywhere. It seemed logical to explore the continent before going back to an East End search or, perish the thought, even farther afield in some as yet unknown country. Stuck amidst the archival casinos of Europe, where luck sometimes trumped science, I decided to take another chance. With the Goddess of History scowling at my rank opportunism, I wrote to national repositories in Belgium, Germany and the Netherlands asking whether they had any record of 'Joseph Lis/Silver' between 1908 and the outbreak of the First World War. The barrels of the great machines began to roll and, when they came to rest some weeks later there, firmly in the frame, against all the odds, were three cherries. Hooray for the home of scientific policing; for the land of Maigret and of Poirot! The Belgian archives had a file covering the period 1909–10 and two photographs!

It got better. The file on Lis was, as the old cliché has it, pure gold. It recorded his passage through Belgium, France, Germany and Holland over several months along with that of a band of jewel thieves and bank robbers he had linked up with. The activities of the gang, composed largely of men and women drawn from his native province, Kielce, provided new insights. Read in conjunction with other files recording impressive heists, it showed how the émigré Russo-Polish underworld had links not only with gangs in London's East End such as the Bessarabians, but with similar groupings all round the Atlantic. A file retrieved from Washington, DC covering the extradition of one of the gang members, Leibus Brjiski, from the United States to Belgium was the spur for rethinking carefully the wider context in which Silver had operated in the historical past, was operating in during the first decade of the twentieth century and, in all probability, continued to operate in the First World War.

The final entry on the Brussels file indicated that he had again eluded continental justice and, by mid-1910, was on his way to Buenos Aires. Now that made sense. Had not his brother been there just twenty-four months earlier? A second foray into the Atlantic was just what I needed to get me to think through 'the bigger picture'. I tracked every reading I could on East Europeans and organised crime in the cities of the western hemisphere. I then attempted to link this to technological advances in the late nineteenth century, such as the spread of the tele-graph and the advent of cheap rail and steamship travel, and came to the predictable conclusion that I was dealing with the story of one man's determined exploration of the Atlantic world. The essay appeared as 'Jewish Marginality in the Atlantic World: Organised Crime in the Era of the Great Migrations, 1880–1914' (*South African Historical Journal*, Vol. 43, Nov. 2000 pp. 96–137). For those blessed with 20–20 vision, the 'discovery' that I was working in an Atlantic-wide context was not worth commenting on, but for me, trapped in the twilight of pragmatic enquiry, it brought a flood of light. I revelled in what seemed like new acuity but my Goddess just smiled. Clio knew better than I, that exposure to too much light after groping about in the dark hardly makes for clear-sightedness.

In the mid-1980s, convinced that Silver had gone to Argentina, I was lured deeper into the Atlantic by lights seen through dense fog. I undertook an initial search in Buenos Aires. It would only be a matter of time before I picked up the scent. It *was* only a matter of time: it took me ten years. It was in the mid-1990s, with the help of an exceptional researcher, Gabriela Braccio, that I worked out a little more clearly what had happened to Silver after he fled Belgium in 1910. But to this day there are some questions – such as his date of entry into Argentina and the timing of his departure – that remain unanswered. Clio, who knew where the *real* clues lay, laughed at my efforts to crack the codes of this master mariner of the underworld.

Throughout the 1980s I searched in vain. Silver was nowhere to be found in Buenos Aires, in the mysterious underworld of the Zwi Migdal. Nor did his name or a variant of it appear in the registers of the criminal courts; a place where you might expect to find a bank robber or safe-cracker. My historical eyesight deteriorated and I cast about ever more frantically for other, more 'logical', sites in the Atlantic world. East European pimps and white slavers were notorious for following the flow of capital: perhaps he had gone to Brazil which drew in thousands of immigrants each year? Or Cuba? What about Cuba? Cuba, with easy access to the United States, was ideal for anyone with an interest in vice and a love of dollars. And what of Mexico, where urban growth offered an ideal retail, perhaps wholesale, market for prostitutes? Could he not have gone to Panama, where some Russo-Polish entrepreneurs of the flesh exploited the market created by the construction of the Canal? Partial, tentative probes in Colon, Havana, Rio de Janeiro and Mexico City – all done without much conviction – failed to produce any answer. My 'theory' about the Atlantic world was, it seemed, no more than an obsession with geography. The source of my inspiration was deficient and in the background I heard Clio chuckling.

C. Wright Mills, in a brilliant essay, warned of the dangers of becoming intoxicated with 'grand theory'. Mine was hardly 'grand', let alone a 'theory', and I should have let go but, like a drunk with a bottle at daybreak, I cradled last night's solace. Every time, I was ready to abandon the demon, a swig would offer renewed reason for hope. After months of fruitless wanderings I abandoned speculation about Buenos Aires. I

returned to basics and concentrated on what I could remember. Silver
had always been attached to his United States citizenship and, when
last seen in Europe, had been travelling on a forged American passport. If he was indeed a creature of the Atlantic world, then surely he
would have returned to the United States and reapplied for a passport
under the name 'Silver' so that he could continue to roam the seas?
And, if he did get a passport, there was surely nothing for it but to
work systematically through those most soul-destroying sources of all
– the manifests of ships calling at port cities in the Atlantic? It was the
counsel of despair but it did stop Clio laughing. She approves of
exhausting searches. That's her style, damn her.

Unwilling to fight on one front, I opened up two lines of attack –
the first exploring passenger lists of ships entering New York between
1910 and 1914; the second probing passport applications, in
Washington, DC. It was guerrilla war; you knew the enemy was out
there somewhere, that you needed to be vigilant at all times, but there
was no guarantee that a satisfactory engagement would follow. A foray
in the forests of documentation uncovered a trail of broken twigs. In
May 1914, Joseph Silver, 'a merchant' – the nomenclature of choice
for white slavers – had disembarked in New York having boarded the
Mauretania in Liverpool. He was back in the Atlantic world and still
active. More tracking flushed him again. In January 1916 he entered
New York City from Bergen, via neutral Norway. It was a significant
find since tracking gangsters during the war was almost impossible and
the *Kristianiasfjord* was a vessel much favoured by activists and spies
of all stripes during the turbulence of the First World War.

But a fox by the foot is a fox only half snared. I hoped that, if I
found an application for a passport, it would provide the cord to bind
him securely. In the end, it did not do so but it did give me an idea
where to continue the search at a time when Europe was drenched in
blood and underworld figures were less likely to be found centre stage.
Whenever streams of international capital and migrant labour were
interrupted, pimps and prostitutes abandoned their old haunts and
followed the armies that heralded the largely male business of war.

For reasons unconnected to war, thousands of men and women
engaged in the 'immoral traffick' had abandoned Argentina in 1913
and repositioned themselves in central and western European cities –
a trend that accelerated as twilight settled over the continent. Silver,
too, moved with rather than against the tides of humanity. A passport

application, in New York in June 1914, offered an interesting new lie. He was, he claimed, born in 'Myslowitz', in German Silesia. It was a fascinating choice. Myslowitz was a transhipment point for white slavers, close to the Austro-Hungarian border, but beyond it lay Kraków and Kielce. It seemed that an ageing Silver was intent on business, but that he may also have been hankering to get back home. This helped clear research pathways for the period after 1914, but did nothing to fill the earlier gap in his career. Where had he been between 1910 and 1914? Love of continuity in the temporal domain is one of the weaknesses that besets drones in the hives of history. I needed – no, demanded – to know what had happened to him after he fled Belgium *before* I explored wartime Europe, a search that had started, in desultory fashion, some years earlier. But She-Who-Knows-All refused to give so much as a hint as to where to start. Her parsimoniousness was trying and, shunning her company, I took to my study and struggled like a mad alchemist to manufacture luck, to produce silver from paper. If I could not track Joseph Lis, I reasoned, then I was better advised to try to find his brother, Jack. Surely the tracks of the younger Lis would, in the fullness of time, lead me to the lair of the sibling?

An old craft formula demanded that I return to what was known, re-examine the facts and extend the lines of reasoning. Jack Lis was last seen in Paris in 1910, but to the extent that he had a 'home' he favoured London. While the older of the Lis brothers clung to an 'American' identity, Jack was more inclined to see himself as English. If ever *he* sought citizenship or a passport, it was likely to be British. Attempts to track him through the usual naturalisation processes and passport applications proved fruitless. Clinging to the only thread I held, I tugged to see if it was attached to anything other than archival fantasies. If Jack was 'British', abroad after 1910 and found himself in trouble, then perhaps some British ambassador or consul out there in the Atlantic world would have brought it to the attention of colleagues in Whitehall? I commissioned a combing of the Foreign Office correspondence registers in the then wonderfully reassuringly named Public Records Office and, amazingly, there it was!

'It', was the most extraordinary thing – both much more and far less than I hoped for. I was like a child on Christmas morning finding wrapping paper hinting at a longed-for treasure only to discover the present itself missing. The registers showed that, in 1913, Sir Henry Lowther, Consul in Santiago de Chile, had written to London requesting that inquiries be made about the criminal histories of the brothers 'Silver' but the surviving 'files' were mere folders – the letters they once contained were gone: for ever. All those warnings about 'grand theory' rang in my ears. Twenty years into a biographical search and I had only just discovered that my subject had once spent three years on the Pacific coastline; in Chile! So captivated by the formalistic dimensions of my Atlantic 'theory' had I become that I had lost all sensitivity to the underlying economic and social realities that bound Silver's universe. Instead of placing my starting point in South America in its *regional* context, I had slipped into seeing Argentina as a self-contained, Atlantic-facing, entity. Instead of focusing on its links with its trans-Andean neighbour and exploring the integrating political economy of crime, I had viewed Argentina as a mere nation-state – the most treacherous of all units of analysis for a historian. It was an error of undergraduate proportions, one that had resulted in years of inefficient searching, of wasted effort.

Chastened, I tried to make up for lost time by exploring the three years the Lis brothers had spent in Santiago and Valparaiso. Everything I uncovered, via a generous and enterprising South American colleague, showed that prostitution and white slavery in Chile were, in essence, an extension of supply lines that could be traced back to Argentina and the Zwi Migdal and then, via the steamship, back across the oceans into central and western Europe. Although based on the Pacific coast, Silver's business remained firmly hooked into the dynamics of the 'Atlantic world'. My error had arisen from being too literal – or as the deconstructionist would have it, too littoral-minded. I had scoured place and structure to the exclusion of process.

Having restored some continuity to Silver's career I was ready to push on and focus on what lay behind his sketchy zigzagging across the Atlantic between late 1914 and early 1916 and onto the partially lit area beyond. In truth, beyond confirming Silver's movements and the fact that he was a 'merchant' – a person buying and selling 'commodities' – the passenger lists had not been very helpful. But even that meagre ration of information, ship biscuit in size, was better than nothing. It spoke of a man in his mid-forties, of a body slowing down, of a mind shifting emphasis from the hectic physical burglar-pimp exploits of youth, to the more cerebral considerations of matching supply and demand in the market-place at a time of great social instability.

In one sense, however, these musings were as much a part of a problem as they were of a solution. If he was a 'merchant' in the 'Atlantic world' during the earlier part of the war – and everything pointed in that direction – he was operating at the supply *and* demand ends of the chain. This meant that he was collecting or recruiting prostitutes and white slaves in parts of central and western Europe that had been over-supplied with prostitutes ever since the industrial revolution, and directing or distributing them to venues somewhere in the central or southern Atlantic where, regardless of status, women remained in great demand. It was a dangerous and fraught practice at the best of times, let alone during the war when commercial shipping was disrupted and vulnerable to enemy attack. The same realities made for an 'import–export' business that was unlikely to have survived the duration of the conflict. What I needed to do was to address the lacunae that existed *between* Silver's arrivals in New York in mid-1914 and early 1916. Given the difficulty of tracing white slavers during the economic and social upheavals of 1914–18, it made sense to focus on his penchant for operating in the western hemisphere. This time the false lights that had so nearly lured me on to the rocks in places like Colon, Havana or Vera Cruz held no attraction. Still smarting from my Chilean mis-adventure, I re-examined the developed locus of underworld power in the south Atlantic – Argentina, Buenos Aires and the Zwi Migdal.

If Silver had *not* returned to Argentina and Chile after 1914, and I was almost certain that he had not, there was only one place where the writ of the Zwi Migdal continued to run and where his business connections would have held some sway – Brazil. And if the Fox had burrowed into Brazil, there was only one place to seek him – Rio de Janeiro. The only consideration that caused me to pause briefly was the question of language. How would he operate in a Lusophone en-vironment? But on reflection this problem, too, was brushed aside. What terrors could Portuguese hold for a man who was in control of good measures of English, German, Polish, Spanish, Russian and Yiddish? I remained confident even though I caught Her raising a quizzical eyebrow.

Casting a net requires more skill than hauling it in; the latter demands patience and strength rather than wit. Twenty years working the coastal shallows of every continent framing the Atlantic produces grudging respect for mundane aspects of the profession. It took an effort to draw the net in and upon examination, the catch was sardine rather than shark. Nevertheless, there, one day in 2002, it lay – quivering silver in the sunlight after its submergence in the murky brine of immigration records. He had entered Rio aboard the *Voltaire* in February 1915 but stayed in the city only briefly. Two months later, days before his forty-seventh birthday, he had boarded the *Alcantara* and joined two other prominent white slavers from Buenos Aires who, like him, were bound for Liverpool. It was hardly a coincidence that the three were making their way to London's East End, and it reconfirmed Silver's ongoing interest in white slavery.

Nothing is more pathetic than a researcher who, having enjoyed success with one technique and devoid of a better idea, works the method to death. I probed shipping manifests and port city records but nothing was forthcoming. Given that he had re-entered Britain in 1915, I was keen to establish his, or his brother's presence. Having failed, I settled on a new ploy. Instead of trying to find him skulking in the shadows of wartime London, I would skip ahead in time to the better-illuminated post-war years. If I did find him I could always double back to fill the gaps in a story which, at almost every turn, already mocked the contours of the finest crafted fiction.

The chances of finding the Fox after 1918 were, I knew, slim. In 1984, a graduate student, Hartwig Stein and a Pole, Rysard Swietek, had helped uncover a clue pointing to his presence in Hamburg in 1917 and on the troubled eastern front in 1918. Fourteen years later, in 1998, another researcher, Dirk Nierhaus helped confirm what had happened to Silver during the closing months of the war. But still I felt the need to be certain. What made a further search appealing was the knowledge that, in 1927, the League of Nations had undertaken extensive research in the Atlantic world to produce a comprehensive, city-by-city report on the 'Traffick in Women and Children'. It was easy enough to determine that Silver did not figure in the main body of the report by name – indeed none of the white slaving fraternity did, since all traffickers were referred to by their initials only. But what if his name or a new alias were to be discovered in the *unpublished* material the 1927 report was based on? It took a trip to Geneva, in 2001, to persuade me that he had not survived the war.

Having completed this 'negative' search, I felt more confident in re-examining his wartime movements in the Atlantic, in Germany and on the eastern front. The 1914 passport application confirmed his intention of operating in, or around, Germany. Nor had I lost sight of the brief unexpected appearance of the Fox in Norway in early 1916 – it was of a piece with someone who, having passed through Hamburg, had embarked at a Baltic or Dutch port under German control. What did this review reveal? The material Stein had found showed that, on 1 March 1917, a military court in Jaroslaw, on the eastern front under Austro-Hungarian control, had asked the police in Hamburg to arrest Jakob Pilat, born in Wolina in 1884 and a certain Filip Skrzat, real name Joseph Lis (but no date of birth), on charges of theft and espionage. Days later the police had passed on the request to colleagues in Gelsenkirchen and, by 18 March, the police in Berlin – who, significantly, possessed a photo of Lis – had joined in the search for the Fox. But at that point the written evidence petered out.

What was to be made of this? Hamburg seemed to fit. The port city, which he had passed through as a sixteen-year-old on his way to London, was within easy reach of the Baltic and close enough to his former prison home in Neumünster for him to have criminal acquaintances in the area. Gelsenkirchen, too, was of a piece. Not only was it in the industrialised Ruhr region but close to his mid-career triumph, the 1910 bank robbery in Aachen. Neither was it surprising, given his history in South West Africa, that the authorities in Berlin should possess a photo of the suspect, 'Josef Lis'. But what was more suggestive still was the fact that the Polish town of Jaroslaw was only 175 kilometres from the Fox's home in Kielce. Could that, too, be coincidence?

The answer to that, in one sense 'final' question, in a twenty-five-year-long search lay in the records of the Austro-Hungarian army, in the Military Archives, Vienna. Finding documentation that matched the German police records could only have been one of Her favours. Conflict along the eastern front was marked by arbitrary actions against individual Jews as well as scores of pogroms. The war unleashed all of central and eastern Europe's anti-Semitic demons, prejudices and stereotypes. While 'Joseph Silver', a police informer with a penchant for larceny, was more than capable of 'theft' and 'espionage' in peacetime, Joseph Lis, a Polish Jew, would have had to have done far less to draw such charges in wartime. What did 'theft' and 'espionage' mean at a time when anti-Semitism acted as Public Prosecutor on both sides of the front? In times of war one man's theft was another's attempt at survival. In the same way class, ethnicity and crisis could transform common knowledge into sensitive information. When it came to 'the Jews', one size fitted all. The records in Vienna, dripping with the silences that mark wartime processes, did not interrogate the elasticities of supposed 'theft' and 'espionage'. What the incomplete documents did confirm was that Lis and four accomplices had been arrested on an unknown date in late 1917, perhaps early 1918, and then been tried and probably sentenced to death.

Clio and the Fox, lovers of ambiguity, were not content to leave the matter there. After the imposition of sentence, there was a flurry of appeals and a petition for clemency emanating from Kielce, in July 1918. It fitted with his argumentative, legalistic predilections but also caused the dispersal of the files that were now untraceable. Clio continues to toy with me. An interview in the early 1980s with one of a handful of Jews from Kielce who survived the Holocaust confirmed that Joseph Lis/Silver had not survived the war, though it was coupled to the totally baseless suggestion that the Fox had died in Brussels, in 1912. Nor are the surviving records of the Austro-Hungarian army helpful. The final entry on his file, after the appeal for clemency from Kielce in the summer of 1918, is fittingly enigmatic. It indicates only that the matter has been 'settled'. In the end just one fragment drawn from an interview with a survivor of Treblinka, and a negative search of records for the 1920s and 1930s, 'prove' that Joseph Lis of Kielce was executed as a spy in 1918.

And perhaps in that messy uncertainty, too, lies truth of a kind. In the background I see Her smiling, still teasing me. Did the Fox really die that summer and, if so, what unknown truths did he take to earth with him? Why was he, and those around him, so determined not to reveal where he had been between 1885 and 1889 when all the circumstantial evidence pointed to London's East End and Whitechapel? Clio called me nearer and then, most unexpectedly, whispered her most jealously guarded secret of all in my ear – she loves questions more than answers; her work is never done.

All the above, using the hit-and-miss methodology I adopted in researching the life of Silver was written months, nay, years, before I again reviewed the evidence and decided – not without misgivings – to try to write a dedicated chapter on the Fox in Whitechapel. Most historians know how chance and craft can produce a defining moment in the life of a book but other readers may be interested to know when I became curious about Jack the Ripper and why it was that I chose to link my material on Lis to events in the East End in the autumn of 1888. There was no single clear-cut moment of discovery when it became apparent to me that Lis, as he was in 1888, was the Ripper.

It was the slow unfolding of my imperfect understanding of Silver's mind and personality that led me to that conclusion. It was a hesitant, cumulative process that took place over years rather than a one-off revelation.

No historian researching London of the mid-1880s can avoid the Whitechapel murders. Lit by the popular and serious literature that flicker behind the slayings, the shadows of the usual suspects move through the historiography. From the moment I established that Lis had gone to England on leaving Kielce in 1884–5, I was aware that his presence there coincided with the murders. But the thought that he might have been connected to the slaughter was the last thing I had in mind at the time. I knew he had an interest in, perhaps an obsession with, prostitutes that must have started at about the time of the Whitechapel murders but as I was unversed in 'Ripperology' or the psychiatric literature, his age at the time – twenty – seemed a disqualification. In the early 1980s I was so preoccupied with just trying to track his movements that I paid scant attention to the growing literature on the murders. At the prompting of my friend, Tim Couzens, I read the Ripper literature solely to develop a feel for time and place.

I never went looking for Jack the Ripper – *he* always came looking for *me*. It was not I who tugged at Silver's sleeve to ask if there was any chance that he was the Ripper; it was Joseph Lis who, through his consistent attempts to conceal his presence in London in 1885–88, aroused my suspicions. Two pieces of evidence made me wonder whether it was not silly to ignore a possible link between Lis and the murders. The first, I encountered early on. In J.C. Smuts's 'Secret Correspondence', Lis allegedly threatened a prostitute by telling her that he would 'open up her belly'. The reference was clear, but it could just have been verbal excess – a dramatic, but ultimately meaningless way of getting a point across to a Victorian prostitute. But then, months later, I discovered that he had been party to an unsuccessful conspiracy to have blue vitriol stuffed into the vagina of a recalcitrant prostitute in German South West Africa. Placed back to back, they forced me to reappraise the East End murders.

I read the secondary literature but, other than developing some sensitivity to the issues of barbers and the name 'Ludwig', found nothing to go on. Like police at the time and historians since, I clutched at such circumstantial evidence as I could find. Contemporary talk about the murderer having been a 'Polish Jew', a description of Lis gleaned from

American prison records, and the birth of an unwanted child in 1888, gave me no reason to *exclude* Lis as a suspect, but it was tough going. When in 2000 I wrote the first draft of the chapter covering his stay in London, I hinted that he could have had motive and opportunity for the killings – that he *may* have been the right man, in the right place, at the right time. I could see bits of the puzzle that fitted but was hardly convinced. On a scale from one to ten, I thought that the chances of his being the Ripper stood at one or two. I took fragments pointing to Ripper-like behaviour and incorporated them into appropriate contexts throughout this book, diluting the evidence and reducing the chances of ever persuading readers that Lis should be considered a leading suspect. There the matter rested for three years while I drafted the remaining chapters of what was already a lengthy study. I decided not to foreground any Ripper angles for fear that they would not only be unpersuasive but would detract from what was an interesting biography in its own right. I wanted Lis's life clear of unsolved murders which authors had been analysing, without success, for more than a century. I was unwilling to trade what I *knew* about Lis for the unknown.

But, as we have noted repeatedly, Clio delights in teasing devotees. Twice she sent bolts of lightning to brighten the dull night sky of my mind. First, while trawling the internet for clues that might help me better understand Lis's strange mind, I chanced upon an article written in 1989 by Gordon Banks exploring the possibility that Don Juan was a psychopath. It reminded me of Hervey Cleckley's classic, *The Mask of Sanity*. It is difficult for me to over-emphasize the effect that a re-reading of Cleckley's work, last encountered as an inattentive undergraduate, had on me. Each chapter read like a historical guide to Lis's behaviour and helped make sense of his inner life. With the mask lifted, I made sense of hundreds of seemingly unrelated bits of evidence accumulated over decades. At last I could understand his relationship with his brother and daughter and behaviour which had seemed irrational. Cleckley pushed me to read modern literature on psychopathy.

Armed with new insights I suppose I should have re-examined the possibility of Lis being linked to the Whitechapel murders. I did not because, having recently worked through the secondary literature, I could find no circumstantial evidence placing him close to the slayings. Even though I knew that Lis sometimes took on different identities and names, I was still looking for him or someone easily identifiable as him. Here, then, was another cardinal error. No professional historian should ever develop new insights, acquire new sensitivities and then not go back and systematically review *all* the evidence at his disposal. Good historical research demands constant reassessment of documentary evidence so that it can be realigned and repositioned with new ways of seeing the subject. I was not good enough to do that. But Clio never deserts the truly faithful; she literally shoved a new possibility under my nose. Ian Phimister, a historian friend who knew about the tentative links I had been exploring, sent me a copy of Evans and Skinner's *The Ultimate Jack the Ripper Source Book: An Illustrated Encyclopaedia.* Clio must have despaired. For several months I did nothing about my unexpected but welcome gift. The book joined others in a pile beside my bed. When I did start reading it, I went about it in the compulsive, intense way that comes readily to those who are obsessive.

Although it is a reference book, if a delightfully well-ordered one, I decided to read all of the encyclopaedia. It gave me nothing new until I got to page 437. There I saw, for the first time, reproduced in its entirety, a newspaper account of the arrest of the suspect, Joseph Isaacs, a Polish Jew. But not even that could nudge me towards Joseph Lis. It was not until I read about Isaacs's impulsive behaviour that I was convinced of the need to probe, systematically, the similarities between Isaacs and Lis. Having the concept of psychopathy to draw on placed me at a huge advantage over police at the time. That, together with evidence about Lis's childhood and behaviour in the thirty years after the Whitechapel murders, encouraged me to speculate that 'Lis' and 'Isaacs' might well be the same person. I revisited the psychological literature – a process that got new focus, urgency and purpose when Milton Shain steered Robert Kaplan, a forensic psychiatrist with a passion for history, in my direction in mid-2004. Kaplan's expert tutoring helped me understand the inner world of serial killers and accurately identify behavioural traits associated with the development of neurosyphilis in a subject like Joseph Lis.

Still there was no epiphany. The advances in my understanding simply highlighted two new problems requiring urgent attention. The first was to try, yet again, to find a fragment of circumstantial evidence that might place Lis in Whitechapel, in 1888. I went back to the Family Records Centre in London and came across the marriage of a young woman, Mandel Lis, to Moses Gourvitch, on 11 March 1888. The FRC does not encourage frivolous enquiries but the name 'Lis' was sufficiently uncommon for me to decide to take a chance. I paid for a copy of the certificate to be forwarded to me, not knowing exactly what it was I wanted from it. The second was the need to reconstruct, far more carefully, the killer's mindset during the murders.

Well, I never did find that one piece of incontrovertible evidence that could convince everyone in the world that Joseph Lis was Jack the Ripper; but twice I sensed the Grail was within reach. One morning, in March 2005, I walked across to the porters' lodge at Magdalen and collected my mail. I opened the letter from the FRC and made the astounding discovery that, at the time of their marriage in March 1888, Gourvitch and Mandel Lis were living in the house of her father, at 35 Plumber's Row, Whitechapel. There, before me, was the most exciting, extraordinary 'coincidence' imaginable. Number 35 Plumber's Row was, presumably, directly opposite number 34 – the very place where Lis's closest friend, Adolph Goldberg, had committed a burglary in late 1887 while living around the corner at 3 Vine Court. Surely it was a place that, at some point or other, the young Joseph Lis had access to? It also reminded me of Martin Fido's observation that, after the murder of Mary Ann Nichols, three streetwalkers had told the police that they suspected a man living not far from Buck's Row, close by Plumber's Row. Furthermore, the route taken by the Ripper after the murder of Catherine Eddowes in Mitre Square, via Goulston Street, was not incompatible with someone looping round back towards Plumber's Row.

The next moment, probably even less convincing for sceptics, came during that same exhilarating term at Magdalen. While re-examining evidence relating to the murders I was alerted to the need to be far more rigorous in my thinking about two broadly related matters. The murderer clearly had a loathing for streetwalkers, as opposed to brothel-based prostitutes. Might it not be profitable to explore the notions of ritual purity, danger and sexual pollution that would inform a nominal Jew, like Silver? I reconstructed the pattern of his interactions with prostitutes and saw, ever more clearly, that he had a well-developed interest in public baths/*mikvot* and that he confined the prostitutes to the point where his brothels became like prisons.

This led to a second line of enquiry – to establish the historical evolution of the way in which adulteresses, like his mother, and prostitutes were treated in Jewish tradition. While exploring L.M. Epstein's *Sex Laws and Customs in Judaism*, I learned that, in ancient times, female transgressors of the law had their noses and ears sliced off; a startling realisation which forced me to re-examine the mutilation of Catherine Eddowes, the fireside butchering of Mary Jane Kelly and the early street attack on Emma Smith. These insights into early 'Jewish' ideas of punishment were, however, of no value unless it could be demonstrated that Silver carried about deep within him medieval notions of justice. The fact that he did indeed invoke wild biblical and other images when under stress added significantly to mounting evidence against him.

For reasons I only partially understand, over a period of several days I came to the conclusion that the 'solution' to the murders did not lie only in mutilation of the victims' sex organs – the preoccupation of most literary detectives – but in the underlying significance of the removal of rings from the fingers of two of the prostitutes and the slicing off of the ears and noses of two other victims. Was it not the seemingly incidental, the trivial and the unexceptional that led to the solution of most murders? I became ever more convinced that the cutting off of the ears and noses was a key component in the serial killer's developing 'signature'. But where had the murderer got his ideas from? I went back to Epstein's *Sex Laws and Customs* to check on what source *he* had been using: it was the Book of Ezekiel.

I took out my copy of the King James version, turned to Ezekiel and read chapters 23 and 24 in amazement and utter disbelief. There, for all to see, in the most widely sold if not read book in the world, were the verses authorising – no, legitimising – the removal of the ears, nose and jewellery of the biblical whore, Aholibah, and a sequence of events that had so many parallels with the murder of Mary Jane Kelly as to be a total revelation. It was a charter for psychopaths and the mutilation of the female body. I had been handed the template of Jack the Ripper's mind and offered a code of perception and motivation. Staggered by these findings, I set about trying to discover the biblical context and meaning of the prophet's writings and Johanna Siebert referred me to David J. Halperin's *Seeking Ezekiel: Text and Psychology*. Halperin's brilliant analysis convinced me that a deeply troubled young Jewish immigrant concerned about sex and pollution and living in the East End, in 1888, might read and identify with the problems and murderous solutions propounded by Ezekiel in the original Masoretic text. How persuasive my own presentation to readers is, time alone will tell. Clio gave me a Fox to chase and, for me, the trail will always end with Joseph Lis, alias Joseph Silver, alias Joseph Isaacs, alias *Jack the Ripper*.

NOTES

Chapter 1: Kielce, 1868–1884

1. N. Davies, *Heart of Europe: A Short History of Poland* (Oxford 1984), pp. 308–311.

2. See J. Pazdur, *Dzieje Kielc, 1864–1939* (Wroclaw 1971), pp. 22–23 and N. Davies, *God's Playground: A History of Poland* (Oxford 1981), pp. 163–177.

3. See A. Eisenbach, *Emancipation of the Jews in Poland* (Oxford 1991), pp. 451–455 and 460–465; and S. Kieniewicz, *The Emancipation of the Polish Peasantry* (Chicago 1969), pp. 170–180; and G. Stephenson, *A History of Russia* (London 1969), pp. 76–87.

4. The early history of Kielce and its Jewish community, although sometimes indifferently translated into English, is best retrieved from several websites. Amongst the most useful of these, in no particular order, are; www.jewishgen.org/krsig/YearOne.html and www.jewishgen.org/krsig/YearTwo.html – Vols. 1 and 2 of the *Journal of the Kielce-Radom Special Interest Group*; www.geocities.com/Hollywood/2082/history4.htm, R. Blumenfeld, *The History of the Kielce Jewish Community*; www.geocities.com/Hollywood/2082/slownjk.htm, K. Urbanski and R. Blumenfeld, Slownjk: *The Dictionary of the Kielce Jews* and the compilation to be found at www.um.kielce.pl/um english/history a.html, *Urzad Miasta Kielce*. Perhaps most important of all for the social historian, however, is www.jewishgen.org/Yizko/kielce/Kie047.htm, *Book of Kielce: History of Kielce from its Founding until its Destruction*. The latter is a most useful translation by W. Blatt and others of the indispensable edited work of P. Cytron, *Sefer Kielce. Toldot Kehilat Kielce: Miyom Hivsuduh V'ad Churbanah* (Tel Aviv, 1957).

5. On the economic development of Kielce and its hinterland see Z. Guldon and A. Massalski, *Historia Kielc do roku 1945* (Kielce 2000), pp. 218–240;

Pazdur, *Dzieje Kielc*, pp. 9–32; and R. Blumenfeld, *History of the Kielce Jewish Community*, Chapter 9, pp. 1–4.

6. See Guldon and Massalski, *Historia Kielc*, p. 218 and Pazdur, *Dzieje Kielc*, pp. 10–11. On Russian garrisons and prostitution see E.J. Bristow, *Prostitution and Prejudice: The Jewish Fight against White Slavery, 1870–1939* (Oxford 1982), pp. 50–52.

7. Early expulsions of Jews in Kielce are outlined, but no sources cited, in Blumenfeld, *History of the Kielce Jewish Community*, Chapter 2, pp. 1–2. See also, sections on the 'Historical Background' and 'Towns in Kielce and Radom Gubernias' in the *Journal of the Kielce-Radom S.I.G.*, and *Urzad Miasta Kielce*, p. 1.

8. On the rise and practice of these various traditions see A. Polonsky, J. Baista and A. Link-Lenczowski (eds), *The Jews in Old Poland, 1000–1795* (London 1984), p. 8; D. Biale, *Eros and the Jews* (New York 1992), pp. 123–130; G.D. Hundert, *The Jews in a Private Polish Town: The Case of Opatów in the Eighteenth Century* (Baltimore 1992), p. 83 and D.K. and D.G. Roskies, *The Shtetl Book: An Introduction to East European Jewish Life and Lore* (New York 1975), p. 39; and D. Soyer, *Jewish Immigrant Associations and American Identity in New York* (London 1997), pp. 10–28. On Kielce itself, Cytron, *Sefer Kielce*, pp. 57–66 and 162–169.

9. On the divisions during the 1863 uprisings see, especially, Chapter 4 of Blumenfeld, *History of the Kielce Jewish Community*, p. 1.

10. On *mauscheln* see S.L. Gilman, *Jewish Self-Hatred: Anti-Semitism and the Hidden Languages of the Jews* (London 1986), pp. 138–139 and 270–305.

11. In a vast literature see, for example, S.H. Dinwiddie, 'Genetics, Antisocial Personality, and Criminal Responsibility', *Bulletin of the American Academy of Psychiatry and Law*, Vol. 24, No. 1, 1996, pp. 95–108; M.G. Gelder, J.J. López-Ibor and N. Andreason (eds), *The New Oxford Textbook of Psychiatry* (Oxford 2000), pp. 807–808; J. Sánchez, 'Social Crises and Psychopathy: Towards a Sociology of the Psychopath', in W.H. Reid, D. Dorr, J.I. Walker and J.W. Bonner III (eds), *Unmasking the Psychopath: Antisocial Personality and Related Syndromes* (New York 1986), pp. 78–97; and E. Simonoff, J. Elander, J. Holmshaw, A. Pickles, R. Murray and M. Rutter, 'Predictors of Antisocial Personality', *The British Journal of Psychiatry*, Vol. 184, 2004, pp. 118–127.

12. Cytron, *Sefer Kielce*, p. 13.

13. Letter to the author from one of Kielce's Holocaust survivors, Mr David Lewartowski of Tel-Aviv, 27 May 2001.

14. Cytron, *Sefer Kielce*, p. 13.

15. On the socialisation of Jewish children in this context see, for example,

L. Landes and M. Zborowski, 'Hypotheses concerning the Eastern European Jewish Family', *Psychiatry*, Vol. 13, No. 4, 1950, pp. 281–328; and M. Zborowski and E. Herzog, *Life is with People: The Culture of the Shtetl* (New York 1952).

16. On smuggling see, for example, Zborowski and Herzog, *The Culture of the Shtetl*, p. 260.

17. On Hannah Lis's presence in Kielce see Poland (Pol.), Voievudskie Arkhivum Panstvove v Kieltsakh – State Archives Kielce (S.A.K.), Zhond Gubernialny Radomski, Vol. 6845, (no pagination). See also Hundert, *The Jews in a Polish Private Town* (London 1992), p. 66.

18. See A. Unterman, *Dictionary of Jewish Folklore and Legend* (London 1991), p. 40.

19. See Cytron, *Sefer Kielce*, p. 13. In the text of the study that follows below, Anzel's name is rendered in the form most frequently encountered in the Polish archival sources – Ansel – and that of his wife's maiden name as 'Kwekzylber' despite the fact that it is frequently also found as 'Kweksylberg'.

20. See Pol., S.A.K., Oprzanysroeyck i handlowych zaeradach w Kieltsakh; Akta m. Kielc sygn 648, eik 1975 and Civil Registers, Checiny, Nos 49 and 49(a). Files pertaining to marriage of Ansel Lis and Hannah Kweksilberg (sometimes rendered Kwekzylber). On divorce more generally see, for example, C.Y. Freeze, *Jewish Marriage and Divorce in Imperial Russia* (Hanover, Mass. 2002), pp. 131–200. On the scholarly pedigree and social standing of Rabbi Tuwia Gutman HaKohen see Cytron, *Sefer Kielce*, p. 154. The reconciliation of Ansel and Hannah Lis, too, would have been in keeping with Hasidic traditions – see, for example, Unterman, *Jewish Folk Lore and Legend*, p. 64.

21. On other factors helping to shape Silver's personality over time see also Chapters 22 and 23 below.

22. These observations are drawn from Landes and Zborowski, 'The East European Family', pp. 453–454. Given Joseph Lis's apparent later concern with the problem of women as pollutants – as expounded by biblical prophets – see also the comments of D. J. Halperin, *Seeking Ezekiel: Text and Psychology* (Pennsylvania State University Press 1993), pp. 105–106.

23. See, for example, Namibia (Nam.), Namibia National Archives (N.N.A.), Windhoek, File GW1 F44/06, Statement by Jack Lis, 27 Dec. 1905.

24. On Joseph and Jack as stepbrothers see the evidence of Samuel Grohus, who probably got the information from Joseph Anker, in 'Silver Sentenced', *The Bloemfontein Post*, 24 Jan. 1903, and for the broader context, Chapter 13 below. On Joseph Silver's portrayal of Jack as a 'maternal half-brother' see below, Chapter 21.

25. See Pazdur, *Dzieje Kielc*, pp. 22 and 57–58.

26. See, for example, Unterman, *Jewish Folklore and Legend*, p. 180.

27. See Pazdur, *Dzieje Kielc*, p. 58. On Joseph as horse trader see below, Chapter 16, and for Jack Lis's army background, Nam., N.N.A., Windhoek, File GW1 F44/06, Statement by Jack Lis, 27 Dec. 1905. For a description of a *shtetl* boyhood see, for example, Zborowski and Herzog, *The Culture of the Shtetl*, pp. 342–345. Short overviews of Russian conscription of Jews into the army are to be found in Bristow, *Prostitution and Prejudice*, pp. 86–87; and D. Soyer, *Jewish Immigrant Associations and American Identity in New York, 1880–1939* (London 1997), p. 17.

28. See, for example, *Gazeta Kielecka*, Nos. 94 and 95, 1879.

29. This account is derived from *Gazeta Kielecka*, 17 Oct. 1879.

30. Pol., S.A.K., Zhond Gubernialny Kieletski, Vidzh, Voiskovo-Politseyny, Vol. 26a, 1879, Ansel Lis to Governor, 16 Oct. 1879.

31. Pol., S.A.K., Zhond Gubernialny Kieletski, Vidzh, Voiskovo-Politseyny, Vol. 26a, 1879, Chief of Police, Kielce, to Governor, 27 Oct. 1879.

32. On the increase in Jewish merchants see Pazdur, *Dzieje Kielc*, pp. 48–49. On Ansel's problems with letters of credit see Pol., S.A.K., Court Registers covering the period 1880–86.

33. See, for examples, Unterman, *Jewish Folklore and Legend*, pp. 40, 147 and 190. See also, Chapter 17 below.

34. *Mishnah*, Megillah, 4:10. See also Halperin, *Seeking Ezekiel*, p. 142.

35. My reading of the book of Ezekiel and, more especially chapters 16 and 23, has been profoundly influenced by Halperin's outstanding *Seeking Ezekiel*, pp. 81–176. See also Chapter 25 below.

36. See especially M. Aronson, 'The anti-Jewish pogroms in Russia in 1881', in J.D. Klier and S. Lambroza (eds), *Pogroms: Anti-Jewish Violence in Modern Russian History* (Cambridge 1992), pp. 41–61. On Bishop Kulinski see, for example, Guldon and Massalski, *Historia Kielc*, p. 218.

37. Or, for the matter, being a Russian and a Jew – see, for example, B. Nathans, *Beyond the Pale: The Jewish Encounter with Late Imperial Russia* (London 2001), pp. 334–339.

38. For examples rooted in the province of Kielce see, Hundert, *The Case of Opatów*, pp. 58 and 102 and, more generally, Zborowski and Herzog, *The Culture of the Shtetl*, pp. 232–235.

39. See also, C. van Onselen, 'Jewish Marginality in the Atlantic World: Organised Crime in the Era of the Great Migrations, 1880–1914', *South African Historical Journal*, Vol. 43, Nov 2000, pp. 120–125; also below, Chapter 22. Significantly it is a Pole, Joseph Conrad, who best captures some of the resulting madnesses in novels such as *The Secret Agent* and *Under Western Eyes*. For specifically non-fictional 'Jewish' examples of the consequences see, for example, R. Pipes, *The Degaev Affair: Terror and Treason in Tsarist Russia* (London 2003); B. Wasserstein, *The Secret*

Lives of Trebitsch Lincoln (London 1988); or Z.A.B. Zeman and W.B. Scharlau, *The Merchant of Revolution: The Life of Alexander Israel Helphand (Parvus)* (London 1965). For some of the same considerations explored from another aspect see also, M. J. Turnbull, *Victims or Villains: Jewish Images in Classic English Detective Fiction* (Bowling Green 1988).

40. See below, Chapter 7.

41. See below, Chapter 18.

42. On Moscovitz see below, Chapter 3 and, on Kleinberg, Chapter 18.

43. Haskel Brietstein's early career and life can be traced in the United Kingdom, Hull, Hull City Archives, Records of the Court of Summary Jurisdiction, Borough of Kingston-upon-Hull, Hersch Haskel Brietstein, 16 March 1887. Early Yiddish theatre had strong links to the Jewish underworld. See, for example, N. Sandrow, *Vagabond Stars: A World History of Yiddish Theatre* (Syracuse 1977), pp. 86–88. See also below, Chapter 20.

44. On Joseph Lis/Silver's subsequent interactions with Brietstein's extended family, see below, Chapters 3, 4 and 8.

45. See below, Chapter 7.

46. See, for example, Halperin, *Seeking Ezekiel*, p. 12.

47. See Bristow, *Prostitution and Prejudice*, p. 101.

48. For an example of a Jewish barber-surgeon at work in the Kielce district in the late eighteenth century see Hundert, *The Case of Opatów*, p. 74, and Chapter 2 below.

49. See Bristow, *Prostitution and Prejudice*, p. 126. On barbershops see for example, T.J Gilfoyle, *City of Eros: New York City* (New York 1992), p. 241 and J. White, *Rothschild Buildings: Life in an East End Tenement Block, 1887–1920* (London 1980), p. 115. On Joseph Lis/Silver's associations with barbershops see below, Chapters 2, 3 and 15.

50. Pol., S.A.K., Kantseliaria Gubernatora Kieletskiego, Vol. 200a, entry for J. Lis, 14 Aug. 1884 (no pagination).

51. See especially Bristow, *Prostitution and Prejudice*, pp. 215–323.

52. See Chapter 23 below.

53. For a description of the routes and modes of travel employed by Jewish emigrants from northern Europe see A. Newman (with the assistance of N. Evans) 'Trains and Shelters and Ships', unpublished paper presented to a meeting of the Jewish Genealogical Society of Great Britain, 1999.

Chapter 2: London, 1885–1889

1. See J. Harris, *Private Lives and Public Spirit: Britain, 1870–1914* (London 1993), pp. 1–32 and E.J. Hobsbawm, *Industry and Empire* (London 1968), pp. 110–127.

2. See, for example, G. O' Neill, *My East End: A History of Cockney London* (London 1999), pp. 1–75.

3. See W.J. Fishman and N. Breach, *The Streets of East London* (London 1979); W.J. Fishman, *East End 1888: A Year in a London Borough amongst the Labouring Poor* (London 1988); G. Stedman Jones, *Outcast London: A Study in the Relationship between Classes in Victorian Society* (Harmondsworth 1971); and J. White, *Rothschild Buildings: Life in an East End Tenement Block, 1887–1920* (London 1980).

4. See D. Feldman, *Englishmen and Jews: Social Relations and Political Culture, 1840–1914* (London 1994), p. 168; Fishman, *East End 1888*, p. 142; D.S. Levy, *Two Gun Cohen: A Biography* (New York 1997), p. 18; and W.D. Rubenstein, *A History of the Jews in the English-speaking World: Great Britain* (London 1996), p. 96.

5. See Fishman, *East End 1888*, pp. 130–135; R. Porter, *London, A Social History* (London 1994), p. 302; and White, *Rothschild Buildings*, pp. 79–82.

6. See Fishman, *East End 1888*, p. 131; W.T. Gidney, *At Home and Abroad: Description of the English and Continental Missions of the London Society for the Promoting of Christianity amongst the Jews* (London 1900), pp. 35–36; and Porter, *London*, p. 302.

7. See United Kingdom (U.K.), London (Lon.), Family Records Centre (F.R.C.), Marriage of Moses Aaron Gourvitch to Mandel Lis of 35 Plumber's Row, 11 March 1888.

8. Some gambling and fencing opportunities appear to have clustered around the Aldgate–Houndsditch areas and many barbershops, boxing and prize-fighting opportunities were often close to where Whitechapel Road gave way to Mile End Road. Both locations were also within walking distance for those intent on preying on labouring women or prostitutes. In 1885 the Jewish Ladies' Society for Preventative and Rescue Work (J.L.S.P.R.W.) erected Charcroft House in Mile End – see E.J. Bristow, *Prostitution and Prejudice: The Jewish Fight against White Slavery* (Oxford 1980), pp. 236–237. In 1895, the successor organisation, the Jewish Association for the Protection of Girls and Women (J.A.P.G.W.) built a shelter for prostitutes, the Sarah Pyke House, in Tenter Street, in Aldgate. Lis, during his second stay in London, in 1895–98, took a room in St Mark's, Aldgate, around the corner from the Sarah Pyke House, and used it as a base while ensnaring Rachel Laskin. Anker took rooms at 4 Osborn Street, from which address he monitored the comings and goings of prostitutes which he and the gang sought to export as 'white slaves' – see below, Chapter 7.

9. See Fishman, *East End 1888*, p. 149; and Stedman Jones, *Outcast London*, pp. 215–217.

10. See Fishman, *East End 1888*, pp. 52, 134 and 152; also White, *Rothschild Buildings*, p. 16.

11. Levy's background is sketched in R. Hallet's, 'Policemen, Pimps and Prostitutes – Public Morality and Police Corruption, Cape Town, 1902–1904', paper presented to the History Workshop Conference, University of the Witwatersrand, 3–7 Feb. 1978, p. 14. See also Chapter 15, below.

12. See L. Sante, *Lures and Snares: Low Life of Old New York* (New York 1991), pp. 156–160.

13. See Fishman, *East End 1888*, pp. 158 and 306. On Tower Hamlets Club see *East London Observer*, 10 Aug. 1899.

14. See below, Chapter 15.

15. See, for example, Fishman, *East End 1888*, p. 302; Levy, *Two-Gun Cohen*, pp. 18–21; O' Neill, *My East End*, p. 62; and White, *Rothschild Buildings*, p. 190. On linkages between boxing, ethnicity and social mobility see J.T. Sammons, *Beyond the Ring: The Role of Boxing in American Society* (Chicago 1980).

16. For descriptions of the facial markings on Lis in 1889 (age 21) and 1899 (age 31) see United States of America (U.S.A.), Albany, Archives of the State of New York (A.S.N.Y.), Admissions Register, Sing Sing Prison, 1889, entry dated 12 Oct. 1889; and Republic of South Africa (R.S.A.), Bloemfontein, L.B.L., Landdrost Bloemfontein, Case No. 144 of 1903, The King versus Joseph Silver, Exhibit 'C', Certified Extract from the Record of the Johannesburg Prison, dated 18 Jan. 1903.

17. U.K., University of Southampton, Hartley Library, Records of the Jewish Welfare Board, Annual Report of the Jewish Association for the Protection of Girls and Women 1899, the case of Rosa Goodman.

18. See G. Thorne, *The Great Acceptance: The Life Story of F.N. Charrington* (London 1913), pp. 153–167.

19. U.S.A., Albany, A.S.N.Y., Admissions Register, Sing Sing Prison, 1889, entry dated 12 Oct. 1889; and F. Moss, *The American Metropolis from Knickerbocker Days to the Present Time: New York City Life in all its Various Phases*, Vol. III, (New York 1897), p. 216, interview with 'J.S.' – Joseph Silver.

20. See below, Chapter 25.

21. All quotes from J.R. Walkowitz, *City of Dreadful Delight: Narratives of Sexual Danger in Late Victorian London* (Chicago 1992), pp. 205–206.

22. See, for example, *East End Advertiser*, 14 Jan. 1888. On youth culture see M. Fido, *The Crimes, Detection and Death of Jack the Ripper* (London 1987), p. 90; Fishman, *East End 1888*, p. 185; and Levy, *Two Gun Cohen*, p. 26.

23. See K. Chesney, *The Victorian Underworld* (Harmondsworth 1972),

p. 376; Fishman, *East End 1888*, p. 122; and D. Thomas, *The Victorian Underworld* (Cambridge 1998), pp. 80–106.

24. See E.J. Bristow, *Vice and Vigilance: Purity Movements in Britain since 1700* (London 1977), pp. 75–85 and 94–105.

25. See Bristow, *Vice and Vigilance*, pp. 94–108; T. Fisher, *Prostitution and the Victorians* (New York 1997), pp. 112–130; Thomas, *Victorian Underworld*, p. 97; Walkowitz, *City of Dreadful Delight*, p. 82; and J.R. Walkowitz, *Prostitution and Victorian Society: Women, Class and the State* (New York 1980), pp. 3–9.

26. See E.W. Stead, *My Father: Personal and Spiritual Reminiscences* (London n.d.) and, on the campaigns culminating in legislative changes, Bristow, *Vice and Vigilance*, pp. 108–110; and Walkowitz, *City of Dreadful Delight*, pp. 11 and 82–86.

27. See *East London Observer*, editions of 8 Oct. 1887, 26 Nov. 1887, 11 Feb. 1888, 25 Feb. 1888 and 3 March 1888. On Charrington's campaigns, more generally, see Fishman, *East End 1888*, pp. 249–255 and Thorne, *The Great Acceptance*, pp. 104–134 and 153–167. On the changes wrought to street prostitution by the Criminal Law Amendment Act of 1885 see Chesney, *Victorian Underworld*, pp. 432–433.

28. See, for examples, 'Alleged Abduction of Two Sisters, *East London Advertiser*, 19 Nov. 1887; or 'The Raid on East End Brothels and 'The Traffic in Foreign Women – a Procuration Case', in the *East London Observer* of 3 March 1888, and 18 Aug. 1888. Also Bristow, *Prostitution and Prejudice*, pp. 236–237, and Fishman, *East End 1888*, pp. 141 and 206.

29. See especially D.J. Halperin, *Seeking Ezekiel: Text and Psychology* (Pennsylvania State University Press 1993), pp. 143–144, and Chapter 25 below.

30. On two occasions Joseph Lis acknowledged that he was the father of Bertha Lis/Silver. The first was in Cape Town, in 1904 – see, R.S.A, Cape Archive Depot (C.A.D.) Cape Town (C.T.), Attorney-General (AG) Vol. 1531, No. 12984, J. Silver to Captain Lorimer, 18 Aug. 1904 and 'The Morality Law', *Cape Argus*, 12 Sept. 1904. The second was in 1905 – see Namibia (Nam.), Namibian National Archives (N.N.A.), Windhoek, File GW1 D56/05, Statement of Joseph Lis before the Imperial Local Police, 13 Sept. 1905. Bertha's suggestion that she was born in 1891, in Kielce (clearly not possible given that her father was in Sing Sing prison at the time) and that her mother's name was 'Rose', is to be found in France (Fr.), Archives Generales de la Police Judiciaire (A.G.P.J.), Paris, Quai des Orfèvres, warrant for the arrest of Bertha Lis, issued by Judge Larcher, 2 Feb. 1909. More plausibly, in 1905, when there was no incentive to lie, she told emigration authorities in Germany that she was born in 1888 – see Germany (Ger.), Staatsarchiv, Hamburg, Verzeichnis der in

den Jahren 1895–1914 aus Hamburg ausgegangenen Auswandererschiffe, Auswanderungsamt 1, VIII, A 4, Band III, *Erna Woermann*. Later that year, she told police in Windhoek that she was born on 26 April 1888, in New York City. That, too, was impossible since Joseph Lis only entered the U.S.A. for the first time in 1889 – see Nam., N.N.A., Windhoek, GW1, File F44/06, Statement signed by 'Bertha Liss', 27 Dec. 1905. Illegitimacy and the abandoning of children were common: see, for example, Fishman, *East End 1888*, p. 126 and Chesney, *Victorian Underworld*, p. 373. As late as 1915, upon entering the United States as an immigrant, Bertha Lis suggested that she was a 'Russian Hebrew' but said that her closest kin was a certain Mrs Dorfin (perhaps her original guardian) residing at 82 Hessel Street, Whitechapel, London – see U.S.A., Ellis Island Immigration Records, List of Passengers, *Philadelphia*, 16 Dec. 1915. This Dorfin appears to have been Mrs Dora Dorfman, wife of the late music hall artist, Osief Dorfman, who at the time of her death was living at 21 Paragon Mansions, Mile End – see U.K., London, F.R.C., Deaths, D. Dorfman, 23 Aug. 1921. The full significance of all this dissembling – to help conceal the period that Joseph Lis spent in London's East End between 1885 and 1889 – is explored in Chapter 25.

31. U.K, Kingston-upon-Hull, Public Library, Hull City Archives, Records of the Court of Summary Jurisdiction, Crown vs. Hersch Haskel Brietstein, 16 March 1887.

32. See Fishman, *East End 1888*, pp. 209 and 223–224.

33. See N. Sandrow, *Vagabond Stars: A World History of Yiddish Theatre* (Syracuse 1977), pp. 70–72.

34. See 'Burglary in Whitechapel', 'Burglary in Whitechapel' and 'Another Burglary' in the *East London Observer* of 7, 14 and 21 Jan. 1888. Also, 'Wholesale Robbery of Overcoats', *Reynold's Newspaper*, 12 Feb. 1888. See also Chapter 25, below.

35. See Fishman *East End 1888*, pp. 2–3, 121–122 and 145–147; also Walkowitz, *City of Dreadful Delight*, pp. 26–29 and 125–131.

36. On Lis's facial features see U.S.A., Albany, A.S.N.Y., Admissions Register, Sing Sing Prison, 1889, entry dated 12 Oct. 1889; and U.S.A., Harrisburg, Pennsylvania State Archives (P.S.A.), R6–15, Microfilm Roll No. 419, Intake, Discharge and Descriptive List of the Western State Penitentiary, Entry for J. Silver, 1 Dec. 1893. On the symptoms and progression of syphilis, see H. Rolleston (ed.), *The British Encyclopedia of Medical Practice* (London 1938), p. 225; K.K. Holmes, 'Spirochetal Diseases', in T.R. Harrison (ed.), *Principles of Internal Medicine* (New York 1977), p. 920; and more especially, W.A. Lishman, *Organic Psychiatry: The Psychological Consequences of Cerebral Disorder* (Oxford 1998), pp. 337–346.

37. On Lis as barber see U.S.A., Harrisburg, P.S.A., R6–15, Microfilm Roll 419, Records of the Western State Penitentiary, Descriptive List; U.S.A., New York City, Municipal Archives of New York City (M.A.N.Y.C.), Court of the General Sessions of the Peace, The People of the State of New York against Joseph Lis, 22 Sept. 1889; R.S.A., C.T. C.A.D., Colonial Office Records, CO 8658, Vol. 22, No. 7/1156, Application for Letters of Naturalisation, Joseph Silver, approved in Executive Council, 29 April 1904; and France, Archives de Paris, Registres des Rôles du Tribunal Correctionel de Paris, Judgment No. 42 706/54 134, 22 May 1909. See also, F. Moss, *The American Metropolis*, p. 216.

38. On Klosowski see H.L. Adam, *The Trial of George Chapman* (London 1930), pp. 1–65; D. Rumbelow, *The Complete Jack the Ripper* (London 1988), pp. 171–175; and, especially, P. Sugden, *The Complete History of Jack the Ripper* (London 2002), pp. 439–466.

39. See S.P. Evans and K. Skinner, *The Ultimate Jack the Ripper Sourcebook: An Illustrated Encyclopedia* (London 2000), pp. 104–105; and Sugden, *The Complete History*, pp. 148–151.

40. Stedman Jones, *Outcast London*, pp. 35, 60, 70 and 77.

41. On barbershops and pimping see Thomas, *Victorian Underworld*, pp. 201–202; and on the High Rips and other gangs, sources in note 22 above.

42. See L.P. Curtis, *Jack the Ripper and the London Press* (London 2001).

43. Sugden, *The Complete History*, p. 31.

44. See P. Begg, *Jack the Ripper: The Facts* (London 2004), pp. 21–38; M. Fido, *The Crimes, Detection, and Death of Jack the Ripper* (London 1987), pp. 15–19; and M. Howells and K. Skinner, *The Ripper Legacy: The Life and Death of Jack the Ripper* (London 1987), p. 2; and Sugden, *The Complete History*, p. 31.

45. See Begg, *The Facts*, pp. 39–53; Evans and Skinner, *The Ultimate*, pp. 22–54; Fido, *Jack the Ripper*, pp. 20–23; and Rumbelow, *The Complete Jack*, pp. 40–42.

46. See 'A Riot against the Jews', *East London Observer*, 15 Sept. 1888 and Sugden, *The Complete History*, p. 121. On the Chapman murder see, Begg, *The Facts*, pp. 65–85; Evans and Skinner, *The Ultimate*, pp. 55–120; Fido, *Jack the Ripper*, pp. 28–38; and Sugden, *The Complete History*, pp. 82–84.

47. See Curtis, *London Press*, p. 21; and Howells and Skinner, *The Ripper Legacy*, p. 13.

48. See Begg, *The Facts*, pp. 136–164; Evans and Skinner, *The Ultimate*, pp. 134–198; and Fido, *Jack the Ripper*, p. 42.

49. See Begg, *The Facts*, pp. 165–183; Evans and Skinner, *The Ultimate*, pp. 199–266; Fido, *Jack the Ripper*, pp. 46–47; and Rumbelow, *The Complete Jack*, pp. 64–65.

50. See Evans and Skinner, *The Ultimate*, p. 238; and Rumbelow, *The Complete Jack*, pp. 6–68. Sugden, *The Complete History*, renders the original graffito as 'The Juwes' (p. 183).

51. See Begg, *The Facts*, pp. 267–313; Evans and Skinner, *The Ultimate*, pp. 370–42; Fido, *Jack the Ripper*, pp. 84–100; and Sugden, *The Complete History*, pp. 333–335.

Chapter 3: New York City, 1889–1891

1. See I. Howe (with the assistance of K. Libo), *The Immigrant Jews of New York, 1881 to the Present* (London 1976), p. 69; and D. Soyer, *Jewish Immigrant Associations and American Identity in New York, 1889–1939* (New York 1997), pp. 5–6.

2. See T.J. Gilfoyle, *City of Eros: New York City, Prostitution and the Commercialization of Sex, 1790–1920* (New York 1992), pp. 28 and 38; A.R. Heinze, *Adapting to Abundance: Jewish Immigrants, Mass Consumption and the Search for an American Identity* (New York 1990), pp. 45 and 98; and I. Howe, *World of our Fathers: The Journey of the East European Jews to America and the Life they Found and Made* (New York 1997), pp. 96–97.

3. See M. Rischin, *The Promised City: New York's Jews, 1870–1914* (Cambridge Mass. 1962), pp. 77–78.

4. See A. Fried, *The Rise and Fall of the Jewish Gangster in America* (New York 1993), p. 28; C.W. Gardner, *The Doctor and the Devil, or Midnight Adventures of Dr Parkhurst* (New York City 1894), pp. 24–27; Gilfoyle, *City of Eros*, pp. 236–239; Heinze, *Adapting to Abundance*, p. 140; I. Howe, *World of our Fathers*, pp. 96–101 and L. Sante, *Low Life: Lures and Snares of Old New York* (New York 1991), pp. 105–140.

5. See D. Czitrom, 'Underworlds and Underdogs: Big Tim Sullivan and Metropolitan Politics in New York, 1889–1913', *Journal of American History*, Vol. 78, No. 2, 1991, pp. 536–558; Gardner, *The Doctor and the Devil*, p. 48; A.F. Harlow, *Old Bowery Days: The Chronicles of a Famous Street* (New York 1931), pp. 397–399; J.W. Joselit, *Our Gang: Jewish Crime and the New York Jewish Community, 1900–1940* (Bloomington 1983), p. 36; and Sante, *Low Life*, pp. 89 and 118.

6. See Fried, *The Jewish Gangster*, pp. 22–23; Howe, *Immigrant Jews*, p. 99; and Sante, *Low Life*, pp. 156–160.

7. See Sante, *Low Life*, pp. 98 and 222.

8. See Gilfoyle, *City of Eros*, pp. 224–232; Heinze, *Adapting to Abundance*, pp. 116–119; Howe, *Immigrant Jews*, pp. 96–98, Sante, *Low Life*, p. 181 and, less reliably and for a later period, G.K. Turner, 'The Daughters of the Poor', *McClure's Magazine*, 1909, pp. 45–61. See also N. Warnke, 'Immigrant Popular Culture as Contested Sphere: Yiddish Music Halls,

the Yiddish Press, and the Processes of Americanization, 1900–1910',
Theatre Journal, Vol. 48, No. 3, 1996, pp. 321–335.

9. See E.J. Bristow, *Prostitution and Prejudice: The Jewish Fight against White
Slavery, 1870–1939* (Oxford 1982), p. 165; M.T. Connelly, *The Response
to Prostitution in the Progressive Era* (Chapel Hill 1980) pp. 62–63; Fried,
The Jewish Gangster, p. 62; Gardner, *The Doctor and the Devil*, p. 46;
Gilfoyle, *City of Eros*, pp. 244–45; Heinze, *Adapting to Abundance*, p.
199; Joselit, *Our Gang*, pp. 9 and 24–25; and Sante, *Low Life*, p. 186.

10. See Bristow, *Prostitution and Prejudice*, p. 71; Joselit, *Our Gang*,
pp. 24–26; G.J. Kneeland, *Commercialised Prostitution in New York City*
(New York 1913), pp. 87–89; F. Moss, *The American Metropolis from
Knickerbocker Days to the Present Time: New York City Life in all its
Various Phases* (New York 1897), p. 164; Sante, *Low Life*, pp. 177–178;
and Turner, 'Daughters of the Poor', pp. 48–49.

11. Sante, *Low Life*, pp. 65 and 210; Gardner, *The Doctor and the Devil*,
p. 12; and Fried, *The Jewish Gangster*, pp. 25–26

12. Sante, *Low Life*, pp. 211–213.

13. See 'No Report from the Jury', *New York Times*, 16 March 1895.

14. Moss, *The American Metropolis*, p. 216.

15. Ibid.

16. Moss, *The American Metropolis*, p. 216.

17. See 'She Frightened the Burglar', *The Star*, 23 Sept. 1889; and 'A Shoplifter's
Bag as a Chest Protector', *The Sun*, 23 Sept. 1889.

18. United States of America (U.S.A.), New York City (N.Y.C.), Municipal
Archives of New York City (M.A.N.Y.C.), Roll. 52, Vol. 16, Part 1,
Minutes of the Court of General Sessions of the Peace, Manhattan, The
People vs. Joseph Liss, 10 Oct. 1889.

19. U.S.A., N.Y.C., M.A.N.Y.C., Grand Jury Indictment Records, Box 373,
File 3490; and Minutes of the Court of the Grand Sessions of the Peace,
Manhattan, The People vs. Adolph Goldberg, 4 Dec. 1889.

20. On 'The Tombs' see Sante, *Low Life*, pp. 244–245.

21. See L.E. Lawes, *Twenty Thousand Years in Sing Sing* (New York 1942), pp.
68–69 and p. 258; and W.D. Lewis, *From Newgate to Dannemora: The Rise
of the Penitentiary in New York, 1796–1848* (Ithaca, 1965), p. 138.

22. U.S.A., Albany, Archives of the State of New York (A.S.N.Y.), Annual
Reports of the Superintendent of State Prisons for 1888, 1889 and 1890.
Also, Lawes, *Sing Sing*, pp. 8, 9, 13–15 and 19, and Lewis, *The Penitentiary
in New York*, pp. 18–22. Sing Sing's downward trajectory is also alluded
to in Caleb Carr's carefully researched historical novel, *The Alienist*
(London 1994), p. 248.

23. On the role of the receiving clerk see Anonymous, *Life in Sing Sing* (New
York 1904), pp. 50–51 and Lewis, *The Penitentiary in New York*, p. 144.

24. U.S.A., Albany, A.S.N.Y., Admissions Register, Sing Sing Prison, 1889, Entry for Joseph Liss, 12 Oct. 1889.

25. Anon., *Life in Sing Sing*, pp. 55–56, 223, 231, 240; Lawes, *Sing Sing*, p. 99; and P.R. Eisenhauer, 'Organizing Discipline: Prison Organization and Penal Theory in 19th Century New York', unpublished D.Phil., University of Pennsylvania, 1988, pp. 166–199.

26. Anon., *Life in Sing Sing*, pp. 53–55, 223; Lawes, *Sing Sing*, pp. 72–73, 86 and 100; and Lewis, *The Penitentiary in New York*, p. 140.

27. Anon., *Life in Sing Sing*, p. 33.

28. Ibid., pp. 28–29 and 231; and Lawes, *Sing Sing*, p. 103.

29. The classic study remains E. Goffman, *Asylums: Essays on the Social Situation of Mental Patients and Other Inmates* (Harmondsworth 1961).

30. Inmates and prison personnel shared notions of 'manliness' as epitomised in physical combat – see, for example, Anon., *Life in Sing Sing*, p. 224.

31. Anon., *Life in Sing Sing*, pp. 240–241. Some sense of immigrant Jews' perceptions of the roles of constitutions, procedures and rules in a modern democratic society can be gleaned from Soyer, *Jewish Immigrant Associations*, pp. 75–76.

32. See U.S.A., N.Y.C., M.A.N.Y.C., Roll 52, Vol. 16, Part 1, Minutes of the Court of General Sessions of the Peace, Manhattan, the People vs Joseph Liss, J.S. Williams, Private Secretary to John R. Fellows, 30 June 1890; and U.S.A., Albany, A.S.N.Y, Governor of New York State, Register of Discharges by Commutation of Sentence, 1891, Entry for Joseph Liss, 15 Sept. 1891.

33. See Moss, *The American Metropolis*, pp. 216–217 in which 'S' (Silver) states that, 'I was going to leave the country but I met a man who was discharged from Prison a week later than I, and . . .'

34. U.S.A., N.Y.C., M.A.N.Y.C., Naturalization Records of the Superior Court, Bundle 487, Record No. 200, Joseph Silver. Frank Miller gave his address as 26 Stanton Street, but the only Frank Miller, 'barber', recorded in Trow's *New York Directory* in the period 1890–93, lived around Tenth and Eleventh Avenues in the vicinity of 49th Street.

35. Moss, *The American Metropolis*, p. 217. See also, U.S.A., N.Y.C., M.A.N.Y.C., Roll 53, First District, Magistrates' Court Docket Books, Entry for Wednesday, 28 Oct. 1891; Roll 2, Part 3, Vol. 5, Minutes of the Court of the General Sessions, 18 Nov. 1891, 'The People vs. Adolph Goldberg impleaded with John Leiss, p. 259; and Grand Jury Indictments, Supreme Court, Box 457, File No. 4204.

Chapter 4: New York City, 1891–1893

1. On the position of the Jewish left at the time see, for example, I. Howe (with the assistance of K. Libo), *The Immigrant Jews of New York, 1881*

to the Present (London 1976), pp. 101–115. For a sketch of the more immediate economic context see K.F. Kasaba, 'New York City: The Underside of the World's Capital', in J. Smith and I. Wallerstein (eds), *Creating and Transforming Households* (Cambridge Mass. 1992), pp. 63–90. For middle-class fears see, amongst others, F. Moss, *The American Metropolis from Knickerbocker Days to the Present Time* (New York 1897), p. 171.

2. See the account by 'J.S.' (Joseph Silver) in Moss, *The American Metropolis*, pp. 217–218.

3. Ibid., p. 218.

4. Ibid., pp. 218–219.

5. Ibid., p. 219.

6. Ibid., p. 218.

7. Ibid., p. 219. Reports on the Sage bombing are to be found in the following editions of the *New York Times*, 'A Crazy Man's Awful Act', 5 Dec. 1891; 'Who was the Assassin?', 6 Dec. 1891; 'Perhaps an Accomplice', 7 Dec. 1891; 'At Work in Sage's Office', 8 Dec. 1891; 'Was Norcross the Dynamiter?', 12 Dec. 1891; 'Russell Sage's Assailant', 13 Dec. 1891; 'Probably Not Norcross', 14 Dec. 1891; 'Identified as Norcross', 15 Dec. 1891; and 'The Norcrosses Affidavits', 16 Dec. 1891.

8. See United States of America (U.S.A.), New York City (N.Y.C.), Municipal Archives of New York City (M.A.N.Y.C), Court of the General Sessions of the Peace, Box 460, File 4227, The People vs. Adolph Fischer and Nelson Trebos, 14 Dec. 1891 and accompanying papers. See also, Moss, *The American Metropolis*, p. 220.

9. Jacobs's background is reconstructed from fragments contained in: U.S.A., N.Y.C., M.A.N.Y.C., Box 457, File 4204, Court of the General Sessions of the Peace, The People vs. Joseph Liss and Adolph Goldberg, 4 Nov. 1891 as well as several newspaper reports. See, amongst others: 'Detectives in Custody', *New York Times*, 28 Feb. 1895; 'Detectives for Pals', *The Press*, 28 Feb. 1895; and 'Two Detectives Nabbed', *The Sun*, 28 Feb. 1895. See also, note 11, immediately below.

10. On Byrnes see, amongst others, J.F. Richardson, *The New York Police, Colonial Times to 1901* (New York 1970), pp. 209–213 and E. Sifakis, *The Encyclopedia of American Crime* (New York 1982), p. 114. On the development of the NYPD see, amongst others, E.R. Ellis, *The Epic of New York City* (New York 1966), p. 432; J. Lardner and T. Reppetto, *NYPD: A City and its Police* (New York 2000), pp. 125–146; F. Morn, *'The Eye that Never Sleeps', A History of the Pinkerton National Detective Agency* (Bloomington 1982), p. 132; Richardson, *The New York Police*, pp. 236–238; M. Rischin, *The Promised City. New York's Jews, 1870–1914*

(Cambridge Mass. 1962), p. 74; and L. Sante, *Lures and Snares, Low Life of Old New York* (New York 1991), pp. 236–250. I have also been privileged to read the first two chapters of a draft manuscript of Daniel Czitrom's, a study that is likely to become the definitive work on the early history of the NYPD.

11. On Jacobs's political work in 1893 see, amongst many others: 'Queen Emma's Trial', *Morning Advertiser*, 10 Aug.; 'Emma Goldman', *New York Press*, 10 Aug.; 'Her Words Quoted' and 'A Blow to Anarchy' in the *New York Recorder*, 5 and 10 Oct.; 'Anarchists Kept in Check', 'Anarchy's Dingy Stronghold' and 'Where do Anarchists Riot' in the *New York Times*, of 20 Aug., 22 Aug. and 24 Aug.; and 'Emma Goldman on Trial', *The Sun*, 5 Oct. For Goldman's own recollections see E. Goldman, *Living my Life, Vol. 1* (New York 1931), pp. 124–127.

12. Trow's *New York Directory, 1892–93*, p. 1317; and *1893–94*, p. 1296. The broader context and the propensity for men such as Lis to 'collaborate' with the authority as 'agents' or 'private detectives' is explored indirectly in C. van Onselen, 'Jewish Marginality in the Atlantic World: Organised Crime in the Era of the Great Migrations', *South African Historical Journal*, No. 43, Nov. 2000, pp. 120–124.

13. The classic primary document outlining the prevailing systems of police corruption in New York City in the mid-1890s is the official report of the Lexow Committee of 1895. For extensive extracts from the Lexow report, and a sensationalised account, see W.T. Stead, *Satan's Invisible World Displayed, or Despairing Democracy: A Study of Greater New York, Review of Reviews Annual* (London 1898).

14. On Lis and the 'Rogues Gallery' see 'Byrnes's Men Accused', in *New York World*, 28 Feb. 1895 and, on Byrnes and the gallery in fictionalised setting, C. Carr, *The Alienist* (New York 1994), pp. 65 and 113. On NYPD police promotions and property see, for example, Stead, *Satan's Invisible World*, p. 59 and pp. 67–77.

15. For examples see, 'Call it a Put-up Job', *New York Mercury*, 28 Feb. 1895; or 'Detectives in Custody', *New York Times*, 28 Feb. 1895. Also, Sante, *Low Life*, pp. 116–117.

16. As reproduced in Moss, *The American Metropolis*, pp. 213–214.

17. See A. Fried, *The Rise and Fall of the Jewish Gangster in America* (New York 1993), pp. 28–29; I. Howe, *World of our Fathers: The Journey of the East European Jews to America and the Life they Found and Made* (New York 1997), p. 100; J. Joselit, *Our Gang: Jewish Crime and the New York Jewish Community, 1900–1940* (New York 1983), pp. 26–27, 108 and 144; and Sante, *Low Life*, pp. 117–118.

18. See Moss, *The American Metropolis*, pp. 164–170, and 238–240; also Sante, *Low Life*, p. 117. On the transformation of the Max Hochstim

Association into the New York Independent Benevolent Association, in 1896, see E.J. Bristow, *Prostitution and Prejudice: The Jewish Fight against White Slavery, 1870–1939* (Oxford 1982), p. 165; Fried, *The Jewish Gangster*, p. 18; and A.A. Goren, *New York Jews and the Quest for Community: The Kehillah Experiment, 1908–1922* (New York 1970), p. 137. See also A.A. Goren, *Saints and Sinners: The Underside of American Jewish History* (Brochure Series of the American Jewish Archives, Number VII, 1988) for a fascinating account of the practices surrounding the burial of Jewish gangsters.

19. Moss, *The American Metropolis*, p. 220. Paragraph based on evidence drawn from F. Cordasco and T.M. Pitkin, *The White Slave Trade and the Immigrants: A Chapter in American Social History* (New York 1981), p. 11; Bristow, *Prostitution and Prejudice*, pp. 151, 165, 170 and 173; T. J. Gilfoyle, *City of Eros: New York City, Prostitution and the Commercialization of Sex, 1790–1920* (New York 1992), p. 247; Moss, *The American Metropolis*, p. 220 and Sante, *Low Life*, p. 118.

20. On the Essex Street Market Court Gang see, amongst others, Cordasco and Pitkin, *White Slave Trade and Immigrants*, pp. 11–12; D. Czitrom, 'Underworlds and Underdogs: Big Tim Sullivan and Metropolitan Politics in New York, 1889–1913', *Journal of American History*, Vol. 78, No. 2, Sept. 1991, pp. 549–550; and Stead, *Satan's Invisible World*, pp. 88–90.

21. See Cordasco and Pitkin, *White Slave Trade and Immigrants*, pp. 11–12; Czitrom, 'Big Tim Sullivan', pp. 549–550; and Gilfoyle, *City of Eros*, p. 261. For Martin Engel putting up the bail for Charles Jacobs and another Tammany Hall politician, Charles Raab, putting up bail for Charles McManus see, 'Byrnes's Men Accused', *New York World*, 28 Feb. 1895.

22. See Bristow, *Prostitution and Prejudice*, p. 151; Czitrom, 'Big Tim Sullivan', pp. 541 and 557; Fried, *The Jewish Gangster*, p. 28; Gilfoyle, *City of Eros*, pp. 257 and 261; Howe, *World of our Fathers*, p. 99; Joselit, *Our Gang*, pp. 26–27; Moss, *The American Metropolis*, p. 168; and Sante, *Low Life*, p. 268.

23. See D. Czitrom, 'Our Police Protectors: Authority and Corruption in Turn of the Century New York', unpublished paper presented to the Organization of American Historians, Chicago, 29 March 1996, pp. 14–17; Fried, *The Jewish Gangster*, pp. 44–46; and Stead, *Satan's Invisible World*, pp. 48–49.

24. See Czitrom, 'Our Police Protectors', pp. 15–16. Also, Ellis, *The Epic of New York City*, pp. 423–424 and Fried, *The Jewish Gangster*, p. 46.

25. C.W. Gardner, *The Doctor and the Devil, or Midnight Adventures of Dr Parkhurst* (New York 1894).

26. See Czitrom, 'Our Police Protectors', pp. 15–17; Ellis, *The Epic of New*

York, pp. 425–429; Fried, *The Jewish Gangster*, pp. 44–50; Gardner, *The Doctor and the Devil*, pp. 86–87; and Sante, *Low Life*, pp. 283–288.

27. See Republic of South Africa, Pretoria, South African National Archives, Z.A.R. Collection, Records of the Supreme Court, ZTPD 3660/1898, The State vs. Joseph Silver and Sam Stein, Affidavit signed by Sadie Wolff, 11 March 1899, p. 2.

Chapter 5: Pittsburgh, 1893–1894

1. See J. Bodnar, R. Simon and M.P. Weber, *Lives of their Own: Blacks, Italians and Poles in Pittsburgh, 1900–1960* (Chicago 1982), pp. 13–15; and F.C. Couvares, *The Remaking of Pittsburgh: Class and Culture in an Industrializing City* (Albany, NY 1984), pp. 84–85.

2. Bodnar, *Lives of their Own*, pp. 13–28 and Couvares, *Remaking of Pittsburgh*, pp. 80–95.

3. Bodnar, *Lives of their Own*, pp. 19–22.

4. See Couvares, *Remaking of Pittsburgh*, p. 86.

5. On the Homestead strike see Bodnar et al, *Lives of their Own*, pp. 16–18; A.G. Burgoyne, *The Homestead Strike of 1892* (Pittsburgh 1894) pp. 146–149; Couvares, *Remaking of Pittsburgh*, p. 83; and for the strike in the larger context of American labour history, G.B. Tindall and D.E. Shi, *America: A Narrative History* (New York 1993), p. 523.

6. Bodnar, *Lives of their Own*, pp. 24–25. Also, J.S. Feldman, 'The Early Migration and Settlement of Jews in Pittsburgh, 1754–1894' (unpublished ms, United Jewish Federation of Pittsburgh, Pennsylvania, 1959), Chapter 4, 'Growth of the East European Jews', pp. 31–41, especially p. 41.

7. See Couvares, *Remaking of Pittsburgh*, pp. 51–61 and 62–79. As Lincoln Steffens put it, Pittsburgh was 'a growing town, too busy for self-government; [with] two not very unequal parties, neither of them well organized'. See L. Steffens, *The Shame of the Cities* (New York 1992), p. 105.

8. Steffens, *Shame of the Cities*, pp. 101–105.

9. Ibid., pp. 114 and 124; and Couvares, *Remaking of Pittsburgh*, pp. 63–67.

10. Steffens, *Shame of the Cities*, p. 107.

11. Ibid., pp. 116–117.

12. Ibid., p. 116.

13. See S.J. Kleinberg, *The Shadow of the Mills: Working Class Families in Pittsburgh, 1870–1907* (Pittsburgh 1989), pp. 166–169.

14. On Wayne's address see J.F. Dieffenbacher's, *Directory of Pittsburgh and Allegheny Cities, 1892*, 37th Annual Issue (Pittsburgh 1892). This is the first date at which there is any record of a Mrs M. Wayne.

15. Leff's public business can be traced, in outline form, through

Dieffenbacher's *Directory of Pittsburgh and Allegheny Cities* for the years 1889 through to 1895 – that is, annual issues 34 to 40. Entries for the years 1894 and 1895, however, show that only his brother, Louis, stayed on at the hotel business in Wylie Avenue.

16. See Republic of South Africa, Pretoria, South African National Archives, Z.A.R. Collection, Records of the Supreme Court, ZTPD 3660/1898, The State vs. Joseph Silver and Sam Stein, Affidavit signed by Sadie Wolff, 11 March 1899. p. 2. On 'Jewish Lightning', see J. Joselit, *Our Gang: Jewish Crime and the New York Jewish Community, 1900–1940* (New York 1983), pp. 36–39.

17. 'A Serious Case', *Pittsburgh Commercial Gazette*, 22 June 1893.

18. On Minnie Wayne's change of marital status compare entries in Dieffenbacher's, *Directory of Pittsburgh and Allegheny Cities* for 1892 and 1893.

19. See 'A Serious Case', *Pittsburgh Commercial Gazette*, 22 June 1893; and 'A Shady Transaction', *Pittsburgh Press*, 22 June 1893.

20. Ibid.

21. U.S.A., University of Pittsburgh, Archives of the Industrial Society, Allegheny Court Dockets, 1864–1926, Vol. 10, 4 April 1893–11 Aug 1894, Court Dockets Register 1893, entry Nos. 871 and 872.

22. For the events leading up to these proceedings see U.S.A., New York City (N.Y.C.), Municipal Archives of the City of New York (M.A.N.Y.C.), Mayor's Papers 1893, Series 89–GTF–14, C.H. Parkhurst and others to James J. Martin, President of the Board of Police Commissioners (n.d.) and Thomas F. Byrnes, Superintendent of Police to The Board of Police, 3 Nov. 1893. For the Society for the Prevention of Crime's version see F. Moss, *The American Metropolis, from Knickerbocker Days to the Present Time: New York City Life in all its Various Phases* (New York City 1897), pp. 237–239.

23. Ibid. See also 'Mobbed by Thugs. Parkhurst Agents Assaulted on the Bowery in Daylight', in the pro-Parkhurst, anti-Tammany, *The World*, 28 Oct. 1893. A further indication of the increasingly supportive attitude that the Parkhurst campaign was evoking amongst sections of middle-class Manhattan can be seen in the editorials which the *New York Times* carried about the Bowery 'riot' – see, for example, the editions of 29 Oct. and 4 Nov. 1893.

24. U.S.A., N.Y.C., M.A.N.Y.C., Minutes of the Court of the General Sessions of the Peace, Manhattan, 1893.

25. 'Silver was Identified', *Pittsburgh Press*, 15 Nov. 1893.

26. On Robb's stalled career prospects see Couvares, *Remaking of Pittsburgh*, p. 93. For the broader political context of the times see P. Kleppner, 'Government, Parties and Voters in Pittsburgh,' in S.P. Hays (ed.), *City*

   at the Point: Essays on the Social History of Pittsburgh (Pittsburgh 1989), pp. 151–163

27. U.S.A., Harrisburg, Pennsylvania State Archives (P.S.A.), Court Records, Pittsburgh, September Sessions 1893, p. 290, Case No. 967, Commonwealth vs. Joseph Silver, Philip Hack, Barney Davis and Casper Leff. See also sometimes inaccurate reports in the *Pittsburgh Press* – 'A Conspiracy Case', 19 Nov. 1893; 'Criminal Court Cases', 20 Nov. 1893; and 'Convicted of Conspiracy', 21 Nov. 1893.

28. U.S.A., Harrisburg, P.S.A., Court Records, Pittsburgh, September Sessions 1893, p. 290, Case No. 967, Commonwealth vs. Joseph Silver and others.

29. Ibid. See also an account which, in the case of Davis is inaccurate, in the *Pittsburgh Press*, 1 Dec. 1893.

30. See E.S. Wright, *A Brief History of the Western State Penitentiary* (Pittsburgh 1909), pp. 97–116.

31. U.S.A., Harrisburg, P.S.A., R6–15, Microfilm Roll 408, Western State Penitentiary, Admissions Register, No. 362, 1 Dec. 1893; and No. 361, Philip Hack; and R6–15, Microfilm Roll 419, Descriptive List, 1 Dec. 1893, No. 3621, Joseph Silver.

32. See T.J. Gilfoyle, *City of Eros: New York City, Prostitution and the Commercialization of Sex, 1790–1920* (New York 1992), pp. 298–300; and M. Shefter, 'The Emergence of the Political Machine: An Alternative View', in W.D. Hawley et al. (eds), *Theoretical Perspectives on Urban Politics* (Englewood Cliffs 1976), especially pp. 38–39.

33. See D. Czitrom, 'Our Police Protectors: Authority and Corruption in Turn of the Century New York', Paper presented to the conference of the Organisation of American Historians, Chicago 1996, pp. 16–19; and Gilfoyle, *City of Eros*, p. 301.

34. Gilfoyle, *City of Eros*, p. 301.

35. See especially Czitrom, 'Our Police Protectors', pp. 17–18; but also E.R. Ellis, *The Epic of New York City* (New York 1977), pp. 429–431; Gilfoyle, *City of Eros*, p. 30; and J.F. Richardson, *The New York Police: Colonial Times to 1901* (New York 1970), pp. 239–240.

36. On Lexow and organised vice on the Jewish Lower East Side see M.T. Connelly, *The Response to Prostitution in the Progressive Era* (Chapel Hill 1980), p. 60; A . Fried, *The Rise and Fall of the Jewish Gangster in America* (New York 1993), pp. 49–53; and Joselit, *Our Gang*, p. 5.

37. See Gilfoyle, *City of Eros*, pp. 268 and 294; L. Sante; *Lures and Snares: Low Life of Old New York* (New York), p. 188; and C. van Onselen, 'Prostitutes and Proletarians', in *Studies in the Social and Economic History of the Witwatersrand, 1886–1914, Vol. 1, New Babylon* (Johannesburg 1982), p. 122.

38. Ibid. There is an easily accessible, albeit dramatised, account of these

events to be found in W.T. Stead's, *Satan's Invisible World Displayed or, Despairing Democracy: A Study of Greater New York,* in *The Review of Reviews' Annual 1898* (London 1898), p. 126.

39. *Report and Proceedings of the Senate Committee to Investigate the Police Department of the City of New York* (Albany 1895), Vol. 1, p. 40.

40. 'The Hebrews Asked for Help', *New York Times,* 17 Oct. 1894.

Chapter 6: New York City, 1895

1. United States of America (U.S.A.), Harrisburg, Pennsylvania State Archives (P.S.A.), RG–15, Microfilm Reel 413, Western State Penitentiary, Discharge Description Docket, Register No. 299–A511, Joseph Silver.

2. See 'Detectives in Custody', *New York Times,* 2 Feb. 1895; 'Two Detectives Nabbed', *The Sun,* 28 Feb. 1895; 'Detectives under Ban', *New York Recorder,* 28 Feb. 1895; 'Call it a Put-up Job', *New York Mercury,* 28 Feb. 1895; and 'The Accused Detectives', *The Sun,* 1 March 1895; and 'Appeal to Grand Jury', *The World,* 1 March 1895.

3. F. Moss, *The American Metropolis, From Knickerbocker Days to the Present Time: New York City Life in its Various Phases* (New York 1897), pp. 157–161.

4. See T.J. Gilfoyle, 'A Pickpocket's Tale: George Appo and the Urban Underworlds of Nineteenth-Century America', *Missouri Review,* Vol. 16, No. 2, 1993, pp. 34–77.

5. See Moss, *The American Metropolis,* pp. 215–220.

6. 'Crooks as Stool Pigeons', *New York Recorder,* 1 March 1895.

7. Moss, *The American Metropolis,* p. 220.

8. 'The Accused Detectives', *The Sun,* 1 March 1895.

9. 'Two Detectives Arrested', *New York Daily Tribune,* 28 Feb. 1895.

10. 'The Accused Detectives', *The Sun,* 1 March 1895.

11. On Silver's 'permit to carry a revolver at New York' and naturalisation papers see, Republic of South Africa (R.S.A.), Pretoria, South African National Archive (S.A.N.A.), Z.A.R. Collection, Johannesburg Landdrost, Public Prosecutor – Incoming, Vol. P. 1040, J. Silver to M. Cleaver, 26 June 1899; and 'Two Detectives Nabbed', *The Sun,* 28 Feb. 1895.

12. 'Two Detectives Nabbed', *The Sun,* 28 Feb. 1895.

13. Ibid. Also 'May Indict Detectives', *New York Times,* 3 March 1895.

14. See 'A Pimpsverien', *Standard & Diggers' News,* 7 Dec. 1898 (Johannesburg, South Africa); also C. van Onselen, 'Prostitutes and Proletarians, 1886–1914', in *Studies in the Social and Economic History of the Witwatersrand, 1886–1914, Vol. 1, New Babylon,* pp. 118–120.

15. 'Detectives under Ban', *New York Recorder,* 28 Feb. 1895.

16. See United Kingdom (U.K.), Family Records Centre (F.R.C.), London, Vol.

197, Marriage of Joseph Silver, 'Detective's Agent', age 27, to Hanna Opticer, 'Spinster', age 25, 24 Oct. 1895; and Namibia (Nam.), Windhoek, Namibian National Archives (N.N.A.), Imperial District Court, Vol. D 56/05, Statement signed by Joseph Lis, 13 Sept. 1905.

17. See R.S.A., Pretoria, S.A.N.A., Z.A.R. Collection, ZTPD 3660/1898, The State vs. Joseph Silver and Sam Stein, statements signed by Lillie Bloom, Sadie Wolff and others, Johannesburg, 8 March 1899.

18. 'Detectives in Custody', New York Times, 28 Feb. 1895; and 'Two Detectives Nabbed', The Sun, 28 Feb. 1895.

19. 'Crooks as Stool Pigeons', New York Recorder, 1 March 1895.

20. The date of the meeting between Jacobs and Lis at his house was later confirmed by Jacobs although, as will become evident below, he claimed that the discussion that took place was concerned with Silver's release from prison and his desire to 'reform'. See 'Detectives in a Fix', Morning Journal, 28 Feb. 1895.

21. 'Byrnes's Men Accused', New York Times, 28 Feb. 1895; 'Two Detectives Nabbed', The Sun, 28 Feb. 1895; and 'Detectives in a Fix', Morning Journal, 28 Feb. 1895.

22. 'Connived at Burglary', The World, 28 Feb. 1895; and 'Two Detectives Nabbed', The Sun, 28 Feb. 1895.

23. 'Two Detectives Nabbed', The Sun, 28 Feb. 1895.

24. 'Appeal to Grand Jury', The World, 1 March 1895.

25. 'Detectives for Pals', The Press, 28 Feb. 1895.

26. This version, supposedly cited from memory by Jacobs, is as reported in 'Two Detectives Nabbed', The Sun, 28 Feb. 1895.

27. 'Parkhurst Agents Accused', New York Times, 10 March 1895.

28. 'Two Detectives Nabbed', The Sun, 28 Feb. 1895.

29. 'Detectives in a Fix', Morning Journal, 28 Feb. 1895; and 'Two Detectives Nabbed', The Sun, 28 Feb. 1895.

30. Ibid.

31. 'Two Detectives Nabbed', The Sun, 28 Feb. 1895; and 'May Indict Detectives', New York Times, 1 March 1895.

32. 'Parkhurst Agents Accused', New York Times, 10 March 1895.

33. 'Two Detectives Nabbed', The Sun, 28 Feb. 1895.

34. 'Detectives under Ban', New York Recorder, 28 Feb. 1895; and 'Two Detectives Nabbed', The Sun, 28 Feb. 1895.

35. 'Detectives under Ban', New York Recorder, 28 Feb. 1895.

36. 'Two Detectives Nabbed', The Sun, 28 Feb. 1895.

37. Ibid.

38. 'Call It a Put-up Job', New York Mercury, 28 Feb. 1895; and 'Two Detectives Nabbed', The Sun, 28 Feb. 1895.

39. 'May Indict Detectives', New York Times, 1 March 1895; 'Grand Jurors

Take It Up', *New York Daily Tribune*, 1 March 1895; 'Call it a Put-up Job', *New York Mercury*, 28 Feb. 1895; and 'Two Detectives Nabbed', *The Sun*, 28 Feb. 1895.

40. The allegation that Lis was 'visited' throughout the night by the two detectives after he was detained is contained in 'Crooks as Stool Pigeons', *New York Recorder*, 1 March 1895. See also 'Two Detectives Arrested: Charged with Being in League with a Robber', *New York Daily Tribune*, 28 Feb. 1895; 'Two Detectives Nabbed', *The Sun*, 28 Feb. 1895; and 'Byrnes's Men Accused', *New York Times*, 28 Feb. 1895.

41. 'Two Detectives Nabbed', *The Sun*, 28 Feb. 1895.

42. 'Grand Jurors Take It Up', *New York Daily Tribune*, 3 March 1895. The fact that Silver had gone missing as far as the SPC was concerned, is reported on 'Call It a Put-up Job', *New York Mercury*, 28 Feb. 1895; also 'May Indict Detectives', *New York Times*, 1 March 1895.

43. 'Two Detectives Nabbed', *The Sun*, 28 Feb. 1895. See also U.S.A., New York City, Municipal Archives of New York City (M.A.N.Y.C.), Register of Complaints, Charge Office, Essex Street Market Court House Police Station, 27 Feb. 1895, complainants Charles Jacobs and Charles McManus.

44. See 'Byrnes's Men Accused', *New York Times*, 28 Feb. 1895; 'Call It a Put-up Job', *New York Mercury*, 28 Feb. 1895; 'Detective under Ban', *New York Recorder*, 28 Feb. 1895; 'Two Detectives Nabbed', 28 Feb. 1895; 'Two Detectives Arrested', *New York Daily Tribune*, 28 Feb. 1895; and 'Detectives for Pals', *The Press*, 28 Feb. 1895.

45. It was brought out in court that Jacobs and McManus had a long association with Silver in various 'unsavoury professions' – see 'Detectives for Pals', *The Press*, 28 Feb. 1895. Jacobs had also been mentioned before the Lexow Committee as collecting money from a brothel-keeper on the Lower East Side, Mrs Augusta Thurow – see *Report and Proceedings of the Senate Committee to Investigate the Police Department of the City of New York* (Albany 1895), Vol. 1, p. 1079, evidence of Mrs A. Thurow; on McManus see, ibid., Vol. 5, p. 5424.

46. Parkhurst's visit to Strong is recorded in 'Will Fight Byrnes', *Morning Advertiser*, 2 Feb. 1895 and an extract from Moss's cross-examination in the police court is contained in Moss, *The American Metropolis*, pp. 212–215.

47. See, amongst others, 'Detectives for Pals', *The Press*, 28 Feb. 1895; 'Detectives in a Fix', *Morning Journal*, 28 Feb. 1895; 'Detectives in Custody', *New York Times*, 28 Feb. 1895; 'Two Detectives Arrested', *New York Daily Tribune*, 28 Feb. 1895; 'Two Detectives Nabbed', *The Sun*, 28 Feb. 1895; and 'Byrnes's Men Accused', *The World*, 28 Feb. 1895.

48. See, for example, 'Lawyer Frank Moss and the New Haven Police Claim

that Developments will be Sensational', *New York Recorder*, 3 March 1895.

49. The letter is reproduced, in full, in 'May Indict Detectives', *New York Times*, 3 March 1895. See also, 'Appeal to Grand Jury', *The World*, 3 March 1895. On Howe & Hummel see, for example, L. Sante, *Lures and Snares: Low Life of Old New York* (New York 1991), pp. 211–214.

50. See 'Grand Jurors Take It Up', *New York Daily Tribune*, 3 March 1895; 'Appeal to Grand Jury', *New York Times*, 1 March 1895; 'Appeal to Grand Jury', *The World*, 1 March 1895; and 'The Charges Dismissed', *New York Daily Tribune*, 2 March 1895.

51. On Nathan see 'Grand Jurors Take It Up', *New York Daily Tribune*, 1 March 1895. On Nathan's evidence before Lexow see, *Report and Proceedings of the Senate Committee*, Vol. 1, pp. 289–300.

52. See 'Appeal to Grand Jury', *The World*, 1 March 1895.

53. Another important encounter centred on the 'Nicolaus–Gould affair – see 'Fought at Close Range', *New York Times*, 14 March 1895. It is significant that the same month saw serious attempts to recirculate copies of the sensationalist testimony arising from the Revd Parkhurst's notorious visit to the brothel of Hattie Adams as part of his campaign against the N.Y.P.D. a few years earlier – see, for example, 'Indictments Might be Found – Mr Comstock on the Spreading of Dr Parkhurst's Testimony', *New York Times*, 28 March 1895.

54. See 'May Indict Detectives', *New York Times*, 1 March 1895.

55. 'Detectives in Custody', *New York Times*, 28 Feb. 1895.

56. 'Grand Jurors Take It Up', *New York Daily Tribune*, 3 March 1895.

57. 'Detectives in a Fix', *Morning Journal*, 28 Feb. 1895; and 'Parkhurst Agents Accused', *New York Times*, 10 March 1895.

58. This comment, although made about the police court hearing that preceded the Grand Jury inquiry, captured some of the public puzzlement that followed on the flurry of charges and counter-charges – see 'Two Detectives Arrested', *New York Daily Tribune*, 28 Feb. 1895.

59. See 'Case Before the Grand Jury', *New York Mercury*, 3 March 1895; and 'The Accused Detectives', *The Sun*, 3 March 1895.

60. 'The Charges Dismissed', *New York Daily Tribune*, 3 March 1895; 'Angel Dennett Turned Down', *New York Mercury*, 3 March 1895; and 'Did not Indict the Detectives', *New York Times*, 4 March 1895.

61. 'Jacobs and McManus Discharged', *New York Times*, 6 March 1895.

62. 'Parkhurst Agents Accused', *New York Times*, 10 March 1895 and 'Fought at Close Range', *New York Times*, 14 March 1895.

63. Ibid. See also, 'No Report from the Jury', *New York Times*, 16 March 1895.

64. Quoted in J.F. Richardson, *The New York Police: Colonial Times to 1901* (New York 1970), p. 250.

65. E. Sifakis, *The Encyclopedia of American Crime* (New York 1982), p. 114.

66. This inference is drawn from Moss who, writing twenty-four months later, noted; 'The Eleventh Precinct swarms with such criminals as the burglar whose story we have indicated [Silver]; but bad as matters still remain in this human sink, it is confidently believed that such settled relations of business between thieves and policemen have been broken up and exist no longer' – Moss, *The American Metropolis*, p. 220.

67. M. Rischin, *The Promised City: New York's Jews, 1870–1914* (Cambridge Mass. 1962), p. 74.

68. See T.J. Gilfoyle, *City of Eros: New York City, Prostitution and the Commercialization of Sex, 1790–1920* (New York 1992), p. 257.

69. See, for example, R.S.A., Pretoria, S.A.N.A., Z.A.R. Collection, ZTPD 3660/1898, The State vs. Joseph Silver and Sam Stein, Affidavit signed by Lillie Bloom, 11 Mar. 1899.

70. See, for example, the case of the Goldberg couple in E.J. Bristow, *Prostitution and Prejudice: The Jewish Fight against White Slavery, 1870–1939* (Oxford 1982), pp. 152–153.

71. See R.S.A., Pretoria, S.A.N.A., Z.A.R. Collection, ZTPD 3660/1898, The State vs. Joseph Silver and Sam Stein, Affidavit signed by Sadie Wolff, 8 March 1899.

72. See U.S.A., Washington, DC, Federal Archives of the United States of America, Records of the Department of State, Passport Applications (RG 59), Vol. 813, Application by Joseph Silver, No. 3212, issued at New York City, 16 Aug. 1895.

Chapter 7: London, 1895–1898

1. For the broader context see, for example, R. Lloyd-Jones and M.J. Lewis, *British Industrial Capitalism since the Industrial Revolution* (London 1998), pp. 82–102; and M. MacKinnon, 'Living Standards, 1870–1914, in R. Floud and D.N. McCloskey, *The Economic History of Britain since 1700* (Cambridge 1994), Vol. 2, pp. 265–289.

2. See also P.J. Cain and A.G. Hopkins, *British Imperialism, Innovation and Expansion, 1688–1914* (London 1993), pp. 276–314 and 369–381.

3. See C. van Onselen, 'Jewish Marginality in the Atlantic World: Organised Crime in the Era of the Great Migrations, 1880–1914', *South African Historical Journal*, No. 43, Nov. 2000, pp. 96–137.

4. See, for example, G. Stedman Jones, *Outcast London: A Study in the Relationship between Classes in Victorian Society* (Harmondsworth 1971).

5. See D.J. Guy, *Sex & Danger in Buenos Aires: Prostitution, Family and Nation in Argentina* (London 1991), pp. 11–12; and E.J. Bristow,

Prostitution and Prejudice: The Jewish Fight against White Slavery, 1870–1930 (Oxford 1982), pp. 236–237.

6. See Bristow, *Prostitution and Prejudice*, pp. 116 and 238.

7. On the progression and stages of syphilis see, for example, D. Hayden *Pox: Genius, Madness, and the Mysteries of Syphilis* (New York 2003), pp. 51–59.

8. See Republic of South Africa. (R.S.A.), Pretoria, South African National Archives (S.A.N.A.), Z.A.R. Collection, ZJB (Landdrost Johannesburg), Vol. 209, Veldkornet, Register van Nuwe Aankomelinge and, R.S.A., Bloemfontein, Free State Archive Depot (F.S.A.D.), Colonial Office Collection C.O., Vol.III, File 4791/02, J. Silver to Commissioner of Police, Bloemfontein, 22 Jan. 1903. It is also worth mentioning that in 1898 Silver's stepbrother the pimp, Jacob ('Jack') Lis, assumed the name 'Jacob Smith' during the period when he was a member of the notorious 'American Club': see below, Chapter 8.

9. On Tsarist conscription of Jewish boys see Bristow, *Prostitution and Prejudice*, pp. 86–88 and N. Davies, *God's Playground: A History of Poland in Two Volumes*, Vol. 2, *1795 to the Present* (Oxford 1981), p. 244. The most accessible guide to regiments serving in the Warsaw Military District is Major W.A. MacBean, General Staff, *Handbook of the Russian Army* (London 1905). Jack Lis's claim of having documentary evidence proving his receipt of a medal during military service can be found in Namibia (Nam.), Windhoek, Namibian National Archives (N.N.A), File GW1 F44/06, signed statement serving before the Imperial District Court at Windhoek, 27 Dec. 1905.

10. See Nam., Windhoek, N.N.A., File GW1 F247/05 statement by Rosa Silberberg made before the Imperial District Court, Windhoek, 27 Oct. 1905. This largely hearsay evidence about Jack Lis's early career fits extremely well with other evidence collected by the police much later in his career.

11. On Beile Fierstein see United Kingdom (U.K.), Southampton, University of Southampton (U.S.), Hartley Library, Papers of the Jewish Association for the Protection of Girls, Women and Children (J.A.P.G.W), Minute Book of the General Committee, 3 May 1900–28 Oct 1901 and Minutes of the Gentleman's Sub-Committee, 8 Nov. 1896. See also, 'Police', *The Times*, 17 Feb. 1898.

12. Sources as in note 11. See also, R.S.A., Bloemfontein, F.S.A.D, CO 140, File 961/03 'Joseph [H]anker & Jack Lis; Request that orders for expulsion of from O.R.C. be issued'.

13. United Kingdom (U.K.), London, Family Records Centre (F.R.C.), Certified Copy of an Entry of Marriage, Certificate No. MX 547185.

14. U.K., London, London Metropolitan Archives (L.M.A.), County of London.

(North) Sessions, Marlborough Police Court, Accused No. 2385142, 1895. For Griffin's various commercial outlets see U.K., London, L.M.A., *The Post Office London Directory for 1895*, p. 1056 and, more generally, T.S. Crawford, *A History of the Umbrella* (New York 1970), pp. 179–192.

15. U.K., London., L.M.A., County of London (North) Sessions, Marlborough Police Court, Accused No. 2385142, 1895. On prison life see, for example, D.T. Hawkings, *Our Criminal Ancestors* (London 1992), pp. 17–23.

16. U.K, London, L.M.A., Central Criminal Court: Calendar of Prisoners for the Session commencing on Monday, 20 April, 1896, Case No. 1, Accused number 2385/44.

17. On Pentonville see, for example, Hawkings, *Criminal Ancestors*, pp. 17–21, and D. Thomas, *The Victorian Underworld* (London 1998), pp. 253–271.

18. R.S.A., Pretoria, S.A.N.A., ZTPD 3660/1898, The State vs Joseph Silver and Sam Stein, Affidavit by Sadie Wolff, 8 March 1899. On the extraordinary mobility of elements in the Atlantic criminal classes see, for example, van Onselen, 'Jewish Marginality', pp. 96–137 or, for a fine case study, B. Macintyre, *The Napoleon of Crime: The Life and Times of Adam Worth, Master Thief* (New York 1997).

19. Anker's betrayal is recorded in U.K., Southampton, U.S., Hartley Library, J.A.P.G.W., Minutes of the Gentlemen's Sub-Committee for the Protection of Girls and Women, 8. Nov. 1896. See also, L.P. Gartner, 'Anglo-Jewry and the Jewish International Traffic in Prostitution, 1885–1914', *Association for Jewish Studies Review*, Vol. 78, 1982–83, pp. 162–164.

20. The acquisitions at 130 and 167 Stamford Street can be traced in U.K., London, L.M.A. *The Post Office London Directory 1897*. See also, Nam., Windhoek, N.N.A., File GWI D56/05, Statement by Joseph Lis before the Imperial Local Police, Windhoek, 13 Sept. 1905 from which it may be deduced that the 'American Hotel' stood at the corner of Stamford Street and Waterloo Road – a prominent site almost directly opposite Waterloo station.

21. See U.K., Southampton, U.S., Hartley Library, J.A.P.G.W., Minutes of the General Committee, 3 May 1900–28 Oct. 1901, Case No. 2 and, 'A Whitechapel Scandal – Saturday Night Scenes', *East London Observer*, 27 Nov. 1897.

22. On the links between Yiddish theatre and the underworld of commercial sex see, for example, N. Sandrow, *Vagabond Stars: A World History of Yiddish Theater* (Syracuse 1977), pp. 87–90.

23. For Hyman and the Johannesburg theatres see *The Post Office London Directory 1897*. On the actors and their Johannesburg context see V. Belling, 'The Golden Years of Yiddish Theatre in South Africa, 1902–1910', *Jewish Affairs*, Rosh Hashana 2000, pp. 7–9; and

S. Jackson, *The Great Barnato* (Harmondsworth 1970) pp. 164 and 226. On Schacht/Finegold's links to prostitution see R.S.A., Pretoria, S.A.N.A., Johannesburg Landdrost Collection (Public Prosecutor), File P. 1940, S. Johnson to Lieut. Murphy, 14 Jan. 1899. On the links between Silver and 'Sam' Wallerstein as pimps with ties to the Empire and other theatres see *Standard & Diggers' News*, 31 Jan. 1899 and 7 Feb. 1899.

24. U.K., Southampton, U.S., Hartley Library, J.A.P.G.W., Minutes of the General Committee, 3 May 1900–28 Oct. 1901, Case No. 2.

25. On the use of this plan and drugs in New York City at the turn of the century see, for example, A. Fried, *The Rise and Fall of the Jewish Gangster in America* (New York 1993), pp. 14–16; or L. Sante, *Low Life: Lures and Snares of Old New York* (New York 1991), p. 108. For an East End example dating back to the time of 'Jack the Ripper' see, 'The Raid on East End Brothels', *East London Observer*, 3 March 1888.

26. The Gordon and Rosenbaum case is reconstructed from the following sources: U.K., London, U.S., Hartley Library, J.A.P.G.W., Annual Report for 1900, Case No. 3. See also the following items drawn from *The People*: 'Revolting Story', 12 Feb. 1898, 'Unusual Charge', 13 Feb. 1898; and 'Old Bailey Trials', 3 April 1898. See also, *The Times*, 'Police', 17 Feb., 25 Feb. and 18 March 1898.

27. Source as in note 26. See also, 'Sequel to the Procuration Case at the West End', *East London Observer* [date unclear].

28. U.K., Southampton, U.S., Hartley Library, J.A.P.G.W, Minute Book of the General Committee, 3 May 1900–28 Oct. 1901, Case No. 3.

29. U.K., Southampton, U.S., Hartley Library J.A.P.G.W., Minutes of the General Committee, 3 May 1900–28 Oct. 1901, Case No. 4; and, 'Police', *The Times*, 25 Feb. 1898, and 'Alleged Procuring of Girls'. *The People*, 27 Feb. 1898.

30. See U.K., London, L.M.A., *Central Criminal Court: Sessions Paper* (1898), Vol. 127, p. 425; and 'Central Criminal Court, 2 April – before the Common Serjeant', *The Times*, 4 April 1898.

31. U.K., Southampton, U.S., Hartley Library, Minute Book of the General Committee, 3 May 1900–28 Oct. 1901, Case No. 4. Also *Central Criminal Court: Sessions Paper* (1898), Vol. 128, p. 687.

32. On Kuhbeck and Stein's move from Stamford Street see 'The Great Ontucht Plot', *Standard & Diggers' News* (Johannesburg), 2 Feb. 1899. The importance of the Union Castle Line for Jewish emigration to South Africa is highlighted in A. Newman, 'The Union Castle Line and Emigration from Eastern Europe to South Africa', unpublished seminar paper University of Southampton, 1998. On Silver and others' bookings aboard the *Ionic* see UK., London, National Archives, Kew, BT, *Ionic*, 8 June 1898.

33. See U.K., Southampton, U.S., Hartley Library, J.A.P.G.W., Annual Report for 1900, Case No. 5; and Bristow, *Prostitution and Prejudice*, p. 206.

34. U.K., Southampton, U.S., Hartley Library, J.A.P.G.W., Minute Book of the General Committee, 3 May 1900–28 Oct. 1901, Case No. 5.

35. Ibid.

36. Poland, State Provincial Archives, Kielce, Governor's Records, National Passport Control and Inspection, Departure and Deportation of Foreigners, 1901.

Chapter 8: Johannesburg, 1898

1. See United Kingdom (U.K.), London, National Archives, Kew, B.T, 'Ionic', 8 June 1898.

2. See U.K., Southampton, University of Southampton, Hartley Library, Jewish Association for the Protection of Girls and Women, Minutes of the General Committee, 3 May 1900–28 Oct. 1901, Case No. 4.

3. For the wider political and economic context, as well as the more imme-diate legal and judicial environment into which Silver and his party were intent upon inserting themselves see C. van Onselen, 'The Modernisation of the Kruger State: F.E.T. Krause, J.C. Smuts and the Struggle for the Control of the Johannesburg Public Prosecutor's Office, 1898–1899', *Law and History Review*, Vol. 21, No. 3, Fall 2003, pp. 483–526.

4. Ibid, pp. 489–490.

5. Ibid. pp. 496–500.

6. See C. van Onselen, *New Babylon, New Nineveh: Everyday Life on the Witwatersrand, 1886–1914* (Johannesburg 2001), p. 110. As the country's most talented novelist of the day put it: 'I think that only to a woman's eyes can it be opened in all its hideousness. It is the women that are most terrible here; but doubtless the mass of ill-gotten wealth attained without labour and squandered with recklessness is the true source of the evil. It attracts the worst class of women to Johannesburg; and it demoralizes those who were not demoralized before' – Olive Schreiner to J.X. Merriman, from Johannesburg, 17 March 1899, in R. Rive (ed.), *Olive Schreiner, Letters 1871–99* (Cape Town 1987), p. 346.

7. See R. Krut, 'The Making of a South African Jewish Community in Johannesburg, 1886–1914', in B. Bozzoli (ed.), *Class, Community and Conflict: South African Perspectives* (Johannesburg 1987), pp. 135–159.

8. 'Peruvian' – this now largely archaic censorious, contemptuous, dismis-sive term of largely unknown provenance was used by middle-class Gentiles and Jews alike to attribute boorish behaviour and/or a lack of cultural refinement to urbanising, male, Polish and Russian Jewish immigrant workers employed in low-status occupations, interacting

largely with indigenous – especially black – peoples, in industrialising southern Africa during the era of the great Atlantic migrations, c. 1881–1914.

The term, in all probability an acronym, has an elusive etymology. Used primarily – but not exclusively – by those South African Jews of real or imagined social standing and education of Anglicised, German or Lithuanian origins to refer to those of lesser status, education and income hailing from eastern Europe, it has been suggested that the term may derive from 'Peruvia' – a distortion of the Latin term 'Poruvia'. (See M.P. Grossman, 'A Study in the Trends and Tendencies of Hebrew and Yiddish Writings in South Africa since the Beginnings of the Early Nineties of the last Century to 1903', 3 vols, unpublished Ph.D. thesis, University of the Witwatersrand, 1973, p. 162.) First used in the *Johannesburg Times*, 1 March 1896. See also, van Onselen, *New Babylon, New Nineveh*, pp. 81–82 and J. Sherman, 'Serving the Natives: Whiteness as the Price of Hospitality in South African Yiddish Literature', *Journal of Southern African Studies*, Vol. 26, No. 3, Sept. 2000, pp. 505–521.

In similar 'top-down' but probably even more misleading fashion, it is implied, or suggested, that the term's origins might owe something to Baron Maurice de Hirsch's colonisation scheme of 1891 which encouraged European Jewish settlement in Latin America. (See J.E. Corbett, *The Owl*, Cape Town, 8 Feb. 1901.) But since use of the term pre-dates the scheme and Hirsch's Jewish Colonisation Association's efforts were confined largely to Atlantic, east-coast, Argentina, rather than Pacific, west-coast, Peru, this does not appear to be either a particularly helpful, or a persuasive explanation. It seems more likely that the origins of the acronym/word are to be found in the somewhat more remote and lived experiences of first-generation Polish and Russian Jewish immigrants in southern African mining centres in the last quarter of the nineteenth century – a more 'bottom-up' explanation. In the diamond mining centre of Kimberley, the Polish and Russian Union – a Jewish social club founded in the 1870s – may have provided the etymological roots of the word. (See Max Sonnenberg, *The Way I Saw It*, Howard Timmins, Cape Town, 1957, p. 52; and M. Shain, *The Roots of Antisemitism in South Africa*, Charlottesville 1994, pp. 27–28.) The term was certainly widely used in Johannesburg after the discovery of gold in 1886 to refer to unskilled East European Yiddish-speaking immigrants employed legally as store assistants in concession stores serving African workers on mining properties, or to itinerant Jewish hawkers and traders (W.F. Bailey, 'The Native Problem in South Africa', *National Review*, No. 28, 1896, p. 546). After the prohibition on the sale of alcohol to Africans in the South African

Republic in 1898, the word was applied to lower-order Polish and Russian Jewish gangster-functionaries in illegal retail and wholesale liquor-selling gangs and syndicates (C. van Onselen, 'Randlords and Rotgut', in *New Babylon, New Nineveh*, pp. 81–82).

It would appear that, although more solidly rooted in white South African culture than elsewhere in the western hemisphere, the term subsequently also found its way back north into the lexicon of contemporary Yiddish usage on both sides of the Atlantic. Thus, the term is recorded in the *Harkavy English-Yiddish Dictionary* (New York City, 1910), p. 451, which would suggest its use in New York City's Lower East Side Jewish community. Similarly its use in London's Jewish East End is noted in J. Gross, *A Double Thread: Growing Up English and Jewish in London* (London 2001), p. 29.

I would like to thank Veronica Belling, Susan Rich and – especially – Milton Shain for their generous advice and assistance in attempting to trace the etymology of the word.

9. On terminology in the organised trade in Atlantic prostitution see, for example, A. Londres, *The Road to Buenos Aires: The White Slave Traffic* (New York 1928), pp. 75 and 170.

10. 'Great Ontucht Plot', *Standard & Diggers' News*, 9 Feb. 1899.

11. On Budner and the Goldbergs in New York City see above, Chapter 6.

12. On Priziger see *Standard & Diggers' News*, 7 Dec. 1898. On Witkofsky see 'The Morality Law – Threats to Kill', *Standard & Diggers' News*, 22 Feb. 1899 and Republic of South Africa (R.S.A.), Cape Town, Cape Archives Depot (C.A.D.), C.T. 11/31, 'Wolf Witkofski' to 'Dear Wife Rosie', 16 Jan. 1902; and B.I. Feldman, 'Social Life of Cape Town Jewry, 1904–1914, with special reference to the Eastern European Immigrant Community', BA (Hons.) thesis, University of Cape Town, 1984, p. 32. On 'Rosie Woolf', who never ever did disappoint Joseph Silver, see 'A Pimpsverein', *Standard & Diggers' News*, 7 Dec. 1898; 'The Seamy Side', *Standard & Diggers' News*, 14 Dec. 1898; and Namibia (Nam.), Windhoek, Namibian National Archives (N.N.A.), GW1 F247/05, Imperial District Court, Case against J. Liss, 10 Jan. 1906, list of witnesses for the defence.

13. See van Onselen, *New Babylon, New Nineveh*, pp. 115–135.

14. Ibid. On Hermann, see also above, Chapter 5.

15. See, for example, 'A Pimpsverein', *Standard & Diggers' News*, 7 Dec. 1898.

16. See van Onselen, 'Krause and Smuts', *Law and History Review*, pp. 493–496 and 511.

17. See also van Onselen, *New Babylon, New Nineveh*, pp. 66–67.

18. For a view of the Bowery Boys prior to Silver's arrival and their subsequent transformation into the American Club see, for example, 'A Reign

of Terror', *Standard & Diggers' News*, 13 July 1897; and 'In Commissioner Street – Brave Show of Revolvers', *Standard & Diggers' News*, 8 Feb. 1898. Also, van Onselen, *New Babylon, New Nineveh*, pp. 127–128.

19. The registration papers of the Speer Medical and Chemical Company and its Articles of Association are to be found in the Republic of South Africa (R.S.A.), Pretoria, Companies House, Proes Street. Brennan's background can be retrieved from reports on court proceedings in the following issues of the *Standard & Diggers' News*: 20 and 23 Feb. 1899; 3, 6, 7, 8 and 17 March 1899. For the role of other, continental, medical doctors in organised prostitution during the 1890s see van Onselen, *New Babylon, New Nineveh*, p. 122.

20. On Corney and Winter see the following items in the *Standard & Diggers' News*, 'The Morality Law', 30 Dec. 1898; 'A Big Row', 25 Jan. 1899; 'The Ontucht Plot', 17 Feb. 1899; 'The Ontucht Scandal', 18 Feb. 1899 and 'Emphatic Repudiation', 20 Feb. 1899.

21. Hardly surprising then that, in the trial that followed in 1899, the managers of both shipping lines were subpoenaed to give evidence – see R.S.A., Pretoria, South African National Archives (S.A.N.A.), ZTPD 3660/1898, The State vs Joseph Silver and Sam Stein, 18 April 1899. By early 1897 the existence of organised traffic in women was known at both the London and Johannesburg ends of this route – see, for example, 'An Infamous Traffic', *Daily Mail* (London) carried in the *Standard & Diggers' News*, 27 April 1897. French and German traffickers also routed 'fresh goods' bound for South Africa through London – for examples, see the *Standard & Diggers' News*, 'Rand Woman Traps', 12 July 1897; 'Decoyed to the Rand', 17 Nov. 1897; and 'The Police Service', 12 Nov. 1898.

22. On early cafés, dancing halls and restaurants as fronts for vice as well as potential points of recruitment for prostitutes see *Delicate Mutters: An Open Letter addressed to Dr F.W. Engelenburg by the Rev. C. Spoelstra* (published by the Transvaal White Cross Purity League, Johannesburg 1896), p. 19 and, for someone who had to deal directly with Silver, S.G. Maritz, *My Lewe en my Strewe* (Pretoria 1939), pp. 8–9. Also, 'A Reign of Terror', *Standard & Diggers' News*, 13 July 1897.

23. On Bernstein, Silver, grocery stores and restaurants in Commissioner and Sauer Streets, see: 'A Pimpsverein', *Standard & Diggers' News*, 7 Dec. 1898. Also, R.S.A., Cape Town, C.A.D., A.G. Vol. 1531, File 12984, Rex vs. Joe Lis alias Joe Silver and Annie Bloem alias Lena Fygenbaum, 23 Aug. 1904, p. 5; and *Cape Argus*, 30 Aug. 1904.

24. See R.S.A., Pretoria, S.A.N.A., South African Constabulary (S.A.C.), Vol. 23, File 8/67 (1908), District Commandant to Secretary, Transvaal Police, 7 Dec. 1908.

25. See R.S.A., Pretoria, S.A.N.A., WLD 5/71, File 135/96, Opposed Applications, Ginsburg and Manesewitz vs. Jack Lis, 6 March 1906.

26. On the dominance of French interests see R.S.A., Pretoria, S.A.N.A., S.P, Vol. 813, DDM 1486/99, KCB 176/99, Acting Chief Detective to Head of the Detective Division, 28 Oct. 1899.

27. See above, Chapter 7.

28. See above, Chapter 7. On Strakiosky and Silver's 'coffee shop' in Germiston see R.S.A., Pretoria, Johannesburg Landdrost's Collection (J.L.C.), The State vs D. Davis (Krakower), M. Rosenberg and H. Rosenchild, Dec. 1898; and 'A Pimpsverein', *Standard & Diggers' News*, 7 Dec. 1898.

29. On Gustav Shakt, alias Schacht alias Finegold see R.S.A., Pretoria, S.A.N.A., J.L.C, Public Prosecutor's Collection – Incoming, Vol. 1940, S. Johnson to Lieut. Murphy, 14 Jan. 1899. Shakt came out to South Africa in 1898 as 'Finegold', at the invitation of a local syndicate interested in providing immigrant Jewry with Yiddish theatre. For the immediate context see V. Belling, 'The Golden Years of Yiddish Theatre in South Africa, 1902–1910', *Jewish Affairs*, Spring 2000, p. 7. On Shakt's later career see Zylbercweig *Lekiskon fun Yidishn Teater* (New York 1959), Vol. 3, cols 2219–25.

30. Silver's business interests in Pretoria are alluded to, in passing, by Rosa Feldman, in Nam., Windhoek, N.N.A., File D 56/05, Imperial District Court, Windhoek, J. Liss, undated statement by R. Feldman, 1905. On 'Borris' – sometimes Baras – Alexander see R.S.A., Pretoria, S.A.N.A., ZTPD, Vol. 3714/1897, The State vs. Joseph Silver and Sam Stein, subpoena, Borris Alexander, 24 April 1899; and 'Obstructing the Police', *Standard & Diggers' News*, 29 July 1897.

31. On Wallerstein's artistic origins see Belling, 'Yiddish Theatre', *Jewish Affairs*, p. 7. For his membership of the American Club, see 'Ontucht Freemasonry', *Standard & Diggers' News*, 7 Feb. 1899. Although poorly developed in comparison with Buenos Aires, where the links between organised 'vice' and the theatre were most pronounced, it would seem that there are at least some similar tendencies to be detected in South Africa at the turn of the century. On Argentina see, for example, N. Sandrow, *Vagabond Stars: A World History of Yiddish Theatre* (Syracuse 1977), pp. 87–89.

32. On Kaplan's earlier work as translator and his later involvement in prostitution and white slavery see 'Rand Morality Law', *Standard & Diggers' News*, 5 Aug. 1898 and R.S.A., Pretoria, S.A.N.A., S.P., Vol. 204, JPR 3499/99, telegram, M. Cleaver to State Attorney, 13 April 1899. For his later role as a clerk in a charge office, and dealings with Silver elsewhere in southern Africa, see R.S.A., Cape Town, C.A.D., A.G. Vol. 1531, Ref. 12984, Rex vs Joe Lis alias Joe Silver and Annie Bloem alias Lena Fygenbaum, 23 Aug. 1904, pp. 11–12.

33. See R.S.A., Pretoria, S.A.N.A., Z.A.R., S.P., Geheime Minute, Vol. 193, File 1197/98, affidavits by H.E. Cuyler and W.A. De Klerk, dated 5 Nov. 1898. Also, the following items in the *Standard & Diggers' News*, 'Ontucht Law', 24 Nov. 1898; 'The Seamy Side', 14 Dec. 1898; 'The Morality Law', 30 Dec. 1898; 'French Tribute', 10 Feb. 1899; 'Great Ontucht Plot', 15 Feb. 1899; 'When Police Fall Out', 16 Feb. 1899; and 'The Ontucht Plot', 17 Feb. 1899.

34. See van Onselen, *New Babylon, New Nineveh*, p. 123 for a fuller list of public corporations willing to profit from commercial sex. For the names of individual landlords involved see *Standard & Diggers' News*, 'The Morality Law', 10 Jan. 1899 and 'The Great Ontucht Plot', 15 Feb. 1899.

35. See 'When Police Fall Out', *Standard & Diggers' News*, 16 Feb. 1899.

36. On the early operation see, for example, 'A Gambling Affair', *Johannesburg Times*, 18 Aug. 1896. On the 'Green House' see van Onselen, *New Babylon, New Nineveh*, p. 121; and below.

37. For the earlier occupants of Sauer Street see, for example, 'A Score of Them' and 'The Nigger as Macquerot' in *Standard & Diggers' News*, 17 Nov. 1896; and van Onselen, *New Babylon, New Nineveh*, p. 122.

38. See R.S.A., Pretoria, S.A.N.A., Z.A.R. Criminal Cases, ZTPD, 3/115, The State vs Lizzie Josephs (Rachel Laskin) for the 'control and management' of a brothel; State vs. Joseph Silver and Sam Stein and State vs. Joseph Silver alias Joe Lees. On payment of protection money by prostitutes see R.S.A., Pretoria, S.A.N.A., ZTPD 3660/1898, affidavit by the hostile Sadie Wolff, 11 March 1899; but see also *Standard & Diggers' News*, 'Ontucht Raid', 10 Jan. 1899; and 'The Great Ontucht Plot', 2 Feb. 1899.

39. See R.S.A., Pretoria, S.A.N.A., Z.A.R. Criminal Cases, ZTPD, 3/1115, The State vs Lizzie Josephs.

40. See 'Ontucht Freemasonry', *Standard & Diggers' News*, 7 Feb. 1899 and van Onselen, *New Babylon, New Nineveh*, p. 129. For the Max Hochstim Association, the Warsaw Burial Society and the wider context for such organisations see C. van Onselen, 'Jewish Marginality in the Atlantic World: Organised Crime in the Era of the Great Migrations, 1880–1914', *South African Historical Journal*, No. 43, Nov. 2000, pp. 109–115. For the deeper roots of urban organisation in Jewish culture see also D. Soyer, *Jewish Immigrant Associations and American Identity in New York, 1880–1939* (Cambridge, Mass. 1997), pp. 20, 59 and 71.

41. See van Onselen, *New Babylon, New Nineveh*, p. 138.

Chapter 9: Johannesburg, 1899

1. See *Zuid Afrikaansche Republiek* (Z.A.R)., Wet No. 23, 1898, to amend and supplement Law No. 2 of 1897, especially clauses 4 and 5.

2. For the broader context and significance of this appointment see C. van Onselen, 'The Modernising of the Kruger State: F.E.T. Krause and J.C. Smuts and the Struggle for the Control of the Johannesburg Public Prosecutor's Office, 1898–99', *Law and History Review*, Vol. 21, No. 3, Fall 2003, pp. 483–525. Also, F.R.M. Cleaver, *A Young South African: A Memoir of Ferrar Reginald Mostyn Cleaver, Advocate and Veldcornet* (Johannesburg 1913), pp. 1–4 [edited by 'His Mother'].

3. Cleaver, *A Young South African*, p 2.

4. See 'The Detective Control', *Standard & Diggers' News*, 18 Nov. 1898.

5. See Cleaver, *A Young South African*, p. 21; also *Standard & Diggers' News*, 'A Pimpsverein', 7 Dec. 1898; and 'When Police Fall Out', 16 Feb. 1899. On the use of private detectives against criminals of East European origin more generally see, C. van Onselen, 'Jewish Marginality in the Atlantic World: Organised Crime in the Era of the Great Migrations, 1880–1914', *South African Historical Journal*, No. 43, Nov. 2001, pp. 120–124.

6. See *Standard & Diggers' News*, 'A Pimpsverein', 7 Dec. 1898; 'The Morality Law', 30 Dec. 1898 and 'The Great Ontucht Plot', 2 Feb. 1899.

7. On Krakower and Lizzie Josephs, battered into taking different positions, see *Standard & Diggers' News*, 'A Pimpsverein', 7 Dec. 1898; and 'The Seamy Side', 14 Dec. 1898.

8. See Republic of South Africa (R.S.A.), Pretoria, South African National Archives (S.A.N.A), Staatsprokureur Z.A.R., Geheime Minute, Vol. 193, File 1197/98, Affidavits by J.J. Donovan, 4 Nov. 1989, and F.E.T. Krause, 5 Nov. 1898. Also, the following items drawn from the *Standard & Diggers' News*, 'Public Morality', 21 Nov. 1898 and 'The Ontucht Law', 24 Nov. 1898. Also, 'The Morality Police', *The Star*, 27 Jan. 1899.

9. See 'The Ontucht Scandal', *Standard & Diggers' News*, 18 Feb. 1899.

10. 'Great Ontucht Plot', *Standard & Diggers' News*, 15 Feb. 1899.

11. See *Standard & Diggers' News*, 'The Ontucht Plot', 17 Feb. 1899; and 'The Ontucht Scandal', 18 Feb. 1899.

12. See, for example, *Standard & Diggers' News*, 'The Seamy Side' 2 Dec. 1898, and 'When Police Fall Out', 16 Feb. 1899.

13. See M. Maritz, *My Lewe en My Strewe* (Pretoria 1938), pp. 6–8; and 'The Seamy Side', *Standard & Diggers' News*, 2 Dec. 1898.

14. For the wider context see van Onselen, 'Krause and Smuts', *Law and History Review*, p. 517.

15. On Maritz in Corney's house see *Standard & Diggers' News*, 'Brewing on Morality Intrigues', 25 Jan. 1899; and 'The Ontucht Scandal', 18 Feb. 1899.

16. See 'The Ontucht Law', *Standard & Diggers' News*, 24 Nov. 1898 and van Onselen, 'Krause and Smuts', *Law and History Review*, pp. 510–511.

17. See 'A Pimpsverein', *Standard & Diggers' News*, 7 Dec. 1898; and van Onselen, 'Krause and Smuts', *Law and History Review*, p. 512.

18. The effects of Lizzie Josephs's 'bicycle fall' were still evident a week later – see, 'The Seamy Side', *Standard & Diggers' News*, 14 Dec. 1898.

19. See especially, 'A Pimpsverein', *Standard & Diggers' News*, 7 Dec. 1898.

20. See *Standard & Diggers' News*, 'The Seamy Side', 14 Dec. 1898; 'Ontucht Raid', 10 Jan. 1899; and 'When Police Fall Out', 16 Feb. 1899.

21. 'The Morality Law', *Standard & Diggers' News*, 28 Sept. 1898 and C. van Onselen, 'Prostitutes and Proletarians: Commercialised Sex in the Changing Social Transformations engendered by Rapid Capitalist Development during the Era of Imperialism', in *New Babylon, New Nineveh: Everyday Life on the Witwatersrand, 1886–1914* (Johannesburg 2001), p. 138.

22. These conflicts are explored in van Onselen, 'Krause and Smuts', *Law and History Review*, p. 512.

23. See Cleaver, *A Young South African*, p. 22 and 'Charge of Procuration', *Standard & Diggers' News*, 30 Dec. 1898 and, for the wider context, van Onselen, 'Krause and Smuts', *Law and History Review*, p. 514, and van Onselen, 'Prostitutes and Proletarians', *New Babylon, New Nineveh*, p. 142.

24. See 'The Morality Police', *The Star*, 27 Jan. 1899; and 'Perjury Epidemic', *Standard & Diggers' News*, 23 March 1899.

25. See *Standard & Diggers' News*, 'Brewing on Morality Intrigues', 25 Jan. 1899; and 'Perjury Epidemic', 23 March 1899. Also, Maritz, *My Lewe en My Strewe*, pp. 6–8.

26. R.S.A., Pretoria, S.A.N.A., Z.A.R. Staatsprokureur, Vol. 195, File 244/99, telegram, '2 P.V.' [Tweede Publieke Vervolger] to Staatsprokureur, 10 Jan. 1899, 11.00 a.m.; and File 251, 2 P.V. to Staatsprokureur, telegram, 12.40. p.m.

27. *Standard & Diggers' News*, 'Ontucht Raid', 10 Jan. 1899; and 'The Seamy Side', 11 Jan. 1899.

28. R.S.A., Pretoria, S.A.N.A., Z.A.R., Staatsprokureur, Vol. 195, File 313/99, Confidential, 2e Pub. Vervolger to Staatsprokureur, telegram, 11 Jan. 1899, 7.35 a.m.; and 2de Pub. Vervolger to Staatsprokureur, telegram, 11 Jan. 1899, 10.20 a.m. Also, *Standard & Diggers' News*, 'Ontucht Raid', 10 Jan. 1899; and 'The Seamy Side', 11 Jan. 1899.

29. 'The Seamy Side', *Standard & Diggers' News*, 11 Jan. 1899. On Nathan see, W.J. De Kock and D.W. Kruger (eds), *Dictionary of South African Biography*, Vol. 2 (Cape Town 1972), p. 509; M. Kaplan and M. Robertson (eds), *Founders and Followers: Johannesburg Jewry, 1887–1915* (Cape Town 1991), p. 146; or *Men of the Times: Pioneers of the Transvaal and Glimpses of South Africa* (The Transvaal Publishing Company 1905), p. 260 [no editor].

30. On the history of the Johannesburg Fort see H.J. Venter, *Die Geskiedenis van die Suid-Afrikaanse Gevanginisstelsel* (Pretoria 1959), pp. 105–125.
31. Cleaver, *A Young South African*, pp. 21–23.
32. See 'Perjury Epidemic', *Standard & Diggers' News*, 23 March 1899.
33. See 'A Pimpsverein', *Standard & Diggers' News*, 7 Dec. 1898.
34. R.S.A., Pretoria, S.A.N.A., Z.A.R., ZTPD 3660/1898, The State vs Joseph Silver and Sam Stein, Affidavit by Public Prosecutor, J.B. Skirving, 11 March 1899; and 'Great Ontucht Plot', *Standard & Diggers' News*, 7 Feb. 1899.
35. R.S.A., Pretoria, S.A.N.A., Z.A.R., Criminal Cases, ZTPD, 3/115, The State vs Lizzie Josephs, p. 359, Affidavit by Lena Landau before F.R.M. Cleaver, 11 Jan. 1899. See also the following in the *Standard & Diggers' News*: 'A Pimpsverein', 7 Dec. 1899 and 'The Great Ontucht Plot', 2 Feb. 1899.
36. R.S.A., Pretoria, S.A.N.A., Z.A.R. Collection, ZTPD 3660/1898, The State vs Joseph Silver and Sam Stein, Affidavit signed by Bessie Weinberg, Sarah Shanegold, Minnie Blum, Bertha Kamfer and Rosie Blank, 1 March 1899.
37. Ibid., Affidavit by J.B. Skirving, 11 Mar. 1899. 'The Morality Law', *Standard & Diggers' News*, 22 Feb. 1899, however, records only attempted assault, threats to kill, attempted bribery, and threats issued to various other female witnesses on, or about, 10 Jan. 1899.
38. Ibid., Affidavit by Lillie Bloom, 8 March 1899.
39. Ibid.
40. Ibid, Affidavit by J.B. Skirving, 11 March 1899 where he writes of '*noodlotige gevolgen*'.
41. R.S.A., Pretoria, S.A.N.A., Z.A.R. Staatsprokureur, Vol. 196, File 580/99, telegram, 2 P.V. to Staatsprokureur, 19 Jan. 1899.
42. See van Onselen, 'Krause and Smuts', *Law and History Review*, pp. 516–522.
43. R.S.A., Pretoria, S.A.N.A., Z.A.R., Johannesburg Archive, Kriminele Landdrost, Inkomende Stukke, 1899–1900, Vol. 1720, J. Silver and S. Stein to the Hon. Mr. Dietzch, 2 Feb. 1899.
44. The original minute books of the American Club have eluded an extensive archival search. Some verbatim extracts from the minutes are, however, to be found in the following items drawn from that scandalously neglected national treasure, now sadly disintegrating, the *Standard & Diggers' News*: 'The Great Ontucht Plot', 2 Feb. 1899; 'Great Ontucht Plot', 7 Feb. 1899; 'Ontucht Freemasonry', 9 Feb. 1899; and 'Great Ontucht Plot', 15 Feb.1899.
45. 'Great Ontucht Plot', *Standard & Diggers' News*, 15 Feb. 1899.
46. 'In Court', *Standard & Diggers' News*, 11 Feb. 1899.
47. R.S.A., Pretoria, S.A.N.A., Z.A.R., ZTPD 3660/99, State vs Joseph Silver

and Sam Stein, Opposed Application in the High Court of the Z.A.R., 14 March 1899.

48. See, Cleaver, *A Young South African*, pp. 18–29; and van Onselen, 'Krause and Smuts', *Law and History Review*, pp. 513–514.

49. 'A Dynasty Overthrown', *Standard & Diggers' News*, 6 April 1899.

50. On Kotzé see W.J. De Kock (ed.), *Die Suid-Afrikaanse Biografiese Woordeboek, Deel 1* (Cape Town 1968), pp. 458–461. It is significant that Kotzé makes no reference to this case at all in an otherwise expansive and comprehensive work – J.G. Kotzé, *Biographical Memoirs and Reminiscences, Vols. 1 and 2* (Cape Town 1941). See also, van Onselen, 'Krause and Smuts', *Law and History Review*, p. 515.

51. C.J. Beyers and J.L. Basson (eds), *Suid-Afrikaanse Biografiese Woordeboek Deel V* (Pretoria 1987), pp. 401–402.

52. R.S.A., Pretoria, S.A.N.A., Z.A.R. Collection, S.P., Vol. 204, File SPR 3499/99. telegram, 2de P.V. to Staatsprokureur, 13 April 1899.

53. As reproduced in Cleaver, *A Young South African*, p. 4.

54. For a list of witnesses in the trial see R.S.A., Pretoria, S.A.N.A., Z.A.R., ZTPD Vol. 3/115 of 1899, also ZTPD 3660/99, State vs Joseph Silver and Sam Stein. On Cohen, Priziger and Strakiosky see the trial records and 'A Pimpsverein', *Standard & Diggers' News*, 7 Dec. 1898.

55. See below, Chapter 20.

56. R.S.A., Pretoria, S.A.N.A., Z.A.R. Collection, ZTPD 3/115, The State vs Joseph Silver; and 'The Silver Case', *Pretoria News*, 29 April 1899. Also, Cleaver, *A Young South African*, p. 23.

57. *Standard & Diggers' News*, 27 April 1899.

58. R.S.A., Pretoria, S.A.N.A., Z.A.R. Collection, ZTPD, 3/115. The State vs Lizzie Josephs.

59. Cleaver, *A Young South African*, p. 3.

60. R.S.A., Pretoria, S.A.N.A., Z.A.R., S.P.O.SPR 5838/99, R 0207/99, Papers of the Officer of the High Court, 22 June 1899.

61. R.S.A., Pretoria, S.A.N.A., Z.A.R., Uitvoerende Raad, U.R. Vol. 102 (1899), 7 June 1899.

62. R.S.A., Pretoria, S.A.N.A., Z.A.R., Collection, Johannesburg Landdrost's Archive, Public Prosecutor – Incoming, Vol. 1940, File 579/99, Joseph Silver to Mr Cleaver, 26 June 1899.

63. R.S.A., Pretoria, S.A.N.A., Z.A.R., Johannesburg Landdrost's Archive, Public Prosecutor – Incoming Correspondence, Vol. 1940, J.T. Lloyd to F.E.T. Krause, 27 Sept. 1899.

64. G. Saron, 'The "Morality Question" in South Africa' (undated and unpublished mss, given to the author by the late Mr Saron). See also, E.J. Bristow, *Prostitution and Prejudice: The Jewish Fight against White Slavery, 1870–1939* (Oxford 1982), p. 243.

65. Van Onselen, 'Prostitutes and Proletarians', *New Babylon, New Nineveh*, pp. 130–131.

66. R.S.A., Pretoria, S.A.N.A., Z.A.R., Johannesburg Landdrost's Archive, Vol. 1824, The State vs. Joseph Silver, evidence presented on 13 and 15 Sept. 1899.

67. On the Ninevites and the role of AmaSilvas see C. van Onselen, 'The Regiment of the Hills: *Umkosi Wezintaba*, the Witwatersrand's Lumpenproletarian Army, 1890–1920', in *New Babylon, New Nineveh*, pp. 368–397; and C. van Onselen, *The Small Matter of a Horse: The Life of 'Nongoloza' Mathebula, 1867–1948* (Johannesburg 1984).

68. R.S.A., Pretoria, S.A.N.A., Z.A.R. Collection, Johannesburg's Landdrost's Archive, Vol. 1824, The State vs. Joseph Silver, sentence recorded on 20 Sept. 1899. But see also items in the *Standard & Diggers' News* of 22 Sept. and 2 Nov. 1899.

69. See *Standard & Diggers' News*, 27 Sept. 1899.

70. Silver: 'I have no marks on my body, and am willing to be examined by a doctor' – 'Morality Law', *The Argus* (Cape Town), 22 Sept. 1904. See also, R.S.A., Cape Town, Cape Archives Depot, A.G. 1531, 12984/04, Rex vs Joe Lis alias Joe Silver and Annie Bloom alias Lena Fygenbaum, 23 Aug. 1904, evidence of Hyman Bernstein, p. 5 and J. Silver, p. 21.

71. Ibid.

Chapter 10: Kimberley, 1900

1. On the military dimensions of the war see, for example, T. Pakenham, *The Boer War* (London 1979). Aspects of Milner's post-war social engineering on the Witwatersrand are sketched in C. van Onselen, *New Babylon, New Nineveh: Everyday Life on the Witwatersrand, 1886–1914* (Johannesburg 2001) but see also D. Denoon, *A Grand Illusion: The Failure of Imperial Policy in the Transvaal Colony during the Period of Reconstruction, 1900–05* (London 1973).

2. For the wider context of these anti-Semitic prejudices, and the social realities they articulated with, see C. van Onselen, 'Jewish Marginality in the Atlantic World: Organised Crime in the Era of the Great Migrations, 1880–1914', *South African Historical Journal*, Vol. 43, Nov. 2000, pp. 124–128. On South Africa and the Cape during the last decade of the nineteenth and first decade of the twentieth centuries see M. Shain, *Jewry and Cape Society: The Origins and Activities of the Jewish Board of Deputies for the Cape Colony* (Historical Publication Society, Cape Town 1983), pp. 1–55.

3. This paragraph is constructed almost entirely from D. Cammack's *The Rand at War, 1899–1902: The Witwatersrand and the Anglo-Boer War* (London 1990) – pp. 108–129.

4. See, for example, H.J. and R.E. Simons, *Class and Colour in South Africa, 1850–1950* (Harmondsworth 1969), pp. 34–51; and W. H. Worger, *South Africa's City of Diamonds: Mine Workers and Monopoly Capitalism in Kimberley, 1867–1895* (New Haven 1987).

5. For a picture of Kimberley on the eve of the siege see H.J. Terblanche, 'Die Beleg van Kimberley', unpublished MA thesis, University of Potchefstroom, 1973, pp. 1–14.

6. On the conflict between Rhodes and Kekewich see, for example, Pakenham, *The Boer War*, pp. 321–328.

7. See S. Jackson, *The Great Barnato* (Harmondsworth 1990), pp. 26–30 and 51–52. Also, L. Cohen, *Reminiscences of Kimberley* (London 1911).

8. Information supplied to the author in a letter, dated 16 July 1998, from Dr J.J. Swart of Bloemfontein who has made an informal study of the city's wartime history based, in part, on reports in the newspapers of the day.

9. Rabinowitz was later one of the subjects of a fascinating exposé, presumably by a disaffected member of the underworld, that was hastily printed and circulated in Johannesburg in 1904–5. See Republic of South Africa (R.S.A.), Johannesburg Public Library, Strange Collection, Anonymous, *Calumniator Morally Masked or The Scandal of Johannesburg* (16 pp.) but see, especially, p. 4.

10. Thus Jacobs's name was mentioned in passing during the Grand Jury investigations in New York City in 1895, when Silver was attempting to implicate Detectives Jacobs and McManus. See 'No Report from the Jury', *New York Times*, 16 March 1895.

11. See United Kingdom (U.K.), Glasgow, Scottish Records Office, SC 1/55/33 Case 45 of 1901.

12. By 1896 there were 200 Japanese prostitutes in India – see, for example, *Japan Weekly Mail*, 30 May 1896. According to Japanese scholars there were already two Japanese prostitutes in Cape Town and, from there, they and others seem to have moved on to the more industrialised cities of Kimberley and Johannesburg. I am indebted to Dr D.C.S. Sissons of the Australian National University for this information.

13. Reconstructed from R.S.A., Cape Town, Cape Archive Depot (C.A.D.), A.G. Vol. 1531/12984, In the Cape Supreme Court of the Colony of the Cape of Good Hope, Joe Lis alias Joe Silver, appellant and Rex, Respondent, evidence of Frank Henry Kingston, Police Sergeant, Kimberley; and Chief of the Detective Department [illegible] to the Secretary, Law Department, Cape Town, 28 Sept. 1904. See also, Case No: 87(2) SA 739 [C], Mr Joseph Silver in account with Louis F. Lezard, Re: Defence charged under section 3, para. A, Act 44 of 1898. See also the evidence of Kingston as reported in 'The Morality Law', *Cape Argus*, 12 Sept. 1904.

14. See 'The Case of Silver', *Diamond Fields' Advertiser*, 17 Nov. 1900.

15. What follows is drawn from various documents, including notes taken during a later court case and the detailed bill subsequently presented for his services by L.F. Lezard. See R.S.A., Cape Town, C.A.D., Case No. 87(2) SA 739 [C] Heard in the High Court of Griqualand, Kimberley, 11 Sept. 1902. The case was also subsequently reported, in a different legal context, in *Reports of Cases decided in the High Court of Kimberley*, Vol. 9, Jan. 1899–Dec. 1904, pp. 224–229, *J. Silver* vs *L.F. Lezard* and reported by P.M. Laurence (hereafter referred to as Case No. 87(2) SA 739 of 1902). On Baier see, M. Henderson (ed.), *Kimberley Year Book and Directory for 1901* (Kimberley 1901), p. 225. The same source confirms the presence of detectives F. Kingsbury and D. Nelson. See also, items in the *Diamond Fields Advertiser* of 28 Sept., 5 Oct., 10 Nov., 17 Nov. and 21 Dec. 1900.

16. See R.S.A., Johannesburg, Library of the South African Jewish Board of Deputies, South African Jewish Sociological and Historical Society, 'Report of an Interview with Mr. Louis Flavian [*sic*] Lezard conducted by Mrs H. Kehr, 18 October 1947.' On the role of Jews in the South African War more generally, see 'Jews and the Anglo-Boer War', *Jewish Affairs*, Spring 1999 and especially pp. 20–21, which outlines the role of Colonel Sir David Harris in the siege of Kimberley.

17. R.S.A., Cape Town, C.A.D., Case No: 87(2) SA 739 [C], Heard in the High Court of Griqualand, Kimberley, 11 Sept. 1902 – especially, 'Mr. Joseph Silver, in account with Louis F. Lezard', 30 Sept. 1902; and hand-written notes, 'Silver vs. Lezard'.

18. Ibid.

19. Ibid.

Chapter 11: Cape Town, 1901–1902

1. The quote is from R. Krut, 'The Making of a South African Jewish Community in Johannesburg, 1886–1914', in B. Bozzoli (ed.), *Class, Community and Conflict: South African Perspectives* (Johannesburg 1987) pp. 134–159; but for the immediate context see M. Shain, 'Diamonds, Pogroms and Undesirables – Anti-alienism and Legislation in the Cape Colony, 1890–1906', *South African Historical Journal*, Vol. 12, Nov. 1980, pp. 13–28. Also, M. Shain, *Jewry and Cape Society: The Origins and Activities of the Jewish Board of Deputies for the Cape Colony* (Historical Publication Society 1983), pp. 15–56.

2. See V. Bickford-Smith, *Ethnic Pride and Racial Prejudice in Victorian Cape Town: Group Identity and Social Practice, 1875–1902* (Cambridge 1995), and more especially, pp. 67–125. Bickford-Smith also points to Polish 'paupers' being singled out as anti-Semitic targets, p. 148.

3. Surprisingly, there is no single dedicated, integrated historical study of District Six. For glimpses of its commercial, residential and social contours, however, see B.I. Feldman, 'Social Life of Cape Town Jewry, 1904–1914, with special reference to the Eastern European Immigrant Community', BA (Hons) thesis, University of Cape Town, 1984. See also W. Nasson, 'She Preferred living in a cave with Harry the Snake-catcher': Towards an Oral History of Popular Leisure and Class Expression in District Six, Cape Town, c. 1920s–1950s', paper presented to the History Workshop Conference, University of the Witwatersrand, 9–14 Feb. 1987.

4. For the context of this legislation see E.B. van Heyningen, 'The Social Evil in the Cape Colony 1868–1902: Prostitution and the Contagious Diseases Acts', *Journal of Southern African Studies*, Vol. 10, No. 2, April 1984, pp. 170–199 and R. Hallett, 'Policemen, Pimps and Prostitutes – Public Morality and Police Corruption, Cape Town, 1902–04', paper presented to the History Workshop Conference, University of the Witwatersrand, 1978. For the prosecution of Max Harris (1904) and Joseph Silver (1905), see Chapter 14 below.

5. Hallett, 'Policemen, Pimps and Prostitutes', pp. 5–6.

6. Ibid., p. 6. See also, Republic of South Africa (R.S.A.), Cape Town, Cape Archives Depot (C.A.D.), Attorney-General (A.G.), 1902, 1019/02, Acting Commissioner of Police, R.M. Crawford, 'Annual Report 1901', to Secretary to the Law Department, Cape Town, 2 Sept. 1902.

7. See R.S.A., Cape Town, C.A.D., Colonial Office (C.O.), Naturalisation Papers 'H' (1899–1903), Vol. 8567, Ref. 22, Part 1, 1903, Application of Max Harris dated 6 Jan. 1903; and C.A.D., Cape Supreme Court, Criminal Records, (C.S.C.C.R.), May–June 1904, Case No. 33, Rex vs. Charteris, evidence of M. Harris pp. 5–6. On Harris's earlier career in Johannesburg see above, Chapter 8.

8. See Rex vs. Charteris, evidence of Leah Wynstock (*sic*), pp. 27–28. Also, R.S.A., Cape Town, C.A.D., C.S.C.C.R., May–June 1904, Case No. 38, Rex. vs Thor Osberg, evidence of Leah Weinstock, p. 17.

9. On the European, London, Milner and Taymouth Castle hotels as clearing houses for police and/or criminal business see Rex vs. Charteris, 1904, p. 25, evidence of M. Harris; Rex vs. Osberg, 1904, p. 47, evidence of T. Osberg and, in the *Cape Times*, the following items – 'The Charteris Case' as reported on in the editions of 24 June, 29 June and 1 July 1904.

10. On Charteris see Hallett, 'Policemen, Pimps and Prostitutes', p. 17; and on his early encounters with Weinstock, Rex vs. Charteris, pp. 27–28, evidence of Leah Weinstock.

11. See, for example, Rex vs Charteris, pp. 5–12, 21–27, evidence of M. Harris; pp. 27–29, evidence of Leah Wynstock; pp. 31–37, evidence of S. Goldstein; and pp. 38–39, evidence of F. Ricardi.

12. Rex vs. Charteris, p. 24; evidence of Max Harris.

13. See M. Zborowski and E. Herzog, *Life is with People: The Culture of the Shtetl* (New York 1952), p. 79.

14. On the Empire Café as an outlet for the illicit sale of liquor see, for example, R.S.A., Cape Town, C.A.D., A.G. 1531/12984, Case no. 6559 of 1904, Rex vs. Joe Lis alias Joseph Silver and Annie Bloem alias Lena Fygenbaum (*sic*), 23 Aug. 1904, p. 13, evidence of Det. Head Constable S. Davis; and Statement by H. Bernstein, dated 23 Aug. 1904.

15. R.S.A., Cape Town, C.A.D., Case No. 87(2) SA 739 [C] Heard in the High Court of Griqualand, Kimberley, 11 Sept. 1902 (Silver vs. Lezard, 1902). The case was also subsequently reported on, in a different context, in *Reports of Cases decided in the High Court of Kimberley*, Vol. 9, Jan. 1899–Dec. 1904, pp. 224–229, J. Silver vs. L.F. Lezard and reported on by P.M. Laurence.

16. Ibid., J. Silver to L.F. Lezzard (*sic*), 22 Feb. 1901.

17. R.S.A., Cape Town, C.A.D., A.G. Vol. 1938, Jan–June 1901, 'Report of District Surgeon or Other Medical Practitioner, or Medical Superintendent of Asylum', 'Lizzie Silver', 26 May 1901.

18. R.S.A., Cape Town, C.A.D., Records of the Cape Supreme Court, Illiquid Case No. 314 of 1905, The Colonial Government vs. Joseph Silver, 28 June 1905, pp. 1–3.

19. See R.S.A., Cape Town, C.A.D., 1/CT–6/402, Case No. 4390 of 1901, Crown vs. Joseph Silver, 27 May 1901. See also, 'Sunday Selling without a Licence', *Cape Argus*, 28 May 1901.

20. The best description of Silver's lifestyle at this time is to be found in R.S.A., Cape Town, C.A.D., CT 11/31, Resident Magistrate's Letters, G. Easton, Insp. C.I.D., to Capt. S. Lorimer, CID, 1 Feb. 1902.

21. See R.S.A., Cape Town, C.A.D., A.G., Vol. 3118, in the Supreme Court of the Colony of the Cape of Good Hope, His Majesty vs. Joseph Davis, 'an artist', and Marguerite De Theiss 'a modiste', Jan. 1902.

22. This paragraph draws extensively from B. Feldman's fine 'Social Life of Cape Town Jewry, 1904–1914' – especially pp. 12–14, 25–31, 54–56 and 66. For a more detailed exposition on Yiddish theatre, including Wallerstein's role, see V. Belling. 'The Golden Years of Yiddish Theatre in South Africa, 1902–1910', *Jewish Affairs*, Spring 2000, especially pp. 9–11.

23. On Koskes see R.S.A., Cape Town, C.A.D., Criminal Sessions of the Supreme Court of the Cape Colony, Attorney-General, James Rose Innes, J. Silver (not 'our' Silver), G.F. Clough and D. Williams, 5 May 1891; A.G. 1531/12984, Rex vs. Joe Lis alias Joe Silver, 30 Aug. 1904, p. 7, evidence of Det. Robert Barber and p. 22, evidence of J. Silver (Rex vs. J. Silver 1904) or, 'The Morality Act – The Silver Case', *South African News*, 16 Sept. 1904. For Silver later denying his presence at Koskes's

see Namibia, National Archives of Namibia, Windhoek, GWL D56/05, J. Lis (Joseph Silver) to 'Dear Brother' (Jack), 28 Jan. 1906.

24. For Silver as scribe see R.S.A., Cape Town, C.A.D., Supreme Court Criminal Records, May–July 1904, Rex vs. Thor Osberg, pp. 19–20, evidence of Lena Bloem. On the barbershop/pimps' post office see Rex vs. J. Silver, 1904, pp. 23–24, evidence of H. Woolf.

25. R.S.A., Bloemfontein, Free State Archive Depot (F.S.A.D.), Colonial Secretary (C.S.), Vol. 206, File 203/03, Sworn Statement, J. Silver, 31 Dec. 1902. For Silver's interactions with Lorimer – said to have commenced in 1902 – see R.S.A., Cape Town, C.A.D., Rex vs. J. Silver and A. Bloem, 1904, p. 15, evidence of Det. Head Cons. S. Davis; and pp. 17–18, evidence of Capt. S. Lorimer.

26. On 'Scotch Jack' in Aberdeen see Scotland, Scottish Records Office, Edinburgh, SCI 1/55/33, Case 45 of 1901. But see also, R.S.A., Bloemfontein, F.S.A.D., C.S, File 479/02. 'American Pimps', Sworn Statement by Annie Bloom, 31 Dec. 1902.

27. See R.S.A., Cape Town, C.A.D., Rex vs. Charteris, pp. 34–35, evidence of S. Goldstein. In 'The Charteris Case', *Cape Times*, 25 June 1904, Goldstein is – incorrectly – reported as having originally come from 'Brazil'.

28. See R.S.A., Cape Town, C.A.D., Rex vs. Osberg, 1904, p. 15, evidence of M. Harris.

29. See R.S.A., Cape Town, C.A.D., Rex vs. Charteris, 1904, p. 33, evidence of S. Goldstein.

30. On Goldstein see 'The Charteris Case', *Cape Times*, 25 June 1904 and, for Silver at the racetrack see, especially, Rex vs. Charteris, p. 21, evidence of M. Harris.

31. There are numerous references to horses, horse trading, the racetrack, policemen and pimps – by all the parties concerned – in the subsequent cases against both Charteris, who was found guilty of corruption, and Osberg, who was not. See R.S.A., Cape Town, C.A.D., Rex vs. Charteris, 1904, pp. 40, 56, 58, 83 and 92; and Rex vs. Osberg, 1904, pp. 44 and 52.

32. R.S.A., Cape Town, C.A.D., C.T. 11/31 (Resident Magistrate), Copy of a letter from W. Wilkoski (*sic*) to 'Dear Wife Rosie', dated 16 Jan. 1902, Cape Town.

33. On 'stuss' see also above, Chapter 2. For Silver's and Goldstein's involvement as 'bankers' while in Cape Town see, for example, Rex vs. Charteris, 1904, p. 26, evidence of M. Harris; and p. 32, evidence of S. Goldstein.

34. On Witkofsky see B. Feldman, 'Social Life of Cape Town Jewry', pp. 32–33; and Hallett, 'Policemen, Pimps and Prostitutes', p. 15.

35. R.S.A., Cape Town, C.A.D., C.T. 11/31, S. Lorimer to Resident Magistrate, Cape Town, 29 Jan. 1902.

36. The richest source on Roach is R.S.A., Pretoria, South African National Archives (S.A.N.A.), Transvaal Colony Archive, Attorney-General Papers (A.G.), L.D. 603, File 637/04, 1904, and, within it, more especially, 'Description Register of Male Prisoner'. In the same collection see also, A.G. File 172/06, 'Return of Persons Convicted in other Countries who have been Dealt with in Transvaal Courts', p. 2. On Roach's connections with Levy in Cape Town see, for example, 'City Police News', *Cape Times*, 17 April 1903.

37. On Beck, aged thirty-two in 1906, see R.S.A., Pretoria, S.A.N.A., A.G. 1909, Transvaal Police – C.I.D., Special Circular No. 10, 'List of Persons deported from the Transvaal under the Prevention of Crimes Ordinance, 1905, p. 2, entry no. 6.

38. On Levy in the Cape, and in London see Hallett, 'Policemen, Pimps and Prostitutes, p. 14.

39. See E.J. Bristow, *Prostitution and Prejudice: The Jewish Fight against White Slavery, 1870–1939* (Oxford 1982), p. 189; and A.R. Heinze, *Adapting to Abundance: Jewish Immigrants, Mass Consumption and the Search for American Identity* (New York 1990), pp. 60–61.

40. R.S.A., Cape Town, C.A.D., A.G. 3118, Resident Magistrates' Papers, Preparatory Examination of Annie Marshall alias Hannah Alexander, 10 May 1902. On the Lock Hospital and its patients, and a brief summary of the Kohler case see also van Heyningen, 'The Social Evil in the Cape Colony', pp. 180–186. Van Heyningen, however, seems unaware of that fact that, in the case of Hannah Alexander, 'the accused was acquitted' and that the evidence of Kohler needs to be dealt with more circumspectly.

41. R.S.A., Cape Town C.A.D., C.S.C.C.R., King vs. Leon Alexander, 24 April 1902.

42. As Lorimer put it in evidence during a later court case: 'The proposal was made by the accused himself' or, as it was reported in the press, 'When the accused [Silver] went to Kimberley he was employed at his own suggestion'. See R.S.A., Cape Town, C.A.D., A.G. 1531, File 12984, Rex vs. Joe Lis alias Joe Silver and Annie Bloem alias Lena Fygenbaum, 23 Aug. 1904, p. 18, evidence of S. Lorimer and 'The Morality Law', *Cape Argus*, 15 Sept. 1904.

43. On the campaign mounted by churchmen, feminists and others see, for example, van Heyningen, 'The Social Evil in the Cape Colony', pp. 181–191; and Hallett, 'Policemen, Pimps and Prostitutes', pp. 3–4.

44. R.S.A., Cape Town, C.A.D., Rex vs. Joe Lis alias Joe Silver, 1904, pp. 17–18; evidence of S. Lorimer and p. 22, evidence of Joseph Silver, which was never contested by the police.

45. Ibid. See also, 'The Morality Laws', *South African News*, 23 Sept. 1904.

This seemingly extraordinary salary is confirmed in a letter from the Chief of the Detectives to the Secretary to the Law Department, Cape Town dated 29 Sept. 1904 – see R.S.A., C.A.D., A.G. 1531, File 12984.

Chapter 12: Kimberley–Bloemfontein, 1902

1. Republic of South Africa (R.S.A.), Cape Town, Cape Archives Depot (C.A.D.), A.G. 1531/12984, Chief of the Detective Department, Kimberley, to the Secretary to the Law Department, 29 Sept. 1904.
2. R.S.A., Cape Town, C.A.D., High Court of Griqualand, Kimberley, Case No. 87 (2), SA 739, Silver vs. Lezard, L.F. Lezard to Coghlan and Coghlan, 28 July 1902.
3. Ibid.
4. R.S.A., Cape Town, C.A.D., Records of the Supreme Court of the Colony of the Cape of Good Hope, Illiquid Case, the Colonial Government vs. Joseph Silver, 28 June 1905, p. 1, evidence of E.J. Rigg.
5. Hirschberg could, apparently, produce discharge papers proving that he had, for some time, been a member of the 'Special Cape Police' – see 'Morality Prosecution', Bloemfontein Post, 7 Jan. 1903.
6. See, The Friend, 8 Jan. 1903.
7. On Vygenbaum's background see above, Chapter 11.
8. See above, Chapter 7.
9. The marriage is recorded in R.S.A., Cape Town, C.A.D., HAWC 1/3/42/1/2, Marriage Register, entry 14 Oct. 1902. On Annie Schwartz see above, Chapter 9.
10. See R.S.A., Bloemfontein, Free State Archives Depot (F.S.A.D.) L.B.L., (Landdrost Bloemfontein), Case No. 144 of 1903, The King vs. Joseph Silver, 24 Jan. 1903, evidence of Joseph Silver (pages unnumbered). On Anker see R.S.A., Bloemfontein, F.S.A.D., Vol. C.O. 140, File 961/03, 'Joseph Hanker (sic) and Jack Lis: Request that orders for the expulsion of, from O.R.C., be issued', Statement by John Egley, 6 Feb. 1903.
11. There are few comprehensive histories of Bloemfontein. Some idea of early development can, however, be gained from a publication which emerged from the office of the town clerk. See, Bloemfontein: A Short Illustrated History (date and publisher unknown). A copy of this publication is held in the library of the University of Cape Town.
12. Ibid., p. 8.
13. Some idea of the life of the local Jewish community on the eve of the South African War can be gleaned from a two-page typescript manuscript held in the library of the South African Jewish Board of Deputies entitled 'Jewish Chronicle', 10 Nov. 1899, p. 12 – 'Jewish Free Staters and the War – Interview with J.H. Levy'.

14. See The King vs. Joseph Silver, 1903, evidence of Joseph Silver.

15. See above, Chapter 7. On Weinberg – 'Annie Fineberg' – during the South African War see, The King versus Joseph Silver, 1903, Statement by Annie Fineberg, 19 Jan. 1903.

16. R.S.A., Bloemfontein, F.S.A.D., C.S. 2364/02, 'Houses of Ill Fame in Towns policed by Municipal Police, 1902', G.D. Gray, Commissioner of Police to the Acting Colonial Secretary, Bloemfontein, 11 July 1902.

17. See 'Wholesale Perjury', Bloemfontein Post, 22 Jan. 1903.

18. Hardly surprisingly, this was not only considered outrageous by religious Jews in the town but even lodged in the memories of some members of the underworld. See R.S.A., Cape Town, C.A.D., A.G. 1531 Ref. 12984, in the Supreme Court of the Colony of the Cape of Good Hope, 22 Sept. 1904, Statement by Hyman Bernstein, 23 Aug. 1904.

19. R.S.A., Bloemfontein, F.S.A.D., C.S. 2364/02, Commissioner of Police to Colonial Secretary, 29 Sept. 1902.

20. On Struzack as 'Director of Cinematographs' see R.S.A., Bloemfontein, F.S.A.D., C.O. Vol. 134 File 539/03, 'Undesirable Characters in Bloemfontein', Affidavit made by Detective John Egley, C.I.D., 22 Jan. 1903. The description of a 'panorama' relies completely on M. Gayford's fascinating 'Geographical Sensitivity', Spectator, 27 July 2002.

21. See R.S.A., Bloemfontein, F.S.A.D., C.O. 206, File 203/03, 'Undesirable Characters in Bloemfontein', Affidavits by B. Struzack and J. Silver, dated 31 Dec. 1902. On the unfortunate Mr Church see, for example, The Friend, 23 Jan. 1903.

22. See The Friend, 6 Jan. 1903; and 'Morality Prosecution', Bloemfontein Post, 7 Jan. 1903.

23. Ibid.

24. 'Morality Prosecution', Bloemfontein Post, 7 Jan. 1903.

25. Silver was later confident enough to summon Egley – unsuccessfully – as a witness for the defence when he was prosecuted. The Reid petition is alluded to in The Friend, 8 Jan. 1903. On Silver being 'used as a means to an end' see, for example, R.S.A., Bloemfontein, F.S.A.D., C.O. Vol. 111, File 4791/02, 'American Pimps', Affidavit by Inspector R. Ovendale, 23 Jan. 1903.

26. For a list and description of some of these see ibid, Affidavit by John Egley, dated 22 Jan. 1903. Significantly, this list does not foreground the role of Joseph Silver.

27. On Wax, see various documents in R.S.A., Bloemfontein, F.S.A.D., C.O. 111 File 4791/02, 'American Pimps'.

28. R.S.A., Bloemfontein, F.S.A.D., C.O. 147, File 1454/03, 'Petition to be got up on behalf of Martin Johnson: J. Silver's Statement concerning former', J. Silver to the Commissioner of Police, Bloemfontein, 22 Feb.

1903. On Dickenfaden, see for example, E.J. Bristow, *Prostitution and Prejudice: The Jewish Fight against White Slavery, 1870–1939* (Oxford 1982), p. 125. On the men who had crossed Silver at the time of his trial in Johannesburg see above, Chapter 9.

29. See, for example, 'Clearing the Issue', *Bloemfontein Post*, 23 Jan. 1903.
30. R.S.A., Bloemfontein, F.S.A.D., C.O. 111, File 4791, 'American Pimps', S. Goldreich to H.F. Wilson, Colonial Secretary, 4 Nov. 1902. For Goldreich's background see, for example, S. Cohen, 'The South African Zionist Federation and the South African Jewish Board of Deputies: Samuel Goldreich and Max Langermann', in M. Kaplan and M. Robertson (eds), *Founders and Followers. Johannesburg Jewry, 1887–1915*, pp. 197–210.
31. See 'A Reign of Terror', *Bloemfontein Post*, 9 Jan. 1903.
32. See R.S.A., Bloemfontein, F.S.A.D., C.O. File 5612/02, J.H. Levy to H.F. Wilson, Colonial Secretary, 9 Dec. 1902. On Levy's background, including his interest in things medical, see typescript manuscript held in the library of the South African Jewish Board of Deputies, Johannesburg, entitled 'Jewish Chronicle', 10 Nov. 1899, p. 12– 'Jewish Free Staters and the War – Interview with J.H. Levy'.
33. See especially, R.S.A., Bloemfontein, F.S.A.D., C.O. 206, File 203/03, 'Undesirable Characters in Bloemfontein', Affidavit by Inspector J.H. Bromley, 8 Jan. 1903.
34. See above, Chapter 11.
35. See affidavit made by George Beck on 23 December 1902, and reproduced in *The Friend*, 19 Jan. 1903.
36. Quotes in this paragraph are from the *Bloemfontein Post*, 25 Nov. 1902; and *The Friend*, 19 Jan. 1903.
37. Ibid.
38. Ibid.
39. 'The Burglary', *Bloemfontein Post*, 26 Nov. 1902.
40. See R.S.A., Bloemfontein, F.S.A.D., C.O. 111 File 479/02, 'American Pimps', Affidavit by Inspector J.H. Bromley, 8 Jan. 1903.

Chapter 13: Bloemfontein, 1903

1. See statements by Beck and Roach as reproduced in *The Friend*, 19 Jan. 1903.
2. Republic of South Africa (R.S.A.), Bloemfontein, Free State Archives (F.S.A.D), C.O. 111, File 4791/02, 'American Pimps', Affidavits by Annie Bloom, Nellie Moore, Bernard Struzack and Joseph Silver, all dated 31 Dec. 1902.
3. See *The Friend*, 6 Jan. 1903.
4. See the *Bloemfontein Post*, 7 Jan. 1903; and *The Friend*, 8 Jan. 1903.

5. See 'A Reign of Terror', *Bloemfontein Post*, 9 Jan. 1903; and 'The Social Evil', *The Friend*, 13 Jan. 1903.

6. For a short schematic introduction to the turbulent politics of the Far East in the 1890s see, for example, G. Stephenson, *A History of Russia*, (London 1969), pp. 284–289.

7. All information on 'James Lee' is extracted from 'The Morality Cases' and 'Lee's Story – He comes from Pekin' carried in the *Bloemfontein Post* on 21 and 23 Jan. 1903.

8. For the emerging context of the South African-Far Eastern connections with organised prostitution and the role of some leading pimps see C. van Onselen, *New Babylon, New Nineveh: Everyday Life on the Witwatersrand, 1886–1914* (Johannesburg 2001), pp. 149–150.

9. See, for example, 'Joe Silver Again', *Bloemfontein Post*, 23 Jan. 1903.

10. The direct speech (emphasis added) was recorded by a court reporter in *The Friend*, 21 Jan. 1903; while the indirect speech is to be found in R.S.A., Bloemfontein, F.S.A.D., L.B.L. (Landdrost Bloemfontein), Case No. 144 of 1903, The King vs. Joseph Silver, 24 Jan. 1903.

11. The apprehension of the press and its agents can be seen in 'Clearing the Issue', *Bloemfontein Press*, 23 Jan. 1903.

12. The state's predicament is perhaps set out most clearly in R.S.A., Bloemfontein, F.S.A.D., C.O. 206, File 203/03, 'Undesirable Characters in Bloemfontein' and, more especially, in the notes of the Attorney-General and Colonial Secretary dated 9 Jan. 1903. In the latter it is noted that, 'What complicates matters is that Silver, who is being used by the Police, is a most notorious scoundrel and the biggest pimp of them all. His game is to get a monopoly of the trade in Bloemfontein and as long as the police treat him as they are doing, he will succeed in this effort.'

13. See *The Friend*, 16 and 17 Jan. 1903.

14. See especially, 'The Reign of Terror', *Bloemfontein Post*, 19 Jan. 1903.

15. See 'Scotch Jack's' version, reported under his trade name at the time, in 'Johnston's [sic] Story', *Bloemfontein Post*, 19 Jan. 1903. See also, *The Friend*, 17 Jan. 1903.

16. See 'Johnston's Story', *The Friend*, 19 Jan. 1903.

17. Ibid.

18. See *The Friend*, 17 Jan. 1903.

19. 'The Reign of Terror', *Bloemfontein Post*, 19 Jan. 1903.

20. See 'Silver before the Court', *Bloemfontein Post*, 19 Jan. 1903; and *The Friend*, 19 Jan. 1903.

21. 'The Morality Muddle', *Bloemfontein Post*, 19 Jan. 1903.

22. See 'Deported from Kimberley', *Bloemfontein Post*, 20 Jan. 1903; 'Bloemfontein Purity Crusade' and 'Telegraphic News – Orange River

Colony', *The Star*, 20 Jan. 1903; and 'A Natal Comment', *Bloemfontein Post*, 21 Jan. 1903.

23. *The Friend*, 19 Jan. 1903.

24. *The Friend*, 20 Jan. 1903.

25. 'Immorality Charges', *Bloemfontein Post*, 20 Jan. 1903.

26. 'Silver in Court', *Bloemfontein Post*, 20 Jan. 1903.

27. Ibid.

28. 'Further Developments', *Bloemfontein Post*, 20 Jan. 1903. It is possible that Alford's initiative may, in turn, have derived from yet another action launched by the Attorney-General and public prosecutor. Earlier the same day, Tuesday, 20 Jan. 1903, Alford – this time under her married name, 'Annie Silver' – had again been charged with keeping a brothel but, in keeping with the traditions of her profession, had produced a medical certificate and failed to appear in court. It seems possible that a prosecution under her married name may, in some unknown way, have had other, indirect, implications for the ownership of the house in Fichardt Street. See also, 'Silver in Court', *Bloemfontein Post*, 20 Jan. 1903.

29. 'The Morality Cases', *Bloemfontein Post*, 21 Jan. 1903; and *The Friend*, 21 Jan. 1903.

30. See *The Friend*, 21 Jan. 1903; and 'Joe Silver Convicted', *Bloemfontein Post*, 21 Jan. 1903. See also, however, R.S.A, Bloemfontein, F.S.A.D, The King vs. Joseph Silver, Case No. 144 of 1903.

31. 'Joe Silver Convicted', *Bloemfontein Post*, 21 Jan. 1903; and 'Wholesale Perjury', *Bloemfontein Post*, 22 Jan. 1903.

32. 'Joe Silver Again', *Bloemfontein Post*, 23 Jan. 1903.

33. See R.S.A., Bloemfontein, F.S.A.D., C.O. 111 File 4791/02, 'American Pimps', Affidavits by J. Egley, 22 Jan. 1903 and R. Ovendale, 23 Jan. 1903.

34. See especially, 'Clearing the Issue', *Bloemfontein Post*, 23 Jan. 1903.

35. 'Joe Silver Again', *Bloemfontein Post*, 23 Jan. 1903; and R.S.A., Bloemfontein, F.S.A.D. Landdrost Bloemfontein, Case No. 172 of 1903, The King vs. Joseph Silver, 23 Jan. 1903.

36. The King vs. Joseph Silver, 23 Jan. 1903; but see also 'Silver Sentenced', *Bloemfontein Post*, 24 Jan. 1903.

37. See, for example, *The Friend*, 30 Jan. 1903.

38. See 'Silver Echoes', *The Friend*, 31 Jan. 1903.

39. R.S.A., Bloemfontein, F.S.A.D., C.O. 140, File 961/03 'Joseph Hanker (*sic*) and Jack Lis: Request that orders for expulsion from O.R.C. be issued', Affidavits by J. Egley, sworn before R. Ovendale, 6 Feb. 1903.

40. Orange River Colony, Ordinance 11 of 1903, 'To Provide for the Suppression of Brothels and Immorality and to Amend the Police Offences Ordinance, 1902'.

41. Transvaal Colony, Ordinance 46 of 1903 for the 'Suppression of Brothels and Immorality'. On the Immorality and Criminal Law Amendment legislation see R. Posel, '"Continental Women" and Durban's "Social Evil"', *Journal of Natal and Zulu History*, Vol. 12, 1989, pp. 1–13.

42. See correspondence and telegrams in R.S.A., Bloemfontein, F.S.A.D., C.O. 143, File No. 1181/03, 'Joseph Silver', covering the period 13 Feb. 1903–28 March 1903.

43. On the trial of Beck and Roach see R.S.A., Bloemfontein, F.S.A.D., HG 4/1/2/1/2, File 8/1903, 20 Feb. 1903. On Beck's subsequent history see R.S.A., Pretoria, South African National Archives (S.A.N.A.), JUS, Transvaal Criminal Investigation Department, Special Circular No. 10, 18 Feb. 1909, *List of Persons deported from the Transvaal under the Prevention of Crimes Ordinance*, 1905, Entry No. 6. On the earlier and later part of Roach's career see, for example, R.S.A., Pretoria, S.A.N.A., L.D. 603, File 637/04, Rex vs. Daniel Roach, 'Housebreaking & Theft'.

44. See R.S.A., Bloemfontein, F.S.A.D., C.O. 111, File 4791/02. 'American Pimps', J. Silver to Commissioner of Police, Bloemfontein, 22 Feb. 1903.

45. On 'Scotch Jack' Jacobs alias 'Martin Johnson' see R.S.A., Pretoria, S.A.N.A., WLD 5/378, File 690/1921, Opposed applications, Martin Johnson, 1903. See especially, Commissioner of Police to The Secretary to the Law Department, 11 April 1903.

46. See especially D. Hayden, *Pox: Genius, Madness and the Mysteries of Syphilis* (New York 2003), pp. 126 and 217.

47. R.S.A., Bloemfontein, F.S.A.D., C.O. 155, 'Joseph Silver: Petition for release from Prison', J. Silver to His Excellency, the Lieutenant-Governor, Orange River Colony, 21 March 1903.

48. 'Joe Silver', *Bloemfontein Post*, 28 April 1903.

Chapter 14: Cape Town, 1903–1904

1. See Republic of South Africa (R.S.A.), Cape Town, Cape Archives Depot (C.A.D.), Attorney-General (A.G.), Vol. 1531, File 12984, Rex vs. Joe Lis alias Joe Silver in the Court of the Resident Magistrate, C.W. Broers, on 30 Aug. 1904, evidence of Robert Barber, p. 7. Also, R.S.A., Cape Town, C.A.D., Cape Supreme Court Criminal Records, May–July 1904, Case no. 38, Rex vs. Thor Osberg, evidence of Lena Bloem (Annie Bloom/Vygenbaum), p. 20.

2. On the petition see Rex vs. Joe Silver 1904, evidence of Joe Silver, p. 21; and as reported in 'Morality Law', *The Argus*, 22 Sept. 1904. On Levy's background see R. Hallett, 'Policemen, Pimps and Prostitutes – Public Morality and Police Corruption, Cape Town 1902–1904', paper presented to the History Workshop Conference, University of the Witwatersrand,

3–7 Feb. 1978, p. 14. On Levy and Roach's business connection see, for example, 'City Police News – Six Months Hard Labour', *Cape Times*, 17 April 1903. On Levy and Silver's ability to work together, see Hallett, 'Policemen, Pimps and Prostitutes', p. 14.

3. The morals police started easing off on their campaign to prosecute *all* brothel-owners as early as March 1903, when the policy was revised so as to pursue only the most 'rowdy' houses. See R.S.A., Cape Town, C.A.D., Cape Supreme Court Criminal Records, Rex vs. David Charteris, Oct. 1904, evidence of Thor Osberg, p. 77. There is a useful overview of the police campaign in the section devoted to 'The Cape Town Police Cleaning up the Vice Spots' in Hallett's, 'Policemen, Pimps and Prostitutes', pp. 5–8.

4. The police were perfectly aware of this. Thus, for example, Harris once claimed in evidence that: 'He (Osberg) afterwards said that there must be some cases because, if there were no cases, he would soon be unable to give me any protection.' See Rex vs. Osberg, 1904, evidence of Max Harris, p. 7.

5. The neatest summary of these properties is to be found in the charge sheet in the case Rex vs. Charteris, 1904. For details of Harris's dealings with the likes of Ricardi and Roytowski see ibid., evidence of M. Harris, pp. 10 and 23; and evidence of Constable A. Irvine, p. 63. On Harris's interactions with men like Goldstein, Mabon (rendered Maybaum in its Yiddish form during the trial) and Roytowski see, for example, ibid., evidence of M. Harris, pp. 12–14 and 33. Also, 'The Charteris Case', *Cape Times*, 24 June 1904; and 'The Osberg Case', 5 and 6 July 1904.

6. See especially 'The Password' in 'The Charteris Case', *Cape Times*, 24 June 1904.

7. There are valuable fragments of evidence about 'French' activities contained in parts of the evidence presented in Rex vs. Charteris, 1904, but a good deal more is contained in the evidence presented in the case of Rex vs. Osberg, 1904.

8. See United States of America, National Archives and Federal Record Centre, Washington, DC, US Immigration and Naturalization Service, Record Group No. 85, No V 52484, 1 – G, Braun European Report, 2 Oct. 1909 (pages unnumbered).

9. See France, Paris, Centre Historique des Archives Nationales, Box BB 18, F/7 14854, 'Trafiquants professionnels signalisés aux ports par notices spéciales, 1913', Notice No. 37, 16 June 1913 and E.J. Bristow, *Prostitution and Prejudice: The Jewish Fight against White Slavery, 1870–1939* (Oxford 1982), p. 265. See also the evidence of Valentine Dufis on 'Dacheau' in Rex vs. Osberg, 1904.

10. Some idea of Hayum's Lakeside operation can be obtained from the evidence of Valentine Dufis in Rex vs. Osberg, 1904, pp. 22–23.

11. On Dempers see R.S.A., Cape Town, C.A.D., CSC 2/2/1/237, No. 98 and, more generally, J. Edwards, *Our Heritage: A History of Caledon* (Cape Town 1979), pp. 17–18 and *Prominent Men of the Cape Colony* (Portland, Maine 1902) p. 49.

12. As reported in the 'Social Purity League' and 'The Morality Act – a Bond M.L.A. fined', in *The Star* (Johannesburg) on 18 July and 28 Aug. 1903.

13. On 'Madame Sarah' a.k.a. Agnes Bach see France, Paris, Centre Historique des Archives Nationales, Box BB 18, F/7/14854, 'Trafiquants profession-nels signalisés aux ports par notices spéciales, 1913', Notice No. 37, 16 June 1913, note on Hayum. On her and Osberg's doings at 12 Muir Street see Rex vs. Osberg, 1904, evidence of Alec Goverovitch, pp. 24–27.

14. On the sale of illicit alcohol at the Alliance Café, 21 Bree Street, see Rex vs. Joe Silver, 1904, pp. 5–6, evidence of Hyman Bernstein. See also, Namibia (Nam.), Windhoek, National Archives of Namibia (N.N.A.) Papers of the Imperial Court, Windhoek, File D 56/05, Statement by Joseph Lis, 13 Sept. 1905.

15. On Rogers's link to the house at 100 Hout Street see Rex vs. Charteris, 1904, p. 12, evidence of Max Harris.

16. Nam., Windhoek, N.N.A., GW1 File F44/06, 'History of Jack Lis alias Silver', S. Lorimer, Inspector in Charge, C.I.D., Cape Town, 22 Feb. 1906.

17. See Rex. vs. Charteris, 1904, p. 23, evidence of Max Harris.

18. See Rex. vs. Charteris, 1904, pp. 1–2, evidence of 'Lena Blume', and 'The Charteris Case', *Cape Times*, 25 June 1904.

19. See Rex vs. Charteris, 1904, pp. 9–11 and 21–22, evidence of Max Harris, pp. 30–31 evidence of Leah Wynstock [*sic*] and p. 84, evidence of David Charteris. See also, 'The Charteris Case', *Cape Times*, 25 June 1904. From a close study of this evidence it would appear that there were several cases involved in this conflict. The outcomes of these proceedings are indirectly alluded to in Rex vs. Charteris, 1904, but I have been unable to track the original documents pertaining to the latter cases. It is also significant that Goldstein used Osberg as his route into the prosecutions brought by Trautman: see ibid.

20. On the Goldstein assault see especially 'The Charteris Case', *Cape Times*, 26 June 1904.

21. On the deportation of Mabon and Rogers, and the ensuing fears in East European underworld circles see, for example, Rex vs. Charteris, 1904, p. 12, evidence of Max Harris, or p. 36, evidence of Solomon Goldstein. Also, 'The Cape Town Police Scandals', *The Star*, 28 June 1904 and 'The Osberg Case', *Cape Times*, 5 July 1904. The fears of Jewish gangsters were not, it later transpired, entirely without foundation. As we shall have occasion to note below, Harris and Hayum were both deported from Cape Town, in 1904, albeit *after* the fall from grace of Charteris

and Osberg. The wider context is outlined in M. Shain, 'Diamonds, Pogroms and Undesirables – Anti-alienism and Legislation in the Cape Colony, 1890–1906', *South African Historical Journal*, Vol. 12, Nov. 1980, pp. 13–28 and, of course, Hallett, 'Policemen, Pimps and Prostitutes'.

22. On the various temporary absences of Goldstein, Harris and Witkofsky see Rex vs. Charteris, 1904, pp. 27–28, evidence of Leah Wynstock [*sic*]; 'The Charteris Case', *Cape Times*, 25 June 1904; and Hallett, 'Policemen, Pimps and Prostitutes', p. 15. For the situation on the Rand at the time see C. van Onselen, *New Babylon, New Nineveh: Everyday Life on the Witwatersrand, 1886–1914* (Johannesburg 2001), pp. 149–153.

23. See R.S.A., Cape Town, C.A.D., Colonial Office (C.O.), Vol. 365, Ref. 22, I.J. Roytowski to the Colonial Secretary of the Cape of Good Hope, 25 Feb. 1904. On the remarks attributed to Roytowski, which come from a less than reliable source, Solomon Goldstein, see Rex vs. Charteris, 1904, pp. 33–34.

24. As Charteris pointed out to Harris, 'he could not protect the Jewish houses any longer, as they were "too rough" and would not pay enough protection money'. See 'The Charteris Case', *Cape Times*, 24 June 1904. On Silver's dealings with Bloom and Rosenblatt ('Mrs Blatt') see, for example, Rex vs. Joe Silver, 1904, pp. 13–16, evidence of Det. Head Constable S. Davis; and Rex vs. Osberg, 1904, pp. 42–47, evidence of Thor Osberg. Rosenblatt, too, was closer to Osberg than Charteris: see ibid.

25. See Rex vs. Joe Silver, 1904, pp. 8–9, evidence of Robert Levy (Private Detective).

26. Ibid. For the names of some of those to be found in the Longmarket and Sydney Street brothels during 1904 see R.S.A., Cape Town, C.A.D., A.G. Vol. 1531, File 12984, Rex vs. 'Susan Josephine' (18 Jan.), 'Marguerite Degland' (15 Feb.), 'Jenny Durant' (31 March), 'Louise de Blean' (13 May), 'Fanny Bloem' (16 May), and 'Marianne de Lorme' (15 June).

27. See R.S.A., Cape Town, C.A.D., Cape Supreme Court, Case No. 314 of 1905, 'Joseph Silver, Illiquid Case', evidence of J. Silver.

28. On out of town visits by Silver to Lakeside and Paarl so as to avoid being served with police notices, and the use of telegrams and other ploys see, for example, Rex vs. Osberg, 1904, pp. 30–34, evidence of the policemen, Alexander Clark and Samuel Davis. Also, 'The Osberg Case', *Cape Times*, 9 July 1904.

29. See Nam., Windhoek, N.N.A., File GW1 D56/06, Statement by Bertha Linczock, 2 Sept. 1905.

30. See Rex vs. Charteris, 1904, p. 22 evidence of Max Harris.

31. On charges of slave-like status see Nam., Windhoek, N.N.A., Windhoek, GWI 56/05, Statement by Rosa Müller (neé Feldmann), 30 Aug. 1905.

See also R.S.A., Cape Town, C.A.D., A.G. Vol. 1531, File 12984, Rex vs. Susan Josephine.

32. See R.S.A., Cape Town, C.A.D., Cape Town Supreme Court, Criminal Case Records, Case No. 20, Rex vs. Jack Lis, Nov. 1904, p. 1, evidence of Morris Gilbert.

33. On Goldstein's involvement in the 'coffee shop' at Bree Street, the significance of which seems to have eluded the police at the time, see Rex. vs. Charteris, 1904, p. 34, evidence of Solomon Goldstein.

34. See especially Rex vs. Charteris, 1904, p. 23, evidence of Max Harris.

35. See Rex vs. Osberg, 1904, p. 36, evidence of Max Harris.

36. Advocate Nightingale, who led the case for the prosecution in Rex vs. Charteris could see at least part of this alliance and once, rather pointedly, asked Solomon Goldstein, 'Did a man named Silver bring you down from Johannesburg to give evidence?' To which, Goldstein replied, 'No'. As reported in 'The Charteris Case', Cape Times, 25 June 1904.

37. Hallett, 'Policemen, Pimps and Prostitutes, Cape Town', p. 8.

38. One T.W.A. Meares, asked to make a false affidavit against Charteris at the height of mid-1904 police corruption cases, was alleged to have been told by Silver that: 'It's all right Tommy. I am well in with Captain Lorimer. I will make it right'. See Rex vs. Charteris, 1904, p. 61.

39. See Hallett, 'Policemen, Pimps and Prostitutes', p. 8.

40. See R.S.A., Cape Town, C.A.D., A.G. 531, File 12984, Case Nos. 517, 1468 and 2866 of 1904.

41. See Rex vs. Charteris, 1904, p. 24, evidence of Max Harris.

42. On Silver's letter of application for naturalisation see R.S.A., Cape Town, C.A.D., C.O. Vol. 8658, File 22 1904/05. The path of the papers through police channels is recorded in R.S.A., Cape Town, C.A.D., A.G. 1624, R.M. Crawford to Sir John Graham, Sec. to Law Dept., 28 Aug. 1905.

43. See Chapter 11 above.

44. The account of the Zeeman case that follows is drawn almost entirely from R. Hallett's, 'Policemen, Pimps and Prostitutes', pp. 9–14. It should, however, be read against the background provided by M. Shain's 'Diamonds, Pogroms and Undesirables.'

45. Hallett, 'Policemen, Pimps and Prostitutes', p. 12.

46. Ibid., pp. 13–14. For the role of the editor of the Jewish Advocate in the sequel to the Zeeman arrest see also Cape Argus, 23 Aug. 1904.

Chapter 15: Cape Town, 1904–1905

1. See R. Hallett, 'Policemen, Pimps and Prostitutes – Public Morality and Police Corruption, Cape Town, 1902–1904', Paper presented to the History Workshop Conference, University of the Witwatersrand, 3–7 Feb. 1978,

pp. 14–15. See also Republic of South Africa (R.S.A.), Cape Town, Cape Archive Depot (C.A.D.) Supreme Court Criminal Records, Rex vs. David Charteris, 1904, pp. 31–32 evidence of Solomon Goldstein. It is possible, however, that this raid was at one of Harris's other outlets – number 7, Caledon Street. See 'Gambling Den Raid', *Cape Argus*, 18 April 1904.

2. Samuel Lorimer died of General Paralysis of the Insane, induced by syphilis, in Valkenberg Hospital, on 13 Nov. 1913. See R.S.A., Cape Town, C.A.D., File HAWC 1/3/9/5/12 (1912–1914).

3. Hallett, 'Policemen, Pimps and Prostitutes', p. 15.

4. Rex vs. Charteris, 1904, p. 31, evidence of Leah Wynstock [*sic*].

5. Harris, an illiterate, sometimes used the Jewish holy days – such as Passover – to orientate himself as to time and place. See, for example, Rex vs. Charteris, 1904, p. 8, evidence of Harris.

6. Rex vs. Charteris, 1904, p. 25, evidence of Harris (emphasis added).

7. As cited in Hallett, 'Policemen, Pimps and Prostitutes', p. 15.

8. Ibid.

9. See Rex vs. Charteris, 1904, pp. 26 and 74, evidence of Harris and Dr H.A. Engelbach.

10. 'The Charteris Case', *Cape Times*, 2 July 1904.

11. Hallett, 'Policemen, Pimps and Prostitutes', p. 17. The description of Goverovitch is that of Osberg.

12. See Rex vs. Charteris, 1904, p. 19, evidence of Lena Bloem; 'The Osberg Case', *Cape Times*, 9 July 1904, and 'The Morality Laws – Silver Again Remanded', *South African News*, 6 Sept. 1904. See also, Namibia (Nam.), Windhoek, Namibian National Archives (N.N.A), File GW 11 D56/05, Statement by Bertha Linczok, 15 Sept. 1905.

13. See R.S.A., Cape Town, C.A.D., Rex vs. Joe Silver, 1904, pp. 6–7, evidence of Detective Head Constable C. Bassett.

14. See Rex vs Silver, 1904, R.S.A., Cape Town, C.A.D., Attorney-General (A.G.), Vol. 1531, File 12984, Rex vs. Joe Lis alias Joe Silver in the Court of the Resident Magistrate, C.W. Broers, on 30 Aug. 1904. p. 19, evidence of W. Muller, Clerk in the Office of the Registrar of Deeds.

15. R.S.A., Cape Town, C.A.D., A.G. Vol. 1518, the Inspector in Charge, C.I.D., S. Davis, to W.B. Shaw, 20 Aug. 1904.

16. The official position, as late as March 1904, was against the use of private detectives – see R.S.A., Cape Town, C.A.D., A.G. Vol. 1442, Part 1, C.J. Munsen to Attorney-General, 15 March 1904 and response. It was the need to deal with Silver that saw this policy reversed – see R.S.A., Cape Town, C.A.D., A.G. Vol. 1518, S. Lorimer to Acting Commander, Urban Police, Cape Town, 20 Aug. 1904; and Rex vs. Silver, 1904, pp. 3–4, evidence of F.C. King, Clerk of the Court.

17. On Robert Levy see Rex vs. Silver, 1904, pp. 8–11, evidence of Levy.

18. On Woolf's barbershop, see above, Chapter 11.
19. Rex vs Silver, 1904, pp. 8–9, evidence of Levy; and pp. 23–24, evidence of Henry Woolf.
20. Rex vs. Silver, 1904, p. 10, evidence of Levy.
21. The original charge, as recorded in R.S.A., Cape Town, C.A.D., A.G. Vol. 1531, File 12984 appears, incorrectly, to suggest that the charge was in terms of 'Act 36 of *1904*'. This should, presumably, have read *1902*.
22. See Rex vs Silver, 1904, J. Silver to Hon. Captain Lorimer, 18 Aug. 1904 (emphasis added).
23. See 'The Jewish Murderer', in S. Gilman, *The Jew's Body* (London 1991), p. 111. The original motto, Gilman informs us, came from C.F.S. Hahnemann, 'the founder of homeopathic medicine'.
24. R.S.A., Cape Town, C.A.D., A.G. Vol. 1518, W.B. Shaw, to the Hon. Attorney-General, 19 Aug. 1904.
25. *Cape Argus*, 23 and 25 Aug. 1904. At a later date, however, Shaw suggested that he – Shaw – could arrange for Annie Bloom to reappear and stand trial. See 'Morality Law', *Cape Argus*, 22 Sept. 1904.
26. R.S.A., Cape Town, C.A.D., A.G. Vol. 1518, Attorney-General to W.B. Shaw Esq., 30 Aug. 1904.
27. See R.S.A., Cape Town, C.A.D., A.G. Vol. 1531/12984, Affidavit sworn before A. Pett, Justice of Peace, 30 Aug. 1904.
28. Rex vs. Silver, 1904, pp. 5–6. Compare this rather amnesic testimony, on 30 Aug., with Bernstein's original, more fulsome and truthful, affidavit in R.S.A., Cape Town, C.A.D., statement by Hyman Bernstein before H.W. Whitehorn, Justice of Peace, 23 Aug. 1904.
29. On the Caledon Street bottle store and its attendant problems, see a score of letters in R.S.A., Cape Town, C.A.D., Vol. T853, File 4660.
30. R.S.A., Cape Town, C.A.D., Vol. C.T. 835, File 4660, Acting Commissioner of Urban Police, R.M. Crawford to the Secretary to the Law Department, 23 Aug. 1904.
31. See R.S.A., Cape Town, C.A.D., Cape Supreme Court Records, Sept.–Nov. 1904, Rex vs. Jack Lis, pp. 1–15, evidence of various parties. See also 'Lis Committed for Trial', *South African News*, 14 Sept. 1904.
32. See, for example, 'Alleged Intimidation', *South African News*, 3 Sept. 1904.
33. In the matter of Rex vs. Silver and the charge of attempting to defeat the ends of justice see the following items: 'Alleged Intimidation', *South African News*, 3 Sept., 'The Course of Justice', *Cape Argus*, 8 Sept. and 'Intimidation Case', *South African News*, 13 Sept. 1904. In the case Rex vs. Jack Lis for attempted murder see, 'Lis Committed for Trial', *South African News*, 14 Sept. 1904 and R.S.A., Cape Town, C.A.D., Cape Town Supreme Court Records, Sept –Nov. 1904, Rex vs. Jack Lis, pp. 1–15, evidence of various parties. In the matter of brothel-keeping, see Rex. vs. Silver, 1904 and items

in the *Cape Argus* d. 15, 23 and 30 Aug. 1904. See also, 'The Morality Laws – Silver Again Remanded', 'The Morality Laws – Silver Again Charged', 'The Morality Act – The Silver Case', 'The Morality Laws – Silver Sentenced' and 'The Case of Joe Silver' – all of which appeared in the *South African News*, on the following dates: 6, 13, 16, 23 Sept. and 25 Oct. 1904. The latter case is also covered in: 'The Morality Law – Silver's Case, Further Evidence To-Day', 'The Morality Law – Silver's Case, a Further Remand' and 'Morality Law – The Silver Case, Accused Gives Evidence', all of which appeared in the *Cape Argus*, of 12, 15 and 22 Sept. 1904.

34. On Polikansky see also above, Chapters 11 and 12. Polikansky, presumably a supplier of cigarettes to the various Lis/Silver cafés and restaurants, was a respected member of Cape Town society.

35. Apparently without a great deal of success: see R.S.A., Cape Town, C.A.D., A.G. Vol. 1591, File 11591, see undated memo. *c.* Dec. 1904 but which also has signatures from Dec. 1905 attached to it.

36. Rex vs. Silver, 1904, pp. 17–18, evidence of Captain S. Lorimer.

37. R.S.A., Cape Town, C.A.D., A.G. Vol. 1531, Ref. 1351/12984, Chief of the Detective Department Kimberley to the Secretary to the Law Department, Cape Town, 29 Sept. 1904.

38. Rex vs. Silver, 1904, p. 21, evidence of J. Silver.

39. See 'The Morality Laws', *South African News*, 23 Sept. 1904; and Rex vs. Silver, 1904.

40. See R.S.A., Pietermaritzburg, KwaZulu-Natal Archives Depot, Vol. 30, Ref. I.R.D. 928/1904, 'Forwards photographs and descriptions of certain undesirables (Pimps) who have been deported from this Colony at their own expenses', 20 Sept. 1904.

41. See Rex vs. Max Harris, 24 July 1905, as recorded in *Law Reports of Cases in the Supreme Court 1905*, (Cape Town 1906), Vol. XV, pp. 582–588.

42. On the appeal see R.S.A., Cape Town, C.A.D., A.G. 1531 File 12984, W. Coulton, 17 Oct. 1904, C.A.D., Cape Supreme Court, C.S.C. 1/1/1/59, Sir J.H. De Villiers, 15 Nov. 1904; and 'The Case of Joe Silver', *South African News*, 25 Oct. 1904.

43. There appear to be no early records for the prison, or any study of early prison life at Tokai. Some idea of the official mind at the time can, however, be gleaned from: 'The Origins of the Reformatory in the Cape Colony, 1882–1910', in L. Chisholm, 'Reformatories and Industrial Schools in South Africa: A Study in Class, Colour and Gender, 1882–1939' (unpublished D.Phil. thesis, University of the Witwatersrand, Johannesburg, 1989), pp. 28–54. On Jack Lis at about this time see, for example, R.S.A., Cape Town, C.A.D., Vol. C.T. 853, Ref. 4660, Acting Secretary to the Assistant Treasurer, 16 Jan. 1905.

44. See United Kingdom, London, National Archives, Kew, MEPO 6/23, Metropolitan Police: Criminal Record Office: Habitual Criminals Registers and Miscellaneous Papers, p. 51.

45. See Nam., Windhoek, N.N.A., GWI D56/05, Statement by Bertha Linczok, [sic] 2 Sept. 1905.

46. See R.S.A., Cape Town, C.A.D., C.O. Vol. 8579, Part I, Letters of Naturalisation, 1903. Also, C.A.D., C.S.C., Vol. 1/1/1/53, 1903, Part 1, Rex vs. H. Parnell, S. Jackson and L. O' Gara.

47. See Nam., Windhoek, N.N.A., GWI D56/05, Statement by Fanny Stein, 2 Sept. 1905; and C202/05, Statement by Rosa Silberberg, 16 Feb. 1906.

48. See Nam, Windhoek, N.N.A., GWI D56/05, Statement by Fanny [Bern]Stein, 2 Sept. 1905; and statements by Gussy Bernstein, 2 Sept. and 6 Oct. 1905. For Silver's version on the sisters and other prostitutes with whom he interacted, see statement by Joseph Lis, 13 Sept. 1905.

49. See Nam., Windhoek, N.N.A., GWI D56/05, Statements by Gertie Abrahams, 13 and 14 Sept. 1905.

50. See R.S.A., Cape Town, C.A.D., Cape Supreme Court, Case No. 314 of 1905, 'Joseph Silver, Illiquid Case'.

51. R.S.A., Cape Town, C.A.D., C.S.C., Case No. 314 of 1905, p. 3, evidence of Joseph Silver. I have had no success in tracing any property deal between Silver and any *shul* in Cape Town at that time.

52. Ibid. It is evident from *Juta's Cape Town & Suburban Directory for the Years 1903–1906* that privately owned baths, some attached to men's hairdressing salons, were not unusual in the city at the time. The Caledon Street Baths appear to have operated briefly in 1903 at 137(a) Caledon Street, moved briefly in 1904 to Roeland Street and then acquired a more permanent outlet at 207 Caledon Street in 1905–6. Silver, presumably, bought into the business in 1904/5. I am indebted to Petrie Le Roux for tracking down these details for me.

53. See R.S.A., Cape Town, C.A.D., A.G. Vol. 1613, Commissioner Urban Police to the Secretary, Law Department, 6 July 1905.

54. See R.S.A., Cape Town, C.A.D., Cape Supreme Court, Case No. 314 of 1905; Note from the Deputy Sheriff's Office, 11 July 1905.

55. R.S.A., Cape Town, C.A.D., A.G. Vol. 1624, R. Crawford to Sir John Graham, 28 Aug. 1905.

56. German Federal Republic, Berlin, Bundesarchiv, Vol. R151F, File FC 5125, J. Lis to His Excellency, the Governor-General of German South West Africa, 18 Jan. 1906.

Chapter 16: Swakopmund, 1905

1. For the wider context see I.R. Phimister, 'Africa Partitioned', *Review*, Vol. 18, Spring 1995, pp. 351–381 and, more especially, p. 370.

2. On nineteenth-century Germany see, for example, D. Blackbourn, *The Fontana History of Germany, 1780–1918* (London 1977), pp. 350–399. On early colonial policy in the region see I. Goldblatt, *History of South West Africa from the Beginning of the Nineteenth Century* (Cape Town 1970), p. 120, and H. Bley, *Namibia under German Rule* (Hamburg 1996).

3. On early resistance see Goldblatt, *History of South West*, pp. 120–149.

4. See T. Dedering, 'The German–Herero War of 1904: Revisionism of Genocide or Imaginary Historiography?', *Journal of Southern African Studies*, Vol. 19, No. 1, March 1993, pp. 80–89; and J.B. Gewald, *Herero Heroes: A Socio-Political History of the Herero of Namibia, 1890–1923* (Ohio 1999).

5. See Goldblatt, *History of South West*, pp. 129–144.

6. See Blackbourn, *History of Germany*, p. 368; and R.V. Pierard, 'The Transportation of White Women to German Southwest Africa, 1898–1914', *Race*, Vol. 12, No. 3, Jan. 1971, pp. 317–322. The Germans were not, of course, alone in this. See K. Ballhatchet, *Race, Sex and Class under the Raj* (London 1980) and, as pertinently, S. Dubow, *Scientific Racism in Modern South Africa* (Johannesburg 1995).

7. This para. is based on Pierard, 'Transportation of White Women', pp. 317–320; Bley, *Namibia under German Rule*, pp. 73–77 and pp. 91–96 on 'colonial aloofness' and 'town and country' in South-West Africa; and N.O. Oermann, *Mission Church and State Relations in South West Africa under German Rule, 1884–1915* (Stuttgart 1999), pp. 213–215.

8. See Namibia (Nam.), Windhoek, Namibian National Archives (N.N.A.), GWI 585, File D80/02, the case against Henri Sourd and others.

9. 'The influx of the Deutsche Colonial troops also brought other problems for the authorities. There were few women and, in the manner of the armies of those days, the authorities established brothels at Swakopmund. Several of these were operated and staffed by Jews from South America.' S. Davis, 'Yiddische Voortrekkers of S.W.A.', *Southern African Jewish Times*, Dec. 1958 p. 46. This is the only published source which I have been able to trace that makes reference to the women coming from Brazil.

10. See U. Massmann, *Swakopmund: A Chronicle of the Town's People, Places and Progress* (Society for Scientific Development and Museums, Swakopmund, Namibia, 1983), p. 46.

11. Ibid., pp. 7–9 and 42.

12. Ibid., pp. 10–17.

13. Ibid., pp. 28–29.

14. Ibid., p. 30.

15. See D. Sorkin, 'The Port Jew: Notes toward a Social Type', *Journal of Jewish Studies*, Vol. 1, No. 1, Spring 1991, pp. 87–97.

16. See *Jewish Chronicle* (London), 17 Nov. 1905, p. 45. I am indebted to Reuben and Naomi Musiker for drawing to my attention this and other items relating to the history of the Jewish community in South West Africa held in the Library of the Board of Deputies, Johannesburg. See also Massmann, *Swakopmund*, p. 70.

17. In this regard South Africans obviously posed rather different questions both of the protectorate itself and of the neighbouring territory. See, for example, T. Dedering, 'The Ferreira Raid of 1906: Boers, Britons and Germans in Southern Africa in the Aftermath of the South African War', *Journal of Southern African Studies*, Vol. 26, No. 1, March 2000, pp. 43–60.

18. On Friedman see S. Davis, 'Lawrence G. Green', in *S.W.A.-Jaarboek 1973* (Windhoek 1973), p. 117; and on Smith, F.C. Metrowich, *Scotty Smith: South Africa's Robin Hood* (Cape Town 1962). On the frontier situation more generally, see T. Dedering, 'The Prophet's War, "War Against the Whites": Shepherd Stuurman in Namibia and South Africa, 1904–1907', *Journal of African History*, Vol. 40, No. 1, 1999 pp. 1–19 and, more especially, p. 4.

19. See Nam, Windhoek, N.N.A., File F 247/05, Statement by Morris Davidson and Rosenmann, Dec. 1905. See also, *Windhuker Nachrichten – Südwestbote*, No. 24, 14 Dec. 1905, p. 2. On Silver's connection to Rosenberg see, for example, Nam., Windhoek, N.N.A., F 247/05, telegram, Joe [Lis/Silver] to Max Rosenberg, 3 Nov. 1905. Also Chapter 15 above.

20. See Nam, Windhoek, N.N.A., GWI, File F44/06, Statement by Sylvia Melchior, 5 April 1906.

21. See *Jewish Chronicle* (London), 17 Nov. 1905, p. 43; M de Saxe (ed.), *The South African Jewish Year Book 1929* (The South African Jewish Historical Society, Johannesburg, 1929), p. 354. On Mande's later, sometimes tempestuous career, see also B.A. Kosmin, *MaJuta: A History of the Jewish Community of Zimbabwe* (Gweru, Zimbabwe 1981), p. 28. On Mande's portrayal of self while in South-West Africa see Nam., Windhoek, N.N.A., File F247/05, Statements by Max Mande, dated 7 and 14 Dec. 1905. On the state of Silver and Mande's financial affairs see Nam. Windhoek, NNA, GWI, F247/05, M. Mande to 'Rachel' (Rosa Silberberg), 6 Dec. 1905. For Silver's hold on Mande see, for example, GWI F247/05, Telegrams, Lis to Weinberg, 3 Nov. 1905; and, more directly, Lis to Monday (*sic*), 10 Nov. 1905.

22. For Mande's various business connections with Lis and Tuchmann see Nam., Windhoek, N.N.A., GWI, File F247/05, Statements by Max Mande, dated 7 and 14 Dec. 1905.

23. See Nam., Windhoek, N.N.A., GWI D56/05, Statements by J. Lis and Rosa Silberberg, 15 Sept. 1905.

24. Gordon's mindset at the time can be traced in Nam., Windhoek, N.N.A., GWI, File D56/05, Statements by Gussy Bernstein on 2 and 15 Sept. 1905; and Rosa Silberberg, 15 Sept. 1905.

25. This was a fact which Silver later attempted, unsuccessfully, to use as the basis for an appeal against his conviction. See Nam., Windhoek, N.N.A., GWI D56/05, Jacques Sanders to the Imperial District Court, Windhoek, 7 Nov. 1905 and marginalia by court officials.

26. See especially Nam., Windhoek, N.N.A., GWI D56/05, Statement by R. Silberberg, 15 Sept. 1905.

27. The rent is recorded in Nam., Windhoek, N.N.A., GWI D56/05, Statement by Joseph Lis, 15 Sept. 1905. But even Lis later acknowledged that the real rent was 1,000 marks per month – see Nam., Windhoek, N.N.A., GWI D56/05, Joseph Lis to the Imperial District Court, Windhoek, 23 Nov 1905, appeal against the findings of the court.

28. Ibid. On Silver's relationship with the Schroeders see especially Nam., Windhoek, N.N.A., GWI F247/05, Joseph Lis to the Hon. Judge, Dr Kornmeyer, 8 Dec. 1905.

29. See Nam., Windhoek, N.N.A., GWI F247/05, Findings of the Court in the case of Joe Lis, 17 Jan. 1906; and GWI D56/05, Statement by Gertie Gordon (Katia Abrahams) 15 Sept., 1905. Also, GWI F247/05, List of charges being investigated against Joe Lies/Lees/Liss, 28 Oct. 1905.

30. Silver, in a statement filled with lies, denied having based himself at the station in this way – see Nam., Windhoek, N.N.A., GWI D56/05, Statement by Joseph Lis, 6 Oct. 1905. This practice, however, matches his previous behaviour, as for example in the case of Margaret Finn in Bloemfontein; see above, Chapter 13. See also GWI F56/05, Statements by Fanny and Gussy Bernstein, and Rosa Müller, 2 Sept. 1905.

31. On Ablowitz see Nam, Windhoek, N.N.A., GWI F247/05, Statements by Simon Ablowitz and Rosa Silberberg, 17 Jan. 1906. See also German Federal Republic (G.F.R.), Berlin, Bundesarchiv, R151F, Joseph Lis to His Excellency, Von Lindequist, 18 Jan. 1906.

32. See Nam, Windhoek, N.N.A., GWI F247/05, Statement by Rosa Silberberg, 28 Oct. 1905.

33. See Nam., Windhoek, N.N.A., GWI FD56/05, Statement by Gertie Gordon (Katia Abrahams), 13 Sept. 1905.

34. See above, Chapters 7 and 8.

35. On the search for the 'bluestone' and the discovery of the sublimate – in a medicine bottle – see Nam., Windhoek, N.N.A., GWI F247/05, instruction to search issued by the investigating magistrate, Dr Kornmeyer, and the report back by officer Steikel, both dated 28 Oct. 1905. See also,

R.H. Driesbach, *Handbook of Poisoning: Prevention, Diagnosis and Treatment* (Los Altos 1980), pp. 234–239.

36. See Nam., Windhoek, N.N.A., GWI File F247/05, Statement by Rosa Silberberg, 27 Oct. 1905.

37. See Nam., Windhoek, N.N.A., GWI 585, File D80/02, The case against Henri Sourd and others.

38. See Nam., Windhoek, N.N.A., GWI 56/05, Statements by Rosa Müller, Fanny Stein (Bernstein), Gussy Bernstein, Bertha Linczock, and Gertie Abrahams/Gordon, between 2 and 13 Sept. 1905.

39. On Silver's interactions and conflict with Walter see Nam., Windhoek, N.N.A., GWI F247/05, Joseph Lis to the Hon. Judge, Dr Kornmeyer, 8 Dec. 1905; and GWI D56/05, Joseph Lis to 'Dear Brother' (Jack), 28 Jan. 1906, in which it is alleged that Walter was in partnership with one Otto Meyer and seeking to monopolise the trade in commercial sex in the town. The latter letter is perhaps also the one that is referred to in GWI F247/05, where it is noted that a letter from Silver to his brother has been held back because it contained 'insults' relating to the 'authorities' and certain 'court officials'. See also, G.F.R., Berlin, Bundesarchiv, R151F, FC 5128, Joseph Lis to His Excellency, von Lindequist, 18 Jan. 1906, for further allegations against Walter.

40. See Nam., Windhoek, N.N.A. GWI D56/05, Imperial District Court, Windhoek, 15 Sept. 1905; and Jacques Sander, Authorisation to represent J. Lis, dated 14 Sept. 1905.

41. On Jack Lis/Silver in 1904–5 see United Kingdom (U.K.), London, London Metropolitan Archives, HO 140/234, County Court of London (North Side of the Thames), Calendar of Prisoners tried at the Adjourned General Session, Clerkenwell, 22 Nov. 1904, under the name 'Hyman Goldstein'. On Regina Weinberg during the same period see Nam., Windhoek, N.N.A., GWI F44/06, Statement by Rosa Müller, dated 10 Feb. 1906.

42. Ibid. See also, Republic of South Africa (R.S.A.), Pretoria, South African National Archives (S.A.N.A.), WLD 5/70, File 103/1906; Opposed Application, Ginsberg and Manesewitz vs. Jack Lis; WLD 5/71 File 135/1906, Opposed Application, Ginsberg and Manesewitz vs. Jack Lis, 27 Feb. 1906; and WLD 39/1906, Illiquid Case, Bernard Ginsberg and Herman Manesewitz vs. David Mehr and Jack Lis, Opposed Application, Ginsberg and Manesewitz vs. Jack Lis, 6 March 1906.

43. On earlier Silver–Weinberg interactions see above, Chapter 13. On Sam Gilbert see Nam., Windhoek, N.N.A., GWI F44/06, Statement by Sylvia Melchior, 5 April 1906; also, R.S.A., KwaZulu-Natal Archives Depot, Pietermaritzburg, I.R.D. Vol. 30, File 928/1904, Criminal Investigation Department – deportations. The latter source points to Jack Lis/Silver

having perhaps first met Gilbert while he was based in Port Elizabeth during the South African War of 1899–1902.

44. The Jewish Cemetery in Swakopmund is commented on in A.T. Shrock, 'Oddities in a Jewish Cemetery', *Jewish Affairs*, March 1965, pp. 10–12.

45. In June 1905, the Chief Medical Officer reported that: 'In Swakopmund there are over 1,000 Herero prisoners, men, women and children. Most of those who arrived here are literally skin and bone' – see, Goldblatt, *History of South West*, p. 147. For the wider picture, however, see T. Dedering, '"A Certain Rigorous Treatment of All Parts of the Nation": The Annihilation of the Herero in German South West Africa, 1904', in M. Levene and P. Roberts (eds), *The Massacre in History* (New York 1999), pp. 205–222.

46. Letter to the author from a former customer at the shop in Kielce, David Lewartowski, 27 May 2001.

47. On Davidson see, for example, Nam., Windhoek, N.N.A., GWI File F247/05, Statement by Morris Davidson, 17 Jan. 1906. For Silver's version of his horse and livestock dealings see ibid., Joseph Lis to the Hon. Judge Dr Kornmeyer, 8 Dec. 1905. See also B. Chatwin, *In Patagonia* (London 1982), pp. 45–47.

48. See Nam., Windhoek, N.N.A., GWI F247/05, J. Lis (Joseph Silver) to the Hon. Judge, Dr Kornmeyer, 8 Dec. 1905.

49. See Nam., Windhoek, N.N.A., GWI F247/05, J. Lis (Joseph Silver) to the Hon. Judge Dr Kornmeyer, 8 Dec. 1905. See also, *Windhuker Nachrichten – Südwestbote*, No. 24, 14 Dec. 1905.

50. See Nam, Windhoek, N.N.A., GWI 585 Files D72/05, Statement by Boesel, and File D80/02.

51. Ibid. See also, *Windhuker Nachrichten – Südwestbote*, No. 24, 14 Dec. 1905.

52. See Nam., Windhoek, N.N.A., GWI F 247/05, J. Lis to the Hon. Judge Dr Kornmeyer, 8 Dec. 1905.

Chapter 17: *Windhoek, 1905–1906*

1. This paragraph is constructed from a series of a dozen letters, telegrams and statements over the period 12–30 Oct. 1905 which are to be found in Nam (Nam.), Windhoek, Namibian National Archives (N.N.A.), File GWI F247/05. On use of this code see R. Deacon, *A History of the Russian Secret Service* (London 1971), p. 89.

2. Paragraph constructed from: Nam., Windhoek, N.N.A., GWI F247/05, Senior Lieutenant, Karibib (name indecipherable) to Imperial Justice Official, Windhoek, 6 Dec. 1905; also statements by W. Ewert, R. Silberberg and R. Weinberg, all dated 27 Oct. 1905; and German

Federal Republic (G.F.R.) Berlin, Bundesarchiv, R151, FC 5175, J. Lis (Joseph Silver) to His Excellency, von Lindequist, Governor of German South West Africa, 18 Jan. 1906.

3. Nam., Windhoek, N.N.A., GWI F247/05; see, especially, statement by R. Silberberg, 27 Oct. 1905.

4. Nam., Windhoek, N.N.A., GWI D56/05, George Easton, Inspector-in-Charge, Criminal Investigation Department, Cape Town to German Consul-General, 30 Oct. 1903.

5. See Nam., Windhoek, N.N.A., GWI F247/05, Warrant for the arrest of Joseph Lis, 20 Oct. 1905.

6. All these exchanges are recorded in Nam., Windhoek, N.N.A., GWI F247/05. For Silver's truncated account of these developments, and his manifest frustration at not having succeeded in being released on 'bail', see G.F.R., Berlin, Bundesarchiv, R151, FC 5175, Joseph Lis to His Excellency von Lindequist, Governor of German South West Africa, 18 Jan. 1906.

7. As quoted in I. Goldblatt, *History of South West Africa from the Beginning of the Nineteenth Century* (Cape Town, 1970), p. 146.

8. Nam., Windhoek, N.N.A., GWI F247/05.

9. Nam., Windhoek, N.N.A., GWI F247/05, 'Joseph', Jakalswater to Gertie Gordon, Windhoek, 2 Nov. 1905.

10. All three are to be found in Nam., Windhoek, N.N.A., GWI F247/05.

11. See *Windhuker Nachrichten – Südwestbote*, 14 Dec. 1905.

12. Nam., Windhoek, N.N.A., GWI F247/05, The Director of the Central Prison, Rüstow, to Imperial District Court, Windhoek, 10 June 1907 offers detailed accounts of the time Silver spent in prison prior to that date.

13. Ibid., Rosa Silberberg to 'My Dear Husband', undated, but apparently translated on 6 Dec. 1905.

14. Nam., Windhoek, N.N.A., GWI F247/05, District Administrator to Police Captain, Windhoek, 4 Nov. 1905.

15. See Nam., Windhoek, N.N.A., GWI F247/05.

16. An outline of the case and the reasons supporting the judgment are to be found in Nam., Windhoek, N.N.A., GWI D56/05.

17. Ibid. See also, *Windhuker Nachrichten – Südwestbote*, No. 24, 14 Dec. 1905.

18. Both communications are to be found in Nam., Windhoek, N.N.A., GWI F247/05.

19. This paragraph is based on correspondence to be found in Nam., Windhoek, N.N.A., GWI F 2476/05 and, to a lesser extent, File C202/05.

20. See Nam., Windhoek, N.N.A., GWI F247/05, Imperial District Judge Kornmeyer to the Imperial District Court, Swakopmund, 8 Dec. 1905; and Statement by Max Mande, 14 Dec. 1905. On the alleged intervention of community leaders see GWI F44/06, Statement by Lina Ebener, 28 March 1906.

21. See Nam., Windhoek, N.N.A., File C202/05, Case No. 202/05, Civil Process, Lis & Phellep (Krell) vs. Frau Rosa Silberberg; 13 Dec. 1905 and pertinent papers following.

22. See Nam., Windhoek, N.N.A., GWI F44.06, Statements by Jack and Lifka (Rifka) Lis, 27 Dec. 1905; and order by Boesel to Rabe, 27 Dec. 1905. See also GWI 247/05, Note on file by Boesel, 15 Nov. 1905.

23. See Nam., Windhoek, N.N.A., GWI F44/06, Warrant for the arrest of Jack Lis, 6 Jan. 1906 and the supporting statements on which this charge was based.

24. The crisis within the greater Lis family occasioned in part by the Pasenau house can be traced in Nam., Windhoek, N.N.A., GWI F44/06 – amongst others in a telegram from W. Tuchmann to Jack Lis, 5 Feb. 1906 and a statement by Sylvia Melchior, 5 April 1906. See also, Nam., Windhoek, N.N.A., File C202/05, Case No. 70 of 1906, Tuchmann vs Joe Lis.

25. See notice of property registration in *Deutsch Südwestafrikanische Zeitung*, No. 16, 18 April 1906. More pertinently, however, see Nam., Windhoek, N.N.A., File C202/05,

26. See Nam., Windhoek, N.N.A., GWI F247/05, J. Lis (Joseph Silver) to the Hon. Judge Dr Kornmeyer, 8 Dec. 1905; and J. Lis (Joseph Silver) to Mr J. Sanders, 13 Dec. 1905.

27. See G.F.R., Berlin, Bundesarchiv, R151F, FC 5125, Joseph Lis to His Excellency von Lindequist, 18 Jan. 1906.

28. For this and the next paragraph see Nam., Windhoek, N.N.A., GWI F247/05, Record of Criminal Proceedings against the trader, Joe Lis, Case 19/05 (emphasis added).

29. Nam., Windhoek, N.N.A., GWI D56/07, J. Lis (Joseph Silver) to Your Honour, Windhoek, 18 Jan. 1906.

30. See G.F.R., Berlin, Bundesarchiv, R151F, FC 5125, J. Lis (Joseph Silver) to His Excellency von Lindequist, 18 Jan. 1906.

31. See Nam., Windhoek, N.N.A., GWI F44/06, District Administrator Strahler to Police Captain, Windhoek, 20 Jan. 1906.

32. See G.F.R., Berlin, Bundesarchiv, FC 5171, J. Lis to His Excellency Baron von Lindequist, 24 Jan. 1906. The metaphor Silver presented offers a rare pointer to Jewish roots. The extended tale, which revolves around the perils accompanying hospitality to outsiders in Sodom, is recorded in many places including A. Unterman (ed.), *Dictionary of Jewish Lore and Legend* (London 1991), p. 169.

33. Nam., Windhoek, N.N.A., GWI F247/05, Note by Sergeant Rahmen, 25 Jan. 1906.

34. Nam., Windhoek, N.N.A., GWI D56/05, J. Lis (Joseph Silver) to 'Dear Brother' (Jack), 28 Jan. 1906.

35. See, for example, Nam., Windhoek, N.N.A., GWI F44/06, Letter from

Bertha Lis to Jack Lis, 5 Feb. 1906; or a telegram from W. Tuchmann to Jack Lis, 5 Feb. 1906.

36. Nam., Windhoek, N.N.A., GWI F247/05 Note by Kornmeyer and receipt signed by 'Gertie Abrahams' (Gordon), 26 Jan. and 1 Feb. 1906.

37. See Nam., Windhoek, N.N.A., GWI F44/06, Kornmeyer to the Imperial General Consul, Cape Town, Baron von Humboldt, 6 Feb. 1906; and Warrant for the Arrest of Jack Lis, signed by Kornmeyer, 6 Feb. 1906. On transportation of Joseph Lis see, G.F.R., Berlin, Bundesarchiv, FC 1516, District Judge, Windhoek, 8 Feb. 1906.

38. Paragraph based on Nam., Windhoek, N.N.A., GWI F44/06, J.A. Rössler, Police, to Kornmeyer, 9 Feb. 1906; Proceedings in the Imperial District Court, Kornmeyer and Müller in attendance, 14 Feb. 1906; and S. Lorimer, Office of Inspector in Charge, C.I.D., Cape Town, 'History of Jack Lis @ Silver', 22 Feb. 1906.

39. See Nam, Windhoek, N.N.A., GWI F44/06, Statements by Lina Ebener, Windhoek, dated 28 March 1906; and Sylvia Melchior, Windhoek, 5 April 1906. Both respondents previously of Swakopmund.

40. Ibid.

41. See Nam., Windhoek, N.N.A., GWI F247/05, Dr Bonard to Kornmeyer, the Imperial District Court, Windhoek, 26 March 1906.

42. Ibid.

43. The launching of the *Bürgermeister* is reported on in *Hamburger Nachrichten*, No. 50, 28 Feb. 1902.

44. See G.F.R., Berlin, Bundesarchiv, R901, No. 27831, Instructions for the Transportation of Prisoners, 19 Aug. 1903.

45. See Nam., Windhoek, N.N.A., GWI F44/06, Gustav Stein, London, to the 'Head Office' of the German Colonial Society, Berlin, undated but received 8 March 1906.

46. See various items of correspondence in Nam., Windhoek, N.N.A., GWI F247/05.

47. See Nam., Windhoek, N.N.A., GWI F44/06, Bohme, Lüderitz, to Kornmeyer, Windhoek, 30 March 1906; and Statement by Lina Ebener, 28 March 1906.

48. Nam., Windhoek, N.N.A., GWI F44/06, *Uebersetzung*, 11 May 1906.

49. See Nam., Windhoek, N.N.A., C202/05, Case 70 of 1906, Statement by Baker, legal representative of Jack Lis, 16 May 1906.

50. See Republic of South Africa (R.S.A.), Pretoria, South African National Archives (S.A.N.A.) WLD 39/1906, Illiquid Case, Bernard Guinsberg and Herman Manesewitz (Plaintiffs) vs. David Mehr and Jack Lis (Defendants), 19 March 1906. This records a judgment for the plaintiffs, the ejection from the premises of Mehr, and an award of damages and costs of £105 against Jack Lis.

51. Nam, Windhoek, N.N.A., GWI F44/06, J. Lis to the Imperial District Court, Windhoek, 14 April 1906.

52. Most of this conflict can be traced in Nam., Windhoek, N.N.A., F11/06, C202/05, Case No. 202/05 and Case No. F80/06

53. See Nam., Windhoek, N.N.A., Civil Case No. 70 of 1906, W. Tuchmann vs. Jack Lis, 17 May 1906.

54. Nam., Windhoek, N.N.A., GWI F44/06, Bäker, Swakopmund, to the Imperial District Court, Windhoek, 14 May 1906.

55. Nam., Windhoek, N.N.A., GWI F44/06, Note by Imperial District Justice, Kornmeyer, 26 May 1906.

56. Nam., Windhoek, N.N.A., GWI F2407/05, Imperial District Administration, Swakopmund, to Imperial District Administrator, Boesel, 14 June 1906.

57. R.S.A., Pietermaritzburg, KwaZulu-Natal Archives Depot, IRD Vol. 52, IRD 658/1906.

Chapter 18: Neumünster and Paris, 1908–1909

1. On the opening of the prison see T. Grunau, '50 Jahre Strafvollzug in Neumünster', Schleswig-Holsteinischse Anzeigen für des Jahr 1955, p. 346.

2. See Namibia (Nam.), Windhoek, Namibian National Archives (N.N.A.), Chief Treasurer, Windhoek to the Trader, Joseph Lis, Neumünster Central Prison, 13 Sept. 1907.

3. On syphilis and hair loss see, for example, A. Friedli, P. Chavaz and M. Harms, 'Alopecia Syphilitica: Report on two Cases in Geneva', Dermatology, Vol. 202, No. 4, 2001, p. 376.

4. See Nam., Windhoek, N.N.A., F. 2407/05, Rüstow, Central Prison Neumünster, to Imperial District Court, Windhoek, 22 Sept. 1909.

5. See F. Caron, An Economic History of Modern France (London 1979), pp. 135–136; J.H. Clapham, The Economic Development of France and Germany, 1815–1914 (Cambridge 1966), pp. 168–169; and G. Wright, 'Economy: Structure and Trends, 1870–1914' in France in Modern Times: 1760 to the Present (London 1962), pp. 343–365.

6. See D. Weinberg, "Heureux comme Dieu en France": 'East European Jewish Immigrants in Paris, 1881–1914', in J. Frankel (ed.) Studies in Contemporary Jewry (Bloomington 1984), pp. 26–41 and in the same source P. Hyman, 'From Dreyfus to Vichy: The Remaking of French Jewry, 1906–1939,' pp. 62–72. A fascinating and very different dimension to the wider context of Jewish vulnerability is to be found in D. Biale, Power and Powerlessness in Jewish History (New York 1987), pp. 138–139.

7. On the emptying of the French countryside during the belle époque see

Clapham, *Economic Development of France and Germany*, pp. 168–169; and on the decline of formal employment in the clothing and textile industries, Caron, *Economic History of Modern France*, pp. 145–146.

8. See Weinberg, 'East European Jewish Immigrants in Paris', p. 40.

9. See E.J. Bristow, *Prostitution and Prejudice: The Jewish Fight against White Slavery, 1870–1939* (Oxford 1982), p. 265; Weinberg, 'East European Jewish Immigrants in Paris', pp. 30–31; and Hyman, 'The Remaking of French Jewry', pp. 66–67.

10. See M.T. Connelly, *The Response to Prostitution in the Progressive Era* (Chapel Hill 1980), p. 49.

11. See United States of America (U.S.A.), Washington, DC, National Archives (N.A.), Record Group 85, V 5284 1–G, Marcus Braun, 'Report on European "White Slave" Traffick in Relation to American Immigration Laws', 2 Oct. 1909.

12. On Apaches in New York City see G.K. Turner's notorious muck-raking article, 'The Daughters of the Poor', *McClure's Magazine*, No. 34, 1909, p. 60; I.L. Allen, *The City in Slang: New York Life and Popular Speech* (Oxford 1993), p. 212; and, in fictionalised form but said to be based on contemporary court cases and information elicited from the police, A. H. Lewis, *The Apaches of New York* (New York 1912). For Buenos Aires, see the incomparable 'Los Apacaes', *Fray Mocho*, No. 3, 17 May 1912. At about the same time, 'Apaches' with a specific brief to 'frighten the children' started appearing in Cape Town's 'coloured' community's annual New Year minstrel parade, the Coon Carnival; see Denis-Constant Martin, 'Cape Town's Coon Carnival: A Site for the Confrontation of Opposed Coloured Identities', unpublished paper presented to the Interdisciplinary Seminar, University of Pretoria, 12 Oct. 2000, p. 5. In Paris, P. Drachline and C. Petit-Castelli, *Casque d'or et les apaches* (Renaudot 1990).

13. See B. Macintyre's delightful *The Napoleon of Crime: The Life and Times of Adam Worth, Master Thief* (New York 1997), especially pp. 47–57.

14. Easily the most notorious such fence was the formidable Frederika 'Marm' Mandelbaum and her family. See ibid., pp. 29–36 and 205–206. See also Luc Sante, *Low Life: Lures and Snares of Old New York* (New York 1991), pp. 210–211.

15. See Anonymous, *Calumniator Morally Masked, or The Scandal of Johannesburg* (n.d. but *c.* 1904), p. 5; housed in the Strange Collection, Johannesburg Public Library, Republic of South Africa.

16. As it did for another white slaver trafficker from Kielce, Moses Sztunke. Sztunke left Poland illegally in 1907 and went to Paris, where he was resident for some months before making his way to New York, Buenos Aires and Bahia Blanca between 1910 and 1914. See Poland, Voievudskie

Arkhwum Panstovove v Kieltsakh, Wyolziat Sledezy, Kielecki, sygn.6, Senor M. Schtuncke, Cale Mitre 522, Bahia Blanca, 5 May 1910; and other police correspondence, Kielce-Kraków. Other white slavers from Kielce active on the continent during this period include the tailor Chaim Benamowitz: see *Bericht über die Deutsche National-konferenz zu internationaler Bekämpfung des Madchenhandles*, Herausgegeben von Deutschen Nationalkomittee, 1908, p. 103.

17. See 'Undesirable Alien', *Hampshire Telegraph*, 24 Aug. 1907. The marriage to Neinstein is recorded in Belgium (Belg.), Brussels, Algemeen Rijksarchief, (A.R.), Police des Etrangers, File 8892 322, Leibus Brjiski, Police Commissioner, Antwerp, 28 May 1913.

18. On Leibus Cohen and Sarah Haberberg see various documents in Belg., Brussels, A.R., Police des Etrangers, File 934 796, 1913, Sarah Haberberg.

19. See Belg., Brussels, A.R., Brussels, Police des Etrangers, File 930 733, Joseph Silver, Public Prosecutor, Liège, to Minister of Justice, Brussels, 20 Dec. 1910. See also (U.S.A.), Washington, DC, N.A., Department of State, C.8.6, No. 7, US Legation, Belgium, Notes to the Belgian Government, 15 Jan. 1910–14 Dec. 1911, (Deportation of Leibus Brjiski), evidence presented to J.A. Bonjean, Examining Magistrate, Liège, 20 March 1910.

20. See, also, Belg., Brussels, A.R., Brjiski 8892–322, Prosecutor, Liège to the Ministry of Justice, Brussels, 21 Dec. 1910; United Kingdom (U.K.), London, National Archives, N.A., Kew, Mepo 6/23, Provincial Cases, entry for Moritz Booter alias Morris Klemburg, 31 May 1910 – store breaking, Liverpool; and 'Juzgados de Instructcion – Asociacion Ilicita', 'Mauricio @Moses Klein', *Gaceto del Foro*, (Buenos Aires), 1 Nov. 1930.

21. See U.K., London, N.A., Kew, BT 271554, Ships' Manifest for *Arraguaya* bound for Buenos Aires, 14 June 1907; and Argentina (Arg.), Buenos Aires, Centro de Estudios Migratorios Latinoamericanos (C.E.M.L.A) (Latin American Centre for Migration Studies), Immigration Records, *Arraguaya*, 6 July 1907.

22. See J.R. Scobie, *Argentina: A City and a Nation* (London 1978); D.J. Guy, *Sex and Danger in Buenos Aires: Prostitution, Family and Nation in Argentina* (London 1991), p. 106. See also V.A. Mirelman, 'The Jews in Argentina, 1890–1930: Assimilation and Particularism', unpublished D.Phil., University of Columbia, 1973, pp. 1–57.

23. For all its sensationalist moralising, the magnificently presented, illustrated and photographed Juan José Soiza Reilly's 'Los Apacaes', *Fray Mocho*, Issue 3, 17 May 1912 remains central – not least because it also contains a portrait of 'Jack Liss' and others who worked with him in 1908.

24. For Buenos Aires in comparative perspective see C. van Onselen, 'Jewish Marginality in the Atlantic World: Organised Crime in the Era of the Great Migrations, 1880–1914', *South African Historical Journal*, No. 43,

Nov. 2000, pp. 96–137. On the Zwi Migdal see, for example, Bristow, *Prostitution and Prejudice*. For some ward-specific examples of processes and places alluded to in this para. see various items in the following editions of the Buenos Aires *Tribuna*: 12 April 1909, 12 and 13 May 1909, 30 Sept. 1909, 12 Sept. 1910, 12 Nov. 1910, 15 Aug. and 17 Oct. 1911, 1 and 18 May 1912.

25. See Reilly, 'Los Apacaes'.

26. Ibid. See also Argentina (Arg.), Buenos Aires, Archives of the Argentine Federal Police (A.A.F.P.), Police Notebook Precinct (PNP) 3, No. 189, 28 Feb.–7 May 1908, p. 285. Such 'Jewish'–'Italian' co-operation was, of course, later seen as a distinctive feature of the organisation of the Mafia in the United States: see, for example, 'The Italian Alliance', in D. Eisenberg, U. Dan and E. Landau, *Meyer Lansky: Mogul of the Mob* (London 1979), pp. 51–57.

27. Arg., Buenos Aires, A.A.F.P., PNP 4, No. 94, 1 May–4 June 1908, p. 36; and 'Police News', *Tribuna*, 4 May 1908.

28. See Arg., Buenos Aires, A.A.F.P., PNP 3, No. 188, 24 Feb. –5 April 1908, entries on p. 124 and, more especially, p. 361; also, in retrospect, a report in *La Prensa*, 3 March 1912.

29. On the Cellini robbery and the events that followed, see the precinct note-book, in Arg., Buenos Aires, A.A.F.P., PNP 4, No. 94, 1 May–4 June 1908, p. 36; and, on 'Jenny de Liss's' and the maidservant Elena Kaisman's internment in the women's section of a prison run by Catholic nuns, Arg., Buenos Aires, Penitentiary Archive, Entry Register, Unit 3, Letter to the Mother Superior, 8 July 1908 from person unknown, signature illegible. Also, 'Police News' in *Tribuna* of 4 May and 10 June, 1908; and, for a retrospect of unknown accuracy, *La Prensa*, 3 March 1912.

30. Jack Lis was still in prison until at least the second week of the month; see 'Police News', *Tribuna*, 10 June 1908. The subsequent fate of the 'Apaches' involved in the notorious Cellini robbery and its long-running court sequel can be deduced from *La Prensa*, 3 March 1912. Unfortunately, the file containing the original court proceedings against Jack Lis and others has been destroyed, or lost, but an index card, in Arg., Buenos Aires, Archives of the Palace of Justice, records it as File No. 499 of 1908.

31. On Mendel Cohen's links to diamond workers in Antwerp see U.S.A., Washington, DC, N.A., Department of State, C.8.6, No. 7, U.S. Legation, Belgium, Notes to the Belgian Government, 15 Jan. 1910–14 Dec. 1911 (Deportation of Leibus Brjiski), evidence presented to J.A. Bonjean, Examining Magistrate, Liège, 20 March 1910.

32. On the possibility of uncle–niece marriage in *shtetl* society see R. Landes and M. Zborowski, 'Hypotheses concerning the East European Jewish

Family', in *Psychiatry*, William Alanson White Psychiatric Foundation, Vol. 4, No. 13, Nov. 1950, p. 461.

33. See Weinberg, 'East European Jewish Immigrants in Paris', p. 48.

34. See France (Fr.), Paris, Archives Départementale de Paris (A.D.P), Registres d'information du parquet, Series D2U7, Register No. 23, entry date 9 Jan. 1909.

35. See C. Beavan, *Fingerprints: The Origins of Crime Detection and the Murder Case that Launched Forensic Science* (New York 2001), pp. 74–82.

36. Fr., Paris, Archives General de la Police Judiciare (A.G.P.D.), No. 378.967, Silver Berthe, 2 Feb. 1909.

37. See Fr., Paris, A.D.P., Registres d' Information du Parquet, Series D2U7, Register No. 27, entry dated 4 June 1909.

38. See Belg., Brussels, A.R., Police des Etrangers, File 934 796, Sarah Haberberg.

39. See items in *Le Petit Parisien* and *Le Petit Journal*, 4 April 1909.

40. On Segalowicz, see a note by Le Procureur Général dated 21 April 1910, on Dossier No. 800 relating to the possible extradition of Cohen L. and Silver J. in Fr., Paris, Archives Nationales (A.N.), B.B. 18/14078.

41. See Belg. Brussels, A.R., Police des Etrangers, File 930 733, Silver 930 733, Chief Commissioner of Police, Brussels to Director General, Public Security, 16 June 1910.

42. See 'The Jewellery Shop Burglars', *Le Petit Parisien*, 9 April 1909.

43. Fr., Paris, A.D.P., Registres d'Information du Parquet, Series D2U7, Register No. 27, entry dated 8 April 1909.

44. See M. Fize, *Une Prison dans la Ville: Histoire de la prison modéle de La Santé per époque 1867–1914* (Paris 1983).

45. See Fr., Paris, A.D.P, Registres d' Information du Parquet, Series D2U7, Register No. 27, Case No. 42706/5434, 27 May 1909.

46. See Fr., Paris, A.D.P, Registres d' Information du Parquet, Series D2U7, Register No. 27, entry date, Appeal 796, No. 4678 of 1909, 15 Nov. 1909.

Chapter 19: Antwerp, Brussels, Liège and Aachen, 1909–1910

1. P.J. Stead, *Pioneers in Policing* (London 1977), pp. 280–296.

2. See United States of America (U.S.A.), Washington, DC, National Archives (N.A.), Record Group 84, Department of State, Diplomatic Post Records, Belgium Vol. 18, Notes from Belgium Government, 19 Jan. 1901–16 Oct. 1911, Evidence taken before J.A. Bonjean, Examining Magistrate, District of Liège and Registrar Alfred Muschart, 20 March 1910, Extradition of Leibus Brjiski.

3. For a generalised account of the Antwerp underworld at the time see

U.S.A., Washington, DC, N.A., Record Group No. 85, Department of Commerce and Labor, 1–G, File V 52484, Braun European Report, 2 Oct. 1909.

4. See Belgium (Belg.), Brussels, Algemeen Rijksarchief (A.R.), Brussels, Police des Etrangers, File 930 733 – Joseph Silver, Aix-la-Chapelle, Police Headquarters, 2nd Division, Publication No. 1644, 11 May 1910.

5. U.S.A., Washington, DC, N.A., Record Group 85, Extradition of Leibus Brjiski, 1910, Evidence of A. Deprelle, policeman, before J.A. Bonjean and A. Muschart, Court House, Liège, on 17 Jan. and 20 March 1910.

6. Ibid.

7. U.S.A., Washington DC, N.A., Record Group 85, Extradition of Leibus Brjiski, 1910, J.A. Bonjean, Matter No. 20 – Report accompanying the warrant, 13 May. 1910. See also, Belg., Brussels, A.R., Brussels, Police des Etrangers, File 8892 322 – Leibus Brjiski.

8. On Stoermak Mottel see U.S.A., Washington, DC, N.A, Record Group 85, Extradition of Leibus Brjiski, 1910, Evidence of A. Deprelle, policeman, before J.A. Bonjean, Liège, 20 March 1910. On the Herlichs see, for example, Le Patriote (Brussels), 5 April 1910.

9. U.S.A., Washington, DC, N.A., Record Group 85, Extradition of Leibus Brjiski, 1910, Evidence of A. Deprelle before J.A. Bonjean, Liège, 20 and 21 March 1910.

10. On the original informing from London see U.S.A., Washington, DC, N.A., Record Group 85, Extradition of Leibus Brjiski, 1910, J.A. Bonjean to Director-General, Special Investigation Bureau, Department of Justice, Brussels, 19 Jan. 1910.

11. See Belg., Brussels, A.R., File 8892 322 – Leibus Brjiski; unsigned letter to Chief of Police, Munich, 23 Jan. 1911.

12. See, for example, P. Marnham, The Man Who Wasn't Maigret: A Portrait of Georges Simenon (London 1992), pp. 34–35. Interestingly enough, Georges Simenon's mother also took in a Jewish student from Odessa, 'Paula Feinstein', as a boarder in the family home at about this time to help make ends meet.

13. See U.S.A., Washington, DC, N.A., Record Group 85, Extradition of Leibus Brjiski, 1910, Evidence of Selma Kunze, Maurice Beckermann and Joseph Schyns before Examining Magistrate, J.A. Bonjean, in Liège on 18 March 1910.

14. Ibid.

15. See U.S.A., Washington, DC, N.A., Record Group 85, Extradition of Leibus Brjiski, 1910, Evidence of François Marck before Examining Magistrate, J.A. Bonjean, 7 Jan. 1910.

16. Ibid., Evidence of E. Marck before Examining Magistrate, J.A. Bonjean, 7 Jan. 1910; and A. Deprelle, policeman, 20 March 1910.

17. See A. Hochschild, *King Leopold's Ghost* (Oxford 1999). On Leopold's funeral see N. Ascherson, *The King Incorporated: Leopold II in the Age of Trusts* (New York 1964), p. 298.

18. See U.S.A., Washington, DC, N.A., Record Group 85, Extradition of Leibus Brjiski, 1910, evidence of Philomene Eussen, Valerie Bayi and Jeanne Patout before Examining Magistrate, J.A. Bonjean, on 7, 12 and 20 Jan. 1910.

19. Ibid. See especially J.A. Bonjean to the Minister of Foreign Affairs, Count Pierre van der Straten, 13 May 1910.

20. See item 31, 'A List of the Valuables stolen to the prejudice of Messrs. Marck Bros, Liège, during the night of 6–7 January, 1910, with quoted values as at 7 Jan., 1910', in U.S.A., Washington, DC, N.A., Record Group 85, Extradition of Leibus Brjiski, 1910.

21. See F.P. Wensley, *Forty Years of Scotland Yard: The Record of a Lifetime's Service in the Criminal Investigation Department* (New York 1933), pp. 111–113. It is not clear whether the establishment that Brjiski and his accomplices took refuge in, the Odessa, was the bar-restaurant with the same name earlier presided over by Joseph Weinstein at the height of Bessarabian-Odessian gang warfare. See F. Linnane, *London's Underworld: Three Centuries of Vice and Crime* (London 2003), pp. 105–107. On crime and the commercialised sex trade in Odessa on the Black Sea, in 1909, see also U.S.A., Washington, DC, N.A., Braun Report 1909, pp. 45–46.

22. On Fosel Codet and the Odessa Saloon see U.S.A., Washington, DC, N.A., Record Group 85, Extradition of Leibus Brjiski, 1910, Evidence of A. Deprelle, policeman, before J.A. Bonjean, 6 Feb. 1910.

23. Ibid.; Item 20, 'Report accompanying the Warrant', J.A Bonjean, 13 May 1910. Also, evidence of A. Deprelle, policeman, before J.A. Bonjean, 20 March 1910. Also, *Etoile Belge*, 9 April 1910.

24. U.S.A., Washington, DC, N.A., Record Group 85, Extradition of Leibus Brjiski, 1910, Translation, 'Dear Nephew' to 'My Dear Uncle, Wolf Sametband', 27 Jan. 1910.

25. See, Marnham, *The Man Who Wasn't Maigret*, pp. 10–70.

26. See especially, Item 20, 'Inventory of Papers – A True Copy of the Evidence upon which the Warrant was Issued', in U.S.A., Washington DC, N.A., Record Group 85, Extradition of Leibus Brjiski, 1910.

27. See Belg., Brussels, A.R., File 930 733 – Joseph Silver, Chief Commissioner of Police to Director-General, Public Security, Brussels, 19 June 1910.

28. See Linnane, *London's Underworld*, p. 103.

29. In the absence of other evidence this account of the actual burglary is taken from 'Le Vol de la rue Neuve', *Etoile Belge*, 9 April 1904.

30. Ibid. On the value of the jewellery taken see, for example, Belg., Brussels,

A.R., Brussels, Police des Etrangers, File 934 796 – Sarah Haberberg, the Assistant Commissioner of Police, New Scotland Yard, to the Director of Public Security, Brussels, 22 Feb. 1911.

31. See 'Une Bijouterie dévalisée à Bruxelles', *Le Patriote*, 5 April 1910.

32. See especially *Le Patriote*, 5 April 1910 but also 'Trois Individus sont arrêtés en Allemagne', *La Dernière Heure*, 5 April 1910.

33. See N. Davies and R. Moorhouse, *Microcosm: Portrait of a Central European City* (London 2002), pp. 306–325.

34. Ibid.

35. *La Dernière Heure*, 5 April 1910; *Le Patriote*, 5 April 1910; and *Etoile Belge*, 9 April 1910.

36. On the British refusal to extradite Mendel Cohen and Moritz Kleinberg see, for example, Belg., Brussels, A.R., File 930–733, Joseph Silver, Public Prosecutor, Liège, to the Minister of Justice, Brussels, 20 Dec. 1910.

37. See 'Le Vol de la rue Neuve' and, more especially, 'Cohen et C', in *Etoile Belge*, of 9 and 17 April 1910.

38. See Belg., Brussels, A.R., File 934–796, Sarah Haberberg, Le Procureur du Roi to Le Directeur Général de la Sûreté Publique, Brussels, 23 March 1911; and File 8892–322, Leibus Brjiski, Commissioner of Police, Brussels, to Assistant Commissioner of Police, Convict Supervision Office, New Scotland Yard, London, 15 May 1911.

39. See U.S.A., Washington, DC, N.A., Record Group 85, Extradition of Leibus Brjiski, 1910, Item No. 20, 'Report Accompanying the Warrant', J.A. Bonjean, Liège, 13 May 1910.

40. Ibid. Also Belg., Brussels, A.R., File 8892–322, Leibus Brjiski, Bulletin, Parquet de la Cour D'Appel de Liège, 24 July 1911.

41. See Belg., Brussels, A.R., File 934–796, Sarah Haberberg, Le Procureur du Roi to Le Directeur Général de la Sûreté, Brussels, 5 Oct. 1910; and Tribunal de Bruxelles, 18 July 1913.

42. The original letter from New Scotland Yard to the police in Aachen/Aix la Chapelle was not copied to the Sûreté in Brussels and is, therefore, not to be found in the file on Silver in the records of the Police des Etrangèrs in Belgium; File 930–733. The police in Aachen were, however, also in contact with the *gendarmerie* in France who were taking an increasing – if belated – interest in Silver. The surviving French sources thus contain more information about the original tip-off from London than do those in Belgium or Germany. See especially, France, Paris, Archives Nationales, BB 18/14078, Dossier No. 800, Extradition, Ministère des Affaires Etrangères à Monsieur le Ministre de la Justice, Direction des Affaires Criminelles et des Grâces, 28 June 1910.

43. On Yiddish as a 'secret language' and the history of its reception in Germany see S.L. Gilman, *Jewish Self-Hatred: Anti-Semitism and the*

Hidden Language of the Jews (London 1986) and, more especially, ibid., 'The Language of Thieves', pp. 68–86. On the very mixed reception that East European Jews received in western Europe see J. Wertheimer, *Unwelcome Strangers: East European Jews in Imperial Germany* (Oxford 1987), pp. 143–161.

44. See L. Abrams, 'Prostitutes in Imperial Germany, 1870–1918: Working Girls or Social Outcasts', in R.J. Evans (ed.), *The German Underworld: Deviants and Outcasts* (London 1988), pp. 190–196.

45. Belg., Brussels, A.R., Police des Etrangers, File 930–733, Joseph Silver, Ausschrebung, Aachen, 11 May 1910. For the immediate context of regular urban policing in the Ruhr at the time see E. G. Spencer, 'State Powers and Local Interests in Prussian Cities: Police in the Düsseldorf District, 1848–1914', *Central European History*, No. 3, 1986, pp. 293–313.

46. Belg., Brussels, A.R., Police des Etrangers, File 930–733, Joseph Silver, Ausschrebung, Aachen, 11 May 1910.

47. Belg., Brussels, A.R., Police des Etrangers, File 930–733, Joseph Silver, Chief Commissioner of Police, 2nd Division to Director-General for Public Security, 17 May 1910. See also items in *Echo der Gegenwart*, 17 and 18 May 1910.

48. See Belg., Brussels, A.R., Police des Etrangers, File 930–733, Joseph Silver.

Chapter 20: Buenos Aires, 1910

1. See D. Rock, *Politics in Argentina, 1890–1930: The Rise and Fall of Radicalism* (Cambridge 1975), pp. 2–10; and, more especially, his *Argentina, 1516–1987: From Spanish Colonization to Alfonsin* (Berkeley 1987), pp. 162–172. Also, J.R. Scobie, *Argentina: A City and a Nation* (Oxford 1971), pp. 112–135.

2. See D.C.M. Platt, 'Canada and Argentina: The First Preference of the British Investor, 1904–14', *Journal of Commonwealth and Imperial History*, Vol. 13, No. 3, May 1985, pp. 77–92.

3. On immigration flows, Jewish immigration and the influx of East European gangsters see, amongst others, the following: H. Avni, *Argentina & the Jews: A History of Jewish Immigration* (London 1991), pp. 25, 37 and 45–92, E.J. Bristow, *Prostitution and Prejudice: The Jewish Fight against White Slavery, 1870–1939* (Oxford 1982), pp. 111–145, D.S. Castro, *The Development and Politics of Argentine Immigration Policy, 1852–1914* (San Francisco 1991), pp. 221–255, D.J. Guy, *Sex & Danger in Buenos Aires: Prostitution, Family and Nation in Argentina* (London 1991), pp. 106 and 120, and V.A. Mirelman, 'The Jews in Argentina, 1890–1930: Assimilation and Particularism', Ph.D. dissertation, University of Columbia, 1973, pp. 15–16.

4. See Rock, *Argentina, 1516–1987*, pp. 172–176 and Scobie, *A City and a Nation*, pp. 32–35.

5. See Avni, *Argentina & The Jews*, pp. 47–48 and 82–91; Castro, *Immigration Policy*, pp. 242–253; and Rock, *Politics in Argentina*, pp. 68–91.

6. Avni, *Argentina & the Jews*, pp. 47–51. For the most insightful and suggestive treatment of the development of Jewish anarchism in Buenos Aires, however, see J. C. Moya, 'The Positive Side of Stereotypes: Jewish Anarchists in Early-twentieth-century Buenos Aires', *Jewish History*, Vol. 18, 2004, pp. 19–48.

7. See Castro, *Immigration Policy*, pp. 252–253.

8. See Avni, *Argentina & the Jews*, pp. 49–50; Castro, *Immigration Policy*, pp. 245–246; and most pertinently, Moya, 'Jewish Anarchists in Buenos Aires', pp. 31–34.

9. On the importance of the events of 1909–10 see Avni, *Argentina & the Jews*, p. 50; Rock, *Argentina, 1516–1987*, pp. 186–187; and especially, Moya, 'Jewish Anarchists in Buenos Aires', p. 37.

10. See Castro, *Immigration Policy*, pp. 248–250 and Rock, *Politics in Argentina*, pp. 86–92.

11. See Guy, *Sex & Danger*, pp. 72–73.

12. In the same paradoxical way Jews were seen, simultaneously, as 'compulsive capitalists and anti-capitalist radicals': Moya, 'Jewish Anarchists in Buenos Aires', p. 19.

13. See Bristow, *Prostitution and Prejudice*, pp. 114–124 and, even more pertinently, V.A. Mirelman, 'The Jewish Community versus Crime: The Case of White Slavery in Buenos Aires', *Jewish Social Studies*, Vol. 46, 1984, pp. 152–159. On the police, 'who were overwhelmingly native-born and who shared the ethnic prejudices of their fellow citizens', see J.K. Blackwelder and L.L. Johnson, 'Changing Criminal Patterns in Buenos Aires, 1890 to 1914', *Journal of Latin American Studies*, Vol. 14, Part 2, 1982 p. 367.

14. See especially, Moya, 'Jewish Anarchists in Buenos Aires', p. 22.

15. See, for example, R. Deacon, *A History of the Russian Secret Service* (London 1972), p. 94.

16. For an example of early infiltration and later expulsion of pimps and white slavers from reform-minded organisations see, for example, 'The Campaign against the White Slave Trade', *Fray Mocho* (Buenos Aires), No. 55, 16 May 1913. Also, Guy, *Sex & Danger*, pp. 27–28.

17. On the expulsion from Rio see G. Freyre, *Order and Progress: Brazil from Monarchy to Republic* (New York 1970), pp. 57–62; and on their arrival in Buenos Aires, Mirleman, 'The Jewish Community versus Crime', p. 149. See also Avni, *Argentina & the Jews*, pp. 25 and 37.

18. On pimps and clubs in pre-1890 Buenos Aires, see Guy, *Sex & Danger*, pp. 17 and 102.

19. See Mirelman, 'The Jews in Argentina', pp. 356–358; and 'The Jewish Community versus Crime', p. 153.

20. See Mirelman, 'The Jews in Argentina', pp. 315–318 and, more generally, N. Sandrow, *Vagabond Stars: A World History of Yiddish Theatre* (Syracuse 1977), pp. 87–89.

21. Guy, *Sex & Danger*, p. 46.

22. See, for example, the reported expulsion of the pimps from the racetrack in *Tribuna*, 17 Oct. 1911.

23. On these campaigns see Guy, *Sex & Danger*, p. 19 and, more especially, Mirelman's excellent, 'The Jewish Community versus Crime', p. 156. See also *Tribuna*, 12 April 1909.

24. The case was reported on in the 'Police News' section of *Tribuna*, 12 and 13 May 1909.

25. On the foundation of the Warsaw Society see G. Bra, *La Organización Negra: La Increíble Historia de la Zwi Migdal* (Buenos Aires 1999), pp. 25 and 30–31; and 'La Mutual de los Rufianes', *Todo es Historio*, No. 121, 1999 pp. 75–91. On the collaborative purchase of land see Guy, *Sex & Danger*, p. 22.

26. For a list of the names detained see Argentina (Arg.), Buenos Aires, Archives of the Argentine Federal Police (A.A.F.P.), Police Notebook, Precinct 3 (PNP 3), No. 213, 7 Nov.–19 Dec. 1909), p. 80. This list, even when compared with that which appeared in *Gaceta del Foro* on 1 Nov. 1930 providing names of those alleged to be Zwi Migdal members, shows some overlap despite the passage of more than two decades. The police were also having difficulty distinguishing between anarchists and pimps – see especially Moya, 'Jewish Anarchists in Buenos Aires', pp. 22 and 37.

27. On the organisation of the Warsaw society see Bra, *La Organización Negra*; M.A. Kaplan, *The Jewish Feminist Movement in Germany: The Campaigns of the Jüdischer Frauenbund, 1904–1938* (London 1979), p. 109; and A. Londres, *The Road to Buenos Ayres* (New York 1918). On the lawyers see, for example, various reports carried during the campaign waged by *El Censor* during the period 12 Aug.–May 1906 and in *Tribuna* of 30 July, 19 Aug. and 4 Sept. 1908.

28. On Finn see Arg., Buenos Aires, A.A.F.P., PNP 3, No. 213, 7 Nov.–19 Dec. 1909; and on Hendler, *El Censor*, 25 Oct. 1905.

29. Information about Steiman's early career supplied by Buenos Aires police to colleagues in Valparaíso, Chile, along with a photo of him and two female associates, is to be found in 'La trata de Blancas en Chile', *Revista de la Policia*, Year VII, Issue 92, Sept. 1913, pp. 38–44. See also, Arg., Buenos Aires, Argentine National Archives (A.N.A.), Ministry of Foreign

Affairs, Chile 1912, Box 1297, various documents from Vice-Consul, Santiago, Salvador Nicosia Santiago to the Under-Secretary, Ministry of Foreign Affairs, between 14 June and 13 July 1912. See also, Bra, *La Organización Negra*, pp. 30–31.

30. For information on Steiman and the notoriety of No. 1987 Lavalle spread over three decades see items in the following issues of *El Censor*, 12 Aug., 9 Sept. and 25 Oct. 1905. Also *El Censor* of 18 Dec. 1913 and *La Prensa*, 24 May 1930. On naturalisation of anarchists and pimps see Moya, 'Jewish Anarchists in Buenos Aires', p. 23.

31. On Steiman's status as a police spy see, Arg., Buenos Aires, A.N.A., Ministry of Foreign Affairs, Chile 1912, Box 1297, various documents from Vice-Consul, Santiago, Salvador Nicosia Santiago to the Under-Secretary, Ministry of Foreign Affairs, between 14 June and 13 July 1912. On the anarchist assassin of Falcón. Arg., Buenos Aires, A.N.A., A.G.N. Tribunal, Criminal R–5, 'Radovizky, Simón por homicidio en las personas de Falcón Ramón', 1909. On the Russian/anarchist library see Moya, 'Jewish Anarchists in Buenos Aires', p. 31.

32. For the reported view of Chief of the Buenos Aires Criminal Investigation Division, Rossi, on Silver and Steiman see an interview with the Chief of Police, Santiago, as reported in *El Mercurio* (Santiago), 19 Dec. 1912.

33. For a graphic description of the journey between Santiago and Buenos Aires, and a sense of the excitement at the time, see A. Gallardo, 'A través de los Andes: Desde el Pacifico al Atlántico en 36 horas', *Revista del Ferrocarril Central Argentino*, 1912, pp. 684–686.

Chapter 21: Santiago–Valparaiso, 1910–1912

1. This sketch of the development of the Chilean economy is almost wholly derived from S. Collier and W.F. Sater, *A History of Chile, 1808–1994* (Cambridge 1996), pp. 156–170.

2. Ibid., pp. 170–178 and, on purportedly widespread anti-Semitism, pp. 172–173.

3. Collier and Sater, *A History of Chile*, pp. 173–178.

4. Ibid, pp. 195–196.

5. Collier and Sater, *A History of Chile*, p. 184.

6. See Chile, Santiago, National Archives (N.A.), Records of the Third Criminal Court of Santiago 1912, (CC 3/San./1912), presided over by Juan Bianchi Tupper. These currently unsorted and uncatalogued records, including a file on proceedings initiated in this court by Joseph Silver in Dec. 1912, are held in the basement of the National Archives. I am deeply indebted to Carlos Cousino and Jaime Rosenblitt for their generous assistance in tracing and making available to me copies of the proceedings.

7. On the presence of Rosa Kantor at 284 Merced Street, the Hotel Venecia, as well as that of another of the women who hailed from France, Rosa Liberona Marin, see Chile, Santiago, N.A., CC3/San./1912, Statements made before Judge J. Bianchi Tupper and E.A. Gundian, 18 Dec. 1912. For the fuller story, recounted at a moment of national panic about such matters see, for example, 'A Victim Speaks', *La Unión*, 24 Oct. 1913; or 'One of the Apache's or Caftan's Victims', *El Mercurio*, 24 Oct. 1913.

8. 'The White Slave Trade in Chile', *Police Review: Valparaiso*, Year VII, No. 91, Aug. 1913, pp. 55–64 and No. 95, Dec. 1913, pp. 50–53. Also, 'A Victim Speaks', *La Unión*, 24 Oct. 1913.

9. Ibid.

10. See 'The White Slave Trade in Chile', *Police Review: Valparaiso*, Year VII, No. 92, Sept. 1913 pp. 38–44.

11. For the Argentine context see J.C. Moya, 'The Positive Side of Stereotypes: Jewish Anarchists in Early Twentieth-century Buenos Aires', *Jewish History*, Vol. 18, 2004, pp. 191–148. On the changing moral climate in the Chilean capital see, A. de Ramón, 'Securidad y Moralidad Publicas', in A. de Ramón y P. Gross (compliadores), *Santiago de Chile: Caracteristicas Historico Ambientales, 1891–1924* (London 1985), pp. 39–62; and, A.G. Escobedo, *La Prostitución en Santiago, 1813–1931* (Santiago 1994), pp. 118–123.

12. See Escobedo, *La Prostitución en Santiago*, p. 118. By late 1912, with public anxieties being aroused by a press campaign that was to gain full momentum some months later, it was estimated that there were thirty-eight hardened gangsters, *tenebrosos*, controlling over 200 prostitutes in Santiago and Valparaiso; see 'White Slave Trade: An Established Industry in Chile', *El Mercurio*, 22 Dec. 1912. On conflict and rivalries between brothel-owners see, for example, 'Apaches in Santiago de Chile', *El Mercurio*, 19 Dec. 1912.

13. On Jack Lis's successful appeal in the Cellini case and subsequent arrival see Argentina, Buenos Aires, *La Prensa*, 3 March 1912, and Centro de Estudios Migratorios Latinoamericanos (C.E.M.L.A.), Immigration Records, *Amazon*, 7 Sept. 1912.

14. On Steiman's unpaid police bills in Buenos Aires see, 'White Slave Trade: An Established Industry in Chile', *El Mercurio*, 22 Dec. 1912.

15. See Chile, Santiago, N.A., CC3/San./1912, Statement made before the Judges of the Third Criminal Court by E.J. Castro, C.I.D., Santiago Police, 16 Dec. 1912. See also 'Apaches in Santiago de Chile', *El Mercurio*, 19 Dec. 1912. For another example of an anonymous pamphlet, drawn from the circle of 'Russian' gangsters in which Silver moved while in South Africa, see above, Chapter 10.

16. See Chile, Santiago, N.A., CC 3/San./1912, Statement made before the Judges

of the Third Criminal Court by E.J. Castro, C.I.D., Santiago Police, 16
Dec. 1912. See also, United Kingdom (U.K.) London (Lon.), National
Archives (N.A.), Kew, Foreign Office (F.O.), Vol. 369/1557, No. 17696,
Henry Crofton Lowther, Santiago, to Sir Edward Grey, Whitehall, 3 Feb.
1913.

17. See Chile, Santiago, N.A., CC 3/San./1912, Statement made before the
Judges of the Third Criminal Court by E.J. Castro, C.I.D., Santiago Police,
16 Dec. 1912.

18. On Steiman as informer first in Argentina, and then later in Chile, see
Argentina (Arg.), Buenos Aires, Argentine National Archives (A.N.A.),
Ministry of Foreign Affairs (F.O.), Chile 1912, Box 1297, Salvador Nicosia,
Vice-Consul, Santiago de Chile, to the Under-Secretary, Ministry of Foreign
Affairs, 14 June 1912.

19. Ibid.

20. See Chile, Santiago, N.A., CC3/San./1912, Statement made before the
Judges of the Third Criminal Court by E.J. Castro, C.I.D., Santiago Police,
16 Dec. 1912 ; and 'New Brothels', *Police Review: Valparaiso,* Year VII,
No. 92, Sept. 1913 pp. 38–44.

21. See Chile, Santiago, N.A., CC3/San./1912, Statement made before the
Judges of the Third Criminal Court by E.J. Castro, C.I.D., Santiago Police,
16 Dec. 1912.

22. Ibid.

23. On Dubois see C. Droguett, *Todas esas Muertes* (Madrid 1971), pp. 13–14.
On Lis in Valparaiso see Chile, Santiago, N.A., CC3/San./1912, Statement
made before the Judges of the Third Criminal Court by E.J. Castro, C.I.D.,
Santiago Police, 16 Dec. 1912. There is also a version, reasonably accu-
rate, of the context in a report on 'Apaches in Santiago de Chile', *El
Mercurio,* 19 Dec. 1912.

24. See Chile, Santiago, N.A., CC3/San./1912, Statement made before the
Judges of the Third Criminal Court by E.J. Castro, C.I.D., Santiago Police,
16 Dec. 1912.

25. See ibid where Alamos's letter of 29 Nov. 1912 is reproduced in its
entirety.

26. There is a wonderful statement, in Silver's own words, dated 13 Dec.
1912, to be found in Chile, Santiago., N.A., CC3/San./1912, Statement
made before the Judge of the Third Criminal Court.

27. Ibid. (emphasis added).

28. See H.L. Adam, *Trial of George Chapman* (London 1930), pp. 63–64.

29. See Chile, Santiago., N.A., CC3/San./1912, Statement made by J. Silver
before the Judges of the Third Criminal Court, 13 Dec. 1912 (emphasis
added).

30. 'Apaches in Santiago de Chile'?, *El Mercurio,* 29 Dec. 1912.

31. See 'Police News' and 'The Robbery at the Munóz Arce Hnos. Exchange', *El Mercurio*, 24 and 25 Dec. 1912.

32. U.K., London, Family Records Centre, Birth Certificate of Monthy [*sic*] Lis, born to Jack Lis ('Dealer in Jewellery') and Bertha Lis (née Lis), Flat 2, No. 162 Charing Cross Road, London, 14 Aug. 1914.

33. See U.K., London, N.A., F.O. Vol. 369/1557, No. 17696, Henry Crofton Lowther, Santiago, to Sir Edward Grey, Whitehall, 3 Feb. 1913.

34. See U.K., London., N.A., F.O. Vol. 369/1557, No. 236 215/2, E. Blackwell, Home Office to Under-Secretary of State, Foreign Office, Whitehall, 15 April 1913. See also Chapter 7 above.

35. Ibid. See also, Chapter 7 above.

36. See 'Around the Courts' in *El Mercurio* of 11,18 and 29 April 1913; also 'Pursuit of the Ruffians', *La Unión*, 26 Oct. 1913.

37. On the Argentine and Chilean economies on the eve of the First World War see D. Rock, *Argentina, 1516–1987: From Spanish Colonization to Alfonsin* (Berkeley 1987), p. 193 and Collier and Sater, *A History of Chile, 1808–1994*, pp. 156–170.

Chapter 22: Valparaiso–Santiago, 1913

1. See 'The White Slave Trade in Chile', *Police Review: Valparaiso*, Year VII, No. 91, Aug. 1913, pp. 55–64; and 'White Slave Trade' (continued), *Police Review: Valparaiso*, Year VII, No. 92, Sept. 1913, pp. 38–44.

2. See 'White Slave Trade: An Established Industry in Chile', *El Mercurio*, 22 Dec. 1912.

3. See ibid. Also, 'White Slave Trade', *Police Review: Valparaiso*, No. 92.

4. See especially 'White Slave Trade', *El Mercurio*, 29 March 1913.

5. On the Rabout case see 'White Slave Trade', *Police Review: Valparaiso*, No. 91.

6. See 'White Slave Trade: An Established Industry in Chile', *El Mercurio*, 22 Dec. 1912.

7. 'The White Slave Trade in Chile', *Police Review: Valparaiso*, Year VII, No. 86, March 1913, pp. 28–32.

8. See above, Chapter 20.

9. The early stages of the story can be tracked in the Buenos Aires press of the day. See, amongst others, items carried in *El Dia*, *La Prensa* and *Tribuna* of 8 and 18 Dec. 1912. I am indebted to Gabriela Braccio for drawing my attention to these references.

10. See 'The White Slave Trade in Chile', *Police Review: Valparaiso*, No. 86, p. 28 and, above, Chapter 20.

11. 'White Slave Trade', *El Mercurio*, 29 March 1913.

12. Ibid.

13. See *Police Review: Valparaiso*, No. 92.

14. See 'The Caftan Steiman', *La Unión* (Santiago), 4 Aug. 1913.

15. Identical versions of Kantor's statement are to be found in 'A Victim Speaks', *La Unión*, 24 Oct. 1913 and 'One of the Apache's or Caftan's Victims', *El Mercurio*, 24 Oct. 1913. For further, independent verification of Kantor and Lieberona's presence first in Santiago, and later in Valparaiso, see also Chile, Santiago., N.A., CC3/San./1912, Statements made before Judge J. Bianchi Tupper and E.A. Gundian, 18 Dec. 1912.

16. Ibid.

17. *Police Review: Valparaiso*, No. 92.

18. *La Unión*, 8 Oct. 1913 (emphasis added).

19. *La Unión*, 8 Oct. 1913; and *Las Ultimas Noticias*, 18 Oct. 1913.

20. 'A Caftan Caught', *La Unión*, 25 Oct. 1913.

21. 'The Pursuit of the Ruffians', *La Unión*, 26 Oct. 1913.

22. See, for example, 'mysterious' disappearances of at least five teenage girls from 'humble' homes as reported in *Las Ultimas Noticias* of 10 and 24 Oct. 1913.

23. 'A New "Apache" Feat', *Las Ultimas Noticias*, 24 Oct. 1913.

24. All of the examples are drawn from *Las Ultimas Noticias* of 27 Oct. 1913. Nor was the great terror confined to the capital. On the same day, in the same issue, it was reported that in Chillan, 'Every visiting foreigner is closely observed by his neighbours and, if they have any suspicion of dishonesty, they insult and threaten him.'

25. *La Unión*, 10 Oct. 1913.

26. See *El Mercurio* of 10 and 20 Oct. 1913.

27. *El Mercurio*, 24 and 25 Oct. 1913.

28. The trickle of factual information from the police started with a report, 'The Alarm and the Police', in *El Mercurio*, 29 Oct. 1913 and this was eventually followed by fuller disclosure the following week: see, 'Caftans in Santiago', *La Unión*, 4 Nov. 1913. *El Mercurio*, angered by the scarcity of official information, was of the view that the police perhaps had an interest in 'keeping the neighbourhood alarms ringing'.

29. See correspondence in Argentina, Buenos Aires, Argentine National Archives, Ministry of Foreign Affairs, Chile 1912, Box 1297, Dec. 1912.

30. See Argentina, *Gaceta de Foro*, 1 Nov. 1930, where his police file is listed as number 309.

Chapter 23: London, New York and Rio de Janeiro, 1914–1916

1. See United States of America (U.S.A.), New York City, Ellis Island Records, Passenger manifests, 'Philadelphia', 16 Dec. 1915.

2. On German economic and social development in the late nineteenth and

early twentieth centuries see D. Blackbourn, *Fontana History of Germany, 1780–1918* (London 1997); and on the causes of the war J. Joll, *The Origins of the First World War* (London 1984). Perhaps the most concise, integrated and readable recent history of the war is M. Howard's *The First World War* (Oxford 2002).

3. Howard, *The First World War*, p. 21.

4. On the 1905 Aliens Act see W.D. Rubinstein, *A History of the Jews in the English-Speaking World: Great Britain* (London 1996), pp. 154–157; and on the spy scare A.J.A. Morris, *The Scaremongers: The Advocacy of War and Re-armament, 1896–1914* (London 1984), pp. 98–110 and 148–63.

5. In this instance, which was the precursor to the famous siege of Sidney Street, there was indeed cause for concern. For the wider context and its significance see, for example, R. Spence, *Trust No One: The Secret World of Sidney Reilly* (Los Angeles 2002), pp. 131–132.

6. See D. Feldman, *Englishmen and Jews: Social Relations and Political Culture, 1840–1914* (London 1994), pp. 359–362. For the wider perspective see W.J. Fishman, *East End Jewish Radicals, 1875–1914* (London 1975) and, on the immediate subject, pp. 287–291. For some of the continuities in anti-Semitism in the English context see also, T. Kushner, 'The Impact of British Anti-Semitism, 1918–1945', in D. Cesarani (ed.), *The Making of Modern Anglo-Jewry* (Oxford 1990), pp. 191–208.

7. The British police, too, were becoming better organised and focused on the most oppressive dimensions of the trade in commercial sex. See, United Kingdom, London, National Archives (N.A.), Kew, MEPO 2/1312, *White Slave Traffic*, New Scotland Yard, 12 June 1913; and T. Kushner, 'Sex and Semitism: Jewish Women in Britain in War and Peace', in P. Panyani (ed.), *Minorities in Wartime: National and Racial Groupings in Europe, North America and Australia during World Wars* (Oxford 1993), pp. 118–132.

8. See N.R.P. Bonsor, *North Atlantic Seaway: An Illustrated History of the Passenger Services linking the Old World with the New*, Vol. 1 (London 1975), pp. 102–103 and 107; also R.V. Gibbs, *British Passenger Liners of the Five Oceans: A Record of the British Passenger Lines and their Liners from 1838 to the Present Day* (London 1963), p. 179.

9. See U.K., London, N.A., BT 27/836, Outgoing Passengers, Liverpool, *Mauretania*, 16 May 1914.

10. See M.T. Connelly, *The Response to Prostitution in the Progressive Era* (Chapel Hill 1980), pp. 48–50; and T.J. Gilfoyle, *City of Eros: New York City, Prostitution and the Commercialization of Sex, 1790–1920* (New York City 1992), pp. 308–310.

11. See E.J. Bristow, *Prostitution and Prejudice: The Jewish Fight against*

White Slavery, 1870–1939 (London 1982), pp. 167–168; A.A. Goren, *New York Jews and the Quest for Community: The Kehillah Experiment, 1908-1922* (New York 1970), pp. 59–60; and J.W. Joselit, *Our Gang: Jewish Crime and the New York Jewish Community* (Bloomington 1983), pp. 10, 81–85.

12. For the wider perspective see C. van Onselen, 'Jewish Marginality in the Atlantic World: Organised Crime in the Era of the Great Migrations, 1880–1914', *South African Historical Journal*, No. 43, Nov. 2000, pp. 111–12.

13. On the links between the Rosenthal murder and the Bureau for Social Morals see Joselit, *Our Gang*, pp. 81–82 and Goren, *New York Jews*, pp. 59–60. On 'vice' see a work first published in 1913, G.J. Kneeland's, *Commercialised Prostitution in New York City* (Montclair 1969); and for a fictionalised view of other, contemporary underworld characters, A.H. Lewis, *The Apaches of New York* (New York 1912).

14. See U.S.A., Washington, DC, National Archives (N.A.), Records Administration No. 36337, 10W2, Roll 218, R10, C166, DR 2, passport application of J. Silver, 29 June 1914.

15. The network of white slavers operating out of Myslowitz – which included a certain unknown 'Silberman' during the latter half of 1913 – extended to the emigration halls of Hamburg itself where several members of the Zwi Migdal had relocated. The wider operation was, if not fully infiltrated then informed on by Józef Brodzki an agent of the Russian secret police. On Brodzki's return to Warsaw in 1914, the Okhrana decided to report on the Hamburg–Myslowitz operations in a series of articles in 'The Horizon'. See 'Ghenna Emigracji', *Widnokrag* (Warsaw), nos. 10, 11 and 12 of 1914. See also Bristow, *Prostitution and Prejudice*, p. 130.

16. See Bristow, *Prostitution and Prejudice*, pp. 130–131, 255.

17. See U.K., London, N.A., BT/26/581, Incoming Passengers, *Aquitania*, New York–Liverpool, 7 July 1914; and Gibbs, *British Passenger Liners*, p. 199.

18. See, for example, Howard, *The First World War*, pp. 26–31 and 32–40.

19. U.K., London, Family Records Centre (F.R.C.), Registration of the birth of Bernard Lis, in the sub-district of North Hackney, 6 April 1915.

20. U.K., London, F.R.C., Registration of the birth of Monthy [*sic*] Lis, on 22 Sept. 1913, in the sub-district of St Giles and Bloomsbury. See also note 26 below. Monty's name, the clerk noted at the time, was spelt 'Monthy' on the certificate at the insistence of the father, Jack Lis.

21. U.K., London, N.A., BT 27/858, Out-Going Passengers, *Philadelphia*, Liverpool, 2 Jan. 1915. On the role of the *City of Paris* in Silver's earlier adventures see Chapter 6, above.

22. See Brazil (Bra.), Rio de Janeiro, Arquivo Nacional (A.N.), Fundo:

DPMAF/RJ, CODES, Vapor *Voltaire*, 12 Feb. 1915. The *Voltaire* was later sunk by the German raider *Möwe*, west of Fastnet, on 2 Dec. 1916. On wartime movements see, for example, I. Vincent, *Bodies and Souls: The Tragic Plight of Three Jewish Women Forced into Prostitution in the Americas* (New York 2005), pp. 115 and 129.

23. See above, Chapter 16, and Bra., Rio de Janeiro, Arquivo Casa Rui Barbosa, N. Hoffbauer, 'Relacao das Mulherese que exercem o meretricio em zona 12, Distrito Policial', 1923. On the private lives of prostitutes in Rio de Janeiro see, especially, Vincent, *Bodies and Souls*, pp. 100–115.

24. See Bra., Rio de Janeiro, A.N., Fundo: DPMAF/RJ, CODES, Vapor *Voltaire*, 12 Feb. 1915.

25. U.K., London., N.A., Kew, BT 26/605, Incoming Passengers, *Alcantara*, Liverpool, 6 March 1915. The *Alcantara*, fitted with refrigerated cargo space for the Argentine meat trade, was converted to an armed merchant cruiser and sunk in the Skaggerak on 29 Feb. 1916. The street directories for London for the period 1912–17 reveal that nearby buildings, such as Charing Cross Mansions, housed several theatre costumiers and furriers with French or Jewish names but reveal no long-term residence by Bertha Lis/Silver although, from other sources, it is clear that she had been using the address for several years.

26. On French women in Rio de Janeiro at the time see G. Freyere, *Order and Progress: Brazil from Monarchy to Republic* (New York 1970), pp. 58–60.

27. See, Bristow, *Prostitution and Prejudice*, p. 141, Freyere, *Order and Progress*. pp. 57–62; D. Guy, *Sex & Danger in Buenos Aires: Prostitution, Family and Nation in Argentina* (London 1991), p. 34; and especially J. Lesser, *Welcoming the Undesirables: Brazil and the Jewish Question* (London 1995), pp. 34–39. There is an extensive literature on prostitution in Brazil and Rio de Janeiro available in Portuguese including L. Medeiros de Menezes, *Os estrangeiros e o comércio do prazer nas ruas do Rio, 1890–1930* (Rio de Janeiro 1992). Most pertinent, however, is B. Kushnir's *Baile de Máscaras, Mulheres Judias e Prostituica: As Polacs e suas Associacoes de Ajuda Mútia* (Rio de Janeiro 1996) and Vincent, *Bodies and Souls*, p. 209.

28. Vincent, *Bodies and Souls*, p. 209.

29. See S. Caulfield, 'The Birth of Mangue: Race, Nation and the Politics of Prostitution in Rio de Janeiro, 1850–1942', in D. Balderson and D.J. Guy (eds), *Sex and Sexuality in Latin America* (New York 1997), pp. 86–100.

30. U.K., London, N.A., Kew, BT 26/605, Incoming Passengers, *Amazon*, Liverpool 3 April 1915. See also, Vincent, *Bodies and Souls*, p. 72.

31. U.K., London, N.A., Kew, BT 27/865, Outgoing Passengers, Liverpool,

Philadelphia, 8 Dec. 1915. The Ellis Island immigration records give Bertha's age as 38 rather than 28 and she is listed as 'Bertle' rather than Bertha. The correct details are reflected in the *Philadelphia*'s manifest.

32. See, for example, Spence, *Trust No One*, p. 127.

33. U.S.A., New York City, National Archives, North-East Branch, Varick Street, Incoming Passengers, New York City, *Kristianiafjord*, 23 Jan. 1916. On Boston and 'vice' see Bristow, *Prostitution and Prejudice*, pp. 153 and 177.

34. See B. Wasserstein, *The Secret Lives of Trebitsch Lincoln* (London 1988) and Spence, *Trust No One*, pp. 126–127. The speculation here is that Lincoln was, albeit to a lesser degree, like Silver, afflicted with an 'Antisocial Personality Disorder' if not psychopathy. Wasserstein, for example, refers to Trebitsch as having an 'inverted moral sense' (p. 117). Interestingly, Sidney Reilly, too, shared several such symptoms – including, possibly, the capacity for murder: see Spence, *Trust No One*, pp. 16 and 30. The historical context and genesis of specifically 'Jewish' psychopathologies during the late nineteenth century are hinted at in S. L. Gilman, *Jewish Self-hatred: Anti Semitism and the Hidden Language of the Jews* (London 1986) pp. 286–308. Reilly, Silver and Trebitsch – three 'Jewish' spies and/or police informers at various stages in their careers – are the subject of a planned essay.

35. See Spence, *Trust No One*, especially pp. 63 and 85.

36. There is a list of the names of places and persons recorded by Schoenfeld to be found in Israel, in the Central Archives of the Jewish People, Jerusalem, Judah Magnus Collection, New York City, File D3/1768, p. 126, 'List supplied to the Police Commissioner of the City of New York between 1 June and 1 Dec. 1914' by the Jewish Community. On protection money and horse-poisoners see, for example, Joselit, *Our Gang*, pp. 39–40 and on Schoenfeld, Goren, *New York Jews*, pp. 162–163 and 170–171.

37. See above, Chapter 7.

Chapter 24: Jaroslaw, 1917–1918

1. See The American Jewish Committee, *The Jews in the Eastern War Zone* (New York 1916), pp. 7–10; D. Blackbourn, *The Fontana History of Germany, 1780–1918* (London 1997), pp. 287–301; and J. Wertheimer, *Unwelcome Strangers. East European Jews in Imperial Germany* (Oxford 1987), pp. 77–88.

2. See, for example, *Jews in the Eastern War Zone*, pp. 41–66. For an example closer to Silver's home see 'The Diary of Rabbi Jeruzalimski from the Days of the First World War', translated from the Yiddish by J. Landau

in P. Cytron (ed.), *Sefer Kielce: Toldot Kehilat Kielce, Miyom Hivsuduh V'ad Churbanah* (Tel Aviv 1957) pp. 271–295. This invaluable source, the 'Book of Kielce', can also be consulted, in English, at www.jewishgen.org/Yizkor/kielce'Kie271.htm.

3. See *Jews in the Eastern War Zone* pp. 9–85. Also E.J. Bristow, *Prostitution and Prejudice: The Jewish Fight against White Slavery, 1870–1939* (Oxford 1982), p. 284.

4. On the mobility of Jewish prostitutes in Russia at the time, see *Jews in the Eastern War Zone*, p. 32; and for the overall growth in prostitution, Bristow, *Prostitution and Prejudice*, p. 285.

5. Ibid., p. 285.

6. Ibid., p. 286.

7. On the earliest months of the war in Kielce see 'The Diary of Rabbi Jeruzalimski', *Sefer Kielce*, pp. 271–295, and on the pogrom that came with the assumption of Polish independence, pp. 51–56. For similar anti-Semitic horrors elsewhere along the eastern front see also J. Reed, *War in Eastern Europe: Travels through the Balkans in 1915* (London 1994).

8. *Sefer Kielce*, pp. 159 and 272.

9. See 'The Diary of Rabbi Jeruzalimski', *Sefer Kielce*, pp. 271–295. For an accessible account of conflict around Kielce during the opening months of the campaign see G. Jukes, *The First World War: The Eastern Front, 1914–1918* (Oxford 2002), pp. 22–29. For the classic account, however, see N. Stone, *The Eastern Front, 1914–1917* (London 1998), pp. 92–121. On Jewish refugees in Kielce – both the city and the province bearing the same name – see *Jews in the Eastern War Zone*, pp. 101–111.

10. On the retaking of Przemysl by the Central Powers see B.H. Liddell Hart, *History of the First World War* (London 1982), p. 147.

11. See *Sefer Kielce*, pp. 13–14; and on the influence of the Hasidic tradition within the community, ibid., pp. 154–169.

12. Rabbi Abraham Abele was the son of the community's first rabbi, Tuwia Gutman – see *Sefer Kielce*, p. 165.

13. On the changing fortunes of Przemysl during the First World War see Jukes, *The Eastern Front*, pp. 32–35 and Stone, *The Eastern Front*, pp. 78–96, 114–116 and 142. Also Reed, *War in Eastern Europe*, p. 91.

14. For an example of cross-border activities by Jews opposed to the Russians – a more frequent occurrence it would seem than the other way round on the eastern front during the war – see D.E. Showalter, *Tannenburg: Clash of Empires* (Hamden 1991), pp. 101–102; and Stone, *The Eastern Front*, pp. 134–135 and 296–297.

15. See Germany, Staatsarchiv Hamburg, Polizei behörde Hamburg, Abteilung 1V M (Meldeamt); Tagebuch vom 21.10.1916 bis 7.6.1917, No. 14880–149000/16 und 11541/17.

16. See Poland, Warsaw, Archiwum Glowne Akt Dawnych, K.u.K., Divisionsgericht, Przemysl, Nameverzeichniss zu Dst/ Register, 1917–1918, 'L'/1918. Since the same source also carries an entry for 1917, in 'L'/1917, also undated, it is possible that Lis faced two – separate – hearings.

17. See Austria, Vienna, Österreichisches Staatsarchiv (O.S.), Kriegsarchiv, Gouvernements-Inspektorat, Kielce, Durchläufer Nr. 641/JR, 1/08/1918.

18. Austria, Vienna, O.S., Kriegsarchiv, Gouvernements-Inspektorat, Kielce, Akt mit der Pers. – Nr. 17.582/J.R 31.10.1918.

Chapter 25: Silver's Secrets: Whitechapel, 1888

1. For an accessible, but already dated list of creative and other works centred around the Whitechapel murders, see M. Whitehead and M. Rivett, *The Pocket Essential Jack the Ripper* (Harpenden 2001), pp. 79–92.

2. Aaron Kosminski, Charles Ludwig, Severin Klosowski/George Chapman and, of course, Joseph Lis/Silver were all either barbers or barbers' assistants. Some of the reasons why barbershops sometimes sustained microsociological climates conducive to the cultivation of misogyny are alluded to in Chapters 1 and 2 above.

3. See P. Begg, *Jack the Ripper: The Facts* (London 2004), pp. 417–418; and P. Sugden, *The Complete History of Jack the Ripper* (London 2002), p. 468.

4. Begg, *The Facts*, p. 418.

5. Ibid., p. ix. Notwithstanding these and other observations below, the most disciplined, thoughtful and professional of the recent studies are clearly Begg, *The Facts* and Sugden, *The Complete History*. They complement the earlier, richly suggestive, work of M. Fido, *The Crimes, Detection and Death of Jack the Ripper* (London 1987).

6. Begg, *The Facts*, pp. ix and 418.

7. Sugden, *The Complete History*, p. 468.

8. Ibid. But even the basically sympathetic Sugden is uncertain how much weight should be accorded to advances in psychological research. 'We hear a lot about insanity, medical knowledge, cruelty to women and the like,' he admonishes, but precious little about *evidence*' (p. 468, emphasis in the original). For him, such interpretations remain suspect unless they can be linked directly to existing, hard, empirical evidence. 'We cannot accuse anyone of crimes like those of Jack the Ripper', he opines, 'without clear and positive evidence to back us up' (p. xxiv). At first glance this appears to be a reasonable position. In reality, it poses an extreme test which, as currently formulated, will never get us off the well-worn empiricist treadmill. It diminishes the possibility of using psychological guidelines to help

identify a plausible suspect and then develop a person-specific profile which can be tested against historically verifiable psychiatric evidence and existing data. The relevance and quality of evidence – 'clear and positive' – cannot be determined *a priori*. Its status can only be tested against the explanatory power of the theory underpinning it. In this study of Joseph Silver, advances and insights in forensic psychiatry have been used to ask new questions of old data so as to foreground a well known, existing, suspect – 'Joseph Isaacs' – whose behaviour and movements are compatible with what is already known about the East End murders. This approach lends new relevance to old, seemingly incomprehensible, empirical evidence.

9. The context, details and sources for these various documentary frauds are to be found in Chapters 3, 6 and 23 above. On Lis and Goldberg's admission to being in London, in early 1889, see above, Chapter 3.

10. See above, Chapter 6 and F. Moss, *The American Metropolis, From Knickerbocker Days to the Present Time: New York City Life in its Various Phases* (New York 1897), p. 217.

11. On Bertha's various deceptions as to place and date of birth see above, Chapters 16, 17, 18 and 23.

12. In an extensive literature see, for example, V.J. Gerberth and R.N. Turco, 'Antisocial Personality Disorder, Sexual Sadism, Malignant Narcissism and Serial Murder', *Journal of Forensic Sciences*, Vol. 4, No. 1, 1997, pp. 49–60; B.R. Johnson and J. Becker, 'Natural Born Killers? The Development of the Sexually Sadistic Serial Killer', *Journal of the American Academy, Psychiatry and Law*, Vol. 25, No. 3, 1997, pp. 335–348 and M.H. Stone, 'Serial Sexual Homicide: Biological, Psychological and Sociological Aspects', *Journal of Personality Disorders*, Vol. 15, No. 1, 2001, pp. 1–18.

13. See R.P. Brittain, 'The Sadistic Murderer', *Medicine, Science and the Law*, Vol. 10, 1970, pp. 198–207; R. Langevin, 'A Study of the Psychosexual Characteristics of Sex Killers: Can We Identify Them Before It Is Too Late?', *International Journal of Offender Therapy and Comparative Criminology*, Vol. 47, No. 4, 2003, pp. 367–382; M.MacCulloch, N. Gray and A. Watt, 'Brittain's Sadistic Murderer Syndrome Reconsidered: An Associative Account of the Aetiology of Sadistic Sexual Fantasy', *Journal of Forensic Psychiatry*, Vol. 11, No. 2, 2000, pp. 401–408; and M.J. MacCulloch, P.R. Snowden, P.J.W. Wood and H.E. Mills, 'Sadistic Fantasy, Sadistic Behaviour and Offending', *British Journal of Psychiatry*, Vol. 143, 1983, pp. 20–29.

14. See Langevin, 'Characteristics of Sex Killers', p. 373.

15. See H. Cleckley, *The Mask of Sanity: An Attempt to Clarify Some Issues about the So-called Psychopathic Personality* (St Louis, 1976, 5th edition;

first edition, 1941 and 1950 edition); and R.D. Hare, *Manual for the Hare Psychopathy Checklist-Revised* (Toronto 1991).

16. 'Most psychopaths (with the exception of those who somehow manage to plow their way through life without coming into formal or prolonged contact with the criminal justice system) meet the criteria for A.S.P.D., but most individuals with A.S.P.D. are not psychopaths.' - R.D. Hare, 'Psychopathy and Antisocial Personality Disorder: A Case of Diagnostic Confusion', *Psychiatric Times*, Vol. 13, No. 2, Feb. 1996, pp. 1–2.

17. See M. G. Gelder, J.J. López-Ibor and N. Andreasen (eds), *New Oxford Textbook of Psychiatry, Vol. 1* (Oxford 2000), pp. 931–936; and B.J. Sadock and V.A. Sadock (eds), *Kaplan and Sadock's Synopsis of Psychiatry, Ninth Edition* (New York 1998), pp. 807–808. See also: S.H. Dinwiddie, 'Genetics, Antisocial Personality and Criminal Responsibility', *Bulletin of American Academy, Psychiatry and Law*, Vol. 24, No. 1, 1996, pp. 95–108; J.J. Lindenthal, '*Abi Gezunt*: Health and the Eastern European Jewish Immigrant', *American Jewish History*, Vol. 4, No. 70, 1981, pp. 420–441; H. Markel, '*Di Golden Medina* (The Golden Land): Historical Perspectives of Eugenics and the East European (Ashkenazi) Jewish-American Community, 1880–1925', *Health-Matrix: Journal of Law-Medicine*, Vol. 7, No. 1, 1997, pp. 49–64; J. Sánchez, 'Social Crises and Psychopathy: Towards a Sociology of the Psychopath', in W.H. Reid, D. Dorr, J.I. Walker and J.W. Bonner (eds), *Unmasking the Psychopath: Antisocial Personality and Related Syndromes* (New York 1986), pp. 78–97; and E. Simonoff, J. Elander, J. Holmshaw, A. Pickles, R. Murray and M. Rutter, 'Predictors of Antisocial Personality', *British Journal of Psychiatry*, No. 184, 2004, pp. 118–127.

18. See especially Cleckley, *The Mask of Sanity* (St Louis, 1950 edition), pp. 424–428.

19. These observations are taken – in order cited – from Sadock, *Synopsis of Psychiatry*, p. 808; and Gelder *et al*, *Oxford Textbook of Psychiatry*, p. 933.

20. Hare, *Manual for the Hare Psychopathy Checklist-Revised*.

21. This summary is derived from K. Dewhurst, 'The Neurosyphilitic Psychoses Today', *British Journal of Psychiatry*, Vol. 115, 1969, pp. 31–38; M.C. Roberts and R.A. Emsley, 'Psychiatric Manifestations of Neurosyphilis', *South African Medical Journal*, Vol. 82, Nov. 1982, pp. 335–337; and, especially, W.A. Lishman, *Organic Psychiatry: The Psychological Consequences of Cerebral Disorder* (Oxford 1998), pp. 336–346. On irregularities in handwriting as a sign of syphilis see D. Hayden, *Pox: Genius, Madness and the Mysteries of Syphilis* (New York, 2003), pp. 56, 126 and 217; and the original, classic, study, E. Kraeplin, *General Paresis* (New York 1913).

22. This line of argument follows that of M. Douglas, *Purity and Danger: An Analysis of the Concepts of Pollution and Taboo* (London 1966). In 1898, Lis, as Joseph Silver, appeared at a public meeting suggesting that prostitutes should be sent to 'reformatory institutions or, failing that, be *confined to a particular locality within the city*' – 'The Morality Law', *Standard & Diggers' News*, 28 Sept. 1898 (emphasis added).

23. Ezekiel, 23: 37. Lis's darkest thoughts about blood, child abuse, pollution and women – as will become increasingly evident as the argument below unfolds – appear to have been drawn, in disproportionate measure, from the Book of Ezekiel. My reading of Lis's behaviour and mindset in this, and in its wider, murderous dimension, owes most to my reading of D.J. Halperin's brilliant *Seeking Ezekiel: Text and Psychology* (The Pennsylvania State University Press, 1993), pp. 162–163.

24. Examples of his more expansive behaviour can be traced in London (1895–98), in Johannesburg (1898–99), in Bloemfontein, (1902–3) and, perhaps most strikingly of all, in German South West Africa during 1905–6. See above, Chapters, 7, 8, 9, 13, 16 and 17.

25. See also, Halperin, *Seeking Ezekiel*, p. 218.

26. Ibid. pp. 164–165.

27. This, too, is compatible with a reading of the prophet; see ibid. pp. 58–73.

28. See Chapter 1, above, on the role of the Torah and Jewish folklore – *aggadah* – in the life of the young Lis. On the importance of fatherlessness in the development of serial killers see, amongst others, Stone, 'Serial Sexual Homicide', p. 10. Also, E. Simonoff, J. Elander, J. Holmshaw, A. Pickles, E. Murray and M. Rutter, 'Predictors of Antisocial Personality: Continuities from Childhood to Adult Life', *British Journal of Psychiatry*, Vol. 184, 2004, pp. 118–127.

29. On custom, names and Jewish marriages see M. Zborowski and E. Herzog, *Life is with People: The Culture of the Shtetl* (New York 1952), p. 272. On the centrality of mother–son relationships and 'the transfer of affect from mother to females in general or to a particular female' in sex murderers see especially, E. Revitch, 'Sex Murder and the Potential Sex Murderer', *Diseases of the Nervous System*, Vol. 26, No. 10, Oct. 1965, pp. 640–648.

30. See Chapters 11–15 above where Vygenbaum often appears as 'Bloom' or 'Bloem'. An 'Annie Bloom' does appear amongst the names of prostitutes active in the Transvaal in 1907–8 but since there is also a known pimp by the name of Bloom present at the time it is not clear that this 'Annie Bloom' was Silver's ex-wife. See R.S.A., Pretoria, S.A.N.A., A.G. 172/06, 'Return of Brothels at Johannesburg and Pretoria', 21 May 1907; and S.A.C., Vol. 22 File 8/67, 'List of Persons who Habitually take Houses for Brothels', 1908.

31. Gerberth and Turco, 'Serial Murder', p. 56.

32. Stone, 'Serial Sexual Homicide', p. 8.

33. As Brittain puts it in 'The Sadistic Murderer' at p. 202: 'Such a man has, frequently, a strong ambivalent relationship to his mother, both loving and hating her.'

34. Begg, The Facts, p. 225.

35. Ibid. p. 226.

36. It would also have been part of an important subtext in Ezekiel which seems to have shaped some of his behaviour in Whitechapel. See Halperin, Seeking Ezekiel, pp. 133–135.

37. Brittain, 'The Sadistic Murderer', p. 205.

38. See E.R. Watson, Adolf Beck, 1877–1906 (London 1925), pp. 1–19.

39. On Charles Ludwig see, for example, Begg, The Facts, pp. 130–131.

40. See H.L. Adam, Trial of George Chapman (London 1930), pp. 1–23. On Klosowski's markedly psychopathic tendencies see ibid. pp. 37–40 and Sugden, The Complete History, pp. 441–448.

41. See especially Kraeplin, General Paresis, pp. 24–27; and Hayden, Pox, p. 57.

42. See Chapter 17 above.

43. For the immediate, wider, context of this threat see above, Chapter 13 (emphasis added).

44. See Halperin, Seeking Ezekiel, pp. 102–108 and 151–154. Also, 2 Sam. 11: 2–4.

45. See A. Unterman, Dictionary of Jewish Lore and Legend (London 1997), p. 134.

46. Leviticus, 15: 18.

47. See above, Chapters 15, 16 and 22.

48. For the wider context, see Chapter 9.

49. See above, Chapter 16. The possibility that the Ripper had been infected with a venereal disease was not, of course, lost on observers at the time; see for example, Begg, The Facts, p. 225.

50. It is incorrect to suggest as does R. Castleden in Serial Killers (London 2005), p. 7 that, 'A serial murderer goes on killing until stopped. A peculiarity of serial killing is that there is often a lull, a cooling off period that may go on for months or even years during which no killing happens, and then the killing starts again.' There are plenty of examples, including modern ones, in which the killing does stop. See, for example, Mendoza, Killers on the Loose, pp. 23–43, or for the example cited involving prostitutes in London, D. Thomas, Villains' Paradise (London 2005), pp. 290–291.

51. See, for example, Mendoza, Killers on the Loose, p. 45.

52. See above, Chapters 3 and 23.

53. D.G. Dutton and G. Kerry, 'Modus Operandi and Personality Disorder in Incarcerated Spousal Killers', *International Journal of Law and Psychiatry*, Vol. 22, Nos 3–4, 1999, p. 295.

54. See Chapter 2, above.

55. *Mamzers* 'cannot intermarry freely with other members of the community, since a *mamzer* may not enter "the congregation of the Lord"' (Deut. 23:3) – see Unterman, *Jewish Lore*, p. 126. It was, of course, one of history's many ironies that, in the moral maelstrom that the Lises found themselves in, Hannah Lis's *mamzer*, Jack, was eventually to marry Joseph Lis's illegitimate child, Bertha.

56. See Fido, *The Crimes of Jack the Ripper*, p. 16. Concerns about ways in which the locality and doorstep robbery differed from what might typically be expected from the Ripper are discussed in Begg, *The Facts*, p. 28.

57. In this regard see, especially, the fate of the biblical whore, Oholibah, at the hands of an 'international mob': Halperin, *Seeking Ezekiel*. p. 155.

58. Ibid.

59. See Begg, *The Facts*, p. 29.

60. Ibid., p. 30.

61. See S.P. Evans and K. Skinner, *The Ultimate Jack the Ripper Source Book* (London 2000), pp. 433–434.

62. See especially, Chapter 9, above.

63. See especially, Chapter 7, above.

64. Sugden, *The Complete History*, p. 1.

65. On Lis's version of his introduction to burglary see Moss, *The American Metropolis*, p. 216. On the importance and significance of local knowledge for serial killers see, for example, S. Lundrigan and D. Canter, 'Research Report: Spatial Patterns of Serial Murder: An Analysis of Disposal Site Location Choice', *Behavioral Sciences and the Law*, Vol. 19, 2001, pp. 595–610.

66. Ezekiel, 23: 36.

67. On picquerism, and 'signatures' of serial killers see – despite several alarming errors of detail – R.D. Keppel, J.G. Weiss, K.M. Brown and K. Welch, 'The Jack the Ripper Murders: A *Modus Operandi* and Signature Analysis of the 1888–1891 Whitechapel Murders', *Journal of Investigative Psychology and Offender Profiling*, Vol. 2, 2005, pp. 15–17. On the murder itself see, for example, Begg, *The Facts*, pp. 34–35 and Sugden, *The Complete History*, pp. 14–35.

68. See, for example, Keppel *et al.*, '*Modus Operandi* and Signature Analysis', p. 19.

69. This paragraph is based largely on Begg, *The Facts*, pp. 47–53 and

Sugden, *The Complete History*, pp. 53–56; the quotation is from Begg, p. 50. But see also Fido, *The Crimes of Jack the Ripper*, pp. 20–23; Keppel *et al.*, 'Modus Operandi and Signature Analysis', pp. 4–6; and D. Rumbelow, *The Complete Jack the Ripper* (London 1988), pp. 4–42.

70. Ezekiel, 23: 26.

71. Sugden, *The Complete History*, p. 100.

72. See Begg, *The Facts*, pp. 65–85 and, more especially, p. 79.

73. See Unterman, *Jewish Lore*, pp. 40 and 180.

74. Begg, *The Facts*, p. 80.

75. See Keppel *et al.*, 'Modus Operandi and Signature Analysis', pp. 6–7.

76. Begg, *The Facts*, p. 80.

77. Ibid., p. 76.

78. Report from the *Echo*, 20 Sept. 1888, as reproduced in Fido, *The Crimes of Jack the Ripper*, pp. 210–211 (emphasis added).

79. Fido was clearly alert to this possibility and, while concentrating on another possible suspect, has long pointed to the area around Plumber's Row as a possible base for the Ripper. See Fido, *The Crimes of Jack the Ripper*, map facing p. 28 and pp. 210–11, 217.

80. Sugden, *The Complete History*, p. 121. On the role of the press in the Whitechapel murders see L. Perry Curtis Jnr's excellent *Jack the Ripper and the London Press* (London 2001).

81. See U.K., Oxford, New Bodleian Library, W.T. Gidney, *The History of the London Society for Promoting Christianity amongst the Jews* (London 1908), especially Chapter 42; and DEP.CMJ.E. 17, 'The Thirty-Second Report of the Wanderers' Home, or Temporary Asylum for Inquiring or Believing Jews and Jewesses in Distress or Difficulty, 1885/86'. On Lincoln's use of the society, a decade later, see B. Wasserstein, *The Secret Lives of Trebitsch Lincoln* (London 1988), pp. 14–17. Within the broader context it is perhaps also important to remember Lis's later work with the Revd Charles Parkhurst and the Society for the Prevention of Crime in New York City in 1895.

82. The *Star* (London), of 14 Sept. 1888, reported how 'The Workers' Friend, the Hebrew Socialist paper, of this week announces that as a protest against the Jewish religion and the Day of Atonement, the Jewish Socialists and Freethinkers have organised a banquet for tomorrow . . .' For these renunciations of religion and the public disturbance that followed, see R.J. McLaughlin, 'Interpreting "Lipski"', *Ripperologist*, March 2003, pp. 3–6. It is also interesting to note that, in 1895, Lis chose to work for the Revd Charles Parkhurst who appears to have run a mission to convert the Jews to Christianity on Manhattan's Lower East Side. This, in turn, needs to be put into the context of Lis's hatred of Judaism and God-fearing Jews: see below.

83. Sugden, *The Complete History*, p. 171.

84. Evans and Skinner, *The Ultimate*, p. 228.

85. Begg, *The Facts*, pp. 150 and 153.

86. Ibid., p. 177.

87. Evans and Skinner, *The Ultimate*, p. 228.

88. Sugden, *The Complete History*, p. 178.

89. Begg, *The Facts*, p. 177.

90. Sugden, *The Complete History*, p. 178.

91. Evans and Skinner, *The Ultimate*, p. 228; and Begg, *The Facts*, p. 177.

92. Ezekiel, 23: 25 (emphasis added).

93. Begg, *The Facts*, pp. 172 and 177.

94. See Evans and Skinner, *The Ultimate*, pp. 222–223 and 243. On the role of the *shabbos goi* see, for examples, Unterman, *Jewish Lore*, p. 178.

95. Begg, *The Facts*, p. 168.

96. See J.J. Eddelstone, *Jack the Ripper: An Encyclopedia* (London 2002), p. 278.

97. See Evans and Skinner, *The Ultimate*, pp. 164, 170 and 174.

98. In this connection see also the broadly apposite arguments and comments developed by Fido in *The Crimes of Jack the Ripper*, pp. 214–217, although applying to another suspect often in the same quarter.

99. See J. White's splendid *Rothschild Buildings: Life in an East End Tenement Block, 1887–1920* (London 1980), p. 118.

100. Ibid., pp. 48–49.

101. Ezekiel, 36: 25.

102. Evans and Skinner, *The Ultimate*, pp. 262.

103. See U.K., Oxford, New Bodleian Library, Papers of the Church Ministry among the Jews, DEP.CMJ.E.17, 'The Thirty-Second Report of the Wanderers' Home, or Temporary Asylum for Inquiring or Believing Jews and Jewesses in Distress or Difficulty, 1885/86'.

104. See S.L. Gilman, *Jewish Self-Hatred: Anti-Semitism and the Hidden Language of the Jews* (London 1986), pp. 1–21 and 42–52.

105. D. Assaf, *The Regal Way: The Life and Times of Rabbi Israel of Ruzhin* (Stanford 2002), p. 25.

106. See also Unterman, *Jewish Lore*, pp. 20–21.

107. Assaf, *The Regal Way*, pp. 105–116; and the entry on 'capital punishment' in Unterman, *Jewish Lore*, p. 44.

108. See above, Chapter 22.

109. See L.M. Epstein, *Sex Laws and Custom in Judaism* (New York 1948), pp. 17 and 175 (emphasis added).

110. See the important discussion about the cases of 'Fairy Fay' and Margaret Hayes as outlined in Begg, *The Facts*, pp. 21–25.

111. As quoted ibid., *The Facts*, pp. 346–347.

112. Ibid., p. 267.

113. Evidence of Julia Venturney as reproduced in Evans and Skinner, *The Ultimate*, p. 407.

114. Evidence of Julia Venturney and Joseph Barnett as reproduced in Evans and Skinner, *The Ultimate*, pp. 416 and 409–410.

115. See Barnett's evidence as reproduced in Evans and Skinner, *The Ultimate*, p. 410. The reconstruction of Kelly's early life is taken almost entirely from Begg, *The Facts*, pp. 267–272, and Sugden, *The Complete History*, pp. 307–309.

116. Begg, *The Facts*, p. 298. Sugden, too, in *The Complete History*, shows admirable awareness of the potential importance of this connection; however, understandably, he concludes, 'But we know next to nothing about this or any other of Mary's early relationships' (p. 309). It is only with the benefit of hindsight, having unravelled the importance of the Book of Ezekiel in the murder of Mary Jane Kelly that one can go back and infer what the nature of the relationship between Kelly and Joe III might have been.

117. Evans and Skinner, *The Ultimate*, p. 419.

118. These accounts of the night of the murder are taken from Begg, *The Facts*, pp. 267–287; and Sugden, *The Complete History*, pp. 325–339.

119. Begg, *The Facts*, p. 292 (emphasis added).

120. Sugden, *The Complete History*, p. 315.

121. Ibid., pp. 318–319.

122. Evans and Skinner, *The Ultimate*, p. 417 (emphasis added).

123. Ezekiel, 24: 10–13.

124. Ezekiel, 24: 16.

125. Evans and Skinner, *The Ultimate*, p. 402.

126. See the *London Evening News*, 8 Dec. 1888 and *Manchester Evening News*, 10 Dec. 1888 as reproduced in the invaluable Evans and Skinner, *The Ultimate*, pp. 438–439.

127. Eddelstone, *An Encyclopedia*, p. 277. For another such overlapping, composite, picture see, for example, Sugden, *The Complete History*, p. 468.

128. Report on an 'Examination of documents at the National Archives, Windhoek', by S. Grandin, Professional Graphologist and Forensic Handwriting Examiner, 11 Nov. 2004. (Report in the possession of the author.)

129. On the letter to Lusk see, for example, Begg, *The Facts*, pp. 209–216. See also, S.P. Evans and K. Skinner, *Jack the Ripper, Letters from Hell* (Stroud 2001).

130. See D. McKie, *Jabez: The Rise and Fall of a Victorian Rogue* (London 2004), pp. 230–234 and 248; and *Weekly Dispatch* (London) 18 Nov, 1906. Dr. F.V. Engelenburg, editor of the Pretoria *Volksstem*, who took

a close interest in issues of public morality and prostitution, also specu-
lated that the Ripper might have been in Johannesburg, but in 1889. See
F.V. Engelenburg, 'A Transvaal View of the South African Question',
North American Review, Vol. 165, No. 525, Oct. 1899, p. 483.

131. *United Kingdom, 1881 Census.*

132. *Northern Daily Telegraph*, 7 Dec. 1888, as reproduced in Evans and
Skinner, *The Ultimate*, p. 437.

133. *London Evening News*, 8 Dec. 1888, as reproduced in Evans and Skinner,
The Ultimate, p. 438.

134. United Kingdom (U.K.), London, London Metropolitan Archives (L.M.A.),
County of London North, *Calendars of Convictions and Depositions 1889*,
2 Jan. 1889 – prosecution by Julius Levenson/Levenshon for theft of a
watch. From the depositions in this case, held in the MSJ/CD series, it
would seem that Isaacs was earlier prosecuted in the Barnet Police Court
on 12 Nov. (three days after the murder of Kelly) and – somewhat
puzzlingly – again, on 17 Dec. 1888, in the same court, by 'John Bennet'
for an offence that is unspecified.

135. 'The Whitechapel Murders', *London Evening News*, 8 Dec. 1888, as reproduced in Evans and Skinner, *The Ultimate*, p. 438.

136. Ibid.

137. U.K., London, L.M.A., MSJ/CD, Depositions, 2 Jan. 1889.

138. Ibid.

139. *London Evening News*, 8 Dec. 1888, as reproduced in Evans and Skinner,
The Ultimate, p. 438. There is an identical report, taken from a news
agency, reproduced in *The Times*, dated 8 Dec. 1888. The latter is not
carried in Evans and Skinner who, unfortunately, appear not to have
recorded convictions and depositions relating to Joseph Isaacs as recorded
in the London Metropolitan Archives.

140. *Northern Daily Telegraph*, 7 Dec. 1888, as reproduced in Evans and
Skinner, *The Ultimate*, pp. 437–438.

141. See reports from the *Northern Daily Telegraph* (7 Dec. 1888) and *London
Evening News* (8 Dec. 1888) as reproduced in *The Ultimate*, pp. 437–438.

142. *Manchester Evening News* 19 Dec. 1888, as reproduced in Evans and
Skinner, *The Ultimate*, p. 439.

143. On John Isaacs and his burglaries, see U.K., London, L.M.A., MSJ/CD
Depositions, J. Isaacs, 2 June (in box marked July 1887) and 21 Jan.
1888 (in box marked Feb/1, 1888). There was a second J. Isaacs, alias
'John Lazarus', active in London from 1884 to 1887 who – sentenced to
five years' penal servitude in Nov. 1887 – partly pre-dated Lis, and
appears to have been a less likely 'model' for Lis. The latter Isaacs's criminal career can also be tracked through the 'Calendars of Conviction and
Depositions' housed in the L.M.A. for the period 1884–87.

144. Genesis 22 : 1–12.
145. See especially Halperin, *Seeking Ezekiel,* pp. 167–172.
146. See, for example, Begg, *The Facts*, p. 302.
147. Ibid. p. 313 (emphasis in the original).
148. See, 'Wholesale Robbery of Overcoats', *Reynold's Newspaper*, 12 Feb. 1888.
149. On the police during this period of frenetic activity see, for example, Sugden, *The Complete History*, p. 345.
150. This is confirmed by the report in the *Northern Daily Telegraph*, 7 Dec. 1888.
151. Begg, *The Facts*, p. 314.
152. Evans and Skinner, *The Ultimate*, p. 401.
153. See Sugden, *The Complete History*, especially pp. 91–92, 102, 244–245, 369–370.
154. Whitehead and Rivett, *The Pocket Jack*, p. 66.
155. Eddelstone, *An Encyclopedia*, pp. 276–277.
156. For a list of the usual suspects see, for example, Whitehead and Rivett, *The Pocket Jack*, pp. 66–78.
157. Ibid, p. 11.

SELECT BIBLIOGRAPHY

MANUSCRIPT SOURCES

Official

Argentina
Archives of the Argentine Federal Police, Buenos Aires
PNP Series (Police Notebook Precinct) Vol. 3, File No. 188; Vol. 3, File No. 189 and Vol. 4, No. 94
Archives of the Palace of Justice, Buenos Aires
Index card record of File No. 499 of 1908
Argentine National Archives, Buenos Aires
Ministry of Foreign Affairs, Chile 1912, Box 1297
AGN Tribunal, Criminal, R–5
Latin American Centre for Migration Studies, Buenos Aires
Migration Records, Incoming ships' manifests
Penitentiary Archive, Buenos Aires
Entry Register, Unit 3

Austria
Österreichisches Staatsarchiv, Vienna
Kriegsarchiv, Gouvernements-Inspektorat, Kielce, Durchlaufer Nr. 641/JR, 1/08/1918
Kriegsarchiv, Gouvernements-Inspektorat, Kielce, Akt mit der Pers. – Nr. 17.582/J.R.

Belgium
Algemeen Rijksarchief, Brussels
File 8892 322; File 930 733; File 8892 322; File 934 796

Brazil

Arquivo Nacional, Rio de Janeiro
Fundo: DPMAF/RJ, CODES, 1915
Arquivo Casa Rui Barbosa, Rio de Janeiro
N. Hoffbauer, 'Relacao das Mulherese que exercem o meretricio em zona 12, Distrito Policial', 1923

Chile

National Archives, Santiago
Records of the Third Criminal Court of Santiago 1912, (CC3/San./1912) (uncatalogued)

France

Archives Générales de la Police Judiciaire, Paris
Warrant for the arrest of Bertha Silver, issued by Judge Larcher, dated 2 Feb. 1909, No. 378.967; Series D2U7, Register No. 27
Centre Historique des Archives Nationales
Box BB 18, F/7 14854; Notice No. 37
Archives Nationales, Paris
BB 18/14078, Dossier No. 800
Archives de Paris, Paris
Registres des Roles du Tribunal Correctional de Paris, Judgment No. 42 706/54, 22 May 1909
Registres des Roles du Tribunal Correctional de Paris, Judgment No. 42 706/54 134
Archives Départmentale de Paris, Paris
Registres d'information du parquet, Series D2U7, Register No. 23; and Register No. 27; Series 2Y14, Vol. 398, La Santé, Register 57

German South West Africa

National Archives, Windhoek
Kaizerliches Bezirksgericht Windhoek (Windhoek District Court), 1890–1915
GWI, F44/06; D56/05; F247/05; GWI 585, File D80/02; D72/05; F11.06; C202/05

Germany

Bundesarchiv, Berlin
Vol. R151F; File FC 5125; FC 5178; FC 5171 and FC 5128, R901, No. 27831
Staatsarchiv, Hamburg
Die Polizei behörde Hamburg, Abteilung IV M (Meldeamt); Tagebuch vom 21.10.1916 bis 7.6.1917, No. 14880–149000/16 und 11541/17
Verzeichnis der in den Jahren 1895–1914 aus Hamburg Ausgegangenen

Auswandererschiffe, Auswanderungsamt 1, VIII, A 4, Band III

Israel
Central Archives of the Jewish People, Jerusalem
Judah Magnus Collection, New York City, File D3/1768, 1 June–1 Dec. 1914

Poland
State Archives Kielce, Kielce
Akta Notariuse Gidlewskiego, Sygn 19, 1886, Poz. 320
SAK, Oprzanysroeyck I handlowych zaeradach w Kieltsakh; Akta m. Kielc sygn 648
SAK, Kantseliaria Gubernatora Kieletskiego, Vol. 200a, 14 Aug. 1884
Zhond Gubernialny Radomski, Vol. 6845
Zhond Gubernialny Kieletski, Vidzh, Voiskovo-Politseyny, Vol. 26a, 1879
Wojewoolzkie Archive, Warsaw
Wyolziat Sledezy, Kielecki, sygn.6, 1910
Archivum Glowne, Warsaw
Akt Dawnych, K.u.K., Divisionsgericht, Przemysl, Nameverzeichniss zu Dst/ Register, 1917–1918, 'L"/1918
Voievudskie Arkhivum, Warsaw
Kantseliara Gubernatora Kieletskiego, Zhond Gubernialny Radomski, Zhond Gubernialny Kieletski, Vidzh

Republic of South Africa
Cape Archive Depot, Cape Town
AG Series (Attorney-General Records, Colony of the Cape of Good Hope), Vol. 1531, File 12984; Vol. 1518; Vol. 1591, Vol. 1613; Vol. 1624; Vol. 1902, File 1019/02 and Vol. 1938
CO Series (Colonial Office), Vol. 22, No. 7/1156; Vol 365, Ref. 22 and Vol. 8658
CO Series (Naturalisation Papers) Vol. 8567, Ref. 22, Part 1 (1903); Vol. 8658, File 22, 1904/05 and Vol. 8579
CSC Series (Cape Supreme Court Records) Case Nos. 314 of 1904/1905; 1/1/1/59, 1904 and 1/1/1/53, 1903
CSCCR Series (Cape Supreme Court Criminal Records), Case No. 33, Case No. 38
CT Series (Records of the Resident Magistrate, Cape Town), Vol. 835, File 4660.
HAWC Series (Registers of Deaths and Marriages).
Records of the High Court of Griqualand, Kimberley
Records of the Landdrost Port Elizabeth
Free State Archives Depot, Bloemfontein
CO Series (Colonial Office), Vol. 140, File 961–03; Vol. 134, File 539/03; Vol. 206, File 203/03; Vol. 111, File 4791/02; Vol. 140, File 961/03; Vol. 143,

File No. 1181/03; Vol. 147, File 1454/03 and Vol. 155, File 5612/02.
CS Series (Colonial Secretary)
LBL Series (Landdrost Bloemfontein)
HG 4/1/2/1/2, File 8/1903, 20 Feb. 1903
KwaZulu-Natal Archives Depot, Pietermaritzburg
IRD Series (Criminal Investigation Department – Deportations), Vol. 03, File
928/1904 and Vol. 52, File 658/1906
Transvaal Archive Depot, Pretoria
AG Series (Attorney-General, Transvaal Police, Transvaal Colony Archives).
JLC Series (Johannesburg Landdrost Collection), Public Prosecutor, Incoming,
Vol. P1040, File P1940, 1899
JLC Series (Kriminele Landdrost, Inkomende Stukke), Vol. 1720, 1824 (1899)
JLC (Public Prosecutor's Collection – Incoming) Vol. 1940, File 579/99
JUS Series (Transvaal Criminal Investigation Department)
SAC Series (South African Constabulary) Vol. 23, File 8/67
SP Series (Staatsprokureur of the Zuid-Afrikaansche Republiek) File SPR
5838/99; File R0207/99; File SPR 5838/99; File R 0207/99 Vol. 813, DDM
1486/99; Vol. 204, JPR 3499/99; Vol. 193, File 1197/98; Vol. 193, File
244/99; Vol. 193, File 313/99; Vol. 196, File 580/99
UR Series (Uitvoerende Raad, Zuid-Afrikaansche Republiek), Vol. 102 (1899)
WLD Series (Witwatersrand Local Division) Vol. 5/71, File 135/96; Vol.
5/378, File 690/1921; Vol. 603, File 637/04; Vol. 5/70, File 103/1906;
Vol 39/1906
ZTPD Series (Records of the Supreme Court of the Zuid-Afrikaansche
Republiek), Vol. 3660/1898
ZTPD Series, (Criminal Cases) Vol. 3/115; Vol. 3714/1897
ZJB (Landdrost Johannesburg), Veldkornet, Register van Nuwe Aankomelinge,
Vol. 209

United Kingdom
Family Records Centre, London
Records of Births, Deaths and Marriages: Marriage of Moses Aaron Gourvitch
to Mandel Lis of 35 Plumber's Row, 11 March 1888; Marriage of Joseph
Silver, 'Detective's Agent', age 27, to Hanna Opticer, 'Spinster', age 25, 24
Oct. 1895; Birth Registration Monty Lis, 14 Aug. 1913; Birth Registration
Bernard Lis, 6 April 1915; Certified Copy of an Entry of Marriage, Certificate
No. MX 54718, Dorfman; Death, D. Dorfman, Aug. 1921
Hull City Archives, Kingston-upon-Hull
Records of the Court of Summary Jurisdiction, 1887
London Metropolitan Archives, London
County of London North, Calendars of Convictions and Depositions, 1889
Central Criminal Court, Calendar of Prisoners, 1896

Central Criminal Court, Sessions Paper, Vols 127 & 128, 1898
HO 140/234, County Court of London (North Side of the Thames), Calendar
of Prisoners tried at the Adjourned General Session, Clerkenwell, 1904
MJ/CP/B36, Middlesex Calendar of Prisoners
MJ/SR/5764, Indictment no. 70, Sessional Roll
Marlborough Police Court Records, County of London (North) Sessions, 1895
MSJ/CD Series, Depositions 1885–1889
National Archives, London, Kew
BT Series (Board of Trade, United Kingdom), Incoming and Outgoing Passenger
Manifests
FO Series (Foreign Office) Vol. 369/1557, No. 17696; No. 236 215/2
MEPO Series (Metropolitan Police, London) 6/32; 2/1312
Scottish Records Office, Glasgow
SC 1/55/33 Case 45 of 1901

United States of America
Archives of the State of New York, Albany
Annual Reports of the Superintendent of State Prisons, 1888–1890
Governor of New York State, Register of Discharge by Commutation of
Sentence, 1891
Inmate Admissions Register, Sing Sing Prison, Oct. 1889
Municipal Archives of the City of New York, New York
Court of General Sessions of the Peace, Box 460, File 4227, 1891; Box 457,
File 4205, 1891; Box 373, File 3490, 1889; Box 457, File 4204, 1895
First District, Magistrate's Court Docket Books, Roll 53, 1891
MP (Mayor's Papers), Series 89/GTF/14, 1893
NR (Naturalisation Records of the Superior Court), Bundle 487, Record No.
200
Minutes of the Court of General Sessions of the Peace, Manhattan, Roll 52,
Vol. 16, Part 1, 1893
Register of Complaints, Charge Office, Essex Street Market Court House Police
Station, 1895
*National Archives of the United States of America and Federal Record Centre,
Washington DC*
Department of State, US Legation, Belgium C.8.6, No. 7
Department of State, Diplomatic Post Records, Belgium, Record Group 84
Department of State, Passport Applications, RG 59, Vol. 813, 1895
Department of Commerce and Labour, Record Group 85, 1–G, File V52484;
Records Administration No. 36337, 10W2, Roll 218, R10, C166,
DR 2
Report on European 'White Slave' Traffic in relation to American Immigration
Laws, 2 Oct. 1909 by Marcus Braun, Record Group 85, Vol. 5284 1–G

Pennsylvania State Archives, Harrisburg
Admissions Register, Western State Penitentiary, R6–15 (Microfilm) Roll 408,
   No. 361 and 362; Roll 419, No. 3621
Discharge Description Docket, Western State Penitentiary, RG–15 (Microfilm),
   Roll 413, Register No. 299–A511, 1894
Court Records, Pittsburgh, September Sessions 1893
Minutes of the Court of the General Sessions 1893
GJI (Grand Jury Indictments, Supreme Court)
United States National Archives & Record Administration, North East Region,
   New York
Incoming Passengers, New York City, 1916–1918

Unofficial

Republic of South Africa
Companies House, Proes Street, Pretoria
The Registration Papers of the Speer Medical and Chemical Company and
   'Articles of Association'
Library of the South African Jewish Board of Deputies, Johannesburg
South African Jewish Sociological and Historical Society, 'Report of an Interview
   with Mr Louis Flavian [sic] Lezard conducted by Mrs H. Kehr', 18 Oct.
   1947

United Kingdom
University of Southampton, Hartley Library
Records of the Jewish Welfare Board, UK
JAPGW Annual Report for 1900
JAPGW Minutes of the Gentlemen's Sub-committee for the Protection of Girls
   and Women, Nov. 1896
JAPGW Minutes of the General Committee, 3 May 1900–28 Oct. 1900
JAPGW Papers, 1901

United States of America
Archives of the Industrial Society, University of Pittsburgh
Allegheny Court Dockets, Vol. 10, 1864–1926, April 1893
Court Dockets Register, 871–872, 1893

PRINTED PRIMARY SOURCES

Official Records

Deutschen Nationalkomittee: *Bericht über die Deutsche National-Konferenz zu Internationaler Bekämpfung des Mädchenhaldels*, Herausgegeben 1908

Law Reports of the Cases in the Cape Town Supreme Court 1905, Vol. XV, pp. 582–588

Lexow Committee, *Report and Proceedings of the Senate Committee to Investigate the Police Department of the City of New York*, Albany 1895, Vols 1–5.

Orange River Colony, *Ordinance 2 of 1903*, 'To Provide for the Suppression of Brothels and Immorality and to Amend the Police Offences Ordinance of 1902'

Reports of the Cases Decided in the High Court of Kimberley, Vol. 9, Jan. 1899–Dec. 1904

Transvaal Colony, *Ordinance 46 of 1903*, 'Suppression of Brothels and Immorality'

Zuid-Afrikaansche Republiek, *Wet No. 23, 1898, to amend and supplement Law No. 2 of 1897'*

Newspapers and Periodicals

Argentina
El Censor
Gaceto del Foro
La Prensa
Las Ultimas Noticias
Tribuna

Belgium
Etoile Belge
La Dernière Heure
Le Patriote

Chile
El Mercurio
La Unión
Las Ultimas Noticias

France
Le Petit Parisien
Le Petit Journal

Germany
Echo der Gegenwart
Hamburger Nachrichten

German South West Africa
Deutsch Südwestafrika Zeitung
Windhuker Nachrichten (Südwestbote)

Israel
The Jerusalem Report

Japan
Japan Weekly Mail

Poland
Gazeta Kielecka
Widnokrag

Republic of South Africa
Bloemfontein Post
Bloemfontein Press
Cape Times
Diamond Fields' Advertiser
Eastern Province Herald
Johannesburg Times
South African News
Standard & Diggers' News
The Argus
The Friend
The Looker-On
The Star
Volksstem

United Kingdom
East London Advertiser
East London Observer
Hampshire Telegraph

London Evening News
Manchester Evening News
Northern Daily Telegraph
Reynolds' Newspaper
The Hull News
The People
Weekly Dispatch

United States of America
Morning Journal
New York Daily
New York Mercury
New York Press
New York Times
New York World
Pittsburgh Commercial Gazette
The Morning Journal
The New York Recorder
The Pittsburgh Press
The Press
The Sun
The World

SECONDARY SOURCES

Dictionaries and Directories

Beyers, C.J. and Basson, J.L. (eds), Suid-Afrikaanse Biografiese Woordeboek, Deel V, Pretoria 1987

De Kock, W.J. (ed.), Die Suid-Afrikaanse Biografiese Woordeboek, Deel I, Cape Town 1968

De Kock, W.J. and Kruger, D.W. (eds), Dictionary of South African Biography, Vol. II, Cape Town 1972

Dieffenbacher, J.F., Directory of Pittsburgh and Allegheny Cities 1889–1895, (Annual Issues 34–40)

The Post Office London Directory, 1895–98

Trow's New York Directory, 1890–94

Unterman, A., Dictionary of Jewish Lore and Legend, London 1991

Urbanski, K., Leksykon: Dziejòw Ludnosci Zydowskiej Kielc 1789–1999, Kraków 2000

Urbanski, K. and Blumenfeld R., The Dictionary of the Kielce Jews, Kielce 1995

Zylbercweig, Z., Lekiskon fun Yidishn Teatre, Vol. 3, New York 1959

Select Books

Adam, H.L., *Trial of George Chapman*, London 1930

American Jewish Committee, *The Jews in the Eastern War Zone*, New York, 1916

Anonymous, *Life in Sing Sing*, New York 1904

Ascherson, N., *The King Incorporated: Leopold II in the Age of Trusts*, New York 1964

Avni, H., *Argentina & The Jews: A History of Jewish Immigration*, London 1991

Begg, P., *Jack the Ripper: The Facts*, London 2004

Biale, D., *Eros and the Jews*, New York 1992

Bickford-Smith, V., *Ethnic Pride and Racial Prejudice in Victorian Cape Town, Group Identity and Social Practice, 1875–1902*, Cambridge 1995

Blackbourn, D., *The Fontana History of Germany, 1780–1918*, London 1997

Bley, H., *Namibia under German Rule*, Hamburg 1996

Bodnar, J., Simon, R. and Weber, M.P., *Lives of their Own: Blacks, Italians and Poles in Pittsburgh, 1900–1960*, Chicago 1982

Bourgoyne, A.G., *The Homestead Strike of 1892*, Pittsburgh 1893

Bra, G., *La Organización Negra: La Increible Historia de la Zwi Migdal*, Buenos Aires 1999

Bristow, E.J., *Prostitution and Prejudice, The Jewish Fight against White Slavery, 1870–1939*, Oxford 1982

Bristow, E.J., *Vice and Vigilance: Purity Movements in Britain since 1700*, London 1977

Cain, P.J. and Hopkins, A.G., *British Imperialism, Innovation and Expansion, 1688–1914*, London 1993

Cammack, D., *The Rand at War, 1899–1902: The Witwatersrand and the Anglo-Boer War*, London 1990

Caron, F., *An Economic History of Modern France*, London 1979

Castro, D.S., *The Development and Politics of Argentine Immigration Policy, 1852–1914*, San Francisco 1991

Chesney, K., *The Victorian Underworld*, Harmondsworth 1972

Clapham, J.H., *The Economic Development of France and Germany, 1815–1914*, Cambridge 1966

Cleaver, F.R.M. (edited by 'His Mother'), *A Young South African: A Memoir of Ferrar Reginald Mostyn Cleaver; Advocate and Veldcornet*, Johannesburg 1913

Cleckley, H., *The Mask of Sanity: An Attempt to Clarify some Issues about the so-called Psychopathic Personality*, St Louis 1950

Collier, S. and Sater, W.F., *A History of Chile, 1808–1994*, Cambridge 1996

Connelly, M.T., *The Response to Prostitution in the Progressive Era*, Chapel Hill 1980

Cordasco, F. and Pitkin, T.M., *The White Slave Trade and the Immigrants: A Chapter in American Social History*, New York 1981

Couvares, F.C., *The Remaking of Pittsburgh: Class and Culture in an Industrializing City*, Albany 1984

Curtis, L.P., *Jack the Ripper and the London Press*, London 2001

Cytron, P., *Sefer Kielce: Toldot Kehilat Kielce, Miyom Hivsuduh V'ad Churbanah*, Tel Aviv 1957

Davies, N., *God's Playground: A History of Poland in Two Volumes, Vol. II, 1795 to the Present*, Oxford 1981

Davies, N., *Heart of Europe: A Short History of Poland*, New York 1984

Douglas, M., *Purity and Danger: An Analysis of the Concepts of Pollution and Taboo*, London 1966

Eddlestone, J.J., *Jack the Ripper, An Encyclopaedia*, London 2002

Eisenbach, A., *Emancipation of the Jews in Poland*, Oxford 1991

Ellis, E.R., *The Epic of New York City*, New York 1966

Epstein, L.M., *Sex Laws and Customs in Judaism*, New York 1948

Escobedo, A.G., *La Prostitución en Santiago, 1813–1931*, Santiago 1994

Evans, S.P. and Skinner, K., *Jack the Ripper, Letters from Hell*, Stroud 2001

Evans, S.P. and Skinner, K., *The Ultimate Jack the Ripper Source Book: An Illustrated Encyclopaedia*, London 2000

Feldman, D., *Englishman and Jews; Social Relations and Political Culture, 1840–1914*, London 1994

Fido, M., *The Crimes, Detection and Death of Jack the Ripper*, London 1987

Fisher, T., *Prostitution and the Victorians*, New York 1997

Fishman, W.J., *East End 1888: A Year in a London Borough amongst the Labouring Poor*, London 1988

Fishman, W.J., *East End Jewish Radicals, 1875–1914*, London 1975

Fishman, W.J. and Breach, N., *The Streets of East London*, London 1979

Freeze, C.Y., *Jewish Marriage and Divorce in Imperial Russia*, Hanover Mass. 2002

Freyre, G., *Order and Progress: Brazil from Monarchy to Republic*, New York 1970

Fried, A., *The Rise and Fall of the Jewish Gangster in America*, New York 1993

Gardner, C.W., *The Doctor and the Devil, or Midnight Adventures of Dr Parkhurst*, New York City 1894

Gelder, M.G., López-Ibor, J.J. and Andreasen, N. (eds), *New Oxford Textbook of Psychiatry*, Oxford 2000

Gewald, J.B., *Herero Heroes: A Socio-political History of the Herero of Namibia, 1890–1923*, Ohio 1999

Gilfoyle, T.J., *City of Eros: New York City, Prostitution and the Commercialization of Sex, 1790–1920*, New York 1992

Gilman, S.L., *Jewish Self-hatred: Anti Semitism and the Hidden Language of the Jews*, London 1986

Goldblatt, I., *History of South West Africa from the Beginning of the Nineteenth Century*, Cape Town 1970

Goren, A.A., *New York Jews and the Quest for Community: The Kehillah Experiment, 1908–1922*, New York 1970

Gross, J., *A Double Thread: Growing up English and Jewish in London*, London 2001

Guldon, Z. and Massalski, A., *Historia Kielc do roku 1945*, Kielce 2000

Guy, D.J., *Sex & Danger in Buenos Aires: Prostitution, Family and Nation in Argentina*, London 1991

Halperin, D.J. *Seeking Ezekiel: Text and Psychology* (The Pennsylvania State University Press 1993).

Hare, R.D., *Manual for the Hare Psychopathy Checklist – Revised*, Toronto 1991

Hayden, D., *Pox: Genius, Madness and the Mysteries of Syphilis*, New York 2003

Heinze, A.R., *Adapting to Abundance: Jewish Immigrants, Mass Consumption, and the Search for American Identity*, New York 1990

Hobsbawm, E.J., *Industry and Empire*, London 1968

Hochschild, A., *King Leopold's Ghost*, Oxford 1999

Howard, M., *The First World War*, Oxford 2002

Howe, I. (with the assistance of Libo, K.), *The Immigrant Jews of New York, 1881 to the Present*, London 1976

Howe, I., *World of Our Fathers: The Journey of East European Jews to America and the Life They Found and Made*, New York 1997

Howells, M. and Skinner, K., *The Ripper Legacy: The Life and Death of Jack the Ripper*, London 1987

Hyman, P., *From Dreyfus to Vichy: The Remaking of French Jewry, 1906–1939*, New York 1979

Joll, J., *The Origins of the First World War*, London 1984

Joselit, J.W., *Our Gang: Jewish Crime and the New York Jewish Community, 1900–1940*, Bloomington 1983

Jukes, G., *The First World War: The Eastern Front, 1914–1918*, Oxford 2002

Kaplan, M.A., *The Jewish Feminist Movement in Germany: The Campaigns of the Jüdischer Frauenbund, 1904–1938*, London 1979

Kleinberg, S.J., *The Shadow of the Mills: Working Class Families in Pittsburgh, 1870–1907*, Pittsburgh 1989

Kneeland, G.J., *Commercialised Prostitution in New York City*, New York 1913

Kraepelin, E. *General Paresis* (New York 1913)

Lardner, J. and Reppetto, T., *NYPD: A City and its Police*, New York 2000

Lawes, L.E., *Twenty Thousand Years in Sing Sing*, New York 1942

Lesser, J., *Welcoming the Undesirables: Brazil and the Jewish Question*, London 1995

Lewis, W.D., *From Newgate to Dannemora. The Rise of the Penitentiary in New York, 1796–1848*, Ithaca 1965

Liddell Hart, B.H., *History of the First World War*, London 1982

Linnane, F., *London's Underworld: Three Centuries of Vice and Crime*, London 2003

Lishman, W.A., *Organic Psychiatry: The Psychological Consequences of Cerebral Disorder*, Oxford 1998

Lloyd-Jones, R. and Lewis, M.J., *British Industrial Capitalism since the Industrial Revolution*, London 1998

Londres, A., *The Road to Buenos Aires: The White Slave Traffic*, New York 1928

Macintyre, B., *The Napoleon of Crime: The Life and Times of Adam Worth, Master Thief*, New York 1997

Maritz, S.G., *My Lewe en Strewe*, Pretoria 1939

Massmann, U., *Swakopmund: A Chronicle of the Town's People, Places and Progress*, Swakopmund 1983

McKie, D., *Jabez: The Rise and Fall of a Victorian Rogue*, London 2004

Mendoza, A., *Killers on the Loose: Unsolved Cases of Serial Murder*, London 2000

Morn, F., *'The Eye That Never Sleeps': A History of the Pinkerton National Detective Agency*, Bloomington 1982

Moss, F., *The American Metropolis from Knickerbocker Days to the Present Time: New York City Life in all its Various Phases*, New York 1897

Nathans, B., *Beyond the Pale: The Jewish Encounter with Late Imperial Russia*, London 2001

Oermann, N.O., *Mission Church and State Relations in South West Africa under German Rule, 1884–1915*, Stuttgart 1999

Opalski, M. and Bartal, I., *Poles and Jews, A Failed Brotherhood*, Hanover 1992

Pakenham, T., *The Boer War*, London 1979

Panyani, P. (ed.), *Minorities in Wartime: National and Racial Groupings in Europe, North America and Australia during World Wars*, Oxford 1993

Pazdur, J., *Dzieje Kielc, 1864–1939*, Warsaw 1971

Polonsky, A., Basista, J. and Link-Lenczowski, A. (eds), *The Jews of Old Poland, 1000–1795*, London 1984

Porter, R., *London, A Social History*, London 1994

Reed, J., *War in Eastern Europe: Travels through the Balkans in 1915*, London 1994

Richardson, J.F., *The New York Police, Colonial Times to 1901*, New York 1970

Rischin, M., *The Promised City: New York's Jews, 1870–1914*, Cambridge Mass. 1962

Rock, D., *Argentina, 1516–1987: From Spanish Colonization to Alfonsin*, Berkeley 1987

Rock, D., *Politics in Argentina, 1890–1930: The Rise and Fall of Radicalism*, Cambridge 1975

Roskies, D.K. and Roskies, D.G., *The Shtetl Book: An Introduction to East European Jewish Life and Lore*, New York 1975

Roth, C. and Widoger, G. (eds), *Encyclopaedia Judaica, Vol. 10*, Jerusalem 1971

Rubinstein, W.D., *A History of the Jews in the English-speaking World: Great Britain*, London 1996

Rumbelow, D., *The Complete Jack the Ripper*, London 1988

Sadock, B.J. and Alcott Sadock, V.A., *Kaplan and Sadock's Synopsis of Psychiatry: Behavioural Sciences/Clinical Psychiatry, 9th Edition*, New York 1998

Sandrow, N., *Vagabond Stars: A World History of Yiddish Theatre*, Syracuse 1977

Sante, L., *Low Life: Lures and Snares of Old New York*, New York 1991

Scobie, J.R., *Argentina: A City and a Nation*, London 1978

Shain, M., *Jewry and Cape Society: The Origins and Activities of the Jewish Board of Deputies for the Cape Colony*, Cape Town 1983

Shain, M., *The Roots of Antisemitism in South Africa*, Charlottesville 1994

Sifakis, E., *The Encyclopedia of American Crime*, New York 1982

Sonnenberg, M., *The Way I Saw It*, Cape Town 1957

Soyer, D., *Jewish Immigrant Associations and American Identity in New York, 1880–1939*, London 1997

Stead, P.J., *Pioneers in Policing*, London 1977

Stedman Jones, G., *Outcast London: A Study in the Relationships between Classes in Victorian Society*, Harmondsworth 1971

Steffens, L., *The Shame of the Cities*, New York 1992

Stephenson, G., *A History of Russia*, London 1969

Stone, N., *The Eastern Front, 1914–1917*, London 1998

Sugden, P., *The Complete History of Jack the Ripper*, London 2002

Thomas, D., *The Victorian Underworld*, New York 1998

Tindall, G.B. and Shi, D.E., *America: A Narrative History*, New York 1993

Transvaal White Cross Purity League, *Delicate Matters: An Open Letter Addressed to Dr F.W. Engelenburg by the Rev. C. Spoelstra*, Johannesburg 1896

Turnbull, M.J., *Victims or Villains: Jewish Images in Classic English Detective Fiction*, Bowling Green 1988

Van Onselen, C., *New Babylon, New Nineveh: Everyday Life on the Witwatersrand, 1886–1914*, Johannesburg 2001

Van Onselen, C., *The Small Matter of a Horse: The Life of 'Nongoloza' Mathebula, 1867–1948*, Johannesburg 1984

Vincent, I., *Bodies and Souls: The Tragic Plight of Three Jewish Women Forced into Prostitution in the Americas* (New York 2005)

Walkowitz, J.R., *City of Dreadful Delight: Narratives of Sexual Danger in Late-Victorian London*, Chicago 1992

Walkowitz, J.R., *Prostitution and Victorian Society: Women, Class and the State*, New York 1980

Wasserstein, B., *The Secret Lives of Trebitsch Lincoln*, London 1988

Watson, E.R., *Adolf Beck, 1877–1906*, London 1925

Wertheimer, J., *Unwelcome Strangers: East European Jews in Imperial Germany*, Oxford 1987

White, J., *Rothschild Buildings: Life in an East End Tenement Block, 1887–1920*. London 1980

Worger, W.H., *South Africa's City of Diamonds: Mine Workers and Monopoly Capitalism in Kimberley, 1867–1895*, New Haven 1987

Wright, E.S., *A Brief History of the Western State Penitentiary*, Pittsburgh 1909

Wright, G., *France in Modern Times: 1760 to the Present*, London 1962

Zborowski, M. and Herzog, E. *Life is with People: The Culture of the Shtetl*, New York 1952

Articles and Chapters in Books

Abrahams, L., 'Prostitutes in Imperial Germany, 1870–1918: Working Girls or Social Outcasts', in Evans, R.J. (ed.), *The German Underworld: Deviants and Outcasts*, London 1988, pp. 190–196

Aronson, M., 'The Anti-Jewish Pogroms in Russia in 1881,' in Klier, J.D. and Lambroza, S. (eds), *Pogroms: Anti-Jewish Violence in Modern Russian History*, Cambridge 1992, pp. 41–61

Belling, V., 'The Golden Years of Yiddish Theatre in South Africa, 1902–1910', *Jewish Affairs*, Rosh Hoshana 2000, pp. 7–14

Biale, D., 'Childhood, Marriage and the Family in the Eastern European Jewish Enlightenment', in Cohen, S.M. and Hyman, P.E. (eds), *The Jewish Family, Myths and Reality*, New York 1986, pp. 45–61

Blackwelder, J.K. and Johnson, L.L., 'Changing Criminal Patterns in Buenos Aires, 1890–1914', *Journal of Latin American Studies*, Vol. 14, Part 2, 1982 pp. 359–379

Bra, G., 'La Mutual de los Rufianes', *Todo es Historio*, No. 121, 1999, pp. 75–91

Brittain, R.P., 'The Sadistic Murderer', *Medicine, Science and the Law*, No. 10, 1970, pp. 198–207

Caulfield, S., 'The Birth of Mangue: Race, Nation and the Politics of Prostitution in Rio de Janeiro, 1850–1942', in Balderson, D. and Guy, D.J. (eds), *Sex and Sexuality in Latin America*, New York 1997, pp. 86–100

Czitrom, D., 'Underworlds and Underdogs: Big Tim Sullivan and Metropolitan

Politics in New York, 1889–1913', *Journal of American History*, Vol. 78, No. 2, 1991 pp. 536–558

Davis, S., 'Yiddische Voortrekkers of SWA.', *Southern African Jewish Times*, Dec. 1958 p. 46

Dedering, T., '"A Certain Rigorous Treatment of All Parts of the Nation": The Annihilation of the Herero in German South West Africa, 1904', in Levene, M. and Roberts, P. (eds), *The Massacre in History*. New York 1999, pp. 205–222

Dedering, T., 'The Ferreira Raid of 1906: Boers, Britons and Germans in Southern Africa in the Aftermath of the South African War', *Journal of Southern African Studies*, Vol. 26, No. 1, March 2000, pp. 43–60

Dedering, T., 'The German–Herero War of 1904: Revisionism of Genocide or Imaginary Historiography', *Journal of Southern African Studies*, Vol. 19, No. 1, 1993 pp. 80–89.

Dedering, T., 'The Prophet's War, "War Against the Whites": Shepherd Stuurman in Namibia and South Africa, 1904–1907', *Journal of African History*, Vol. 40, No. 1, 1999, pp. 1–19.

De La Fuente Silva, H., 'The White Slave Trade in Chile', *Police Review*, Valparaiso, Year VII No. 86, March 1913, pp. 28–32; No. 91, Aug. 1913, pp. 55–64; No. 92, Sept. 1913, pp. 38–44 and No. 95, Dec. 1913, pp. 42–9

De Ramón, A., 'Securidad y Moralidad Publicas', in De Ramón, A. and Gross, P. (eds), *Santiago de Chile: Caracteristicas Historico Ambientales, 1891–1924*, London 1985, pp. 39–62

Dewhurst, K., 'The Neurosyphilitic Psychoses Today', *British Journal of Psychiatry*, No. 115, 1969, pp. 31–38

Dinwiddie, S.H., 'Genetics, Antisocial Personality and Criminal Responsibility', *Bulletin of American Academy, Psychiatry and Law*, Vol. 24, No. 1, 1996, pp. 95–108

Dutton, D.G. and Kerry, G., 'Modus Operandi and Personality Disorder in Incarcerated Spousal Killers', *International Journal of Law and Psychiatry*, Vol. 22, Nos 3–4, 1999, pp. 287–299

Friedli, A., Chavaz, P. and Harms, M., 'Alopecia Syphilitica: Report of Two Cases in Geneva', *Dermatology*, 2001, Vol. 202, No. 4, p. 376

Gartner, L.P., 'Anglo-Jewry and the Jewish International Traffic in Prostitution, 1885–1914', *Association for Jewish Studies Review*, Vol. 78, 1982–83, pp. 129–178

Geberth, V.J. and Turco, R.N., 'Antisocial Personality Disorder, Sexual Sadism, Malignant Narcissism and Serial Murder', *Journal of Forensic Sciences*, Vol. 4, No. 1, 1997, pp. 49–60

Gilfoyle, T.J., 'A Pickpocket's Tale: George Appo and the Urban Underworlds of Nineteenth Century America', *Missouri Review*, Vol. 16, No. 2, 1993, pp. 34–77

Glovka, E., 'State Power and Local Interests', in *Central European History*, Vol. 3, 1986, pp. 293–313

Goren, A.A., 'Saints and Sinners: The Underside of American Jewish History', *Brochure Series of the American Jewish Archives*, No. 7, 1988, pp. 1–28

Hare, R.D., 'Psychopathy and Antisocial Personality Disorder: A Case of Diagnostic Confusion', *Psychiatric Times*, Vol. 13, No. 2, Feb. 1996, pp. 39–40

Holmes, K.K., 'Spirochetal Diseases', in Harrison, T.R. (ed.), *Principles of Internal Medicine*, New York, 9th edition, 1980, pp. 716–726

Johnson, B.R. and Becker, J., 'Natural Born Killers? The Development of the Sexually Sadistic Serial Killer', *Journal of the American Academy, Psychiatry and Law*, Vol. 25, No. 3, 1997, pp. 335–348

Keppel, R.D., Weiss, J.G., Brown, K.M. and Welch, K., 'The Jack the Ripper Murders: A Modus Operandi and Signature Analysis of the 1888–1891 Whitechapel Murders', *Journal of Investigative Psychology and Offender Profiling*, No. 2, 2005, pp. 1–25

Kleppner, P., 'Government, Parties and Voters in Pittsburgh', in Hays, S.P. (ed.), *City at the Point: Essays on the Social History of Pittsburgh*, Pittsburgh 1989, pp. 151–163

Krut, R., 'The Making of the South African Jewish Community in Johannesburg, 1886–1914', in Bozzoli, B. (ed.), *Class, Community and Conflict: South African Perspectives*, Johannesburg 1987, pp. 135–159

Kushner, T., 'The Impact of British Anti-Semitism, 1918–1945', in Cesarani, D. (ed.), *The Making of Modern Anglo-Jewry*, Oxford 1990, pp. 191–208

Kushner, T., 'Sex and Semitism: Jewish Women in Britain in War and Peace', in Panyani, P. (ed.), *Minorities in Wartime: National and Racial Groupings in Europe, North America and Australia during World Wars*, Oxford 1993, pp. 118–132

Landau, J., 'The Diary of Rabbi Jeruzalimski from the Days in the First World War', in Cytron, P. (ed.), *Sefer Kielce: Toldot Kehilat Kielce, Miyom Hivsuduh V'ad Churbanah*, Tel Aviv 1957, pp. 271–295

Landes, R. and Zborowski, M., 'Hypotheses concerning the East European Jewish Family', *Psychiatry*, Vol. 4, No. 13, Nov. 1950, pp. 447–463

Langevin, R., 'A Study of the Psychosexual Characteristics of Sex Killers: Can We Identify Them Before It Is Too Late', *International Journal of Offender Therapy and Comparative Criminology*, 2003, pp. 366–382

Lindenthal, J.J., 'Abi Gezunt: Health and the Eastern European Jewish Immigrant', *American Jewish History*, Vol. 4, No. 70, 1981, pp. 420–441

Lundrigan, S. and Canter, D., 'Research Report: Spatial Patterns of Serial Murder; An Analysis of Disposal Site Location Choice', *Behavioural Sciences and the Law*, No. 19, 2001, pp. 595–610

MacCulloch, M.J., Gray, N. and Watt, A., 'Britain's Sadistic Murderer Syndrome Reconsidered: An Associative Account of the Aetiology of

Sadistic Sexual Fantasy', *Journal of Forensic Psychiatry*, Vol. 11, No. 2, 2000, pp. 401–408

MacCulloch, M.J., Snowden, P.R., Wood, P.J.W. and Mills, H.E., 'Sadistic Fantasy, Sadistic Behaviour and Offending', *British Journal of Psychiatry*, No. 143, 1983, pp. 20–29

MacKinnon, M., 'Living Standards, 1870–1914', in Floud, R. and McCloskey, D.N., *The Economic History of Britain since 1700, Vol. 2*, Cambridge 1994, pp. 265–289

Markel, H., '*Di Golden Medina*: Historical Perspectives of Eugenics and the East European (Ashkenazi) Jewish-American Community, 1880–1925', *Health-Matrix: Journal of Law-Medicine*, Vol. 7, No. 1, 1997, pp. 49–64

McLaughlin, R.J., 'Interpreting "Lipski"', *Ripperologist*, March 2003, pp. 3–6

Mirelman, V.A., 'The Jewish Community versus Crime: The Case of White Slavery in Buenos Aires', *Jewish Social Studies*, Vol. 46, 1984, pp. 1–57

Moya, J.C., 'The Positive Side of Stereotypes: Jewish Anarchists in Early-Twentieth-Century Buenos Aires', *Jewish History*, Vol. 18, 2004, pp. 19–48

Pierard, R.V., 'The Transportation of White Women to German South West Africa, 1898–1914', *Race*, Vol. 12, No. 3, Jan. 1971, pp. 317–322

Platt, D.C.M., 'Canada and Argentina: The First Preference of the British Investor, 1904–14', *Journal of Commonwealth and Imperial History*, Vol. 13, No. 3, May 1985, pp. 77–92

Posel, R., '"Continental Women" and Durban's "Social Evil"', *Journal of Natal and Zulu History*, Vol. 12, 1989, pp. 1–13

Reilly, J.J.S., 'Los Apaches' *Fray Mocho*, No. 3, 17 May 1912

Revitch, E., 'Sex Murder and the Potential Sex Murderer', *Diseases of the Nervous System*, Vol. 26, No. 10, Oct. 1965, pp. 640–648

Roberts, M.C. and Emsley, R.A., 'Psychiatric Manifestations of Neurosyphilis', *South African Medical Journal*, Vol. 82, Nov. 1982, pp. 335–337

Rubinstein, W.D., 'The Hunt for Jack the Ripper', *History Today*, Vol. 50, No. 5, May 2000, pp. 10–19

Sanchez, J., 'Social Crises and Psychopathy: Towards a Sociology of the Psychopath', in Reid, W.H., Dorr, D., Walker, J.I. and Bonner J.W., *Unmasking the Psychopath: Antisocial Personality and Related Syndromes*, New York, 1986, pp. 78–97

Shain, M., 'Diamonds, Pogroms and Undesirables – Anti-alienism and Legislation in the Cape Colony, 1890–1906', *South African Historical Journal*, Vol. 12, Nov. 1980, pp. 13–28

Sherman, J., 'Serving the Natives: Whiteness and the Price of Hospitality in South African Yiddish Literature', *Journal of Southern African Studies*, Vol. 26, No. 3, Sept. 2000, pp. 505–521

Simonoff, E., Elander, J., Holmshaw, J., Pickels, A., Murray, R. and Rutter, M., 'Predictors of Antisocial Personality: Continuities from Childhood to

Adult Life', *British Journal of Psychiatry*, No. 184, 2004, pp. 118–127

Sorkin, D., 'The Port Jew: Notes toward a Social Type', *Journal of Jewish Studies*, Vol. 1, No. 1, Spring 1999, pp. 87–97

Spencer, E.G., 'State Powers and Local Interests in Prussian Cities: Police in the Düsseldorf District, 1848–1914', *Central European History*, No. 3, 1986, pp. 293–313

Stead, W.T., 'Satan's Invisible World Displayed or Despairing Democracy: A Study of Greater New York', *Review of Reviews Annual*, London 1898, pp. 57–158

Steinlauf, M.F.C., 'Fear of Purim: Y.L. Peretz and the Canonization of Yiddish Theatre', *Jewish Social Studies*, Vol. 1, No. 3, Spring 1995, pp. 46–65

Stone, M.H., 'Serial Sexual Homicide: Biological, Psychological and Sociological Aspects', *Journal of Personality Disorders*, Vol. 15, No. 1, 2001, pp. 1–18

Turner, G.K., 'The Daughters of the Poor', *McClure's Magazine*, No. 34, 1909, pp. 45–61

Van Heyningen, E.B., 'The Social Evil in the Cape Colony 1868–1902: Prostitution and the "Contagious Diseases Act"', *Journal of Southern African Studies*, Vol. 10, No. 2, April 1984, pp. 170–199

Van Onselen, C., 'Jewish Marginality in the Atlantic World: Organised Crime in the Era of the Great Migrations 1880–1914', *South African Historical Journal*, No. 43, Nov. 2000, pp. 96–137

Van Onselen, C., 'The Modernisation of the Kruger State: F.E.T. Krause, J.C. Smuts and the Struggle for the Control of the Johannesburg Public Prosecutor's Office, 1898–1899', *Law and History Review*, Vol. 21, No. 3, Fall 2003, pp. 483–526

Warnke, N., 'Immigrant Popular Culture as Contested Sphere: Yiddish Music Halls, the Yiddish Press and the Processes of Americanization, 1900–1910', *Theatre Journal*, Vol. 48, No. 3, 1996 pp. 321–335

Weinberg, D., '"Heureux comme Dieu en France!": East European Jewish Immigrants in Paris, 1881–1914', in Frankel, J. (ed.), *Studies in Contemporary Jewry*, Bloomington, 1984, pp. 26–54

Select Websites

www.geocities.com/Hollywood/2082/history1.htm. (The History of Kielce Jewish Community)

www.geocities.com/Hollywood/2082/history4.htm (The History of Kielce Jewish Community)

www.geocities.com/Hollywood/2082/slownjk.htm (The History of Kielce Jewish Community)

www.jewishgen.org/Yizkor/kielce'Kie271.htm (The Book of Kielce)

www.jewishgen.org/krsig/YearOne.html (The Journal of the Kielce-Radom Special Interest Group)

www.jewishgen.org/krsig/YearTwo.html (The Journal of the Kielce-Radom Special Interest Group)
www.umkielce.pl/um-english/history-a.html (Urzad Miasta Kielce)

Select Unpublished Articles and Dissertations

Czitrom, D., 'Our Police Protectors: Authority and Corruption in Turn of the Century New York', unpublished paper presented to the Organization of American Historians, Chicago, 29 March 1996

Feldman, B.I., 'Social Life of Cape Town Jewry, 1904–1914, with special reference to the Eastern European Immigrant Community', BA (Hons.) thesis, University of Cape Town 1984

Hallett, R., 'Policemen, Pimps and Prostitutes – Public Morality and Police Corruption, Cape Town, 1902–1904,' paper presented to the History Workshop Conference, University of the Witwatersrand, 3–7 Feb. 1978

Mirelman, V.A., 'The Jews in Argentina, 1890–1930, Assimilation and Particularism', unpublished D.Phil., University of Columbia, 1973

Newman, A., 'The Union Castle Line and Emigration from Eastern Europe to South Africa', unpublished seminar paper, University of Southampton, 1988

Newman, A. (with the assistance of N. Evans), 'Trains and Shelters and Ships', unpublished seminar paper, 1998, presented to a meeting of the Jewish Genealogical Society of Great Britain, 1999

Saron, G., 'The "Mortality Question" in South Africa' unpublished and undated mss.

ACKNOWLEDGEMENTS

The research for this book started, almost in a fit of absent-mindedness, in 1978 and never stopped, even when I digressed to work on another project for several years. In 1999, June Sinclair was instrumental in my joining the University of Pretoria and for securing for me conditions of employment and a working environment in which a project of this nature could be pursued in the most professional manner possible. Without her assistance and encouragement, along with that of Professors Johan van Zyl and Calie Pistorius, the two Vice Chancellors with whom it has been my pleasure to work, this protracted project would never have been brought to completion. Modern university administrators chant mantras about scholarship, the search for truth and the importance of the book (as opposed to the article), but seldom understand its implications. Few researchers believe them since doing so requires trust, as well as an investment in time and money that the same bureaucratic Brahmins are called upon to avoid in the name of a dull factory-like efficiency. The University of Pretoria has provided me with a research home without parallel. If there is merit in this work, most of the credit belongs to a far-sighted, supportive institution and my colleagues.

I have a special affection for the University of Oxford and it is fitting that this book was brought to a completion there. I would like to thank the managers of the Oppenheimer Fund for a grant which allowed me to complete my research there in 2005. There can be no finer setting in which to write than Magdalen College and my attachment there as a Visiting Fellow allowed me to focus on the work at an important time. I am indebted to the President and Fellows for their assistance and hospitality.

Research, surely the most satisfying of all intellectual activities, is something that can be done, undertaken or conducted. The largest part of the work for this book, the subject of whom made it his life's work to conceal, dissemble and lie, was done by me and undertaken in many settings using a wide range of sources. But some of the most valuable labour was merely conducted by me, at a distance. I held the baton, but the music that flowed came from a superbly talented, international, ensemble. Many years ago Jerzy Szczepánski played a crucial role in initiating this study. Without his assistance and enthusiasm nothing would have followed. John Stoner, so able and so thorough, retrieved fragments of Silver's life in New York City and Pittsburgh that enriched the study; as did Hartwig Stein in Berlin, Georgina Hamilton in London, Alide Dasnois in Paris, and William Martins in Rio de Janeiro. The chapters on Santiago and Valparaiso would not have been possible were it not for the support of the generous Carlos Cousino and help of Jaime Rosenblitt. I cannot stress sufficiently how much my understanding of the way in which members of the international underworld operated in Buenos Aires owes to Gabriela Braccio. She is one of those rare researchers who can put together imaginative links in ways that elude lesser mortals. I would be delighted if all of these talented colleagues approve of the score.

If history is another country, it is best visited with knowledgeable guides. Ed Bristow has supported my enquiries into the nature of the 'white slave' traffick for longer than he would care to remember. It was Josh Brown, patient and ever helpful, who pointed me in the direction of Dan Czitrom. Nobody could possibly know more about the career politics and characters of New York City and its Police Department than does he. Likewise, John Hinshaw advised me to seek the counsel of Joel Tarr and Joe Trotter, who then helped me find my way around some of Pittsburgh's past. Understanding Poland, let alone the history of the Jews in that country, is an undertaking which I will never master. Any sense in the way I have approached these topics owes much to one of my tutors-at-a-distance, Antony Polonsky. There is no one of Jewish descent, alive or dead, who Saul Issroff either does not know personally, or does not know how to trace in two moves. Robert Kaplan is a fine forensic psychiatrist and has great sensitivity to the problems that arise when an historian gropes his way towards psycho-biography. None of these remarkable people are responsible for the errors that might still lurk in this work. I do hope, however, that colleagues and friends will see how their advice and guidance have moulded this study into a more rounded shape than it might otherwise have been.

I am chronically anaemic when writing – a real desk dracula – forever in need of the red juices of advice, encouragement, help and support. Unsuspecting colleagues and friends, now all slightly paler of hue, include Keith Beavon, Helen Bradford, Jim Campbell, Bill Hamilton, Bill Johnson, Jeanette Kruger, Milton Shain and June Sinclair. I would also like to record my thanks to Beth Humphries, Ros Porter, Elisabeth Sifton and Will Sulkin. They have all been generous with critical suggestions and professional insights, and their sharp observations have saved me from many sloppy formulations. There are others, I fear, who have been bled quite dry. None were more encouraging, or understanding of the scale I was working on, than Tim Couzens, Patrick Pearson, Ian Phimister and Stanley Trapido. Without my friends' curiosity and unbridled enthusiasm for this project it would have died with the completion of each draft chapter. It would be remiss of me, however, if I were not to single out Paul la Hausse, a remarkably talented historian, for having given his all both to assist and to spur me on. Paul has the enviable ability to squeeze liquid from the hardest archival rocks, a sharp eye for telling detail, and an irrepressible enthusiasm for the genre of biography which he commands with authority, persuasiveness and skill.

I must record my thanks to my sister, Cherie, for her unflagging support in this and other endeavours. She will appreciate why I would have so liked for my father and mother to have been around to see the conclusion of a project which they, too, urged on in their own inimitable ways. She too would understand why I say that its those that venture closest to the fire who are most likely to be burnt. None have been more vulnerable to the unpredictable changes emanating from the sudden chills of disappointment, the smouldering embers of frustration, or the searing flames of impatience than my supportive wife, Belinda, and our children, Gareth, Jessica and Matthew. My family have all heard of, read about, and had to live with Joseph Silver in ways that nobody else has had to. I have often been away on journeys of the mind or, worse still, on far-off travels. My indebtedness to them is truly without measure.

I am aware, however, that there are hundreds of others who have helped in thousands of ways to bring this project to a satisfactory conclusion.

*   *   *

It is difficult to conceive of any book that is, in any meaningful way, single-authored. In truth, there is no such thing. All authors rely to a greater or lesser extent on the specialist assistance and advice provided by archivists, librarians, translators and other specialists. A work such as this, set on four continents, in a dozen countries and drawing on accounts and sources couched in more than a half-dozen languages, offers an extreme example of the debts that an author can incur in researching and writing history.

Every person listed here contributed, in some way, to the jigsaw portrait of Joseph Silver that eventually emerged. Some may recognise the piece they handed me, others not, but without their contribution to the collective, the project would never have come to fruition. I wish to thank each of these acquaintances, administrators, assistants, friends, and colleagues for their assistance. If I have, inadvertently, failed to include the name of anybody, I apologise most sincerely and, if I have somehow misplaced the piece they handed me, I likewise crave their indulgence. The pieces were theirs, the picture that emerged mine only and I would not like them to feel in any way responsible for errors of emphasis, fact or interpretation. Those are all mine.

A. M. Adam, E. Allina-Pisano, V. Allison, G. Alroey, A. Amarilla, A. Angell, H. Antkiewicz, M. and A. Arpey, E. Ashton, J. Ashton, M. Aspell, A. A. Atmore, A. Auchnie, J. Auslander, H. Avni, D. Bach, J. Back, E. Baez, D. Baker, Z. M. Baker, E. M. Barba, S. Bardwell, M. Barnard, N. C. Barros, B. L. Basberg, K.S.O. Beavon, C. Beck, W. Beinart, V. Belling, C. G. Belsunce, J. Bergh, J. Berkowitz, A. Bezuidenhout, D. Biale, T.B. Bialoronski, A. Bischof, K. Bliss, A. Block, R. Blumenfeld, E. Bolocco, H. D. Boonin, B. Bozzoli, G. Braccio, H. Bradford, F. Brenner, G. Briscoe, E. Bristow, A. Broder, J. Brown, J. J. Bukowczyk, J. Bushnel, J. Buzási, J.T. Campbell, R.F. Campusano, H. Carlson, W. Carmichael, A. Carr, A. Carroll, J. Carter, S. Caulfield, D. Cesarani, P. Cheifitz, G. Chowdharay-Best, A.S. Clausen, K. Cobb, E. Coetzee, N. Colman, J. Copans, E. Corri, C. Cousino, T. Coutinho, T.J. Couzens, K. Couzens-Bohlin, M. Crook, J.M.D. Crossey and D.J. Czitrom, J.A. Da Silva, A. Dasnois, C. Dasnois, L. Davidson, P.K. Davies, C.L. Davis, D. Davis, J. Davis, L.B.E. Davis, M. Davis, S. De Kozlowski, L. De la Torre, R. De Lauro, L. De Mecheleer, I. Delic, L.T. Demas, C. Dengate, Y.M. Deprez, G. Devos, J. Duffy, B.S. Duncan, K. Duncan, S. Eagle, J. Elkin, D.T. Elliott, R. Ellis, S. Ellis, J.E. Evans, R.J. Evans,

B. Fausto, D. Feldman, J. Feldman, J.S. Feldman, A. Ferrari, P. Fievet, I. Filatova, S. Frankental, A. Garlicki, A. Gartner, L.P. Gartner, S. Garton, I. Gaseb, N.S. Gast, V. Gatrell, S.P. Gawe, C. Gazmuri, J. Gennari, A. Gieysztor, T. Gilfoyle, H. Giliomee, N. Glickman, B. Godsell, G. Godsell, S. Godsell, D. Goldblatt, D. Goldey, L. Goldsmith, A.A. Goren, E. Gouws, L. Graham, G. Grannum, E. Grausz, A. Graves, N. Green, G. Greenberg, S. Greenberg, K. Griffin, B. Groeblinghoff, A.M. Grundlingh, T. Gudbrandson, R. Gulden, L. Gurowitz, M. Gustafson, D. Guy, J. Guy, M. Guy, M. Hall, R. Hallet, O. Halvorsen, G. Hamilton, M. Harradine, P. Harries, K. Harris, F.K. Haviland, E. Haxhaj, J. Heine, J. Hellig, R. Hill, W. Hillebrecht, A. Hingeston, E. Hingeston, J. Hinshaw, P. Hodgson, E. Hoffman, R. Hood, C. Howell, B. Howlett, M. Huggins, N. Humphries, G.D. Hundert, D.M. Hunter, M. Hussey, S. Issroff, E. Iversen, A. Jacobs, C. Jacobs, D. James, J. Jansen, W. Jaromiński, K.U. Joerss, B. Johnson, M.M. Johnson, R.W. Johnson, S.M. Johnson, B. Jonson, C. Jooste, E. Kahn, S. Kahn, R. Kaplan, L.G. Karper, L. Kartashova, E. Katz, S. Kassow, J.A.D. Koekemoer, F. Korn, B.A. Kosmin, T. Krogh, G. Krozewski, J. Kruger, L. Krupnak, R. Krut, T. Kushner, B. Kwiatkowski, G. Kynoch, D. La Cava, P. La Hausse, E. Laclau, M. L. Lange, P.M. Larson, E. Le Roux, P. Le Roux, W. Ledochowski, F.E. Leese, A. Legocki, M. Leon, H. Lepper, J. Lesser, S.N. Levy, D. Lewartowski, B. Lewin, A. Lichtenstein, A. Lincoln, B. Lis, H. Lis, J. Lis, J. Lis, B. Liss, D. Liss, H. Liss, P.S. Liss, H.O. Lissoary, S. Littlejohns, A.M. Lloyd, G. Luke, J. Malan, W. Malan, B. Malauzat, R. Manekin, C. Mann, R. Mann, E.A. Mantzaris, W. Markiewicz, W. Martins, I. Masing-Delic, M. Matsuki, M. Maubrey, H. Melber, R.S. Mendez, E. Messina, B. Michler, J.N. Mienie, J. Miles, A.M. Modro, T.A. Modro, S. Mofokeng, D. Monney, C. Moody, R. Morgenstern, R. Morrell, M.J. Moya, N. Mulry, K.M. Murphy, B.K. Murray, I.G. Murray, N. Musiker R. Musiker N. Naro, B. Nasson, Y. Nedrebo, A.N. Newman, A.N. Newsome, I. Niehaus, D. Nierhaus, R.W. O'Hara, R. Oller, C. Oppetit, R. Oren A. Palmer, A. Peacock, P. Pearson, L. Peeters, B. Pejovic, A. Penkalla, J. Penvenne, D. Philips, S. Phillips, I.R. Phimister, J. Pieterse, G.H. Pirie, A. Polonsky, R. Posel, J.H. Potgieter, L. Prager, N. Priscill, N. Quam-Wickham, A. Rädel, M. Rago, R.L. Rees, S. Rich, R. Robboy, K. Robson, A.E.M. Rodrigues, P. Romero, D. Rosenberg, J. Rosenblitt, M. Rosman, X. Rousseaux, S. Rowoldt, W.D. Rubinstein, B. Ruibal, S. Rutland, S. Ryszard, R. Sadowski, H. Salamon, L. Samarbakhsh-Liberge, R. Samuel, J.D. Sarna, G. Saron, E. Sawicki, B.

Schaefer, G. Schirge, B.J. Schulman, B. Scott, A. Scufflaire, I.C. Selavan, M. Shain, R. Shaulis, G. Shepherd, J. Sherman, G. Shimoni, S.W. Siegel, J. Sielemann, E. Sifton, L. Sigel, A. Silvera, J. Silvester, J.D. Sinclair, F. Singer, M. Singer, C.G. Siperman de Kohanoff, D.C.S. Sissons, W. Siwinski, J.D. Skepper, R.W. Slatta, D. Smith, H. Smith, J. Smith, S. Socolow, P. Söldenwagner, D. Sotker, H.A. Spalding, B. Spies, S. Stampfer, P.A. Stanbridge, G. Starn, P. Steege, H. Stein, M. Steinlauf, C. Stern, K. Stern, S. Steven, G. Stewart, J.C. Stoner, F. Stovel, A. Summers, B. Sverdloff, J.J. Swart, J. Szczepański, P. Tabensky, E. Tandeter, J. Tarr, M.M. Taylor, K. Tenfelde, D. Thelen, L. Thiesen, E.F. Thompson, J. Thompson, B. Thrift, L.A. Tomko, R. Torok-Apro, B. Trapido, S. Trapido, J.A. Trost, J.W. Trotter, S. Tuback, D. Tucker, K. Urbanski F. Van Anrooij, P. van der Spuy, W. van Huyssteen, L. van Niekerk, G. van Onselen, J. van Onselen, M. van Onselen, H. van Vuuren, D. Vangheluwe, J. Vellut, G. Verbeeck, A. Victoria, A. Viduarreta, L. Vincent, R. Vincent, B. von der Haar, M. Vovelle, E. Wakin, T. Walichnowski, J. Wall, J. Waynberg, N. Westcott, K.J. Westmancoat, M. M. White, P. White, Z.T. Wierzbicki, M.A. Wihtol de Wenden, B. Willan, E. Williams, M.Y. Williams, W.G. Williams, R. Wilson Kane, S. Wilson, C. Winckler de Lucchesi, H. Winnicka, L.J. Witkowsky, F. Wolff, H. Wolfram, C.M. Woolgar, M. Wright, L. Wulff, E.L. Yabsley, B. Zachary and C. Zimring.

Finally, in my time I have researched, studied and tried to write history in depressingly grey as well as pleasant green settings. I have also worked under minority as well as majoritarian forms of nationalism. The former, in my experience, has nothing whatsoever to commend it and the latter a good deal less than its protagonists would have one believe. Nationalism, exclusivist by nature and guarded by zealots, tends to marginalise not only outsiders but sections of its own citizenry. This book, rooted in the experiences of the Atlantic World, is for metics everywhere.

Charles van Onselen
University of Pretoria
October 2006

INDEX